Re

BEHAVIORAL A
OF ADULT DISORDERS

THE GUILFORD
BEHAVIORAL ASSESSMENT SERIES
John D. Cone and Rosemery O. Nelson, Editors

Behavioral Assessment of Adult Disorders
David H. Barlow, Editor

Behavioral Assessment of Childhood Disorders
Eric J. Mash and Leif G. Terdal, Editors

BEHAVIORAL ASSESSMENT OF ADULT DISORDERS

Edited by

David H. Barlow

STATE UNIVERSITY OF NEW YORK AT ALBANY

THE GUILFORD PRESS

NEW YORK   LONDON

©1981 The Guilford Press, New York
A Division of Guilford Publications, Inc.
200 Park Avenue South, New York, N.Y. 10003

Printed in the United States of America

Library of Congress Cataloging in Publication Data
Main entry under title:

Behavioral assessment of adult disorders.
(The Guilford behavioral assessment series)
Bibliography: p.
Includes indexes.
1. Mental illness—Diagnosis. 2. Personality assessment. 3. Psychology, Pathological —Classification. I. Barlow, David H. II. Series: Guilford behavioral assessment series. [DNLM: 1. Mental disorders—Classification. 2. Mental disorders—Diagnosis. 3. Social behavior disorders—Classification. 4. Social behavior disorders—Diagnosis. 5. Behavior therapy—Methods. 6. Models, Psychological. 7. Psychotherapy—Methods. WM420 B41794]
RC469.B43   616.85′82   80-14673
ISBN 0-89862-901-2 p
ISBN 0-89862-140-2

CONTRIBUTORS

STEWART AGRAS, M.D. Department of Psychiatry, Stanford University School of Medicine, Stanford, California

DAVID H. BARLOW, Ph.D. Department of Psychology, State University of New York at Albany, Albany, New York

EDWARD B. BLANCHARD, Ph.D. Department of Psychology, State University of New York at Albany, Albany, New York

THOMAS J. BOLL, Ph.D. Department of Psychology, University of Health Sciences, The Chicago Medical School, North Chicago, Illinois

KELLY D. BROWNELL, Ph.D. Department of Psychiatry, University of Pennsylvania School of Medicine, Philadelphia, Pennsylvania

JAMES P. CURRAN, Ph.D. Brown University Medical School and Veterans Administration Medical Center, Providence, Rhode Island

MERCEDES DALLAS, M.A. Department of Psychology, The University of Iowa, Iowa City, Iowa

RICHARD W. ELWOOD, B.A. Department of Psychology, The University of Iowa, Iowa City, Iowa

NEIL S. JACOBSON, Ph.D. Department of Psychology, University of Washington, Seattle, Washington

JAMES D. LANGE, Ph.D. Psychology Service, Veterans Administration Medical Center, Providence, Rhode Island

WANDA M. L. LEE, Ph.D. Psychology Department, University of Oregon, Eugene, Oregon

PETER M. LEWINSOHN, Ph.D. Psychology Department, University of Oregon, Eugene, Oregon

MATIG R. MAVISSAKALIAN, M.D. Western Psychiatric Institute and Clinic, University of Pittsburgh School of Medicine, Pittsburgh, Pennsylvania

PETER M. MILLER, Ph.D. Sea Pines Behavioral Institute, Sea Pines Plantation, Hilton Head Island, South Carolina

PETER E. NATHAN, Ph.D. Graduate School of Applied and Professional Psychology, Rutgers University, Piscataway, New Jersey

JOHN M. NEALE, Ph.D. Department of Psychology, State University of New York at Stony Brook, Stony Brook, New York

ROSEMERY O. NELSON, Ph.D. Department of Psychology, The University of North Carolina at Greensboro, Greensboro, North Carolina

THOMAS F. OLTMANNS, Ph.D. Department of Psychology, Indiana University, Bloomington, Indiana

C. BARR TAYLOR, M.D. Department of Psychiatry, Stanford University School of Medicine, Stanford, California

HAROLD W. WESSBERG, Ph.D. Brown University Medical School and Veterans Administration Medical Center, Providence, Rhode Island

JOHN P. WINCZE, Ph.D. Psychology Service, Veterans Administration Medical Center, and Department of Psychiatry and Human Behavior, Brown University, Providence, Rhode Island

PREFACE

The signs and signals from Washington and elsewhere around the country are crystal clear. For psychotherapists and behavior therapists everywhere, the decade of the '80s will be the age of accountability. Those who can become accountable, both to their clients as well as to government agencies and third-party payers, will succeed and prosper, while those who cannot will come upon hard times. More important, however, will be the advances forthcoming to our science and to our clinical practice from a more empirical approach to the assessment of human behavioral problems. There is little doubt that the very heart of the kind of accountability demanded in the years ahead will be accurate classification and assessment and, in particular, the demonstration of improvement through repeated administration of "state-of-the-art" assessment procedures. The purpose of this book is to advance us several steps toward that goal.

This book, unlike most of its predecessors, is not a book on how to do behavioral assessment, listing the various procedures available at this time and the philosophies underlying them. The purpose of this book is to provide an up-to-date, state-of-the-art description of the assessment procedures and strategies for the most common adult clinical problems which will help the clinician achieve accountability.

Although controversial and unpopular in many settings, the advent of DSM-III is bound to affect all of us in our practice, and there are few who will disagree that at the very least it is an improvement over its predecessor. Furthermore, the DSM-III will undoubtedly become an important part of the process of accountability in the years ahead. Thus, the first chapter is a statement on the relationship between behavioral assessment and DSM-III. I was very fortunate indeed to have one of our most distinguished colleagues in this area, Peter Nathan, contribute this chapter. The second chapter, reviewing strategies of behavioral assessment, describes how the various classifications in DSM-III can provide a jumping-off point for the more complex process of assessment, including the use of those procedures which can demonstrate effectiveness of given techniques over time. While the remaining chapters reflect the expertise of their authors, each follows a common outline in order to communicate the most information to the clinician and clinical researcher. After an initial statement on the relationship of classification, and in most cases DSM-III, to the focal problem of the chapter, a model or mini-theory is presented which guides assessment of the particular problem by answering the question, "What should be assessed?" These models are implicit in all assessment and treatment, and by making them explicit, the rationale for assessing some aspects of the problem and not others should become apparent (e.g., the assessment of physiologic responding in phobia but not affective disorders). In most cases these are decisions that follow the initial act of classification by DSM-III or other means. The remainder of each chapter then describes specific procedures for assessment and their implementation. Finally, the implications of assessment for treatment are discussed, since a functional relationship between assessment and treatment is a hallmark of behavioral assessment; and, in most chapters, cases are provided illustrating the whole process.

With its focus on the variety of clinical problems one is likely to encounter and its emphasis on the strategic integration of DSM-III and functionally analytic behavioral assessment, this book should prove useful to clinicians, clinical researchers, and students in the mental-health professions. If for some reason it is not useful, Sallie Morgan and Martha Viglietta, who worked extremely hard on the numerous details involved in putting this book together, will be extremely disappointed. I will take full responsibility for their frustration, and thank them anyway for a seemingly endless and often monotonous effort. If this book accurately anticipates trends in the coming decade, as I think it does, then they should share equally in the gratitude of anyone who finds the book useful. I would like to express deep appreciation to Jodi Weinstein and Annemarie Infantino for making the index as thoroughly complete and useful as it is. Finally, it is with great pleasure, and with considerable respect and love, that I dedicate this book to Doris E. Barlow, for her dedication and her vision.

D.H.B.

Albany, New York

CONTENTS

1

Symptomatic Diagnosis and Behavioral Assessment: A Synthesis?

PETER E. NATHAN

The Data

On his first visit to the Veterans Administration Outpatient Clinic, Charles informed the intake worker that he hadn't been able to keep a job since his discharge from the Army a few months before, that his parents didn't like him moping around the house, and that he hoped the people at the Clinic could help him get a job he could keep. During his second visit, Charles showed some of the behaviors which prevented him from keeping jobs and getting along with people. A person whose parents had been insistent on teaching their only child to be independent and self-reliant, Charles had grown up never really trusting anyone. The suspiciousness his parents taught him, compounded by a few experiences of his own — in the Army, mostly — had made him question every order a supervisor or employer gave, every offer of friendship an acquaintance made — and every effort his new therapist made to build rapport. Small wonder that Charles had remained in no job for more than six weeks and had never had a friend he could feel close to. Compounding Charles's trust problems were vaguely threatening voices, unaccompanied by visible people, which reinforced his skewed view of the world. "Trust nobody," they said, or "Tell him what you think of him," or "He's a son of a bitch"—or

Peter E. Nathan, Graduate School of Applied and Professional Psychology, Rutgers University, Piscataway, New Jersey.

worse. Never insistent despite their message or intrusive despite their persistence, Charles's voices reinforced his concerns about relating very closely to other people as well as his fears that schemes to deprive him of his place in society had been hatched somewhere, by someone.

Arnold's problem was as embarrassing and stupid as it was disabling. So great was his fear of being enclosed, of being in places from which he could not see the world outside, that he visited the metropolitan area to the north as rarely as possible; such visits entailed long, painful minutes of panic in the tunnels which feed the city and in the elevators which serve its skyscrapers. And because friends, relatives, and business associates lived and worked in the city, the distress Arnold felt on making the trip extended even beyond the anxiety and fear he experienced. Knowing that his symptoms prevented him from seeing people who meant something to him made things a lot worse. It was important that Arnold call on his business contacts in the city; it was pleasant to spend time with old friends; it was obligatory to visit family members. Yet all had to be severely curtailed because of Arnold's stupid, unreasoning, blind panic. And what was supremely puzzling was that his feelings were so unreasonable; the tunnels linking New Jersey and Manhattan were unlikely to cave in and modern elevators rarely fell down, and so there was no objective reason to panic.

The Dilemma

All the other chapters of this book detail the place of behavioral assessment in understanding and treating behavioral disorders. The purpose of this chapter is different, however. It is written to engage the reader in earnest consideration of the place of symptomatic—nonbehavioral—diagnosis (based on the recently revised *Diagnostic and Statistical Manual of Mental Disorders* [DSM-III, 1980] of the American Psychiatric Association) in the armamentarium of the behavior therapist; specifically, to assess its role in the process of behavioral assessment. What place, you might ask, can such a notoriously unreliable and useless pursuit as symptomatic diagnosis have in assessment? What place, especially, in the hands of the behavior therapist, a person whose commitment to the empirical has led to a more reliable and useful system, behavioral assessment?

Yet the issue is not so clear-cut. Consider the two brief clinical histories that introduced this chapter. Despite their brevity, the descriptions are sufficient to enable both "traditional" diagnoses and behavioral assessments. To what extent do either or both tell us what we need to know to help Charles and Arnold?

Solutions

Charles merits the diagnosis of schizophrenic disorder, almost certainly of the paranoid variety. This diagnosis, a reliable one on which there would clearly be widespread agreement, is based on observation in Charles's behavior of several DMS-III "operational criteria" for schizophrenia, including poorly formed paranoid delusions and auditory hallucinations, both of which impair job functioning and social relations, as well as chronicity of these and other symptoms extending beyond six months. In fact, Charles had experienced his symptoms for years, though not always at their present intensity.

A behavioral analysis of Charles's behavior is more difficult, in part because behavioral views on the causes of the psychoses (e.g., Bandura, 1968; Ullmann & Krasner, 1975) have not been particularly convincing. Bandura observed that delusions and hallucinations, in common with other typical stigmata of schizophrenia, are both directly reinforced and indirectly modeled by parents and others. Ullmann and Krasner wrote that schizophrenic behavior is the product of "failure of reinforcement for a sequence of behavior," such that the schizophrenic person ultimately learns to stop paying attention to environmental cues after repeated failure of reinforcement—again, most often at the hands of parents. Since Charles's parents were neither deviant nor withdrawn, though their interactions with Charles were emotionally charged because Charles often distorted them, neither behavioral view of Charles's dysfunctional behavior represents an easy "fit."

An analysis of Charles's behavior according to a behavioral schema less dependent on generalized assumptions about etiology, more focused on immediate relations between a behavior and its causes (Tharp & Wetzel, 1969), yields the following:

1. *Antecedent events.* Though Charles complained of his voices and reported on his delusions of persecution most when things had been going particularly badly for him, the delusions and hallucinations were in fact always with him, as were his sense

of social isolation and inability to think clearly. Hence, a specific set of antecedent events associated with increases in the delusional and hallucinatory behavior could not be identified.

2. *Maintaining stimuli*. Charles's parents and doctor paid more attention to him when he talked of his suspicions and voices. It could be said, then, that their attention served as contingent reinforcement for Charles's reports. The actual frequency of these experiences, however, was unaffected by the attention paid to them, in contrast to Charles's spontaneous self-reports, which varied directly with others' interest in them.

3. *Potentials for remediation*. For a time, Charles's parents consulted a local behavior therapist, who told them to ignore Charles's delusional and hallucinatory reports. Following his advice, Charles's parents shortly observed that Charles had begun to give progressively fewer and fewer self-reports. As a result, his parents asked him a few days later whether he still heard voices and distrusted people around him. Charles replied that he still heard the voices and feared for his safety as much as ever but had stopped talking about them because he now believed that his parents had joined in the conspiracy to wear him down. He was relieved when his parents assured him they were not conspirators, and more so when they started asking about his symptomatic behavior again, contrary to the therapist's advice.

Arnold's DSM-III diagnosis is anxiety disorder, specifically, agoraphobia with panic attacks. Diagnostic criteria for the latter diagnosis from DSM-III include (1) efforts to avoid being alone or in situations where help is not readily available (Arnold was most disabled by the drive through the tunnel when he was alone); (2) pervasive, incapacitating fear resulting in avoidance, where possible, of closed or open spaces (Arnold was most afraid of tunnels but disliked elevators and windowless rooms as well; whenever possible he avoided such places even when they were associated with reinforcing events or people); (3) marked anxiety when facing or experiencing feared situations (Arnold experienced heart palpitations, broke out in a cold sweat, and had a sense of impending doom when confronted with tunnels, elevators, or enclosed spaces); (4) phobic behavior not symptomatic of other psychological or psychiatric disorders (Arnold functioned effectively and well when he was not anticipating or experiencing a trip through a tunnel or on an elevator).

The prevailing behavioral view of phobic behavior until recently saw it as respondent behavior conditioned early in life by traumatic exposure to a stimulus, the unconditioned response to which is fear and anxiety; typically, these responses ultimately generalize to similar situations and events. This view has been Joseph Wolpe's explanation (1969) for the development of phobic behavior. This view assumes that phobic behavior is more or less "automatically" acquired when the right components of the Pavlovian conditioning process are present. It also assumes that subsequent phobic attacks are more or less "automatically" experienced whenever the conditioned stimulus is present, regardless of the person's state of mind. An alternative view of phobic behavior, one that has gained widespread acceptance in recent years and conforms better to the specifics of Arnold's behavior, is that of cognitive social learning theory. As conceptualized by Bandura (1977a, 1977b) and Wilson (1980), respondent conditioning is not an automatic process, but rather is self-activated on the basis of learned expectations. This position accurately reflects the fact that Arnold's panic in tunnels and elevators was compounded by cognitions—thoughts—dwelling on the disastrous impact these places had had on him in the past. That is, Arnold was his own worst enemy when it came to tunnels because he always made his anxiety and fear much worse by rehearsing the trip several times in his imagination—to mounting panic—before he experienced it in fact.

Cognitive variables also played an important role in efforts to remediate Arnold's problem. On the advice of a colleague, a behavior therapist whose acceptance of cognitive social learning theory led her to attend to the impact of cognitions on psychopathology, Arnold spent the greater part of three successive mornings traveling under railroad bridges, then in short vehicular tunnels, and finally through a long tunnel to the city in the company of a friend who modeled relaxation, joviality, and keen anticipation of a forthcoming lunch in the city. The friend also told a series of diverting risque jokes. At the conclusion of this intensive treatment experience, Arnold reported that he could traverse tunnels with far greater ease, especially when he made the conscious (cognitive) effort to recall the pleasure of the company of his friend and their interaction during the trip.

Conclusions: Reliability

The newest edition of the *Diagnostic and Statistical Manual* (DSM-III) has addressed one of the most pressing problems posed by its predecessors, the low reliability of symptomatic diagnoses, by providing operational criteria that effectively define each diagnosis (Schacht & Nathan, 1977). By contrast, the reliability of behavioral analysis, when it extends beyond repetitive recording of target symptoms to focus, more ambitiously, on functional relationships among environmental and cognitive determinants of behavior, remains uncertain (Hersen, 1976; Salzinger, 1978).

DSM-III's operational criteria take the form of a series of specific statements listing and describing the diagnostic cues—disordered behaviors—which must be observed in order to justify a diagnosis. Empirically derived, for the most part, from research diagnostic criteria generated by Feighner, Robins, Guze, Woodruff, Winokur, and Muñoz (1972) and Spitzer, Endicott, and Robins (1975), the operational criteria are more likely for that reason to reflect replicable clusters of behaviors characteristic of recognizable groups of psychiatric patients. Requiring clinicians to agree on a set of criteria for a diagnosis is likely to enhance diagnostic reliability, defined as the extent to which two or more clinicians can agree on a diagnosis, given that the clinicians can agree on how to elicit and chronicle those criteria. That the criteria were extensively field-tested prior to publication of the *Diagnostic Manual*—at more than 100 psychiatric facilities around the country—adds to assurance that all reasonable steps have been taken to ensure the greatest possible reliability of diagnosis from these criteria.

Reliability of behavior rating scales and discrete behavioral observation is also generally high. Prior to development of DSM-III's operational criteria, most behavior therapists who set out to observe carefully defined target behaviors in a systematic way (for example, frequency of stuttering or instances of verbal aggression) almost certainly did so with consistently higher reliability than those who observed behavior for the purposes of a DSM-II psychiatric diagnosis. With publication of DSM-III, the gap in reliability between behavioral and psychiatric observation has narrowed, though it is probably still true that many of the discrete behavioral units assessed by behavior therapists will yield the highest reliabilities.

It is when behavior therapists and "traditional" diagnosticians attempt summary statements, however, that the latter may now have an edge in reliability they did not have before. As is well known, the reliability of summary diagnostic statements from DSM-II has been low. Although agreement on certain major DSM-II categories (e.g., psychosis as against nonpsychosis) was quite high (in the neighborhood of .70), agreement on other major disorders (e.g., neurosis as against personality disorder) or within a major diagnostic category (e.g., among the subtypes of schizophrenia, neurosis, or personality disorder) was very low (Greenberg, 1977; Matarazzo, 1978). The reliability of DSM-III summary statements is likely to be a good deal higher because the new operational criteria delimit major classes of dysfunction from one another and differentiate among dysfunction subtypes as well. The diagnoses given Charles and Arnold were made much easier, and more reliable, by virtue of operational criteria from DSM-III; they effectively ruled out alternative diagnoses, even closely related ones like schizophreniform disorder and anxiety disorder, and reduced each ultimate diagnostic choice to but a single one.

By contrast, efforts to formulate replicable behavioral analyses of Charles's and Arnold's behavior were hampered by the absence of guidelines on how to set about identifying crucial environmental or cognitive influences on behavior and, once done, on how to coalesce these observations into behavioral analyses. Even our assessment of Arnold's behavior, which appeared straightforward, was hampered by uncertainty over whether to adopt Tharp and Wetzel's broad operant paradigm (we rejected their scheme because we could not identify the maintaining stimuli for Arnold's phobic behavior), Wolpe's more narrow respondent model (but what was the source of the original conditioned fear response and how did it generalize to tunnels?), or the contemporary social learning view espoused by Wilson and Bandura (even the cognitive social learning model is obscure on how one is to allocate assessment responsibility among the principal modes of learning). That we chose the latter was more a function of our conviction that Charles's cognitions played an important role in his phobic behavior than of consensus.

We conclude, then, that the new revision of the *Diagnostic and Statistical Manual* (1980) has yielded a document that enables the diagnostician to do almost as well as the well-trained, conscientious behavior therapist in recording discrete units of maladaptive behavior — symptoms — and very likely a good deal better than that when called upon to put forth a summary statement (a DSM-III diagnosis on the one hand, a behavioral analysis on the other).

Conclusions: Utility

Let us turn now to the differential usefulness of assessment or diagnosis, which is the most critical issue to be dealt with in this chapter.

Again, if conventional wisdom can be a guide, symptomatic diagnoses are rarely useful for treatment planning, presumably their most important potential use. Here too our hypothetical patients are instructive. The DSM-III label given Arnold—anxiety disorder, agoraphobia with panic attacks—is only of limited utility. Though most readers of this book are likely to agree that behavioral procedures, including systematic desensitization, have proven useful in confronting phobic behavior, that belief is not a widespread one among nonbehavioral clinicians. Hence, the label is not universally helpful for treatment planning. By contrast, the DSM-III label given Charles—schizophrenia, paranoid type—is more generally useful since the phenothiazine drugs have been treatments of choice for schizophrenic behavior since the late 1950s. Hence, with these two patients, symptomatic diagnosis bats .500.

Behavioral assessment achieves about the same batting average, despite the focus of the behavioral assessor on making his or her product maximally relevant to treatment. Because behavioral views of the etiology of the psychoses have gained little acceptance, they have not helped guide development of useful assessment approaches to these disorders. Choosing Bandura's, Ullmann and Krasner's, or Tharp and Wetzel's assessment schemas does not change things much; Charles's delusions and hallucinations do not bear the kind of functional relationship to his environment that enables behavioral assessment to lead naturally and effectively to behavioral treatment.

By contrast, behavioral assessment of Arnold's phobic behavior was a great help in treatment planning. Correctly recognizing the central role that Arnold's cognitions about his phobias played in maintaining them—his obsessional cognitive elaboration of the physiological events which had accompanied prior episodes of phobic behavior invariably amplified those to come before Arnold ever entered a tunnel or an elevator—Arnold's colleague recommended behavioral procedures that interrupted the chain of cognitions which had so successfully maintained the phobias.

Despite the efforts of the drafters of DSM-III to increase its utility—by requiring the coding of each patient's behavior along five dimensions rather than, as before, only one—DSM-III's symptomatic diagnosis continues to pose utility problems. Even though clinicians will now rate severity of psychosocial stressors during the year preceding the consultation (Axis 4) as well as the highest level of adaptive functioning during the same year (Axis 5), the direct relevance of these evaluations—and their reliability—remains to be established.

By contrast, behavioral analyses are more often useful—even given their diversity in terms of conceptual basis and the absence of guidelines for choosing among them on being confronted with one or another assessment problem—because they enable one to focus on the factors that maintain the maladaptive behavior. At the same time, it is necessary to add the caveat that diagnosis and behavioral analysis have utility only to the extent that valid treatments exist. Because a range of promising behavioral treatments do exist for many of the nonpsychotic behaviors, behavioral analysis has potential utility for them. The absence of such treatments for the psychotic disorders renders the utility of behavioral analysis moot with those disorders—and enables DSM-III diagnosis to prove sufficient for the purposes of planning treatment for these disorders.

My admiration for the newly developed virtues of DSM-III has led to criticism of behavioral assessment. I must confess to disappointment at the slow pace with which empirical confirmation of behavioral efforts to assess has proceeded—at the delay in realization of the promise of behavioral analysis. Yet I continue to believe in the potential of behavioral assessment and have grown increasingly pessimistic about the ultimate worth of symptomatic diagnosis, as in DSM-III. Accordingly, while acknowledging that DSM-III is probably at the state-of-the-art of symptomatic diagnosis at the present time, neither DSM-III nor its successors will be able to achieve the kind of ultimate utility that assessment based on something other than symptomatic behavior promises.

Basing a system for categorizing dysfunctional behavior on a chronicling of deviations from normality, as does DSM-III, derives from the tradition in physical medicine (Begelman, 1975; Nathan, 1967). Useful in that context (knowing that someone has tuberculosis is of inestimable value in assigning a rational treatment plan), symptomatic diagnosis is much less useful with the so-called psychiatric disorders, especially the nonpsychotic ones for which proven treatments do not exist. Moreover, it is possible that treatments of universal efficacy, those to which all individuals within a given category will respond, will never be found because of the diversity of etiologies of these disorders. Behavioral analysis may be the only categorization system capable of identifying the environmental and cognitive variables necessary to change, variables which have less to do with "symptoms" than with the factors on which these symptomatic behaviors are contingent.

What is necessary, though, is rededication to efforts to systematize behavioral assessment methods, to maximize their reliability, to broaden their salience to a full range of environmental and cognitive factors, and to measure their utility in treatment-planning. While the practical limitations posed by these goals are formidable (for example, what is the full range of determinants of dysfunctional behavior? Are sufficiently robust treatment methods in existence against which to test behavioral analyses for utility?), the goals are wholly worthwhile.

Symptomatic Diagnosis and Behavioral Assessment: A Synthesis

We conclude, then, that symptomatic diagnosis and behavioral assessment now rate about equal in reliability and in utility. We also conclude that the utility of symptomatic diagnoses is greatest with the psychotic disorders for which drug treatment is the treatment of choice; drugs like the phenothiazines, the tricyclic antidepressants, and lithium carbonate are effective more or less indiscriminately across a given diagnostic category's symptomatology. By contrast, the greater individual specificity of behavioral assessment proves most useful when applied to the nonpsychotic disorders for which a clear treatment of choice does not exist; in such cases a behavioral assessment can provide direction to treatment that a descriptive label conferred by symptomatic diagnosis cannot.

In practice, symptomatic diagnosis and behavioral assessment together sometimes work better than either alone. Had Charles's hallucinations or delusions been maintained, even in part, by parental attention, a behavioral assessment might have directed a behavioral treatment approach capable of augmenting drug treatment. And though Arnold's treatment was not facilitated by his symptomatic diagnosis, the increased descriptive precision of DSM-III's operational criteria provided the behavior therapist who advised Arnold with a much better idea of the precise form his phobic behavior took. That made it easier to relate his cognitive activities before traveling to the symptomatic behavior that accompanied his travels.

Do the diagnostician and the behavioral assessor have things to teach each other? In our judgment — and at this point in time — yes, indeed!

References

Bandura, A. A social learning interpretation of psychological dysfunctions. In P. London & D. Rosenhan (Eds.), *Foundations of abnormal psychology*. New York: Holt, Rinehart, & Winston, 1968.

Bandura, A. *A social learning theory*. Englewood Cliffs, NJ: Prentice-Hall, 1977.(a)

Bandura, A. Self-efficacy: Toward a unifying theory of behavioral change. *Psychological Review*, 1977, *84*, 191–215. (b)

Begelman, D. A. Ethical and legal issues in behavior modification. In M. Hersen, R. M. Eisler, & P. M. Miller (Eds.), *Progress in behavior modification* (Vol. 1). New York: Academic Press, 1975.

Diagnostic and statistical manual of mental disorders (3rd ed.). Washington, D.C.: American Psychiatric Association, 1980.

Feighner, J. P., Robins, E., Guze, S. B., Woodruff, R. A., Winokur, G., & Muñoz, R. Diagnostic criteria for use in psychiatric research. *Archives of General Psychiatry*, 1972, *26*, 57–63.

Greenberg, J. How accurate is psychiatry? *Science News*, 1977, *112*, 28–29.

Hersen, M. Historical perspectives in behavioral assessment. In M. Hersen & A. S. Bellack (Eds.), *Behavioral assessment: A practical handbook*. Oxford: Pergamon Press, 1976.

Matarazzo, J. B. The interview: Its reliability and validity in psychiatric diagnosis. In B. B. Wolman (Ed.), *Clinical diagnosis of mental disorders: A handbook*. New York: Plenum Publishing Corp., 1978.

Nathan, P. E. *Cues, decisions, and diagnoses*. New York: Academic Press, 1967.

Salzinger, K. A behavioral analysis of diagnosis. In R. L. Spitzer & D. F. Klein (Eds.), *Critical issues in psychiatric diagnosis*. New York: Raven Press, 1978.

Schacht, T., & Nathan, P. E. But is it good for the psychologists? Appraisal and status of DSM-III. *American Psychologist*, 1977, *32*, 1017–1025.

Spitzer, R. L., Endicott, J. F., & Robins, E. Clinical criteria for psychiatric diagnosis and DSM-III. *American Journal of Psychiatry*, 1975, *132*, 1187–1192.

Tharp, R. G., & Wetzel, R. J. *Behavior modification in the natural environment*. New York: Academic Press, 1969.

Ullmann, L. P., & Krasner, L. *A psychological approach to abnormal behavior* (2nd ed.). Englewood Cliffs, NJ: Prentice-Hall, 1975.

Wilson, G. T. Cognitive factors in life-style changes: A social learning perspective. In P. O. Davidson & S. M. Davidson (Eds.), *Behavioral medicine: Changing health life styles*. New York: Brunner/Mazel, 1980.

Wolpe, J. *The practice of behavior therapy*. New York: Pergamon Press, 1969.

2

Behavioral Assessment: Basic Strategies and Initial Procedures

ROSEMERY O. NELSON
DAVID H. BARLOW

Basic Strategies in Behavioral Assessment

The purpose of this chapter is to provide an overview of behavioral assessment with typical adult clients. Questions addressed include: How does a behavioral assessor conclude that a particular client has a specific problem? In other words, what makes a clinician decide that another chapter of this book describing the assessment of a specific disorder is applicable to a particular client? How does DSM-III (the American Psychiatric Association's third edition of the *Diagnostic and Statistical Manual of Mental Disorders*, 1980) relate to behavioral assessment? Is the mental status examination useful in behavioral assessment? How are behavioral assessment and abnormal psychology related? How are target behaviors—that is, behaviors designated for alteration—selected? How can a functional analysis be performed during adult assessment? What behavioral-assessment techniques are suitable for work with adults? How are assessment and treatment related? Can research be performed in typical adult treat-

Rosemery O. Nelson. Department of Psychology, The University of North Carolina at Greensboro, Greensboro, North Carolina.
David H. Barlow. Department of Psychology, State University of New York at Albany, Albany, New York.

ment settings? How does the clinician know that an interview is effective?

In attempting to answer these questions, this overview of behavioral assessment with adult clients adopts three basic strategies. The first strategy is the use of the SORC model. SORC is Goldfried and Sprafkin's acronym (1976) which summarizes the critical content of behavioral assessment: the target behaviors or responses (R) to be altered, and the organismic (O) and environmental (S-C) controlling variables. Organismic variables are individual differences that the client brings to the assessment situation. These individual differences are the result of inter- and intrasubject psychological variability and of past learning history. Current environmental variables can be conceptualized as those stimuli (S) present in the problematic situation and those positive and negative consequences (C) causing the target behaviors to be both maintained and troublesome. SORC is a convenient summary of the content of behavioral assessment. In other words, SORC summarizes what the behavioral assessor needs to learn about the client and his or her problems.

A second basic strategy is procedural. The procedure of behavioral assessment can be conceptualized as a funnel (see Hawkins, 1979). Initially, a broad range of information is gathered about the client. The client's functioning in many life areas is considered until suitable target behaviors are selected. Eventually, the assessment funnel narrows and more specific information is sought; specifically, the variables controlling the target behaviors are determined, a treatment is selected, and changes in the target behaviors produced by this treatment are evaluated. In Peterson's words (1968), this funnel strategy begins with the "scanning operation" and is followed by an extended inquiry, periodic reappraisal, and follow-up.

A third basic strategy is the adoption of the distinction between nomothetic conclusions and idiographic applications. Nomothetic conclusions are those generalizations which apply to many people. Idiographic applications individualize these conclusions so that they are unique to a specific person. Nomothetic conclusions, useful for this chapter, include the following: clients have problematic responses that are controlled by organismic and environmental variables (a nomothetic conclusion summarized by the acronym SORC); typical or frequent response covariations are summarized by diagnostic categories; research in abnormal psychology has identified typical or frequently recurring controlling variables for certain problematic responses; and clinical research has identified treatment strategies that are frequently successful with particular problematic responses. These nomothetic conclusions are useful because they summarize a wealth of clinical and research information, because they can prompt and guide a clinician's behavior, and because they can facilitate communication among clinicians. While nomothetic conclusions provide suggestions about a specific client, a successful assessment and treatment require an idiographic application of these conclusions. Nomothetic conclusions suggest response covariations, controlling variables, and treatment strategies, but these conclusions must be individualized or applied idiographically to determine what particular responses covary in a specific client, what are the particular controlling variables for these particular responses, and what is the best treatment strategy to use in this particular situation.

Armed with these three basic strategies, the SORC model, the funnel procedure, and the idiographic–nomothetic distinction, the behavioral assessor may undertake the goals of behavioral assessment. These goals are identification and classification of the target behaviors or problem, determination of the organismic and environmental controlling variables, design of a treatment program, and evaluation of the success of this treatment program.

Identification of Target Behaviors

THE BEHAVIORAL INTERVIEW

The initial contact with the adult client in most settings consists of a series of interviews. During these interviews, the target behaviors are identified, the controlling variables are determined, and an intervention program is planned. More detailed information about the structure and content of the interview from a behavioral perspective is given by Haynes (1978), Linehan (1977), Meyer, Liddell, and Lyons (1977), and Morganstern (1976). The immediate focus is to describe how the interview is used to select the target behavior, using both the content of the clients' verbalizations and other behavior which the client exhibits in the interview setting.

CONTENT OF CLIENT'S VERBALIZATION

The client is first asked to describe his or her presenting complaints, prompted by interview questions such as "What seems to be

the problem?" or "What made you decide to come to the mental
health center?" A common assessment error is to select as the major
target behavior the first identifiable problem, especially one for
which an intervention is readily available. A frequently cited example
of this potential error is Lazarus's case (1971) of a client who reported
a bridge phobia. The client was indeed reluctant to cross the bridge,
but only because of what lay on the other side: his job and his fear of
self and maternal criticism. Selecting the bridge phobia as the target
behavior would have resulted in failure.

To prevent this common error of prematurely selecting a target
behavior, it seems best to rely on the funnel strategy described above.
A wide range of life areas should first be discussed with the client.
Even though many of these areas may turn out to be nonproblematic,
broad assessment is nonetheless a wise investment because identification of all problematic areas is crucial to assessment and successful intervention. In performing this broad assessment, the interviewer may
find structured interview guidelines to be useful, such as those developed by Kanfer and Saslow (1969), by Wolpe (1969), and by Lazarus (1973). Another structured interview developed by Angle, Ellinwood, Hay, Johnsen, and Hay (1977) contains questions about 26 life
areas; for example, employment, primary relations, sleep, tension,
and self-management. To save the assessor's time, this last interview is
available in a computerized format; that is, the questions are presented on a video terminal and the client responds by pressing type-
writerlike keys.

After a wide range of potentially problematic areas have been
surveyed, the funnel begins to narrow to more specific target behaviors. The typical client has been described by Mischel (1968) as a
trait theorist. Hence, the task of the assessor is to persuade the client
to describe vague, general complaints ("It's my nerves," or "Nothing's
right anymore") in more concrete behavioral terms ("my heart races
and I feel like I can't breathe"; or "I'm always telling myself that I'm
a failure"). Interviewing strategies to pinpoint behaviors include
questions such as, "Can you give me an example?" or "Different people mean different things when they say they are depressed; what is it
like when you are depressed?" When the client persists in being
vague, other useful questions are: "Tell me what a typical day for you
is like; let's start with getting up," or "What happened to cause you to
telephone for this appointment?"

In addition to encouraging a specific description, the assessor should keep in mind the "triple response mode." Most behaviorists now regard all organismic activity as behavior, including overt motor behavior, physiological–emotional behavior, and cognitive–verbal behavior. Because these three response systems do not necessarily covary (Lang, 1968), it is important to assess the client's problems in all three response systems. This assessment can occur in the interview situation by asking the client to report what he or she *does* in the criterion situation ("If others were watching you, what would they see?"), how he or she *feels* in the criterion situation ("How does your body react?"), and what he or she is *thinking* in the criterion situation ("If there were a little man inside your head, what would he hear you say to yourself?").

To help ensure that the client will specify target behaviors in all three response systems, the assessor may utilize structured interview guides. These guides differ from the structured interviews noted above in that they assess only a specific problem area, whereas the more general interview guides assess a wide range of life areas. Examples of these more specific structured guides include Stuart's guide for marital problems (1969) or Haynes, Griffin, Mooney, and Parise's guide for psychophysiological problems (1975).

MENTAL-STATUS EXAMINATION

While the content of the client's verbalizations is certainly important in helping to determine the target behavior, so are other client behaviors exhibited during the interview situation. When the assessor observes and categorizes the variety of behaviors emitted by the client, he or she is performing a mental-status examination.

Those not familiar with the formal mental-status exam might assume that it is a structured "test" of some sort, with adequate psychometric properties designed to answer specific questions such as degree and scope of thought disorder or organicity. But it is far from that. The essentials of the mental-status exam are ongoing in almost every interpersonal encounter, as when one observes, "He looks really down today," or "His clothes are about ten years out of date," or "He talks very fast." For the mental status is not a formal test, but rather the observation of overt behavior which occurs when any one person interacts with another. Therefore, all of us, clinician and nonclinician alike, are continually performing mental-status exams in the course of our daily lives. A well-performed mental-status exam, how-

ever, can contribute in a major way to the pinpointing of relevant target behaviors and problems which become appropriate candidates for
later intervention.

Much has been written about the mental-status exam, including
outlines for categorizing these behavioral observations (Noyes & Kolb,
1963; Slater & Roth, 1969; Freedman, Kaplan, & Sadock, 1975).

To illustrate this process, abbreviated transcripts from two clients recently seen in one of our offices (DHB) are presented.

The first client was a 24-year-old male, neatly dressed in working
clothes, who was referred for evaluation and possible treatment of a
variety of fears and anxiety centering around his marriage.

CLINICIAN: What sort of problems have been troubling you during the past month?
CLIENT: I'm beginning to have a lot of marital problems. I was
married about six months ago, but I've been really tense around
the house and we've been having a lot of arguments.
CLINICIAN: Is this something recent?
CLIENT: Well, it wasn't too bad at first, but it's been worse lately. I've also been really uptight on my job, and I haven't been getting my work done.

Further questioning revealed the client worked in an auto-body re-
pair shop and that he had married a very young (17-year-old) woman
over the objections of both parents. During the intial 10 minutes of
the interview the client seemed generally tense and anxious and
talked while looking down at the floor, making little eye contact. After approximately the first five minutes, the client began closing his
eyes for periods of approximately two to three seconds, and this was
always accompanied by a slight contraction or "twitching" of his right
leg.

CLINICIAN: When you feel uptight at work, is it the same kind of
feeling that you have at home?
CLIENT: Pretty much. I just can't seem to concentrate, and lots
of times I lose track of what my wife's saying to me, which makes
her mad and then we'll have a big fight.
CLINICIAN: Are you thinking about something else when you lose
your concentration?
CLIENT: Oh, I don't know. I guess I just worry a lot.
CLINICIAN: What do you find yourself worrying about most of
the time?
CLIENT: Well, I worry about getting fired and then not being

able to support my family. A lot of the time I feel like I'm going to catch something. You know, get sick and not be able to work. Basically I guess I'm afraid of getting sick and then failing at my job and in my marriage, and having my parents and her parents both telling me what an ass I was for getting married in the first place.

Further exploration of marital and job situations and fears of inadequacy continued to be accompanied by occasional closing of the eyes and leg twitches.

CLINICIAN: Are you aware that once in a while you're closing your eyes while you're telling me this?

CLIENT: Not all the time, but I know I do it.

CLINICIAN: Do you know how long you've been doing that?

CLIENT: Oh, I don't know, maybe a year or two.

CLINICIAN: Are you thinking about anything when you close your eyes?

CLIENT: Well, actually I'm trying *not* to think about something.

CLINICIAN: What do you mean?

CLIENT: Well, I have these really frightening and stupid thoughts, and. . . . It's hard to even talk about it.

CLINICIAN: The thoughts are frightening?

CLIENT: Yes. I keep thinking I'm going to take a fit, and I'm just trying to get that out of my mind.

CLINICIAN: Could you tell me more about this fit.

CLIENT: Well, you know, it's those terrible things where people fall down and they froth at the mouth, and their tongues come out, and they shake all over. You know, seizures. I think they call it epilepsy.

CLINICIAN: And you're trying to get these thoughts out of your mind?

CLIENT: Oh, I do everything possible to get those thoughts out of my mind as quickly as I can.

CLINICIAN: I've noticed you moving your leg when you close your eyes. Is that part of it?

CLIENT: Yes. I've noticed if I really jerk my leg and pray real hard for a little while the thought will go away.

This greatly abbreviated transcript provides an example of observations from a mental-status exam; in this case observations of gross motor behavior during an interview, leading the clinician in a somewhat different direction than was indicated by the content of the interview itself. Further exploration revealed a well-developed obsessional thought process consisting of intrusive thoughts of seizures which were triggered by a number of antecedent stimuli such as seeing the letter "E" for epilepsy, hearing certain specific letters or words on the car radio, as well as a variety of other antecedents at home and at work. Fears of inadequacy and failure and lack of concentration accompanied by vague reports of fears of illness were, in fact, secondary to this massive obsessional process which was causing difficulty at work and at home. Nevertheless, this had not come out in previous therapy, which had concentrated on problems surrounding the client's recent marriage — and the occurrence of a simple motor behavior during the interview provided the clue. Obviously, in the context of a good relationship, this material might have been volunteered eventually, but owing to extreme fears of discussing this material, which in itself served as an antecedent, and owing to a variety of misconceptions about seizures, the patient had not volunteered this information up until this time.

The second case involved a 20-year-old male, recently released from the Army, who was referred from a psychiatrist in another state for evaluation of sexual problems.

CLINICIAN: What seems to be the problem?
CLIENT: I'm a homosexual.
CLINICIAN: You're a homosexual?
CLIENT: Yes, and I want to be straight. Who wants to be queer?
CLINICIAN: Do you have any homosexual friends or lovers?
CLIENT: No, I wouldn't get near them.
CLINICIAN: How often do you engage in homosexual behavior?
CLIENT: Well, I haven't as of yet, but it's no secret that I'm homosexual and it's just a matter of time before it happens, I suppose.
CLINICIAN: Do you have somebody specifically in mind? Are you attracted to somebody?
CLIENT: No, but others are attracted to me. I can tell by the way they look at me.
CLINICIAN: The way they look at you?
CLIENT: Yes, the look in their eyes.
CLINICIAN: Has anyone ever actually approached you or said anything to you about being homosexual?
CLIENT: No, not to me; they wouldn't dare. But I know they talk about me behind my back.
CLINICIAN: How do you know that?

CLIENT: Well, sometimes the guys will be talking in the next room and the only thing they could be talking about is that I'm queer.

Although further evaluation revealed no evidence of homosexual arousal patterns, fantasies, or behavior, and a rather well-developed and reasonably strong pattern of heterosexual arousal, the client's thought processes, as illustrated in the abbreviated transcript above, revealed clear ideas of reference. These ideas of reference were strong and pervasive in that most events or activities ongoing in the client's environment were interpreted as referring to his homosexuality. This pattern of verbalization (or thinking) was clearly at odds with reports of behavior relative to homosexuality and came to constitute the major target for intervention. Examination of thought processes, including rate of speech, continuity of thought, and finally patterns of thought, often involving ideas of reference or delusions, as in this case, constitute a major part of the mental-status exam categorized under the rather broad heading of thought disorders. Once again, then, the mental-status exam led to further evaluation of a behavioral problem quite different from the problem as initially stated by the client (see Chapter 4).

These case examples each provide, in their own way, instances of the use of the mental-status exam and how these behavioral observations interact with direct reports from the client during the initial interview. Mental-status exams have been outlined in great detail in some books, as noted above (e.g., Freedman *et al.*, 1975; Slater & Roth, 1969; Noyes & Kolb, 1963), but a standardized extension of the mental-status exam, complete with reliability data and sample questions, called the Present State Exam, has been published by Wing, Cooper, and Sartorius (1974). Many of these sources go into much greater detail than would be useful here. But the brief outline presented below, with some sample questions from Wing *et al.* (1974), covers the essentials of an outline for categorizing behavioral observations during the initial interview.

Typically, the mental-status exam is divided into five major parts:

1. appearance and behavior
2. thought processes
3. mood and affect
4. intellectual functioning
5. sensorium

Appearance and Behavior. Any overt motor behaviors, such as those observed in the first case, are included under this topic. Also included are the client's dress, physical appearance, gait, posture, and facial expression. Slow and effortful motor behavior, sometimes referred to as psychomotor retardation, may indicate severe depression (see Chapter 5).

Thought Processes. Observation of thought processes is, of course, made through the patient's speech. While different models for mental status examinations propose several different ways of categorizing observations of thought processes, the overriding principle, once again, is that one is observing the patterns or form of verbalizations rather than concentrating on the particular problems the client may be offering. The most obvious example is the case of delusions. If the client blurts out that the FBI is after him or her and continues with a similar pattern of statements, the target for a fuller assessment is obviously not the client's ability to deal with FBI interrogations, but rather the strength and persistence of delusional statements.

In our opinion, thought processes can be most conveniently and productively categorized in three ways: (1) Production of speech: the rate or flow of speech is the most important observation here. Is speech pressured (overly fast or retarded)? (2) Continuity: does the client's speech proceed in an orderly process toward a goal? Looseness of associations is the best-known example of disturbances of continuity, but other relevant patterns worthy of observation and categorization include perseveration, the presence of clang associations, neologisms, or persistent blocking. If there is some question about continuity or rate of speech, Wing *et al.* (1974) suggest the following standard questions: "Can you think clearly or is there any interference with your thoughts? Do your thoughts tend to be muddled or slow?" Preliminary observations, along with answers to these questions, should assist the clinician in deciding whether or not to pursue further assessment. (3) This category, once again, does not necessarily refer to target behaviors volunteered by the client, but rather to reoccurring patterns of content, such as delusions, hallucinations, or illusions. Ideas of reference and ideas of influence may be observed, as well as depersonalization or derealization. Observation of any of these patterns may lead to further assessment of psychotic thought processes (see Chapter 4). On the other hand, perceptual disturbances, which also fall into this category, including hallucinations and illusions, particularly visual and tactile hallucinations (for example, insects crawling on skin), may contribute to a decision to further assess possible organicity (see Chapter 3). Wing *et al.* (1974) suggest a series of questions to enable further observation of these disorders, and a sampling will be presented here with follow-up questions in parentheses. Two questions which tap depersonalization or derealization are: "Have you had the feeling recently that things around you were unreal (as though everything was an imitation of reality, like a stage set with people acting instead of being themselves)?" "Have you yourself felt unreal, as though you were not a person, not in the living world?" A standard question to uncover possible hallucinations, variations of which are used by most clinicians in almost every initial interview, is the following: "I should like to ask you a routine question which we ask of everybody. Do you ever seem to hear noises or voices when there is no one about and nothing else to explain it? Is that true of visions or other unusual experiences which some people have (touch, taste, pain, smell, temperature, etc.)?" A standard question to elicit possible delusional thought processes would be the following: "Can you think quite clearly, or is there any interference with your thoughts? (Are you in full control of your thoughts?) (Can people read your mind?) (Is anything like hypnotism or telepathy going on?)" This, of course, may be followed by a series of more specific questions tapping delusions of control, reference, persecution, and so on.

Mood and Affect. It was noted above that observation of mood occurs in almost every interpersonal context and forms a major category of the mental status exam during the initial interview. Does the client look "down in the dumps"? Do his or her verbalizations indicate a mood of depression or hopelessness? How pervasive is this mood? On the other hand, the client may display exaggerated elation. Affect refers to the appropriateness of the emotional expression to the content of verbalizations. Does the client report that his mother just died and laugh? Does she report that she just won the Irish Sweepstakes and cry? There might be good reasons for the affect connected to these statements which would be uncovered by further questions, but more likely the affect would be judged inappropriate. The most common observation is a flat affect whereby reports of critical and emotional life events are verbalized with no emotion whatsoever. Standard preliminary questions, as suggested by Wing *et al.* (1974) to determine depressive thoughts, include the following: "Do you keep reasonably cheerful or have you been very depressed or low-spirited lately? Have you cried at all? (When did you last really enjoy doing anything?) How do you see the future? (Has life seemed quite hope-less?) Have you felt that life wasn't worth living? (Did you ever feel like ending it all?)." This last question, of course, should be asked routinely in any initial interview.

Preliminary signs of elation can be followed up with these standard questions: "Have you sometimes felt particularly cheerful and on top of the world without any particular reason? Have you felt particularly full of energy lately or full of exciting ideas? (Do things seem to go too slowly for you?) (Do you need less sleep than usual?) Do you find yourself extremely active, but not getting tired? Have you developed new interests lately?" Positive indications in any of these areas should lead to further assessment of possible affective disorders (see Chapter 5).

Intellectual Functioning. Clinicians typically make some rough estimates of the client's intelligence. This includes the ability to abstract in the presence or absence of memory deficits.

Sensorium. This last section of the mental-status exam is a particularly important precursor to possible further evaluation of organically based disorders and refers to the client's general awareness of his or her surroundings. The standard questions here include such items as "What is the date? What year is this? Where are you?" A "clear sensorium" is the cryptic notation frequently seen in case records indicating that the client is oriented × 3, which refers to person, place, and situation.

NON-INTERVIEW TECHNIQUES TO SELECT TARGET BEHAVIORS

Based on behavioral interviewing including both the content of the client's verbalizations and other client behaviors exhibited during the interview (the mental-status exam), the assessor makes a preliminary determination of the target behaviors. Other assessment techniques may also be used to help specify the target behaviors in each of the three response systems. One of these techniques is the use of questionnaires in which the client reports his or her behaviors, thoughts, or feelings. Examples of these questionnaires are the Sexual Interaction Inventory (LoPiccolo & Steger, 1974) used in the assessment of sexual dysfunctions and a series of questionnaires designed by Cautela (Cautela & Upper, 1976), such as the Alcohol Questionnaire, Drug Questionnaire, and Eating Habits Questionnaire. Reviews of such questionnaires have been provided by Bellack and Hersen (1977), Haynes (1978), and Tasto (1977).

Another useful assessment technique is self-monitoring, in which the client observes and records problematic behaviors as they occur in his or her own environment (Kazdin, 1974; McFall, 1977b; Nelson, 1977). Self-monitoring can be used to help select the target behavior; for example, when the client feels "bad" or "nervous," he or she can write or record on a tape recorder a description of the exact feelings, thoughts, and actions occurring at the time (as well as environmental circumstances surrounding these responses). The client can also rate the intensity of his or her responses by using a rating scale or a behavioral "thermometer." Self-monitoring has the advantages not only of being convenient and concurrent with events as they are occurring, but also of providing information on responses to which only the client has access; for example, paranoid ideation or headaches.

Another useful assessment technique is role-playing, or asking the client to respond as he or she usually would but within a contrived situation in the clinic (McFall, 1977a; Nay, 1977). Generally, the therapist or other clinic staff serve as role-playing partners. Contrived situations are frequently used to assess interpersonal skills; for example, those of lonely people attempting to increase their social interactions; of people in need of assertion training; or of people with difficult marriages. Contrived situations are also sometimes used to assess fear or anxiety. In some cases, the feared object can actually be presented, as in Lang and Lazovik's Behavioral Avoidance Test for small-animal fears (1963) or in Paul's test (1966), in which clients with public-speaking anxiety were asked to give a speech before a small audience. In other cases, the feared object can be presented by means of slides (Burchardt & Levis, 1977).

Other assessment techniques which are less frequently employed but may nonetheless be useful include the following: With the client's consent, persons who are familiar with the client may be interviewed. This strategy may be useful when the client is paranoid (and hence is not reporting events as others see them), is depressed (and hence may have a low rate of verbal behavior), is schizophrenic (and hence may not be able to communicate in the usual fashion), or is experiencing sexual or marital difficulties (and hence the partner's reports would be important). Psychophysiological recordings may be useful in specifying and measuring physiological–emotional responses; for example, with sexual disorders, with psychophysiological problems such as headache, or with anxiety responses (Epstein, 1976; Geer, 1977; Kallman & Feuerstein, 1977; Lang, 1977). IQ testing may occasionally be useful, as exemplified in two cases treated by one of our (R.N.'s) interns. In one case, the female client was diagnosed as having an "inadequate personality" because she was unemployed and engaged in only simple tasks with members of her own household. An IQ test revealed that she was moderately retarded. The target behavior changed from the client's activities to her relatives' expectations. In another case, an attempt was made to teach an obese female some basic facts about nutrition and Stuart and Davis's weight-control program (1972). Her "lack of cooperation" was reinterpreted when an IQ test revealed moderate retardation. She became very cooperative when the weight-control program was limited to self-monitoring the intake of bread, the client's favorite food, a task she could readily handle.

THE ROLE OF DIAGNOSIS AND RESPONSE COVARIATION

Thus far in this discussion on selecting target behaviors, the implication might be that each client presents unique target behaviors. Returning to the nomothetic–idiographic distinction made earlier, in one sense this uniqueness is valid, and in another sense, it is not. Problematic behaviors do tend to covary in systematic ways. For example, the usual signs of depression are: (1) feelings of hopelessness and worthlessness; (2) suicidal thoughts or attempts; (3) loss of interest in life; (4) self-reproach or guilt; (5) physiological signs, such as anorexia, weight loss, sleep pattern disturbances, impotence, constipation, and anergia; and (6) motoric signs, such as depressed face, slow speech, and psychomotor retardation (Barlow, 1977b, p. 298). This list does not mean that *each* depressed client will show *all* of these behaviors or show them in precisely the *same* way; hence the need for idiographic assessment. But this list does mean that responses like these do indeed tend to covary; hence the nomothetic label of depression (see Chapter 5). Other common patterns of response covariations are given other diagnostic labels and are described in detail in abnormal psychology textbooks and in DSM-III (*Diagnostic and Statistical Manual of Mental Disorders*, 3rd edition, American Psychiatric Association, 1980).

Given that such response covariations exist, why is it important for behavioral assessors to know about them and to label them, especially in terms of traditional diagnostic categories? There are two main reasons for our advocation of their use. The first is that behavioral assessors live in a larger world in which we are badly outnumbered. Thus, in order to communicate with others, it is important to share their terminology. Such communication is important in describing our clients in journal articles or in professional referrals, in classifying clients for insurance or accountability purposes, and in grant proposals. The second reason is that as scientists we may find useful the findings of abnormal psychology as well as the findings of behavior therapy. Nomothetic response covariations do seem to describe the clinical reality of clients. Thus, when a client begins to describe or to show some of the behaviors characteristic of a depressive episode, for example, he or she is sufficiently likely to show other related characteristics worthwhile. In addition to suggesting further target behaviors, diagnoses are useful in suggesting categories of controlling variables. It is well known that various abnormal behaviors are more or less subject to organismic as opposed to environmental control. For example, when a client exhibits schizophrenic behaviors, certain types of controlling variables are suggested. Assessment would contain questions about familial history of schizophrenia or of institutionalization, age when the schizophrenic behaviors first occurred, and a description of the client's behavior prior to the occurrence of the schizophrenic behaviors (see Chapter 4). In another example, depressive behaviors may suggest both environmental variables (e.g., sudden environmental changes, loss of reinforcers) and organismic variables (e.g., familial history of manic–depressive psychosis or an inadequate repertoire of social skills to obtain or maintain sufficient reinforcers; (see Chapter 12). In yet another example, anxiety responses may suggest both environmental-controlling variables (e.g., antecedent stimuli in whose presence anxiety increases, positive consequent stimuli encouraging anxiety responses, negative consequent stimuli which make the anxiety problematic) and organismic-controlling variables (e.g., the client's history of anxiety responses and the client's overall or "state" level of nervousness). Therefore, diagnoses are useful in suggesting responses that covary and typical controlling variables. Diagnoses are also useful in suggesting treatments that have been found to be effective with similar problems. For example, schizophrenics generally respond to a drug regime consisting of phenothiazines and to social skills training. In another example, phobics generally respond to modeling or exposure treatments. In yet another example, a depressed client may respond to antidepressant medication, to modification of irrational cognitions, to social skills training, and to a structured program of increasing pleasant activities. Again, it must be stressed that diagnoses provide only *nomothetic suggestions* about response covariation, controlling variables, and effective treatments. An idiographic assessment must also be performed to determine the behaviors, controlling variables, and probable treatment for this particular client.

Our preference for DSM-III as opposed to an idiosyncratic behavioral classification schema is readily apparent, although several such schemata have been proposed (Adams, Doster, & Calhoun, 1977; Cautela & Upper, 1975; Dengrove, 1972; Ferster, 1967; Suinn, 1970). Our reasons are twofold and have been mentioned briefly in Chapter 1. First, as noted earlier, the use of DSM-III permits communication with a much larger scientific community. Second, DSM-III seems to be a vast improvement over DSM-II in that the former is largely atheoretical and demonstrates good reliability (see the reliability figures for the Research Diagnostic Criteria, upon which DSM-III was partially based, reported by Spitzer, Endicott, & Robins, 1978).

To determine an appropriate diagnostic level, the clinician must consider several factors. First, the assessor must have a broad knowledge of abnormal psychology to know which responses typically covary (e.g., in depression, these responses typically covary: loss of interest or pleasure, sleep disturbance, appetite disturbance, change in weight, psychomotor retardation or agitation, cognitive disturbance, decreased energy, a feeling of worthlessness or guilt, and thoughts of death or suicide). Second, the clinician must conduct a careful assessment to determine which of these responses are occurring in a particular client. Finally, the assessor must be familiar with the diagnostic criteria of DSM-III (e.g., the above response covariation would be labeled "major depressive disorder"). Generally, use of these factors has been summarized under the rubric of "clinical judgment." Attempts have been made, however, to formalize the decision-making process used in reaching a diagnosis. Endicott and Spitzer (1978) developed a standardized interview called the Schedule for Affective Disorders and Schizophrenia (SADS) to interface with the Research Diagnostic Criteria, mentioned above as a partial basis for DSM-III. For DSM-II, Nathan (1967) elaborated decision-making rules which the clinician could follow in reaching a diagnosis. In addition, computer programs have been written to produce a diagnosis based on input information. Information based on the Current and Past Psychopathology Scales (CAPPS) (Endicott & Spitzer, 1972) was utilized by a computer program called DIAGNO II (Spitzer & Endicott, 1969) to produce a DSM-II diagnosis. Similarly, information based on the Present State Examination (PSE) (Wing, Birley, Cooper, Graham, & Isaacs, 1967) was utilized by a computer program called CATEGO (Wing, et al., 1974) to result in a diagnosis. Most clinicians, however, do not use such formalized procedures, computerized or not, but instead rely on "clinical judgment" to determine an appropriate diagnostic label. Nonetheless, the resultant diagnosis may provide useful nomothetic suggestions of response covariations, controlling variables, and intervention strategies.

SELECTING AMONG ALTERNATIVE TARGET BEHAVIORS

The specific target behaviors that are selected involve a value judgment by both the therapist and client (Myerson & Hayes, 1978). A large number of philosophical and empirical guidelines have been proposed, however, to influence this value judgment as previously summarized by Nelson and Hayes (1979). Among the philosophical guidelines are: (1) behavior should be altered if it is dangerous to the client or to others in the environment; (2) target behaviors should be selected which maximize the client's reinforcers (Krasner, 1969); (3) increasing the frequency of desirable behaviors should be selected as a goal rather than making undesirable behaviors decrease (Goldiamond, 1974; McFall, 1976); and (4) target behaviors should maximize the flexibility of the client's repertoire to achieve long-term individual and social benefits (Myerson & Hayes, 1978). Among the empirical guidelines are: (1) the collection of normative data (Kazdin, 1977; Nelson & Bowles, 1975); (2) the use of task analysis and of developmental norms (Hawkins, 1975); (3) subjective ratings by community volunteers regarding which behaviors and rates thereof are important (Wolf, 1978); (4) regression equations to determine which specific behaviors best predict the important criterion behaviors (e.g., Cobb, 1972); and (5) the known groups method (McFall, 1976), by which specific behaviors are identified that differentiate two established groups.

If several socially desirable target behaviors have been identified, a remaining question is where intervention should begin. As previously summarized by Nelson and Hayes (1979), several guidelines have

been offered: (1) alter the most irritating behavior first (Tharp &
Wetzel, 1969); (2) alter first a behavior that is relatively easy to
change (O'Leary, 1972); (3) alter behaviors that will produce thera-
peutically beneficial response generalization (e.g., Hay, Hay, &
Nelson, 1977); and (4) when responses exist as part of a longer chain,
alter first the responses at the beginning of the chain (Angle, Hay,
Hay, & Ellinwood, 1977).

Identification of Controlling Variables

The first step in a behavioral assessment is to identify the target behaviors. The second step is to identify the variables that control the
occurrence of those behaviors. Generally, two classes of controlling
variables are considered. Current environmental variables include
antecedent and consequent stimuli, the S and C in Goldfried and
Sprafkin's SORC model (1976). Organismic variables, the O, include
individual differences produced by physiology and by past learning.
In other words, the organismic variables are those characteristics that
the client brings to the problematic situation which can be described
in terms of their antecedent and consequent stimuli.

The reasons for identifying the controlling variables of the target
behaviors are twofold. First, in what might be termed "conceptual
validity" (Nelson & Hayes, 1979), determination of the controlling
variables enhances our understanding of abnormal psychology. As
scientists, the findings from each individual case can confirm or
heuristically disconfirm the nomothetic principles currently held as
valid. Bijou, Peterson, and Ault (1968) distinguish two kinds of
research: descriptive and experimental. Descriptive research presents
a static or structural phenomenon; for example, identification of
responses that covary. Experimental research determines *why* these
phenomena occur; for example, identification of the controlling variables that determine the response covariation. A complete understanding of clinical phenomena requires both descriptive and experimental findings.

In addition to enhancing our understanding of abnormal behavior, identification of controlling variables is generally thought to be
crucial in the design of successful intervention programs. For example, before an anxious client is subjected to systematic desensitization,
the antecedent stimuli producing anxious responses must be iden-

tified and included in the imaginal hierarchy. As another example, if depressed responses are being maintained by social attention (positive consequent stimuli), then the persons providing that attention must be identified so that their behavior can be altered as part of the intervention package. While it may be true that identification of controlling variables enhances treatment success, it has not been *demonstrated* that such identification is required in each case (Haynes, 1979; O'Leary, 1972). In other words, the "treatment validity" of the functional analysis has not been experimentally verified (Nelson & Hayes, 1979). It may be feasible, for example, to implement a package treatment for each depressed client, rather than spending the hours required to perform an individualized assessment and to design an individualized treatment. In the meantime, however, it is assumed that a functional analysis—that is, identification of the variables of which this response is a function—is crucial to successful intervention. It is further assumed that if the controlling variables are not altered, then the problematic response cannot change.

ORGANISMIC VARIABLES

Organismic variables are the individual differences produced by inter- or intrasubject alterations in physiology and by past learning history. Behavioral assessment focuses on those organismic variables which enhance our understanding of the occurrence of the target behaviors and our ability to alter those behaviors. The particular organismic variables to assess in each individual case are frequently suggested by the nature of the target behavior, or, as noted above, by the resultant diagnosis assigned to the specific responses that covary.

Physiological variables are important in many types of abnormal behavior. Sometimes, identification of physiological variables is important for understanding the abnormal behavior, even though the physiological variables cannot be directly altered; for example, with some organic brain syndromes. At other times, identification of physiological variables not only improves our understanding of the target behavior but also suggests particular treatment. With schizophrenia, for example, which is believed to have a genetic basis, the current treatment of choice is phenothiazine maintenance coupled with behavioral training, perhaps for self-help or social skills. With some disorders, physiological controlling variables may be directly altered. Some cases of sexual dysfunction, for example, may be related to a gynecological disorder or to a partner's unkempt bodily state, both of which could be directly treated. As another example, a deficit in social interaction might be related to obesity or to other aspects of a culturally devalued appearance which could itself become the focus of intervention.

Physiological controlling variables may be assessed in several ways. During assessment interviews, the client may verbally reveal these variables; for example, by describing a recurrent cyclical pattern of depressive episodes seemingly unrelated to environmental events, characteristic perhaps of manic–depressive personality or psychosis. The client is also observed during the assessment interviews in the mental-status exam described above. During these interviews, certain aspects of physiology may be noted; for example, obesity or facial features or grimaces of pain. With the client's permission, information about physiological variables may be obtained by interviewing collaterals or through medical records. Physical examinations specific to the target behavior and to the hypothesized physiological controlling variables may also be suggested to the client; for example, a physical examination for hypoglycemia whose symptoms sometimes resemble anxiety responses.

Past learning history is generally assessed by interviewing the client or perhaps collaterals who know the client well, or by examination of past case records. Knowledge of the client's past learning history would certainly seem important in understanding the current target behaviors and may also be useful in the design of the intervention program. The duration of the problem may predict the probability of treatment success. A therapist can teach an old dog new tricks, but it's harder to do so because the old tricks have been rewarded many times. It is generally held that the probability of treatment success is greater for sexual deviants who have had some prior heterosexual success than for those who have not (Feldman & Mac-Culloch, 1965), possibly because only deviant arousal needs to be suppressed, as opposed to also teaching appropriate arousal and appropriate heterosocial skills (Barlow & Abel, 1976). Sometimes, knowledge of past learning history is very important in determining the current environmental maintaining variables. Wolpe's interviewing of a client (Wolpe, 1958) whose presenting problem was pervasive anxiety revealed an incident in his past in which he had been both sexually attracted to and repulsed by a woman with whom he had intercourse at night in a hotel room. Since the room lights were off, only the dark outlines of objects were visible. The pervasive anxiety was assessed to worsen around sexual stimuli and dark heavy objects. Thus information about the client's past revealed clues as to current antecedent stimuli. Information about the past may also help determine current maintaining consequent stimuli. For example, in some personality disorders, the client has a life-long history of reinforcement for performing a particular "role"; that is, the martyr role or the sick role. Chances are that there are rich social reinforcers for maintenance of this role, in addition perhaps to the presence of a limited repertoire with few alternative roles.

ENVIRONMENTAL VARIABLES

Current environmental variables include the stimuli that precede and follow the problematic response. Since behavior is situation-specific (Mischel, 1968), identification of these specific stimuli is generally believed to be important in both understanding and altering target behavior. The nature of the target behaviors frequently suggests categories of controlling variables to assess. For example, with an anxious client, assessment would focus on stimuli in whose presence anxiety increases, as well as on environmental consequences to anxiety reactions. As another example, with a depressed client, assessment would focus on recent changes in the environment or in the client which may have produced decreases in available reinforcers, as well as on the client's repertoire of self-verbalizations and of alternative reinforcer-obtaining behaviors. The nature of the target behavior may also suggest the *degree* of environmental control influencing the response. For example, it is generally assumed that there is less environmental control of psychotic behavior (schizophrenia, manic–depressive psychosis) than of neurotic behavior (anxiety reactions, depression).

In assessing consequent stimuli, two categories of consequences must be considered: the positive consequences that are maintaining the problematic responses and the negative consequences that make them problematic. In the terms of Mowrer's neurotic paradox (1950), abnormal behaviors may be both "self-perpetuating" (i.e., have positive consequences) and "self-defeating" (i.e., have negative consequences). Given the gradient of reinforcement, since the short-term positive consequences may be more powerful than long-term negative consequences, one function of intervention may be to cue the client to the long-term negative consequences.

Current antecedent and consequent stimuli may be assessed in several ways. During the interview, the client may be asked if there are any situations, time of day, places, or people which seem to make the presenting problem worse or better. The client may also be asked what happens after the problematic response occurs. Frequently, a client reports that the problem has been recurring for a number of months or years. Asking a question like "What made you seek help now?" is often helpful in pinpointing current environmental determinants of the problem. In addition to interviewing, other assessment techniques may also be useful in identifying antecedents and consequences. A diary format can be used during self-monitoring, in which the client indicates the events surrounding each instance of the target behavior (Nelson, 1977). A number of questionnaires have been developed whose primary function is to identify antecedent stimuli (e.g., the Fear Survey Schedule [Geer, 1965]; the College Self-Expression Scale [Galassi, DeLo, Galassi, & Bastien, 1974]) or to identify consequent stimuli (e.g., the Pleasant Events Schedule [Lewinsohn & Libet, 1972]; the Reinforcement Survey Schedule [Cautela & Kastenbaum, 1967]). During role-playing, the stimuli included in the scenario may be varied to determine controlling variables, particularly in the assessment of interpersonal problems (McFall, 1977b; Nay, 1977). The effects of various stimuli on physiological arousal can be determined by presenting these stimuli in contrived situations in the clinic. This procedure is particularly useful in the assessment of anxiety under the rubric of behavioral avoidance tests (e.g., Borkovec, Weerts, & Bernstein, 1977) and in the assessment of sexual disorders to assess deviant and appropriate arousal (e.g., Barlow, 1977a). The effects of various stimuli on physiological arousal can also be determined in the natural environment by means of radio telemetry.

Design of Intervention

The first two goals of behavioral assessment are to identify the target behavior and to determine its controlling variables. The third goal is to design an intervention program with a high probability of success. Selection of an intervention program is guided by the particular target behavior and the specific controlling variables that have previously been identified.

The nature of the target behavior provides nomothetic suggestions for treatment. Most successful treatment techniques are well known for their success *with particular disorders*. As noted earlier, schizophrenics generally respond to phenothiazines and to social skills training; phobics generally respond to modeling or exposure treatments; depressed persons may respond to tricyclic drugs, to modification of irrational cognitions, to social-skills training, and to a structured program of increasing pleasant activities. Identification of particular target responses within the disorder further narrows treatment options. For example, with a sexually deviant client, four subclasses of responses are examined: appropriate sexual arousal, deviant sexual arousal, heterosexual skills, and gender-appropriate behavior (Barlow, 1977a; see also Chapter 10); identification of the particular target responses for each client suggests different treatment strategies. Similarly, for the client with difficulties in social interactions, several alternative approaches are available: anxiety-reduction procedures, social skills training procedures, modification or irrational cognitions, practice dating, alteration of appearance, and discrimination training in selecting appropriate partners. Selection among these alternative approaches is guided by the specific responses identified in the client (Curran, 1977).

Identification of controlling variables also is influential in treatment selection. In the case of sexual deviancy noted above, for example, the stimuli controlling sexual arousal suggest different treatment approaches if the stimuli are judged to be appropriate or deviant (Barlow, 1977a). In a rare empirical demonstration of the interaction between treatment choice and controlling stimuli, Meichenbaum, Gilmore, and Fedoravicius (1971) showed that subjects who were generally anxious in interpersonal situations responded better to a cognitive therapy designed to modify irrational self-verbalizations, while subjects whose anxiety was limited to a public-speaking situation responded better to systematic desensitization. Choice of treatment is influenced by the very complex functional analyses performed with drug abusers by Angle *et al.* (1977). Following the identification of each client's problem areas through a computerized intake interview, these problem areas are summarized in the form of a diagram depicting the hypothesized functional relationship among the various problem areas. Intervention is begun at points likely to produce the greatest client benefit.

While nomothetic guidelines are available, there is a great need for research to explicate how these nomothetic guidelines may best be applied to the individual client (Lick & Katkin, 1976). Information is needed not only to determine which treatment has the best probability of success, but also on how best to present the treatment to the client. In the meantime, most behavioral assessors seem to move from the nomothetic to the idiographic level in treatment selection by means of trial-and-error implementation of alternative procedures, each of which has some undetermined probability of success.

Evaluation of Treatment Success

After the first three goals of behavioral assessment have been accomplished — that is, the target behavior has been selected, the controlling variables have been identified, and a treatment plan has been designed — the last assessment goal begins: evaluating the success of the implemented treatment. There are two critical elements to this evaluation: selection of an appropriate single subject design and selection of practical dependent measures.

The most commonly used evaluation in the clinical setting is the A-B design, where A stands for baseline and B stands for intervention. Repeated measurements taken during baseline and intervention permit an evaluation of *change* to occur. However, such case studies have no internal validity; that is, the *cause* of change cannot be attributed with any certainty to the intervention strategy because alternative explanations are not systematically eliminated. Despite the lack of causal demonstration, clinicians may be satisfied with empirical evidence that improvement has indeed occurred.

Several single-subject designs with internal validity are described by Hersen and Barlow (1976). Chief among these are the reversal or withdrawal design, represented by A-B-A-B, in which the intervention is systematically implemented and withdrawn. Because of ethical concerns in withdrawing an effective treatment and because of practical concerns in reversing the effects of some treatments, especially those producing new learning, a more popular single-subject design in clinical settings is the multiple-baseline design. In this design, the same treatment must be implemented but at different points in time with either different target behaviors (e.g., different irrational negative verbalizations in the depressed client) or with the same target behavior in different settings (e.g., headaches at home and at work). In both the reversal and multiple-baseline designs, internal validity is obtained by demonstrating that improvements occurred each time but only when the treatment was implemented. Improvements can then be attributed to the treatment with some certainty because it is unlikely that another efficacious event covaried each time with treatment implementation. A new single-subject design permits the effectiveness of two different intervention programs to be compared within a single client. In the alternating treatments design, two (or more) interventions are implemented during different blocks of time (Barlow & Hayes, 1979). The interventions must be assigned to blocks of time on a random basis. Consistent differences in effectiveness are then examined. Again, internal validity is present because it is unlikely that an extraneous efficacious factor covaried each time with treatment; rather, greater success is attributed to one of two treatments with a high degree of certainty.

A great variety of alternative dependent measures are available for use in the clinic setting. Therapist imagination can produce even more. One available dependent measure is self-monitored data (Nelson, 1977). The client may use a diary format in which significant events are entered into a notebook or onto a structured form, or the client may keep quantitative records of frequency, duration, or self-ratings. A depressed client, for example, could self-record the amount of exercise obtained, the number of chores completed, and the number of social outings undertaken. Another alternative dependent measure is having the client fill out at weekly or biweekly intervals the same self-report questionnaire, for example, the Beck Depression Inventory (see Bellack & Hersen, 1977). While these self-report questionnaires are standardized, self-reports to idiosyncratic items may be obtained by using a card-sort procedure in which stimulus items are written on index cards and are then rated or sorted at regular intervals. Another alternative dependent measure is direct observations of the client, either in the home by means of the client's cohabitants (e.g., sleep patterns in the insomniacal or depressed client) or in the clinic. In the clinic, the therapist can quantify particular behaviors that occur during the therapy session either by quantifying during the session itself or subsequently from audio or video tapes. For example, the number of ticlike movements in an anxious client could be counted either directly in the therapy session or subsequently from videotape. Relatedly, the same contrived setting could be presented regularly to the client, and repeated physiological or observational data taken (e.g., having a couple with marital difficul-

ties discuss a sensitive topic and then coding the communication patterns used). Videotapes of the client's motor and verbal responses
from both baseline and intervention sessions could be presented in a
random sequence to raters or observers to control for sequence effects
in the resultant data. Finally, indirect dependent measures can also
be used. These indirect measures include archival data, such as days
absent from work, and permanent product data, such as weight lost
or gained.

Summary and Conclusions

Three basic strategies were described as useful to behavioral assessment. First, the content of behavioral assessment is summarized by
the SORC acronym (Goldfried & Sprafkin, 1976): stimulus–organism–
response–consequence. Second, the procedure of behavioral assessment can be likened to a funnel, in which initially a broad range of
information, and then more and more specific information, is
gathered. Third, an assumption of behavioral assessment is that
nomothetic principles and findings are useful for idiographic application.

Within this context, the four goals of behavioral assessment were
presented. First, the target behavior is identified. The most frequently used technique in adult clinical settings is the interview. During the
interview, information is provided not only by the content of the
client's verbal behavior but also by the client's appearance and other
behavior in the interview setting (mental-status exam). Covariation in
the client's problematic responses can be usefully summarized by
means of a diagnostic label. Recognition of this utility is seen in the
organizational schema of the chapters of this book, which are differentiated by means of diagnostic labels. Diagnoses are useful in relating the client's behavior to the findings of abnormal psychology.
Diagnoses suggest typical controlling variables for the behavioral
assessor to investigate idiographically with the particular client, the
second goal of behavioral assessment. Identification of organismic
(physiology and past learning history) and current environmental
(antecedent and consequent) controlling variables contributes not only to our understanding of abnormal behavior but also to its ameliora-
tion. The nature of the target behavior and the identified controlling
variables suggest intervention strategies that are likely to be suc-

cessful. The third goal of behavioral assessment is to choose among these alternatives and to design an intervention program. The last goal is to evaluate the success of that intervention program, which requires the collection of dependent measures within a single-subject design. The remaining chapters of this book demonstrate how the goals of behavioral assessment can be accomplished with different problematic behaviors.

References

Adams, H. E., Doster, J. A., & Calhoun, K. S. A psychologically based system of response classification. In A. R. Ciminero, K. S. Calhoun, & H. E. Adams (Eds.), *Handbook of behavioral assessment*. New York: John Wiley & Sons, 1977.

Angle, H. V., Ellinwood, E. H., Hay, W. M., Johnsen, T., & Hay, L. R. Computer-aided interviewing in comprehensive behavioral assessment. *Behavior Therapy*, 1977, *8*, 747–754.

Angle, H. V., Hay, L. R., Hay, W. M., & Ellinwood, E. H. Computer-assisted behavioral assessment. In J. D. Cone & R. P. Hawkins (Eds.), *Behavioral assessment: New directions in clinical psychology*. New York: Brunner/Mazel, 1977.

Barlow, D. H. Assessment of sexual behavior. In A. R. Ciminero, K. S. Calhoun, & H. E. Adams (Eds.), *Handbook of behavioral assessment*. New York: John Wiley & Sons, 1977. (a)

Barlow, D. H. Behavioral assessment in clinical settings: Developing issues. In J. D. Cone & R. P. Hawkins (Eds.), *Behavioral assessment: New directions in clinical psychology*. New York: Brunner/Mazel, 1977. (b)

Barlow, D. H., & Abel, G. G. Sexual deviation. In W. E. Craighead, A. E. Kazdin, & M. J. Mahoney (Eds.), *Behavior modification: Principles, issues, and applications*. Boston: Houghton Mifflin, 1976.

Barlow, D. H., & Hayes, S. C. Alternating treatments design: One strategy for comparing the effects of two treatments in a single subject. *Journal of Applied Behavior Analysis*, 1979, *12*, 199–210.

Bellack, A. S., & Hersen, M. Self-report inventories in behavioral assessment. In J. D. Cone & R. P. Hawkins (Eds.), *Behavioral assessment: New directions in clinical psychology*. New York: Brunner/Mazel, 1977.

Bijou, S. W., Peterson, R. F., & Ault, M. H. A method to integrate descriptive and experimental studies at the level of data and empirical concepts. *Journal of Applied Behavior Analysis*, 1968, *1*, 175–191.

Borkovec, T. D., Weerts, T. C., & Bernstein, D. A. Assessment of anxiety. In A. R. Ciminero, K. S. Calhoun, & H. E. Adams (Eds.), *Handbook of behavioral assessment*. New York: John Wiley & Sons, 1977.

Burchardt, C. J., & Levis, D. J. The utility of presenting slides of phobic stimulus in the context of the behavioral avoidance procedure. *Behavior Therapy*, 1977, *8*, 340–346.

Cautela, J. R., & Kastenbaum, R. A. Reinforcement Survey Schedule for use in therapy, training, and research. *Psychological Reports*, 1967, *29*, 1115–1130.

Cautela, J. R., & Upper, D. The process of individual behavior therapy. In M. Hersen, R. M. Eisler, & P. M. Miller (Eds.), *Progress in behavior modification* (Vol. 1). New York: Academic Press, 1975.

Cautela, J. R., & Upper, D. The behavioral inventory battery: The use of self-report measures in behavioral analysis and therapy. In M. Hersen & A. S. Bellack (Eds.), *Behavioral assessment: A practical handbook.* New York: Pergamon Press, 1976.

Cobb, J. A. The relationship of discrete classroom behaviors to fourth-grade academic achievement. *Journal of Educational Psychology,* 1972, *63,* 74–80.

Curran, J. P. Skills training as an approach to the treatment of heterosexual-social anxiety: A review. *Psychological Bulletin,* 1977, *84,* 140–157.

Dengrove, E. Practical behavioral diagnosis. In A. A. Lazarus (Ed.), *Clinical behavior therapy.* New York: Brunner/Mazel, 1972.

Diagnostic and statistical manual of mental disorders (3rd ed.). Washington, D.C.: American Psychiatric Association, 1980.

Endicott, J., & Spitzer, R. L. Current and past psychopathology scales (CAPPS). *Archives of General Psychiatry,* 1972, *27,* 678–687.

Endicott, J., & Spitzer, R. L. A diagnostic interview: The Schedule for Affective Disorders and Schizophrenia. *Archives of General Psychiatry,* 1978, *35,* 837–844.

Epstein, L. H. Psychophysiological measurement in assessment. In M. Hersen & A. S. Bellack (Eds.), *Behavioral assessment: A practical handbook.* New York: Pergamon Press, 1976.

Feldman, M. P., & MacCulloch, M. J. The application of anticipatory avoidance learning to the treatment of homosexuality: I. Theory, technique, and preliminary results. *Behaviour Research and Therapy,* 1965, *3,* 165–183.

Ferster, C. B. Classification of behavioral pathology. In L. Krasner & L. P. Ullman (Eds.), *Research in behavior modification.* New York: Holt, Rinehart, & Winston, 1967.

Freedman, A. M., Kaplan, H. I., & Sadock, B. J. *Comprehensive textbook of psychiatry/II* (Vol. 1). Baltimore: Williams & Wilkins, 1975.

Galassi, J. P., DeLo, J. S., Galassi, M. D., & Bastien, S. The College Self-Expression Scale: A measure of assertiveness. *Behavior Therapy,* 1974, *5,* 165–171.

Geer, J. H. The development of a scale to measure fear. *Behaviour Research and Therapy,* 1965, *3,* 45–53.

Geer, J. H. Sexual functioning: Some data and speculations on psychophysiological assessment. In J. D. Cone & R. P. Hawkins (Eds.), *Behavioral assessment: New directions in clinical psychology.* New York: Brunner/Mazel, 1977.

Goldfried, M. R., & Sprafkin, J. N. Behavioral personality assessment. In J. T. Spence, R. C. Carson, & J. W. Thibaut (Eds.), *Behavioral approaches to therapy.* Morristown, NJ: General Learning Press, 1976.

Goldiamond, I. Toward a constructional approach to social problems: Ethical and constitutional issues raised by applied behavior analysis. *Behaviorism,* 1974, *2,* 1–85.

Hawkins, R. P. Who decided *that* he was the problem? Two stages of responsibility for applied behavior analysts. In W. S. Wood (Ed.), *Issues in evaluating behavior modification.* Champaign, IL: Research Press, 1975.

Hawkins, R. P. The functions of assessment: Implications for selection and development of devices for assessing repertoires in clinical, educational, and other settings. *Journal of Applied Behavior Analysis,* 1979, *12,* 501–516.

Hay, W. M., Hay, L. R., & Nelson, R. P. Direct and collateral changes in on-task and academic behavior resulting from on-task versus academic contingencies. *Behavior Therapy,* 1977, *8,* 431–441.

Haynes, S. N. *Principles of behavioral assessment.* New York: Gardner Press, 1978.

Haynes, S. N. Behavioral variance, individual differences, and trait theory in a behavioral construct system: A reappraisal. *Behavior Assessment,* 1979, *1,* 41–50.

Haynes, S. N., Griffin, P., Mooney, D., & Parise, M. Electromyographic biofeedback and relaxation instructions in the treatment of muscle contraction headaches. *Behavior Therapy*, 1975, *6*, 672-678.

Hersen, M., & Barlow, D. H. *Single case experimental designs: Strategies for studying behavior change*. New York: Pergamon Press, 1976.

Kallman, W. M., & Feuerstein, M. Psychophysiological procedures. In A. R. Ciminero, K. S. Calhoun, & H. E. Adams (Eds.), *Handbook of behavioral assessment*. New York: John Wiley & Sons, 1977.

Kanfer, F. H., & Saslow, G. Behavioral diagnosis. In C. M. Franks (Ed.), *Behavior therapy: Appraisal and status*. New York: McGraw-Hill, 1969.

Kazdin, A. E. Self-monitoring and behavior change. In M. J. Mahoney & C. E. Thoresen (Eds.), *Self-control: Power to the person*. Monterey, CA: Brooks/Cole, 1974.

Kazdin, A. E. Assessing the clinical or applied importance of behavior change through social validation. *Behavior Modification*, 1977, *1*, 427-452.

Krasner, L. Behavior modification—values and training: The perspective of a psychologist. In C. M. Franks (Ed.), *Behavior therapy: Appraisal and status*. New York: McGraw-Hill, 1969.

Lang, P. J. Physiological assessment of anxiety and fear. In J. D. Cone & R. P. Hawkins (Eds.), *Behavioral assessment: New directions in clinical psychology*. New York: Brunner/Mazel, 1977.

Lang, P. J., & Lazovik, A. D. Experimental desensitization of a phobia. *Journal of Abnormal and Social Psychology*, 1963, *66*, 519-525.

Lazarus, A. A. *Behavior therapy and beyond*. New York: McGraw-Hill, 1971.

Lazarus, A. A. Multimodal behavior therapy: Treating the "BASIC ID." *Journal of Nervous and Mental Disease*, 1973, *156*, 404-411.

Lewinsohn, P. M., & Libet, J. Pleasant events, activity schedules, and depression. *Journal of Abnormal Psychology*, 1972, *79*, 291-295.

Lick, J. R., & Katkin, E. S. Assessment of anxiety and fear. In M. Hersen & A. S. Bellack (Eds.), *Behavioral assessment: A practical handbook*. New York: Pergamon Press, 1976.

Linehan, M. M. Issues in behavioral interviewing. In J. D. Cone & R. P. Hawkins (Eds.), *Behavioral assessment: New directions in clinical psychology*. New York: Brunner/Mazel, 1977.

LoPiccolo, J., & Steger, J. C. The Sexual Interaction Inventory: A new instrument for assessment of sexual dysfunctions. *Archives of Sexual Behavior*, 1974, *3*, 585-595.

McFall, R. M. Behavioral training: A skill-acquisition approach to clinical problems. In J. T. Spence, R. C. Carson, & J. W. Thibaut (Eds.), *Behavioral approaches to therapy*. Morristown, NJ: General Learning Press, 1976.

McFall, R. M. Analogue methods in behavioral assessment: Issues and prospects. In J. D. Cone & R. P. Hawkins (Eds.), *Behavioral assessment: New directions in clinical psychology*. New York: Brunner/Mazel, 1977. (a)

McFall, R. M. Parameters of self-monitoring. In R. B. Stuart (Ed.), *Behavioral self-management: Strategies, techniques, and outcomes*. New York: Brunner/Mazel, 1977. (b)

Meichenbaum, D., Gilmore, J. B., & Fedoravicius, A. Group insight versus group desensitization in treating speech anxiety. *Journal of Consulting and Clinical Psychology*, 1971, *36*, 410-421.

Meyer, V., Liddell, A., & Lyons, M. Behavioral interviews. In A. R Ciminero, K. S. Calhoun, & H. E. Adams (Eds.), *Handbook of behavioral assessment*. New York: John Wiley & Sons, 1977.

Mischel, W. *Personality and assessment.* New York: John Wiley & Sons, 1968.

Morganstern, K. P. Behavioral interviewing: The initial stages of assessment. In M. Hersen & A. S. Bellack (Eds.), *Behavioral assessment: A practical handbook.* New York: Pergamon Press, 1976.

Mowrer, O. H. *Learning theory and personality dynamics.* New York: Ronald Press, 1950.

Myerson, W. A., & Hayes, S. C. Controlling the clinician for the client's benefit. In J. E. Krapfl & E. A. Vargas (Eds.), *Behaviorism and ethics.* Kalamazoo, MI: Behaviordelia, 1978.

Nathan, P. E. *Cues, decisions, diagnoses.* New York: Academic Press, 1967.

Nay, W. R. Analogue measures. In A. R. Ciminero, K. S. Calhoun, & H. E. Adams (Eds.), *Handbook of behavioral assessment.* New York: John Wiley & Sons, 1977.

Nelson, R. O. Assessment and therapeutic functions of self-monitoring. In M. Hersen, R. M. Eisler, & P. M. Miller (Eds.), *Progress in behavior modification* (Vol. 5). New York: Academic Press, 1977.

Nelson, R. O., & Bowles, P. E. The best of two worlds—observations with norms. *Journal of School Psychology,* 1975, *13,* 3-9.

Nelson, R. O., & Hayes, S. C. Some current dimensions of behavioral assessment. *Behavioral Assessment,* 1979, *1,* 1-16.

Noyes, A. P., & Kolb, L. C. *Modern clinical psychiatry* (6th ed.). Philadelphia: W.B. Saunders, 1963.

O'Leary, K. D. The assessment of psychopathology in children. In H. C. Quay & J. S. Werry (Eds.), *Psychopathological disorders of childhood.* New York: John Wiley & Sons, 1972.

Paul, G. L. *Insight vs. desensitization in psychotherapy.* Stanford: Stanford University Press, 1966.

Peterson, D. R. *The clinical study of social behavior.* New York: Appleton-Century-Crofts, 1968.

Slater, E., & Roth, M. *Clinical psychiatry* (3rd ed.). Baltimore: Williams & Wilkins, 1969.

Spitzer, R. L., & Endicott, J. DIAGNO II: Further developments in a computer program for psychiatric diagnosis. *American Journal of Psychiatry,* 1969, *125,* 12-21.

Spitzer, R. L., Endicott, J., & Robins, E. Research diagnostic criteria. *Archives of General Psychiatry,* 1978, *35,* 773-782.

Stuart, R. B. Operant-interpersonal treatment of marital discord. *Journal of Consulting and Clinical Psychology,* 1969, *33,* 675-682.

Stuart, R. B., & Davis, B. *Slim chance in a fat world.* Champaign, IL: Research Press, 1972.

Suinn, R. M. (Ed.). *Fundamentals of behavior pathology.* New York: John Wiley & Sons, 1970.

Tasto, D. L. Self-report schedules and inventories. In A. R. Ciminero, K. S. Calhoun, & H. E. Adams (Eds.), *Handbook of behavioral assessment.* New York: John Wiley & Sons, 1977.

Tharp, R. G., & Wetzel, R. J. *Behavior modification in the natural environment.* New York: Academic Press, 1969.

Wing, J. K., Birley, J. L. T., Cooper, J. E., Graham, P., & Isaacs, A. D. Reliability of a procedure for measuring and classifying present psychiatric state. *British Journal of Psychiatry,* 1967, *113,* 499-515.

Wing, J. K., Cooper, J. E., & Sartorius, N. *The measurement and classification of psychiatric symptoms.* Cambridge, England: Cambridge University Press, 1974.

Wolf, M. M. Social validity: the case for subjective measurement or how applied behavior analysis is finding its heart. *Journal of Applied Behavior Analysis,* 1978, *11,* 202-214.

Wolpe, J. *Psychotherapy by reciprocal inhibition.* Stanford: Stanford University Press, 1958.

Wolpe, J. *The practice of behavior therapy.* New York: Pergamon Press, 1969.

CHAPTER

3

Assessment

of Neuropsychological Disorders

THOMAS J. BOLL

The role of the brain as the organ of the mind has been
recognized for several centuries. It has long been recognized that damage to the brain can have a profoundly altering affect on a wide range of human behaviors. It is
only more recently, however, that systematic investigations of brain-behavior relationships have been translated into a series of procedures and understandings that
are available in practical form for use by behavioral
clinicians.

BOLL (1981)

This chapter will describe briefly the relevance of brain functions to
normal and aberrant human behavior. A model or guide for selection
of assessment procedures and a description of multiple inferential
methods for their interpretation will be presented. A sample of such
procedures is presented, followed by a description of their clinical applicability, and demonstrated validity related to several neurological
and behavioral conditions. Finally, a case example of the ability of
such procedures to identify, describe, and contribute to intervention
is provided.

Thomas J. Boll. Department of Psychology, University of Health Sciences, The Chicago Medical School, North Chicago, Illinois.

Brain as the Organ of the Mind

Recognition of the brain as the organ of the mind forces consideration of neuropsychological issues that go beyond identification of damage or disorder. The mind is relevant to the full range of considerations that make up the practice of clinical psychology. Differing degrees of ability in one or another area of mental function determine —in part, at least—those things in which we excel or fail, those we enjoy or merely endure, and not least, how we are perceived by others. The brain, as the biological referent for our mental organization, plays a role through its differential organization across individuals, in these same areas of life. This is not to suggest that all of the more usual psychosocial factors typically considered to influence individual behavior and personality style are irrelevant or even necessarily of secondary importance. It is meant to suggest, however, that the art and science of understanding human behavior has developed almost to the exclusion of consideration of the brain as a relevant factor. Such exclusion, or at least oversight, has caused us to remain largely ignorant of a factor in human life and functioning now being shown to have relevance for adjustmental (Rutter, 1977), academic (Rourke, 1981), intellectual (Boll, 1981), occupational (Newman, Heaton, & Lehman, 1978), and emotional (Galin, 1977) development and functioning. Risk factors for learning problems, cognitive style differences between the sexes (Restak, 1979), and even between persons of differing ethnic or cultural backgrounds (Martindale, 1978), and differences in recovery potential following brain impairment have been associated with differing organization within the normal brain. In light of work with both animals and humans, the entire field of individual differences among normals can hardly be discussed without reference to the role of brain organization and such issues as response style, activity level, and differing reinforcement preference (Boll, 1978; Rosenbaum, 1970; Willerman, 1970). That such discussions do in fact take place among psychologists without consideration of the role of the brain underscores our extreme tardiness in establishing what is a recent and rapidly spreading requirement for study in this area as part of professional preparation (Golden & Kuperman, 1980).

It is not accurate to indicate that the role of the brain in human behavior has been entirely ignored. A behavioral analysis of our approach to brain function might easily lead the observer to conclude that the normal brain has no function of interest to the behavioral clinician. When damaged, however, it appears to spring magically to life, demanding attention or at least identification. But even here, the most typical reactions of psychologists have been to attend just long enough to label it damaged and then, without more than a fleeting attempt to discuss the human implications of this damage, hurriedly return to more traditional issues having to do with people and the way they behave.

It is necessary to agree that the normal brain is in fact relevant to human behavior in ways that can and do impinge on people's lives and can and should impinge on the clinician's practice if a discussion of the effects of damage to this organ can begin in its proper context. Just as the normal brain is important to human function, so too is the brain relevant after damage has occurred to some portion of it. The area of the brain destroyed is usually, at most, partly responsible for resulting behavior changes and disordered functions. The influence of the damage on the otherwise intact portions and the functions of those portions in the absence of the part itself is responsible for a significant portion of the patient's behavioral repertoire, both normal and impaired. Hughlings Jackson (1898) stated:

> There are other ways of studying nervous maladies, for example, they are dissolutions, that is as they are reversals of Evolution of this or that part of the nervous system, that is, as they are departures from normal states. In these investigations we do not abandon clinical work: we must study nervous maladies by type first of all. One advantage of considering nervous maladies as dissolutions, is, that in so doing we are obliged in each case to deal with the diseased part as a flaw in the whole nervous system; we thus have to take into account the undamaged remainder and the evolution still going on in it. Apart from these applications of the doctrines of evolution and dissolution, I would urge as I have often done, that a great part of symptomatologies in nervous maladies with negative lesions is the outcome of activities of undamaged, healthy, structures—that that part is a problem, not in pathology, but in physiology. (p. 422)

This interplay of damaged and normal brain tissue as each, separately and together, subserve human performance suggests one of the many complexities which must be recognized in any clinical attempt to measure, diagnose, or describe the psychological effects of brain damage. Reference to the effects of such damage through unitary concepts such as organicity make no sense anatomically or neuropathologically. The use of naive terms to describe measurement devices—that is, tests of organicity—or the behavioral effects of brain impairment—that is, organic brain syndrome—is entirely misleading. Just as there is no neuropathological unity across brain damage, so there is no unity in its behavioral effects. Lashley stated: "It should be a fundamental principle of neural interpretation of psychological functions that the nervous activities are as complex as psychological activities which they constitute" (Cobb, 1960, p. xx). The psychologists' corollary to this dictum suggests, "our methods for assessing behavioral change should be as complex as the brain which subserves these behaviors and behavioral changes" (Boll, 1978, p. 602). It is beyond the scope of this discussion to detail brain anatomy or its pathology in order to emphasize this point. Discussions of geography of the brain by Lezak (1976) and neuropathology as related to behavioral deficits by Boll (1978) serve as reasonable starting points for further study in this area.

It is important to describe, at least briefly, some aspects of the organization of human abilities as these relate to brain organization, which will necessitate some reference to brain structure. Location of an ability in any part of the brain could imply more than one thing. It could suggest that a particular part of the brain produces or is responsible for that single behavior. It might also mean that damage to a particular part of the brain results in an absence or defect in that behavior. Associating a behavior with a particular part of the brain could be taken to mean that other parts of the brain are not involved in its expression when the brain is intact, or damaged, or both. It further suggests that the brain is organized into areas of discrete function uncomfortably reminiscent of the phrenologists' ideas of location of human faculties identifiable through measurements of various portions of the skull. It is not unduly harsh to modern-day traditional clinical procedures in this area, however, to point out that even the phrenologists at whom we scoff for their naivete had a concept of brain behavior relationships that was not only more differentiated and complex but also closer to findings of modern science than the unitary model of damage and dysfunction still in evidence in the current practice of many clinical behavioral scientists.

The most common anatomical organizational scheme for the brain is to recognize its division into two practically identical halves: the right and left cerebral hemispheres. Within each hemisphere four areas or lobes are identified. These are the frontal, parietal, temporal, and occipital lobes, differentiated from each other by their position within their respective hemispheres and separated by relatively arbitrarily chosen neuroanatomical landmarks. This type of demarcation anatomically and the association of certain psychological abilities to one or another of these lobes can be seen as artificial by realizing that these areas were identified originally not for their anatomical or functional specificity or organization, but in order to identify areas of the brain underlying the several bones of the skull carrying the same name. Lobar divisions are not functional divisions (Bailey, 1955). While damage to certain areas does produce similar symptoms, the interaction within hemispheres, and in many cases the bihemispheric representation of higher human functions, must be taken into account when assessing the relationship between a brain lesion and behavior. The organization of human ability between the left and the right cerebral hemisphere is summarized in Table 1.

LEFT-HEMISPHERE FUNCTIONS

The rule of contralateral organization of motor and sensory functions, while not complete and subject to various qualifications (Boll, 1974), is sufficiently universal and applicable to most tasks requiring motor skills as to render it a reasonable generalization. Language abilities represent the human capacity most notably associated with functions of the left cerebral hemisphere. A superb article by Hardyck and Petrinovich (1977) details the exceptions applicable primarily to some left-handers. For the vast majority of right-handers and most left-handed persons this manner of organization applies.

Table 1
Brain–Behavior Organization

Left cerebral hemisphere	Right cerebral hemisphere
Right-sided motor functions	Left-sided motor functions
Right-sided sensory functions	Left-sided sensory functions
Language	Visual perception
Arithmetic	Auditory nonverbal perception
Right–left orientation	Tactile perception
	Spatial mathematics

This is not to say that the right hemisphere either cannot or does not play a role in language in both normal and damaged brains. Children who have one cerebral hemisphere removed in infancy develop language independent of which cerebral hemisphere was removed. Ability to understand language with either hemisphere has been documented (Gazzaniga, 1970; Hecaen & Ajuriaguerra, 1964), and recovery of language following stroke has been reported to be subserved by the previously nonlanguage hemisphere (Smith, 1975). Included with language-related abilities subject to disruption following left cerebral hemisphere lesions are right-left orientation and the ability to perform arithmetic calculations.

RIGHT-HEMISPHERE FUNCTIONS

The previously mentioned contralateral organization of motor and sensory activities indicates that the right cerebral hemisphere is largely responsible for the left-sided motor and sensory functions. There are also many higher-level psychological actions tied to a greater or lesser extent to the integrity of the right cerebral hemisphere. Mathematics restricted to arithmetic calculation is probably primarily dependent upon left-hemisphere functions. Advanced mathmatical processes with significant spatial requirements such as geometry and analytical calculus depend on a type of internal visualization and three-dimensional preception most adequately provided by the right cerebral hemisphere. Individuals who are gifted at graduate-level mathematics but poor at arithmetic manipulation, and others who calculate well through algebra but find geometry a total roadblock, may be expressing their own neuropsychological organizational strengths and weaknesses.

The right cerebral hemisphere, like the left, has one area of function for which it is most famous: perception. Despite its fame, however, the complexity and diversity of functions represented under the term perception is all too seldom appreciated. The undifferentiated use of such terms as "perceptual disorder" and the frequent reliance upon samples of one subset of one mode of perceptual ability as sufficient to assess the presence or absence of impairment of any type of brain function represent examples of this lack of appreciation of the complexity of our perceptual functions. As Table 1 indicates, in oversimplified summary form, there are three major modes of perceptual functioning readily subject to psychological–behavioral measurement procedures: visual, auditory, and tactile.

The visual mode of perceptual performance has received the lion's share of attention in psychological measurement. Nowhere is this more true than in the efforts to determine presence or absence of "organicity." It should be apparent in Table 1 that perception is only one aspect of the human behavioral repertoire. What the table cannot indicate, but what is equally correct, is that it is quite possible to experience mild or even serious brain disruption from many types of damaging conditions or events involving large portions of the brain which seriously compromise many aspects of human performance and not have any perceptual problem, much less just a visual perceptual problem of the spatial variety (Russell, 1976; Smith, 1975; Boll, 1978; and Bruell & Albee, 1962). It is equally possible to have a visuospatial perceptual deficit (which in the final analysis may well reflect upon an aspect of brain organization) and not have any identifiable neurological disorder or brain damage. In the latter case, designation of such a person as brain damaged is not merely incorrect, but could be medically and vocationally harmful and even deprive the person of forms of treatment (psychotherapy) needed for situations totally independent of his or her "perceptual problem."

Within the visual mode, receptive and expressive visuospatial competence is one subset of abilities. Recognition of human faces (visual–social perception), while related, can be quite impaired following discrete brain lesions without significant visuospatial disruption. Even in this differentiated subset, Berent (1977) has shown that some forms of visual–social perception are mediated by primarily right posterior cerebral hemisphere function, while another form (recognition of facial expression and social meaning) is more disrupted following left cerebral hemisphere damage.

Auditory perception has been subject to less investigation and our conclusion about organization of functions must be even more tentative. There is little argument that nonverbal auditory stimuli — that is, tones, musical notes — are managed with reduced competence following right-hemisphere (particularly in the region of the temporal lobe) damage. Another ability, perhaps of greater relevance to daily life, but only partially explored, is the recognition and appreciation of differences in common environmental sounds. Disability in this area would render common acts such as driving, distinguishing the phone from the doorbell, or determining whether a dropped glass broke or bounced, impossible, thus making even routine situations hazardous and confusing. It doesn't take undue imagination to recognize that a person with such defect might respond in an anxious, perplexed, withdrawn, inappropriate manner in many situations. Treatment aimed at intellectual or emotional insight or relearning new response patterns without recognizing the source (etiology) of the behavioral deviation could not hope to be effective.

Tactile and kinesthetic performances also appear to be the special (but not exclusive) responsibility of the right hemisphere. Behaviors observed under this seemingly innocent type of function range from simple recognition of touch and shapes (Boll, 1974; Semmes, 1968) to body-image disruptions and hysterical disorders (Galin, 1974, 1977). One's ability to recognize shapes and objects and to determine where on one's own body stimulus has occurred are included within tactile perception and differentiated from more strictly contralaterally organized tactile sensation. Kinesthetic cues derived from throughout the body allow coordinated action of the body in space. Athletic competence may well be, in part, a reflection of fortunate organization of brain functions, with particular reference to the right cerebral hemisphere. Tasks such as tone perception, shape and body-part recognition, kinesthetically based motor learning, and other nonvisually dependent activities represent an important portion of what our brain does for us each day and, of course, what we are at risk of losing following damage to that brain. Some recognition of this fact by behavioral clinicians faced with the question of psychological assessment of brain functions seems appropriate.

The absence from our discussion of other readily identifiable and major areas of higher cognitive activity such as memory reflects the complex nature of such functions, and not their independence from brain integrity. Memory is dependent in part on its material content; that is, verbal or figural. The area of brian in which damage is likely to produce a particular type of memory deficit, however, cannot be determined from the content alone. The modality of memory (visual, auditory) is a second factor in determining its brain–behavior relationship, as is length (immediate, short-term, long-term, remote) (Boll, 1978; Milner, 1962, 1967, 1968; Russell, 1975; Samuels, Butters, & Fedio, 1972). Review of this major psychological area has recently been prepared by Russell (1981). Memory, like intelligence, perception, or brain integrity itself, can no longer responsibly be referred to as a unitary entity in which someone is deficient. Such oversimplified generalizations not only fail in the provision of correct information, but also suggest incorrect understandings upon which patient care may be predicated. The current state of the science and art of clinical neuropsychology is sufficiently advanced and promulgated that such errors are no longer professionally acceptable or excusable.

Role of Assessment

If use of tests to arrive at binary decisions such as presence or absence of organicity is not appropriate, what is the role of psychology in assessment and diagnosis of patients with neurological disorder, and what represents a reasonable way to proceed in filling this role? The approach to neuropsychological or brain-behavior relationship questions proposed here is developmental or normative rather than dichotomous. Its goal is primarily descriptive and inclusive rather than diagnostic or selective. The neuropsychological model goes beyond a search for and focus upon pathology. The inclusion of tasks subject to normative rather than simply dichotomous evaluation allows for comments about areas and degrees of health or excellence as well as impairment and deficiency. It is the interaction of human ability in the way this interaction expresses itself in human behavior as it is influenced by the organization and integrity of the brain that is being assessed. Reliance on one or even a series of single variables or tasks, considered in sequence, can hardly be held to adequately describe brain function.

> It seems entirely conceivable that the principal correlates of brain lesions may be reflected in alterations of relationships among the behavioral variables and if this does turn out to be the case, it obviously will have been necessary to have used a sufficient number of variables to study their interrelationships and configurations (Reitan, 1974, p. 22).

The areas of human ability included on a neuropsychological evaluation can be sought by reference to the brief schema presented in Table 1. Many areas have been suggested as primary by authors writing well before the emergence of neuropsychology as a clinical subspecialty. Nominations included intelligence (Fulton, 1933), attention (Franz, 1907), highest integrative functions (Chapman & Wolff, 1959), reasoning (Rylander, 1939), and imagination (Freeman & Watt, 1942). More contemporary nominations include receptive and expressive language, stored information and experience, problem solving, learning, abstraction, sensory functions—including tactile, auditory, and visual — simple and complex motor skills, memory in its several aspects, and visual, auditory and tactile perception (Boll, 1978; Davison, 1974; Reitan, 1966a, 1966b; Smith, 1975).

Factors in Test Choice

Whatever tests one chooses in constructing neuropsychological evaluation procedures, several general principles can serve as a guide. Tests are not, after all, good or bad, but merely vehicles to elicit samples of behavior. It is long past time to end the search for that magic test which will tap the one human ability central to and reflective of all aspects of brain function (Spreen & Benton, 1965). Even if such were a conceptual possibility, it would have such limited psychological utility that little justification would exist for its use outside of the desire to affect a presence/absence dichotomy. Such dichotomy, lacking neurological or psychological significance or meaning, would hardly serve as a base for recommendation of use of such a procedure in clinical settings. Short of seeking a magic behavioral wand, the characteristics of an individual clinical setting may cause one to choose tests which are: (1) available in alternative forms; (2) narrow band; that is, tap a single ability; (3) broad band; that is, dependent upon several human abilities such as motor, visual, perceptual, and learning abilities to reform the task; (4) standardized on similar populations; (5) appropriate across a wide age range; (6) portable; and (7) objectively scored. This list could be expanded indefinitely. It should be added that whichever tests are chosen, organization of the battery in a way that allows simultaneous interpretation of performance applying several inferential schemes will add power and efficiency and enhance the potential for application of both clinical and actuarial methods found most likely to maximize validity (Filskov & Goldstein, 1974; Goldstein, Deysach, & Kleinknecht, 1973).

Multiple Methods of Clinical Inference

The amount of clinically useful information obtained from neuropsychological evaluation depends upon two factors. First, the behavior measured must represent a reasonably comprehensive sample of the patient's behavioral repertoire from the simplest psychological functions to the most complex. The behaviors should include multiple modalities of response and type of material or content. Second, the greater the opportunity for evaluating the behavior from more than one perspective, the better. What may seem normal in one context may on the basis of other information indicate considerable deficit, the meaning of which should depend on the independent significance of the behavior and the significance it obtains in comparison with all other behaviors examined.

LEVEL OF PERFORMANCE

This inferential method attends to how well or poorly a person has performed, usually expressed in numerical terms, cast for its interpretation against the performance of others in the normal population. The adequacy of one's behavior may also be assessed with reference to persons in clinical populations such as mentally retarded or brain-damaged individuals. Such information is clinically useful because it permits a continuum of behavior including that which is superior, and it is not tied to identification of pathology for its meaning or clinical utility. Normative data allow placement of individuals at various percentiles within comparative populations providing considerable information in such situations as academic achievement and developmental progress in one or more psychological areas. Such data do not indicate whether or not the patient has ever been better or worse than he or she is now, and give no clue as to the possibility for continued decline or improvement.

In fact, attendence solely to level has encouraged confusion between the terms average and normal. It is not uncommon, for instance, to hear that a child with an IQ of 100 has normal intelligence. It is, however, impossible to tell whether a particular level achieved is indeed normal. If, following an injury, one experienced an IQ drop from 140 to 100, that IQ would not be normal and the patient would most likely know he or she was less able, even if that person's psychologist did not. It has been commonly held that patients with Parkinson's Disesase had essentially unimpaired cognitive ability on the basis of frequently reported IQs in the average range. Reitan and Boll (1971) demonstrated that these average IQs, while present, were actually more than 15 points lower than matched persons without this disease, and were therefore far from normal.

Another application of level of performance to interpret func-

tioning is through cut-off scores. Various cut-off scores relating to
level of performance are employed to categorize people as retarded or
brain-damaged or schizophrenic. While these scores have some clinical utility and considerable group validity, they tend to overlook an
important issue. Performance falling in the "brain-damaged range" is
not, perforce, due to brain damage. The name does not make it so.
There are many reasons beyond the label on the cut-off score why an
individual patient may perform poorly. These include anxiety, disin-
clination, motivation to appear impaired, physical illness, and medication, to name only a few. While these may be recognized by the
clinician, they are not identified by the patient's level of performance.

PATTERN OF PERFORMANCE

Once two scores have been obtained, it is possible to analyze pattern as well as level of performance. Use of this inferential method depends upon the number of different tests administered and the
known expected relationships between and among these tests. Reliance upon tasks assessing essentially the same type of human behavior
(visual perception or verbal memory, for instance) reduces the opportunities for comparison, whereas increased task diversity (motor,
perceptual, conceptual) increases it. Clinical pattern analysis depends also upon known relationships. A battery with which considerable experience has been obtained enhances such an inferential
method, whereas changes in make-up of the neuropsychological battery reduces the likelihood that such relationships will ever be established. Some tests, such as the Wechsler Intelligence Scales, allow for
internal pattern analysis, greatly enhancing the interpretation of the
level of performance achieved. Comparison of performance on the
Wechsler Scale to tests more dependent upon current learning ability
and mental flexibility (Halstead's Category Test) allows assessment of
cognitive deterioration from previously more adequate levels. Additional data, particularly of a motor and sensory nature, greatly enhance the validity of opinions about the contribution of neurological
factors, as opposed to psychosituational factors (anxiety, nonbio-
logical depression) to current mental defects. In so aiding discovery of
etiology, knowledge about prognosis (in the case of deteriorating
CNS, the prognosis is not good even if depression is ameliorated) and
treatment (one must recognize the role of actual deficits in producing

depression and alter one's environment to allow adaptation and reduce instances of failure) is also enhanced.

SPECIFIC SIGNS OF IMPAIRMENT

As the description suggests, this inferential method is not oriented toward strength as well as defect. Certain behaviors are not compatible with normality and, when they occur, suggest deficit or pathology, and not merely a comparatively lesser degree of adequacy. Such behaviors are all or none. Because of this orientation toward deficit identification, false positives must be minimized in the selection of tasks. Such tasks are frequently performed adequately by persons found, through other means, to be impaired (high false negatives), and absence of such signs cannot be read as proof of health or normality. While such behaviors are subject to a type of quantification through assignment to categories or levels of impairment based upon subjective (but reliable) clinical ratings (Russell, Neuringer, & Goldstein, 1970), they are more typically assessed without attempts at scoring. Certain types of verbalizations or perceptual difficulties on the Rorschach (pathognomonic signs) and performance on examinations for aphasia or reproduction of spatial designs are examples of the type of behaviors often subsumed under this inferential approach. Certain difficulties, such as paralysis, inability to name common objects, hallucinations, are never normal and their presence, while not frequent, is convincing evidence of pathology. The etiology and clinical impact on the patient's life of this pathology rests for its determination on complete evaluation, but such behaviors are never construed as a variant of normal.

COMPARATIVE EFFICIENCY OF
THE TWO SIDES OF THE BODY

In addition to providing a separate interpretative approach to the data, this method has the advantage of forcing the use of tasks not routinely employed. These tasks most commonly assess lower level psychological abilities, such as motor speed, strength, coordination, tactile perceptual acuity, and sensory integrity. This addition, in turn, provides information about level of performance on tasks in a wider variety of ability areas and enhances the richness of pattern evaluation.

There is little to suggest that negative factors in one's environment, motivational deficiencies, or affective disruption will exert behavioral affect on one side of the body to a greater extent than on the other. The developmental variability normal during childhood makes attributing level and even unusual patterns of performance to any one of the several possible underlying difficulties an extremely hazardous undertaking. The addition of motor and sensory perceptual tasks and the comparison of the child with him- or herself through right- versus left-side performance has been shown to increase the validity of this type of data interpretation (Boll & Reitan, 1972; Reitan & Boll, 1973).

Neuropsychological Assessment Procedures

Selection of psychological tests providing behavioral samples in the areas mentioned earlier and chosen to maximize the complementary use of several available methods of inference has made it possible for neuropsychologists to validly describe behavioral correlates of brain impairment with a degree of differentiation that includes lateralization, type, and chronicity of the impairment (Filskov & Goldstein, 1974; Reitan, 1964). While other samples of tests have been found to possess comparable validity, the tests included in the neuropsychological assessment most closely associated with the research of Halstead and Reitan will be described as a model for the types of procedures involved and their clinical applications.

THE WECHSLER SCALES OF INTELLIGENCE

The validity of the Wechsler Scales in the context of neuropsychological evaluation have been recently reviewed (Boll, 1978). The Wechsler Scales, in providing three summary measures and 11 individual subtest scores, are subject to analysis, both with respect to level of performance and pattern of ability strengths and weaknesses. The Wechsler Scales for Adults relies heavily upon Type B or crystalized intelligence (past learning and experience as opposed to current problem-solving skills) which, while generally sensitive to the impairing effects of brain damage, as a general rule shows lesser deterioration than do tasks most heavily dependent upon Type A or fluid intellectual processes (learning and problem solving). The Wechsler

Scale provides considerable data about the patient's ability to utilize previously learned verbal skills, to present at least a facade of intellectual adequacy, and to solve certain visual–spatial tasks. It allows comparison with age mates on tasks associated with such important environmental variables as educational and occupational achievement. No single test procedure, no matter how complex or psychometrically excellent, can be seen as a sufficiently adequate sample of human behavior to stand alone as an assessment of brain–behavior relationships. This test, particularly through attention to its various subcomponents, provides an excellent traditional assessment of past and current cognitive functioning. In the context of a complete evaluation it provides information about differential adequacy of verbal and visuospatial capabilities. This is of considerable importance when addressing questions of lateralization as well as type of brain impairment, once independent sources of information have determined neurological deficit to be present.

WIDE-RANGE ACHIEVEMENT TEST

This brief sample of word recognition, spelling, writing, and arithmetic computation provides not only an estimate of current functional literacy and past academic achievements, but also considerable evidence of relevance to educational level in assessing types of abilities which have been compromised following impairment of brain functions. One of the most frequent reasons for performing neuropsychological evaluation is to determine the behavioral consequences of known cerebral events for rehabilitation, return to occupational or academic competition, or determination of degree and nature of deficit in the context of litigation. Such information, of immediate pertinence to a wide variety of day-to-day activities, adds a great deal to data primarily focused on assessing the process rather than the content of psychological activities.

APHASIA SCREENING BATTERY

The relationship of brain damage to impairment of language functions was initially outlined by Dax in 1836 (see Broca), Broca in 1861, and Wernicke in 1874. As with any complex human ability, considerable time and effort can, and in many instances must, be spent in detailed analysis of the subtleties of disordered language function that falls within the overall category of aphasia. Perhaps the single most adequate examination strategy is that outlined by Goodglass and Kaplan (1972) and referred to as the Boston Diagnostic Aphasia Examination. A considerably briefer screening evaluation designed for inclusion in one comprehensive set of neuropsychological procedures is a modification of the Halstead–Wepman Aphasia Screening Battery. This simply administered test, requiring approximately 15 minutes, provides data about the patient's ability in the areas of expressive and receptive language function, including the ability to name objects, spell, read, identify numbers and letters, write, perform arithmetic calculations, enunciate, repeat, identify body parts, perform simple motor actions on command, understand the meaning of verbal communications, follow directions, and differentiate left from right. This test also provides an evaluation of the patient's ability to reproduce the spatial aspects of a variety of geometric shapes. This provides, in brief form, not only a set of procedures more sensitive to certain linguistic and visuospatial deficits than those provided by the Wechsler Scale, but also a set of tasks with known sensitivity to functions of both right or left cerebral hemisphere. Deficits on these tasks represent specific signs of impairment without resorting to available scoring procedures.

MOTOR EXAMINATION

Examination of motor functions not only provides information about human abilities relevant to a wide variety of day-to-day activities, but also adds data not routinely obtained in more traditional clinical psychological examinations. It also provides the opportunity for comparison of the relative efficiency of functioning of one side of the body versus the other.

STRENGTH OF GRIP TEST

This procedure utilizes a hand dynamometer of the plunger type to assess strength of both the right and left upper extremity. As with all motor measures, the preferred side of the body is examined first. Expectation is for the preferred hand to be approximately 10% stronger than the nonpreferred hand.

FINGER OSCILLATION TEST

This measure of motor speed, which forms part of the Halstead Battery, provides a measure of pure motor speed for both the right and the left sides of the body. The patient's task is to depress, as rapidly as possible, a key attached to a counter and to continue in this fashion for a 10-second period. The score for each hand is the average of five consecutive trials.

TACTUAL PERFORMANCE TEST: PSYCHOMOTOR COMPONENT

The Tactual Performance Test, which is part of the original Halstead Battery, is a form-board problem-solving procedure requiring utilization of tactile and kinesthetic cues to guide motor response in the absence of visual information. This procedure utilizes a modification of the Seguin–Goddard Form Board. The patient performs the tasks with the preferred hand followed by the nonpreferred hand, with a third trial allowing the use of both hands working together. The scores on this task are the times required for each of the three trials, with the expectation that normally functioning individuals will perform the entire task in less than 15 minutes. Because of the learning component of this procedure, performance should be more rapid with each successive trial, with improvements on the order of 30 to 40% from trials 1 to 2 and 2 to 3 being expected.

SENSORY EXAMINATION (VISUAL, TACTILE, AND AUDITORY)

Sensory examination through tactile, auditory, and visual sensory channels is included not only to determine whether specific impediments to proceeding with other forms of examinations are present, but also to obtain information about unilateral sensory functioning across these three important modalities. Following determination that unilateral stimulation can be adequately recognized, bilateral simultaneous presentation is initiated, placing one side of the body and contralateral brain functions in competition with the other. If stimuli are presented, such as light touch in a simultaneous fashion to each hand, the patient is expected to respond "both." If the patient responds, "right hand," this suggests that while he or she has been able to demonstrate unilateral recognition of left-handed stimuli, this recognition is no longer possible when expected to occur simultaneously with recognition of stimuli to the right hand. This is referred to as suppression or imperception, which may be indicative of a lesion in the cerebral hemispheres across from the side of the body on which a failure to perceive occurred.

TACTILE PERCEPTUAL EXAMINATION

TACTILE FINGER LOCALIZATION TEST

Patients are required to identify, without use of visual cues, which finger has received unilateral light touch, and this is repeated until each finger of each hand has been stimulated four times, for a total of 20 trials on each hand. The score is the number of errors made in finger recognition for each hand.

FINGERTIP NUMBER-WRITING PERCEPTION

Again, without reference to visual clues, the subject is required to recognize a number written on his or her fingertips by the examiner. The number 3, 4, 5, and 6 are written on each finger of each hand, for a total of 20 trials on each side of the body.

TACTILE FORM RECOGNITION TEST

Four geometric shapes (a cross, square, triangle, or circle) are placed, one at a time, in the hand of the patient, which is hidden from view by a small form board. On the board in front of the patient are the same four shapes. The patient's task is to point with his or her free hand to the shape being held by the hidden hand without being required to name the shape. Each shape is presented to each hand twice, for a total of eight trials per hand. The score on this task is the number of errors and the total response time per hand for recognition of the eight shapes.

Total administration time for the motor, sensory, and tactile perceptual examination is less than thirty minutes. These procedures are appropriate for individuals ages five through adulthood, and their validity individually and in the context of a neuropsychological battery has recently been reviewed (Boll, 1978).

Examination of Higher-Level Cognitive Functions

Procedures originally developed by Halstead and documented as to their clinical validity and utility by Reitan make up the bulk of this portion of the examination. These procedures requiring reliance upon problem solving, mental flexibility, learning, attentional abilities, and several aspects of memory, but minimally dependent upon past background experience, have been demonstrated to be particularly sensitive to the effects of brain impairment of a wide variety of types, locations, and degrees of severity. This has been found to be the case even in individuals whose psychometric levels are in the average and, in some instances, even the superior range.

CATEGORY TEST

The Category Test developed by Halstead presents 208 stimuli divided into seven subtests. The stimuli are presented by means of a slide projection apparatus, to which the subject responds by pulling one of four answer levers. Correct answers are greeted with a pleasant-sounding doorbell, and incorrect responses cause a rather harsh buzzer to sound. The task requires utilization of trial and error and hypothesis-testing behavior to find a solution to a problem, maintain that solution in mind, and apply it consistently throughout an entire subtest. This test requires considerable mental flexibility and learning efficiency, and deficits in this area often correspond to complaints of patients and relatives about impairments in memory. Individuals experiencing difficulty on this task often behave in somewhat self-defeating ways, indicating that they are less than normally able to anticipate the consequences of their actions or to modify them effectively once they have realized that this is necessary.

MEMORY AND LOCALIZATION COMPONENTS OF THE TACTUAL PERFORMANCE TEST

This task, assessing incidental and short-term tactile figural memory, is but one of several procedures in this overall examination scheme, assessing an aspect of memory functions. Following completion of the three psychomotor trials on the Tactual Performance Test, the patient is instructed to draw a picture of the board and place each of the blocks in its correct location without ever having seen it before, during, or after the examination. The patient is scored on the number of shapes correctly remembered and the number correctly located on the board.

SEASHORE RHYTHM TEST

This procedure, which is one subtest of Seashore's Test of Musical Talent, presents, via tape recording, 30 pairs of matched beats. The subject's task is to identify these matched pairs as the same or different. The auditory nonverbal perceptual task requires, in addition, the ability to concentrate over a period of time.

SPEECH SOUNDS PERCEPTION TEST

The Speech Sounds Perception Test developed by Halstead is also presented by a tape recorder. Sixty nonsense words, such as weeg and leeng, are presented. The subject's task is to listen to each word and identify, from among four choices on a piece of paper, which nonsense word has been spoken. This auditory visual–verbal perceptual test also requires considerable concentration ability.

TRAIL-MAKING TEST: PARTS A AND B

Trail-Making Test, Part A, requires the subject to connect a series of circles distributed on a sheet of paper. Inside each circle is a number from 1 to 25, and the patient's task is to connect the numbers in ascending order as rapidly as possible.

Trail-Making Test, Part B, also requires the connection of 25 circles distributed on a piece of paper. In Part B, however, the circles are identified with numbers 1 through 13 or letters A through L. The subject's task is to alternate between numbers and letters, proceeding to connect each of the 25 circles; for instances, 1-A, 2-B, 3-C, and so on. This test taps number and letter recognition, visual sorting, motor speed, mental flexibility, and the ability to maintain two separate requirements of a task simultaneously in mind while alternating between them.

Administration time for the higher-cognitive (Halstead–Reitan Battery) portion of the overall neuropsychological examination is approximately two hours in most outpatient settings. Detailed descriptions of each of these procedures, with appropriate modifications for children ages 9 through 14 and 5 through 8, has recently been reported (Boll, 1981). The overall time for administration of the entire neuropsychological procedures described above varies considerably, depending upon the physical and mental condition of the patient. It is extremely unusual, even with an inpatient population dominated by individuals from a neurosurgical service, to require more than a single day to complete the entire exam, including the Wechsler, aphasia, sensory-perceptual, and academic procedures. The usual time requirement for outpatient adults and the majority of inpatients is five to six hours. Examination of children can usually be accomplished in four to five hours, and in many instances less time is required. The use of highly trained neuropsychology technicians greatly enhances not only the adequacy of the examination procedures, but the efficiency of the overall evaluative effort.

Candidates for and Purpose of Neuropsychological Assessment

The persons to be evaluated can be described best by a discussion of the clinical purposes of such an examination. The two principal and not mutually exclusive purposes for neuropsychological assessment (and almost any other type of examination) are diagnosis and description.

Diagnosis is aimed at determination of the existence of some pathological entity, either hypothetical, in the case of neurosis; normative, in the case of retardation; or biological, in the case of brain damage. Integral to this determination is elucidation of the nature of that entity, or at least its salient (and preferably provable) characteristics which link it to the patient's difficulties. It is not enough to simply state at that because someone has brain damage, his or her psychological difficulties are due to brain damage. Such an attempt was made by Geschwind (1975), who cited a series of cases whose initial treatment focused on the psychosocial situational aspects of their behavioral difficulties and who were later found to have not just brain damage but medically significant neurological disorders. The unusual and sensational nature of such cases suggest the low frequency with which they occur. Nothing in their citation proves the behavioral disorders were, in fact, due to the coexisting neurological disorder. Knowledge of the relationship between static damage or even medically significant brain disease or recent trauma and psychological functions does not suggest that such conditions cause specific types of emotional disorder (Boll, Heaton, & Reitan, 1974; Rutter, 1977). Experience in three active neuropsychological laboratories (Indianapolis, Charlottesville, Seattle), over the last ten years indicates that it is rare indeed to obtain evidence for a medically significant neurological condition in patients who are not already undergoing simultaneous evaluation on the basis of signs or complaints that such disorder may be present. Another important reason for infrequency of neuropsychological identification of disorders not concurrently suspected is this laboratory's requirement that persons whose complaints include the suggestion of medically significant disorders are referred to physicians, typically neurologists and neurological surgeons, but also general physicians, depending upon the referral complaint. Complaints such as nausea, vomiting, dizziness, headache, numbness, loss of motor function, pain, blackouts, ictal episodes, tunnel vision, or loss of sight on a temporary basis strongly suggest the need for medical attention for evaluation and subsequent treatment. As part of such evaluation, neuropsychological examination is quite appropriate in many instances and is frequently performed to aid diagnosis and to provide information enhancing the completeness and appropriateness of medical and/or behavioral intervention.

Rendering of a diagnostic opinion, like any other clinical act, should be done not only by persons trained in that area and aware of the validity of their procedures, but also for the purpose of benefitting the patient diagnosed. The diagnosis of presence of brain damage or organicity should by now be recognized as at best meaningless and at worst harmful to the patient (Boll, 1978, 1980; Smith, 1975). A diagnosis that describes more than the presence of a disorder but provides information about the characteristics of that disorder which impinge on the patient's life and functions is of considerable clinical value. Even in situations where other diagnostic procedures (physical examinations, X rays, electroencephalograms, and the like) have documented the neurological characteristics of a patient's problem, nothing has been understood about the behavioral consequences of that problem from those studies. The ability to validly assess the condition of the brain through behavioral procedures not only adds to the chain of neurological inference that never rests on a single test, but also provides a type of clinical material not otherwise available about conditions whose impact on a person's day-to-day existence cannot be overestimated.

Provision of such examination is a complex task requiring time, technical competence, and specific professional training. Artificial time constraints make no more sense and are no more professionally tolerable in clinical psychology than in surgery. Shortcuts have no place in clinical practice. Because of the complex nature of the issues involved, if a practitioner is not trained to perform the evaluation, such should be the response. One cannot "fake it" with biofeedback, surgery, or neuropsychology and conduct responsible practice. It has been difficult in all professions to move from generalist to specialist and for generalists to recognize the areas in which consultation is appropriate. Not too many years ago, barbers and physicians extracted teeth. Today, within the independent profession of dentistry, general training supplemented by fellowship specialization is provided for those who wish to focus on extraction. So, too, is psychology, general knowledge and awareness are not synonymous with professional competence in every possible specialized area from biofeedback to psychoanalysis. A little bit of neuropsychological examination is like a few days of psychoanalysis or "trying behavior mod for a while" — not likely to be very effective.

Despite my position that the primary role of a clinical neuropsychologist is not that of a neurodiagnostician, there are, nevertheless, many circumstances in which diagnosis is both validly and appropriately accomplished independent of, or in conjunction with, the diagnostic efforts of colleagues in psychology and medicine. That it is possible to assess, through behavioral evaluation, the organic integrity of brain functions with respect to presence of disorder, its location, and type has been impressively and repeatedly demonstrated (Filskov & Goldstein, 1974; Goldstein et al., 1973; Matthews, Shaw, & Kløve, 1966; Reitan, 1964; Russell et al., 1970; Schreiber, Goldman, Kleinman, Goldfader, & Snow, 1976).

In the course of neurological evaluation, results from physical examinations may be equivocal. This may produce a dilemma as to whether to proceed with more definitive tests which carry with them risks of considerable discomfort and, in rare instances, death, or to follow the patient's progress, risking, in turn, a worsening of the condition before it is satisfactorily identified. Because such decisions typically rest upon data gathered in sequence from several sources, the inclusion of neuropsychological evaluation before moving to more hazardous procedures is common practice in many settings (DeJong, 1967). In an excellent study typical of those procedures from his clinical laboratory, Matthews and his colleagues examined, as part of the total neurological work-up, patients whose presenting complaints suggested the possibility of serious neurological disorder (Matthews *et al.*, 1966). Among these patients, some were determined to have cerebral damage, while others were found to have difficulties based on other than central-nervous-system dysfunction. While keeping in mind Teubers' dictim that absence of evidence is not evidence of absence, Matthews *et al.* set out to evaluate the performance of neuropsychological evaluation in identifying those patients with and without evidence of central-nervous-system dysfunction within this population of persons with confusing and worrisome presenting complaints. Such patients are far more typical of day-to-day practice than are those in whom the diagnosis is obvious for all to easily identify. The ability to aid in correct identification of such patients would represent an impressive clinical service. Matthews *et al.* found employment of clinical and actuarial analysis of their neuropsychological battery provided accurate information about the type of disorder responsible for the patients' complaints. They indicated that reliance upon clinical or actuarial approaches alone led to uncomfortably diminished results. They then commented that use of any one of their procedures alone, even though it possessed impressive group validity, produced an abundance of false positives and false negatives.

The ability of neuropsychological procedures to contribute to the overall chain of neurological decision making and its possession of independent validity in the hands of trained professionals was impressively documented by Susan Filskov and Steven Goldstein in what has become a standard reference article in the field (Filskov & Goldstein, 1974). Patients for whom definite, final neurological diagnostic criterion information was available and who had undergone neuropsychological examination were reviewed to determine the accuracy of neuropsychological inference. In no instance in their sample were patients without brain damage designated as neurologically impaired. Within the patients with brain damage, Table 2 indicates the level of accuracy of diagnosis obtained (not simply presence or absence of brain damage, but for type of brain damage and, where appropriate, lateralization of type of damage within the cerebral hemispheres).

For certain questions and neurological conditions, the diagnostic role of the neuropsychological evaluation is all but indispensable. A condition of brain damage can be known to exist following serious head injury and yet visual and electroencephalographic and tomo-

Table 2
Proportion of Correct Statements as to Identification of Cerebral
Impairment, Lateralization, and Neuropathological Process,
by Procedure and Sample Size[a]

	Identification		Lateralization		Neuropatholog- ical process	
	P	n	P	n	P	n
Neuropsychological battery	1.00	89	.89	84	.85	78
Brain scan	.40	76	.36	72	.32	72
Flow	.70	16	.69	16	.66	15
EEG	.60	78	.52	66	.35	55
Angiogram	.85	48	.85	48	.85	48
Pneumoencephalogram	.80	10	.80	10	.86	7
X ray	.16	38	.16	38	.16	38

[a]Reprinted by permission of the American Psychological Association from S. B. Filskov and S. G. Goldstein, Diagnostic Validity of the Halstead-Reitan Neuropsychological Battery, *Journal of Consulting and Clinical Psychology*, 1974, *42*, 382-388. Copyright 1974 by the American Psychological Association.

graphic documentation of the damage may not be forthcoming. This may be true immediately after the injury, and even more commonly a short time following such traumatically induced brain impairment. The ability, on an independent basis, of neuropsychological examination to document the occurrence of a head injury provides valid grounds on which determination of damages in situations of litigation have been made. This ability to identify the existence and etiology of behavioral changes, not incidentally, contributes directly to immediate and long-term patient care and rehabilitation and allows objective monitoring of real recovery of function over time (Smith, 1975; Boll, 1978). In Luria's words,

> the restricted limits of regular neurological symptoms is a result of some very important facts: lesions of the *highest* (secondary or tertiary) zones of the cortex — which are considered as specifically human parts of hemispheres — do not result, as a rule, in any elementry sensory or motor deficits and remain inaccessible for classical neurological ex-

amination. They are associated with alterations of very complex behavioral processes (cognitive processes, elaboration of complex programs of behavior and their control), and that is why one has to establish new complex methods that could be used to study dysfunctional disorders evoked by their injuries. It is thus necessary to apply methods of neuropsychology for local diagnosis of lesions of these complex cortical zones. (Luria, 1973, p. 959).

Patients for whom the initial complaint is depression represent an instance of the type referred to by Luria. Such patients often do not appear seriously cognitively incapacitated on a mental-status examination, particularly after the depression has been taken into account. So, too, such examinations as the physical–neurological, electroencephalogram, and X ray are then negative, and even a CAT scan may produce no more than questionable signs of atrophy, which is possibly associated with the patient's age. In many settings CAT scans are not available, and referral to another setting is not likely without more indication than is usually available. If, however, significant cognitive deterioration beyond that attributable to depression can be documented, such a referral and other types of procedures can be justified to increase the likelihood of obtaining a correct diagnosis. A patient who cannot function because of primary depression may spontaneously improve or benefit from psychological or psychopharmacologic intervention. A patient who is secondarily depressed due to recognition of increasing incapacity must be approached rather differently psychologically and pharmacologically. Requirements for a different coping strategy to be employed by the patient, and particularly his or her family, issues of prognosis for return to work, and the management of personal affairs depend upon understanding the nature of the disorder. We recently examined a 42-year-old business executive whose persistent complaints of motor and sensory difficulties in his limbs and back without clinical evidence of mental impairment led to speculation of peripheral neuropathy in a bright, aggressive man who was overinvested in his physical condition. Neuropsychological examination revealed not only the complained-of motor and sensory deficits, but tactile and visual perceptual problems, memory impairment (verbal and nonverbal, immediate, short-term, and incidental) and learning and problem-solving difficulties characteristic of a moderately mentally disabled man despite the presence of above-average (but quite likely also reduced) IQ scores. The neuropsychological impression was of diffuse impairment of brain functions consistent with slowly progressive neurological disease affecting functioning at the level of the cerebral hemispheres. The referring neurologist questioned the patient and family members more closely, and determined that many of the critical areas of the business operation had been gradually taken over by subordinates. Further examination also revealed a diligent effort on the part of the patient and his family to deny any disability in this man whose primary functions were now oriented toward use of his still-good verbal facade and outgoing personal style in a personal-relations function highly valued in his type of business. Further diagnostic efforts to identify the source of these neuropsychological impairments resulted in a diagnosis of multiple sclerosis. Certainly the treatment regime for a bright businessman overinvolved in his peripheral physical symptoms can be seen as quite different for patient and family from that designed for a young man anticipating significant and increasing mental and physical difficulties on the basis of multiple sclerosis.

This is not a case of our being right and someone else being wrong or of our getting there first with the correct answer. It is an example of the complementary use of physical and behavioral evaluation in the determination of the nature of the patient's disorder, the physical and the all-too-often overlooked psychological–behavioral expression and consequences of that disorder, and the most appropriate medical–psychosocial intervention strategy for the patient's entire situation.

The request for neuropsychological evaluation as a means of obtaining a description of the psychological behavioral strengths and weaknesses of a patient is most common and allows the best expression of the uniqueness of the professional contribution that neuropsychologists are prepared to offer. The validity of neuropsychological evaluation support its diagnostic capability. But validity, like diagnosis, must not be pursued for its own sake. A set of procedures has value as its validity allows us to do something with it. In addition to its support of our contribution to a clearer understanding of the integrity of the cerebral hemispheres, the validity of the procedures supports the psychological–behavioral descriptions that the examination generates. There is nothing exclusively neurological about these procedures. Their association with neurology comes from the attempt, most fully developed by Ralph M. Reitan, to tie the significance of these behaviors to a biological base. This biological base can be seen as just as valid in discussing the differential psychological competencies of normal as well as brain-damaged persons. There is no restriction of these procedures to patients at risk for neurological damage.

While these procedures have demonstrated particular relevance with this group where research has focused its attention, the use of these procedures as a *comprehensive ability evaluation* in a variety of clinical contexts is entirely appropriate as well. Without reference to brain damage, these procedures have been employed to develop understandings about the relationship between differential patterns of psychological functioning in academic achievement (Rourke, 1975; Reitan & Boll, 1973). Evaluations of general psychological strength and weakness prior to placement in vocational programs, and assessments of persons labeled mentally retarded for purposes of finding the most appropriate areas for training for occupational skills, frequently require the kind of comprehensive ability coverage provided by neuropsychological evaluation. In such instances, reliance upon IQ is not sufficient, as motor skills may represent the best vocational strength. Understanding the content of these strengths and weaknesses and what they represent when considered together for a single person is a task well-suited to the neuropsychological battery. The most frequent referral questions pertain to patients whose neurological status is not in doubt on the basis of already accomplished medical–neurological examinations. Despite the known diagnosis, the implications now and in the future of the brain disorder for psychological functions is not subject to an answer from traditional neurological procedures.

Head injury, a condition in which neuropsychology plays a diagnostic role, also represents a type of disorder ideally suited to benefit from neuropsychological description. The most common psychological–behavioral difficulties following head injury are in areas least obvious to routine clinical inspection or traditional psychometric measurements. These deficits include higher-level complex problem-solving, mental flexibility, concept formation, new learning, and recent as opposed to distant or historical memory. These same skills are also the slowest to recover. Difficulties in these areas of a moderate and even severe nature are frequently seen in patients whose physical appearance, social conversation, and even IQ scores suggest normality. Such invisible deficits can be highly disruptive to the patient and family alike. The failures they produce are often attributed to motivation or emotional problems because nothing of a cognitive nature appears amiss. This deficit may also escape detection in the nondemanding environment of the hospital and very early convalescent period. The appearance of normal health and ability may result in return, too early, to cognitively demanding work or school activities requiring just the abilities in which the patient is temporarily most deficient. The consequences of this include predictable failure with concurrent increased anxiety, decreased self-concept, and frequently depression, fear of reattempting tasks once recovery has taken place, and significant family stress created by misunderstood behavioral alterations. Such consequences are far worse and more long-lasting than are the direct consequences of the head injury.

The role of neuropsychological evaluation is to determine the presence and type of psychological deficits which have occurred. If such deficits appear, knowledge about expected recovery and current level of ability in several areas allows the neuropsychologist to provide information to the patient about what difficulties to expect and what inconsistencies to anticipate, and the proper understanding about their origin. Initial recommendations and plans for timing of return to work or school are subject to modification following repeat examinations, usually conducted at six-month intervals. Three-month or even shorter intervals are appropriate, depending upon the initial severity of the damage, rapidity of recovery, and requirements in the patient's life situation. Patients are typically followed for 12 to 18 months after a head injury, at which time, for most patients, recovery is complete and the remaining difficulties are likely to persist or improve at a significantly slower rate.

Evaluation before and after neurosurgical intervention serves two purposes. Such examinations provide data about the patient's cognitive sequelae from their neurological disorder and allow assessment of the quality of survival with communication to the patient and/or family of realistic functioning expectations after a "successful" surgical experience. Such examinations have also been important in documenting the psychological benefits of a procedure designed not to aid mental functions, but to prevent or delay cerebral-vascular accidents — endarterectomy.

Data from several neuropsychological labs suggest that at least 40 to 50% of patients can expect significant cognitive improvement following this procedure (Goldstein, Kleinknecht, & Gallo, 1970; King, Gideon, Haynes, Dempsey, & Jenkins, 1977). Such improvement would not have been recognized or documented unless comprehensive ability evaluations using validated neuropsychological procedures had been routinely performed with this population of patients. The value of this neurosurgical procedure would have continued to be determined without reference to behavioral issues so critical to life functioning long after one has been discharged from the hospital.

Baseline examination of patients in the early stages of conditions known to be characterized by neurological deterioration should be routine in any medical setting. While such patients frequently show normal IQs, their ability to handle financial affairs, hold jobs, and live independently require constant reevaluation (Reitan & Boll, 1971; Boll et al., 1974). In many instances their neurological–behavioral progress can be monitored through neuropsychological examination while simultaneously providing an update on a broad range of the patient's adaptive capabilities. Understanding by patient and family that forgetfulness, inconsistency, confusion, misunderstanding, poor judgment, self-defeating and even hurtful behavior are due to real brain impairment and associated cognitive loss and not ill will or emotional disturbance, while still uncomfortable, is routinely received with relief. This produces an increased willingness within the family to modify the environment and the expectations of the patient. It allows for development of ways of interacting designed to prevent areas of difficulty, and reduces the tendency to ignore or become angry at the patient. As stress tends to make impaired persons behave even less adequately, failure to understand the nature of the problems and modify the environment to minimize difficulties raises stress and exacerbates the problems. The role of the clinical psychologist is central to this sort of follow-up evaluation and management intervention.

LITIGATION

Brain damage resulting in physical and psychological disability, particularly as a result of traumatic injury, often results in the need for a determination of the amount of loss and the relationship of the loss to present and future disability (Black, Shepard, & Walker, 1975). Such issues, frequently involving civil litigation, are resolved, often in part and on occasion totally, on the basis of neuropsychological evaluation of extent of loss, amount of recovery, and degree of residual deficit. Use of a battery providing a sufficient sample of human behavior to adequately address such issues is the first step. Reliance upon multiple methods of inference applied across multiple areas of function aids greatly in assessing change, even from the results of a single examination. Independent demonstration of validity (correctly identifying the deficits as due to head injury) and accurate assessment of expectations for change when tested across time not only provide data for patient care, but document that the descriptions provided reflect brain–behavior relationships without significant contamination from other factors not directly related to the situation at hand. Such issues as premorbid emotional disturbances, and motivation to obtain large settlements by enhancement of deficits are difficulties neuropsychologists face in interpreting their data. A recent article by Heaton, Smith, Lehman, and Vogt (1978) discusses the issue of malingering and demonstrates the validity of neuropsychological procedures in separating head-injury patients from malingerers.

Emotional disturbance, especially predating brain injury, may represent a tempting, even convincing, scapegoat for posttraumatic difficulties, especially if these difficulties are not accompanied by impressive physical injuries—a situation common to head injury with or without emotional disturbance. The following case provides an example of the ability of clinical/actuarial interpretation of neuropsychological evaluation to detect neurological impairment in a generally very bright, emotionally disturbed patient. This identification was confirmed by subsequent neuroradiologic investigation, and neuropharmacologic treatment proved successful in controlling the most impairing behavioral symptoms which were, in fact, a form of epilepsy, and not hysterical behavior, as was at first assumed. The neuropsychological evaluation led to the recognition that such impairment, while relatively mild and coexisting with very good abilities in some areas, was, in fact, central to the patient's premorbid area of occupational endeavor and therefore disabling.

Clinical Case

The patient, Larry L., was a 20-year-old single male who four years previously had graduated from high school and college at age 16. He was most notably a mathematical wizard, and for three years prior to his accident, pursued a career as a mathematician while attending graduate school part time. For much of his life he had been a social isolate who had received psychiatric treatment on several occasions, and at the time of his accident, was again in psychotherapy. His most pronounced symptoms were chronic social isolation and chronic depression. Nine months prior to our examination, he was involved in an auto accident in which he was a passenger. Following the accident, he was unconscious for several hours but showed no physical–neurological deficits upon examination two weeks after the injury. Throughout the nine months prior to our examination, he complained of difficulties which had not been part of his complaint repertoire prior to that time. These included headaches, gray spells short of blacking out, difficulty with reading, occasional dizziness, and periods of confusion. His most disabling complaint was a periodic total inability to solve mathematical problems. This disability was sufficiently inconsistent that on occasions he was able to complete half of a task with considerable brilliance and then not only be unable to finish the rest of it, but be left with no idea as to how he had solved the probems that he had just completed. This prevented him from performing his job, which was not only his source of financial support, but his sole personal–emotional investment and his entire claim to personal adequacy and self-worth. Larry was referred because of the belief shared by his lawyer and psychiatrist, despite his obvious significant emotional difficulties, that his complaints were not part of that package. They felt he experienced difficulties which began after the head injury but which had not been shown to be neurological in origin on the basis of examinations to that time. Prior to our examination, physical neurological and electroencephalographic examinations were interpreted as normal. Results of the neuropsychological evaluation, which were interpreted initially without knowledge of Larry's medical history, produced findings and conclusions reported below. The data from which these conclusions were drawn appear in Figures 1, 2, and 3.

The Wechsler Adult Intelligence Scale was administered, and Larry obtained a Verbal IQ that fell within the superior range (142). His general fund of information, vocabulary development, and ability to recall and utilize previously learned verbal information were all distinctly superior, placing his general skills in this area easily within the upper 1% of the general population. He obtained a Performance IQ that also fell within the superior range. Larry demonstrated some considerable unevenness and disruptiveness in these skills, however, with two demonstrations of ability in this area falling in the average to below-average range. Such inconsistency between verbal and performance skills is not unusual in itself in an extremely intelligent individual. The inconsistency within his visuospatial problem-solving abilities, when coupled with the verbal versus perceptual skill differ-

PATIENT __LARRY L.__   AGE _20_ SEX _M_ DATE TESTED _8-28_

HOSPITAL STATUS _O P_   EDUCATION _16_ HANDEDNESS _R_

OCCUPATION_____   REFERRED BY_____

Halstead's Neuropsychological Battery			Wechsler Intelligence Scale for Adults	
Category Test	Total _39_		VIQ	_142_
			PIQ	_122_
Tactual Performance Test			FS IQ	
RH _8.3_ LH _9.5_	Time	_19.2_	Information	_16_
BH _1.4_	Memory	_9_	Comprehension	_18_
	Localization	_6_	Arithmetic	_16_
			Similarities	_19_
Speech Perception Test		_11_	Digit Span	_15_
			Vocabulary	_16_
Seashore Rhythm Test		_5_	Digit Symbol	_15_
Raw score _26_			Picture Completion	_18_
			Block Design	_15_
Finger Oscillation Test			Picture Arrangement	_11_
Dominant hand _53_			Object Assembly	_7_
Non-dominant hand _38_				

_0.3_ Halstead Impairment Index

Aphasic & Perceptual Tests				Lateral Dominance Tests		
Aphasia:				Hand	R _7_	L____
				Eye	R _2_	L____
Sensory Suppression			Trails Test	Foot	R _2_	L____
	Right	Left				
Visual	_0_	_0_	A _25_	Handwriting		
Auditory	_2_	_1_			R _13_ L _88_	
Tactile	_1_	_7_	B _59_			
Finger Agnosia	_4_	_3_		Grip		
Finger-tip writing	_7_	_4_			R _35_ kg. L _29_ kg.	
Tactile forms	_0_	_0_				

Figure 1
Neuropsychological examination — adult.

ences, however, is suggestive of some degree of disruptiveness and inconsistency that falls outside of normal expectation.

An aphasia screening battery was administered and no specific aphasic deficits were noted. Larry did demonstrate some mild tendency toward difficulty with complex language usage which involved arithmetic computation, spelling, and grasping the general significance of verbally expressed ideas. This difficulty, while mild in itself, is slightly greater than would be expected from an individual with

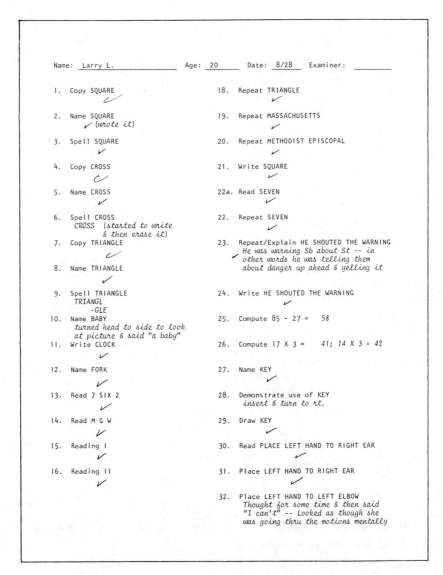

Figure 2
Aphasia screening test—form for adults and older children.

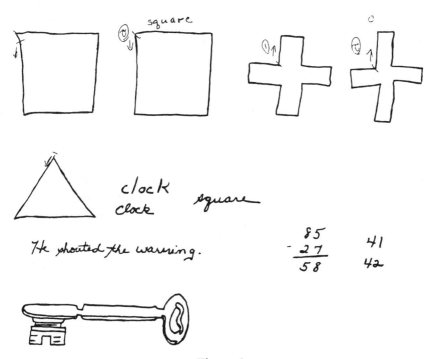

Figure 3
Aphasia screening test — patient's productions.

such superior verbal abilities. He also demonstrated a very mild constructional dyspraxia.

A battery of sensory perceptual measures was administered, and Larry demonstrated mild bilateral difficulty on measures of tactile and auditory bilateral simultaneous stimulation. He demonstrated mild to moderate finger agnosia and astereognosis bilaterally. These findings also fall outside of normal limits and suggest some degree of disruptiveness, not only in attention to and concentration on simple and complex tasks, but also in actual tactile–perceptual skills, which is quite consistent with that seen in individuals who have sustained some mild bilateral impairment of brain functions.

A motor battery was administered, and again Larry demonstrated a reasonably adequate level of motor strength and motor speed. On both of these measures, however, his left upper extremity was significantly weaker than would be expected in relation to the right, even considering his strong right-handedness. On a measure of complex psychomotor problem-solving in which tactile and kinesthetic cues must be utilized in a learning procedure without the benefit of visual information, he demonstrated bilateral difficulties. Here, too, his left upper extremity was significantly less able than his right, completing a consistent picture of left-sided tactile–perceptual, kinesthetic, and motor deficiency that falls outside of normal expectations for an individual with even average general mental and motor abilities.

The Halstead Neuropsychological Test Battery was administered, and on this measure of higher-level cognitive functioning, Larry obtained an impairment index of .3. This falls within the normal range. His skills in the areas of learning, attention, concentration, problem solving, and memory were all well within normal limits. His higher-level mental processes, including abstraction ability, concept formation, and ability to benefit from trial-and-error experience to form hypotheses and to behave in a mentally efficient manner when attending to even relatively difficult tasks, were all at least average to somewhat above average. None of his performances, however, revealed the level of mental superiority suggested by his psychometric abilities, suggesting that he may well be slightly less able than has previously been the case. His performance is, however, still well within average limits. This indicates that he has sufficient ability to subserve entirely adequate day-to-day performances in almost all tasks.

From a neurological point of view, despite the fact that Larry is able to demonstrate exceedingly excellent abilities in a variety of areas and essentially average abilities in most others, he nevertheless, demonstrates a variety and degree of difficulty in certain types of functioning that would appear to be inconsistent with entirely normal brain functions. His perceptual difficulties of a visuospatial as well as a tactile and kinesthetic nature, when coupled with the specific motor deficits noted with the left as compared with the right upper extremity, are quite consistent with that seen in individuals who have sustained some degree of impairment, particularly affecting functions subserved by the right cerebral hemisphere and very probably primarily involving functions of the frontal and temporal areas of that hemisphere. His general mild difficulty in higher-level cognitive functions, when coupled with very mild inefficiency in language usage despite excellent acquisition of language abilities, is also consistent with some decline from previously more able levels and may well be reflective of similar types of brain changes referable to the left cerebral hemisphere, albeit of a somewhat milder nature. Such behavioral changes are most characteristic of conditions that are not found to be rapidly progressive but that are rather static in nature and of a sufficiently mild degree as to be unlikely to produce abnormalities on such procedures as physical–neurological examination. Such a pattern of inconsistent performance affecting lower- and higher-level psychological ability—in this instance associated with dysfunctions primarily referable to the right frontal temporal area—is quite consistent with that seen in individuals who have sustained mild static impairment at the level of the cerebral hemispheres on the basis of a closed head injury.

From a neurological point of view, Larry's general abilities, while possibly somewhat decreased from a previously more adequate level, nevertheless should be quite sufficient in most areas to subserve entirely normal performances in his environment. His relatively reduced adequacy in complex problem-solving skills may well be a source of disruption if his primary day-to-day activities are heavily involved with complex analytic thinking, academic pursuits, and demands for higher-level cognitive activity. In such instances, this patient may well notice a subjective decrease in ability which may compromise his ability to perform such tasks. This compromise in important life activities, when coupled with the absence of obvious deficits to explain it, can be very disruptive and disconcerting both to the patient and to those around him, producing misunderstandings and additional sources of stress likely to further exacerbate adjustment difficulties.

From a personality point of view, Larry appears to be highly psychologically upset, anxious, and at least moderately, if not severely, depressed at the current time. He appears to be experiencing considerable difficulty in maintaining intact coping skills. He appears prone to high levels of social isolation and instances of cognitive disorganization, and seems currently under high degrees of psychological stress, tension, and subjective discomfort. While this high level of psychological disruptiveness may be sufficient to account for some subjective symptoms and may well interact with his very real cognitive deficits to enhance behavioral difficulties, it is necessary to recognize the critical importance of the abilities lost to individuals of superior mental endowment which cannot be dismissed as entirely due to affective disruption.

Following the completion of this independent report, the total clinical data were reviewed in consultation with his psychiatrist and attorney, and the decision was made to pursue more vigorously additional neurological diagnostic activity at a distant center noted for its work in this area. The results of the pneumoencephalogram and enhanced computerized axial tomographic scan revealed atrophy of the temporal lobe manifested by the enlargement of the temporal horn of the lateral ventrical, which included part of the right frontal lobe. Following this examination, seizure medication was initiated and his "spells" declined from an average of six to an average of one per day. Psychological intervention, including behavioral techniques for the management of headache, was also successful, although this patient's basic personality style and the presence of difficulties with social adjustment persisted.

Such a clinical example illustrates the combined diagnostic and descriptive use of neuropsychological evaluation in collaboration with medical-neurological diagnostic and intervention strategies as well as those of a psychotherapeutic nature. The correspondence of neurologic and neuropsychologic information lead to initiation of treatment. This treatment remediated most of the difficulties which occurred following his head injury. It did not magically produce a well-adjusted individual, but did have several positive effects. Understanding the source of the difficulty allowed remediation of symptoms and discomfort by pharmacologic and psychologic intervention. They also provided the patient with an explanation for the particular cognitive difficulties experienced. While painful, this made clear the necessity for a modification in his career pattern which would not have been acceptable without an adequate explanation as to its necessity.

The need for well-validated remediation procedures is also illustrated by the above case example. While research in this area is actively under way (Barth & Boll, 1980; Cleeland, 1980; Diller & Gordon, 1981), this most assuredly represents the current most important frontier of neuropsychological research.

ACKNOWLEDGMENT

Preparation of this chapter and supporting research were funded in part by the National Institute of Neurological and Communicative Disorders and Stroke, Contracts NO1-NS-5-2329 and NO1-NS-7-2373.

References

Bailey, P. Symposium on the temporal lobe. *American Medical Association Archives of Neurology and Psychiatry*, 1955, *74*, 568-569.

Barth, J., & Boll, T. J. Rehabilitation and treatment of central nervous system dysfunction: A behavioral medicine perspective. In L. A. Bradley & C. Prokov (Eds.), *Medical psychology: A new perspective.* New York: Academic Press, 1980.

Berent, S. Functional asymmetry of the human brain in the recognition of faces. *Neuropsychologia*, 1977, *15*, 829-831.

Boll, T. J. Behavioral correlates of cerebral damage in children aged 9-14. In R. M. Reitan & L. A. Davison (Eds.), *Clinical neuropsychology: Current status and application.* Washington, D. C.: V. H. Winston & Sons, 1974.

Boll, T. J. Diagnosing brain impairment. In B. B. Wolman (Ed.), *Clinical diagnosis of mental disorder* (Vol. 18). New York: Plenum Publishing Corp. 1978.

Boll, T. J. The Halstead-Reitan Neuropsychology Battery. In S. Filskov & T. J. Boll (Eds.), *Handbook of human clinical neuropsychology.* New York: John Wiley & Sons, 1981.

Boll, T. J., Heaton, R., & Reitan, R. M. Neuropsychological and emotional correlates of Huntington's chorea. *Journal of Nervous and Mental Disease*, 1974, *158*, 61-69.

Boll, T. J., & Reitan, R. M. Motor and tactile-perceptual deficits in brain-damaged children. *Perceptual and Motor Skills*, 1972, *34*, 343-350.

Black, P., Shepard, R. H., & Walker, A. E. Outcome of head trauma: Age and posttraumatic seizures. In R. Porter & D. FitzSimmons (Eds.), *Outcome of severe damage to the central nervous system* (Ciba Foundation Symposium 34). Amsterdam: Elsevier, 1975.

Broca, T. Sur la faculté de la langage articulé. *Bulletin de la Société d'Anthropologie*, 1861, *6*, 493.

Bruell, J. H., & Albee, G. W. Higher intellectual functions in a patient with hemispherectomy for tumors. *Journal of Consulting and Clinical Psychology*, 1962, *26*, 90.

Chapman, L., & Wolff, H. G. The cerebral hemispheres and the highest integrated functions of man. *American Medical Association Archives of Neurology*, 1959, *1*, 357.

Cleeland, C. S. Biofeedback as a clinical tool: Its use with the neurologically impaired patient. In S. Filskov & T. J. Boll (Eds.), *Handbook of human clinical neuropsychology.* New York: John Wiley & Sons, 1980.

Cobb, S. A. A salute for neurologists. In F. A. Beech, D. O. Hebb, C. T. Morgan, & H. W. Nissen (Eds.), *The neuropsychology of Lashley.* New York: McGraw-Hill, 1960.

Davison, L. A. Current status of clinical neuropsychology. In R. M. Reitan & L. A. Davison (Eds.), *Clinical neuropsychology: Current status and applications.* Washington, D.C.: V. H. Winston & Sons, 1974.

DeJong, R. N. *The neurologic examination.* New York: Hoeber, 1967.

Diller, L., & Gordon, W. A. Rehabilitation and clinical neuropsychology. In S. Filskov & T. J. Boll (Eds.), *Handbook of human clinical neuropsychology.* New York: John Wiley & Sons, 1981.

Filskov, S. B., & Goldstein, S. G. Diagnostic validity of the Halstead-Reitan Neuropsychological Battery. *Journal of Consulting and Clinical Psychology*, 1974, *42*, 383-388.

Franz, S. I. On the functions of the cerebrum: The frontal lobes. *Archives of Psychology*, 1907, *2*, 1.

Freeman, W., & Watt, J. *Psychosurgery*. Springfield, IL: Charles C. Thomas, 1942.

Fulton, J. F. *Functional localization in the frontal lobes and cerebellum*. Oxford: Clarendon Press, 1933.

Galin, D. Implications for psychiatry of left and right cerebral specialization. *Archives of General Psychiatry*, 1974, *31*, 572-583.

Galin, D. Lateral specialization and psychiatric issues: Speculations on development and the evolution of consciousness. *Annals of the New York Academy of Science*, 1977, *299*, 397-411.

Gazzaniga, M. S. *The bisected brain*. New York: Appleton-Century-Crofts, 1970.

Geschwind, M. The borderline of neurology and psychiatry: Some common misconceptions. In D. S. Benson & D. Bloomer (Eds.), *Psychiatric aspects of neurological disease*. New York: Grune & Stratton, 1975.

Golden, C. J., & Kuperman, S. J. Graduate training in clinical neuropsychology. *Professional Psychology*, 1980, *11*, 55-63.

Goldstein, S. G., Deysach, R. E., & Kleinknecht, R. A. Effect of experience and amount of information on identification of cerebral impairment. *Journal of Consulting and Clinical Psychology*, 1973, *41*, 30-34.

Goldstein, S. G., Kleinknecht, R. A., & Gallo, A. E. Neuropsychological changes associated with carotid endarterectomy. *Cortex*, 1970, *6*, 308-322.

Goodglass, H., & Kaplan, E. *The assessment of aphasia and related disorders*. Philadelphia: Lea & Febiger, 1972.

Hardyck, C., & Petrinovich, L. F. Left-handedness. *Psychological Bulletin*, 1977, *84*, 385-404.

Heaton, R. J., Smith, H. H., Lehman, R. A., & Vogt, A. T. Prospects for faking believable deficits on neuropsychological testing. *Journal of Consulting and Clinical Psychology*, 1978, *46*, 892-900.

Hecaen, H., & Ajuriaguerra, J. *Left handedness*. New York: Grune & Stratton, 1964.

Jackson, J. H. Relations of different divisions of the central nervous system to one another and to parts of the body. In J. Taylor (Ed.), *Selected writings of John Hughlings Jackson* (Vol. 2). New York: Basic Books, 1932. (Originally published, 1898.)

King, G. D., Gideon, D. A., Haynes, C. D., Dempsey, R. L., & Jenkins, C. W. Intellectual and personality changes associated with carotid endarterectomy. *Journal of Clinical Psychology*, 1977, *33*, 215-220.

Lezak, M. *Neuropsychological assessment*. New York: Oxford University Press, 1976.

Luria, A. R. Neuropsychological studies in the USSR: Part I. *Proceedings of the National Academy of Sciences*, 1973, *70*, 959.

Martindale, C. Hemisphere asymmetry and Jewish intelligence test patterns. *Journal of Consulting and Clinical Psychology*, 1978, *46*, 1299-1301.

Matthews, C. G., Shaw, D. J., & Kløve, H. Psychological test performances in "pseudoneurologic" subjects. *Cortex*, 1966, *11*, 244-253.

Milner, B. Laterality effects in audition. In V. B. Mountcastle (Ed.), *Interhemispheric relations and cerebral dominance*. Baltimore: Johns Hopkins University Press, 1962.

Milner, B. Brain mechanisms suggested by studies of temporal lobes. In F. L. Darley (Ed.), *Brain mechanisms underlying speech and language*. New York: Grune & Stratton, 1967.

Milner, B. Visual retention and recall after right temporal excision in man. *Neuropsychologica*, 1968, *6*, 191-210.

Newman, O. S., Heaton, R. K., & Lehman, R. A. Neuropsychological and MMPI correlates of patients' future employment characteristics. *Perceptual and Motor Skills*, 1978, *46*, 635-642.

Reitan, R. M. Psychological deficits resulting from cerebral lesions in man. In J. M. Warren & K. Akert (Eds.), *The frontal granular cortex and behavior*. New York: McGraw-Hill, 1964.

Reitan, R. M. Problems and prospects in studying the psychological correlates of brain lesions. *Cortex*, 1966, *2*, 127-154. (a)

Reitan, R.M. A research program on the psychological effects of brain lesions in human beings. In N. R. Ellis (Ed.), *International review of research in mental retardation*. New York: Academic Press, 1966. (b)

Reitan, R. M. Methodological problems in clinical neuropsychology. In R. M. Reitan & L. Davison (Eds.), *Clinical neuropsychology: Current status and application*. Washington, D.C.: V. H. Winston & Sons, 1974.

Reitan, R. M., & Boll, T. J. Intellectual and cognitive functions in Parkinson's disease. *Journal of Consulting and Clinical Psychology*, 1971, *37*, 364-369.

Reitan, R. M., & Boll, T. J. Neuropsychological correlates of minimal brain dysfunction. *Annals of the New York Academy of Science*, 1973, *205*, 65-88.

Restak, R. *The brain: The last frontier*. New York: Doubleday, 1979.

Rosenbaum, A. L. Neuropsychologic outcome of children born via the occiput posterior position. In C. R. Angel & E. A. Bering (Eds.), *Physical trauma as an etiological agent in mental retardation*. Bethesda: National Institute of Neurological Diseases and Stroke, 1970.

Rourke, B. P. Brain-behavior relationships in children with learning disabilities. *American Psychologist*, 1975, *30*, 911-920.

Rourke, B. P. Neuropsychological assessment of children with learning disabilities. In S. Filskov & T. J. Boll (Eds.), *Handbook of human clinical neuropsychology*. New York: John Wiley & Sons, 1981.

Russell, E. W. Multiple scoring method for assessment of complex memory functions. *Journal of Consulting and Clinical Psychology*, 1975, *43*, 800-809.

Russell, E. W. The Bender-Gestalt and the Halstead-Reitan Battery: A case study. *Journal of Clinical Psychology*, 1976, *32*, 355-361.

Russell, E. W. The pathology and clinical examination of memory. In S. Filskov & T. J. Boll (Eds.), *Handbook of human clinical neuropsychology*. New York: John Wiley & Sons, 1981.

Russell, E. W., Neuringer, C., & Goldstein, G. *Assessment of brain damage: A neuropsychological key approach*. New York: Wiley-Interscience, 1970.

Rutter, M. Brain damage syndromes in childhood: Concepts and findings. *Journal of Child Psychology and Psychiatry*, 1977, *18*, 1-21.

Rylander, G. *Personality changes after operation on the frontal lobes: A clinical study of 32 cases*. Copenhagen: Munksgaard, 1939.

Samuels, I., Butters, N., & Fedio, P. Short-term memory disorders following temporal removals in humans. *Cortex*, 1972, *8*, 283-298.

Schreiber, D. J., Goldman, H., Kleinman, K. F., Goldfader, P. R., & Snow, M. Y. The relationship between independent neuropsychological and neurological detection and localization of cerebral impairment. *Journal of Nervous and Mental Disease*, 1976, *162*, 360-365.

Semmes, J. Hemispheric specialization: A possible clue to mechanism. *Neuropsychologia*, 1968, *6*, 11-26.

Smith, A. Neuropsychological testing in neurological disorders. In W. J. Friedlander (Ed.), *Advances in neurology* (Vol. 7). New York: Raven Press, 1975.

Spreen, O. J., & Benton, A. C. Development norms for 15 neuropsychological tests ages 6 to 15. *Cortex,* 1965, *5,* 171–191.

Wernicke, C. *Der Aphosische Symptom en Complex.* Breslan: Max Cohn and Wergent, 1874.

Willerman, L. Fetal head position during delivery and intelligence. In C. R. Angel & E. A. Bering (Eds.), *Physical trauma as an etiological agent in mental retardation.* Bethesda: National Institute of Neurological Diseases and Stroke, 1970.

CHAPTER

4

Assessment of Schizophrenia

JOHN M. NEALE
THOMAS F. OLTMANNS

Implicit in early writings on schizophrenia, like those of Kraepelin and Bleuler, was the idea that schizophrenia is a disease. Although this disease viewpoint still persists, it is equally clear that it is a difficult position to defend, particularly because of the ambiguity which surrounds the definition of "disease" itself (Kendell, 1975; Meehl, 1972). Schizophrenia has also been conceptualized as a learned social role (e.g., Scheff, 1966), as a strategy for coping with an untenable life situation (Laing, 1969), and as a group of more or less independent maladaptive responses that are produced and maintained by reinforcement from the patient's environment (Ullmann & Krasner, 1968). There is much less than total agreement on how to think about schizophrenia.

Our solution to this problem is to regard schizophrenia as a scientific construct. (A closely related alternative is the notion of a "syndrome" [e.g., Spitzer, Sheehy, & Endicott, 1977], although we believe that the construct approach is preferable in some ways [see Neale & Oltmanns, 1980].) By taking this tack we avoid a premature emphasis on any single model of schizophrenia. And there is no implication that any particular type of information (e.g., current symptoms vs. history) should be especially emphasized in attempts to define the

John M. Neale. Department of Psychology, State University of New York at Stony Brook, Stony Brook, New York.
Thomas F. Oltmanns. Department of Psychology, Indiana University, Bloomington, Indiana.

construct. Questions concerning schizophrenia can then be placed in
the more general context of defining and validating scientific constructs. As to definitional issues, we regard the schizophrenia construct as open but capable of being partially defined via a series of
measurement operations (cf. Hempel, 1958). Further definition and
validation of the construct then involves specifying the network of
lawful relationships into which the construct enters (Cronbach &
Meehl's nomological network [1955]).

When schizophrenia is seen as an open, scientific construct, the
assessment enterprise becomes central to our understanding of the
disorder, particularly as overt behaviors are related to other referents
(e.g., prognosis, family history, and so on) associated with it. In contrast to the disease model, which assumes a static set of clearly defined
symptoms, the construct approach does not assign a priori significance to any particular behaviors. The relevance of specific symptoms is determined empirically by relating them to other factors such
as treatment response. The construct approach does emphasize the
importance of the individual's specific behavior, unlike labeling
theory, which focuses almost exclusively on the social context in
which it takes place. Seen from the construct perspective, the phenomena associated with the labeling process are interesting but nevertheless secondary to our understanding of the etiology and treatment
of schizophrenia. Both the construct approach and the behavioral
formulation are concerned with the careful observation of overt
behaviors, but they share little else in common. Operantly oriented
clinicians have generally been interested in the identification of isolated maladaptive behaviors (e.g., incoherent speech) and the manipulation of environmental contingencies which presumably maintain
such responses. When schizophrenia is viewed as a hypothetical construct, specific symptoms may be seen as the various manifestations of
internal mediating variables, including biological and cognitive processes. The construct perspective also raises assessment issues which are
beyond the realm of a simple learning viewpoint. One such example
is the search for endophenotypic traits which may signal the presence
of a genetically based vulnerability to the disorder. Thus, overall, the
construct approach has several advantages over other ways of conceptualizing schizophrenia. It is empirically based, concerned with a
variety of biological and environmental events, and flexible enough
to handle the obvious complexity of the phenomena associated with
schizophrenia.

Given the foregoing arguments, the question of the assessment of schizophrenia becomes very broad. A definition of the construct could be approached, for example, by assessments of observable behavior, verbal report, biochemical markers, presence of a positive family history for the disorder, response to treatment, and history and course, to mention only a small subset of the possibilities. Most of these measurement operations hinge on data obtained from investigations relying on behaviorally defined groups of schizophrenics. For example, given a diagnosis of schizophrenia, the presence of a positive family history, good response to phenothiazines, and a history of poor premorbid adjustment could all be seen as corroborating the diagnostic decision. But none of these variables are currently given as much weight as the patient's behavior in the initial diagnostic assessment. Thus, to bring our task within manageable limits we have chosen to focus most of our discussion on the data which are presently of paramount importance: current behavior, history, and course. (Some writers [e.g., Cromwell, 1975] would argue that current behavior [e.g., symptoms] will never prove adequate in assessing schizophrenia. While these arguments have merit, the alternatives [e.g., laboratory tests] have not yet been sufficiently validated to warrant detailed discussion.)

We will first discuss some of the history of the schizophrenia concept, describing how tremendous differences in the definition of the term emerged. This discussion will be followed by a consideration of two recent developments in assessment procedures: structured interview schedules and specific diagnostic criteria. Finally, we will present contemporary data concerning the primary behavioral features which are related to the construct.

Survey of Diagnostic Concepts

HISTORY OF THE CONCEPT

The foundation for modern conceptions of schizophrenia was laid in the nineteenth century. The famous French physician Pinel, for example, applied the term *la manie* to most patients. Yet, another group, also viewed as insane but not showing the same degree of affective excess, were said to have *la démence* — dementia, presumably without a strong emotional component. At about the same time, the

British physician Haslam (1809) described what appeared to be similar patients who displayed "a state which cannot be termed maniacal or melancholic: a state of complete insanity, yet unaccompanied by furious or depressing passions." Later in the century, Morel applied the term dementia praecox (*démence précoce*) to similar patients. Catatonia was described as a separate disease in 1874 by Kahlbaum, who noted both the clinical features and the typical cyclic course. Hecker (1871), a student of Kahlbaum's, published a monograph on hebephrenia which stressed the symptomatology and deteriorating course. The beginning of what we may view as "the modern period," though, comes with the work of Emil Kraepelin (1855–1926) and his delineation of the concept *dementia praecox*.

In the fourth edition of his famous textbook of psychiatry (1893), Kraepelin had used the term dementia praecox in a narrow sense to refer to patients who fit Hecker's description of hebephrenia. He grouped dementia praecox together with catatonia and dementia paranoides under "processes of dementing." The title of this chapter was changed to "Dementia Praecox" in the fifth edition (1896) of his text, thus indicating a shift in Kraepelin's conception of the disorder. The full-blown concept of dementia praecox was first presented in a paper titled "The Diagnosis and Prognosis of Dementia Praecox" which was delivered to the 29th Congress of Southwestern German Psychiatry in Heidelberg in 1898. Two major groups of endogenous (internally produced) psychoses were differentiated: manic–depressive illness and dementia praecox. (Paraphrenia was also proposed by Kraepelin as a diagnosis for cases with less severe intellectual deterioration and more pronounced delusions.) Dementia praecox now included several of the diagnostic concepts which had previously been regarded as distinct entities (e.g., catatonia, hebephrenia, dementia paranoides). The term dementia praecox is itself descriptive of two major features of the disorder: an early onset (praecox) and a progressive intellectual deterioration (dementia). Among the major symptoms that Kraepelin saw in such patients were hallucinations, delusions, negativism, attentional difficulties, stereotyped behaviors, and emotional dysfunctions. Thus, Kraepelin focused on both course and symptoms in defining the disorder, although he often emphasized the former over the latter.

In proposing a unitary dementia praecox concept, Kraepelin had brought together several disorders which had been described earlier in the century. But Kraepelin also recognized the behavioral heterogeneity of patients included in the diagnosis. Therefore, dementia praecox was further divided into subtypes, depending on the prominence of particular symptoms. In early editions of his text, three subcategories were proposed. In the paranoid type, delusions were predominant. In the catatonic type, motor dysfunctions were most obvious, and in the hebephrenic type, emotional incongruity was the major feature. Later, following Bleuler's lead, Kraepelin added a fourth category, the simple type, for which no single symptom was paramount.

Kraepelin did not move much beyond a descriptive level. In the eighth edition of his textbook, for example, he grouped the symptoms of dementia praecox into 36 major categories, each of which contained hundreds of individual behaviors. Little effort was made to interrelate the symptoms. Kraepelin stated only that they all reflected dementia and a loss of the usual unity between thinking, feeling, and acting.

In contrast to Kraepelin's descriptive approach, the viewpoint of the next major figure, Eugen Bleuler (1857-1939), represented both a specific attempt to define the "core" of the disorder and a move away from Kraepelin's emphasis on prognosis in diagnosis. Bleuler broke with Kraepelin on two major points, believing that the disorder in question did not necessarily have an early onset or an inevitable progression toward dementia. Thus Bleuler was much less attentive to the *course* of the disorder than was Kraepelin, and the label dementia praecox was no longer considered appropriate. In 1911, Bleuler proposed his own term, *schizophrenia,* to capture what he viewed as the essential feature of the disorder.

Psychoanalytic theory had a major influence on Bleuler's view of schizophrenia. First, he thought that Freudian concepts could account for the specific content of symptoms such as delusions and hallucinations. (See, for example, his 1906 paper. Also relevant here is Bleuler's association with C. G. Jung, who was also at the Borgholzli Clinic in Zurich and whose 1906 paper was a classic attempt to apply Freudian theory to dementia praecox.) Second, and even more importantly, Bleuler was led to attempt for schizophrenia what Freud had tried to accomplish for the neuroses — to specify underlying processes which were at the root of the various behavioral disturbances shown by schizophrenic patients.

Bleuler, like Kraepelin, had noted the wide variety of disturbance displayed by schizophrenic patients. But Bleuler went much further than Kraepelin in trying to specify a common denominator or essential property which would tie the types together. The metaphorical concept he used for this purpose was the "breaking of associative threads." For Bleuler, associative threads linked together not only words but thoughts. Thus, goal-directed, efficient thinking and communication were possible only when these hypothetical structures were intact. The notion that associative threads are disrupted in schizophrenics was then used to "account" for other problems. The attentional difficulties displayed by schizophrenics, for example, were viewed by Bleuler as resulting from a loss of purposeful direction in thought which in turn led to passive responding to immediately present environmental stimuli. In a similar vein, blocking, a seeming total loss of communication, was seen as a complete disruption in the associative threads for the current topic.

BLEULER'S AND KRAEPELIN'S CONTEMPORARY INFLUENCE

Kraepelin's writings fostered a narrow definition of schizophrenia and an emphasis on description. Although he recognized that a small percentage of patients who originally manifested symptoms of dementia praecox did not deteriorate, he preferred to limit this diagnostic category to only those patients who had a poor prognosis. Bleuler's work, in contrast, led to a broader concept of schizophrenia and a more pronounced theoretical emphasis. He placed patients with a good prognosis in his group of schizophrenias and even proposed the existence of "latent" schizophrenia, a term to be applied to patients who have the disorder but do not manifest overt schizophrenic symptoms. In addition, he included as schizophrenic "many atypical melancholias, and manias of other schools, especially hysterical melancholias and manias, most hallucinatory confusions, some 'nervous' people and compulsive and impulsive patients, and many prison psychoses" (1923, p. 436). Furthermore, the fundamental symptoms (the famous four "A's") which he outlined were less clearly defined than the symptoms which Kraepelin emphasized, and their identification often depended upon unreliable clinical inferences.

Bleuler has had a great influence on the American concept of schizophrenia. The breadth of the concept has been considerably extended. At the New York State Psychiatric Institute, for example, about 20% of patients were diagnosed schizophrenic in the 1930s.

This figure increased through the 1940s, and in 1952 peaked at a remarkable 80% (Kuriansky, Deming, & Gurland, 1974). The reasons for this increase are not hard to find; several prominent figures in the history of American psychiatry have broadened the concept of schizophrenia and also diverted attention from the process of differential diagnosis.

Adolf Meyer (1866–1950), considered by many to have been the dean of American psychiatry (e.g., Zilboorg, 1941), argued that diagnostic categories were often arbitrary and artificial (e.g., Meyer, 1917, 1926). Although Meyer visited Kraepelin in Heidelberg in 1896 and was influential in introducing American psychiatrists to the concept of dementia praecox, he was not enthusiastic about the diagnostic process and placed greater emphasis on the *individual* characteristics of each patient. His approach to schizophrenia was flexible and did not rely on either specific pathognomonic symptoms or progressive deterioration for a definition of the disorder.

Following Meyer's lead, a number of influential American investigators suggested the addition of further schizophrenic subtypes. For example, in 1933, Kasanin described a series of nine patients who had all been assigned diagnoses of dementia praecox. They had all demonstrated an acute onset of the disorder followed by a relatively rapid recovery. Noting that their symptoms represented a combination of schizophrenic and affective components, Kasanin suggested the term "schizoaffective psychosis" to describe these patients' disturbance. This category subsequently became part of the American concept of schizophrenia (DSM-I, 1952).

The schizophrenia category was further expanded by Hoch and his colleagues, who argued that schizophrenia often "masquerades" as other disorders. They suggested the terms "pseudoneurotic schizophrenia" (Hoch & Polatin, 1949) and "pseudopsychopathic schizophrenia" (Hoch & Dunaif, 1955) to describe anxious, withdrawn persons with serious interpersonal problems who also have neurotic and psychopathic symptoms. Hoch argued that while these patients often lacked more classic symptoms of schizophrenia, they would reveal, upon closer examination, the cognitive and emotional disorganization which he considered the hallmark of the disorder. Thus, in the Bleulerian tradition, his emphasis was on inferred dynamics rather than overt symptoms. In fact, Hoch reported that only 20% of a large group of pseudoneurotic schizophrenics developed *overt* schizophrenic symptoms during a 5- to 20-year follow-up study (Hoch, Cottell,

Strahl, & Pennes, 1962). As a result of such arguments, many patients who would otherwise have been diagnosed as suffering from neuroses, affective disorders, or personality disturbances came to be considered schizophrenic.

In the 1960s and 1970s the process-reactive dimension was another key feature in maintaining the breadth of the schizophrenia concept in the United States. Process (or poor premorbid) versus reactive (or good premorbid) schizophrenics are most often distinguished by measures of social and sexual adjustment prior to the onset of the disorder (e.g., the Phillips scale, 1953). The process-reactive distinction is strongly related to prognosis: reactives are more likely than process patients to have only an episodic problem and have good prognoses. In addition, the development of the disorder differs between the two groups. The process schizophrenic shows a slow, insidiously developing deterioration. The reactive, in contrast, shows a rapid onset, typically preceded by some environmental stress. Process schizophrenia, then, may be equated with Kraepelin's original description of dementia praecox, and the inclusion of reactive patients in the definition of schizophrenia helped keep the American concept broad.

A prevailing interest in treatment also served to broaden the American conception of schizophrenia. Both Bleuler and Meyer had rejected the notion that deterioration was an inherent element of the disorder, thus allowing the possibility of recovery and intervention. Harry Stack Sullivan (1892-1949) shared this optimistic view and became the first major theorist to develop a systematic approach to the psychological treatment of schizophrenia. Sullivan's psychoanalytic approach emphasized the *underlying* emotional and cognitive factors which seemed to motivate what Sullivan saw as the schizophrenic's withdrawal from interpersonal relationships. Behavior did not play an important role in his definition of the disorder. In fact, he maintained that there were *no* fundamental criteria for the disorder (1928).

By way of contrast, the European concept of schizophrenia has remained narrower than the American view. In the study mentioned earlier (Kuriansky *et al.*, 1974), the percentage of patients diagnosed schizophrenic at the Maudsley Hospital in London remained relatively constant (at 20%) over a 40-year period. In Europe, borderline cases are *not* diagnosed schizophrenic, and differentiations are made between nuclear (Frank, 1932) or true (Langfeldt, 1937) schizophrenia and schizophreniform psychosis. Langfeldt (1937), for example, compared schizophrenic patients with a deteriorating course to those who had recovered. A favorable outcome was found to be related to an acute onset, presence of precipitating stress, confusion, affective symptoms, and a family history of depression. These widespread differences led him to argue that these recovered patients were not classically schizophrenic and he proposed the diagnosis of schizophreniform psychosis for them. In the United States, a similar pattern of differences has been found between process and reactive schizophrenics (e.g., Phillips, 1968). Despite the many differences, however, both types of patients have continued to be regarded as schizophrenic in America.

The continued influence of Kraepelin's narrow, descriptive approach in Europe can also be seen in the diagnostic system advocated by Schneider (1959), a prominent figure in German psychiatry. Schneider proposed a set of "first-rank symptoms," a list of eleven disturbances which are thought to be pathognomonic of schizophrenia. (Schneider, although an intellectual descendant of Kraepelin, did not emphasize the course of the disorder as an essential diagnostic feature. In fact, he specifically stated that first-rank symptoms could *not* be used to determine the patient's prognosis [p. 142].) Rather than relying on highly inferential judgments made by the interviewer, Schneider emphasized the need for a careful exploration of the specific features of the patient's phenomenological experience. He believed that he had identified a set of symptoms which should be given preference over other features in the diagnosis of schizophrenia.

The first three symptoms listed by Schneider are types of auditory hallucinations: hearing voices speaking your thoughts aloud (audible thoughts), hearing voices talking about you in the third person (voices conversing), and hearing voices describing your behavior (voices commenting). The fourth first-rank symptom discussed by Schneider is concerned with "hallucinations of a somatic character." These experiences, known as somatic passivity, involve the patient's perception of interference with functions. This interference is often seen by the patient as being the work of external forces.

The next three first-rank symptoms are concerned with disturbed thinking. Schneider disagreed with Bleuler on this topic. (Schneider also argued that ambivalence and blunted or inadequate affective response were elusive concepts which were not important diagnostically [p. 119].) He proposed that "thought blocking" and "disjointed thinking" are not useful criteria for the diagnosis of schizophrenia because they are commonly observed in normal people and in other psychiatric disorders. Schneider noted three particularly meaningful forms of thought disturbance: thought withdrawal, thought insertion, and thought diffusion (or broadcasting). These phenomena were not considered to be mutually exclusive. Indeed, Schneider mentioned one patient who believed that her thoughts were withdrawn by her father following an earlier episode of thought diffusion.

Having considered disturbances of perception and thought, Schneider turned to a discussion of delusional phenomena, which he separated into two forms: delusional perception and delusional notion. The latter form of delusion included such phenomena as simple ideas of persecution and grandiosity. These symptoms were not regarded as being of primary diagnostic significance. Delusional perception, on the other hand, was considered by Schneider to be of "exceptional diagnostic importance." It is defined as the attribution of special, *personal* significance to a routine innocuous perception in the absence of reasonable justification. (Because it is based on a normal perception, this symptom was seen as belonging to the area of thought disturbance rather than perceptual disturbance.) Schneider noted that the inferred significance was almost always of an urgent nature.

The remaining first-rank symptoms consist of feelings, impulses, and motor actions which are experienced as imposed and controlled from outside the body. Schneider emphasized the importance of such beliefs in alien control but cautioned against the misinterpretation of patients' metaphorical references and superstitious ideas which might resemble such symptoms.

Schneider's list of symptoms is clearly very specific. He did allow for the occasional appearance of these symptoms in other psychotic disorders and did not insist on their presence to justify a diagnosis of schizophrenia. Nevertheless, he did argue that when these symptoms were present, they should be given first priority in the diagnosis of schizophrenia. Other criteria which cannot be "incontestably established" were given little importance by Schneider. For this reason, many of the patients who would be considered schizophrenic by Bleulerian criteria would be excluded from that diagnosis by Schneider. First-rank symptoms have played an important role in the development of contemporary European conceptions of schizophrenia and have been instrumental in the maintenance of the Kraepelinian tradition.

The results of the diagnostic differences that we have outlined between America and Europe have been studied empirically in a series of investigations conducted through the U.S.-U.K. Cross National Project (Cooper, Kendell, Gurland, Sharpe, Copeland, & Simon, 1972). In one part of the overall investigation, consecutive admissions to several hospitals in London and New York were interviewed by project staff who later reached a consensual diagnosis based on the International Classification of Diseases (ICD) and the British *Glossary of Mental Disorders* (General Register Office, 1968). (We will discuss these criteria later in the chapter.) These diagnoses were then compared with those made on the same patients by the staffs of the respective institutions.

The rate of schizophrenia diagnoses made by project staff was about the same for the New York and London patients (see Table 1). In contrast, examining the diagnoses made by the staffs of each institution, we see a great preponderence of schizophrenic diagnoses in New York. The difference between New York and project diagnoses can be further illustrated by examining project diagnoses of patients diagnosed as schizophrenic by the American hospital staff. As can be seen in Table 2, a substantial proportion of New York schizophrenics were diagnosed as having an affective illness by the project staff. Looking at American diagnoses in relation to project diagnoses, we

Table 1
Results of the U.S.–U.K. Diagnostic Project[a]

	New York		London	
	Hospital diagnosis	Project diagnosis	Hospital diagnosis	Project diagnosis
Schizophrenia	118	56	59	61
Affective illness	13	62	68	76
Neurosis	5	3	10	7
Personality disorder	2	8	8	5
Other	54	63	29	25
TOTAL	192	192	174	174

[a]From data of Cooper *et al.* (1972).

Table 2
**Project Diagnoses of Patients Diagnosed as Schizophrenic
by New York Hospital Staff[a]**

Project diagnosis	n
Schizophrenia	50
Affective illness	42
Neurosis	3
Personality disorder	5
Other	18
TOTAL	118

[a]From data of Cooper *et al.* (1972).

find that many patients in all project categories were regarded as schizophrenic in New York. *"Sixty-three percent of those with a project diagnosis of depressive psychosis, 91 percent of those with a project diagnosis of mania, 69 percent of those with a project diagnosis of neurosis, and 63 percent of those with a project diagnosis of personality disorder all have hospital diagnoses of schizophrenia"* (Cooper *et al.*, 1972, p. 104). Thus, the American concept of schizophrenia (or at least the New York concept) was shown to be considerably broader than that used either by project staff or by hospital staff in London. (There is considerable variation within the U.S. in the breadth of the schizophrenia concept. For example, groups of psychiatrists in California and in St. Louis utilize criteria somewhat closer to U.K. standards [Sharpe, Gurland, Fleiss, Kendell, Cooper, & Copeland, 1974].)

The U.S.-U.K. Cross National Project clearly illustrates the distinction between broad and narrow conceptions of schizophrenia. The Bleulerian approach to diagnosing schizophrenia, which has prevailed in the United States, places a principal emphasis upon the presence of certain cognitive and emotional disturbances which are loosely defined and sometimes difficult to identify. Specific symptoms, such as hallucinations and delusions, are not given as much weight. Consequently, a wide range of patients are included in this definition of schizophrenia. European diagnosticians, on the other hand, have generally followed the tradition established by Kraepelin and have excluded from a diagnosis of schizophrenia either those patients who have a good prognosis (Langfeldt, 1937) or those patients who do not manifest specific overt symptoms (Schneider, 1959).

CURRENT DIAGNOSTIC CRITERIA

There are currently several different diagnostic systems which are utilized by practicing clinicians and research investigators in various parts of the world. Two formalized diagnostic statements about schizophrenia have gained widespread acceptance: the American Psychiatric Association's *Diagnostic and Statistical Manual* (DSM-II, 1968) and the British *Glossary* (1968). (Although DSM-III has now been published, we present DSM-II because most American research on schizophrenia has been based on it.) Their criteria for schizophrenia are presented in Table 3. Both systems place schizophrenia within the more general category of functional psychoses. The British *Glossary* does not attempt a specific overall definition of psychosis (this apparent shortcoming is more than compensated for by its more extensive definition of schizophrenia). DSM-II, in contrast, does provide such a general definition:

> Patients are described as psychotic when their mental functioning is sufficiently impaired to interfere grossly with their capacity to meet the ordinary demands of life. The distortion may result from a serious distortion in their capacity to recognize reality. Hallucinations and delusions, for example, may distort their perceptions. Alterations of mood may be so profound that the patient's capacity to respond appropriately is grossly impaired. Deficits in perception, language and memory may be so severe that the patient's capacity for mental grasp of his situation is effectively lost. (p. 23)

Beyond these introductory comments, the DSM-II definition is quite brief and involves only the simplest mention of several putative features of the disorder: (1) thought disorder including delusions and hallucinations, (2) mood disorders such as ambivalence, constricted or inappropriate responsiveness, and (3) behavioral features such as regression and withdrawal. Some equally brief theoretical comments are made along with these descriptions. Delusions and hallucinations are labeled as "self-protective" and viewed as due to a disturbance in concept formation which in turn produced misinterpretation of reality. This causal hypothesis — disorder in concept formation ⟶ misperception of reality ⟶ delusions and hallucinations — is totally unsubstantiated.

Table 3
Formal Definitions of Schizophrenia

DSM-II (1968)	British *Glossary* (1968)
This large category includes a group of disorders manifested by characteristic disturbances of thinking, mood, and behavior. Disturbances in thinking are marked by alterations of concept formation which may lead to misinterpretation of reality and sometimes to delusions and hallucinations, which frequently appear psychologically self-protective. Corollary mood changes include ambivalent, constricted and inappropriate emotional responsiveness and loss of empathy with others. Behavior may be withdrawn, regressive, and bizarre. . . .	Under this heading are included those illnesses which are characterized from the outset by a fundamental disturbance of the personality involving its most basic functions, which give the normal person his feeling of individuality, uniqueness and self-direction. The schizophrenic disturbance shows itself in an utterly unfamiliar experience, *in a setting of evidently clear consciousness,*[a] whereby the person's inmost life, thoughts, feelings and acts are known to or shared by others, accompanied (or followed a very short time later) by explanatory delusions that the patient's thoughts, etc., are influenced by outside forces which may be natural or supernatural; these ideas and passivity experiences frequently assume bizarre form. Hallucinations are common, predominately auditory, in the form of "voices" which may comment on the patient's thoughts and actions, and somatic or tactile, and unpleasant sensations which the patient may be unable to describe in ordinary language and which again usually lead to delusional interpretation. An important symptom of schizophrenia, not however evident in all cases, is a curious disturbance of thinking, which is usually prominent, in which peripheral, marginal, and irrelevant features of a total concept, inhibited in normal directed mental activity, are brought to the forefront and utilized in place of the elements relevant and appropriate to a given situation. Thus thinking becomes vague, elliptical and obscure and its

Table 3 *(continued)*

DSM-II (1968)	British *Glossary* (1968)
	expression in speech often incomprehensible. Sudden breaks in the flow of thought ("blocking") are frequent, and there is difficulty in retaining thoughts, which is often interpreted delusionally as "thought withdrawal" by outside agencies. Hearing one's thoughts spoken aloud is common and is believed to be diagnostically significant. Perception is also disturbed so that irrelevant features of a percept become all-important and, accompanied by passivity feelings, lead the patient to believe that everyday objects and situations, e.g., statements in the press, possess a special, usually sinister, meaning especially intended for him. The affective state becomes capricious and often inappropriate to a given situation. It should, moreover, be borne in mind that a minority of cases showing the foregoing features clear up apparently without residual defect.

[a]Consciousness may be slightly impaired temporarily in an "acute schizophrenic episode" (295.4).

The definition in the British *Glossary* is much more complete and descriptive. Characteristic delusions and hallucinations are described in some detail. Likewise, thought disorder is not simply mentioned but described, and the important point is made that thought disturbances do *not* occur in all schizophrenic patients. Finally, it is noted that schizophrenic symptomatology must occur in the context of a state of clear consciousness, thus distinguishing this psychosis from those, usually caused by organic illness or toxic states, wherein consciousness is clouded.

There are several criteria by which these two approaches to the diagnosis of schizophrenia may be evaluated. Reliability is a particularly important one because it sets a limit on the validity of the construct. Clearly, a construct that cannot be identified consistently cannot possess systematic meaning or importance (Hempel, 1961). One useful measure of reliability is kappa, an index of interrater agreement which is corrected for the expected rate of chance agreement (Cohen, 1960). A kappa value of zero indicates that the raters agree at exactly the level expected by chance. Improvements on the chance rate, up to a perfect rate of $+1.0$, are reflected in positive kappa scores. Negative values reflect less than chance agreement. Spitzer and Fleiss (1974) have assembled kappa values for several studies of diagnostic reliability published prior to 1972. The kappa values which they report for diagnoses of schizophrenia are presented in Table 4 along with data from additional studies reported after Spitzer and Fleiss conducted their review. The rather modest kappa values presented in this table indicate that schizophrenia can be diagnosed with some degree of reliability. But they also leave some room for improvement. (The range of values [.27 – .77] is striking. A number of factors such as the method of data collection [interviews vs. case folders] and the experience of the raters are important sources of variance in these studies. A complete discussion of these points is beyond the scope of this chapter.)

Table 4
Reliability of Diagnosing Schizophrenia

Study	Kappa	Sample size	Diagnostic criteria
Schmidt and Fonda (1956)[a]	.77	426	DSM-I
Beck et al. (1962)[a]	.42	153	DSM-I
Sandifer et al. (1964)[a]	.68	91	DSM-I
Cooper et al. (1972)[a]	.60	424	ICD-8
Blashfield (1973)	.27	[b]	DSM-II
Kety (1974)	.67	364	DSM-II
Kuriansky et al. (1974)	.48	120	DSM-II

[a]Kappa values presented in Spitzer and Fleiss (1974)
[b]The sample in this study was composed of 71 computer-generated stimuli, or "artificial patients."

One approach to this diagnostic problem is to examine the sources of disagreement. Beck and his colleagues in Philadelphia conducted just such an investigation (Ward, Beck, Mendelson, Mock, & Erbaugh, 1962). They reexamined the data from their original study (included in Table 4) to identify major problem areas. Meeting again after they had completed the interviews and made their initial diagnoses, the clinicians found three major reasons why they had not always reached the same determination. First, accounting for 5% of the disagreements, *were inconsistencies on the part of the patient.* The second major group of diagnostic disagreements (32.5%) were attributed to *inconsistencies on the part of the diagnostician.* Differences in interview techniques, in judging the importance of particular symptoms, and in interpreting the same pathology constituted most of these inconsistencies. The third and largest group of disagreements (62.5%) were considered to stem from *inadequacies of the diagnostic system.* The diagnosticians found the criteria unclear. Either too fine distinctions were required, or the classification system seemingly forced the diagnostician to choose a major category that was not specific enough.

These data have motivated two major developments aimed at the improvement of diagnostic procedures. First, structured interview schedules have been developed to guide the clinician in the collection of information regarding symptomatology and social history. Second, more specific criteria have been proposed to simplify the process of diagnostic decision-making and to eliminate many of the ambiguities present in earlier systems such as DSM-II.

Contemporary Diagnostic Methods

STRUCTURED MENTAL-STATUS INTERVIEWS

Several research teams have constructed formal interview schedules (e.g., Burdock & Hardesty, 1969; Spitzer & Endicott, 1968; Spitzer & Endicott, 1978). There are two such interviews that are in widespread current use: the Present State Exam (PSE) and the Schedule for Affective Disorders and Schizophrenia (SADS). The PSE has been carefully tested and modified through nine editions (Wing, Cooper, & Sartorius, 1974) and was utilized in both the Cross-National Project and the International Pilot Study of Schizophrenia

(World Health Organization, 1973). It is intended to be used as a guide for conducting an assessment of the patient's *current* mental status. The manual lists over 500 questions which are designed to elicit information which will allow the interviewer to rate 107 symptoms based on the patient's self-report. Many of the questions and definitions of items depend heavily on the work of Schneider (1959). Delusions and hallucinatory experiences, for example, are covered in great detail. Having asked the recommended questions for each item, the interviewer is encouraged to follow up any interesting or suggestive leads with additional questions in order to define the specific nature and degree of each symptom. Symptoms are rated on a scale ranging from 0 (not present) to 2 (present in severe form). Sample items are presented in Figure 1.

In addition to recording this type of self-reported symptoms, the PSE provides an opportunity to make direct observations of the patient's behavior, affect, and speech. Ratings are made on such topics as agitation, mannerisms and posturing, irritability, blunted affect, incoherence, and flight of ideas. An important feature of the PSE is the extensive definitions which are provided for various symptoms. A glossary of descriptive terms and instructions for ratings is provided to clarify the assessment procedure. The glossary items which correspond to the questions in Figure 1 are presented in Figure 2. These specific definitions facilitate the reliability with which the interview can be employed.

The interrater reliability of the PSE is indeed impressive. Kendell, Everitt, Cooper, Sartorius, and David (1968) reported a detailed examination of the extent of agreement between ratings made by an interviewer following the PSE and a subsequent observer who viewed a videotape of the same interview. Reliability estimates for specific items were, for the most part, highly acceptable although mean kappa values for items based on the patient's verbal report were significantly higher than corresponding values for items based on the interviewer's observations (.76 and .49, respectively). In many forms of analysis based on PSE interviews, individual items are grouped into sections which reflect major areas of functioning, for instance, general anxiety, depressed mood, and perceptual disturbances. The specific reliabilities of the 23 sections studied by Kendell and his colleagues are presented in Table 5. The average correlations between ratings made by the interviewer and the observer was .84 for these item groups. Comparable values have been reported by Luria and McHugh (1974).

Do you ever seem to hear your own thoughts repeated or echoed?
(What is that like? How do you explain it?)
(Where does it come from?)
RATE THOUGHT ECHO OR COMMENTARY. ☐ (57)

   1 = Thought echo. If any doubt, rate (8) or (0).
   2 = Subject experiences alien thoughts related to his own thoughts, that is, associations or comments on his own thoughts. Not hallucinations.

Do you ever experience your thoughts stopping quite unexpectedly so that there are none left in your mind, even when your thoughts were flowing freely before?
(What is that like?)
(How often does it occur? What is it due to?)

Do your thoughts ever seem to be taken out of your head, as though some external person or force were removing them?
(Can you give an example?)
(How do you explain it?)
RATE THOUGHT BLOCK OR WITHDRAWAL. ☐ (58)

   1 = Thought block. Do not include if due to anxiety or lack of concentration; only if it occurs totally unexpectedly when thoughts are flowing freely. One single occasion is not sufficient for rating. *Be very critical in rating this symptom.*
   2 = Delusional explanation that thoughts are withdrawn.

Can anyone read your thoughts?
(How do you know? How do you explain it?)
RATE DELUSION OF THOUGHTS BEING READ: *Only if subject does not mean that people can infer his thoughts from his acions.*
(Do not include subject reading thoughts of other people → 76.) ☐ (59)

   1 = "Partial" delusion. Subject entertains the possibility that thoughts might be read but is not certain about it. Exclude if subcultural explanation.
   2 = Full delusion. Exclude if subcultural explanation. The term "thought reading" is commonly used to mean the ability to tell what someone is thinking from the way they behave—this use should be excluded.

Figure 1

Sample items from the Present State Exam. Reprinted by permission from Wing *et al.* (1974, pp. 208-209). Copyright 1974, Cambridge University Press.

Diagnostic decisions based on information collected with the PSE are also highly reliable. During the development of the PSE, two interviewers each saw 172 patients. Using 11 major diagnostic groups, complete agreement was obtained in 84% of the cases, ranging from a low of 50% for personality disorders to a high of 92% for schizo-

57. THOUGHT ECHO OR COMMENTARY

See definition of "thought insertion" (No. 55): the general remarks apply also to the present symptom which is often rated positively on insufficient evidence.

The subject experiences his own thought as repeated or echoed (not just spoken aloud = 56) with very little interval between the original and the echo. Rate this situation (1). The repetition may not be a simple echo, however, but subtly or grossly changed in quality.

If the subject experiences alien thoughts in association with his own, or as comments upon his own, rate (2). This experience is very rare but, when it occurs, the subject can describe it exactly. It is not the same as voices commenting on the subject's thoughts (No. 64).

58. THOUGHT BLOCK OR THOUGHT WITHDRAWAL

Thought block is extremely rare and should only be rated present when the examiner is quite sure it is present. If there is any doubt, it is probably *not* present. The subject experiences a sudden stopping of his thoughts, quite unexpectedly, while they are flowing freely, and in the absence of anxiety. When it occurs it is fairly dramatic and it happens on several occasions. Rate this (1).

Although the subject may be unable to describe pure thought block, it is very recognizable in the form of an explanatory delusion of thought withdrawal. The subject says that his thoughts have been removed from his head so that he has no thoughts.

Distinguish from the somewhat similar delusion of depersonalization (No. 90) in which the subject may say that he has no thought, but not that his thoughts have suddenly stopped or that they have withdrawn. It is the element of withdrawal which makes the symptom recognizable—rate (2). Withdrawal may be present without thought block being experienced.

Distinguish also from thought broadcast or sharing (No. 56) in which the subject still has plenty of thoughts but experiences them as being available to others beside himself.

59. DELUSIONS OF THOUGHT BEING READ

This is usually an explanatory delusion. Often it goes with delusions of reference or misinterpretation, which require some explanation of how other people know so much about the subject's future movements. It may be an elaboration of thought broadcast, thought insertion, auditory hallucinations, delusions of control, delusion of persecution, or delusions of influence. It can even occur with expansive delusions (the subject wishing to explain how Einstein, for example, stole his original ideas). The symptom is therefore in no way diagnostic. It is most important that it should not be mistaken for diagnostically more important symptoms such as thought insertion or broadcast.

If the subject merely entertains the possibility that his thought might be read but is not certain about it, rate (1). Rate delusional conviction (2).

Exclude those who think that people can read their thoughts as a result of belonging to a group that practices "thought reading"—this would be rated (1) or (2) on symptom No. 83.

Figure 2

Glossary items from the PSE to accompany the questions in Figure 1. Reprinted by permission from Wing *et al.* (1974, pp. 162-164). Copyright 1974, Cambridge University Press.

phrenia (Wing, Birley, Cooper, Graham, & Isaacs, 1967). Of the 16% disagreements, 7% were actually partial agreements (e.g., nonpsychotic depression [retarded] vs. nonpsychotic depression [other]). Thus, given a more careful and probing assessment, even of current symptomatology alone, quite impressive diagnostic reliability can be achieved.

Although the data on the PSE are impressive, it has two draw-

Table 5
Reliability of Section Scores Based on Item Groups from the PSE[a]

Item group	Product-moment correlations between interviewer and observer
Worry	.83
Tension	.93
General anxiety	.93
Situational anxiety	.58
Phobic avoidance	.81
Autonomic symptoms	.97
Slowed thinking	.80
Retardation	.85
Ideas of reference	.86
Self-opinion	.88
Depression of mood	.84
Signs of depression	.62
Somatic symptoms	.85
Irritability	.92
Elevation of mood	.85
Obsessional symptoms	.93
Interests	.86
Concentration	.94
Depersonalization	.96
Perceptual disturbance	.81
Memory	.85
Insight	.79
Abnormal motor behavior	.72

[a]Reprinted by permission from Kendell *et al.* (1968).

backs. First, training for most people is hard to come by and there are no specific training materials available. Second, the PSE, as its name implies, assesses current state only and has no history section. Historical data may be of importance in distinguishing between schizophrenia and recurrent brief episodes of reactive psychosis. The Schedule of Affective Disorders and Schizophrenia (SADS) provides a solution to both these problems (Spitzer & Endicott, 1978).

The SADS is an extensive structured interview broken into current and historical sections. Many symptoms are rated on a six-point scale of severity, while others follow the three-point present/absent ratings seen in the PSE. The points anchoring each scale are well described. Sample items are presented in Figure 3. Notice again that the SADS features a detailed inquiry into characteristic features of schizophrenia. It is not sufficient, for example, to merely rate the presence or absence of hallucinations. Rather, the questions must probe in depth the content of hallucinatory experiences. Training materials which accompany the SADS include case records to be rated and videotapes. Definitions of many key terms are included in the Research Diagnostic Criteria, a set of operationalizations of diagnostic criteria for most diagnoses. As with the PSE, diagnostic reliability using the SADS is impressive (Endicott & Spitzer, 1978). Intraclass correlation coefficients based on summary scale scores for independent raters viewing the same interview are presented in Table 6. The value for "delusions–hallucinations," which is perhaps the most important factor in arriving at a diagnosis of schizophrenia, was .97. Test–retest reliability, shown in the same table and determined in a separate set of interviews, was also substantial. Thus, the SADS is another very useful interview schedule which can be used to collect information about the patient's current and past mental status.

In sum, both the PSE and the SADS provide a good data base on which to make a diagnosis. One area — behavior ratings — though, requires more comment. Previously we noted that the reliability of the ratings of observable behavior was lower than that for ratings of a patient's verbal reports. But one of the key features of schizophrenia, flat affect, requires such a judgment. Because of this low reliability, the Feighner, Robins, Guze, Woodruff, Winokur, and Muñoz (1972) diagnostic criteria did not include flat affect and in DSM-III, flat affect plays a minor role in the diagnosis of schizophrenia. Both the PSE and the SADS, however, contain only a single item pertaining to

Figure 3

Sample items from the SADS interview. Reprinted by permission from Spitzer and Endicott (1978).

HALLUCINATIONS

Hallucinations are perceptions in the absence of identifiable external stimulation. For the purpose of this assessment, hallucinations are recorded here only if they occurred when the subject was fully awake, and neither febrile nor under the influence of alcohol or some drug. Hallucinations should not be confused with illusions, in which an external stimulus is misperceived, or normal thought processes which are exceptionally vivid. Always get the subject to describe the perception in detail. A rating of "suspected" indicates that the rater suspects, but is not certain, that the subject has experienced the particular kind of hallucination noted, as, for example, when it is not clear if the subject is describing an illusion rather than a true hallucination. If the hallucination occurred in the setting of a "religious experience," inquire to determine if this is an expected perception that is idiosyncratic to the subject.

If there is no evidence from the case record, informants, or from your interview to suggest hallucinations, ask the following questions and any others from the section on hallucinations which you think are appropriate.

Has there been anything unusual about the way things looked, or sounded, or smelled?

Have you heard voices or other things that weren't there or that other people couldn't hear, or seen things that were not there?

☐ If there is still no evidence to suggest hallucinations, check here and skip to Bizarre Behavior, p. 32.

Experienced auditory hallucinations of voices, noises, music, etc. (Do not include if limited to hearing name being called.)

0	No information
1	Absent
2	Suspected or likely
3	Definite

The (sounds, voices) that you said you heard, did you hear them outside your head, through your ears, or did they come from inside your head?

Could you hear what the voice was saying?

(Did it talk about you or repeat your thoughts?)

Did you hear anything else? What about noises?

(*continued*)

Figure 1 *(continued)*

Auditory hallucinations in which a voice keeps up a running commentary on the subject's behaviors or thoughts as they occur.	0	No information
	1	Absent
Did the voice describe or comment upon what you were doing or thinking?	2	Suspected or likely
	3	Definite
Auditory hallunications in which 2 or more voices converse with each other.	0	No information
	1	Absent
Did you hear 2 or more voices talking with each other?	2	Suspected or likely
	3	Definite
Nonaffective Verbal Hallucinations Spoken to the Subject. A voice or voices are heard by the subject speaking directly to him, the content of which is unrelated to depressed or elated mood (although he may be depressed or elated at the time). Rate absent if limited to voices saying only one or two words. Examples: A woman heard voices telling her that she was having a baby and should go to the hospital. A man heard a voice telling him he was being watched by his neighbors for signs of perversion.	0	No information
	1	Absent
	2	Suspected or likely
	3	Definite

CHARACTERISTICS OF HALLUCINATIONS OF ANY TYPE

The following items should be rated for the period when the subject had the hallucinations.

Severity of hallucinations of any type. (It may also include hallucinations not listed above.) Consider conviction in reality of hallucination, preoccupation, and effects on his actions.

(Did you ever think . . . was your imagination?)

(What did you do about it?)

0	No information
1	Definitely no hallucinations
2	Suspected or likely
3	Definitely present, but subject is generally aware that it is his imagination and is usually able to ignore it
4	Generally believes in the reality of the hallucination but it has little, if any, influence on his behavior
5	Convinced his hallucination is real and it has a significant effect on his actions, for example, locks doors to keep pursuers, whom he hears, away from him
6	Actions based on hallucinations have major impact on him or others, for example, converses with voices so much that he is unable to work

Skip to Bizarre Behavior, p. 32.

111

Table 6
Coefficients of Reliability for Summary Scales of the Schedule for
Affective Disorders and Schizophrenia (SADS)[a]

| Summary scales | Intraclass r | | Internal consistency[b] ($n = 150$) |
	Joint interview ($n = 150$)	Test–retest ($n = 60$)	
Depressive mood and ideation	.95	.78	.87
Endogenous features	.96	.83	.80
Depressive-associated features	.96	.88	.79
Suicidal ideation and behavior	.97	.83	.80
Anxiety	.94	.67	.58
Manic syndrome	.99	.93	.97
Delusions–hallucinations	.97	.91	.87
Formal thought disorder	.82	.49	.47

[a]Reprinted by permission from Endicott and Spitzer (1978).
[b]Cronbach's alpha.

this feature. Perhaps adequate reliability could be achieved by drawing on a classic principle for psychometric theory—increasing test length. Abrams and Taylor (1978) have attempted this by developing a 16-item scale of emotional blunting (see Table 7). (Note that some of the items [e.g., 7, 11, 16] appear to have little validity as indices of the blunted affect construct. Furthermore, Abrams and Taylor did not report any measures of internal consistency, so we are unable to determine if all the items in the scale are indeed relevant to the construct.)

In their paper, Abrams and Taylor report on the reliability of the scale in a sample of 30 patients who were sequentially interviewed by two diagnosticians. The reliability of individual items ranged from .32 to .76 (weighted kappa). More importantly, the overall reliability of the scale was .78. A group of 13 physicians who observed seven interviews also yielded an acceptable reliability figure for the entire scale (.77). Thus, it may be possible to improve on the SADS and the PSE in this area.

SPECIFIC DIAGNOSTIC CRITERIA

Once reliable information has been collected concerning the patient's current status, the diagnostician must know how to combine these data to arrive at a diagnosis. What symptoms must be present to indicate schizophrenia? What phenomena should exclude a patient from that category? The DSM-II is rather vague on these points. The

Table 7
Abrams and Taylor's Scale for Assessing Blunted Affect[a]

Item	Rating[b]			kW
Affect				
1. Absent, shallow, incongruous mood	0	1	2	.55
2. Constricted affect (narrow range)	0	1	2	.41
3. Unvarying affect (lacks modulation)	0	1	2	.73
4. Unrelated affect (lacks warmth, empathy)	0	1	2	.43
Behavior				
5. Expressionless face	0	1	2	.68
6. Unvarying, monotonous voice	0	1	2	.68
7. Seclusive/withdrawn, avoids social contact	0	1	2	.65
8. Lacks social graces (negligent dress, ill-mannered, unbathed)	0	1	2	.32
9. Difficult to excite emotions/unresponsive	0	1	2	.68
10. Lacks spontaneity	0	1	2	.73
11. Causeless, silly laughter/silly disposition	0	1	2	.32
12. Indifferent to surroundings (staff, visitors, patients, physical environs)	0	1	2	.74
Thought content				
13. Indifference/lack of affection for family, friends	0	1	2	.57
14. Indifference/unconcern for own present situation	0	1	2	.51
15. Indifference/unconcern for own future (lacks plans, ambition, desires, drive)	0	1	2	.76
16. Paucity of thought (unable to elaborate on answers)	0	1	2	.51
Total score_____				

[a]Reprinted by permission from Abrams and Taylor (1978). Copyright 1978, the American Psychiatric Association.
[b]0 = absent, 1 = slight or doubtful, 2 = clearly present.

manual describes *typical* features of schizophrenia but does not specify exactly what the boundaries of that construct are. Several groups of investigators have suggested specific sets of criteria which may improve on current formal diagnostic systems in this regard. We will discuss one of these suggested sets of criteria, the Research Diagnostic Criteria (RDC), which is currently being used by numerous investigators and which is also the foundation for DSM-III (Spitzer *et al.*, 1977).

The RDC (Spitzer, Endicott, & Robins, 1978) are presented in Table 8. These criteria are an outgrowth of the earlier work of the Renard Hospital Group (e.g., Feighner *et al.*, 1972). The major differences are that in the RDC (1) the period of illness is no longer required to be six months in length; (2) delusions, hallucinations, and thought disorder are more clearly specified; and (3) several of the Renard criteria (e.g., unmarried) are omitted. In introducing their criteria, Spitzer and his colleagues note that while they do not exclude patients whose symptoms remit shortly after onset, they do intend to exclude many borderline-type patients as well as patients with principal affective symptoms.

The system has notable clarity and precision. First, the diagnostic terms are well defined in an accompanying manual. Second, and for the first time, rather precise information is presented to the diagnostician concerning just what is required for a diagnosis of schizophrenia. As can be seen from Table 8, the symptoms in the "A" section are drawn heavily from Schneider. But the system is more comprehensive than Schneider's in that it specifies exclusion criteria (e.g., symptoms of a major affective illness), and allows that the diagnosis of schizophrenia could be made in the absence of any first-rank symptom. The two symptoms required from group A, for example, could be grandiose delusions and formal thought disorder. Unfortunately, the utility of individual components of the RDC have not yet been investigated. It is not known, for example, whether some symptoms from group A are more telling than others or whether the presence of two of them is an optimal criterion. But initial work does suggest that the system achieves very adequate levels of diagnostic reliability. Spitzer *et al.* (1978), for example, report that interjudge agreement (kappa) for independent raters viewing the same interview with 68 newly admitted patients, using the RDC criteria for schizophrenia, was .80. In a subsequent study using a test–retest format with an additional 60 patients, the kappa coefficient for schizophrenia was .65.

A striking contrast between RDC and DSM-II diagnoses is illus-

Table 8
Research Diagnostic Criteria for Schizophrenia[a]

There are many different approaches to the diagnosis of Schizophrenia. The approach taken here avoids limiting the diagnosis to cases with a chronic or deteriorating course. It includes subjects who would not be considered schizophrenic by many, particularly those subtyped as "acute." However, the criteria are designed to screen out subjects frequently given clinical diagnosis such as: borderline schizophrenia, brief hysterical, or situational psychoses and paranoid states. Subjects with a full depressive or manic syndrome which overlaps active psychotic symptoms are excluded and are diagnosed as either Schizoaffective Disorder, Major Depressive Disorder, or Manic Disorder. If the symptoms in A occur only during periods of alcohol or drug use or withdrawal from them, the diagnosis should be Other Psychiatric Disorder because of the likely organic etiology of the symptoms.

A through C are required for the period of illness being considered.

A. During an active phase of the illness (may or may not now be present) at least two of the following are required for definite and one for probable:
1. Thought broadcasting, insertion, or withdrawal (as defined in this manual).
2. Delusions of being controlled (or influenced), other bizarre delusions, or multiple delusions (as defined in this manual).
3. Somatic, grandiose, religious, nihilistic, or other delusions without persecutory or jealous content lasting at least one week.
4. Delusions of any type if accompanied by hallucinations of any type for at least one week.
5. Auditory hallucinations in which either a voice keeps up a running commentary on the subject's behaviors or thoughts as they occur, or two or more voices converse with each other.
6. Nonaffective verbal hallucinations (as defined in this manual) spoken to the subject.
7. Hallucinations of any type throughout the day for several days or intermittently for at least one month.
8. Definite instances of marked formal thought disorder (as defined in this manual) accompanied by either blunted or inappropriate affect, delusions or hallucinations of any type, or grossly disorganized behavior.

B. Signs of the illness have lasted at least two weeks from the onset of a noticeable change in the subject's usual condition (current signs of the illness may not now meet criterion A and may be residual symptoms only, such as extreme social withdrawal, blunted or inappropriate affect, mild formal thought disorder, or unusual thoughts or perceptual experiences).

C. At no time during the *active* period (delusions, hallucinations, marked formal thought disorder, bizarre behavior, etc.) of illness being considered did the subject meet the full criteria for either probable or definite manic or depressive syndrome (criteria A and B under Major Depressive or Manic Disorders) to such a degree that it was a *prominent* part of the illness. (See criteria for Depressive Syndrome Superimposed on Residual Schizophrenia.)

[a]Reprinted by permission from Spitzer *et al.* (1978).

115

trated by Strauss and Gift (1977), who contrasted several approaches to the diagnosis of schizophrenia using a sample of 272 first-admission patients. They found that 53 of these patients were considered schizophrenic according to DSM-II criteria. But only 4 of these 272 patients met the RDC for schizophrenia! What happened to the other patients? Of the 272, 68 were considered "schizoaffective disorder, depressed" by the RDC. Thus, by defining a smaller, more homogeneous group of patients in the schizophrenia category, the RDC may create, or expand, other problematic categories. Nevertheless, the specificity with which the diagnoses are made represents a significant improvement over past systems. The RDC obviously do not solve the problem of schizophrenia, but they do ensure that researchers who define a sample of patients using these criteria will be able to compare their results with those of other investigators who have also employed the RDC.

As Strauss and his colleagues have suggested, the selection of an optimal set of criteria for schizophrenia is a problem to be answered by further empirical research. Contemporary investigators would be well advised to collect extensive descriptive information on each patient and then compare their results utilizing several different sets of criteria in a flexible approach to the diagnostic dilemma.

Major Symptoms of the Disorder

CURRENT BEHAVIORAL REFERENTS

Thus far we have examined the history of the concept of schizophrenia as well as several of the major approaches to its diagnosis. We turn now to an evaluation of the major behavioral referents of schizophrenia. Our intent here is not to evaluate diagnostic *systems*, but to assess the relationship between discrete behaviors and the diagnosis. In other words, what are the major behavioral referents of the concept of schizophrenia?

The most promising data available come from the International Pilot Study of Schizophrenia sponsored by the World Health Organization (Sartorius, Shapiro, & Jablonsky, 1974). At the outset of this project, field research centers were established in nine countries: China, Colombia, Czechoslovakia, Denmark, England, India, Nigeria, the United States, and the Soviet Union. Psychiatrists from participating institutions were first brought together for training in selected assessment instruments. Then all team members returned to their institutions and evaluated newly admitted patients there. Patients were initially screened to rule out those outside of the usual age of risk for schizophrenia and those who had signs of organicity, drug abuse, mental retardation, or a long-standing psychosis. The only criterion for inclusion in the study was the presence of typical signs of psychosis. The primary assessment instrument was Wing's PSE. All together, 1202 patients were evaluated. The patients were diagnosed by clinicians involved in the assessment and by CATEGO, a computer diagnostic system associated with the PSE. Finally, based on symptom profiles from the PSE, patients were divided into groups with similar patterns of symptomatology. Of the ten groups thus formed, three contained primarily schizophrenics (as determined by diagnoses).

To try to specify the behavioral referents of schizophrenia, we will focus on an unambigous group—those patients designated schizophrenic by all three diagnostic methods. Table 9 presents the prominent behavioral features of this group. The symptoms are based on PSE units which include groups of items reflecting facets of a single problem. As can be seen from the table, there were twelve features found in 50% or more of the schizophrenic sample. Individual

Table 9
Prominent Features of Schizophrenia from the IPSS

Feature	Percentage of schizophrenics
Lack of insight	97
Auditory hallucinations	74
Verbal hallucinations	70
Ideas of reference	70
Delusions of reference	70
Suspiciousness	66
Flat affect	66
Voices speaking to patient	65
Delusional mood	64
Delusions of persecution	64
Inadequate description of problem	64
Thought alienation	52
Thoughts spoken aloud	50

features ranged from a high of 97% for lack of insight to a low of 50% for thoughts spoken aloud.

The previous analysis tells us what problems were frequent among schizophrenics. But these symptoms could also be common among members of other diagnostic groups and thus of little significance for *differential* diagnosis. A different approach to characterizing the symptoms of schizophrenia was taken by Carpenter, Strauss, and Bartko (1974). These investigators first contrasted the IPSS schizophrenics and nonschizophrenics on each of the PSE's 443 items. One hundred and fifty variables were found to discriminate between the groups, and these were reduced to 69 by eliminating redundancies. Next, a discriminant function analysis was applied using these 69 variables. The best discriminating equation was found to contain the 12 variables shown in Table 10. Variables with minus signs were those whose presence weighted *against* a diagnosis of schizophrenia.

We are now in a position to offer a specification of what seem to be the most salient behavior features of schizophrenia. We have grouped them into five major categories:

1. *Thought.* The disturbances here may be divided into problems of the *form* of thought and of its *content*. Examples of the former include incoherence (the understandibility of speech is impaired due to lack of logical connections, grammatical distortions, and the like), loosening of associations, and poverty of speech content (stereotyped repetitions, vagueness). Disorders of the content of thought refer primarily to delusions. Although the possibilities are virtually limitless, primary emphasis should be placed on the Schneiderian categories of thought insertion, thought withdrawal, and delusions of control. Strauss and Carpenter's (1974) results also highlight the importance of widespread, bizarre, and nihilistic delusions. Another important problem which we place here is lack of insight; the patient has little appreciation that any disorder exists.

2. *Perception.* The primary difficulty here is hallucinations, particularly auditory ones such as hearing one's thoughts spoken aloud, or hearing voices discussing or commenting on one's behavior or speaking directly to oneself.

3. *Affect and Emotion.* The data point toward flat affect as a hallmark of schizophrenia. Emotional incongruity, viewed as

Table 10
Twelve Symptoms Which Formed
the Best Discriminating Function for Schizophrenics

Items to provide data on the 12 discriminating sysmptoms

1. Restricted affect. *(i)* Blank expressionless face; *(ii)* very little or no emotion shown when delusional or normal material is discussed that would usually bring out emotion.

2. Poor insight. Overall rating of insight (is patient aware that he has problems?).

3. Hearing one's thoughts aloud. *(i)* Do you feel your thoughts are being broadcasted or transmitted, so that everyone knows what you are thinking? *(ii)* Do you ever seem to hear your thoughts spoken aloud (almost as if someone standing nearby could hear them)?

4. Waking early — Have you been waking early in the morning and remaining awake (rate positive if awakens over one hour earlier than usual)? Absence of symptoms counts toward the diagnosis of schizophrenia.

5. Poor rapport. Did the interviewer find it possible to establish good rapport with the patient during the interview?

6. Other difficulties in rapport.

7. Depressed facies — Sad or depressed facial expression.

8. Elation — Elated, joyous mood.

9. Widespread delusions. Are patient's delusions very widespread? How many areas in the patient's life are interpreted delusionally?

10. Incoherent speech. *(i)* free and spontaneous flow of incoherent speech, unreliable information; *(ii)* was the information obtained in this interview credible or not?

11. Bizarre delusions. Are the delusions comprehensible?

12. Nihilistic delusions. *(i)* Do you feel that your body is decaying or rotting? *(ii)* Do you feel that some part of your body is missing, for example, your head, brain, or arms? *(iii)* Do you ever have the feeling that you do not exist at all; that you are dead, dissolved?

an important feature of hebephrenia, may be important for a small group of patients but does not have widespread applicability.

4. *Motor Disorder.* Although catatonic schizophrenia is a somewhat rare category, motor disturbances predominate in this type. These problems include the maintenance of rigid pos-

tures, waxy flexibility, and/or seemingly purposeless and stereotyped motoric excitement. In the IPSS these motoric disturbances were found in about 5% of schizophrenics. The comparison figures for psychotic depressives and manic-depressives were 1% and 1.5%, respectively.

5. *Disorders in Interpersonal Relations.* Many schizophrenics have a history of seclusiveness, withdrawal, and interpersonal incompetence. This pattern led Bleuler to speak of schizophrenics as having withdrawn from reality. Interview studies of schizophrenics also rate them as having little rapport with the interviewer.

In addition to these positive characteristics, we must consider exclusionary features. Symptomatology that is most likely due to organic disease and/or drug abuse must not be used to justify a diagnosis of schizophrenia. The former of these two confounds is dealt with by the "clear sensorium" restriction (see, for example, the British *Glossary*), the latter presumably by an inquiry into possible drug abuse. A more thorny issue is the patient who combines the features of schizophrenia with those of affective illness. Three major possibilities exist: (1) such patients are a variant of "true" schizophrenia; (2) such patients are a variant of affective disorder; and (3) such patients have a distinct "third psychosis." Some would exclude such patients (primarily the schizoaffectives) from the schizophrenia category (e.g., the RDC of Spitzer, Endicott, & Robins). And there is some evidence to support this division. Schizoaffectives, for example, show a preponderance of affectively ill first-degree relatives instead of the usual increased rate for schizophrenia (Welner, Croughan, & Robins, 1974). But other work suggests that schizophrenics and patients with affective psychosis are not readily differentiated on the basis of affective expression (Kendell & Gourlay, 1970). Furthermore, the differentiation between schizophrenia and affective psychosis in the IPSS was best achieved not by affective symptoms but by the increased prevalence of Schneiderian features in the schizophrenics. Data such as these led Wing to formulate a hierarchical diagnostic model in which the presence of affective symptoms does not rule out schizophrenia *if Schneiderian symptoms are also present* (Wing et al., 1974). Thus, the status of schizoaffective patients is currently a matter of controversy and the decision to include or exclude such patients will depend on the needs of the individual investigator.

Conclusion

Our current definition of schizophrenia is incomplete. Nevertheless, it does appear to be a meaningful construct that can be identified with acceptable reliability. In the foregoing analysis, we have tried to present a set of characteristic features, recognizing that none of them are uniquely linked to the disorder. Patients diagnosed as schizophrenic should display some subset of these features, although none of them, either singly or in combination, provides a totally explicit definition of schizophrenia. (This apparent ambiguity should not be seen as particularly alarming, given that many useful classes are polythetic rather than monothetic in nature. For example, there are no specific features which exhaustively define the class, mammals, but it is nevertheless a useful zoological entity.) As to validity, the schizophrenia construct is indeed embedded, with at least moderate levels of associative linkage, in a large and expanding network of relationships. We will consider one of these, treatment response, as an illustration.

A vast literature exists testifying to the efficacy of phenothiazines and several other neuroleptics with schizophrenic patients (see, for example, Klein & Davis, 1969); they seem to have a beneficial effect on acute symptoms (e.g., Cole, 1964) and they also increase the probability that some patients will be able to stay out of the hospital after they have been released (Davis, Gosenfeld, & Tsai, 1976). Although these studies are not flawless from a methodological standpoint (Mac-Donald & Tobias, 1976; Marholin & Phillips, 1976; Tobias & Mac-Donald, 1974), the cumulative weight of the evidence favors the conclusion that medication does have beneficial effects for a substantial percentage of schizophrenic patients. Since these drugs are apparently not effective in treating nonschizophrenic patients (manics may be an exception), the diagnostic decision plays an important role in the formulation of a treatment plan.

Future research will undoubtedly improve on our current state of knowledge in this area. For example, although many schizophrenic patients respond favorably to phenothiazines, others do not. Several groups of investigators have attempted to identify patient characteristics that will predict response to medication, but their results have been inconsistent (e.g., Goldstein, 1970; Klein & Rosen, 1973; May, VanPutten, Yale, Potepan, Jenden, Fairchild, Goldstein, & Dixon,

1976). The relationship between specific sets of diagnostic criteria and drug response is another important unanswered question. Thus, at the present time, the decision that a particular patient is schizophrenic implies that antischizophrenic medication *may* be beneficial.

The use of maintenance medication is another difficult issue. Although specific drugs do help prevent the need for rehospitalization (e.g., Hogarty, Goldberg, Schooler, Ulrich, & the Collaborative Study Group, 1974) in a substantial number of patients, as many as 60% of schizophrenic outpatients may be able to "survive" in the community without medication (Gardos & Cole, 1976). Furthermore, most controlled studies have reported that placebo patients who avoided rehospitalization were as well adjusted as those who were receiving medication. Given that there are serious side-effects associated with the long-term use of antischizophrenic medication (e.g., tardive dyskinesia), drug-free trials may be extremely informative. If the patient's behavior should deteriorate, most studies indicate that it can be restabilized by the resumption of medication.

As in the case of acute disturbances, there are currently no known patient characteristics that predict response to, or need for, maintenance medication. There is some evidence that the utility of medication depends on the interaction between patient characteristics (past psychotic symptoms) and environmental variables. Following discharge from the hospital, patients who return to a noncritical, nonhostile family environment exhibit a very low rate of relapse, regardless of whether or not they receive maintenance medication. On the other hand, antischizophrenic drugs do have a positive effect in patients who return to a family in which one or more members has previously expressed negative feelings about the patient (Brown, Birley, & Wing, 1972; Vaughn & Leff, 1976). Thus, the clinician must be concerned with a careful assessment of the patient's social environment as well as specific overt behaviors.

Antischizophrenic drugs do seem to relieve particular symptoms, and they also reduce the risk of readmission to the hospital. They do not, however, provide patients with needed social and occupational skills, nor do they resolve interpersonal difficulties in the patient's family and social sphere. Although problems such as these may not figure specifically in the diagnostic decision itself (as do symptoms such as hallucinations), there is considerable evidence that schizophrenics are often poorly adjusted in these areas (e.g., Keith, Gunderson, Reifman, Buchsbaum, & Mosher, 1976), and they should be considered in the design of a comprehensive treatment program. A conventional functional assessment of these problems can be seen as a useful, or perhaps necessary, supplement to a diagnostic interview in this regard. Several investigators have reported beneficial effects produced by skill-training programs carried out within a social-learning framework (e.g., Bellack, Hersen, & Turner, 1976; Goldsmith & McFall, 1975). The most notable effort in this regard has been reported by Paul and Lentz (1977), who were able to demonstrate considerable success with a social-learning problem aimed at the development of useful self-care and interpersonal skills and the reduction of disruptive behavior.

Despite the apparent utility of such direct behavioral programs, it would be naive to assume that they can be employed indiscriminantly with all patients. In other words, the special needs and possible limitations of schizophrenic patients must be taken into consideration. There are, indeed, some interesting data which indicate that the utility of active psychosocial intervention with schizophrenic outpatients depends on whether or not the patients also receive maintenance medication. Hogarty and his colleagues in the NIMH Collaborative Aftercare Study conducted a careful evaluation of the effects of medication with and without supplementary psychosocial intervention. (The results of the NIMH study are somewhat at odds with the study reported by Paul and Lentz [1977], in which the social-learning program was quite successful with patients who were, for the most part, off drugs. This discrepancy is probably owing to the fact that patients who demonstrated a positive response to medication were screened out of the Paul and Lentz study before it began [see their discussion of their subject-selection problems]. It may also be, however, that the two psychosocial programs differ on important dimensions.) The latter program consisted of intensive problem-solving casework done by psychiatric social workers on an outpatient basis. Hogarty, Goldberg, and the Collaborative Study Group (1973) and Hogarty et al. (1974) found that those patients who received medication were less likely to be rehospitalized than placebo patients; the psychosocial program was ineffective in this regard, either by itself or in combination with drugs. A somewhat different picture emerged when the data were examined for only those patients in each group who managed to stay out of the hospital for at least two years. In the drug group, those patients who also received psychosocial treatment were better adjusted than those who did not. Exactly the opposite pattern was found for placebo patients; those who received psycho-social treatment were not as well adjusted as those who received medication alone. One explanation for this interesting interaction may be that some schizophrenic patients are not able to cope with the added stress associated with an active psychosocial treatment program. The main point is that, as in the case of medication, psychosocial interventions may be beneficial for some patients and, under certain circumstances, harmful to others. The identification of patient characteristics and environmental factors that more accurately predict a positive response to specific forms of medication, psychosocial treatment, and various combinations of the two modalities is a challenge for future research.

In summary, certain general probability statements are reliably associated with the schizophrenia construct. For example, if a patient exhibits certain symptoms (e.g., auditory hallucinations or bizarre delusions together with signs of incoherent speech and blunted affect), it is likely that the patient will respond favorably to antischizophrenic medication. On the other hand, it would be a mistake to rely solely on the use of medication, for two principal reasons. First, some patients improve significantly without medication (or, perhaps, in spite of it). While these patients cannot be specifically identified at the present time, assessment efforts aimed at the prediction of medication response should focus on the social environment as well as individual patient characteristics. Second, the problems encountered by schizophrenics range well beyond the small number of behaviors by which these patients are identified. Meaningful treatment programs must therefore address issues such as social and occupational adjustment as well as the remediation of specific symptoms. It is hoped that as we come to understand the schizophrenia construct more fully, we will be in a better position to predict which combinations of specific pharmacological and psychosocial programs will be beneficial for which particular patients.

We have argued that schizophrenia is a meaningful construct and that certain empirically defined relationships between overt behaviors and treatment response should be recognized by the practicing clinician. On the other hand, even after trying to specify "characteristic symptoms," we are left with a class whose members display considerable heterogeneity. Schizophrenics, even carefully defined and assessed, still show much variability in prognosis and treatment response. Symptoms themselves are not good predictors of these other variables (see Pope & Lipinski, 1978). In recent research, for example, neither the presence of Schneider's first-rank symptoms nor Langfelt's narrow criteria for schizophrenia was found to predict prognosis (Strauss & Carpenter, 1974; Taylor & Abrams, 1975). These data are compatible with several alternative explanations. It may be that our current general definition of the schizophrenia construct includes several different disorders which may or may not be etiologically related (as Bleuler suggested many decades ago). Prognosis could also be the product of a single general predisposition to the disorder and a complex interaction of environmental (nongenetic) events which are currently insufficiently understood. The common features of the disorder may be appreciated, and prognosis more easily predicted, when these factors are clarified. In any case, we do not believe that the obvious variability associated with schizophrenia should be taken to imply that the construct is meaningless or that it should be abandoned. On the contrary, future progress depends upon a careful expansion of our knowledge of the network of relationships between behavioral, biological, and environmental events which currently define schizophrenia.

References

Abrams, R., & Taylor, M. A. A rating scale for emotional blunting. *American Journal of Psychiatry*, 1978, *135*, 226–229.

Beck, A. T., Ward, C. H., Mendelson, M., Mock, J. E., & Erbaugh, J. K. Reliability of psychiatric diagnosis II: A study of consistency of clinical judgments and ratings. *American Journal of Psychiatry*, 1962, *119*, 351–357.

Bellack, A. S., Hersen, M., & Turner, S. M. Generalization effects of social skills training in chronic schizophrenics: An experimental analysis. *Behaviour Research and Therapy*, 1976, *14*, 391–398.

Blashfield, R. K. An evaluation of the DSM-II classification of schizophrenia as a nomenclature. *Journal of Abnormal Psychology*, 1973, *82*, 352–389.

Bleuler, E. *Lehrbruch der psychiatrie* (4th ed.). Berlin: Springer, 1923.

Brown, G. W., Birley, J. L. T., & Wing, J. K. Influence of family life on the course of schizophrenic disorders: A replication. *British Journal of Psychiatry*, 1972, *121*, 241–258.

Burdock, E. I., & Hardesty, A. S. *Structured clinical interview manual*. New York: Springer, 1969.

Carpenter, W. T., Strauss, J. S., & Bartko, J. J. Use of signs and symptoms for the identification of schizophrenic patients. *Schizophrenia Bulletin*, 1974, *2*, 37–49.

Cohen, J. A. A coefficient of agreement for nominal scales. *Educational and Psychological Measurement*, 1960, *20*, 37–46.

Cole, J. O. Phenothiazine treatment in acute schizophrenia. *Archives of General Psychiatry*, 1964, *10*, 246–261.

Cooper, J. E., Kendell, R. E., Gurland, B. J., Sharpe, L., Copeland, J. R. M., & Simon, R. *Psychiatric diagnosis in New York and London.* London: Oxford University Press, 1972.

Cromwell, R. L. Assessment of schizophrenia. In M. R. Rosezweig & L. W. Porter (Eds.), *Annual review of psychology.* Palo Alto: Annual Reviews, 1975.

Cronbach, L. J., & Meehl, P. E. Construct validity in psychological tests. *Psychological Bulletin,* 1955, *52,* 281–302.

Davis, J. M., Gosenfeld, L., & Tsai, C. C. Maintenance antipsychotic drugs do prevent relapse: A reply to Tobias and MacDonald. *Psychological Bulletin,* 1976, *83,* 431–447.

Diagnostic and statistical manual of mental disorders (2nd ed.). Washington, D.C.: American Psychiatric Association, 1968.

Endicott, J., & Spitzer, R. L. A diagnostic interview: The Schedule for Affective Disorders and Schizophrenia. *Archives of General Psychiatry,* 1978, *35,* 837–844.

Feighner, J. P., Robins, E., Guze, S. B., Woodruff, R. A., Winokur, G., & Muñoz, R. Diagnostic criteria for use in psychiatric research. *Archives of General Psychiatry,* 1972, *26,* 57–63.

Frank, J. Psychoanalyse und psychiatrie. *Sammlung psychoanalytischer aufsatze,* 1932, 99–102.

Gardos, G., & Cole, J. O. Maintenance antipsychotic therapy: Is the cure worse than the disease? *American Journal of Psychiatry,* 1976, *133,* 32–36.

A glossary of mental disorders. London: General Register Office, 1968.

Goldsmith, J. B., & McFall, R. M. Development and evaluation of an interpersonal skill-training program for psychiatric inpatients. *Journal of Abnormal Psychology,* 1975, *84,* 51–58.

Goldstein, M. J. Premorbid adjustment, paranoid status, and patterns of response to phenothiazine in acute schizophrenia. *Schizophrenia Bulletin,* 1970, *1,* 24–37.

Haslam, J. *Observations on madness and melancholy.* London: Hayden, 1809.

Hecker, E. Die hebephrenie. *Archiv für Pathologiscohe Anatomie und Physiologie und Klinische Medizin,* 1871, *52,* 394–429.

Hempel, C. G. The theoretician's dilemma. In H. Feigl, M. Scriven, & G. Maxwell (Eds.), *Minnesota studies in the philosophy of science* (Vol. 2.). Minneapolis: University of Minnesota Press, 1958.

Hempel, C. G. Introduction to problems of taxonomy. In J. Zubin (Ed.), *Field studies in the mental disorders.* New York: Grune & Stratton, 1961.

Hoch, P. H., Cottell, J. P., Strahl, M. O., & Pennes, H. H. The course and outcome of pseudoneurotic schizophrenia. *American Journal of Psychiatry,* 1962, *119,* 106–115.

Hoch, P. H., & Dunaif, S. L. Pseudopsychopathic schizophrenia. In P. H. Hoch & J. Zubin (Eds.), *Psychiatry and the law.* New York: Grune & Stratton, 1955.

Hoch, P. H., & Polatin, P. Pseudoneurotic forms of schizophrenia. *Psychiatric Quarterly,* 1949, *23,* 248–276.

Hogarty, G. E., Goldberg, S. C. & the Collaborative Study Group. Drug and sociotherapy in the aftercare of schizophrenic patients: One-year relapse rates. *Archives of General Psychiatry,* 1973, *28,* 54–64.

Hogarty, G. E., Goldberg, S. C., Schooler, N. R., Ulrich, R. F., & the Collaborative Study Group. Drug and sociotherapy in the aftercare of schizophrenic patients: II. Two-year relapse rates. *Archives of General Psychiatry,* 1974, *31,* 603–608.

Jung, C. G. The psychology of dementia praecox. *Nervous and Mental Disease Monographs Series* No. 3, 1936. (Originally published, 1906.)

Kahlbaum, K. L. *Die katatonie oder das spannungsirresein.* Berlin: Hirschwald, 1874.

Keith, S. J., Gunderson, J. G., Reifman, A., Buchsbaum, S., & Mosher, L. Special report: Schizophrenia 1976. *Schizophrenia Bulletin,* 1976, *2,* 509-565.

Kendell, R. E. *The role of diagnosis in psychiatry.* London: Blackwell, 1975.

Kendell, R. E., Everitt, B., Cooper, J. E., Sartorius, N., & David, M. E. Reliability of the Present State Examination. *Social Psychiatry,* 1968, *3,* 123-129.

Kendell, R. E., & Gourlay, J. The clinical distinction between affective psychoses and schizophrenia. *British Journal of Psychiatry,* 1970, *117,* 261-266.

Kety, S. S. From rationalization to reason. *American Journal of Psychiatry,* 1974, *131,* 957-963.

Klein, D. F., & Davis, J. M. *Diagnosis and drug treatment of psychiatric disorders.* Baltimore: Williams & Wilkins, 1969.

Klein, D. F., & Rosen, B. Premorbid asocial adjustment and response to phenothiazine treatment among schizophrenic inpatients. *Archives of General Psychiatry,* 1973, *29,* 480-485.

Kraepelin, E. *Psychiatrie* (4th ed.). Leipzig: Barth, 1893.

Kraepelin, E. *Psychiatrie* (5th ed.). Leipzig: Barth, 1896.

Kuriansky, J. B., Deming, W. E., & Gurland, B. J. On trends in the diagnosis of schizophrenia. *American Journal of Psychiatry,* 1974, *131,* 402-408.

Laing, R. Is schizophrenia a disease? *International Journal of Social Psychiatry,* 1969, *10,* 184-193.

Langfeldt, G. *The prognosis in schizophrenia and the factors influencing the course of the disease.* Copenhagen: Munksgaard, 1937.

Luria, R. E., & McHugh, P. R. Reliability and clinical utility of the "Wing" Present State Exam. *Archives of General Psychiatry,* 1974, *30,* 866-871.

MacDonald, M. L., & Tobias, L. L. Withdrawal causes relapse? Our response. *Psychological Bulletin,* 1976, *83,* 448-451.

Marholin, D., & Phillips, D. Methodological issues in psychopharmacological research: Chlorpromazine — a case in point. *American Journal of Orthopsychiatry,* 1976, *46,* 477-495.

May, P. R. A., Van Putten, T., Yale, C., Potepan, P., Jenden, D. J., Fairchild, M. D., Goldstein, M. J., & Dixon, W. J. Predicting individual responses to drug treatment in schizophrenia: A test dose model. *Journal of Nervous and Mental Disease,* 1976, *162,* 177-183.

Meehl, P. E. Specific genetic etiology, psychodynamics, and therapeutic nihilism. *International Journal of Mental Health,* 1972, *1,* 10-27.

Meyer, A. The aims and meaning of psychiatric diagnosis. *American Journal of Insanity,* 1917, *74,* 163-168.

Meyer, A. Genetic-dynamic psychology versus nosology. In E. E. Winters (Ed.), *The collected papers of Adolf Meyer* (Vol. 3). Baltimore: John Hopkins University Press, 1951. (Originally published, 1926.)

Neale, J. M., & Oltmanns, T. *Schizophrenia.* N.Y.: John Wiley & Sons, 1980.

Paul, G. L., & Lentz, R. J. *Psychosocial treatment of chronic mental patients.* Cambridge, MA: Harvard University Press, 1977.

Phillips, L. Case history data and prognosis in schizophrenia. *Journal of Nervous and Mental Disease,* 1953, *6,* 515-525.

Phillips, L. *Human adaptation and its failures.* New York: Academic Press, 1968.

Pope, H. G., & Lipinski, J. F. Diagnosis in schizophrenia and manic-depressive illness. *Archives of General Psychiatry,* 1978, *35,* 811-828.

Sandifer, M. G., Pettus, C., & Quade, D. A study of psychiatric diagnosis. *Journal of Nervous and Mental Disease,* 1964, *139,* 350-356.

Sartorius, N., Shapiro, R., & Jablonsky, A. The international pilot study of schizophrenia. *Schizophrenia Bulletin,* 1974, *2,* 21-35.

Scheff, T. J. *Being mentally ill: A sociological theory.* Chicago: Aldine, 1966.

Schmidt, H. O., & Fonda, C. D. The reliability of psychiatric diagnosis: A new look. *Journal of Abnormal and Social Psychology,* 1956, *52,* 262-267.

Schneider, K. *Clinical psychopathology.* New York: Grune & Stratton, 1959.

Sharpe, L., Gurland, B. J., Fleiss, J. L., Kendall, R. E., Cooper, J. E., & Copeland, J. R. M. Some comparisons of American, Canadian and British psychiatrists in their diagnostic concepts. *Canadian Journal of Psychiatry,* 1974, *19,* 235-245.

Spitzer, R. L., & Endicott, J. Diagno: A computer program for psychiatric diagnosis using the differential diagnostic procedure. *Archives of General Psychiatry,* 1968, *18,* 746-756.

Spitzer, R. L., & Endicott, J. *Schedule for affective disorders and schizophrenia (SADS)* (3rd ed.). New York: Biometrics Research, New York State Psychiatric Institute, 1978.

Spitzer, R. L., Endicott, J., & Robins, E. *Research diagnostic criteria (RDC) for a selected group of functional disorders.* New York: Biometrics Research, New York State Psychiatric Institute, 1978.

Spitzer, R. L., & Fleiss, J. L. A re-analysis of the reliability of psychiatric diagnosis. *British Journal of Psychiatry,* 1974, *125,* 341-347.

Spitzer, R. L., Sheehy, M., & Endicott, J. DSM-III: Guiding principles. In V. M. Rakoff, H. C. Stancer, & H. B. Kedward (Eds.), *Psychiatric diagnosis.* New York: Brunner/Mazel, 1977.

Strauss, J. S., & Carpenter, W. T. The prediction of outcome in schizophrenia: II. Relationships between predictor and outcome variables. *Archives of General Psychiatry,* 1974, *31,* 37-42.

Strauss, J. S., & Gift, T. E. Choosing an approach for diagnosing schizophrenia. *Archives of General Psychiatry,* 1977, *34,* 1248-1253.

Sullivan, H. S. Tentative criteria of malignancy in schizophrenia. *American Journal of Psychiatry,* 1928, *7,* 759-782.

Taylor, M. A., & Abrams, R. Manic-depressive illness and good prognosis schizophrenia. *American Journal of Psychiatry,* 1975, *132,* 741-742.

Tobias, L. L., & MacDonald, M. L. Withdrawal of maintenance drugs with long-term hospitalized mental patients: A critical review. *Psychological Bulletin,* 1974, *81,* 107-125.

Ullmann, L., & Krasner, L. *A psychological approach to abnormal behavior.* Englewood Cliffs, NJ: Prentice-Hall, 1968.

Vaughn, C. E., & Leff, J. P. The influence of family and social factors on the course of psychiatric illness: A comparison of schizophrenic and depressed neurotic patients. *British Journal of Psychiatry,* 1976, *129,* 125-137.

Ward, C. H., Beck, A. T., Mendelson, M., Mock, J. E., & Erbaugh, J. K. The psychiatric nomenclature: Reasons for diagnostic disagreement. *Archives of General Psychiatry,* 1962, *7,* 198-205.

Welner, A., Croughan, J. L., & Robins, E. A persistant enigma. *Archives of General Psychiatry,* 1974, *31,* 628-631.

Wing, J. K., Birley, J. T., Cooper, J. E., Graham, P., & Isaacs, A. D. Reliability of a procedure for measuring and classifying "Present Psychiatric State." *British Journal of Psychiatry,* 1967, *113,* 499-515.

Wing, J. K., Cooper, J. E., & Sartorius, N. *The measurement and classification of psychiatric symptoms.* Cambridge, England: Cambridge University Press, 1974.

World Health Organization. *The international pilot study of schizophrenia.* Geneva: World Health Organization, 1973.

Zilboorg, G. *A history of medical psychology.* New York: W. W. Norton, 1941.

CHAPTER

5

Assessment
of Affective Disorders

PETER M. LEWINSOHN
WANDA M. L. LEE

An estimated 4% of the adult population is sufficiently depressed to warrant clinical treatment; the prevalence of depression increases with age (Schmidt, 1974) and it is especially high in females (Silverman, 1968). Even though exact figures of suicide rates among depressed patients are difficult to pinpoint, there is agreement that the probability of self-injurious and suicidal behavior is significantly elevated in depressed populations (Mendels, 1975). Because of the prevalence of depression and its association with suicide, the correct and early recognition of depression is especially important.

The clinical assessment of depressed patients has several related goals:

1. *Differential Diagnosis.* Assessment must first determine whether or not depression is *the,* or at least *a,* problem for the individual. Diagnostic assessment must also allow the clinician to evaluate the severity and the duration of the presenting symptoms; to differentiate between different subtypes of depression; and to establish a baseline for evaluating treatment progress and outcome.

2. *Functional Diagnosis and Identification of Targets for Intervention.* Assessment should also begin to identify specific

Peter M. Lewinsohn and Wanda M. L. Lee. Psychology Department, University of Oregon, Eugene, Oregon.

events and behavior patterns which are functionally related to the person's depression. The goal of assessment at this level is to pinpoint areas of person–environment interaction which may contribute to the patient's depression. Such information should guide in the formulation of a specific treatment plan to change the events and the behavior patterns accounting for the patient's depression and assist in ongoing treatment decisions.

3. *Evaluation.* But diagnosis is not enough. Evaluation is also necessary. Evaluation involves periodic assessment not only of changes in depression level, but also of concomitant changes in the events presumed to be related to the patient's depression. This two-pronged approach to assessment allows the therapist to evaluate the effectiveness of treatment in changing the targeted behavior patterns, and also to determine whether these are accompanied by changes in depression level. For example, a therapist may hypothesize, on the basis of his or her assessments, that the patient's difficulties with assertion are functionally related to his or her depression, and hence, may recommend assertiveness training. Positive change in *both* the patient's social interactions and depression provides support for the original functional diagnosis. If the patient's assertion skills improve but there is no concomitant improvement in depression level (or vice versa), the validity of the original functional diagnosis needs to be questioned. On the other hand, if neither the patient's assertion nor depression change in the expected directions, a different therapy tactic is needed.

Differential Diagnosis

The diagnosis of depression is rendered difficult by the fact that the term "depression" does not have a single, generally accepted set of referents. Consequently, individuals who are labeled depressed are quite heterogeneous. Given this lack of consensus, it is especially important that one explicitly define the criteria which are used to diagnose patients as depressed. The diagnosis of depression is complicated further because (1) some of the symptoms of depression (e.g., irritability, fatigue, lethargy, insomnia, upper gastric intestinal disturbances, headaches, anorexia) occur in more than 40% of general medical patients (Schwab, Bialow, Clemmons, & Holzer, 1966), and (2) a substantial proportion of psychologically depressed individuals have one or more somatic symptoms as their chief complaint (Schwab, Clemmons, Bialow, Duggan, & Davis, 1965). Ruling out organic involvement is thus an important part of the diagnostic process. If significant health problems are present, patients should be asked, as part of the diagnostic process, to consult a physician to clarify the potential importance of these problems for their depression.

Here are two examples.

1. A 50-year-old female complained of depression during the intake interview. Since her symptoms included hyperactivity as well as substantial weight loss even in the context of reported good appetite, the intake worker recommended a thorough medical evaluation. The results indicated a hyperthyroid syndrome.

2. Another patient's depression began after a heart attack. The patient had interpreted his physician's recommendations as calling for a drastic curtailment of his activities. Communication with the physician revealed that a much less severe reduction of activities was intended.

The differential diagnosis of depression can be accomplished with four different but complementary methods: (1) psychiatric diagnosis; (2) symptom ratings; (3) self-report depression scales; (4) observations of overt behavior.

PSYCHIATRIC DIAGNOSIS

Even though behaviorally oriented clinicians, and many others, have questioned the adequacy of psychiatric diagnosis, it is by far the most commonly used diagnostic procedure. Furthermore, there is evidence that with the use of recently developed interview schedules (the *Schedule for Affective Disorders and Schizophrenia* [Endicott & Spitzer, 1978]) and the diagnostic systems (the *Research Diagnostic Criteria* [Spitzer, Endicott, & Robins, 1978]), very good interrater reliability can be achieved.

Psychiatric diagnosis is based on dichotomous (i.e., noncontinuous) distinctions. This framework assumes that the affective disorders represent a number of qualitatively different disorders (Klerman, 1973; Mendels, 1975). At present, no single scheme for subdividing affective disorders has emerged that is either empirically compelling and/or generally acceptable. The major diagnostic schemes currently used are the DSM-II (1968), the DSM-III (1980), and the Research Diagnostic Criteria (RDC) (Spitzer *et al.*, 1978). The main diagnostic categories for affective disorders as classified in these three systems are shown in Table 1. The technical problems of the DSM-II are well

Table 1

Major Affective Disorder Classifications in the DSM-II, DSM-III, and the Research Diagnostic Criteria (RDC)

DSM-II	DSM-III	RDC
Schizophrenia Schizoaffective type	Schizoaffective Disorder	Schizoaffective Disorder
Major Affective Disorder	Affective Disorders	Manic Disorder
Involutional Melancholia	Episodic Affective Disorders	Hypomanic Disorder
Manic–Depressive Illness	Manic Disorder	Bipolar (I) with Mania
Psychotic Depressive Reaction	Major Depressive Disorder	Bipolar (II) with Hypomania
Depressive Neurosis	Bipolar Affective Disorder	Major Depressive Disorder
	Chronic Affective Disorders	Minor Depressive Disorder
	Chronic Hypomanic Disorder	Intermittent Depressive Disorder
	Chronic Depressive Disorder	
	Cyclothymic Disorder	
	Atypical Affective Disorders	
	Atypical Manic Disorder	
	Atypical Depressive Disorder	
	Atypical Bipolar Disorder	

known and need not be repeated in detail. A very serious weakness has been low interrater reliability (e.g., Ward, Beck, Mendelson, Mock, & Erbaugh, 1962), stemming in large part from uncertainty regarding the criteria for specific diagnoses. This lack of clarity in the DSM-II is illustrated, for example, in the definition of a "depressive neurosis" as a disorder which "is manifested by an excessive reaction of depression due to an internal conflict or to an identifiable event such as the loss of a love object or cherished possession" (DSM-II, p. 40). This DSM-II definition is in marked contrast to the RDC definition of Major Depressive Disorder, which is shown in Table 2. Both the RDC and DSM-III attempt to provide clear criteria (number and kinds of symptoms required, severity level, duration, exclusion criteria) for their diagnostic categories. A statistic, kappa, has been developed for measuring how well two (Cohen, 1960) or more (Fleiss, 1971) judges agree beyond the level predicted by chance. As can be seen in Table 3, the kappa coefficients for the RDC categories for affective disorders are quite adequate. It should be kept in mind that such high levels of agreement were attained by raters who were using the interview outline provided by the Schedule of Affective Disorders and Schizophrenia (Endicott & Spitzer, 1978). Use of the latter insured that the diagnosticians had comparable information on which to base their diagnoses.

DSM-II allowed for four "psychotic" depressions (schizoaffective, involutional meloncholia, manic–depressive, psychotic depressive reaction) and for one "neurotic" depression (depressive neurosis).

Involutional melancholia has been eliminated from the newer schemes because there is little rational basis for using a separate diagnostic category simply on the basis of the age of onset of the disorder (Rosenthal, 1968; Beck, 1967). The neurotic versus psychotic depression *dichotomy*, which implied that these were qualitatively different types of disorders, has also been eliminated.

Table 2
Research Diagnostic Criteria (RDC) for Major Depressive Disorders[a]

A. One or more distinct periods with dysphoric mood or pervasive loss of interest or pleasure. The disturbance is characterized by symptoms such as the following: depressed, sad, blue, hopeless, low, down in the dumps, "don't care anymore," or irritable. The disturbance must be prominent and relatively persistent but not necessarily the most dominant symptom. It does not include momentary shifts from one dysphoric mood to another dysphoric mood, for example, anxiety to depression to anger, such as are seen in states of acute psychotic turmoil.

B. At least five of the following symptoms are required to have appeared as part of the episode for definite, and four for probable (for past episodes, because of memory difficulty, one less symptom is required):
   1. Poor appetite or weight loss or increased appetite or weight gain (change of 0.5 kg a week over several weeks or 4.5 kg a year when not dieting). *(continued)*

Table 2 *(continued)*

---

 2. Sleep difficulty or sleeping too much.
 3. Loss of energy, fatigability, or tiredness.
 4. Psychomotor agitation or retardation (but not mere subjective feeling of restlessness or being slowed down).
 5. Loss of interest or pleasure in usual activities, including social contact or sex (not included if limited to a period when delusional or hallucinating). (The loss may or may not be pervasive.)
 6. Feeling of self-reproach or excessive or inappropriate guilt (either may be delusional).
 7. Complaints or evidence of diminished ability to think or concentrate, such as slowed thinking or indecisiveness (do not include if associated with marked formal thought disorder).
 8. Recurrent thoughts of death or suicide, or any suicidal behavior.

C. Duration of dysphoric features: at least one week, beginning with the first noticeable change in the subject's usual condition (definite if lasted more than two weeks, probably if one to two weeks).

D. Sought or was referred for help from someone during the dysphoric period, took medication, or had impairment in functioning with family, at home, at school, at work, or socially.

E. None of the following that suggest schizophrenia is present:
 1. Delusions of being controlled (or influenced), or of thought broadcasting, insertion, or withdrawal (as defined in the RDC manual).
 2. Nonaffective hallucinations of any type (as defined in the RDC manual) throughout a one-week period.
 3. Auditory hallucinations in which either a voice keeps up a running commentary on the subject's behavior or thoughts as they occur, or two or more voices converse with each other.
 4. At some time during the period of illness had more than one month when he or she exhibited no prominent depressive symptoms but had delusions or hallucinations (although typical depressive delusions of guilt, sin, poverty, nihilism, or self-deprecation, or hallucinations with similar content, are not included).
 5. Preoccupation with a delusion or hallucination to the relative exclusion of other symptoms or concerns (other than typical depressive delusions of guilt, sin, poverty, nihilism, self-deprecation, or hallucinations with similar content).
 6. Definite instances of marked formal thought disorder (as defined in the RDC manual), accompanied by either blunted or inappropriate affect, delusions or hallucinations of any type, or grossly disorganized behavior.

F. Does not meet the criteria for schizophrenia, residual subtype.

---

[a]Reprinted by permission from Spitzer *et al.* (1975).

Table 3
Kappa Coefficients of Agreement[a] for Major Affective Disorder
Categories Using the Research Diagnostic Criteria[b]

	Joint interviews		Test–retest (n = 60)
	Study A (n = 68)	Study B (n = 150)	
Present episode only			
Schizoaffective disorder, manic type	c	c	.79
Schizoaffective disorder, depressed type	.86	.85	.73
Manic disorder	.82	.98	.82
Major depressive disorder	.88	.90	.90
Minor depressive disorder	c	.81	c
Lifetime diagnosis			
Schizoaffective disorder manic type	c	c	c
Schizoaffective disorder, depressed type	.94	.87	.70
Manic disorder	.89	.93	.77
Hypomanic disorder	.85	c	.56
Major depressive disorder	.97	.91	.71
Minor depressive disorder	c	.68	c
Labile personality	c	c	.70
Bipolar I	.93	.95	.40
Bipolar II	.79	.85	c
Recurrent unipolar	.81	.83	.80
Intermittent depressive disorder	c	.85	.57

[a]Both probable and definite ratings included as present.
[b]Reprinted by permission from Spitzer et al. (1975).
[c]Less than 5% frequency by either rater.

A separate category for schizoaffective disorders has always been included to reflect the fact that there are some patients who manifest mixtures of affective and schizophrenic symptoms. The question has been whether these patients represent a subtype of schizophrenia, a subtype of affective disorder, or whether a third independent noso-logical entity is necessary. In DSM-II, schizoaffective disorder was re-garded as a subtype of schizophrenia. In DSM-III, and in the RDC, schizoaffective disorder is listed separately. In the DSM-III and RDC usage, the schizoaffective category is reserved for patients who meet criteria for depression (or mania) and who have at least one of the symptoms used to define schizophrenia (e.g., delusions of control or thought broadcasting). The affective syndrome must precede or de-velop concurrently with the schizophrenic symptoms. The develop-ment of a full affective syndrome *following* an established schizo-phrenic syndrome is excluded from this category because affective symptomatology following the development of a psychotic syndrome, which is fairly common, does not appear to have the same favorable prognostic significance as affective symptoms that precede a schizo-phrenic syndrome (DSM-III, 1980).

Patients with manic, and those with a history of both manic and depressive episodes, have always been recognized as a separate diagnos-tic group. The inclusion of manic–depressive disorder among the psychoses in DSM-II required that patients so diagnosed be con-sidered psychotic. Both the DSM-III and RDC have dropped this re-quirement. In DSM-III, a manic episode is defined by the presence of at least one distinct period of elevated, expansive, or irritable mood, associated with a specified number of manic symptoms from among the following: more active and/or talkative than usual; excessive in-volvement in activities without recognizing their high potential for painful consequences (e.g., buying sprees); flight of ideas; inflated self-esteem; decreased need for sleep; and distractibility. Whether or not the patient is also psychotic (defined by the presence of delusions or hallucinations) is indicated with a "level of severity" rating. A diag-nosis of bipolar affective disorder is given to a patient who is currently depressed and who also has a history of one or more manic episodes, or vice versa. The general distinction between unipolar and bipolar depressions is becoming increasingly recognized as important for therapy outcome. There is evidence that these two subgroups differ in response to pharmacological intervention (Morris & Beck, 1974), and that they may have different genetic and/or biochemical bases (Becker, 1977; Cadoret & Tanna, 1977).

DSM-III uses one major category (Affective Disorders) within which three subgroups are distinguished. The first group is termed "Episodic Affective Disorders." The term "episodic" is used to indicate that there is a period of disorder which is clearly distinguishable from previous functioning. The second group is referred to as "Chronic Affective Disorders." The term "chronic" is used to indicate a long-standing disorder (lasting at least two years) which usually does not have a clear onset. The disturbance in mood and related symptoms may be sustained throughout the period or be intermittent. The third group, "Atypical Affective Disorders," are residual categories for individuals with a mood disturbance that cannot be classified as either episodic or chronic. Within each of the three groups, distinctions are made between Manic (Hypomanic), Major Depressive (Unipolar), and Bipolar (Cyclothymic) Disorders, based on whether both manic and depressive episodes are involved, or only one of them is.

In addition to the schizoaffective and the bipolar disorders, the RDC distinguishes among three types of affective disorder: Major Depressive Disorder; Minor Depressive Disorder; and Intermittent Depressive Disorder. The criteria for a diagnosis of Major Depressive Disorder are shown in Table 2. Minor Depressive Disorder is a "weaker" diagnosis in that fewer symptoms are required. A diagnosis of Intermittent Depressive Disorder is made when the individual has been bothered *intermittently,* for a period lasting at least two years, by a depressed mood. This category is distinguished from Major and Minor Depressive Disorders, in which there are clear-cut episodes of a sustained depressed mood preceded by a normal mood. A patient may be given more than one diagnosis when warranted; for instance, a patient may have a current episode of Major Depressive Disorder which was preceded by an Intermittent Depressive Disorder.

To recognize the various subtypes of depressive disorder which have at one time or another been thought to be important, the RDC allows for 11 *nonmutually exclusive* subtypes of Major Depressive Disorder:

1. *Primary:* Depression not preceded by any of a long list of disorders including schizophrenia, alcoholism, and preferential homosexuality.
2. *Secondary:* Depression preceded by a long list of conditions, including serious physical illnesses, which led to major changes in living conditions or which were associated with psychological symptoms (e.g., thyrotoxicosis).
3. *Recurrent unipolar:* For individuals who have *never* met the

criteria for manic disorder, hypomanic disorder, or schizo-affective disorder, manic type; but who have had two or more episodes of major depressive disorder separated by at least two months of return to more-or-less usual functioning.

4. *Psychotic:* For individuals who show evidence of delusions and/or hallucinations and/or depressive stupor (mute and unresponsive).

5. *Incapacitating:* For individuals who, because of the severity of their symptoms, are unable to function either at work or at school, take care of the house for at least one week, feed or clothe themselves, or maintain minimal personal hygiene without assistance.

6. *Endogenous:* Defined on the basis of specific symptoms including the "distinct" quality of depressed mood; that is, depressed mood is perceived as distinctly different from the kind of feeling he or she would have or has had following the death of a loved one.

7. *Agitated:* For patients with symptoms such as pacing, hand-wringing, inability to sit still, pulling or rubbing hair, outbursts of complaining or shouting, talking on and on, and incessant talking.

8. *Retarded:* For patients who show symptoms such as slowed speech, frequent pauses before answering, low or monotonous speech, mutism or markedly decreased speech, and slowed bodily movements.

9. *Situational:* For patients in whom depression has developed after an event or in a situation that seems likely to have contributed to the appearance of the episode at that time.

10. *Simple:* For patients who have not shown any significant signs of psychiatric disturbance in the year prior to the development of the current episode of depression.

The RDC thus provides operational criteria for many subtypes of depression. The fact that these are treated as nonmutually exclusive — that is, patients may meet criteria for more than one subtype — is consistent with some empirical evidence. Lewinsohn, Zeiss, Zeiss, and Haller (1977) present data suggesting that the endogenous and situational subtypes are indeed not mutually exclusive in that there are patients who manifest endogenous symptoms after the occurrence of a stressful life event.

The RDC is the most elaborated and probably the best currently available diagnostic system for the affective disorders. Its use in research studies is recommended so that patient samples can be compared across studies.

SYMPTOM RATINGS

Another way of measuring the presence and severity of the manifestations of depression is through ratings on items presumed to represent the symptoms of depression. Such items and their broader dimensions have been identified in descriptive studies of depressed individuals (e.g., Grinker, Miller, Sabshin, Nunn, & Nunally, 1961). These studies have typically started with a large number of relatively specific symptoms to be rated. These symptoms were then reduced to a smaller number of clusters through factor analysis. While studies have differed in the kinds of observations used, and hence in the kinds of factors finally derived, there is considerable agreement across studies as to the constituents of the depression syndrome. The symptoms of depression may be grouped into six general categories: dysphoria, reduced rate of behavior, social-interactional problems, guilt, material burden, and somatic symptoms. Depressed patients manifest different combinations of these. The diagnostic task involves an evaluation of the presence and severity level of the various components of the depression syndrome in the individual patient.

The central symptom of depression is *dysphoria,* that is, an unpleasant feeling state. Patients use different verbal labels to communicate their dysphoria. Commonly used words are "down," "blue," "depressed," "hopeless," "helpless," "despondent," and "pessimistic." Patients may also feel that they are worthless or useless and may see life as meaningless. Frequently patients describe themselves as deficient or as total failures, particularly in matters of special importance such as intelligence, interpersonal relationships, or vocational competence. Such assertions of inadequacy may be at odds with an objective appraisal of the patient's abilities and achievements. Depressed patients often feel gloomy and pessimistic about the future and feel they have "nothing to look foward to."

In almost all seriously depressed patients there is an objective overall *reduction in the rate with which the patient engages in behaviors of various kinds.* While a few specific behaviors may be markedly elevated (e.g., a patient may spend a great deal of time talking and ruminating about the negative aspects of his or her situation), depressed patients *do* considerably less overall than when they are not depressed. The depressed patient's typical day may consist largely of "sitting around and doing nothing," or engaging in some passive solitary activity such as watching television, eating, or sleeping. Going to work or taking care of daily household chores seems to require an inordinate amount of effort, and in the case of more severely depressed persons, may not occur at all. Frequently the depressed patient reports feeling unmotivated to engage in hobbies or other activities that previously were enjoyable and satisfying. Such activities no longer appeal to the patient and seem like "just another chore" which would require too much effort on his or her part.

Many depressed persons express *concern about their interpersonal relationships*. This concern is expressed in a variety of ways. Some patients are acutely concerned and unhappy about their marital relationships. Marital problems are present in the lives of many depressed patients. Other patients feel uncomfortable and anxious in the presence of people, especially in situations requiring them to interact with more than one or two persons. Still others are dissatisfied with their ability to cope with certain social situations, especially those requiring them to be assertive. Such patients often feel that they are being exploited by others. Finally, some patients express concern about their passivity and general social withdrawal. These patients frequently express contradictory goals with respect to interpersonal relationships. On the other hand, they may complain of feeling very lonely and unloved, while on the other hand, they may express little interest in being with other people.

Some, but by no means all, depressed persons express *feelings of guilt*. Sometimes the patient has a vague feeling that he or she deserves to be punished for "unpardonable" actions. Other patients report guilt because of their presumed inability to assume specific family or job responsibilities. Such persons frequently blame themselves for being a burden to others.

In contrast to those patients who hold themselves primarily accountable for their problems, some depressed patients are prone to *blame their depressed mood upon external causes,* such as a financial setback or a conflict with an employer. Often such patients complain of excessive demands placed upon them by their families or employers and believe their depression could be alleviated if these material problems could somehow be resolved.

Many patients begin by expressing any of a number of *somatic complaints*. Sleep disturbance of some kind is a very common symptom of depression. Depressed patients often report difficulty in falling asleep, or restless sleep with periods of wakefulness throughout the night, or both. A smaller number of patients report early-morning awakening and a subsequent inability to return to sleep. An even smaller number of depressed patients report excessive sleeping. Another common somatic symptom is loss of appetite and subsequent weight loss. Patients report not enjoying their food and, if they live by themselves, not eating regular meals. Other frequent symptoms of depression include chronic fatigue, loss of libido, headaches, and upper gastrointestinal complaints. Finally, some depressed patients describe vague symptoms. They may complain of a constant lump in the throat, an empty feeling throughout the body, or a heavy, sinking feeling in the chest area. The clinician needs to rule out a physical abnormality as a basis for these somatic symptoms prior to concluding that they are symptomatic of depression.

The task of assessing the presence and severity of the phenomena of depression is facilitated by the use of one of several available interviewer rating scales. These scales have been constructed by combining items reflecting characteristic attitudes and symptoms associated with depression. In addition to the obvious advantage of providing quantitative data on pre- and post-treatment functioning, these rating scales have the advantage of providing concrete instances of the behaviors to be rated. Some of these scales have been factor analyzed. It is thus possible to compute factor scores for the various areas of the depression syndrome. Among the better-known scales are the Feelings and Concerns Checklist (Grinker *et al.,* 1961), the Hamilton Rating Scale for Depression (Hamilton, 1960, 1967), and the more global ratings of the Raskin Depression Scales (Raskin, Schulterbrandt, Reatig, Crook, & Odle, 1974). Other similar rating scales are the Psychiatric Judgment of Depression Scale (Overall, 1962), the Depression Rating Scale (Wechsler, Grosser, & Busfield, 1963), and the PPH Depression Scale (Friedman, Cowitz, Cohen, & Granick, 1963). When used by well-trained raters, these scales possess high interrater reliability. They differentiate significantly between depressed and nondepressed patients, and between depressed patients differing with respect to intensity of depression.

In order to be able to rate patients on the above-mentioned scales, it is useful to follow an outline and to ask a number of leading questions designed to evoke the patient's expression of feelings of dysphoria, guilt, and the other components of the depressive syndrome. The Schedule for Affective Disorders and Schizophrenia (Endicott & Spitzer, 1978) provides such a structure and very specific questions. Because of its comprehensiveness, the SADS interview takes between one and two hours. For a somewhat shorter interview (approximately 50 minutes), we have found the following questions and topics particularly useful in eliciting responses that permit a careful assessment of the severity of the patient's depression:

Dysphoria
How is it going (work, school, home life)?
Feeling good or bad about it?
Worried?
Feeling under pressure? From where?
If things are bad, what are the prospects for improvement in the immediate or distant future?
Major happenings during the past year: Best? Worst?
Goals for the future? Expectations for attainment?
Self-description: Good points? Bad points?
Aspects of self that would be desirable to change?
Mood: Ups and downs? How severe and long-lasting are the downs? Any highs?
Any thoughts or ideas about suicide? Previous attempts? Plans?

Reduced Rate of Behavior
Describe a typical day.
Interests and activities that are enjoyable?
Any change from previous level of activity or enjoyment?
Difficulty in initiating action?
Having to exert a lot of effort to do things?
Problems making decisions?

Social-Interactional problems
How involved are you with other people?
Number of close friends? Acquaintances?
Ability to share with friends?
Are relationships a source of discomfort, anxiety, and/or conflict?
Feelings of social adequacy/inadequacy?

Guilt
Religious background? Importance of religion at present?
Concern for welfare of family and friends?
Blame self for present condition?

Perceive self as failure in important responsibilities?

Material Burden
Depression attributed to external problems (e.g., finances, children, demands of relatives or employers)?
If external problems could be resolved, would that affect the depression?

Somatic Manifestations (not attributable to physical condition)
Feeling slow? Tired all the time? Without energy?
Problems sleeping? Difficulty in falling asleep? Waking frequently during the night? Sleep not restful? Problems with waking early in the morning and not being able to get back to sleep? Sleeping more than usual?
How is your appetite? Any weight loss?
Gastrointestinal problems?
Headaches?

FEELINGS AND CONCERNS CHECKLIST
(GRINKER *ET AL.*, 1961)

This instrument is made up of 47 items. Each item is rated on a four-point scale from 0 (not present) to 3 (markedly present). Five factors derived from a factor analysis of 96 depressed patients can be scored separately. The factors may be labeled as follows: Factor 1: Dysphoria (e.g., feels hopeless, helpless, and powerless; feels sad and blue; feels unworthy); Factor 2: Material Burden (e.g., feels problems would be relieved by solving financial, job-related, or other "material" problems; concerned with material loss; feels burdened by the demands of others); Factor 3: Guilt (e.g., concerned with suffering he or she has caused others; expresses concern for the welfare of family and friends); Factor 4: Social Isolation (e.g., feels unloved; feels envious of others); Factor 5: Anxiety (e.g., feels "jittery"; has feelings of tenseness; experiences free-floating anxiety).

A shortened version of this instrument, developed by Lewinsohn and his coworkers (e.g., Lewinsohn & Libet 1972) by excluding items with high factor loadings on more than one of the factors, is shown in Figure 1. It has been used extensively as a screening device for depressed subjects in conjunction with the MMPI. Criteria for their combined use are shown in Table 4. Lewinsohn, Biglan, and Zeiss (1976) report that persons meeting these criteria tend to be primarily unipolar, with depression intensity ranging from moderate to severe.

Date:_____

Participant's Name:_____   Interviewer:_____

0=not present   1=present to   2=present to   3=present to
                 slight extent   moderate extent   marked extent

1. Feels hopeless   0 1 2 3   16. Feels a failure   0 1 2 3
2. Feels that he/she is bearing   17. Concerned with making up for
    troubles   0 1 2 3   wrongs he/she has caused
3. Feels helpless and powerless   0 1 2 3   to others   0 1 2 3
4. Has feelings of tenseness   0 1 2 3   18. Uses depressive behavior
5. Concerned with suffering   for interpersonal gain   0 1 2 3
    that he/she has caused others   0 1 2 3   19. Feels guilt for not assuming
6. Feels problems would be   family, job and/or academic
    relieved by the solving of   responsibilities   0 1 2 3
    certain "material" problems   20. Feels unable to make decisions   0 1 2 3
    (i.e., money, job, etc.)   0 1 2 3   21. Feels unloved   0 1 2 3
7. Feels sad and blue   0 1 2 3   22. Feels burdened by the demands
8. Feels unworthy   0 1 2 3   of others   0 1 2 3
9. Considers self lazy   0 1 2 3   23. Feels "jittery"   0 1 2 3
10. Expresses concern for the   24. Feels unable to act   0 1 2 3
    welfare of family & friends   0 1 2 3   25. Credits problems to excessive
11. Has ideas of committing   family and/or job
    suicide   0 1 2 3   responsibilities   0 1 2 3
12. Concerned with material loss
    (i.e., money, property)   0 1 2 3
13. Feels at "end of rope"   0 1 2 3
14. Feels envious of others   0 1 2 3
15. Experiences free anxiety   0 1 2 3

26. Depression is the   Patient manifests   Depression is about   Depression is
    presenting syndrome.   other symptoms but   equal with other   present but the
                             depression is major.   symptoms.   major symptom is
                                                                           something else.

            5   4   3   2

    Depression is not   There are no
    among the presenting   significant
    symptoms.   presenting symptoms.

            1   0

Factor 1 Score = Items 1+3+7+8+9+13+16+20+24 = _____   ÷ 9 = _____ Dysphoria
Factor 2 Score = Items 6+12+22+25 =   ÷ 4 = _____ Material burden
Factor 3 Score = Items 5+10+17+19 =   _____   ÷ 4 = _____ Guilt
Factor 4 Score = Items 4+15+23 =   ÷ 3 = _____ Anxiety
Factor 5 Score = Items 2+14+18+21 =   _____   ÷ 4 = _____ Social isolation

Grand total   =   _____
Overall mean   = Grand total ÷ 21 =   _____

Figure 1
Short version of the Feelings and Concerns Checklist.

HAMILTON RATING SCALE

This popular interview rating scale consists of 17 items (Hamilton, 1960, 1967). Originally intended for use with patients who have already been diagnosed as having a depressive disorder, it provides a systematic method for quantifying the pattern and severity level of depression symptoms.

SELF-REPORT DEPRESSION SCALES

In attempting to determine if a person is depressed, and if such is the case, the severity of the depression, the clinician may wish to administer a brief questionnaire *before* interviewing the patient. Levitt and Lubin (1975) list 23 self-administered depression scales. Only the more popular ones will be described here. All of them have been shown to correlate significantly with each other (e.g., Beck, 1972; Lubin, 1967; Seitz, 1970; Zung, Richards, & Short, 1965) and to correlate substantially with interview ratings. They differ from each other in terms of the number of items, types of symptoms represented

Table 4
Classification Criteria for Selecting Depressed
and Nondepressed Subjects Combining the MMPI with
the Feelings and Concerns Checklist

Group	Step 1: MMPI (Byrne Scale)	Step 2: Feelings and Concerns Checklist ratings
Depressed	(a) D ≥ 70T (b) D > Pt (c) D > Hy	(a) One or more factor scores > 1.0 (b) Mean factor score > .70 (c) Depression is major presenting psychopathology
Psychiatric control	(a) Hy ≥ 70T or Pt ≥ 70T (b) D < 70T (c) D < Pt-10T or D < Hy-10T	(a) Factor I < .70 (b) Subject rated as manifesting emotional difficulties other than depression
Normal control	(a) L < 60T (b) Clinical scales < 70T	(a) Mean factor score ≤ .35 (b) No factor score < .70

by the items, and the time frame for which ratings are made. Since elderly individuals tend to acknowledge more somatic symptoms such as sleep disturbance, lowered energy level, and poor appetite (Gaitz, 1977), and to check fewer socially undesirable items (Harmatz & Shader, 1975), there is a significant issue as to whether the self-report depression scales are in fact measuring the same phenomena in the elderly as they do in younger persons (Gallagher, McGarvey, Zelinski, & Thompson, 1978). With the exception of the MMPI (Dahlstrom, Welsh, & Dahlstrom, 1972) and the Depression Adjective Checklist (Lubin, 1967) available measuring instruments have not been standardized on elderly samples. Similarly, since there is a consistent tendency for females to obtain higher scores on self-report depression inventories (e.g., Radloff, 1977), separate norms for males and for females should be used whenever possible.

MMPI — DEPRESSION SCALE

The best known of the self-report measures for depression is the D scale of the MMPI. It has been used widely for the measurement of depression for clinical and research purposes. For example, Lewinsohn and his colleagues (e.g., Lewinsohn & Libet, 1972) have used multiple MMPI criteria (shown in Table 4) to define depressed populations for research. The MMPI D scale has also been used as a dependent variable in treatment outcome studies (Fuchs & Rehm, 1977; Shipley & Fazio, 1973; Zeiss, Lewinsohn, & Muñoz, 1979).

The D scale is composed of 60 true–false items. No specific time frame is specified in the MMPI instructions. The items are quite heterogeneous and can be grouped into five subscales which have been termed subjective depression, psychomotor retardation, complaints about physical malfunctioning, mental dullness, and brooding (Harris & Lingoes, 1955). Attempts have been made to develop revised MMPI depression scales with greater internal consistency (Dempsey, 1964) and discriminant validity (Costello & Comrey, 1967), but Dahlstrom et al. (1972) conclude that there is little evidence that these modifications have any clear advantage over the original scale except that they are shorter.

There are several other brief questionnaires which take only a few minutes of the patient's time and which can be scored quickly and easily.

BECK DEPRESSION INVENTORY (BDI)

The BDI was developed by Beck, Ward, Mendelsohn, Mock, and Erbaugh (1961). It consists of 21 items. The BDI can be used as a periodic measure in case studies. It has also often been used as a pre- and posttreatment measure. The time frame for the BDI is "the way you feel today, that is, right now." Beck and Beck (1972) have developed a shorter version of the BDI which has only 13 items. It correlates .96 with the original BDI.

ZUNG SELF-RATING DEPRESSION SCALE (SDS)

The Self-Rating Depression Scale (Zung, 1965, 1973) consists of 20 statements. No specific time frame for rating is indicated in the test instructions. The patient indicates the frequency with which each statement is applicable to him or her on a four-point scale from "none or a little of the time" to "most or all of the time." In scoring this scale, a value of 1, 2, 3, or 4 is assigned to each response, depending upon whether the statement was worded positively or negatively. By multiplying the sum of the scores by 1.25, one obtains an index ranging from 25 to 100. Based upon the results of several studies, Zung suggests the use of the following scale to estimate the degree of the patient's depression: 50–59, mild to moderate; 60–69, moderate to severe; 70 and over, severe.

DEPRESSION ADJECTIVE CHECK LIST (DACL)

The DACL was developed by Lubin (1965, 1967, 1977) and consists of two sets of lists. In set 1, lists A, B, C, and D each contain 32 nonoverlapping adjectives, and the four lists are equivalent; in set 2, lists E, F, and G contain 34 nonoverlapping adjectives, and the three lists are equivalent. The lists are designed to provide a measure of what has been called state depression; that is, the individual's mood at a particular moment in time. The subject is asked, "Check the words which describe *How You Feel Now—Today.*" The availability of alternate forms and their brevity make the DACL especially useful for repeated measurement research. It has been used to measure day-to-day fluctuations in mood level (Lewinsohn & Graf, 1973). The DACL differs from the previously described self-report depression scales in sampling a much more limited range of depression behavior; that is, depressed affect. This is in contrast to the BDI and the SDS, which include items involving overt-motor, physiological, and other cognitive manifestations. The DACL is somewhat less valuable for pre- and posttreatment assessment because of the large day-to-day intrasubject variability of DACL scores.

Of all the self-report depression scales, the DACL has been given the most extensive psychometric development (Lubin, 1977). High split-half, alternative form, and internal consistency reliabilities have been replicated (Lubin, 1967; Lubin & Himelstein, 1976) and a large amount of concurrent validity data has been collected (Lubin, 1967, 1977; Christenfeld, Lubin, & Satin, 1978). Normative data are available for different age groups, including an adolescent sample consisting of persons from 12 through 17 years of age (Lubin & Levitt, 1979). The DACL has been translated into Spanish, Portuguese, French, Hebrew, and Chinese.

CENTER FOR EPIDEMIOLOGIC STUDIES—DEPRESSION SCALE (CES-D)

The CES-D (Radloff, 1977) is a 20-item self-report scale. The CES-D has 20 items which were selected from previously validated scales (e.g, MMPI-D scale, Zung SDS, BDI). The wording of the items is simple. The time frame for rating is clearly specified in the directions and refers to the *past week*. The CES-D was developed to measure depression symptoms in the general population, and extensive normative data are available for this test (Radloff, 1977).

VISUAL ANALOGUE SCALES

An even simpler method of assessing depressed affect is to have patients rate their mood on a line which is defined as representing a continuum from "best mood" to "worst mood." An example of a visual analogue scale used for the daily monitoring of mood (Lewinsohn, Muñoz, Youngren, & Zeiss, 1978) is shown in Figure 2. Psychometric development of visual analogue scales has not been extensive. Aitken (1969), Aitken and Zealley (1970), and Folstein and Luria (1973) list some of the arguments for the use of such scales in clinical settings. Substantial correlations between such mood ratings

Daily Mood Rating Form

Please rate your mood for this day (how good or bad you felt) using the 9-point scale shown. If you felt really great (the best you have ever felt or can imagine yourself feeling), mark 9. If you felt really bad (the worst you have ever felt or can imagine yourself feeling), mark 1. If it was a "so-so" (or mixed) day, mark 5.

If you felt worse than "so-so", mark a number between 2 and 4. If you felt better than "so-so", mark a number between 6 and 9. Remember, a low number signifies that you felt bad and a high number means that you felt good.

```
very                                                      very
depressed _____happy
            1    2    3    4    5    6    7    8    9
```

Enter the date on which you begin your mood ratings in Column 2 and your mood score in Column 3.

Monitoring Day	Date	Mood Score	Monitoring Day	Date	Mood Score
1			26		
2			17		
3			18		
4			19		
5			20		
6			21		
7			22		
8			23		
9			24		
10			25		
11			26		
12			27		
13			28		
14			29		
15			30		

Figure 2

A visual analogue depression scale. Reprinted by permission from Lewinsohn, Muñoz, Youngren, and Zeiss (1978).

and the Hamilton Rating Scale, other global psychiatric ratings, and the Beck Depression Inventory have been reported (Davies, Burrows, & Poynton, 1975; Little & McPhail, 1973; Zealley & Aitken, 1969).

ASSESSMENT OF OVERT BEHAVIOR

The construct of depression includes a variety of relatively specific overt behaviors, and a number of methods have been developed to measure them. A Ward Behavior Checklist for use with hospitalized patients has been described by Williams, Barlow, and Agras (1972). This scale includes simple, easily observable behaviors such as talking, smiling, taking a shower. The presence or absence of each behavior is rated by aides using a time sampling procedure (e.g., once per hour). Excellent interrater reliability (96%) was reported for this scale, which also correlated substantially with the Hamilton Rating Scale for Depression ($r = + .71$) and with the Beck Depression Inventory ($r = + .67$). The Ward Behavior Checklist was used as a dependent variable by Hersen, Eisler, Alford, and Agras (1973).

There have been other attempts to count specific behaviors in depressed patients. Reisinger (1972) used a time sampling method to count the frequency of crying and smiling behavior. Interrater reliability exceeded 90% for observation periods of up to two hours. Liberman and Roberts (1974) distinguished between "depressive" behaviors (defined by behaviors such as crying, complaining about somatic symptoms, pacing, and withdrawal) and "coping behavior" (defined by adaptive actions such as cooking, cleaning house, and attending to the children). Robinson and Lewinsohn (1973a) described a method for counting words, or verbal rate, which was used to increase the speech rate of a 50-year-old chronically depressed man in whom a reduced rate of speech constituted one of the major presenting problems. Johansson, Lewinsohn, and Flippo (1969) and Robinson and Lewinsohn (1973b) used a coding system to partition verbal behavior into discrete response categories in their attempts to increase specific low-rate verbal responses of depressed individiuals.

An elaborate attempt to code the verbal behavior of depressed individuals in interpersonal interactions was developed by Lewinsohn (1976b). The system is shown schematically in Table 5. Behavior interactions are seen as having a source and an object. Actions are followed by reactions which can be coded as either positive (i.e., expres-

Table 5
A System for Coding Verbal Behavior in Interpersonal Interactions[a]

Action		Reaction		
Interactional categories		Positive	Negative	
Psychological complaint	PsyC	Affection	Aff	Criticism	Crit
Somatic complaint	SomC	Approval	App	Disapproval	Disapp
Criticism	Crit	Agree	Agr	Disagree	Disagree
Praise	Pr	Laughter	L+	Ignore	Ign
Information request	I−	Interest	Int	Change topic	ChT
Information giving	I+	Continues talking about topic	ConT	Interrupts	Inter
Personal problem	PP	Physical affection	PhysAff	Physical punishment	Pun
Instrumental problem	IP				
Other people's problem	OP				
Talking about abstract, impersonal, general, etc.	Ta				

Content — Topics	
School	Sch
Self	X, Y, Z
Other people (group, family)	X, Y, Z
Treatment	Rx
Therapist	T
Sex	Sx

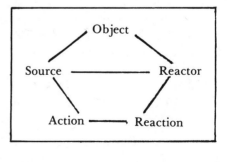

sions of affection, approval, interest) or negative (criticism, disapproval, disinterest). A simplified illustration of an interaction involving four people might be as follows: A makes a statement (an action) which is responded to by B (a reaction). B continues talking (an action), and this is followed by a reaction on the part of C, which in turn is followed by some new action on the part of D, and so on. These kinds of data allow one to focus on individuals in terms of the actions that they emit and the kinds of reactions they elicit. Two observers code all interactional behaviors. The observers pace themselves with an automatic timer which delivers an auditory and visual signal simultaneously every 30 seconds. Differences between raters are conferenced. Interjudge agreement for the major scoring categories has been quite high (Libet & Lewinsohn, 1973). A manual for the coding system has been developed (Lewinsohn, 1976b). This system has been used extensively in coding the behavior of depressed individuals in their own homes and in group therapy situations.

As a result of an extensive analysis of the social-interactional data obtained in five therapy groups and 18 homes, the following social-skill measures emerged as reliable ($r > +.7$) and valid ($p < .02$) in either the group or home situation (Libet, Lewinsohn, & Javorek, 1973).

1. *Activity Level:* Total rate of behavior emitted expressed as the number of actions emitted per hour.
2. *Initiation Level:* Number of actions emitted per hour, given that the individual emitted neither an action nor a reaction in the immediately preceeding time interval; that is, the number of interchanges initiated by the individual.
3. *Silence Level:* Number of time intervals per hour during which the individual is neither an actor nor a reactor.
4. *Action Latency (Action):* Probability of emitting an action in the same or next time interval subsequent to an elicited action.
5. *Action Latency (Reaction):* Probability of emitting an action in the same or next time interval subsequent to an elicited reaction.

McLean, Ogston, and Grauer (1973) describe a simplified method based on Lewinsohn's coding system. Patients were required to make half-hour tape recordings of a discussion of a problem with their spouses at home. These recordings were separated in 30-second intervals and coded for positive and negative initiations and reactions. Interrated agreement was high.

Fuchs and Rehm (1977) videotaped 10-minute segments of inter-action among groups of depressed subjects. The number of state-ments spoken in 10 minutes was counted. Interrater agreement ranged from 83% to 100%, with a mean of 87%.

Kupfer, Detre, Foster, Tucker, and Delgado (1972) describe an apparatus to record activity in inpatient settings. A miniature trans-mitter with a range of 100 feet is worn on a leather wristband. Re-ceivers transform data into pulses which are read out digitally as the number of counts per minute. This measure of psychomotor activity was shown to possess high reliability (e.g., between wrist and ankle transmitters). It has also been shown to be correlated with various sleep parameters such as EEG movement, minutes awake, time asleep, REM time, and REM activity (Kupfer *et al.*, 1972; Kupfer & Foster, 1973; Weiss, Kupfer, Foster, & Delgado, 1974).

ASSESSMENT OF SUICIDE RISK

Any clinician involved in the diagnosis and treatment of de-pressed individuals needs to assess the risk of suicide and take appro-priate preventive steps. It is essential to question depressed patients about any suicidal thoughts or intentions they may have. Often this topic may best be approached by asking the patient if he or she has reached the point where life just doesn't seem worth living any more, or if the patient ever thinks he or she might be better off dead. It is often desirable to ask quite directly if the patient has been thinking about taking his or her own life. If the patient's response is affirma-tive, it is important to determine whether the patient experiences only vague, occasional thoughts about suicide or has more concrete plans.

Several recent studies (Burglass & Horton, 1974; Lettieri, 1974) indicate that on the basis of relatively simple information, one can make quantitative predictions about the probability of serious sui-cidal behavior on the part of a patient. Although the predictive power of some variables differ as a function of age and sex, the fol-lowing elements are predictive for all populations (i.e., their presence increases the probability of suicide): (1) the patient is currently single or recently divorced; (2) the patient has no close friends or relatives in the immediate vicinity and lives alone; (3) the patient has problems involving the use of alcohol; (4) the patient has been arrested and charged with a crime (excluding traffic violations), such as drunken-ness, disorderly conduct, drug abuse, or a sexual offense; (5) the pa-tient has had previous psychiatric treatment; and (6) the patient has

omnipresent suicidal feelings and previous suicidal behavior with a
relatively high degree of lethality. Lethality refers to the degree to
which prior suicidal behaviors *could* have been fatal. In addition, a
pattern of role failure and rejection, confusion, refusal to accept
help, and a history of psychological dependence on another person or
persons are predictive of suicide for older males, among whom the
suicide rate is highest.

Functional Diagnosis and Identification of Targets for Intervention

Functional diagnosis involves pinpointing specific person–environment interactions and events related to a particular patient's depression. This part of the diagnostic process is needed to guide the
formulation of a treatment plan designed to change the events contributing to the patient's depression. The types of events *hypothesized*
to be casually related to depression are, of course, highly influenced
by the particular theory used by the therapist to guide his or her treatment efforts. In general terms, a theory specifies functional relationships between certain antecedent events and the occurrence of
depression. Theories differ in what they regard as the critical antecedent events, and treatment typically is aimed at problem areas
thought to be most critical for the occurrence of depression.

In the last ten years there have been major changes in depression
theory and consequently in the outpatient treatment of depressed individuals. Until the mid-1960s psychoanalytic formulations (Fenichel, 1945; Jacobson, 1971) were predominant. Although details
vary, psychoanalytic formulations of depression emphasize intrapsy-
chic phenomena, and assessment tends to emphasize projective techniques. Currently several psychological theories are most influential:
those that emphasize cognitive events (Abramson, Seligman, & Teasdale, 1976; Beck, 1967; Beck & Rush, 1978; Ellis, 1962; Rehm, 1977;
Seligman, 1975); and those that emphasize social-learning formulations (e.g., Lewinsohn *et al.,* 1976; McLean *et al.,* 1973). For example, cognitive theories emphasize the individual's personal belief
system. Depressives subscribe to "irrational" and overly general beliefs (e.g., one must be perfect all the time; I have no control over my
life; if someone dislikes me, I am not likeable). These kinds of beliefs
are assumed to cause depression. Accordingly, successfully changing
these cognitions to more "realistic" ones should eliminate the depres-

sion. Social-learning formulations (Lewinsohn, Sullivan, & Grosscup, 1980) assume depression and reinforcement to be related phenomena. The primary hypothesis states that a low rate of response-contingent reinforcement constitutes a critical antecedent for the occurrence of depression and that the behavior of depressed individuals does not lead to positive reinforcement to a degree sufficient to maintain their behavior. A corollary hypothesis is that a high rate of punishing experience also causes depression (Grosscup & Lewinsohn, 1980; Lewinsohn & Amenson, 1978; Lewinsohn & Talkington, 1979). Punishment is defined by person–environment interactions with aversive (distressing, upsetting, unpleasant) outcomes.

Beyond theoretical considerations, behavior patterns may be postulated to be functionally related to depression on the basis of three criteria: (1) if the pattern occurs with increased or decreased frequency in depressed vis-a-vis appropriate control groups; (2) if the behavior–environment interaction is present when the person is depressed but is absent or attenuated when the person is not depressed; and (3) if the occurrence of the person–environment interaction covaries with fluctuations in daily mood.

Using the above-mentioned criteria, the following may be listed as functionally related to depression: social-interactional problems, depressive cognitions, low rate of engagement in pleasant activities, and a high rate of occurrence of unpleasant events.

SOCIAL BEHAVIOR: SIGNIFICANCE AND ASSESSMENT

There now appears to be general consensus that depressed persons, as a group, manifest social-interactional problems (e.g., Weissman & Paykel, 1974; Lewinsohn et al., 1976; Youngren & Lewinsohn, 1980). Complaints about various inadequacies in social relationships are frequently among the problems which are identified by the patient. The individual may indicate that his or her relationships at home, in social situations, on the job, or in school are a source of anxiety, are avoided, or are less frequent than desired. In view of this, it is not surprising that many treatments have aimed at increasing assertiveness, positive social impact, and the overall amount of social interaction (Lazarus, 1968; Lewinsohn, Weinstein, & Alper, 1970; Rehm, Fuchs, Roth, Kornblith, & Romano, 1978; Sanchez, Lewinsohn, & Larson, 1980; Wells, Hersen, Bellack, & Himmelhoch, 1977; Zeiss et al., 1979).

At the level of self-report, the following have been found to be associated with depression: (1) infrequent engagement, discomfort, and low levels of obtained pleasure in social activity (Youngren & Lewinsohn, 1980); (2) discomfort in being assertive (Langone, 1979; Sanchez, 1976; Youngren & Lewinsohn, 1980); and (3) discomfort experienced in conjunction with negative cognitions concerning personal interactions (Youngren & Lewinsohn, 1980). Depressed persons tend to feel that they are boring, worry about appearing foolish, feel themselves to be inferior and socially incompetent, and have conflicted interactions with their spouse or partner (Lewinsohn & Talkington, 1979).

At the level of overt interpersonal behavior, depressed persons have been reported to differ from nondepressed persons in their eye contact (Hinchliffe, Lancashire, & Roberts, 1971b; Rutter & Stephens, 1972; Waxer, 1974), speech rate (Hinchliffe, Lancashire, & Roberts, 1971a), facial expressions (Waxer, 1974; Ekman & Bressler, Ekman & Rose, 1965), and hand movements (Ekman & Friesen, 1974). Libet and Lewinsohn (1973) and Libet, Lewinsohn, and Javorek (1973) also found a number of expressive problems associated with depression. Results generally indicated that depressed patients are less active verbally, have a slow response latency, and elicit less social reinforcement from others.

At the level of social impact on others, Coyne (1976) has shown that depressed patients elicit negative affect in others, and as a result, depressed patients are likely to be rejected and avoided. Similarly, Youngren and Lewinsohn (1980) and Lewinsohn, Mischel, Chaplin, and Barton (1980) reported peer- and observer-rated deficiencies in the social competence of depressed persons engaged in group interaction.

Research to date suggests the following: (1) The social behavior of a significant proportion of depressed individuals is unlikely to result in as high a rate of social reinforcement as is true for "normals." (2) It is likely that for these individuals this lower rate of social reinforcement is an important factor in their dysphoria. (3) Specific aspects of the social behavior of depressed individuals which can potentially be used to define goals for behavior change can be identified (Killian, 1971; Lewinsohn et al., 1970; McLean et al., 1973). (4) Not all depressed patients lack social skills. (5) Among patients who have social-interactional problems, there are large individual differences as to their specific nature. It is therefore essential to specifically describe and delineate the particular social-skill problems manifested by a given depressed individual and to focus interventions on the modification of the behaviors relevant to these problems.

Several reviews of the literature relevant to the assessment of social behavior have appeared in the last few years (Arkowitz, Lichtenstein, McGovern, & Hines, 1975; Curran, 1977; Eisler, 1976; Hall, 1977; Sundberg, Snowden, & Reynolds, 1978; Weissman, 1975). In spite of this interest, many issues of critical importance in the assessment of social skill are unresolved (Goldfried & Linehan, 1977), and there is room for improvement and innovation. Social competence, or social adjustment, has typically been measured with social adjustment scales, with self-report measures, or through behavioral observations. For the clinician it is first necessary to identify broad areas of the patient's social behavior which are either viewed as problematic by the patient or which appear likely to be relevant to his or her depression. The clinician might want to systematically examine all of the areas of the individual's life which involve contacts with other people (e.g., in the home, at work, in school, with friends, with strangers,). Three general questions might be asked about each of these areas: (1) Is this relationship a source of anxiety or distress? (2) Does less interaction or contact occur in this relationship than is desired? (3) Are problems in the relationship related to the depression of the patient?

A systematic and quantitative way of accomplishing the above is through one of the available social-adjustment scales. Social-adjustment scales came into use because of interest in assessing the community and social adjustment of patients. Their systematic use with depressed patients may be traced back to the ground-breaking study by Weissman and Paykel (1974). Using their Social Adjustment Scale for evaluating the social adjustment of depressed and nondepressed women, they found that during the acute depressive period, depressed women were rated as more maladjusted than the controls in *all* social roles.

Techniques for the assessment of social adjustment have recently been reviewed by Weissman (1975). Weissman compared 15 currently available scales for assessing social adjustment in terms of their coverage and psychometric properties. Among the better known is the *Social Adjustment Scale* (Weissman & Paykel, 1974), which can be used to rate performance in the areas of work (worker, housewife, or student), social and leisure activities, relationships with extended family, marriage (and as a parent), and economic independence.

Each role area includes assessments of *performance* at tasks, *inter-personal relations, friction,* and *satisfaction* in role.

Another popular social-adjustment rating scale is the *Personal Adjustment and Role Skill Scale,* which has gone through several developmental stages (Ellsworth, 1975). Among the role performance aras evaluated are those of worker, household manager, and parent.

Information needed for the ratings on social-adjustment scales has typically been gathered by a trained interviewer who makes judgments on the basis of an interview with the patient or with a relative or "significant other." Information obtained from patients and from relatives tends to show substantial correlations with each other (Weissman & Bothwell, 1976), but getting independent information from a "significant other," especially the spouse, is often quite valuable in its own right. An alternative to the interview is to have the patient and/or the relative fill out a social adjustment scale. Useful for this purpose is the Social Adjustment Scale Self-Report (Weissman & Bothwell, 1976). This self-report scale takes 15 to 20 minutes to complete. The assessment covers a two-week period. Weissman and Bothwell report substantial agreement between self-report, informant, and interview ratings.

Other self-report inventories of social skill have tended to emphasize "assertiveness," the meaning of which has been extended from the skill of refusing unreasonable requests (McFall & Lillisand, 1971; McFall & Marston, 1970) to more general interpersonal skills, including the expression of both positive and negative feelings as well as the ability to ask for favors, make demands, and initiate and continue conversations (Eisler, Hersen, & Miller, 1973; Hersen, Eisler, & Miller, 1973; Lazarus, 1973). Among the better-known assertiveness inventories are the *Wolpe–Lazarus Assertiveness Questionnaire* (Wolpe & Lazarus, 1966), the *College Self-Expression Scale* (Galassi, Delo, Galassi, & Bastien, 1974), the *Adult Self-Expression Scale* (Gay, Hollandsworth, & Galassi, 1975), the *Rathus Assertiveness Scale* (Rathus, 1973), the *Conflict Resolution Scale* (McFall & Lillisand, 1971), the *Assertion Inventory* (Gambrill & Richey, 1975), and the *Assertiveness Behavior Survey Schedule* (Cautella & Upper, 1976). These scales and more general issues relating to reliability, validity, and social desirability factors have been discussed by Eisler (1976) and by Hall (1977). Newer self-report instruments with potential applications to depressed patients are the *Situations Questionnaire* and

Behavior Inventory developed by Levenson and Gottman (1978) and the *Interpersonal Events Schedule* (IES) described by Youngren and Lewinsohn (1980).

An example of a comprehensive self-report interpersonal inventory is the *Interpersonal Events Schedule* (Youngren, Zeiss, & Lewinsohn, 1975). It consists of a list of 160 items, all of which involve interpersonal activities or cognitions concerning such interactions. Subjects are instructed to complete two ratings on each item. First, the subject is asked to rate the frequency of the event's occurrence during the previous month on a three-point scale. Secondly, the subject is asked to respond to the question, "How did you feel when each event happened during the past month?" on a five-point impact scale. Mean frequency, mean impact, and mean cross-product scores are computed for each scale. The frequency scores are assumed to reflect the rate with which the events occurred during the previous month. The impact scores are assumed to reflect the potential positive or negative reinforcing value of the events. The cross-product scores (obtained by multiplying the frequency and impact ratings for each event summed across all events) are assumed to provide an approximate measure of the response-contingent positive social reinforcement obtained, or of interpersonal aversiveness experienced, during the previous month.

The items are categorized into eight rationally-derived scales. There are 20 items per scale. The Social Activity Scale items involve engaging in an interpersonal conversation or activity (e.g., "having lunch or a coffee break with friends") or being in a situation where others are invariably present (e.g, "going to a service, civic, special interest, or social club meeting"). The Assertion Scale items involve disclosing how one feels toward another person (e.g., "telling a person of the opposite sex that I like him or her"), disclosing one's fear, confusion, or ignorance (e.g., "asking for clarification when I am confused about what someone has said"), soliciting information about others' perceptions (e.g., "taking a definite stand on a controversial issue"), and making and turning down requests (e.g., "turning down a friend's request to borrow money"). All items on the Cognition Scale involve having negative covert thoughts or feelings concerning personal interactions (e.g., "being afraid I will say or do the wrong thing," "feeling rejected by someone"). The Conflict Scale items include arguing (e.g., "having an argument with my spouse or someone

I am romantically involved with") and criticizing or being criticized (e.g., "being criticized by my boss"). The remaining four rationally derived scales all involve giving or receiving responses that are likely to be seen as favorable and reinforcing or as punishing and aversive: Give Positive (e.g., "complimenting someone on his or her creativity"); Receive Positive (e.g., "being praised by someone I admire"); Give Negative (e.g., "frowning or scowling at someone"); and Receive Negative (e.g., "being yelled at by someone important to me").

Test-retest reliability of the IES scales was assessed by computing correlations between one-month and three-month intervals. For the one-month interval, correlations ranged from $+ .44$ to $+ .83$ (average $r = + .67$) for mean frequency scores and from $+ .49$ to $+ .85$ (average $r = + .66$) for mean impact scores. For the three-month interval, correlations ranged from $+ .40$ to $+ .82$ (average $r = + .66$) for mean frequency scores and from $+ .42$ to $+ .85$ (average $r = + .62$) for mean impact scores. The IES has been shown to be highly discriminating between depressed and nondepressed groups (Youngren & Lewinsohn, 1980) and to be sensitive to clinical improvement (Lewinsohn, Youngren, & Grosscup, 1979).

In the behavioral assessment of social behavior, there has been a strong trend toward the use of role playing and/or highly structured social-interactional situations in which to observe the patient. Among the better known role-play procedures is the *Behavioral Role-Playing Assertion Test* (McFall & Marston, 1970); the *Behavioral Assertiveness Test* (Eisler, Miller, & Hersen, 1973); two procedures aimed at assessing the influence of social–interpersonal contexts on assertiveness, the *Behavior in Critical Situations Scale* (Weinman, Gelbart, Wallace, & Post, 1972) and a procedure described by Eisler, Hersen, Miller, and Blanchard (1975); and the *Interpersonal Behavior Role-Playing Test* (Goldsmith & McFall, 1975). Highly structured situations in which the behavior of the patient is assessed while interacting with another person have been used by Arkowitz *et al.*, (1975), by Bryant, Trower, Yardley, Urbieta, and Letemendia (1976) and by Youngren and Lewinsohn (1980). The more open-ended *in vivo* attempts by Lewinsohn and his associates (Lewinsohn, *et al.*, 1970; Libet & Lewinsohn, 1973; Lewinsohn & Shaffer, 1971; Libet *et al.*, 1973) and by McLean *et al.*, (1973) have already been described in the discussion on assessing overt behavior.

COGNITIONS: SIGNIFICANCE AND ASSESSMENT

There is no doubt that the phenomena of depression include cognitive manifestations. Cognitive theorists such as Beck (1967), Ellis and Harper (1961), and Rehm (1976) have each advanced hypotheses which attribute a causal role to cognitions for the occurrence of depression. But they in turn differ among themselves in regard to the *specific* nature of the cognitions which are assumed to lead to depression. There are at least five different ways in which the cognitions presumed to be functionally related to depression have been conceptualized: negative expectancies, cognitive distortions, irrational beliefs, negative thoughts, and attributions about causality. Each of these has led to the development of assessment devices.

NEGATIVE EXPECTANCIES

The construct of expectancy as an important mediator of behavior has been most clearly enunciated by Bandura (1977) and by Rotter (1954). Bandura distinguishes between two kinds of expectancies: efficacy expectations and outcome expectations. Efficacy expectations refer to a person's estimation of his or her ability to perform a given behavior. Outcome expectations refer to a person's estimation of the likely consequences of his or her behavior. The relevance of expectations to depression has been stressed by Beck (1967), who postulates the existence of a "cognitive triad" consisting of negative views of the self, the world, and the future. A number of different tests have been developed to measure expectancies. Weintraub, Segal, and Beck (1974) devised a test consisting of incomplete stories involving a principle character with whom the subject was asked to identify. Subjects completed the stories by selecting one sentence from among several alternatives written so as to represent themes from Beck's description of the cognitive triad. The expected relationship between negative expectancies and depression level was found.

Another instrument designed to assess a respondent's negative expectancies is the *Hopelessness Scale* (Beck, Weissman, Lester, & Trexler, 1974), which consists of 20 true–false items. Eleven of the items are keyed true (example: I might as well give up because I can't make things better for myself) and nine are keyed false (example: I have great faith in the future). The scale was found to have a high degree of internal consistency, showed good correlation with clinical ratings of hopelessness, and was sensitive to changes in the patient's state of depression over time.

The *Subjective Probability Questionnaire* (SPQ) is yet another attempt to operationalize Beck's cognitive triad (Muñoz & Lewinsohn, 1976a). The SPQ consists of 80 statements constructed along three dichotomous and crossed dimensions: self versus world, present versus future, and positive versus negative. Sample statements: "Nuclear warfare will destroy the world by the year 2000" (world, future, negative); "I am more helpful toward others than the average person" (self, present, positive). The respondent indicates on an 11-point scale (0 = 0% probability; 10 = 100% probability) "What you think the chances are that the statement is true or that it will become true." The SPQ has been shown to possess a good test-retest reliability and to discriminate well between depressed and nondepressed samples (Muñoz, 1977).

COGNITIVE DISTORTION

A number of different conceptual distortions have been hypothesized by Beck (1963) to be uniquely associated with depression. These include: arbitrary inference, selective abstraction, overgeneralization, magnification or minimization, and personalization. These conceptual distortions are postulated to cause the depressed individual to distort and to misinterpret his or her experiences. A measure of cognitive distortion in depression has been developed by Hammen and Krantz (1975, 1976). The Hammen and Krantz procedure assesses an individual's interpretations of events depicted in brief stories and measures the presence of a tendency to select the most depressed and distorted (in terms of logical inference based on the information provided in the story) response options. The latter pertain to the central character's feelings, thoughts, and expectations. For example, a depressed–distorted completion to a story about a person who lost an election would be "to shrug it off, feeling I have tried as hard as I could." Depressed individuals have consistently been found to select a greater number of depressed–distorted responses (Hammen & Krantz, 1976).

IRRATIONAL BELIEFS AND DYSFUNCTIONAL ATTITUDES

The idea that irrational beliefs are causally related to the development of depression (and other negative emotional states) is central to the thinking of Albert Ellis (e.g., Ellis & Harper, 1961). Depression in this view occurs when a particular situation triggers an irrational belief. It is the belief rather than the situation which causes the person to overreact emotionally to the latter. A number of scales have been developed to measure the degree to which respondents hold various irrational beliefs (Murphy & Ellis, 1976). These instruments typically include statements reflecting "irrational beliefs" (e.g., "The main goal and purpose of life is achievement and success"), and respondents are asked to indicate their agreement with each belief on a five-point scale. The total score is presumed to be a measure of the degree to which the individual subscribes to irrational beliefs.

Nelson (1977) found a significant correlation between scores on the *Irrational Beliefs Tests* (Jones, 1968) and the Beck Depression Inventory. The *Personal Belief Inventory (PBI)* (Muñoz & Lewinsohn, 1976b) is a modification of a test developed by Hartman (1968). The PBI consists of 30 statements representing irrational beliefs hypothesized to be important for the occurrence of depression. The PBI was found to discriminate well between depressed and nondepressed control groups. A methodologically similar instrument is represented by the *Dysfunctional Attitude Scale* (Weissman & Beck, 1978), which consists of 40 Likert-type items and has two alternate forms. The *Dysfunctional Attitude Scale* also probes the respondent's degree of agreement with beliefs hypothesized by Beck to characterize depressed patients.

Negative Thoughts

Rehm (1977) has developed a self-control theory of depression in which low rates of self-reinforcement and high rates of self-punishment are seen as leading to the low rate of behavior which characterizes depressed patients. The *Cognitive Events Schedule* (CES) (Muñoz & Lewinsohn, 1976c) was intended to probe for the content of thoughts by asking the respondent to report the frequency of occurrence and the emotional impact of each of 160 thoughts during the past 30 days. The frequency of occurrence of each specific thought is rated on a three-point scale and its impact on a five-point scale (1 = very disturbing; 5 = very pleasant). Paralleling the SPQ, CES items were constructed along three dichotomous and crossed dimensions: self versus world, present versus future, and positive versus negative. Two sample items are: "My friends are a great bunch of people" (world, present, positive); "The price of food is going to keep getting higher" (world, future, negative). Depressed individuals have been shown to report a much larger number of negative and a smaller number of positive thoughts than nondepressed controls (Lewinsohn, Muñoz, & Larson, 1978).

ATTRIBUTIONS OF CAUSALITY

The belief that outcomes are independent of responding is central to the learned helplessness theory (Seligman, 1975). Seligman theorizes that this cognition results in the motivational (reduced responding), cognitive (interference with later instrumental learning), and emotional (fear, followed by depression) manifestations of the learned helplessness syndrome, which he assumes to be analogous to clinical depression. Thus, depressed individuals are hypothesized to perceive reinforcement as being outside their own control or noncontingent, that is, as depending on chance, fate, powerful others, or otherwise unpredictable. Locus of control is assumed to be a general cognitive set within this framework and it has typically been measured with the Locus of Control Scale (Rotter, 1966, 1975). More recently attribution theory (Frieze, 1973; Heider, 1958; Weiner & Frieze, 1971) has postulated that in addition to the perceived locus of the cause of an event (i.e., internal vs. external), several other dimensions, such as stable versus unstable, success versus failure, specific versus all-inclusive, mediate the influence of attributions upon behavior. These notions have been incorporated into Learned Helplessness theory (Abramson, *et al.*, 1976). Within this new formulation an individual is hypothesized to be susceptible to depression if he or she makes stable–internal–all-inclusive attributions about failure experiences (I lack intelligence) and external–unstable–specific attributions about success experiences (I was lucky on the math test). The Multidimensional Multiattributional Causality Scale (Lefcourt, 1978) is designed to assess the person's attributions in two types of situations (social and academic). The scale has 48 items written to encompass a four-factor design: internal versus external, ability (task) versus effort (luck), success versus failure, achievement versus affiliation. The scales have had considerable psychometric development and should prove useful in research and perhaps even in clinical application.

ENGAGEMENT IN PLEASANT ACTIVITIES:
SIGNIFICANCE AND ASSESSMENT

It is well established that depressed individuals as a group engage in relatively few activities and in even fewer which are considered to be pleasant or rewarding by them. Thus, for example, the average number of pleasant activities engaged in, and the subjective enjoyability of potentially pleasant events, is lower in depressed than in nondepressed normal and nondepressed psychiatric control subjects (Lewinsohn & Amenson, 1978; Lewinsohn & MacPhillamy, 1974). In another series of studies (Lewinsohn & Libet, 1972; Lewinsohn & Graf, 1973; Grosscup & Lewinsohn, 1980; Rehm, 1978), a significant association between daily mood changes and number of "pleasant" activities engaged in was found.

The patient's rate of engagement in pleasant activities can be assessed in several ways:

1. The patient fills out the Pleasant Events Schedule (MacPhillamy & Lewinsohn, 1971). The PES contains 320 events generated by exhaustively sampling events that were reported to be sources of pleasure by highly diverse samples of people. The schedule calls for two responses to each item. The participant is first asked to rate the frequency of the event's occurrence during the past month on a three-point scale. Second, the participant is asked to rate the subjective enjoyability of each event on a three-point scale. The frequency ratings are assumed to reflect the rate at which the events occurred during the past month. The enjoyability ratings are assumed to reflect the potential reinforcement value of the events for the individual. The sum of the products of the frequency and impact ratings for all the events is assumed to provide an approximate measure of response-contingent positive reinforcement experienced by the individual during the past month. Extensive normative data and results consistent with the construct validity of the scale have been presented elsewhere (Lewinsohn & Amenson, 1978; MacPhillamy & Lewinsohn, 1975).

2. The subject monitors his or her daily rate of engagement in pleasant activities over a period of time through the use of "activity schedules" (Lewinsohn, 1976a; Lewinsohn, Sullivan, & Grosscup, 1980). An activity schedule consists of items judged by the patient to be most pleasant, and the patients is asked to indicate at the end of each day which of the activities he or she performed. With lists of 160

items, the mean daily number of activities for a nondepressed sample is approximately 33 (Lewinsohn & Graf, 1973). The mean for lists of 80 pleasant activities (Lewinsohn, Sullivan, & Grosscup, 1980) was approximately 18. Fuchs and Rehm (1977) employed an activity schedule procedure in a self-control-oriented therapy program. Using the PES as an item pool, a shortened list of 20 classes of reinforcing behavior was constructed. Items on this list, termed the Positive Activity Schedule, were written to emphasize the active role of the subject in producing potential reinforcement.

3. An interesting procedure for monitoring activities has been described by Harmon, Nelson, and Hayes (1978). Their method makes use of a portable timer, which is carried by the patient and is used to cue self-monitoring on a variable interval schedule of one hour. The person is provided with a list of variable intervals used to set the timer and is asked to set the timer for the first interval upon awakening in the morning and reset it for the next interval immediately after being cued. The procedure yields 11 self-recordings per day. When cued, the person is instructed to record a description of his or her activity in addition to a numerical rating of pleasantness from 1 to 5 (1 = this activity is very unpleasant; 5 = this activity is very pleasant). The instructions tell the person, "When the timer elapses, describe what you are doing. Write it down in detail noting where you are, with whom, whether you are talking, and exactly what you are doing." In contrast to the procedure used by the Lewinsohn group, which is not reactive (Lewinsohn, 1976a), the Harmon, Nelson, and Hayes procedure apparently was quite reactive, resulting in substantial increases in engagement in pleasant activities.

AVERSIVE EVENTS: SIGNIFICANCE AND ASSESSMENT

While assessment of pleasant activities has been part of a number of treatment programs for depression (Anton, Dunbar, & Friedman, 1976; Fuchs, & Rehm, 1977; McLean, 1976; Rush, Khatami, & Beck, 1975; Zeiss et al., 1979) relatively little has been done to assess the occurrence of aversive or unpleasant events.

Aversive events have been shown to be related to depression in the following ways:

1. Aversive events have been found to precede the occurrence of clinical depression (Brown, Bhrolchain, & Harris, 1975; Dohrenwend

& Dohrenwend, 1974; Paykel, Myers, Dienelt, Klerman, Lindenthal, & Pepper, 1969). While results have generally been consistent in showing an increase in the occurrence of all disorders, including depression, following an increase in the number of stressful life events, Paykel and his colleagues (1969) found events involving social exits—that is, those involving departures from the social field of the individual (e.g., death of spouse, death of close family member, separation, divorce, family member leaving home, child marrying)—to be uniquely elevated in depressed persons during the six-month period preceding the onset of their depression.

2. Depressed persons have been found to be particularly sensitive to aversive events (Lewinsohn, Lobitz, & Wilson, 1973; Lewinsohn & Talkington, 1979; Libet, Lewinsohn, & Javorek, 1973; Schless, Schwartz, Goetz, & Mendels, 1974; Stewart, 1968).

3. The rate of occurrence of aversive events covaries with dysphoria (Grosscup & Lewinsohn, 1980; Lewinsohn & Talkington, 1979; Rehm, 1978). In one study (Lewinsohn & Talkington, 1979), the types of events uniquely associated with depression fell into the following clusters: (a) *Social Isolation* (e.g., being alone); (b) *Marital Discord* (e.g., arguments with spouse); (c) *Inconveniences* (e.g., having something break or run poorly); (d) *Work Hassle* (e.g., having too much to do); and (e) *Negative Social Interactions* (e.g., being misled, bluffed, or tricked).

The most frequently used assessment device for the occurrence of life events has been the Social Readjustment Rating Scale (SRRS) (Holmes & Rahe, 1967). It consists of 43 items intended to represent fairly common events arising from family, personal, occupational, and financial situations that require or signify changes in ongoing adjustment. The occurrence of the events during the preceding six months is established during an interview. Weights are assigned to each item based on ratings made by a sample of judges (Holmes & Rahe, 1967).

There are many serious methodological and conceptual problems which limit the potential usefulness and theoretical interpretation of results obtained with the SRRS (Rabkin & Struening, 1976). For example, the assignment of constant weights to the items, based on strong convergence by the standardization judges regarding the appropriate weights for particular items, nevertheless assumes that events are equally stressful for everybody, a questionable assumption. Instruments that incorporate refinements suggested by criticisms of the SRRS are the PERI (*Psychiatric Epidemiology Research Interview*) developed by Dohrenwend, Krasnoff, Askenasy, and Dohrenwend (1978), the LES (*Life Experiences Survey*) developed by Sarason, Johnson, and Siegel (1977), and the *Unpleasant Events Schedule* (UES) developed by Lewinsohn and Talkington (1979).

Events for the PERI were selected from a population of events generated by asking respondents, "What was the last major event in your life that, for better or worse, interrupted or changed your usual activities?" A total of 102 events were then rated on the dimension of "change" by a probability-randomized sample from New York City.

The LES is a 57-item self-report measure which asks respondents to indicate events that they have experienced during the past year. Respondents are then asked: (1) to indicate whether they viewed the event as positive or negative at the time; and (2) to rate the impact of the particular event on their life. The LES thus approaches the individualized approach to the measurement of life events advocated by Brown (Brown, 1974; Brown, Sklair, Harris, & Birley, 1973).

The UES consists of 320 events generated on the basis of an extensive search of events considered to be unpleasant, distressing, and aversive by many people. The instructions for the UES call for two responses to each item. The first response rates its frequency of occurrence during the past month on a three-point scale. The second response rates its subjective aversiveness on a three-point scale. The UES schedule includes six nonoverlapping subscales: Health and Well-Being; Achievement — Academic-Job; Domestic and Day-to-Day Inconveniences; Sexual–Marital–Friendship; Legal; Material–Financial. Two additional scales were constructed: a "Social Exits" scale and a "Most Discriminating Items" scale, which consists of 27 items found to discriminate at a very high level of statistical significance between depressed and nondepressed groups. The UES scales generally had very low correlations with the SRRS. Lewinsohn and Talkington (1979) suggest that this lack of correlation between the two scales may reflect a fundamental difference in the types of items comprising the two lists. The SRRS is heavily loaded with past events which are *fortuitous* and *time-limited* (e.g., the sudden accidental death of a close relative) while the UES emphasizes events which Ilfeld (1976a, 1976b, 1977) calls "current social stressors that are patterned into our everyday roles as marital partners, breadwinners, and parents" (Ilfeld, 1977, p. 162). Data on the psychometric properties of the UES, including test-retest reliability, aspects of validity and internal consistency, and relationships with depression, are provided in Lewinsohn and Talkington (1979) and Lewinsohn, Tursky, and Arconad (1979).

The use of daily monitoring of aversive events by patients, with the goal of identifying specific aversive events related to the patient's dysphoria, is described by Grosscup and Lewinsohn (1980) and Lewinsohn, Sullivan, and Grosscup (1980). Patients monitored the occurrence and aversiveness of events on individually constructed lists consisting of 80 events rated as most aversive by the patient. The mean unpleasant events score in a normal population was found to be 5.1 with a standard deviation of 3.9 (Lewinsohn & Talkington, 1979). The daily frequency of events and their correlation with mood was used as feedback to patients and as an aid in formulating and evaluating specific treatment goals aimed at reducing the number and the subjective impact of aversive events in the patients' lives.

Conclusions and Integration

We conceptualize the clinical assessment of persons with affective disorders as a two-pronged process involving differential diagnosis and functional analysis. Differential diagnosis is aimed at the careful initial and periodic assessment of the patient's depression (and/or mania). Functional analysis is aimed at the identification of specific targets for therapeutic intervention and the evaluation of the effects of treatment on the targeted behaviors. Both differential and functional diagnosis are important components of a systematic treatment program offering services to depressed persons.

Great strides have been made in the differential diagnosis of affective disorder. Existing assessment devices have the capacity to generate reliable and replicable data on patients' depression (and/or mania) in terms of specific symptoms, manifestations, severity level, and subtypes. Clinicians and researchers need to select from among the many available procedures. While each has good and weak points, the fact is that many are, to a considerable extent, interchangeable.

An area of weakness concerns the differential diagnosis of depression among the elderly. Clinicians and researchers typically have had considerably less experience in dealing with elderly populations. Differential diagnosis in the elderly is complicated both by the increase in the incidence of physical illness and somatic symptoms with age and by the difficulty in distinguishing the symptoms of depression from those of senile dementia (Epstein, 1976). For example, memory and cognitive impairments are common in both elderly and depressed populations. More work needs to be done to develop instruments appropriate to elderly populations and to standardize existing instruments across the total age range.

Procedures available for the assessment of the events and behavior patterns functionally related to depression are considerably less developed. Various theoretical emphases have focused on different aspects of treatment planning and evaluation and have lead to the development of a wide range of assessment devices. The assessment of assertiveness has received the greatest attention, and the area of general social skill assessment is growing. The development of cognitive assessment instruments is just beginning. There is currently a gap between assessment devices developed for research purposes and the cost-effectiveness of these measures in clinical application. Future efforts are needed to narrow this gap.

Functional analysis, by pinpointing events and behaviors related to the patient's depression, has immediate implications for the treatment of a given patient. An example of a treatment strategy focusing on the low engagement in pleasant activities and on a high rate of occurrence of unpleasant events is described in more detail by Lewinsohn, Sullivan, and Grosscup (1980). Treatment strategies formulated for individuals with cognitive and social-interactional problems have also been formulated (e.g., Beck, Rush, Shaw, & Emery, 1979; Lewinsohn, Muñoz, Youngren, & Zeiss, 1978; McLean & Hakstian, 1979; Rehm *et al.*, 1978).

References

Abramson, L. Y., Seligman, M. E. P., & Teasdale, J. Learned helplessness in humans: Critique and reformulation. *Journal of Abnormal Psychology*, 1967, *86*, 78-97.

Aitken, R. C. B. Measurement of feeling using visual analogue scales. *Proceedings of the Royal Society of Medicine*, 1969, *62*, 989-993.

Aitken, R. C. B., & Zealley, A. K. Measurement of mood. *British Journal of Hospital Medicine*, 1970, *4*, 215-224.

Anton, J. L., Dunbar, J., & Friedman, L. Anticipation training in the treatment of depression. In J. D. Krumboltz & C. E. Thorensen (Eds.), *Counseling methods*. New York: Holt, Rinehart, & Winston, 1976.

Arkowitz, H., Lichtenstein, E., McGovern, K., & Hines, P. The behavioral assessment of social competence in males. *Behavior Therapy*, 1975, *6*, 3-13.

Bandura, A. *Social learning theory*. Englewood Cliffs, NJ: Prentice-Hall, 1977.

Beck, A. T. Thinking and depression: I. Idiosyncratic content and cognitive distortions. *Archives of General Psychiatry*, 1963, *9*, 324-333.

Beck, A. T. *Depression: Clinical, experimental and theoretical aspects*. New York: Harper & Row, 1967.

Beck, A. T. *Depression: Causes and treatment*. Philadelphia: University of Pennsylvania Press, 1972.

Beck, A. T., & Beck, R. W. Screening depressed patients in family practice — A rapid technique. *Postgraduate Medicine*, 1972, *52*, 81-85.

Beck, A. T., & Rush, A. J. Cognitive approaches to depression and suicide. In G. Serban (Ed.), *Cognitive defects in the development of mental illness*. New York: Brunner/Mazel, 1978.

Beck, A. T., Rush, A. J., Shaw, B. F., & Emery, G. *Cognitive therapy of depression*. New York: The Guilford Press, 1979.

Beck, A. T., Ward, C. H., Mendelson, M., Mock, J., & Erbaugh, J. An inventory for measuring depression. *Archives of General Psychiatry*, 1961, *4*, 561-571.

Beck, A. T., Weissman, A., Lester, D., & Trexler, L. The measurement of pessimism: The hopelessness scale. *Journal of Consulting and Clinical Psychology*, 1974, *42*, 861-865.

Becker, J. *Affective disorders*. Morristown, NJ: General Learning Press, 1977.

Brown, G. W. Meaning, measurement and stress of life events. In B. S. Dohrenwend & B. P. Dohrenwend (Eds.), *Stressful life events: Their nature and effects*. New York: John Wiley & Sons, 1974.

Brown, G. W. Bhrolchain, M. N., & Harris, S. Social class and psychiatric disturbance among women in an urban population. *Sociology*, 1975, *9*, 225-254.

Brown, G. W., Sklair, F., Harris, T. O., & Birley, J. L. T. Life events and psychiatric disorder: I. Some methodological issues. *Psychological Medicine*, 1973, *3*, 74-87.

Bryant, B., Trower, P., Yardley, K., Urbieta, H., & Letemendia, F. J. J. A survey of social inadequacy among psychiatric outpatients. *Psychological Medicine*, 1976, *6*, 101-112.

Burglass, D., & Horton, J. A scale for predicting subsequent suicidal behavior. *British Journal of Psychiatry*, 1974, *124*, 573-578.

Cadoret, R. J., & Tanna, V. L. Genetics of affective disorders. In G. Usdin (Ed.), *Depression: Clinical, biological and psychological perspectives*. New York: Brunner/Mazel, 1977.

Cautela, J. R., & Upper, D. The Behavioral Inventory Battery: The use of self-report measures in behavioral analysis and therapy. In M. Hersen & A. S. Bellack (Eds.), *Behavioral assessment: A practical handbook*. Elmsford, NY: Pergamon Press, 1976.

Christenfeld, R., Lubin, B., & Satin, M. Concurrent validity of the Depression Adjective Check List in a normal population. *American Journal of Psychiatry*, 1978, *135*, 582-584.

Cohen, J. A coefficient of agreement for nominal scales. *Educational and Psychological Measurement*, 1960, *20*, 37-46.

Costello, C. G., & Comrey, A. L. Scales for measuring depression and anxiety. *Journal of Psychology*, 1967, *66*, 303-313.

Coyne, J. D. Depression and the response of others. *Journal of Abnormal Psychology*, 1976, *85*, 186-193.

Curran, J. P. Skills training as an approach to the treatment of heterosexual-social anxiety: A review. *Psychological Bulletin*, 1977, *84*, 140–157.

Dahlstrom, W. G., Welsh, G. S., & Dahlstrom, L. E. *An MMPI Handbook.* Minneapolis: University of Minnesota Press, 1972.

Davies, B., Burrows, G., & Poynton, C. A comparative study of four depression rating scales. *Australian and New Zealand Journal of Psychiatry*, 1975, *9*, 21–23.

Dempsey, P. A. Unidimensional depression scale for the MMPI. *Journal of Consulting Psychology*, 1964, *28*, 364–370.

Diagnostic and statistical manual of mental disorders (2nd ed.). Washington, D.C.: American Pychiatric Association, 1968.

Diagnostic and statistical manual of mental disorders (3rd ed.). Washington, D.C.: American Psychiatric Association, 1980.

Dohrenwend, B. S., & Dohrenwend, B. D. *Stressful life events: Their nature and effects.* New York: John Wiley & Sons, 1974.

Dohrenwend, B. S., Krasnoff, L., Askenasy, A. R., & Dohrenwend, B. P. Exemplification of a method for scaling life events: the PERI life events scale. *Journal of Health and Social Behavior*, 1978, *19*, 205–229.

Eisler, R. M. The behavioral assessment of social skills. In M. Hersen & A. S. Bellack (Eds.), *Behavioral assessment.* Oxford: Pergamon Press 1976.

Eisler, R. M., Hersen, M., & Miller, P. M. Effects of modeling on components of assertive behavior. *Journal of Behavior Therapy and Experimental Psychiatry*, 1973, *4*, 1–6.

Eisler, R. M., Hersen, M., Miller, P. M., & Blanchard, E. Situational determinants of assertive behavior. *Journal of Consulting and Clinical Psychology*, 1975, *43*, 303–340.

Eisler, R. M., Miller, P. M., & Hersen, M. Components of assertive behavior. *Journal of Clinical Psychology*, 1973, *29*, 295–299.

Ekman, P., & Bressler, J. *Progress report to National Institute of Mental Health.* Unpublished mimeo, National Institute of Mental Health, 1964.

Ekman, P., & Friesen, W. V. Nonverbal behavior and psychopathology. In R. J. Friedman & M. M. Katz (Eds.), *The psychology of depression: Contemporary theory and research.* New York: John Wiley & Sons, 1974.

Ekman, P., & Rose, D. *Progress report to National Institute of Mental Health.* Unpublished mimeo, National Institute of Mental Health, 1965.

Ellis, A. *Reason and emotion in psychotherapy.* New York: Lyle Stuart, 1962.

Ellis, A., & Harper, R. A. *A guide to rational living.* Hollywood, CA: Wilshire, 1961.

Ellsworth, R. B. Consumer feedback in measuring the effectiveness of mental health programs. In J. Guttentag & E. L. Struening (Eds.), *Handbook of evaluation research.* Beverly Hills: Sage, 1975.

Endicott, J., & Spitzer, R. L. A diagnostic interview: The schedule for affective disorders and schizophrenia. *Archives of General Psychiatry*, 1978, *35*, 837–844.

Epstein, L. J. Symposium on age differentiation in depressive illness—Depression in the elderly. *Journal of Gerontology*, 1976, *31*, 278–282.

Fenichel, O. *The psychoanalytic theory of neurosis.* New York: W. W. Norton, 1945.

Fleiss, J. L. Measuring nominal scale agreement among many raters. *Psychological Bulletin*, 1971, *76*, 378–382.

Folstein, M. F., & Luria, R. Reliability, validity and clinical application of the Visual Analogue Mood Scale. *Psychological Medicine*, 1973, *3*, 479–486.

Friedman, A. S., Cowitz, B., Cohen, H. W., & Granick, S. Syndromes and themes of psychotic depression. *Archives of General Psychiatry*, 1963, *9*, 504-512.

Frieze, I. *Studies of information processing and the attributional process in achievement-related contexts*. Unpublished doctoral dissertation, University of California at Los Angeles, 1973.

Fuchs, C. Z., & Rehm, L. P. A self-control behavior therapy program for depression. *Journal of Consulting and Clinical Psychology*, 1977, *45*, 206-215.

Galassi, J. P., Delo, J. S., Galassi, M. D., & Bastien, S. The College Self-Expression Scale: A measure of assertiveness. *Behavior Therapy*, 1974, *5*, 165-171.

Gallagher, D., McGarvey, W., Zelinski, E., & Thompson, L. W. *Age and factor structure of the Zung Depression Scale*. Paper presented at the 31st annual meeting of the Gerontological Society, Dallas, November 1978.

Gaitz, C. M. Depression in the elderly. In W. Fann, I. Karacan, A. Pokorny, & R. Williams (Eds.), *Phenomenology and treatment of depression*. New York: Spectrum, 1977.

Gambrill, E., & Richey, C. An assertion inventory for use in assessment and research. *Behavior Therapy*, 1975, *6*, 550-561.

Gay, M., Hollandsworth, J. G., Jr., & Galassi, J. P. An assertiveness inventory for adults. *Journal of Counseling Psychology*, 1975, *22*, 340-344.

Goldfried, M. R., & Linehan, M. M. Basic issues in behavioral assessment. In A. R. Ciminero, K. S. Calhoun, & H. E. Adams (Eds.), *Handbook of behavioral assessment*. New York: John Wiley & Sons, 1977.

Goldsmith, J. B., & McFall, R. M. Development and evaluation of an interpersonal skill-training program for psychiatric inpatients. *Journal of Abnormal Psychology*, 1975, *84*, 51-58.

Grinker, R. R., Miller, J., Sabshin, M., Nunn, R., & Nunnally, J. C. *The phenomena of depression*. New York: Paul B. Hoeber, 1961.

Grosscup, S. J., & Lewinsohn, P. M. Unpleasant and pleasant events, and mood. *Journal of Clinical Psychology*, 1980, *36*, 252-259.

Hall, J. R. Assessment of assertiveness. In P. McReynolds (Ed.), *Advances in psychological assessment* (Vol. 4). San Francisco: Jossey-Bass, 1977.

Hamilton, M. A. A rating scale for depression. *Journal of Neurology, Neurosurgery and Psychiatry*, 1960, *23*, 56-61.

Hamilton, M. A. Development of a rating scale for primary depressive illness. *British Journal of Social Clinical Psychology*, 1967, *6*, 278-296.

Hammen, C. L., & Krantz, S. *The Story Completion Test*. Unpublished mimeo, University of California at Los Angeles, 1975.

Hammen, C. L., & Krantz, S. Effect of success and failure on depressive cognitions. *Journal of Abnormal Psychology*, 1976, *85*, 577-586.

Harmatz, J., & Shader, R. Psychopharmacologic investigations in healthy elderly volunteers: MMPI depression scale. *Journal of American Geriatrics Society*, 1975, *23*, 350-354.

Harmon, T. H., Nelson, R. O., & Hayes, S. C. *Self-monitoring of mood versus activity by depressed clients*. Paper presented at the Association for the Advancement of Behavior Therapy, Chicago, November 1978.

Harris, R. E. & Lingoes, J. C. *Subscales of the MMPI: An aid to profile interpretation*. Unpublished manuscript, University of California at San Francisco, 1955.

Hartman, B. J. Sixty revealing questions for 20 minutes. *Rational Living*, 1968, *3*, 7-8.

Heider, F. *The psychology of interpersonal relations*. New York: John Wiley & Sons, 1958.

Hersen, M., Eisler, D., Alford, G., & Agras, W. S. Effects of token economy on neurotic depression: An experimental analysis. *Behavior Therapy*, 1973, *4*, 392-397.

Hersen, M., Eisler, R. M., & Miller, P. M. Development of assertive responses: Clinical, measurement and research considerations. *Behaviour Research and Therapy*, 1973, *11*, 505-521.

Hinchliffe, M., Lancashire, M., & Roberts, F. J. Depression: Defense mechanisms in speech. *British Journal of Psychiatry*, 1971, *118*, 471-472.(a)

Hinchliffe, M., Lancashire, M., & Roberts, F. J. A study of eye contact in depressed and recovered patients. *British Journal of Psychiatry*, 1971, *119*, 213-215.(b)

Holmes, T. H., & Rahe, R. H. The Social Readjustment Rating Scale. *Journal of Psychomatic Research*, 1967, *11*, 213-218.

Ilfeld, F. W. Characteristics of current social stressors. *Psychological Reports*, 1976, *39*, 1231-1247.(a)

Ilfeld, F. W. Methodological issues in relating psychiatric symptoms to social stressors. *Psychological Reports*, 1976, *39*, 1251-1258.(b)

Ilfeld, F. W. Current social stressors and symptoms of depression. *American Journal of Psychiatry*, 1977, *134*, 161-166.

Jacobson, E. *Depression: Comparative studies of normal, neurotic and psychotic conditions.* New York: International Universities Press, 1971.

Johansson, S. L., Lewinsohn, P. M., & Flippo, J. F. *An application of the Premack principle to the verbal behavior of depressed subjects.* Paper presented at the meeting of the Association for the Advancement of Behavior Therapy, Washington, D.C., December 1969.

Jones, R. G. *A factored measure of Ellis's irrational belief systems.* Wichita: Test Systems, Inc., 1968.

Killian, D. H. *The effect of instructions and social reinforcement on selected categories of behavior emitted by depressed persons in a small group setting.* Unpublished doctoral dissertation, University of Oregon, 1971.

Klerman, G. L. Unipolar and bipolar depression. In J. Angst (Ed.), *Classification and prediction of outcome of depression.* Stuttgart, Germany: F. K. Schottauer Verlag, 1973.

Kupfer, D. J., Detre, T. P., Foster, F. G., Tucker, G. J., & Delgado, J. The application of Delgado's telemetric mobility recorder to human studies. *Behavioral Biology*, 1972, *7*, 585-590.

Kupfer, D. J., & Foster, F. G. Sleep and activity in psychotic depression. *Journal of Nervous and Mental Disease*, 1973, *156*, 341-348.

Langone, M. Assertiveness and Lewinsohn's theory of depression: An empirical test. *The Behavior Therapist*, 1979 *2*, 21.

Lazarus, A. A. Learning theory and the treatment of depression. *Behaviour Research and Therapy*, 1968, *6*, 83-89.

Lazarus, A. A. Assertive training: A brief note. *Behavior Therapy*, 1973, *4*, 697-699.

Lefcourt, H. M. Locus of control for specific goals. In L. C. Perlmuter & R. A. Monty (Eds.), *Choice and perceived control.* Hillside, NJ: Lawrence Erlbaum, 1978.

Lettieri, D. J. Research issues in developing prediction scales. In C. Neuringer (Ed.), *Psychological assessment of suicidal risk.* Springfield, IL: Charles C. Thomas, 1974.

Levenson, R. W., & Gottman, J. M. Toward the assessment of social competence. *Journal of Consulting and Clinical Psychology*, 1978, *46*, 453-462.

Levitt, E. E., & Lubin, B. *Depression*. New York: Springer Publishing Co., 1975.

Lewinsohn, P. M. *The Unpleasant Events Schedule: A scale for the measurement of aversive events*. Unpublished mimeo, University of Oregon, 1975.

Lewinsohn, P. M. Activity schedules in the treatment of depression. In C. E. Thoreson & J. D. Krumboltz (Eds.), *Counseling methods*. New York: Holt, Rinehart, & Winston, 1976.(a)

Lewinsohn, P. M. Manual of instructions for behavior ratings used for observation of interpersonal behavior. In E. J. Mash & L. G. Terdal (Eds.), *Behavior therapy assessment*. New York: Springer Publishing Co., 1976.(b)

Lewinsohn, P. M., & Amenson, C. Some relationships between pleasant and unpleasant mood related activities and depression. *Journal of Abnormal Psychology*, 1978, *87*, 644-654.

Lewinsohn, P. M., Biglan, T., & Zeiss, A. Behavioral treatment of depression. In P. Davidson (Ed.), *Behavioral management of anxiety, depression, and pain*. New York: Brunner/Mazel, 1976.

Lewinsohn, P. M., & Graf, M. Pleasant activities and depression. *Journal of Consulting and Clinical Psychology*, 1973, *41*, 261-268.

Lewinsohn, P. M., & Libet, J. Pleasant events, activities schedules, and depression. *Journal of Abnormal Psychology*, 1972, *79*, 291-295.

Lewinsohn, P. M., Lobitz, W. C., & Wilson, S. "Sensitivity" of depressed individuals to aversive stimuli. *Journal of Abnormal Psychology*, 1973, *81*, 259-263.

Lewinsohn, P. M., & MacPhillamy, D. J. The relationship between age and engagement in pleasant activities. *Journal of Gerontology*, 1974, *29*, 290-294.

Lewinsohn, P. M., Mischel, W., Chaplin, W., & Barton, R. Social competence and depression: The role of illusory self-perceptions. *Journal of Abnormal Psychology*, 1980, *89*, 203-212.

Lewinsohn, P. M., Muñoz, R. F., & Larson, D. W. *The measurement of expectancies and other cognitions in depressed individuals*. Paper presented at the meeting of the Association for the Advancement of Behavior Therapy, Chicago, November 1978.

Lewinsohn, P. M., Muñoz, R. F. Youngren, M. A., & Zeiss, A. M. *Control your depression*. Englewood Cliffs, NJ: Prentice-Hall, 1978.

Lewinsohn, P. M., & Shaffer, M. Use of home observations as an integral part of the treatment of depression: Preliminary report and case studies. *Journal of Consulting and Clinical Psychology*, 1971, *37*, 87-94.

Lewinsohn, P. M., Sullivan, J. M., & Grosscup, S. J. Changing reinforcing events: An approach to the treatment of depression. *Psychotherapy: Theory, Research and Practice*, 1980, in press.

Lewinsohn, P. M., & Talkington, J. The measurement of aversive events and relations to depression. Applied Psychological Measurement, 1979, *3*, 83-101.

Lewinsohn, P. M., Tursky, S., & Arconad, M. *The relationship between age and the frequency of occurrence, and the subjective impact, of aversive events*. Unpublished mimeo, University of Oregon, 1979.

Lewinsohn, P. M., Weinstein, M., & Alper, T. A behavioral approach to the group treatment of depressed persons: A methodological contribution. *Journal of Clinical Psychology*, 1970, *26*, 525-532.

Lewinsohn, P. M., Youngren, M. A., & Grosscup, S. J. Reinforcement and depression. In R. A. Depue (Ed.), *The psychobiology of depressive disorders: Implications for the effects of stress*. New York: Academic Press, 1979.

Lewinsohn, P. M., Zeiss, A., Zeiss, R., & Haller, R. Endogeneity and reactivity as orthogonal dimensions in depression. *Journal of Nervous and Mental Disease,* 1977, *164,* 327–332.

Liberman, R. P., & Roberts, J. Contingency management of neurotic depression and marital disharmony. In H. J. Eysenck (Ed.), *Case histories in behavioral therapy.* London: Routledge and Kegan Paul, 1974.

Libet, J., & Lewinsohn, P. M. The concept of social skill with special references to the behavior of depressed persons. *Journal of Consulting and Clinical Psychology,* 1973, *40,* 304–312.

Libet, J. M., Lewinsohn, P. M., & Javorek, F. *The construct of social skill: An empirical study of several behavioral measures on temporal stability, internal structure, validity and situational generalizability.* Unpublished mimeo, University of Oregon, 1973.

Little, J. C., & McPhail, N. I. Measures of depressive mood at monthly intervals. *British Journal of Psychiatry,* 1973, *122,* 447–452.

Lubin, B. Adjective checklists for measurement of depression. *Archives of General Psychiatry,* 1965, *12,* 57–62.

Lubin, B. *Depression Adjective Check Lists: Manual.* San Diego: Educational and Industrial Testing Service, 1967.

Lubin, B. *Bibliography for the Depression Adjective Check Lists: 1966–1977.* San Diego: Educational and Industrial Testing Service, 1977.

Lubin, B., & Himelstein, P. Reliability of the Depression Adjective Check Lists. *Perceptual and Motor Skills,* 1976, *43,* 1037–1038.

Lubin, B., & Levitt, E. E. Norms for the Depression Adjective Check Lists: Age group and sex. *Journal of Consulting and Clinical Psychology,* 1979, *47,* 192.

McFall, R. M., & Lillisand, D. B. Behavior rehearsal with modeling and coaching in assertion training. *Journal of Abnormal Psychology,* 1971, *77,* 313–323.

McFall, R. M., & Marston, A. R. An experimental investigation of behavior rehearsal in assertive training. *Journal of Abnormal Psychology,* 1970, *76,* 295–303.

McLean, P. Therapeutic decision making in the behavioral treatment of depression. In P. O. Davidson (Ed.), *The behavioral management of anxiety, depression and pain.* New York: Brunner/Mazel, 1976.

McLean, P. D., & Hakstian, A. R. Clincal depression: Comparative efficacy of outpatient treatments. *Journal of Consulting and Clinical Psychology,* 1979, *47,* 818–836.

McLean, P. D., Ogston, K., & Grauer, L. A behavioral approach to the treatment of depression. *Journal of Behavioral Therapy and Experimental Psychiatry.* 1973, *4,* 323–330.

MacPhillamy, D. J., & Lewinsohn, P. M. *A scale for the measurement of positive reinforcement.* Unpublished mimeo, University of Oregon, 1971.

MacPhillamy, D. J., & Lewinsohn, P. M. *Manual for the Pleasant Events Schedule.* Unpublished mimeo, University of Oregon, 1975.

Mendels, J. (Ed.). *The psychobiology of depression.* New York: Spectrum Publications, 1975.

Morris, J. B., & Beck, A. T. The efficacy of anti-depressant drugs: A review of research (1958 to 1972). *Archives of General Psychiatry,* 1974, *30,* 667–674.

Muñoz, R. F. *A cognitive approach to the assessment and treatment of depression.* Unpublished doctoral disseratation, University of Oregon, 1977.

Muñoz, R. F., & Lewinsohn, P. M. *The Subjective Probability Questionnaire.* Unpublished mimeo, University of Oregon, 1976.(a)

Muñoz, R. F., & Lewinsohn, P. M. *The Personal Belief Inventory.* Unpublished mimeo, University of Oregon, 1976.(b)

Muñoz, R. F., & Lewinsohn, P. M. *The Cognitive Events Schedule*. Unpublished mimeo, University of Oregon, 1976.(c)

Murphy, R., & Ellis, A. *Rationality scales: A bibliography*. New York: Institute for Rational Living, 1976.

Nelson, R. E. Irrational beliefs in depression. *Journal of Consulting and Clinical Psychology*, 1977, *45*, 1190-1191.

Overall, J. E. Dimensions of manifest depression. *Journal of Psychiatric Research*, 1962, *1*, 239-245.

Paykel, E. S., Meyers, J. K., Dienelt, M. N., Klerman, G. L., Lindenthal, J. J., & Pepper, M. P. Life events and depression: A controlled study. *Archives of General Psychiatry*, 1969, *21*, 753-760.

Rabkin, J. G., & Struening, E. L. Life events, stress, and illness. *Science*, 1976, *194*, 1013-1020.

Radloff, L. S. The CES-D Scale: A self-report depression scale for research in the general population. *Applied Psychological Measurement*, 1977, *1*, 385-401.

Raskin, A., Schulterbrandt, J. G., Reatig, N., Crook, T. H., & Odle, D. Depression subtypes and response to phenelzine, diazepam, and a placebo. *Archives of General Psychiatry*, 1974, *30*, 66-75.

Rathus, S. A. A 30-item schedule for assessing assertive behavior. *Behavior Therapy*, 1973, *4*, 298-406.

Rehm, L. P. Assessment of depression. In M. Hersen & A. S. Bellack (Eds.), *Behavioral assessment*. Oxford: Pergamon Press, 1976.

Rehm, L. P. A self-control model of depression. *Behavior Therapy*, 1977, *8*, 787-804.

Rehm, L. Mood, pleasant events, and unpleasant events: Two pilot studies. *Journal of Consulting and Clinical Psychology*, 1978, *46*, 854-859.

Rehm, L. P., Fuchs, C. Z., Roth, D. M., Kornblith, S. J., Romano, & J. M. *A comparison of self-control and social skills treatments of depression*. Unpublished mimeo, University of Pittsburgh, 1978.

Reisinger, J. J. The treatment of "anxiety-depression" via positive reinforcement and response contingency. *Journal of Applied Behavior Analysis*, 1972, *5*, 125-130.

Robinson, J. C., & Lewinsohn, P. M. Behavior modification of speech characteristics in a chronically depressed man. *Behavior Therapy*, 1973, *4*, 150-152.(a)

Robinson, J. C., & Lewinsohn, P. M. An experimental analysis of a technique based on the Premack principle for changing the verbal behavior of depressed individuals. *Psychological Reports*, 1973, *32*, 199-210.(b)

Rosenthal, S. H. The involutional depressive syndrome. *American Journal of Psychiatry*, 1968, *124*, 21-35.

Rotter, J. B. *Social learning and clinical psychology*. Englewood Cliffs, NJ: Prentice-Hall, 1954.

Rotter, J. B. Generalized expectancies for internal versus external control of reinforcement. *Psychological Monographs*, 1966, *80*, 1-28.

Rotter, J. B. Some problems and misconceptions related to the construct of internal versus external locus of control. *Journal of Consulting and Clinical Psychology*, 1975, *43*, 56-67.

Rush, A. J., Khatami, M., & Beck, A. T. Cognitive and behavior therapy in chronic depression. *Behavior Therapy*, 1975, *6*, 398-404.

Rutter, D. R., & Stephens, G. W. Visual interaction in a group of schizophrenic and depressed patients. *British Journal of Social and Clinical Psychology*, 1972, *11*, 57-65.

Sanchez, V. C. *A comparison of depressed, psychiatric control and normal control subjects on two measures of assertiveness*. Unpublished master's thesis, University of Oregon, 1976.

Sanchez, V. C., Lewinsohn, P. M., & Larson, D. Assertion training: Effectiveness in the treatment of depression. *Journal of Clinical Psychology*, 1980, *36*, 526–529.

Sarason, I. G., Johnson, J. H., & Siegel, J. M. *Assessing the impact of life change: Development of the Life Experiences Survey.* Unpublished mimeo, University of Washington, 1977.

Schless, A. P., Schwartz, L., Goetz, C., & Mendels, J. How depressives view the significance of life events. *British Journal of Psychiatry*, 1974, *125*, 406–410.

Schmidt, C. W. Psychiatric problems of the aged. *Journal of the American Geriatric Society*, 1974, *22*, 355–359.

Schwab, J. J., Bialow, M. R., Clemmons, R. S., & Holzer, C. E. The affective symptomatology of depression in medical inpatients. *Psychosomatics*, 1966, *7*, 214–217.

Schwab, J. J., Clemmons, R. S., Bialow, M., Duggan, V., & Davis, B. A study of somatic symptomatology of depression in medical inpatients. *Psychosomatics*, 1965, *6*, 273–277.

Seitz, R. Five psychological measures of neurotic depression: A correlational study. *Journal of Clinical Psychology*, 1970, *26*, 504–505.

Seligman, M. E. P. *Helplessness.* San Francisco: W. H. Freeman, 1975.

Shipley, C., & Fazio, A. A pilot study of a treatment for psychological depression. *Journal of Abnormal Psychology*, 1973, *82*, 372–376.

Silverman, C. *The epidemiology of depression.* Baltimore: Johns Hopkins University Press, 1968.

Spitzer, R. L., Endicott, J., & Robins, E. *Research Diagnostic Criteria (RDC) for a selected group of functional disorders.* Mimeo, New York State Psychiatric Institute, 1975.

Spitzer, R. L., Endicott, J., & Robins, E. Research Diagnostic Criteria: Rationale and reliability. *Archives of General Psychiatry*, 1978, *35*, 773–782.

Stewart, R. C. *The differential effects of positive and negative social reinforcement upon depressed and nondepressed subjects.* Unpublished master's thesis, University of Oregon, 1968.

Sundberg, N. D., Snowden, L. R., & Reynolds, W. M. Toward assessment of personal competence and incompetence in life situations. *Annual Review of Psychology*, 1978, *29*, 179–223.

Ward, C. H., Beck, A. T., Mendelson, M., Mock, C. E., & Erbaugh, J. K. The psychiatric nomenclature. *Archives of General Psychiatry*, 1962, *7*, 198–205.

Waxer, P. Nonverbal cues for depression. *Journal of Abnormal Psychology*, 1974, *83*, 319–322.

Wechsler, H., Grosser, G., & Busfield, B. The Depression Rating Scale: A quantitative approach to the assessment of depressive symptomatology. *Archives of General Psychiatry*, 1963, *9*, 334–343.

Weiner, B., & Frieze, I. *Perceiving the causes of success and failure.* Morristown, NJ: General Learning Press, 1971.

Weinman, B., Gelbart, P., Wallace, M., & Post, M. Inducing assertive behavior in chronic schizophrenics. *Journal of Consulting and Clinical Psychology*, 1972, *39*, 246–252.

Weintraub, M., Segal, R. M., & Beck, A. T. An investigation of cognition and affect in the depressive experiences of normal men. *Journal of Consulting and Clinical Psychology*, 1974, *42*, 911.

Weiss, B. L., Kupfer, D. J., Foster, F. G., & Delgado, J. Psychomotor activity, sleep, and biogenic amine metabolites in depression. *Biological Psychiatry*, 1974, *9*, 45–53.

Weissman, M. M. The assessment of social adjustment: A review of techniques. *Archives of General Psychiatry*, 1975, *32*, 357-365.

Weissman, A., & Beck, A. T. *Development and validation of the Dysfunctional Attitude Scale*. Paper presented at the annual meeting of the Association for the Advancement of Behavior Therapy, Chicago, December 1978.

Weissman, M. M., & Bothwell, S. Assessment of social adjustment by patient self-report. *Archives of General Psychiatry*, 1976, *33*, 1111-1115.

Weissman, M. M., & Paykel, E. G. *The depressed woman*. Chicago: University of Illinois Press, 1974.

Wells, K. C., Hersen, M., Bellack, A. S. & Himmelhoch, J. *Social skills for training for unipolar depressive females*. Paper presented at the meeting of the Association for the Advancement of Behavior Therapy, Atlanta, December, 1977.

Williams, J. G., Barlow, D. H., & Agras, W. S. Behavioral measurement of severe depression. *Archives of General Psychiatry*, 1972, *72*, 303-337.

Wolpe, J., & Lazarus, A. A. *Behavior therapy techniques*. Oxford: Pergamon Press, 1966.

Youngren, M. A. & Lewinsohn, P. M. The funcational relationship between depression and problematic interpersonal behavior. *Journal of Abnormal Psychology*, 1980, *89*, 334-391.

Youngren, M. A., Zeiss, A. M., & Lewinsohn, P. M. The Interpersonal Events Schedule. Unpublished mimeo, University of Oregon, 1975.

Zealley, A. K. & Aitken, R. C. Measurement of mood. *Proceedings of the Royal Society of Medicine*, 1969, *62*, 993-996.

Zeiss, A. M., Lewinsohn, P. M., & Muñoz, R. F. Nonspecific improvement effects in depression using interpersonal, cognitive, and pleasant events focused treatments. *Journal of Consulting and Clinical Psychology*, 1979, *47*, 427-439.

Zung, W. A self-rating depression scale. *Archives of General Psychiatry*, 1965, *12*, 63-70.

Zung, W. K. From art to science: The diagnosis and treatment of depression. *Archives of General Psychiatry*, 1973, *29*, 328-337.

Zung, W., Richards, C. B., & Short, M. J. Self-rating depression scale in an outpatient clinic. *Archives of General Psychiatry*, 1965, *13*, 508-516.

6

Assessment of Phobia

C. BARR TAYLOR
STEWART AGRAS

The measurement of phobia is largely determined by prevailing concepts of the nature of phobia. For this reason, we will begin with a discussion of the definition and diagnosis of phobia and then construct a model of phobia from which the various measures may be derived. Finally, we will review these various measures and consider their implications for both research and clinical practice.

Definition and Diagnosis

Many early psychiatric taxonomers included some of the specific phobias in their systems. For example, Avicenna described patients with fear of water (hydrophobia) (Menninger, 1963). However, the term phobia was not used in the psychiatric literature until the 19th century, when Westphal (1872) published a report on three male patients with fears of open or public places, a condition which he named agoraphobia. Soon, under the influence of Freud and others working from a psychoanalytic viewpoint, phobias became the object of intensive study. However, the phobia itself was viewed as a symptom of an underlying conflict rather than a problem in its own right (Wachtel, 1977). Thus assessment became a matter of either determining individual psychodynamic influences, measuring aspects of personal-

C. Barr Taylor and Stewart Agras. Department of Psychiatry, Stanford University School of Medicine, Stanford, California.

ity, or determining whether a person was cured, much improved, and so forth. Until recently, the assumptions inherent in the psychodynamic model largely determined the diagnosis of phobia. Thus in the second *Diagnostic and Statistical Manual* (DSM-II) of the American Psychiatric Association (1968) phobias were classified as phobic neurosis with the explicit assumption that

> anxiety is the chief characteristic of the neuroses. It may be felt and expressed directly, or it may be controlled unconsciously and automatically by conversion, displacement and various other psychological mechanisms. Generally, these mechanisms produce symptoms experienced as subjective distress from which the patient desires relief. (p. 39)

However, the limitations of a diagnostic system, largely dependent on untested assumptions, began to outweigh the advantages, and thus a new diagnostic and statistical system which presents a more descriptive and less theoretically based system has now been developed (DSM-III, 1980). According to DSM-III,

> the essential feature [of phobia] is persistent avoidance behavior secondary to irrational fears of a specific object, activity, or situation. Avoidance behavior sometimes takes the form of a compelling desire. . . . More commonly, the individual does actually avoid the feared situation or object. The fear is recognized by the individual as unreasonable and unwarranted by the actual dangerousness of the object, activity, or situation. (Draft, p. G:1)

Then, an individual has either agoraphobia with panic attacks, agoraphobia without panic attacks, social phobia, or simple phobia.

The criteria for agoraphobia without panic attacks, for example, are:

1. The individual avoids being alone or in a situation where he or she cannot get to help or help cannot get to him or her in case of sudden incapacitation.
2. These fears are pervasive and dominate the individual's life so that a large number of situations are entered into only reluctantly or are avoided. The individual avoids at least one of the following situations: (a) closed or open spaces; (b) traveling while alone; (c) traveling more than five miles from home by any means; (d) walking alone; (e) being alone.
3. Marked anxiety is experienced when faced with the potential of being in one of the above situations.
4. The phobic symptoms are not symptomatic of an episode of

Major Depression Disorder, Obsessive-Compulsive Disorder, or Schizophrenia.

Presumably, such operational criteria will not only allow for more accurate diagnosis, but will encourage clinicians to assess phobic behavior along more discrete lines.

Toward a Theory of Phobia: Psychological Concepts

As we have seen, the first "modern theories" of phobia were developed by psychodynamic psychiatrists and psychologists who viewed phobia as a symptom of an underlying process. The flaws in such theories have been well discussed in other publications (e.g., Ullmann & Krasner, 1969) and need not be reviewed here. As we have also seen, a theory which implies an internal dynamic origin of phobia requires measurement of these dynamics and the symptoms hypothesized to stem from such dynamics. Although some clinicians, including Freud, focused at one time or another on aspects of overt phobic behavior, it remained for the behavior therapists to introduce direct measurement of phobic behavior.

The earliest behavioral theory of phobia was based on Mowrer's two-factor theory of learning (Mowrer, 1947). This view postulates that phobias are acquired by classical conditioning in which the future phobic stimulus is paired with a noxious stimulus. While a single intense experience may account for the origins of some phobias, it seems more likely that repeated pairings of milder intensity would more commonly be the case. These pairings would then lead to avoidance of the (now) fear-arousing situation, and such avoidance behavior would be strengthened by anxiety reduction. Stimulus generalization would be expected to occur, thus gradually widening the range of objects, situations, or ideas associated with phobic avoidance.

In this scheme, the critical element of phobic behavior is the physiologic arousal or anxiety which is hypothesized to underlie phobic avoidance behavior, and one might expect that measurement would focus largely on that variable, since phobic avoidance should be highly correlated with physiologic arousal. However, studies have not substantiated that this is always the case. Thus Leitenberg, Agras, Butz, and Wincze (1971) obtained simultaneous measures of heart rate and approach behavior in the feared situation. While parallel reductions in autonomic activity and avoidance behavior were found in some patients, others showed no reduction of heart rate as avoidance lessened, while yet others showed paradoxical effects where heart rate increased and avoidance behavior and self-reported fear lessened.

Similar findings both in animal work and in other human studies were reviewed by Rachman and Hodgson, who termed this phenomenon desynchrony (Rachman & Hodgson, 1974; Hodgson & Rachman, 1974). Bandura (1971) has suggested that changes in the different response systems are coparallel events. If this is so, then both avoidance behavior and physiologic arousal in phobic situations should be measured, since they may represent different aspects of the condition. Moreover, since self-perception, as indicated by report of phobic anxiety or avoidance, may also not correlate well either with physiologic changes or with avoidance behavior, then self-report might be considered as a third aspect of phobic behavior requiring assessment.

An extended theory of phobic behavior, however, must take into account not only physiologic and avoidance behaviors, but also cognitive factors which may modulate these behaviors. For example, Bandura (1977) has suggested that persons perceive their effectiveness in approaching a feared situation based upon prior performance and the estimated difficulty of the forthcoming task, a process he refers to as self-efficacy. In several experiments it appears that the level of self-efficacy nicely predicts future specific performance.

In elaborating a model of phobia it is therefore necessary to take into account the existence of several feedback systems which modulate phobic behavior and may lead to discrepancies between different measures. For example, several factors may modify the impact of the phobic stimulus. Thus, when an agoraphobic is accompanied by someone trusted, then he or she can walk farther from home with less discomfort. Similarly, labeling an intervention as therapy, or experimenter demand to approach a feared situation for the purpose of measurement, may also alter the impact of the phobic stimulus and thus affect both autonomic and avoidance behavior. Demand might, for example, lead a patient to approach nearer to a feared object or situation than usual, but might also cause a raised heart rate.

Phobic behavior is, of course, also attended by consequences, which in turn influence the behavior. Successful approach to the feared situation may, for example, lead to praise and encouragement from it. Several carefully controlled studies (e.g., Agras, Leitenberg, & Barlow, 1968) have showed that social reinforcement may lead to marked improvement in the ability to approach phobic situations. Another consequence of approach or avoidance behavior is the perception of behavior change, otherwise called feedback as to progress. Again, such feedback has been demonstrated to affect performance beneficially (Leitenberg, Agras, Thompson, & Wright, 1968; Leitenberg, Agras, Allen, Butz, & Edwards, 1975).

Such examples do not outline all the various interactions that may occur with all aspects of phobic behavior. However, they do emphasize the need for a feedback model taking into account motor, physiologic, and cognitive components of behavior.

Behavior such as phobic avoidance is both dependent upon and affects physiologic activity. Thus a complete theory of phobia (not yet, alas, possible to elaborate) must take into account both behavioral and biological systems and their interaction. A biological model of anxiety developed by Lader (1974), which integrates physiology, self-report, and internal psychological and physiologic events seems relevant to the interactive model of phobias we are presenting. Lader's model was developed to explain the role of peripheral and central catecholamines in anxiety and to fit anatomical systems to biochemical knowledge. In his model, anxiety is viewed as occurring with changes in peripheral physiology, emotional feelings, and self-report. The changes in emotional feeling are modulated through the limbic system; changes in central nervous system (CNS) arousal also affect emotional feeling, and peripheral physiologic changes are modulated by the dorsal bundle. These various processes interact in complex ways to determine the eventual peripheral, physiologic, and emotional feelings which denote the person's anxiety. The model has interesting theoretical implications for which pharmacologic agents would be most effective in treating various types of anxiety. If, for instance, a person's anxiety is predominantly manifested by peripheral physiologic changes, then a pharmacologic agent such as propranolol, which blocks peripheral autonomic nervous system activity, might be most effective in reducing the anxiety. However, if the anxiety is predominantly CNS, with no apparent changes in peripheral physiology, then agents which affect central catecholamines, such as diazepam (Valium), would be recommended if a drug were the treatment of choice.

In Figure 1 we have elaborated Lader's model to include the motor system and behavior and its consequences. With these refinements the model has relevance to phobias and demonstrates the interactions that occur between systems. A phobic stimulus is appraised through cognitive process and, depending on past experience, perhaps genetic endowment (e.g., ducklings will respond with avoidance behavior to hawklike shadows) may lead to CNS arousal, emotional feeling, and/or verbal report of fear. CNS arousal can in turn lead to peripheral physiologic and biochemical changes, which in turn modify cognitive appraisal. The emotional feeling and CNS arousal may lead to motor behavior (such as avoidance), and the behavior may lead to consequences (such as reinforcement). In turn, the consequences may modify the cognitive appraisal or the phobic stimulus (e.g., the experimenter "reassures the patient"), and the behavior may modify the phobic stimulus (e.g., the patient runs away).

What to Measure

Given an interactive model of phobia, it is clear that no one measure will provide an accurate indication of phobia under all circumstances. In Table 1 we have listed the main sources of measurement for phobias which are implied by this model: self-report, physiologic and biochemical measures, and behavior itself. For completeness we have included personality measures which have frequently been used in studies of phobias. In the next few pages we will review each of the major categories of measurement separately.

SELF-REPORT

GENERAL FEAR INVENTORIES

A variety of fear inventories has been developed to measure phobias. These can be classed into two categories: general fear-assessment instruments and specific fear-assessment instruments.

The first general fear survey (FSS-I) was reported by Lang and Lazovick (1963). This survey listed 50 common fears to be rated by subjects on a seven-point scale. This was followed by a subsequent scale (Fear Survey Schedule-III) developed by Wolpe and Lang

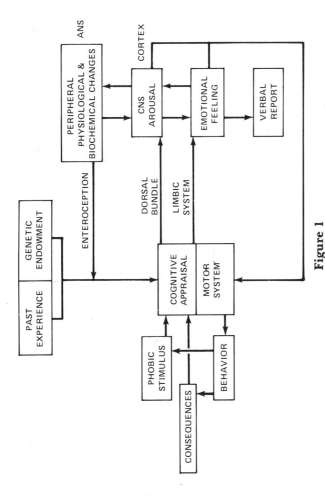

Figure 1

An interactive model for phobias. The various parameters illustrated above interact to determine the final verbal report, peripheral physiologic changes, and behavior which occur with a phobic stimulus. These parameters influence each other: for instance, behavior leads to consequences; cognitive appraisal effects emotional feeling. As therapy progresses, the relative importance of a particular parameter as an assessment measure may change. For instance, verbal report of fear of a phobic stimulus may be modified by the demand characteristics of the experimental situation, while peripheral, physiologic, and biochemical changes remain unchanged. Each of these parameters may also be influenced simultaneously but in different ways by other factors while a phobic stimulus is presented. For instance, a peripheral autonomic blocking agent may reduce autonomic nervous system (ANS) activity while a phobic stimulus is presented.

187

Table 1
Source of Measurement of Phobic Behavior

Self-report
  General fear inventories
  Specific fear inventories
  Self-report hierarchies (including self-efficacy)
  Self-monitoring
Personality measures
Physiologic and biochemical measures
  Skin conductance
  Heart rate
Behavior
  In vitro
  In vivo

(1964), which consisted of 75 items rated on a five-point Likert-type scale. The items were derived from the fears that Wolpe saw most commonly in clinical practice and were subdivided into the following subcategories: animal, tissue damage and illness, death or associated stimuli, noises, and miscellaneous. Geer (1965) added another fear survey (FSS-II), which consisted of 51 items. (Geer's fear survey is known as FSS-II despite publication after Wolpe and Lang's FSS-III.) Many other general fear schedules have been devised by augmenting or combining some of the existing schedules.

The psychometric properties of these inventories have not been extensively studied, with the exception of FSS-II. With the FSS-II, Geer (1965) found the internal consistency reliability for college students to be an overall r of $+.94$, a female r of $+.83$, and a male r of $+.93$. Hersen (1971) reported an internal consistency reliability of .97 with psychiatry inpatients on the FSS-II and of .98 for males, females, and combined groups with the FSS-III. Using the TSS-I, a 100-item inventory compiled from the FSS-I and -III, Braun and Reynolds (1969) found a test–retest reliability estimate for college students of .88 for males and .85 for females. In an interesting study, Cooke (1966) found that the test–retest reliability of a sample of untreated male and female subjects showed that the reliability for the total FSS was .90 but an *r* of only + .65 for some specific fears. And most alarming, Suinn (1969) found that test–retest reliability for an undergraduate sample of subjects was .72, and an overall 10-point decrement of fear occurred on the second testing. Reliability of these fear surveys is particularly disturbing considering how commonly they are used in studies as outcome measures. Cooke's study even suggests that their usefulness for specific fears may be questionable.

CORRELATION OF FSS AND OTHER MEASURES

The FSS has been given simultaneously with many other measures. In reviewing the correlations obtaining between FSS and other measures, Hersen (1973) found only moderate associations (ranging between an *r* of + .27 and + .60) between FSS measures and anxiety measures in 15 studies. One study (Lang & Lazovick, 1963) obtained an *r* of + .80 between the FSS-I and the Taylor Manifest Anxiety Scale on a highly selected group treated for snake phobia. In his review, Hersen (1973) also noted that many of the general fear surveys tap into the same factors, and that the most parsimonious approach is to use a survey which compiles without duplicating items of other scales. Geer (1965) undertook direct tests of fearfulness of the subjects who rated themselves as having high or low fear on several items of the FSS-II. The self-report of fear correlated with actual behavior in the feared situation with some items but not others. For instance, male subjects reporting fear of dogs consistently touched dogs when tested. On the other hand, subjects with a high fear of speaking before a group spoke at a reduced rate and evidenced lengthier silences than low-fear subjects. Cooke (1966) found a correlation of .35 between a "look, touch, and hold" step of an approach task and responses of "very much afraid of laboratory rats" on a modified FSS. Lang (1968) reports a low negative correlation ($r = -.26$) between snake phobia ratings on the FSS and overt avoidance on a behavioral test. Fazio (1969) found significant negative correlations between amount of self-reported fear on the FSS-III and degree of approach toward a harmless insect. These and other studies suggest that general fear inventories have poor correlations with fear as measured by avoidance, a finding that fits well with the interactive model of phobia outlined previously.

SPECIFIC FEAR INVENTORIES

Another approach to the self-report of fears is to measure specific fears. Three approaches to measuring specific fears have emerged: specific fear surveys, self-report hierarchies, and self-monitoring diaries.

The first report of the use of a "fear thermometer," a self-report instrument used to measure fear, was made by Walk (1956). To evaluate the fear of trainees required to make a pharachute jump from a 34-foot tower, each trainee was asked to place a mark on a thermometer-like figure divided into 10 equal parts, with the height of the mark indicating the degree of fear experienced. Walk (1956) found that subjects' responses on his fear thermometer accurately predicted behavioral performance on a parachute jump. Parachuters who passed the course had rated themselves significantly less fearful than those who failed. Since then the fear thermometer has been used in a variety of studies.

Other instruments have been developed to measure self-report of specific fears. These fear surveys generally measure aspects of cognitive, behavioral, and/or physiologic manifestations of anxiety. Unlike the fear surveys which are used as a general guide in planning treatment, these instruments are often used as outcome measures. Klorman, Weerts, Hastings, Melamed, and Lang (1974) studied the psychometric properties of three specific fear questionnaires, the snake questionnaire (SNAQ), spider questionnaire (SPQ), and the mutilation questionnaire (MQ). Of the 851 females and 456 males tested, the distributions were positively skewed and leptokurtic with the same general distribution across males and females on all three measures. In general, the tests demonstrated high internal consistency and test-retest reliability. There was also evidence of external validity. The authors suggest that the instruments can serve a useful purpose for subject screening. Interested readers can find examples of these self-report measures for fear of snakes and spiders (Lang, Melamed, & Hart, 1970) mutilation (Hastings, 1971) heights (Baker, Cohen, & Saunders, 1973), tests (Alpert & Haber, 1960; Sarason, 1957), and heterosexual dating (Twentyman & McFall, 1975).

In one study, Lick and Sushinsky (1975) had separate groups of college students rate their fear of rats and snakes in various stimulus conditions. A week later these same subjects were asked to approach a rat or snake in these same situations. They found that correlations were highest between the students' actual behavior and their self-report when the self-report questions accurately described the real situations, a finding that should be remembered when constructing new scales to measure fear.

SELF-REPORT HIERARCHIES

Lick and Sushinsky's study (1975) also suggests the importance of developing inventories to directly characterize a person's fears. A number of techniques have been developed to help a subject record his fears very specifically. The self-rating form used by Marks's group (Marks, Hallam, Connolly, & Philpott, 1977) in one study can be seen in Figure 2.

These self-report measures have the subject rate the phobia on a numeric scale from 0 to n. Different scale ranges may not be comparable, for instance, in one study (Teasdale, Walsh, Lancashire, & Matthews, 1977), the 0-8 scale of Watson and Marks (1971) was compared with the 1-5 scale of Gelder and Marks (1966). When both measures were administered before treatment, a significant difference was found between them, even when one scale was converted numerically to the other. Larger treatment effects were found with the 0-8 scale than with the 1-5 scale.

Another approach to self-report is to develop a hierarchy of specific situations associated with a particular phobia. Bandura (1977) has developed a number of such hierarchies. An example is given in Figure 3. To understand why Bandura chose to measure these variables, it is important to consider in greater detail some aspects of his theoretical approach to phobia. Bandura wondered why a person will undertake a particular therapeutic task and what factors might relate to persistence in that task, even when experiencing unpleasant physiologic events and consequences. For Bandura, a person's self-efficacy is largely related to persistence in the face of obstacles or aversive experiences. The stronger the perceived self-efficacy, the more vigorous and persistent the effort. Bandura even hypothesizes that individuals with low self-efficacy in a particular task may make negative self-referrent thoughts (e.g., "I can't do this"), which may impede success. Bandura's self-efficacy theory also presents a different theoretical orientation to the cause of anxiety than the theories previously mentioned. From the social learning perspective, it is mainly per-

SELF-RATING: PHOBIC TARGETS Name _____ Date _____

On the scales below place an X in the space which best describes your feelings about each of the two phobic situations.

Phobia 1   Phobia 2

0	I have no uneasiness in this situation	0
1		1
2	I feel uneasy but do not avoid it	2
3		3
4	I feel definitely afraid and tend to avoid it	4
5		5
6	I have a strong fear of the situation and avoid it if at all possible	6
7		7
8	I am extremely afraid of this situation and I always avoid it	8

Figure 2

The phobic rating system used by Marks *et al.* (1977). The detailed instructions for the form are included in his book. Reprinted by permission from Marks *et al.* (1977).

10
quite
uncertain   20   30   40   50
moderately
certain   60   70   80   90   100
certain

Can do   Confidence

AIRPORTS and FLYING

Drive to airport with partner

Approach airport with partner and drive around the departure area

Park in airport garage, remain observing people for several minutes

Park in airport garage, enter Terminal with partner, and remain for several minutes

Enter Terminal alone and remain for several minutes, browsing and observing

Enter a grounded plane with partner

Enter a grounded plane with partner and remain buckled in seat for several minutes

Enter a grounded plane alone and remain inside for several minutes

Enter a grounded plane, browse and then remain buckled in seat for 10 minutes

Take a short flight (20 minutes) with partner

Take a short flight alone

Take a flight alone to Los Angeles

Figure 3

Self-efficacy hierarchy developed by Bandura for airplane phobias.

ceived inefficacy in coping with potentially aversive events that makes them fearsome.

The issue of self-efficacy becomes very relevant, then, to a previous behavior.[1] A subject may only perform phobic tasks he feels confident he can accomplish. A personalized hierarchy permits individuals to rate their confidence in approaching a feared situation under very specific stimulus conditions. This same hierarchy may be useful in predicting what the subject will do in an actual phobic situation.

A third approach to specific fear evaluation is *self-monitoring*. The methodology and techniques of self-monitoring are well described in other publications (McFall, 1977). While self-monitoring has been used to record a person's anxiety, it has not, for the most part, been used with specific fears.

PERSONALITY MEASURES

Many personality tests have been used together with some of the phobic measures mentioned above. In a review of 43 phobic studies, Agras and Jacob (1980) found that 23 different personality scales were used, the most frequent being the Eysenck Personality Inventory (EPI), which was used in three studies. They found that personality measures were the least sensitive method for discriminating between treatments, suggesting that they have little usefulness for the asessment of phobias.

PHYSIOLOGIC MEASURES

It is generally assumed that real or imagined contact with a phobic stimulus is associated with physiologic arousal. Physiologic recordings have been taken while a patient imagines a phobic situation, talks about phobias, or is exposed to the phobic situation itself. The same physiologic measures used to measure anxiety and fear in gen-

---

[1]There is an intriguing similarity between Bandura's self-efficacy theory and a model of stress proposed by the physiologist, Henry (Henry & Stephens, 1977). Henry suggests that an animal's perceived control relative to a particular demand is central to the type of behavior and physiologic response the animal will undergo. When experiencing a threat, an animal may actively engage in fight or flight with concomitant limbic sympathetic adrenal medullary arousal or conservation withdrawal with concomitant activation of the pituitary hypothalamic adrenal cortical system. The former appears behaviorally as an active response, the latter as withdrawal-avoidance. An animal's past learning largely determines his response. Henry might argue that an animal who "feels" efficacious will engage in fight or flight.

eral have been used with phobias, although heart rate and galvanic skin response (GSR) have been most commonly used.

A general problem in using physiologic measures is the rapid adaptation that tends to occur in physiologic systems, making serial measures difficult to interpret. Moreover, most phobic individuals will not expose themselves to highly fear-arousing stimuli before treatment, so that pre–post measures taken in the same situation are difficult to obtain. Thus a subject may show low levels of skin conductance or heart rate at the beginning of treatment and increased levels following treatment. The latter may, however, indicate that the subject is actually confronting the feared situation.

SKIN CONDUCTANCE

The techniques used to measure skin conductance have been well described elsewhere (Lykken & Venables, 1971). Skin conductance is measured either in terms of absolute levels of skin resistance or spontaneous fluctuations. Subjects exhibiting extreme arousal to a phobic situation will show rapid habituation to the same stimulus both within and across sessions (Mathews, 1971). Nevertheless, several studies have shown that phobic subjects show larger skin-conductance responses to phobic-stimulus objects than to nonphobic-stimulus objects, and that phobic subjects show greater responses to the same stimulus than nonphobic subjects (Geer, 1966; Wilson, 1967). This is true for both real and imagined stimulus objects (Barber and Hahn, 1964; Barlow, Agras, Leitenberg, & Wincze, 1970; Craig, 1968).

Agras and Jacob (1980) found that GSR was a poor measure for discriminating within-group treatment outcome. (The study will be presented in more detail later.)

HEART RATE

The other commonly used measure is heart rate. Heart rate can be accurately and easily obtained, both in clinical and ambulatory settings. In general, heart rate increases with increased sympathetic activity, and the heart rate reported for some subjects experiencing phobic situations is comparable to high rates of physical activity.

One problem, however, with heart rate as an outcome measure is that fear may lead to acute heart-rate reduction. Some individuals exhibit marked bradycardia when confronted with a fearful situation. The bradycardia results from parasympathetic stimulation of the heart through vagus nerve activity; parasympathetic activity is usually short lived and will override sympathetic activation (Koelle, 1966).

On the positive side, heart rate may offer the possibility of continuous measurement in actual phobic situations. For instance, Taylor (1977) measured spider-phobic heart-rate responses to outdoor spider stimuli.

OTHER MEASURES

Other measures of autonomic arousal have not been widely used with phobic subjects. Forearm blood flow, temperature, EMG, and blood pressure have all been widely used to measure anxiety and fear in general, but with the possible exception of forearm blood flow, these measures do not seem to have any advantage over skin conductance and heart rate.

To date, physiologic measures of phobia have focused on peripheral physiology. As suggested in Figure 1, central physiologic processes play an important role in processing phobic stimuli and may offer a relevant source of measurement as techniques to measure CNS processes are developed. For instance, it is possible to use EEG activity to measure CNS arousal.

The interactive model outlined earlier also suggested that biochemical measures might be used in the assessment of phobias (e.g., Curtis, 1976). Catecholamines, which reflect peripheral autonomic-nervous-system activity, have been demonstrated to increase dramatically in some fearful settings (e.g., public speaking), but have not been studied with phobic subjects per se (Taggart, Carruthers, & Somerville, 1973). Cortisol, which reflects activity in the hypothalamic-pituitary-adrenal cortical system, has been demonstrated to show changes in fearful situations (Mason, Maher, Hartley, Mougey, Perlow, & Jones, 1976). Such biochemical measures are more useful for theoretical studies than clinical or outcome assessment at this stage of their development.

IN VITRO BEHAVIORAL MEASURES

Direct behavioral assessment of phobia was first used in a controlled outcome study by Lazarus (1961). Unfortunately, in that study, Lazarus used different pre–post measures of acrophobia; thus the change score for the behavioral measure was not reported. Since then, a number of behavioral tests have been devised. The pioneering work with analogues of phobia such as analogue snake fears was reported by Lang and Lazovik (1963). In that study, subjects were given instructions to progressively approach and, if possible, handle a caged snake. The subjects approached the snake before and after treatment, and change in the distance of approach was used as an outcome measure. This procedure has been used with many phobias (examples are provided in Table 2), and is known as the behavioral approach test (BAT). It does not seem to make much difference whether or not the subjects approach the feared object or the object is brought closer to them (Borkovec & Craighead, 1971). Live phobic objects produced more avoidance than dead ones (Feist & Rosenthal, 1973).

While most of the BAT studies thus far discussed have involved the subject approaching a *feared situation,* other studies have attempted to replicate or stimulate a feared situation (see Table 2). For instance, Öst (1978) used flashing neon lights and tape recordings to replicate a storm. Claustrophobia has been measured by using a small, closed room. Agoraphobia has been measured by monitoring the dis-

Table 2
In Vitro Behavioral Measures

Phobia	Example
Small animals	Live snakes (Bandura, Jeffery, & Gadjos, 1975; Russell & Mathews, 1975)
	Cats (Whitehead, Robinson, Blackwell, & Stutz, 1978)
	Dogs (MacDonald, 1975; Kroll, 1975)
Insects	Live spiders (Taylor, 1977; Whitehead *et al.,* 1978
Height	Ladder (Lazarus, 1961)
Closed space	Closet (Leitenberg *et al.,* 1970)
	Elevator (Nesbitt, 1973)
Storms	Tape recordings of storms, flashing neon lamps (Öst, 1978)
Medical objects and situations	Needles (Taylor, Ferguson, & Wermuth, 1977)

tance a subject walks from a designated point, acrophobia by how high a patient is able to climb a ladder, mountain, or stairs. The recent development of electronically controlled tropical-environment rooms will permit the measuring of subjects experiencing fear of paradise.

The use of direct measures of behavior, while attractive in theory, has several problems. First, the *demand characteristics* of the experiment may have a major impact on the subject's performance; some subjects, knowing they will be expected to improve at the time of the postmeasure, may not perform as well on the pretests. The *instructions* are also important. Instructions emphasizing the critical importance of maximum approach produce nearer approach on a BAT than less demanding instructions (Bernstein, 1973; Bernstein & Neitzel, 1973). Subjects may also perceive the test situation as less threatening than a real situation, based on the implicit notion that the experimenter would not subject them to danger. In an old experiment used to determine the effects of a fear-arousing situation on catecholamines, Ax (1953) told subjects that his machinery was malfunctioning and implied that the subject might get shocked. This deception produced significant arousal in subjects who had been exposed to an already fearful situation.

The exposure to the fear-arousing situation may also produce improvement or changes in phobic behavior. A severe claustrophobic was asked to enter a small room and to leave when she felt at all fearful (Leitenberg, Agras, Edwards, Thompson, & Wincze, 1970). However, the patient was able to stay for progressively longer periods of time in the room, apparently because the baseline measurement had a therapeutic effect. *Finally,* and perhaps most important, there is a realization, reinforced by some studies, that successful performance in a BAT may not reflect actual performance in phobic situations. Lick and Unger (1975) studied two animal-phobic subjects who manifested improvement on the BAT. The first was a 22-year-old female with a lifelong fear of snakes. Following a short period of systematic desensitization, she was able to approach a caged snake and lift the cage. She reported little fear when doing this. However, when the therapist then took the snake from the cage and put it on the floor, "the subject reacted with visible terror. She trembled, screamed and demanded that the snake be returned to the cage" (p. 865). This case and others like it, that have been reported, emphasize the importance of developing natural *in vivo* observations of phobic behaviors and of *not* equating the stimulus properties of caged snakes and snakes out of cages.

IN VIVO BEHAVIORAL MEASURES

A number of studies have reported that the behavior of subjects in real-life situations usually follows treatment in the phobic situation. For instance, agoraphobic subjects have been accompanied outside, spider phobics have been asked to touch spider environs, bridge phobics have been observed crossing bridges, and so forth. Telemetric assessment or ambulatory monitoring of subjects offers the possibility of following heart rates in a variety of settings. Taylor (1977) required subjects with spider phobias to return with a phobic object. Inevitably, such measurement procedures produce some reactive effects, since the subject is aware that the therapist is observing his behavior, and this observation may instill a certain confidence. Such measures are probably more useful as outcome measures than pre–post measures, since compliance with the instructions may have a major therapeutic effect, as mentioned above.

The Relative Sensitivity of the Different Measures of Fear and Phobia

Agras and Jacob (1980) have recently compared the relative sensitivity of the different measures used to assess phobias. An estimate of the utility of a measure can be determined from studies in which the same clinical change was assessed by different measures. The sensitivity of such measures can be compared by using a standardized index of sensitivity which takes into account both the magnitude of change and the error term without being affected by the sample size. The effect size for the independent test t-test (d) can serve this purpose. d is defined as the ratio between the magnitude of the obtained difference and the pooled within-group standard deviation (Cohen, 1977). Agras and Jacob found three studies with a total of six groups in which the treatment effects were assessed by the same nine variables: ratings (on a nine-point scale) of anxiety for the main phobia by client and therapist, ratings of avoidance for the main phobia by client and therapist, the same ratings for supplementary phobias, and *in vivo* measurement of the main phobia. d was calculated for each of these measures for each of the groups. It appeared that client ratings of the main phobia were the most sensitive to change, followed by *in vivo* behavioral measurements. The FSS was found to be less sensitive than *in vivo* performance measures. The authors then extended this finding by determining the proportion of studies in which each major class of measures (client ratings, *in vivo* performance, or FSS) discriminated between treatment conditions or showed a pre–post change at or above the .05 level of significance. These proportions are displayed in Figure 4. As can be seen, *in vivo* performance measures showed the best ability to discriminate between treatments, followed by self-report of the intensity of the main phobia. Direct behavioral measures also showed the best ability to identify change from the beginning to end of treatment, followed closely by the FSS. From this perspective, the sensitivity of measures of phobia can be ranked as follows, from least to most sensitive; personality measures, FSS, assessor's ratings of the main phobia, heart-rate measurement, client ratings of the main phobia, and behavioral measures.

COMPARISONS BETWEEN SELF-REPORT, THERAPIST, AND ASSESSOR RATINGS

As seen in the preceding pages, self-ratings are an integral part of the measurement of phobia. On the other hand, research workers have been concerned with the reliability of such reports, since they are influenced by factors such as experimenter demand or wishful thinking. Therapist ratings do not seem more trustworthy in this regard, since the therapist may have a vested interest in reporting favorable treatment effects. A way to test these concerns empirically is to determine the correlation between the ratings from these two sources, with ratings made by an independent observer who is uninvolved in the treatment and does not know which treatment the subject has received. Several studies reported such correlations, although it should be noted that such agreement is often not reported for the specific study but for the method in general on the basis of old data. Correlations between patient self-report and therapist report ranged from .53 to .83; between patient and assessor, .62 and .90; and between therapist and assessor, .59 to .88. These correlations were generally regarded as being satisfactory in the papers reviewed. However, given the observed variations in agreement between studies, it is necessary for agreement between the different observers to be estimated and re-

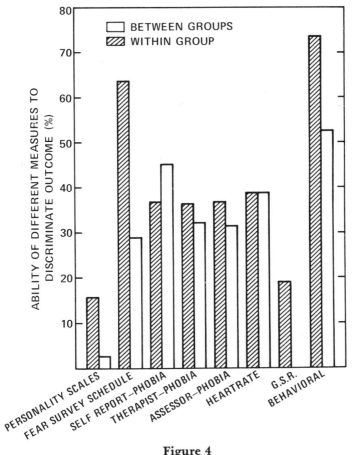

Figure 4
The proportion of phobia studies using a particular class of measurement
(e.g., client rating) which discriminated between treatment conditions or
showed a pre-post change at or above the .05 level of significance.

ported separately for each study. In this way the reader can form a
better estimate of the degree of confidence to place upon the particular study.

Another way to view agreement is to consider studies which used
all three methods to assess the main phobia and to compare outcomes
between the methods. Agras and Jacob (1980) analyzed 10 studies
which included self-report, therapist, and assessor ratings. There was
perfect agreement among all three measures in five of the 10 studies.

No method appears to be more or less sensitive than the others, and remarkably little would have been lost if only patient self-report had been used as an outcome measure. This, of course, is true only if it can be assumed that the reliability was being assessed. Thus, a cautious researcher should probably continue to obtain all three ratings, but if reliability is high, use the average of these three as one dependent variable. This will decrease error variance and, in addition, circumvent the problem of spurious significant findings because of a large number of statistical tests.

Some Special Problems in the Measurement of Specific Phobias

SOCIAL PHOBIA

Individuals with social phobia avoid social stimuli. Unfortunately, such stimuli are so complex that developing specific evaluation techniques is difficult. There has been the assumption that change in an individual with social phobia should be directed at improving a person's set of social skills rather than desensitizing or exposing him to a particular social situation. Accordingly, assessment has tended to focus on a person's set of skills more than his social fears. However, to measure social fear, a number of structured inventories, similar in concept to other fear inventories, have been developed. For instance, Watson and Friend (1969) developed the Social Avoidance Distress Scale (SAS) to measure the experience of discomfort in social situations and the Fear of Negative Evaluation (FNE) to assess the degree to which the respondent fears negative social evaluation. The physiologic measures employed in assessing social phobia are identical to those discussed before.

In the behavioral literature, the measurement of social skills fits into the assertiveness-training literature and will not be discussed here. The same sources of measurement applicable to phobias are also applicable to social skills, including self-report inventories, *in vitro* monitoring of social skills, and *in vivo* measurement (e.g., natural environment partners, and so on).

CANCER PHOBIA

Cancer phobia raises a problem of assessment. Since cancer phobics are mostly afraid of internal stimuli, which they interpret as indicating cancer, self-report is the cornerstone of assessment, although cancer phobics may also avoid situations where they fear they may "catch" cancer and pursue repetitive and needless medical work-ups. The avoidance and the extent of work-ups can both be measured.

AIRPLANE PHOBIA

Another phobia difficult to measure is airplane phobia. Although it is possible to simulate airplane stimuli through artificial cockpits or airplane-cabin models, the phobic person may readily distinguish this setting from the real one. It is always possible that a snake may escape from a cage, but it is very unlikely that a simulated cockpit will take off from the ground. Also, unlike phobias such as claustrophobia or acrophobia, where the baseline measure may have therapeutic impact (Leitenberg et al., 1971), there is no escape once the subject has begun exposure. It is possible for a claustrophobic to leave a closed room or an acrophobic to descend rapidly from the heights, but an airplane phobic cannot jump out of an airplane once it has taken off. Thus the treatment (taking off), which may have phobic subjects participate in an actual plane flight, necessarily contaminates the baseline measure and may falsely suggest successful treatment. In this case, only subjects who actually make plane flights following therapy can be considered as improved. Perhaps airline computer records could be used creatively to measure the progress of airplane phobics in making flights.

Assessment as Therapy

Many clinicians do not use objective measures in their treatment of phobic clients, feeling perhaps that such measures confer no benefit to their patient and that the cost involved is not offset by the usefulness of such measures. However, assessment may in fact have a therapeutic impact in at least three ways. First, assessment provides feedback of various kinds. For instance, the subjects may learn that their physiology is not vastly perturbed by encountering the phobic simuli or that they are progressing in their ability to face their feared situation from session to session. Such feedback has, of course, been shown to be of some therapeutic benefit in phobics (Leitenberg et al., 1975). Second, assessment may indicate that the feared situation is not really to be feared. For instance, the therapist may model calmness and re-

assurance when encountering the same stimuli as the subject. Moreover, a large body of research indicates that exposure to the feared
situation may be one of the critical procedures in overcoming fear
and phobia (Agras *et al.*, 1968; Leitenberg *et al.*, 1975). Finally, precise measurements of progress allow many occasions for the therapist
to reinforce behavior in the feared situation. What is a reactive nui-
sance in the experimental measurement of phobia becomes a therapeutic asset in the clinic.

   Assessment may also have therapeutic usefulness in other ways.
If certain types of phobias are more amenable to one type of treatment than others, then assessment may play a key role in diagnosis.
The rather cavalier and arbitrary methods of diagnosing phobias
should be replaced by clearly defined criteria (like DSM-III), backed
up by assessment of self-reported, physiologic, and actual behavior in
various aspects of the phobic situation. Such a procedure may help to
sort out which phobias are best treated by which procedures. Thus, a
subject exhibiting physiologic arousal may require a different approach from a subject who shows no such arousal; a subject who
shows 100% confidence on a number of phobic tasks on Bandura's
hierarchy (see earlier discussion of self-report hierarchies) may not
need to engage in these subtasks, making therapy more efficient.
And, again, a subject who shows improved self-report or behavior but
no change in physiologic arousal after treatment, or reduction in
physiologic arousal and self-report but no behavior change, may require more treatment. We do not know which change in these systems
predicts future change in actual phobic situations. In all these areas
the assessment of the phobia has clear therapeutic uses.

Summary

We have argued that the most useful view of phobic behavior is an interactive model which takes into account what we know about behavior and the functioning of the human nervous system. In this model,
phobic behavior is affected by an interaction among the phobic stimulus, cognitive appraisal of the stimulus, CNS arousal, peripheral
physiologic and biochemical changes. These same factors influence
emotional feeling and verbal report. Phobic behavior is attended by
consequences which, in turn, influence behavior. Such a model suggests that single measures of phobia cannot possibly represent the

condition, since some measures may show improvement while others worsen, depending upon interactions within the variables specified. The types of measures that seem necessary are those which tap phobic avoidance behavior, physiologic arousal, and self-perception. Behavioral measures, client ratings of their phobia, and heart-rate measures are the most sensitive measures of treatment effects. However, methodologic problems exist within each of these major categories. Self-report is significantly influenced by the conditions of the self-report, physiologic and biochemical measures reflect a variety of external and internal process simultaneously, and behavioral avoidance is influenced by the stimulus conditions of the test. But stimuli vary widely. The caged snake in the laboratory and the wiggling horror encountered on a picnic are two different stimuli; and the phobic behavior in each may be quite different. Such methodologic problems lead us to conclude that we can only see phobia through a glass darkly. Nonetheless, significant advances in measurement have been made which the researchers ignore at their peril. Moreover, we await the day when the advances in measurement in the context of research impact clinical practice to the benefit of both clinician and client.

References

Agras, W. S., & Jacob, R. Phobia: Nature and measurement. In M. Mavissakalian & D. H. Barlow (Eds.), *Phobia: Psychological and pharmacological treatment.* New York: Guilford Press, 1980.

Agras, W. S., Leitenberg, H., & Barlow, D. H. Social reinforcement in the modification of agoraphobia. *Archives of General Psychiatry*, 1968, *19*, 423–427.

Alpert, R., & Haber, R. M. Anxiety in academic achievement situations. *Journal of Abnormal and Social Psychology*, 1960, *61*, 207–215.

Ax, A. F. The physiological differentiation between fear and anger in humans. *Psychosomatic Medicine*, 1953, *15*, 433–442.

Bandura, A. *Principles of behavior modification.* New York: Holt, Rinehart, & Winston, 1971.

Bandura, A. Self-efficacy: toward a unifying theory of behavioral change. *Psychological Review*, 1977, *84*, 191–215.

Bandura, A., Jeffery, R. W., & Gadjos, E. Generalizing change through participant modeling with self-directed mastery. *Behaviour Research and Therapy*, 1975, *13*, 141–152.

Baker, B. L., Cohen, D. C., & Saunders, J. T. Self-directed desensitization for acrophobia. *Behaviour Research and Therapy*, 1973, *11*, 79–89.

Barber, T. X., & Hahn, K. W. Experimental studies in "hypnotic" behavior: Physiological and subjective effects of imagined pain. *Journal of Nervous and Mental Disease*, 1964, *139*, 416–425.

Barlow, D. H., Agras, W. S., Leitenberg, H., & Wincze, J. P. An experimental analysis of the effectiveness of "shaping" in reducing maladaptive avoidance behavior: An analogue study. *Behaviour Research and Therapy*, 1970, *8*, 165–173.

Bernstein, D. A. Situational factors in behavioral fear assessment: A progress report. *Behavior Therapy*, 1973, *4*, 41–48.

Bernstein, D. A., & Neitzel, M. T. Procedural variation in behavior avoidance tests. *Journal of Consulting and Clinical Psychology*, 1973, *41*, 165–174.

Borkovec, T. D., & Craighead, W. E. The comparison of two methods of assessing fear and avoidance behavior. *Behaviour Research and Therapy*, 1971, *9*, 285–291.

Braun, P. R., & Reynolds, D. N. A factor analysis of a 100-item fear survey inventory. *Behaviour Research and Therapy*, 1969, *7*, 399–402.

Cohen, J. *Statistical power analysis for the behavioral sciences* (rev. ed.). New York: Academic Press, 1977.

Cooke, G. The efficacy of two desensitization procedures: An analogue study. *Behaviour Research and Therapy*, 1966, *4*, 17–24.

Craig, K. D. Physiological arousal as a function of imagined, vicarious, and direct stress experiences. *Journal of Abnormal Psychology*, 1968, *73*, 513–520.

Curtis, G. C. Are nocturnal cortisol spikes in depressed patients due to stress? In E. J. Sachar (Ed.), *Hormones, behavior and psychopathology*. New York: Raven Press, 1976.

Diagnostic and statistical manual of mental disorders (2nd ed.). Washington, D.C.: American Psychiatric Association, 1968.

Diagnostic and statistical manual of mental disorders (3rd ed.). Washington, D.C.: American Psychiatric Association, 1980.

Fazio, A. Verbal and overt behavioral assessment of a specific fear. *Journal of Consulting and Clinical Psychology*, 1969, *33*, 705–709.

Feist, J. R., & Rosenthal, T. L. Serpent versus surrogate and other determinants of runaway fear differences. *Behaviour Research and Therapy*, 1973, *11*, 483–489.

Geer, J. H. The development of a scale to measure fear. *Behaviour Research and Therapy*, 1965, *3*, 45–53.

Geer, J. H. Fear and autonomic arousal. *Journal of Abnormal Psychology*, 1966, *71*, 253–255.

Gelder, M. G., & Marks, I. M. Severe agoraphobia: A controlled prospective trial of behavior therapy. *British Journal of Psychiatry*, 1966, *112*, 309–320.

Hastings, J. E. *Cardiac and cortical responses to affective stimuli in a reaction time task*. Unpublished doctoral dissertation, University of Wisconsin, 1971.

Henry, J. P., & Stephens, P. M. *Stress, health and the social environment: A sociobiological approach to medicine*, New York: Springer Publishing Co., 1977.

Hersen, M. Fear scale norms for an inpatient population. *Journal of Clinical Psychology*, 1971, *27*, 375–378.

Hersen, M. Self-assessment of fear. *Behavior Therapy*, 1973, *4*, 241–257.

Hodgson, R., & Rachman, S. Desynchrony in measures of fear. *Behaviour Research and Therapy*, 1974, *2*, 319–326.

Klorman, R., Weerts, T. C., Hastings, J. E., Melamed, B. G., & Lang, P. J. Psychometric description of some specific fear questionnaires. *Behavior Therapy*, 1974, *5*, 401–409.

Koelle, G. B. Neurohumoral transmission and the autonomic nervous system. In L. S. Goodman & A. Gilman (Eds.), *The pharmacological basis of therapeutics* (3rd ed.). New York: Macmillan, 1966.

Kroll, H. W. Rapid therapy of a dog phobia by a feeding procedure, *Journal of Behavior Therapy and Experimental Psychiatry*, 1975, *6*, 325–326.

Lader, M. The peripheral and central role of the catecholamines in the mechanisms of anxiety. *International Pharmo-psychiatry,* 1974, *9,* 125-137.

Lang, P. J. Fear reduction and fear behavior: Problems in treating a construct. In J. M. Shlien (Ed.), *Research in psychotherapy* (Vol. 3). Washington, D.C.: American Psychological Association, 1968.

Lang, P. J., & Lazovik, A. D. Experimental desensitization of a phobia. *Journal of Abnormal and Social Psychology,* 1963, *66,* 519-525.

Lang, P. J., Melamed, B. G., & Hart, J. A psychophysiological analysis of fear modification using an automated desensitization procedure. *Journal of Abnormal Psychology,* 1970, *76,* 220-234.

Lazarus, A. A. Group therapy of phobic disorders by systematic desensitization. *Journal of Abnormal Social Psychology,* 1961, *63,* 504-510.

Leitenberg, H., Agras, W. S., Allen, R., Butz, R., & Edwards, J. Feedback and therapist praise during treatment of phobia. *Journal of Consulting and Clinical Psychology,* 1975, *43,* 396-404.

Leitenberg, H., Agras, W. S., Butz, R., & Wincze, J. Relationship between heart rate and behavioral change during the treatment of phobias. *Journal of Abnormal Psychology,* 1971, *78,* 59-68.

Leitenberg, H., Agras, W. S., Edwards, J. A., Thomson, L. E., & Wincze, J. P. Practice as a psychotherapeutic variable: An experimental analysis within single cases. *Journal of Psychiatric Research,* 1970, *7,* 215-225.

Leitenberg, H., Agras, W. S., Thompson, L. E., & Wright, D. E. Feedback in behavior modification: An experimental analysis in two phobic cases. *Journal of Applied Behavior Analysis,* 1968, *1,* 131-137.

Lick, J. R., & Sushinsky, L. *Specificity of fear survey schedule items and the prediction of avoidance behavior.* Unpublished manuscript, State University of New York at Buffalo, 1975.

Lick, J. R., & Unger, T. External validity of laboratory fear assessment: Implications from two case studies. *Journal of Consulting and Clinical Psychology,* 1975, *43,* 864-866.

Lykken, D. T., & Venables, P. M. Direct measure of skin conductance: A proposal for standardization. *Psychophysiology,* 1971, *8,* 656-672.

Marks, I. M., Hallam, R. S., Connolly, J., & Philpott, R. *Nursing in behavioral psychotherapy.* London: Royal College of Nursing, 1977.

Mason, J. W., Maher, J. T., Hartley, L. H., Mougey, E. H., Perlow, M. J., & Jones, L. G. Selectivity of corticosteroid and catecholamine responses to various natural stimuli. In G. Serban (Ed.), *Psychopathology of human adaptation.* New York: Plenum, 1976.

Mathews, A. M. Psychophysiological approaches to the investigation of desensitization and related procedures. *Psychological Bulletin,* 1971, *76,* 73-90.

McDonald, M. L. Multiple impact behavior therapy in a child's dog phobia. *Journal of Behavior Therapy and Experimental Psychiatry,* 1975, *6,* 317-322.

McFall, R. M. Parameters of self-monitoring. In R. B. Stuart (Ed.), *Behavioral self-management: Strategies, techniques, and outcomes.* New York: Brunner/Mazel, 1977.

Menninger, K. *The vital balance.* New York: Viking, 1963.

Mowrer, O. H. On the dual nature of learning: A reinterpretation of "conditioning" and "problem solving." *Harvard Educational Review,* 1947, *17,* 102-148.

Nesbitt, E. B. An escalator phobia overcome in one session of flooding *in vivo. Journal of Behavior Therapy and Experimental Psychiatry,* 1973, *4,* 405-406.

Öst, L. Behavior therapy of thunder and lightening phobias. *Behaviour Research and Therapy*, 1978, *16*, 197–207.

Rachman, S., & Hodgson, R. I. Synchrony and desynchrony in fear and avoidance. *Behaviour Research and Therapy*, 1974, *12*, 311–318.

Russell, R. K., & Matthews, C. O. Cue-controlled relaxation in *in vivo* desensitization of a snake phobia. *Journal of Behavior Therapy and Experimental Psychiatry*, 1975, *6*, 46–51.

Sarason, I. G. Test anxiety, general anxiety, and intellectual performance. *Journal of Consulting Psychology*, 1957, *21*, 485–490.

Suinn, R. M. Changes in non-treated subjects over time: Data on a fear survey schedule and the test anxiety scale. *Behaviour Research and Therapy*, 1969, *7*, 205–206.

Taggart, P., Carruthers, M., & Somerville, W. Electrocardiogram, plasma catecholamines, and lipid and their modification by oxprenalol when speaking before an audience. *Lancet, 1973, 2*, 341.

Taylor, C. B. Heart-rate changes in improved spider-phobic patients. *Psychological Reports*, 1977, *41*, 667–671.

Taylor, C. B., Ferguson, J., & Wermuth, B. Simple techniques to treat medical phobias. *Postgraduate Medical Journal*, 1977, *53*, 28–32.

Teasdale, J. D., Walsh, P. A., Lancashire, M., & Mathews, A. M. Group exposure for agoraphobics: A replication study. *British Journal of Psychiatry*, 1977, *130*, 186–193.

Twentyman, C. T., & McFall, R. M. Behavioral training of social skills in shy males. *Journal of Consulting and Clinical Psychology*, 1975, *43*, 384–395.

Ullmann, L. P., & Krasner, L. A. *A psychological approach to abnormal behavior.* Englewood Cliffs, NJ: Prentice-Hall, 1969.

Wachtel, P. L. *Psychoanalysis and behavior therapy.* New York: Basic Books, 1977.

Walk, R. D. Self-ratings of fear in a fear-invoking situation. *Journal of Abnormal and Social Psychology*, 1956, *52*, 171–178.

Watson, D., & Friend, R. Measurement of social–evaluative anxiety. *Journal of Consulting and Clinical Psychology*, 1969, *33*, 448–457.

Watson, J. P., & Marks, I. M. Relevant and irrelevant fear in flooding: A crossover study of phobic patients. *Behaviour Research and Therapy*, 1971, *2*, 275–293.

Westphal, C. Die Agoraphobie: eine neuropathische Erscheinung. *Archiv fuer Psychiatrie Nervenkrankherten*, 1872, *138*.

Whitehead, W., Robinson, A., Blackwell, B., & Stutz, R. M. Flooding treatment phobias: Does chronic diazepam increase effectiveness? *Journal of Behavior Therapy and Experimental Psychiatry*, 1978, *9*, 219–226.

Wilson, G. D. GSR responses to fear-related stimuli. *Perceptual and Motor Skills*, 1967, *24*, 401–402.

Wolpe, J., & Lang, P. J. A fear survey schedule for use in behavior therapy. *Behaviour Research and Therapy*, 1964, *2*, 27–30.

7

Assessment of

Obsessive-Compulsive Disorders

MATIG R. MAVISSAKALIAN

DAVID H. BARLOW

Obsessive-compulsive neurosis is the least common of all the neuroses and yet it represents one of the best-recognized syndromes in clinical psychiatry and psychology. Following a statement made by Aubrey Lewis in 1957 that "the clinical phenomena have been well recognized and described for over a half a century and little new information has accumulated in recent years regarding the treatment and course of the [obsessional] illness" (Lewis, 1957, p. 157), and perhaps stirred by his remarks as well as his pioneering work with obsessionals, a number of studies dealing with the natural history, clinical course, and prognostic factors of obsessive-compulsive neurosis have appeared recently in the literature. The natural history of obsessional neurosis has been reviewed comprehensively by Allen Black (1974); hence, a detailed review of the literature will not be repeated here. Instead, the following schematized profile of the obsessional patient and the course of the disorder is presented to highlight the important and relevant findings.

The typical obsessional patient is likely to develop persisting

Matig R. Mavissakalian. Western Psychiatric Institute and Clinic, University of Pittsburgh School of Medicine, Pittsburgh, Pennsylvania.
David H. Barlow. Department of Psychology, State University of New York at Albany, Albany, New York.

symptoms in his or her early 20s. The patient, however, will seek professional help on the average of two years later. If precipitating factors are found, they are most likely to be of a sexual and marital nature, related to pregnancy and delivery or to illness or death of a near relative. The patient is likely to be of high intelligence and belong to the middle or upper socioeconomic classes. Family history of mental illness and history of symptoms in childhood are unlikely to differentiate the patient from other neurotics. However, most patients will report that the initial onset of their obsessional symptoms occurred between the ages of 10 and 15 years and that they followed a slowly progressive, sometimes fluctuating course, punctuated with exacerbations. The outcome of the disorder cannot be predicted, but the individual may be among the approximately 60% of those with this condition who improve, sometimes, even to an asymptomatic level regardless of mode of treatment and follow-up. Finally, there is less than 3% chance that a schizophrenic syndrome will evolve in time.

Diagnosis

The definition of obsessional symptoms generally agreed upon and followed by most authors is that of a recurrent or persistent idea, thought, image, feeling, impulse, or movement which is accompanied by a sense of subjective compulsion and the desire to resist it; the event being recognized by the individual as foreign to his or her personality and as an abnormality into which the individual has insight. Thus, the new edition of the *Diagnostic and Statistical Manual of Mental Disorders* (DSM-III) (1980) required the following diagnostic features for a primary diagnosis of obsessive–compulsive disorder:

1. Obsessions and/or compulsions. Obsessions are recurrent, persistent ideas, thoughts, images, or impulses which are ego-alien. Compulsions are behaviors that are not experienced as the outcome of the individual's own volition, but are accompanied by a sense of subjective compulsion and a desire to resist.
2. The individual recognizes the senselessness of the behavior.
3. The obsessions or compulsions have a significant effect on the individual's life adjustment.

4. The obsessions or compulsions are not associated with an underlying schizophrenic condition, organic brain syndrome, or major affective disorder.

RELATIONSHIP TO DEPRESSION

The relationship between obsessive–compulsive disorders and depression is a complex one and deserves elaboration. First, it is most common in obsessive–compulsive neurotics to find feelings of discouragement, helplessness, a sense of defeat, and hopelessness in the face of chronic difficulties and symptoms. This, of course, is a secondary depression (or reactive depression) and usually does not require treatment in its own right, but improves as the primary obsessive–compulsive condition improves. However, recent data would suggest that an improvement of this mild-to-moderate reactive depression does not always follow substantial reduction in the obsessive–compulsive disorder (Marks *et al.*, 1975).

Second, the initial onset of obsessive–compulsive symptoms occurs in the face of difficult and often "depressing" life situations and in the context of depressed mood. Thus Mellett (1974), in a detailed study of 20 obsessional patients, provided information that depression, rather than anxiety, is more fundamentally related to obsessive–compulsive disorders and that the onset of obsessive–compulsive symptoms coincided with depression in all the patients studied.

Gittleson (1966a, 1966b) has studied the relationship of obsessions to severe (psychotic) depression and found important clinical differences depending on the premorbid existence or absence of obsessions. Of interest is the finding that by and large, obsessions which develop *de novo* in the course of depression improve with resolution of the depression. However, it was found that 3 out of 85 patients whose obsessional symptoms started in the context of the depression retained their obsessions permanently. On the other hand, the majority of patients whose obsessions antedated the episode of depression retained their obsessions following the resolution of the depression, with 13.5% of these cases showing a permanent worsening of their obsessions. An interesting and somewhat unexpected finding was that 13% of the cases exhibiting obsessions prior to the depression lost their obsessions during the depression.

Finally, in recent years a number of researchers (Collins, 1973;

Rack, 1973) have reported successful treatment results with chlorimipramine (Anafranil) a tricyclic antidepressant agent, as the primary
treatment for obsessive–compulsive disorders. Some studies (Wyndowe, Solyom, & Ananth, 1975) have suggested that chlorimipramine might possess a primary specific antiobsessive effect. However,
Rachman, Cobb, Grey, McDonald, Mawson, Sartory, and Stern
(1979) found no evidence of direct antiobsessive effect due to chlorimipramine.

In the light of these observations made in different centers and
by various investigators, the existence of a close and complex relationship between depression and obsessive–compulsive disorders seems
unquestionable. Although the nature of this relationship remains
largely unclear, it strongly suggests that in the assessment of obsessive–compulsive disorders, the assessment of depression and mood
changes can no longer be overlooked.

Prognostic Factors

To date, some evidence exists for the effectiveness, more or less, of
three different forms of treatment of obsessive–compulsive disorders.

1. Psychosurgery in the form of bilateral stereotactic tractotomy
   or subcodate tractotomy (Bridges, Goktepe, & Maratos, 1973)
   and stereotactic limbic leucotomy (Mitchell-Heggs, Kelly, &
   Richardson, 1976) has resulted in clinically substantial improvement of 67% of 24 patients and 89% of 66 patients respectively, the latter reporting a 67% rate of freedom from
   symptoms.
2. Psychopharmachological treatment with chlorimipramine
   (Anafranil) has resulted in unexpected success with both oral
   and intravenous administration (van Renynghe de Voxvrie,
   1968; Collins, 1973; Waxman, 1975; Marshall & Micev, 1975;
   Wyndowe et al., 1975). Rack (1973), for example, reports
   60% excellent to good results in 21 primary obsessional patients. However, the majority of these reports are anecdotal
   and deal with a heterogeneous patient population, and therefore are at best tentative.
3. A newly developed behavioral method of treatment consisting
   essentially of prolonged *in vivo* exposure (flooding) and
   response prevention has evidenced results of approximately
   70% improvement rate over a two-year follow-up period

(Marks *et al.*, 1975). A number of other authors have shown similarly encouraging results (Levy & Meyer, 1971; Boersma, Den Hengst, Dekker, & Emmelkamp, 1976; Foa & Goldstein, 1978).

Although the studies of the natural history of obsessive–compulsive disorders have somewhat diminished the overall pessimism concerning the outcome of patients with this syndrome, and although the newer methods of psychopharmacological and behavioral treatments call for added optimism and might make recourse to psychosurgery less frequent, it becomes apparent that these results should be considered tentative since good controlled studies have not been done and sample size in the outcome studies is small.

In an effort to deal with the frustrating finding of nearly one-third of unimproved patients in most studies, investigators have tried to find accurate prognostic variables that might differentiate the patients with good outcome from those with a poor outcome. These efforts have led, for the most part, to inconsistent and, not infrequently, contradictory findings (Black, 1974). It appears that short duration of symptoms before treatment, the presence of precipitating factors, and cases with phobic ruminative symptoms are considered favorable prognostic indicators. In contrast, a severe clinical state, presence of motor symptoms (compulsions, rituals), and a positive history of childhood symptoms are considered prognostically unfavorable.

Recently, Akhtar, Wig, Varma, Pershad, and Verma (1975) attempted to relate the phenomenology of obsessive–compulsive symptoms to prognosis. The only significant finding was that the absence of compulsions was associated with good prognosis. In addition, they suggested that distinctly different phenomenological forms of compulsions might have important prognostic implications. This will be discussed in greater detail later in the chapter. Bridges *et al.* (1973), reporting a three-year follow-up study of 24 patients with obsessional neurosis treated with psychosurgery, failed to find a significant correlation between symptomatology and outcome. As expected, short duration of illness and onset associated with pregnancy carried a good prognosis. The presence of prominent depression also appeared to improve prognosis. Marks *et al.* (1975), reporting a two-year follow-up study on 20 patients with obsessive–compulsive neurosis treated with exposure and response prevention, failed to find a meaningful prognostic pattern except to state that significant improvement at the end of three weeks' treatment was maintained at a two-year follow-up.

Finally, a recent article (Foa, 1979) suggests that two factors are responsible for failure in treating obsessive–compulsive neurotics. Four out of the 10 patients who failed to improve despite full cooperation with treatment were found to manifest a strong conviction that their obsessional fears were realistic. Another four were found to be severely depressed, and the remaining two showed evidence of both severe depression and "overvalued ideas." Of additional interest was the finding that all of these 10 patients failed to habituate; patients who held their fears to be realistic showed habituation within sessions but failed to transfer gains from session to session and therefore failed to generalize, whereas depressed patients did not even show evidence of within-session habituation.

The need for further research exploring prognostic variables cannot be overemphasized. In the absence of clear-cut clues in this respect, comprehensive measures and longitudinal assessments become essential in the search for factors differentiating between successful outcome and failure.

Phenomenology (Descriptive Studies)

Sir Aubrey Lewis was among the first to study the distinctive characteristics of obsessive–compulsive symptoms, and his views have been largely retained in modern-day textbooks. It is only recently that investigators have started scrutinizing and even sometimes challenging them.

According to Lewis (1957), obsessive–compulsive symptoms have two essential components; namely, compulsion and resistance. "The essence of an obsession is the fruitless struggle against a disturbance that seems isolated from the rest of mental activity" (p. 157); and "the indispensible subjective component of an obsession lies in the consciousness of the patient: to him it is an act of will, which he cannot help making, to try and suppress or destroy the unwelcome intruder upon his mental integrity; but the effort is always in vain" (p. 158).

Based largely on his vast clinical experience, Lewis (1957) also offered a functional classification of obsessional symptoms which went beyond the mere subdivision of obsessional phenomena into different forms and content.

Obsessions can conveniently be divided into primary and secondary. An example would be first the insistent feeling that he is dirty — that is the primary phenomenon. And then there is the impulse to wash — the secondary phenomenon, developed in order to obtain relief from the primary disturbance. The second phenomenon can be regarded as defensive and aimed at preventing or relieving tension. They can themselves be obsessional, that is, the patient has to struggle against them and may indeed develop rituals or tricks against them in turn; or, they may remain neutral and unresisted, they may indeed be prized for their protective efficiency. . . . The secondary phenomenon is, as a rule, resisted (or accepted) according to the extent to which it offends against familiar, social, hygenic or moral cannons of conduct. (p. 158)

Rachman (1973) has further characterized the distinguishing features of Lewis's primary phenomena, which are often called obsessive ruminations or simply obsessions. Again based largely on clinical experience, Rachman found that obsessions have a fantastic and irrational quality, have an aggressive and/or abhorrent content, are egodystonic (foreign to the person's value system), and are resisted. He also observed that patients often feel guilty as a direct result of having had the thoughts and that they frequently are uncertain about the reality of the content of their ruminations.

Similarly, Walker (1973) has elaborated on the distinguishing characteristic features of Lewis's secondary phenomena, also called compulsions or rituals. She observes that obsessional rituals are purposive actions (unlike tics). They are performed in accordance with rules and are designed to bring about or prevent a future state of affairs (unlike sexual deviations); the ritual is not connected by a rational (sensible) justification to the state of affairs it is designed to bring about (unlike normal behavior). Obsessional rituals, Walker contends, usually fail to reduce anxiety and are performed multiple times and usually occur in the absence of objective danger (unlike superstitious and religious rituals).

In a recent study of obsessive-compulsive neurosis, Nutter, Jens, and Mavissakalian (submitted for publication) conducted a systematic phenomenological analysis of obsessive-compulsive symptomatology based on chart reviews of 21 hospitalized obsessive-compulsive patients and interviews of nine obsessive-compulsive outpatients. All patients met the diagnostic criteria of obsessive-compulsive neurosis for use in psychiatric research proposed by Feighner, Robins, Guze, Woodruff, Winokur, and Muñoz (1972). The presence of the various distinguishing features of obsessions and compulsions proposed by Rachman

(1973) and Walker (1973), respectively, were noted. As can be seen, the findings corroborate and lend support to the original definitions offered by Rachman and Walker. The only notable exception was that contrary to Walker's definition, performing the ritual reduces anxiety in seven out of eight outpatients interviewed. Unfortunately, 17 out of the 21 charts were deficient in information in this respect. The issue of the anxiety-producing function of compulsions remains a controversial one, and we will have many occasions in this chapter to return to it.

Recently, Akhtar *et al.* (1975) conducted a phenomenological analysis of symptoms in 82 obsessional neurotics based on data collected during structured interviews. Unlike most other studies, they used operational definitions for obsessions and compulsions and studied the form, content, and number of the different obsessive–compulsive symptoms.

Their definition of an obsession was that of "an anxiety-provoking psychic phenomenon that recurs in spite of the patient's resisting it and regarding it as alien to himself and at times clearly absurd" (p. 343). In this way they identified five distinct and one miscellaneous form of obsessions. The most commonly encountered forms were, in decreasing order, obsessive doubts, obsessive thinking, obsessive fears, obsessive impulses, and obsessive images. They highlight the difference between the four most commonly encountered forms by this example; "A woman who worries about her child's safety might have an obsessive doubt (has something happened to him?), or an obsessive fear (something might happen to him because of my negligence), or an obsessive image (over and over I see him drowning!), or obsessional thinking (if he plays outside he might catch cold that might turn into pneumonia, and if that goes undiagnosed, then . . .)" (p. 345). They emphasize that in the example given above, despite the similarity of thought content, the form of the obsessional symptom is different.

As for the content of obsessional symptoms, they found that the subject of dirt and contamination was the most frequent, followed by aggression and violence, religion, and sex.

Akhtar and his associates (1975) defined compulsion as "a reluctantly performed voluntary act that temporarily reduces the anxiety aroused by an obsession" (p. 343), and identified two categories of compulsions which they termed yielding (when the compulsive act gives expression to the underlying obsessive urge), and controlling (when the compulsive act tends to divert the underlying obsession without giving expression to it). They thus found that 24% of their sample had no compulsions, 61% had yielding compulsions, and 6% had controlling compulsions. Only 9% of their patients had both types of compulsions, and these were the only patients to have multiple compulsions which contrasted with a larger proportion (nearly 50%) of the sample found to have multiple obsessions.

As mentioned earlier, Akhtar *et al.* (1975) also attempted to relate their phenomenological findings to outcome, and they tentatively suggested that controlling compulsions might have a better prognosis than yielding compulsions.

Stern and Cobb (1978), in a phenomenological study of 45 obsessive–compulsive neurotics, aimed at classifying symptomatology into behavioral forms, in contrast to the emphasis placed on cognitive forms by Akhtar and his associates (1975). These authors also used operational definitions for each subdivision of compulsive behavior and thus identified four primary behavioral forms.

Fifty-one percent of patients had cleaning rituals. As an example, Stern and Cobb state the case of a woman who washed her hands for at least five minutes, as many as 40 times during the course of a day. The authors found that neither the total number of times nor the total time spent washing was characteristic of this behavior; rather, "the patient's aim was to achieve a state of bodily cleanliness which would give her satisfaction" (p. 235).

Fifty-one percent had avoiding rituals, and the authors found these to be similar to the avoidance behavior manifested in phobic disorders. Repeating rituals were found in 40% of the patients, and the authors point that the essential characteristic of this form of ritual is "to do things by numbers, regardless of the type of activity being carried out" (p. 234). The fourth primary behavioral form was found in 38% of the patients, and consisted of checking rituals. The characteristic of this form of compulsion was described as "going back to check actions performed."

Three other minor forms were also identified; namely, (1) slowness (of motor actions as if they were carried in slow motion), (2) completeness (with the aim of doing things properly), and (3) meticulousness (a concern that objects be arranged in specific order). These minor forms, although phenomenologically distinct, seem to create a specific clinical problem, which is that simple tasks take up a great deal of time in the patient's everyday life. Whether these minor forms constitute hypertrophied obsessional traits or distinct obsessional

symptoms is a question not yet settled. However, they seem to constitute what Rachman (1974) has called primary obsessional slowness, a
topic to which we will return later.

Stern and Cobb (1978) found that only 8 out of the 45 patients
had a single behavioral type of ritual, with 50% having a mixture of
three or more types. A surprisingly small number (30%) of the patients demonstrated great resistance to performing the ritual (resistance, however, was found to be marked with repeating type of
rituals). On the other hand, 65% of the patients recognized the senselessness of their rituals. This latter finding led the authors to recommend that in diagnosing obsessive-compulsive neurosis, the patient's
feelings that their rituals are senseless should be emphasized as much
as, if not more than, their resistance to them.

Other interesting findings from this study were that 31% of the
patients confined their rituals to one place; in the majority of the
cases, this was the home. The type of ritual affecting and disturbing
the family the most was found to be cleaning rituals. Although the
presence of another person was found not to reduce rituals, being
reassured helped prevent the ritual in 42% of the patients.

Finally, the most common ideational content associated with the
rituals had to do with dirt and contamination (38% of the patients),
and the most common underlying theme was that of causing harm
either to self or to others.

Four types of obsessive-compulsive complaints have been recently described by Hodgson and Rachman (1977). These authors, using
a factor-analytic technique, classified obsessive-compulsive complaints into two major and two minor types. The two major ones are
checking and washing, which were found in 52% and 48% of the patients respectively. Hodgson and Rachman called the minor types
slowness and doubting rituals. Slowness was characterized by slow repetitive behavior, with little or no anxiety and no persistant ruminations, and was found in 52% of the patients. Doubting, which was
present in 60% of the patients, was characterized by never being certain that the performance of the ritual was properly done, as well as
by doubts about daily activities. The authors also found that the majority of the patients had more than one type of obsessional complaint.

Before summarizing the findings of the phenomenological assessment of obsessive-compulsive symptoms, a recent study comparing
abnormal and normal obsessions should be mentioned. Rachman

and DeSilva (1978) conducted an exploratory study into the occurrence and nature of obsessions in a nonpatient population. Obsessions were operationally defined as "repetitive, unwanted, intrusive thoughts of internal origin," and it was found that 80% of 124 normal subjects experienced obsessions, with one-third having only obsessional thoughts and one-seventh having only obsessional impulses, while more than 50% had both obsessional thoughts and urges.

Subsequently Rachman and DeSilva (1978) compared the distinguishing features between the obsessions of normals and the obsessions of eight obsessive–compulsive patients. They found that normal and abnormal obsessions are similar in form and content, in meaningfulness (they were not felt to be senseless), and in their relationship to mood (they were associated with depression and anxiety). What differentiated abnormal obsessions from the obsessions experienced by a normal population was that abnormal obsessions last longer, produce more discomfort, and are more ego-alien, more often and more strongly resisted and harder to dismiss, and provoke more urges to neutralize.

The phenomenological studies discussed thus far have dealt with defining and identifying different forms and contents of obsessive–compulsive symptoms, have attempted to differentiate the characteristics of clinical obsessions from "normal" obsessions and of obsessional rituals from other behaviors. Most have been based on observations and data gathered in interviews and questionnaires. However, the functional relationship between the primary and secondary obsessional phenomena — that is, obsessions and compulsions; specifically, the question of whether the performance of the ritual leads to a decrease or an increase in the anxiety/discomfort and dysphoria accompanying the obsession — remains untouched in these studies. It is to this interesting and controversial issue that we will turn next.

Behavioral Analysis

Beech and Liddell (1974) have maintained, on the basis of close observation and interviewing of patients, that rituals increase the anxiety/discomfort that accompany obsessions. "First there is a strong tendency for the mood of patients to show increasing deterioration as their ritual proceeds, and on a good proportion of occasions the patient will terminate his ritual in a considerably more distressed state than that in which be began. Secondly, as a matter of empirical fact, the interruption of a ritual has a generally beneficial effect upon mood" (Beech, 1971). Other investigators (Wolpe, 1958; Reed, 1968) have made similar observations and commented on the anxiety-elevating potential of compulsions.

An excellent example of an attempt to systematically investigate mood changes accompanying ritualistic behavior is reported by Walker and Beech (1969). By careful, detailed interviewing, direct observation, and systematic ratings of mood (hostility, depression, and anxiety), these investigators concluded that some rituals cause mood to deteriorate and that the interruption of a ritual could have a beneficial effect on mood. Both of these findings contradicted traditionally held views that compulsions have an anxiety-reducing function and that one should not interrupt the ritual for fear of acutely exacerbating the patient's dysphoric mood.

Rachman and his associates (Hodgson & Rachman, 1972; Roper, Rachman, & Hodgson, 1973; Roper & Rachman, 1976), in a series of elegant experiments, addressed the question of whether the performance of the obsessive–compulsive ritual decreases òr increases anxiety/discomfort provoked by exposing the patients to situations which produce strong urges to perform the ritual. In the first study (Hodgson & Rachman, 1972), twelve obsessive–compulsive hand washers took part in four experimental manipulations to assess the effect on subjective levels of anxiety and distress measured on standardized subjective rating scales of the following conditions: (1) touching a contaminated object, (2) hand washing immediately after the contamination, (3) delaying a hand wash by 30 minutes, (4) hand washing after the thirty-minute delay, and (5) interrupting the handwashing ritual. Their results indicated that touching a contaminated object does produce an increase in subjective anxiety and discomfort, and that the completion of the ritual produces a reduction of the anxiety and discomfort to baseline precontamination levels. In addition, they demonstrated that interruption of a compulsive ritual does not have an effect on anxiety and discomfort.

The second experiment (Roper et al., 1973) was similarly designed and carried on with 12 obsessional checkers. Although the overall results replicated the findings with the washers of the previous experiment, the following differences were noted: (1) the checkers experienced a lower level of anxiety/discomfort than the washers when provoked, (2) there was a significant increase in anxiety/discomfort following the half-hour delay period following provocation with the checkers, and (3) five patients reported increase in anxiety/discomfort after completion of the ritual on at least one occasion during the experiment. Because of these differences, a third experiment (Roper & Rachman, 1976) with twelve checkers was carried out in the patient's home under two experimental conditions, one with the experimenter present and the other in his absence. They found that the pattern of response closely followed that of the compulsive washers. The performance of the checking ritual produced a decrease in anxiety/discomfort. The levels of anxiety/discomfort were higher in the experimenter-absent condition, and the time taken to complete the checking ritual was also longer in this condition. These findings firmly support the anxiety-reduction hypotheses of compulsive behavior, at least in the two most commonly found forms; namely, compulsive hand washing and compulsive checking.

In a further experiment with eleven obsessive–compulsive checkers, Rachmen, DeSilva, and Roper (1976) studied the fate of anxiety/discomfort and of urges to check over a three-hour period immediately following provocation. In the control condition, a checking ritual immediately followed provocation, whereas in the experimental condition, checking was absolutely prevented for a three-hour period following provocation. Thus the experimenters found that the checking ritual in the control condition resulted in a marked decrease in anxiety/discomfort and dissipation or urges to check. In the experimental condition where checking was prevented, Rachman *et al.* found a marked decline of anxiety/discomfort and dissipation of urges to check after the first hour of response prevention. In addition, they observed further decline during the second and third hours of response prevention. Furthermore, the decline in anxiety/discomfort and urges to perform a ritual were found to run parallel courses, with urges dissipating slightly faster than anxiety/discomfort.

This series of experiments clearly demonstrates that, at least with obsessional washes and checkers, the performance of rituals is followed by a decline of the urges to engage in the ritual and a decrease in anxiety/discomfort caused by the obsessions. However, the fact remains that compulsions and rituals can produce an increment in anxiety/discomfort or cause deterioration of mood, as was previously mentioned (Walker & Beech, 1969; Beech, 1971; Beech & Liddell, 1974). These investigators have studied this problem very closely, and offer interesting explanations hinging essentially on the obsessionals' difficulty with decision making. It would seem that when the patient cannot decide when to stop his or her ritual or when the ritual has fulfilled its purpose (has been completed) and continues to be performed over and over, this would cause a deterioration of mood and increase anxiety/discomfort.

To complicate matters, the observation has been made by several investigators that rituals can also become autonomous of underlying obsessions and have little effect on the prevailing level of anxiety/discomfort. Thus Walton and Mather (1963) hypothesized that the disassociations of rituals from anxiety/discomfort-producing obsessions would tend to occur mainly in the chronic stages of the obsessive-compulsive illness. Marks, Crowe, Drewe, Young, and Dewhurst (1969) gave an illustration of this phenomenon when the washing rituals of a patient continued to occur despite the successful desensitization of the obsessional fear of contamination. More recently, Rachman (1974) studied ten patients with extensive rituals and reported that only "four out of ten said that they have experienced adverse reaction (increased tension and irritability and loss of concentration) when placed under a time pressure by someone else" (pp. 11-12). These are the patients whose rituals conform to the behavioral type of slowness mentioned earlier, which consists of spending long periods of time on the simplest of tasks, such as getting dressed, shaving, showering, and brushing teeth.

It becomes evident that our understanding of the role of anxiety in obsessive-compulsive disorders, with their varied and rich phenomenological forms, and our understanding of the functional link between obsessions and compulsion, needs much further elucidation through experimental investigations. Especially indicated would seem to be the psychophysiological assessment of obsessive-compulsive phenomena.

Psychophysiological Assessment

The psychophysiological assessment of obsessive-compulsive phenomena is yet in its infancy. Unfortunately, very little systematic work has been done in this area despite the relative abundance of psychophysiological research in anxiety and phobias (Lader & Mathews, 1968; Mathews, 1971; Van Egeren, Feather, & Hein, 1971; Boulougouris, Marks, & Marset, 1971; Marks & Hudson, 1973).

The few studies reported by Boulougouris and his associates (Boulougouris & Bassiakos, 1973; Rabavilas & Boulougouris, 1974; Boulougouris, Rabavilas, & Stefanis, 1977) are among the best of the psychophysiological assessments of obsessive–compulsive neurosis. Their experimental work has shown consistently that autonomic activity as measured by heart rate and GSR (skin conductance and spontaneous fluctuations) increases significantly when the patient is engaged in obsessional behavior as compared to neutral behavior. Although these are their major findings, their approach to the assessment of obsessional behavior and a certain number of observations they make are germane to the subject of assessment of obsessive–compulsive disorder and therefore will be discussed briefly.

First, the multiple test stimuli used, as well as their controls, are the following: (1) spontaneous (fantasy) occurrence of the main obsession contrasted to a neutral fantasy; (2) therapists' description of the main obsessional scene contrasted to a neutral scene; (3) actual touching of contaminated object versus touching a neutral object; (4) flooding condition, during which the patient is asked to touch the contaminated object or to rehearse the distressing, unacceptable thoughts with their disastrous consequences. The usefulness of these multiple-test situations is reflected in the following observations. Boulougouris and Bassiakos (1973) state: "contrary to our expectations, the fantasy scenes and flooding talks increased autonomic arousal more on some measures than the 'touch' of a contaminated object" (p. 230). Similarly, Boulougouris *et al.* (1977) found that in the spontaneous obsessive fantasy condition habituation of heart rate and GSR responses was less compared to the therapist's description of obsessional scenes and the flooding conditions. The exact meaning of these differences is not yet clear; however, they seem to suggest that in obsessive–compulsive neurosis, internally presented stimuli (obsessive fantasy) are different from externally presented stimuli, and they may be more resistant to change.

Psychophysiological studies of compulsive behavior are even more scarce. Carr (1971) reported reduction of autonomic activity following performances of rituals. Recently, Hornsveld, Kraaimaat, and Van Dam-Baggen (1979) conducted a psychophysiological study in 6 patients with obsessive fears of contamination and handwashing rituals, using as a control 12 psychiatric inpatients without obsessive–compulsive symptoms. More specifically, the researchers were interested in studying and comparing the effects of anticipation and the actual act of touching a feared dirt stimulus on subjective and physiological measures of anxiety/distress. In addition, they explored the differences between neutral (unprovoked) handwashing and handwashing after touching the dirt stimulus both within and between the two groups of patients.

Every subject participating in this study went through the same five experimental conditions in the following order: (1) neutral handwashing: subjects were asked to wash their hands in preparation for the application of the electrodes; (2) relaxation: this phase lasted ten minutes and served as a baseline; (3) anticipation: patients were shown the dirt stimulus to be touched. The dirt stimulus for each patient was individualized and selected from the midpoint of a hierarchy of dirty objects scaled from 0 to 100; (4) touching of the contaminated object; and (5) provoked handwashing, which followed the touching of the dirt stimulus. Subjective anxiety/distress was measured on a five-point self-rating scale and assessed at each experimental phase. Physiological measures consisted of heart rate, which was also assessed in all the experimental conditions, and GSR (skin conductance level and spontaneous fluctuations), which was assessed in conditions 2, 3, and 4 only. Their major findings could be summarized as follows: (1) Anticipation of dirt stimulus increased anxiety/discomfort in both subjective and physiological measures in obsessive-compulsive patients as well as in the control patients. (2) The actual touching of a dirt stimulus also increased autonomic activity in both groups of patients, but resulted in an increase of subjective distress only in the obsessive-compulsive patients. (3) Spontaneous fluctuations were significantly greater in the obsessive-compulsive group during anticipation and actual touching conditions, but no differences regarding heart rate and skin conductance level were found between the groups. (4) Handwashing after touching the feared dirt stimulus (compulsive handwashing) resulted in a reduction of subjective distress in the obsessive-compulsive group. (5) On the other hand, heart-rate differences were not found between the first and last fifteen seconds of handwashing after contamination. Unfortunately, skin conductance measures, which might have been more sensitive to change in autonomic reactivity, were not taken during handwashing. (6) In addition to the psychophysiological measures, a number of specific features of handwashing behavior were observed and compared, but no major and significant differences emerged. For example, the duration of neutral handwashing and handwashing after contamination was essentially the same both within and between groups. However, obsessive–compulsive patients had a tendency to wash their hands more extensively as well as to use more total rubbing and ringing movements than the control patients.

In a recent pilot study, Grayson, Nutter, and Mavissakalian (in press), using heart rate as their sole psychophysiological measure, found interesting differences in the following four experimental conditions: (1) phobic scene in which subjects imagine performing the feared task without engaging in their compulsive ritual (e.g., touching a contaminated object without taking a shower), (2) compulsive scenes in which subjects imagined engaging in the compulsive ritual without provocation (e.g., taking a shower), (3) phobic/compulsive scenes in which subjects imagine performing a feared task and then engaging in their ritual (e.g., touching a contaminated object and then taking a shower), and (4) a neutral scene. The content of the scenes was individualized for each subject.

The subjects were five obsessive–compulsives involved in outpatient treatment at the time of the study. All subjects met the diagnostic criteria proposed by Feighner *et al.* (1972) for psychiatric research. Each subject underwent the four experimental conditions outlined above, each condition consisting of a 30-second visualization of a scene immediately following a 20-second oral presentation by the experimenter and instructions to imagine the same scene. There was a 40-second rest period between conditions to allow a return to baseline. Each experimental condition was presented three times in a counterbalanced fashion. Beat-by-beat heart rate was monitored during each of the 30-second experimental conditions and was converted to second-by-second heart rate.

Heart-rate wave form—that is, heart rate plotted over time—has been recognized as the most reliable measure of the orienting response (OR). The OR is a short latency response characterized by an initial heart rate deceleration occurring at stimulus onset and lasting for two to three seconds. The defense response (DR) has been described as an initial heart-rate acceleration followed by a deceleration and than a secondary acceleration, all occurring within 10–15 seconds. Recent experimental findings (Hare, 1972; Hare & Blevings, 1975; Grayson, 1979) would suggest that DR responses will occur with the presentation of emotionally laden stimuli such as phobic and obsessional stimuli, whereas orienting responses will occur with a neutral stimulus.

The results showed that subjects responded to neutral scenes with orienting type of heart-rate responses. ORs also tended to characterize compulsive scenes, although the initial heart-rate deceleration was smaller in both size and duration compared to the neutral scene. The phobic scenes tended to elicit DR type of responses. Most interesting was the heart-rate response to the phobic compulsive scenes. An initial heart-rate acceleration was followed by a series of short latency decelerations and accelerations in which heart rate tended to increase over time. The virtual absence of a decelerative component suggests that the phobic compulsive scenes elicited fully developed DRs.

The results of this study should be interpreted with caution. Tentatively, they suggest that subjects perceived the total complex of obsessive–compulsive symptomatology as more anxiety-producing or more aversive, perhaps, owing to the implied failure in the scenes to cope with the phobic situation without giving in to the compulsion. Alternatively, they might suggest that the combined phobic/compulsive scenes resulted in greater avoidance, and hence decreased processing of the stimulus (Sokolov, 1963). Most interesting, however, is the finding that the combined obsessive–compulsive scene differed in its effect on heart rate from both the phobic (obsessional) scene and the compulsive scene presented separately.

Clearly the need for further psychophysiological research in the study of obsessive–compulsive phenomena is apparent. The psychophysical study of the functional relationships of obsessions and compulsions needs to be pursued. The controversy surrounding the anxiety-reducing function of compulsion needs clarification and psychophysiological as well as behavioral determination. Only in this way will we be able to validate the various conceptualizations of obsessive–compulsive phenomena, and the role of anxiety in this syndrome, conceptualizations which thus far have been based on anecdotal and clinical impressions and which are as varied as the rich phenomenology of obsessive–compulsive neurosis.

Mavissakalian (1979) recently developed a unitary formulation and functional classification of obsessive–compulsive phenomena which serves as a summary of the material presented thus far in the chapter. The proposed formulation assumes a functional equivalence between motoric and cognitive obsessive–compulsive phenomena and defines these phenomena according to their psychophysiological properties. Recently Rachman (1976) made a distinction between obsessional thoughts that act as "noxious stimuli" and thoughts that attempt to neutralize the noxious stimuli, and proposed that we assume a functional equivalence between compulsive checking and cleaning rituals, requests for reassurance, and "neutralizing rituals" (cognitive rituals) on the basis that all of these constitute attempts to neutralize obsessions which are anxiety/ discomfort-producing. It is hoped which much of the confusion that has arisen from the interchangeable use of the terms rituals, compulsions, and similarly, obsessions and ruminations, will dissipate with the following functional definition of obsessive–compulsive phenomena.

1. Obsessions are internal noxious stimuli in the form of repetitive, intrusive, and unacceptable thoughts, images, feelings, and impulses that the person finds ego-alien, resists, and attempts to dismiss. Obsessions can be spontaneous and/or provoked by environmental events. As reviewed earlier, there is clinical, phenomenological, and physiological evidence in support of this notion.

2. Compulsions are behaviors which attempt to counter and neutralize the obsessions and reduce subjective anxiety/discomfort associated with them. They may be purely cognitive or motoric or can be a combination of both. Compulsive washing and checking are typical examples of this type of obsessive–compulsive phenomenon; however, according to this current definition, silent praying or any other cognitive event (such as a magical word) would be also classified here. More simply put, compulsions as defined here are anxiety-reducing.

3. Obsessionalized compulsions are compulsions which, instead of reducing the anxiety/discomfort accompanying obsessions, produce an increment of anxiety and discomfort. Since they generate anxiety/discomfort or a deterioration of mood, they will be considered functionally as obsessions. They can be viewed as unsuccessful compulsions or failed compulsions or secondary obsessions although the label "obsessionalized compulsions" is preferred because it accurately reflects the functional conception and the functional status of this phenomenon. Obsessionalized compulsions can also be cognitive or motoric or a combination of the two.

4. Rituals are stereotyped behaviors which take an inordinately long amount of time during the patient's waking hours. Their prime characteristic is that they have become functionally autonomous of anxiety/discomfort and have lost all apparent connection to obsessions.

This functional formulation of obsessive-compulsive phenomena, by transcending content and typology as well as the difference between cognitive and motoric obsessional behavior, provides a parsimonious yet encompassing framework to explain obsessive-compulsive phenomena. It has the added advantage of unifying our approach to the study and treatment of obsessive-compulsive neurosis whether the clinical presentation is primarily one of ruminations or motoric compulsions. The two behavioral treatment modalities — namely, exposure and response prevention — could be targeted to the anxiety-provoking and anxiety-reducing phenomena respectively. Indeed, recent findings (Foa, Steketee, & Milby, 1980) suggest that prolonged exposure is more effective in reducing anxiety/discomfort associated with obsessions than it is in changing compulsive behavior; and inversely, response prevention diminishes compulsive behavior more than it effects anxiety/discomfort associated with obsessions.

Furthermore, according to the present formulation, one would not think of prolonged exposure or of response prevention as treatments of choice for functionally autonomous rituals. Indeed, a treatment consisting of shaping, pacing, and prompting procedures has been already suggested and found to be moderately effective in the treatment of patients with primary obsessional slowness (Rachman, 1974). In a few cases of ritualized obsessional thinking, the authors have used symptom scheduling, which consists of instructing the patient to indulge in the obsessive thinking for a predetermined period of time which is gradually decreased in length and frequency; this was found to be clinically helpful.

Much research is obviously needed to advance our understanding of obsessive-compulsive neurosis. The need for further psychophysiological and behavioral research of obsessive-compulsive phenomena and the functional relationship of obsessions and compulsions is apparent, and it is hoped that the material reviewed in this chapter and the proposed functional classification will encourage future research in that direction.

Assessment Tools

The preceding sections have emphasized a comprehensive approach to the study of obsessive-compulsive neurosis. In contrast, the focus of this last section will be sharply directed on measures of change of obsessive–compulsive symptoms. Thus the omission of measures of depression, personality inventories, and assessment of general adjustment from the following pages should be seen in this perspective.

Guided by controlled studies published in the last decade and which investigated a clinical population of obsessive–compulsives, we can classify assessment measures of obsessive–compulsive disorder in the following three groups: (1) self-report measures: these include symptom checklists and clinical rating scales; (2) *in vivo* behavioral measures: these include performance tests and direct observation and quantification of behavior; and (3) physiological measures: heart rate and GSR (skin conductance level and spontaneous fluctuations).

SELF-REPORT MEASURES

SYMPTOM CHECKLIST

The most commonly used symptom checklist appears to be the Leyton Obsessional Inventory (LOI), which was originated by Cooper (1970). The LOI is comprised of 69 items, of which 47 relate to obsessional symptoms and 27 to obsessive–compulsive personality traits. The questions regarding the symptoms provide a comprehensive coverage of common obsessional symptomatology with the exception of terrible and horrible obsessional thoughts and compulsive hand washing.

In addition to a total symptom score, the LOI provides a way of assessing a total resistance and interference score. Resistance refers to the degree to which the patient resists the obsessional thought or action, and as such is centrally relevant to the obsessional disorder. The interference score measures the degree of handicap the symptoms cause in the patient's everyday functioning.

Despite the fact that neither the reliability nor the validity of the LOI has been determined, a number of independent investigators have shown marked and significant pre–post differences in the symptom and interference scores (Marks *et al.*, 1975; Boersma *et al.*, 1976; Emmelkamp & Kraanen, 1977; Hackman & McLean, 1975; Foa & Goldstein, 1978).

The Lynfield Obsessional/Compulsive Questionnaire (Allen & Tune, 1975) is a 20-item variant of the LOI and is presented as a paper-and-pencil test. It also taps ruminations, which were neglected in the LOI. The patient rates each item on a five-point scale as to resistance and interference, and this yields a total resistance and interference score. The procedure, however, fails to provide a symptom score, which is a clear shortcoming. The reliability and validity of the questionnaire have not been tested and the Lynfield Questionnaire has not yet found the extensive usage that LOI enjoys.

The Maudsley Obsessional/Compulsive Inventory (MOC) is a 30-item questionnaire developed by Hodgson and Rachman (1977) as a result of their extensive experience in the assessment and treatment of obsessional disorders. The MOC provides a total score as well as four subtotals referring to each of the following types of obsessional complaints: (1) checking, (2) washing, (3) doubting, and (4) slowness. This questionnaire possesses good test–retest reliability and correlates well with total LOI scores and is sensitive to changes after treatment. Unfortunately, the questionnaire does not address obsessional ruminations.

More clinical use of the MOC should be encouraged because the inventory is short and easily administered and because total scores and scores for checking and washing are reliable. The value of the doubting and slowness scores, however, remains uncertain.

Recently Philpott (1975) has proposed another obsessive–compulsive checklist. Unlike the previous questionnaires, however, this form is completed by the therapist when interviewing the patient, and rates 62 different activities according to degree of impairment. In addition to providing a total impairment score regarding the obsessive–compulsive disorder, this checklist is an excellent interviewing aid.

CLINICAL RATING SCALES

Clinical rating scales are the most commonly used self-report method in the assessment of obsessive–compulsive disorders. The reason for their frequent use seems to stem from the ease with which they can be construed and administered and to the fact that they are sensitive to clinical improvement (Marks et al., 1975; Boersma et al., 1976; Foa & Goldstein, 1978).

Different scale ranges have been used varying from one–five- to zero–eight-point scales, but it appears that the nine-point scale is more sensitive to treatment effect than the five-point scale, at least in the case of phobias (Teasdale, Walsh, Lancashire, & Mathews,

1977). In few instances, visual analogue scales consisting of hundred-millimeter lines have been used (Levy & Meyer, 1971).

The wide variety of dimensions assessed by clinical scales indicates their extreme versatility. Thus obsessional symptoms have been rated for phobic anxiety and/or avoidance, for degree of distress felt from obsessive thoughts or rituals, for time consumed by preoccupation with obsessions or rituals, and for symptom severity. However, despite their extensive use in obsessive–compulsive neurosis, neither the reliability nor the validity of these clinical rating scales has been adequately tested.

RECORD KEEPING (DIARIES)

A somewhat less frequently used self-report method consists of asking the patient to keep an ongoing record of targeted thoughts or behaviors. Mills, Agras, Barlow, and Mills (1973) asked their patients to mark down every time they experienced the "urge" to wash their hands. They thus obtained a measure of daily frequency of this particular obsessional symptom. Boersma et al. (1976) asked their patients to note the occurrence and duration of targeted compulsive behaviors on prerecorded observation forms for a period of one week at pretreatment, posttreatment and follow-up assessments. The same procedure was used by Emmelkamp and Kraanen (1977), who also supplied mechanical counting devices and stop watches to the patients to help them in their task. Hackman and McLean (1975) asked their patients to record at the end of every half-hour in a sample day whether rituals or obsessional thoughts had or had not occurred. Thus they derived a measure of the daily frequency of symptoms.

It is surprising that frequency counts of target behaviors have been used so rarely in clinical studies. Since a major aim of therapeutic intervention is to decrease the frequency of and time consumed by obsessive–compulsive behaviors, it behooves clinicians and researchers alike to develop and refine assessment tools to measure frequency and duration of obsessive–compulsive symptoms.

In conclusion, self-report measures are practical and helpful in assessing change. However, their reliability and validity is uncertain, and changes should always be double checked with more objective measures, including corraboration by reports from the patient's environment.

BEHAVIORAL MEASURES

PERFORMANCE TESTS

Direct behavioral assessment of change in obsessive–compulsive symptoms has been reported extremely rarely. Rachman and his colleagues (Rachman, Hodgson, & Marks, 1971; Hodgson, Rachman, & Marks, 1972; Rachman, Marks, & Hodgson, 1973; Roper, Rachman, & Marks, 1975) are the only ones who have assessed their patients' approach/avoidance behavior under controlled situations. These performance tests were essentially identical to the avoidance tests commonly used in the assessment of phobias.

In their earlier studies these investigators asked their patients to undertake approximately 10 activities which they usually avoided because of their obsessions. For example, a patient with an obsessional fear of contamination from germs would be asked to touch rubbish. The researchers derived an avoidance score which consisted of the percentage of items failed. In addition, they asked their patients to rate the degree of anxiety felt while carrying out their most difficult task on a 0–100 SUDS scale. These behavioral measures revealed significant pre- and posttreatment effects.

More recently, Rachman and his colleagues (Rachman *et al.,* 1979) have slightly modified their method of administering and scoring behavioral-avoidance tests to obsessive–compulsive patients. Five tasks are chosen which usually give rise to rituals. The performance is rated 1 when executed, 0 when the task has been avoided, and gives a maximum score of 5 on performance. Discomfort in carrying out the task is rated on a zero-to-eight scale by the assessor, giving a maximum discomfort score of 40 per patient. However, there is no firm evidence that assessor rating of subjective discomfort is superior to patient ratings of same (Agras & Jacob, 1980).

Another example of a different type of performance test comes from Turner, Hersen, Bellack, and Wells, (1979). In this case the investigators were not concerned with phobic anxiety or avoidance but with ritualistic behavior per se. The patient was a 44-year-old man who had repetition compulsions (carrying on behaviors in a sequence or series of sevens) which consumed several hours of his time. Time spent on a task was targeted, and since the patient was a psychologist, time required to administer and score the WAIS was measured and showed a reduction with treatment.

Even fewer are reports of behavioral measures in the case of obsessional ruminations, an admittedly difficult undertaking often amenable only to indirect measures. The few reports have used psychophysiological measures and hence will be presented in the discussion of physiological measures.

OBJECTIVE MEASURES OF BEHAVIOR

Reported objective measures of behavioral change in obsessive-compulsive patients are extremely rare. The two most obvious reasons for this dearth in the literature seem to be that direct observation of change is both time-consuming and might require a special monitoring apparatus.

Mills *et al.* (1973) built a washing pen enclosing the only sink available in the patient's room. A cumulative recorder was connected to the underside of the gated pen and activated by the patient approaching the sink. This provided a 24-hour daily record of the frequency of handwashing. These same investigators also used video equipment to monitor the patient's bedtime ritualistic behavior. Two different methods of direct observation are reported by Turner *et al.* (1979). In the first instance, nurses and aides directly observed and recorded time spent in bathing and grooming activities on a daily basis. In the second instance, the presence or absence or ritualistic behavior was directly observed and recorded at fifteen-minute intervals on a 24-hour basis.

PHYSIOLOGICAL MEASURES

The use of physiological measures to assess change in obsessive-compulsive phenomena has been limited. An early attempt (Stern, Lipsedge, & Marks, 1973) to study treatment effect on physiological measures in 10 obsessive-compulsive patients with predominant ruminations treated with thought-stopping failed. Even in the subgroup of patients who responded clinically, changes in heart rate and GSR (conductance level and spontaneous fluctuations) could not be detected.

Boulougouris and Bassiakos (1973), in a pilot study of three obsessive-compulsive patients treated with flooding, were successful in demonstrating pre-post differences in heart rate and spontaneous fluctuations of skin conductance. (For details of their procedure,

especially the different test stimuli used, see earlier discussion in section on psychophysiological assessment).

Finally, Boulougouris *et al.* (1977), using the same procedure as
in the previous study, found significant changes in heart rate, spontaneous fluctuations of skin conductance, and maximum deflection
of skin conductance when they assessed the combined treatment effects of four different variants of flooding in 12 obsessive–compulsive
patients. However, despite the reduction in physiological arousal
after treatment, obsessive–compulsive stimuli continued to be significantly discriminated from neutral stimuli on heart rate and GSR
measures.

Concluding Remarks

It has become customary, indeed ritualistic, to end a review with
pleas and exhortations for future research in the specific field in question. Such a need obviously exists for obsessive–compulsive disorders
as well. It is hoped, however, that future researchers appreciate the
difficulties and efforts of the investigators of the past two decades.
Through their painstaking work we now have a growing understanding and a fairly good basis from which to tackle new challenges in the
study and treatment of obsessive–compulsive disorders. Most important would seem to be the development and application of precise
and comprehensive assessment procedures in clinical, phenomenological, behavioral, and physiological dimensions, to allow the emergence of new and meaningful findings.

Of particular importance are further investigations of the relationship among the three response systems: subjective, behavioral,
and physiological, since, unlike the other major anxiety-based disorder, phobia, the patterns of discordance and desynchrony are not
clear. Other investigators (see Chapter 6) have noted that different
patterns of responding among the three response systems may have
implications for treatment in that phobics with strong physiological
but weak behavioral components of fear might benefit from a different treatment approach than those with some other pattern. Since
this work is proving fruitful in the investigation of the assessment of
phobia, similar investigations with obsessive–compulsive disorders
might also have implications for treatment. This is complicated, however, by the uncertain relationship among obsessions, compulsions, or

rituals mentioned above. It the model suggested above ultimately bears some relation to reality, then functional assessment of the particular type of obsessions, compulsions, or rituals will imply a specific combination of treatments. Further development in the area of assessment is likely to have major implications for this very difficult disorder.

Based on the progress made in the past decade in the study of obsessive-compulsive disorders, the future indeed looks bright and justifiably holds promise for obsessive-compulsive patients.

References

Agras, S., & Jacob, R. Phobia: Nature and measurement. In M. Mavissakalian & D. H. Barlow (Eds.), *Phobia: Psychological and pharmacological treatment.* New York: Guilford Press, 1980.

Akhtar, S., Wig, N. N., Varma, V. K., Pershad, D., & Verma, S. K. A phenomenological analysis of symptoms in obsessive-compulsive neurosis. *British Journal of Psychiatry*, 1975, *127*, 342-348.

Allen, J. J., & Tune, G. S. The Lynfield Obsessional/Compulsive Questionnaires. *Scottish Medical Journal*, 1975, *20*, 21-24.

Beech, H. R. Ritualistic activity in obsessional patients. *Journal of Psychosomatic Research*, 1971, *15*, 417-422.

Beech, H. R., & Liddell, A. Decision making, mood states and ritualistic behavior among obsessional patients. In H. R. Beech (Ed.), *Obsessional states.* London: Methuen, 1974.

Black, A. The natural history of obsessional patients. In H. R. Beech (Ed.), *Obsessional states.* London: Methuen, 1974.

Boersma, K., Den Hengst, S., Dekker, J., & Emmelkamp, P. Exposure and response prevention in the natural environment: A comparison with obsessive-compulsive patients. *Behaviour Research and Therapy*, 1976, *14*, 19-24.

Boulougouris, J. C., & Bassiakos, L. Prolonged flooding in cases with obsessive-compulsive neurosis. *Behaviour Research and Therapy*, 1973, *11*, 227-231.

Boulougouris, J. C., Marks, I. M., & Marset, P. Superiority of flooding (implosion) to desensitisation for reducing pathological fear. *Behaviour Research and Therapy*, 1971, *9*, 7-16.

Boulougouris, J. C., Rabavilas, A. D., & Stefanis, C. Psychophysiological responses in obsessive-compulsive patients. *Behaviour Research and Therapy*, 1977, *15*, 221-230.

Bridges, P. K., Goktepe, E. O., & Maratos, J. A comparative review of patients with obsessional neurosis and with depression treated by psychosurgery. *British Journal of Psychiatry*, 1973, *123*, 663-674.

Carr, A. T. Compulsive neurosis: Two psychophysiological studies. *Bulletin of the British Psychological Society*, 1971, *24*, 256-257.

Collins, G. H. The use of parenteral and oral chloemipramine (anafranil) in the treatment of depressive states. *British Journal of Psychiatry*, 1973, *122*, 189-190.

Cooper, J. The Leyton Obsessional Inventory. *Psychological Medicine*, 1970, *1*, 48-64.

Diagnostic and statistical manual of mental disorders (3rd ed.). Washington, D.C.: American Psychiatric Association, 1980.

Emmelkamp, P. M. G., & Kraanen, J. Therapist-controlled exposure *in vivo* versus self-controlled exposure *in vivo:* A comparison with obsessive-compulsive patients. *Behaviour Research and Therapy*, 1977, *15*, 491-495.

Feighner, J. P., Robins, E., Guze, S. B., Woodruff, R. A., Winokur, G., & Muñoz, R. Diagnostic criteria for use in psychiatric research. *Archives of General Psychiatry*, 1972, *26*, 57-63.

Foa, E. B. Failure in treating obsessive-compulsive. *Behaviour Research and Therapy*, 1979, *17*, 169-176.

Foa, E. B., & Goldstein, A. Continuous exposure and complete response prevention in the treatment of obsessive-compulsive neurosis. *Behavior Therapy*, 1978, *9*, 821-829.

Foa, E. B., Steketee, G. S., & Milby, M. B. Differential effects of exposure and response prevention in obsessive-compulsive washers. *Journal of Consulting and Clinical Psychology*, 1980, *48*, 71-79.

Gittleson, N. L. The effect of obsessions on depressive psychosis. *British Journal of Psychiatry*, 1966, *112*, 253-259. (a)

Gittleson, N. L. The fate of obsessions in depressive psychosis. *British Journal of Psychiatry*, 1966, *112*, 705-708. (b)

Grayson, J. *The elicitation and habituation of orienting and defensive responses in phobic simagery and the incremental stimulus intensity affect.* Unpublished doctoral dissertation, University of Iowa, 1979.

Grayson, J., Nutter, D., & Mavissakalian, M. Psychophysiological assessment of obsessive-compulsive neurosis. *Behaviour Research and Therapy*, in press.

Hackman, A., & McLean, C. A comparison of flooding and thought stopping in the treatment of obsessional neurosis. *Behaviour Research and Therapy*, 1975, *13*, 263-269.

Hare, R. D. Cardiovascular components of orienting and defensive responses. *Psychophysiology*, 1972, *9*, 606-614.

Hare, R. D., & Blevings, G. Conditioned orienting and defensive responses. *Psychophysiology*, 1975, *12*, 289-297.

Hodgson, R. J., & Rachman, S. The effects of contamination and washing in obsessional patients. *Behaviour Research and Therapy*, 1972, *10*, 111-117.

Hodgson, R. J., & Rachman, S. Obsessional-compulsive complaints. *Behaviour Research and Therapy*, 1977, *15*, 389-395.

Hodgson, R., Rachman, S., & Marks, I. M. The treatment of chronic obsessive-compulsive neurosis: Follow-up and further findings. *Behaviour Research and Therapy*, 1972, *10*, 181-189.

Hornsveld, R. H.J., Kraaimaat, F. W., & Van Dam-Baggen, R. M. J. Anxiety/discomfort and handwashing in obsessive-compulsive and pyschiatric control patients. *Behaviour Research and Therapy*, 1979, *17*, 223-228.

Lader, M. H., & Mathews, A. M. A physiological model of phobic anxiety and desensitization. *Behaviour Research and Therapy*, 1968, *6*, 411-421.

Levy, R., & Meyer, V. Ritual prevention in obsessional patients. *Proceedings of the Royal Society of Medicine*, 1971, *64*, 1115-1120.

Lewis, A. Obsessional illness. *Acta Neuropsiquiatrica Argentinia*, 1957, *3*, 323-335.

Marks, I. M., Crowe, M., Drewe, E., Young, J., & Dewhurst, W. G. Obsessive-compulsive neurosis in identical twins. *British Journal of Psychiatry*, 1969, *115*, 991-998.

Marks, I. M., Hodgson, R., & Rachman, S. Treatment of chronic obsessive-compulsive neurosis by *in vivo* exposure. A two-year follow-up and issues in treatment. *British Journal of Psychiatry*, 1975, *127*, 349-364.

Marks, I. M., & Hudson, J. Physiological aspects of neutral and phobic imagery: Further observations. *British Journal of Psychiatry*, 1973, *122*, 567–572.

Marshall, W. K., & Micev, V. The role of intravenous clomipramine in the treatment of obsessional and phobic disorders. *Scottish Medical Journal*, 1975, *20*, 49–53.

Mathews, A. M. Psychophysiological approaches to the investigation of desensitization and related procedures. *Psychological Bulletin*, 1971, *76*, 73–91.

Mavissakalian, M. Functional classification of obsessive-compulsive phenomena. *Journal of Behavioral Assessment*, 1979, *1*, 271–279.

Mellett, P. G. The clinical problem. In H. R. Beech (Ed.), *Obsessional states*. London: Methuen, 1974.

Mills, H. L., Agras, W. S., Barlow, D. H., & Mills, J. R. Compulsive rituals treated by response prevention. *Archives of General Psychiatry*, 1973, *28*, 524–529.

Mitchell-Heggs, N., Kelly, D., & Richardson, A. Stereotactic limbic leucotomy—a follow-up at 16 months. *British Journal of Psychiatry*, 1976, *128*, 226–240.

Nutter, D., Jens, K., Mavissakalian, M. The phenomenology of obsessive-compulsive neurosis (an American study). Submitted for publication.

Philpott, R. Recent advances in the behavioural measurement of obsessional illness. Difficulties common to these and other measures. *Scottish Medical Journal*, 1975, *20*, 33–40.

Rabavilas, A. D., & Boulougouris, J. C. Physiological accompaniments of ruminations, flooding and thought-stopping in obsessive patients. *Behaviour Research and Therapy*, 1974, *12*, 239–243.

Rachman, S. Some similarities and differences between obsessional ruminations and morbid preoccupations. *Canadian Psychiatric Association Journal*, 1973, *18*,71–73.

Rachman, S. Primary obsessional slowness. *Behaviour Research and Therapy*, 1974, *12*, 9–18.

Rachman, S. The modification of obsessions: A new formulation. *Behaviour Research and Therapy*, 1976, *14*, 437–443.

Rachman, S., Cobb, J., Grey, S., MacDonald, B., Mawson, D., Sartory, G., & Stern, R. The behavioural treatment of obsessive-compulsive disorders, with and without clomipramine. *Behaviour Research and Therapy*, 1979, *17*, 465–478.

Rachman, S., & DeSilva, P. Abnormal and normal obsessions. *Behaviour Research and Therapy*, 1978, *16*, 233–248.

Rachman, S., DeSilva, P., & Roper, G. The spontaneous decay of compulsive urges. *Behaviour Research and Therapy*, 1976, *14*, 445–453.

Rachman, S., Hodgson, R., & Marks, I. M. The treatment of chronic obsessive-compulsive neurosis. *Behaviour Research and Therapy*, 1971, *9*, 237–247.

Rachman, S., Marks, I. M., & Hodgson, R. The treatment of obsessive-compulsive neurotics by modeling and flooding *in vivo*. *Behaviour Research and Therapy*, 1973, *11*, 463–471.

Rack, P. H. Clomipramine (anafranil) in the treatment of obsessional states with special reference to the Leyton Obsessional Inventory. *Journal of International Medical Research*, 1973, *1*, 397–402.

Reed, G. F. Some formal qualities of obsessional thinking. *Psychiatric Clinic*, 1968, *1*, 382–392.

Roper, G., & Rachman, S. Obsessional-compulsive checking: Experimental replication and development. *Behaviour Research and Therapy*, 1976, *14*, 25–32.

Roper, G., Rachman, S., & Hodgson, R. An experiment on obsessional checking. *Behaviour Research and Therapy*, 1973, *11*, 271–277.

Roper, G., Rachman, S., & Marks, I. Passive and participant modeling in exposure treatment of obsessive-compulsive neurotics. *Behaviour Research and Therapy*, 1975, *13*, 271–279.

Sokolov, E. *Perception and the conditioned reflex.* New York: Macmillan, 1963.

Stern, R. S., & Cobb, J. P. Phenomenology of obsessive–compulsive neurosis. *British Journal of Psychiatry,* 1978, *132,* 233–239.

Stern, R. S., Lipsedge, M. S., & Marks, I. M. Obsessive ruminations: A controlled trial of thought-stopping technique. *Behaviour Research and Therapy,* 1973, *11,* 659–662.

Teasdale, J. D., Walsh, P. A., Lancashire, M., & Mathews, A. M. Group exposure for agoraphobics: A replication study. *British Journal of Psychiatry,* 1977, *130,* 186–193.

Turner, S. M., Hersen, M., Bellack, A. S., & Wells, K. C. Behavioral treatment of obsessive–compulsive neurosis. *Behaviour Research and Therapy,* 1979, *17,* 95–106.

Van Egeren, L. F., Feather, B. W., & Hein, P. L. Desensitization of phobias: Some psychophysiological propositions. *Psychophysiology,* 1971, *8,* 213–228.

Van Renynghe de Voxvrie, G. L'anafranil (G 34586) dans l'obsession. *Acta Neurologica Belgica,* 1968, *68,* 787–792.

Walker, V. J. Explanation in obsessional neurosis. *British Journal of Psychiatry,* 1973, *123,* 675–680.

Walker, V. J., & Beech, H. R. Mood state and the ritualistic behavior of obsessional patients. *British Journal of Psychiatry,* 1969, *115,* 1261–1268.

Walton, D., & Mather, M. D. The application of learning principles to the treatment of obsessive–compulsive states in the acute and chronic phases of illness. *Behaviour Research and Therapy,* 1963, *1,* 163–174.

Waxman, D. An investigation into the use of anafranil in phobic and obsessional disorders. *Scottish Medical Journal,* 1975, *20,* 61–66.

Wolpe, J. *Psychotherapy by reciprocal inhibition.* Stanford: Stanford University Press, 1958.

Wyndowe, J., Solyom, L., & Ananth, J. Anafranil in obsessive–compulsive neurosis. *Current Therapeutic Research,* 1975, *18,* 611–617.

8

Behavioral Assessment
of Psychophysiologic Disorders

EDWARD B. BLANCHARD

The two terms "psychosomatic" and "psychophysiologic" disorders have come to be used more or less interchangeably, with the latter being the more current term. The area is replete with the philosophical problem of possible mind–body dualism; however, this chapter will not attempt to resolve that issue or explicitly take a position on that problem. Instead, it is assumed that psychological stimuli can have physiologic effects or can lead to physiologic responses. At the naive experiential level almost everyone has observed, or possibly experienced, the warming of the face in response to certain social situations which are generally labeled "embarrassing"; also almost everyone has been aware of the sweatiness of the palms and the increased rate and contractility of the heart in situations which could be labeled stressful or frightening, such as having narrowly avoided an automobile accident or in preparing to give a speech before an evaluative audience.

In psychophysiologic disorders, the physiologic response to the psychological stimuli has led to what is generally agreed upon to be a "disease" state. Thus, at a very general level, when I refer to psychophysiologic disorders, I mean those disorders in which physiologic responses are outside of the normal, adaptive, homeostatic range and instead are in the abnormal, or maladaptive, or diseased range. It is further assumed that psychological stimuli or factors have played a

Edward B. Blanchard. Department of Psychology, State University of New York at Albany, Albany, New York.

major role in this disordered physiological state either as initiators or maintainers of the disordered physiological responses.

A more technical definition of psychophysiologic disorders is provided by the now defunct DSM-II:

> 305 Psychophysiologic disorders: This group of disorders is character-ized by physical symptoms that are caused by emotional factors and in-volve a single organ system, usually under autonomic nervous system innervation. The physiological changes involved are those that normal-ly accompany certain emotional states, but in these disorders the changes are more intense and sustained. The individual may not be consciously aware of his emotional state. If there is an additional psy-chiatric disorder, it should be diagnosed separately whether or not it is presumed to contribute to the physical disorder. The specific disorders should be named and classified in one of the following categories. (p. 46)

Although reified and codified in DSM-II, psychophysiologic dis-orders did not fare as well in DSM-III. They almost disappeared from DSM-III and were relegated to the status of nondiagnosis (DSM-III, Draft, 1978, p. Q:1): "This category does not, by itself, constitute a diagnosis. Rather, it documents on Axis I the certainty with which the clinician judges psychological factors to be contributory to the in-itiation, or exacerbation of a physical disorder." The position taken by DSM-III is probably more realistic in that is is difficult to prove that "a physical symptom" is "caused by emotional factors." Whether the change in nomenclature was sparked by realism or by a desire for a better accommodation of psychiatry to the rest of medicine is not known.

Although the deemphasis by DSM-III of psychophysiologic dis-orders might lead one to infer that they no longer exist in any num-ber, this is far from the case. As data from Schwab, Fennell, and Warheit (1974) indicate, as much as half of the population suffers from some type of psychophysiologic disorder.

It is important to keep in mind the distinction between psycho-physiologic disorders and conversion disorders, or, in the terminology of DSM-III, somatoform disorders. A key feature to always keep in mind in both the assessment and treatment of psychophysiologic disorders is that there is a *real* lesion with the psychophysiologic dis-order, that there is a genuine pathophysiology, that the physiology of the individual is, in fact, disordered or outside of normal or adaptive limits.

I have found Table 1 helpful in distinguishing among several kinds of problems: psychophysiologic disorders, conversion disorders, depression, and other physical disorders. This table lists several of the dimensions on which these four classes of disorders may vary.

Examining the material in Table 1, one can begin to see some of the typical distinctions among psychophysiologic disorders, other physical disorders, and conversion disorders. To emphasize again, in the psychophysiologic disorder there is real, or genuinely disordered, physiology; there is a real lesion. The presence of a specific psychological conflict antedating the onset of the disorder is less clear-cut in the psychophysiologic disorder than in the conversion disorder. It is seen as a necessary condition in the conversion disorder. As will become more apparent later in this chapter, in the psychophysiologic disorder, rather than a single conflict, there is more likely to be a series of conflicts or an ongoing conflict which leads to the psychophysiologic disorder.

The role of a so-called "secondary gains" also distinguishes

Table 1
Differentiation of Psychophysiologic Disorders from
Hysterical Conversion Reactions

Class of disorder	Presence of specific precipitating psychological "conflict"	Presence of pathophysiology or physical lesion	Presence of "Sick role" "anxiety" or distress over symptoms	"Sick role" or presence of "secondary gains"	Removal of secondary gains leads to decrease in symptoms
Physical illness	0	+	+	+	0
Psychophysiologic disorder	0[a]	+	+	+	0
Conversion reaction	+	0	0	+ +	+
Malingering	+	0	+	+ +	+
Depression	0 or +[b]	0	+	+	0 or +[b]

[a]There is usually a long-standing conflict or series of conflicts in psychophysiologic disorders.
[b]This depends on the type of depressive disorders.

among these disorders. There are secondary gains for almost anyone in our society who adopts the "sick role" or who sees the physician for some type of disorder. Thus, for the patient with the psychophysiologic disorder there is the same level of secondary gains as for patients with other physical disorders. An important aspect to consider is that elimination of the secondary gains or the environmental reinforcement is not likely to lead to a cessation of the symptoms in the psychophysiologic disorder, whereas it may very well do that with the conversion disorder. One would not expect the blood pressure of the hypertensive patient to be decreased or the crater in the stomach lining of the ulcer patient to heal merely because solicitous concern by his or her family was removed from the patient with a psychophysiologic disorder. However, as Blanchard and Hersen (1976) have shown, extinction, or the removal of social reinforcement, can have pronounced effects on conversion disorders.

A final point I want to make here, and which I will repeatedly emphasize, is that the patient with the psychophysiologic disorder has a genuine medical disorder which upon occasion can be a genuine medical emergency. The duodenal ulcer that perforates is a medical disorder and can lead to extreme morbidity and even mortality if not treated. An obvious implication of this point is that the nonphysician therapist who opts to work with patients with psychophysiologic disorders is well advised always to work in close cooperation with the medical practitioner.

Models of Psychophysiologic Disorders

The older, more traditional model of psychophysiologic disorders is epitomized by the work of Franz Alexander and represents the application of psychoanalytic thought to psychophysiologic disorders (Alexander, 1950). This model emphasized three factors: (1) organ weakness, or a biological predisposition to develop a certain disorder, (2) a particular kind of personality type or style in line with the traditional analytic view of personality development and character types, and (3) a specific kind of psychological conflict which was viewed, of course, as being unconscious.

Alexander's work was highly influential; however, upon close empirical examination, it has not held up as a general theory or model of psychophysiologic disorders. Problems arose in that all patients with a particular disorder did not show the specified personality styles, nor did everyone with that personality style develop a particular kind of psychophysiologic disorder. Moreover, it was quite often not possible to find the specific psychological conflict, which Alexander's theory had specified, present in patients with certain kinds of disorders; conversely, patients with a particular kind of conflict did not always develop the specific kind of disorder. What remain from Alexander's monumental work are very astute clinical observations and material which can be of potential value in dealing with classes of psychophysiologic patients. Thus one may be especially on guard for certain kinds of maladaptive personality characteristics or habitual ways of interacting and for certain kinds of interpersonal conflicts within certain classes of patients, and can expect to find a higher incidence of these problems in patients with one disorder rather than the other.

Newer work illustrated by Lipowski (1977) and Weiner (1977) had indicated an acceptance of an interactive, or general systems, or biopsychosocial model of psychophysiologic disorders. Both of these major theorists pay allegiance to the insights of Alexander but emphasize the need to consider the interaction of various traditional spheres such as the biological or physiological and the psychological in understanding the etiology of psychophysiologic disorders and also as ways of leading to treatment implications for them.

Another interesting development in this field is the implication of the work of Holmes and Rahe (1967) and others who suggest that all illness may be psychophysiologic. The seminal work on the effects of stress, or life change, on illness could lead to the general conclusion that psychosocial factors, particularly life change or having to adapt to change, predispose individuals to all varieties of illness (Rahe, Floistad, Bergen, Ringdal, Gerhardt, Gunderson, & Arthur, 1974). This type of grandiose thinking, while useful in terms of medical education and reminding the practitioners of medicine to keep psychosocial factors in mind, is probably not of great heuristic value, at least in the short run. Medicine in this century has made its major advances through becoming more and more aligned with the physical sciences and through the understanding of the biochemical and physiological mechanisms involved in the normal body and in the diseased state. To throw this over for an entirely psychophysiologic approach would be foolish. However, it is of value to point out that there may be psychological "first causes" in many disease states or in the etiology of many disease states. This would be in contrast to a purely genetic or biological-determinism model. The life-change work also illustrates the potential value of the life-change score derived from Holmes and Rahe's work in the assessment of psychophysiologic disorders. Use of their scale is probably a useful adjunct in information in assessing the patient and planning treatment, as will be noted later.

In line with the theme of this volume, I will next propose a working model for psychophysiologic disorders and then, I hope, show how this model is useful in designing intervention and treatment strategies. The model could be considered a form of organ weakness model in that it looks like the diagram presented in Figure 1.

Thus in this model I accept the notion that in most, if not all, psychophysiologic disorders, there is a physiologic predisposition to develop the particular disorder. The patient with bronchial asthma tends to have an airway which is more sensitive to allergens and other materials than the normal individual. The individual with essential hypertension will tend to have a genetic loading or family history of hypertension and to begin to show elevation in blood pressure earlier than his or her peers. The individual with ulcerative colitis has a more irritable digestive track than another individual. I have thus taken as an article of faith, which is in need of further research, that most of the physiologic predispositions are due to genetic factors with which the individual is endowed.

Given this predisposed individual, the model next assumes that various types of stimuli, such as life changes, and especially interpersonal conflicts, will lead to increased physiologic arousal. This arousal

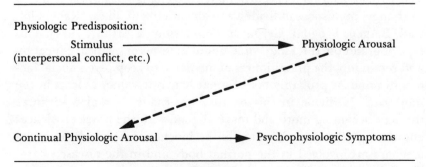

Figure 1
Model of psychophysiologic disorders.

is mediated primarily by the sympathetic nervous system, but not entirely so. Thus an implication of this model is that the headache-prone individual would be more likely to show increases in muscle tension (for the muscle-contraction headache) or increases in cranial vascular activity (for the migrainous individual). With continued arousal due either to serial conflicts or to unresolved conflicts, one finds the development of the psychophysiologic symptoms.

Assessment and the Treatment Approach

It is taken as a given that the strategies and procedures used for the assessment of a particular kind of disorder are determined in large part by the treatment procedures which are to be employed. This point has been made repeatedly in this volume and is one of its themes. Most patients suffering from psychophysiologic disorders will be treated initially by the general medical community, utilizing traditional medical approaches. Assessment within the traditional medical realm is typically a three-part affair: a history including the elicitation of symptoms, the physical examination, and laboratory diagnostic tests. The physician, having arrived at a diagnosis, will typically then implement a traditional medical treatment involving drugs and some instructions, including suggestions for modifications of behavior. To avoid either talking in vague generalities about all psychophysiologic disorders or composing a chapter equivalent to the length of this book by giving detailed descriptions for many psychophysiologic disorders, I have chosen to focus much of the remainder of this chapter around one category of psychophysiologic disorder, *headache*. It is my hope that the general principles will not be lost in the details of the example.

Thus, for the disorders which are to be an example in this chapter, headaches, the standard medical procedures involved in diagnosis would consist of a history in which the patient would describe symptoms of the headache, a physical examination with particular attention paid to the neurological examination, and various laboratory tests including, typically, a clinical EEG, skull X rays, brain scan, and possibly a CAT scan. In addition, various chemical tests would be done on blood samples.

The traditional medical treatment for headaches would then

follow the diagnostic work-up and could include the prescription of different drugs for vascular and/or muscle-contraction headaches. For the vascular headaches this would typically be an ergotamine derivative or possibly other kinds of drugs; for muscle-contraction headaches, the drug treatment might very well be some type of minor tranquilizer or muscle relaxant such as one of the benzodiazepines like Librium or Valium. For the latter category there might also be the recommendation that the individual try to relax more and not worry as much.

In addition to these two classes of headaches, which account for the vast bulk of headache complaints that physicians will attend to, there are many other possible causes of headache which could be identified by this general medical-diagnosis approach. For example, the patient could have a brain tumor which might be revealed in the EEG or in the brain scan, he or she could be suffering from other kinds of cerebral vascular disorders, from extremely elevated blood pressure, from eye strain, and other problems. Thus headache is associated with many other kinds of medical disorders. The physician, from his or her diagnostic work-up, would then implement treatment appropriate to the type of headache.

In summary, then, the physician utilizes a tripartite diagnostic schema to enable him or her to arrive at a diagnosis, and then implements treatment which would primarily involve the use of drugs and/ or surgery, with the possibility of some suggestions and instructions for behavior change.

A behavioral treatment approach, on the other hand, would of necessity emphasize some different aspects in assessment. For one thing, many of the diagnostic tools used by the physician are not readily available to the behavioral practitioner. Thus one treads on shaky ground in performing a physical examination, both because of ethical concerns and because of a lack of expertise. Secondly, many of the laboratory diagnostic procedures are not open to prescription by the nonphysician behaviorist.

It is imperative, from my point of view, for the nonphysician behaviorist to start with the physician's findings. One must always keep in mind that with psychophysiologic disorders there is real pathophysiology; there are real lesions. So for the nonphysician behaviorist involved in the assessment and treatment of psychophysiologic disorders, a close collaborative arrangement with a physician is a first order of business. If there is no formal collaborative arrangement, the behaviorist is well advised to refer the patient to his or her physician for a traditional medical work-up before embarking upon a behavioral assessment.

One of the fears which haunts me, and should haunt most non-physicians involved in the assessment and treatment of psychophysiologic disorders, is the attempt to treat, through psychological or behavioral means, headaches secondary to brain tumor. There is always the dangerous possibility of engaging in psychological treatment for a physiologic disorder which, if detected early enough, might be readily treatable by traditional medical means, but which, if treatment is delayed long enough, becomes untreatable and results in severe morbidity or mortality. Thus, if there is a first rule in behavioral assessment of psychophysiologic disorders, it is *to have the patient seen by a competent physician* first, or at least concurrently.

BEHAVIORAL ASSESSMENT PROCEDURES

Returning to my first premise that the treatment approach will determine the assessment procedures, I am assuming that within behavioral assessment and treatment of psychophysiologic disorders there are two general treatment approaches. The first approach is termed *palliative*. By this I mean, consistent with my model of psychophysiologic disorders, the treatment is intended to *reduce* the reaction or the overall level of arousal of the individual to the stressor. This approach then emphasizes *reaction* to symptoms and attempts to give the individual treatment for that reactive component.

The second treatment approach I have labeled *preventive*. In this approach the key features are (1) to teach the patient to recognize sources of conflict, or stress, and their concomitant physiologic arousal, and then (2) to learn more adaptive means of coping with them. Overall the goal is to *prevent* the excessive physiologic arousal to the conflict either through reducing or eliminating the conflicts or through very early detection of arousal and prevention of its occurrence. Since many of the conflicts tend to be interpersonal, it then follows that assessment of ability to handle and deal effectively with interpersonal conflict becomes a part of the overall assessment approach. Means for coping with the conflicts and with the subsequent psychophysiologic arousal would include various behavioral procedures as well as various cognitive procedures. These will be discussed in more detail later. A comprehensive assessment and treatment approach should, of course, use a combination of these two approaches, palliative and preventive.

More details on the behavioral treatment of psychophysiologic disorders can be found in three recent review articles (on cardiovascular disorders [Blanchard & Miller, 1977]; or general psychophysiologic disorders [Blanchard & Ahles, 1979a]; and on headaches [Blanchard, Ahles, & Shaw, 1979]). In this chapter I am excluding consideration of some disorders which have typically been subsumed under the psychophysiologic disorder category such as sexual dysfunction, which can be seen as a genitourinary disorder, and obesity and anorexia nervosa, which can be seen as gastrointestinal disorders. I am also omitting a disorder which is not easily classified but might be considered a psychophysiologic disorder of the central nervous system, namely, sleep disorders.

Actual Assessment Procedures

In this section I shall lay out some of the actual procedures used in the behavioral assessment of psychophysiologic disorders and illustrate the general principles with details from the assessment of two kinds of headaches. The organizing scheme for the behavioral assessment of psychophysiologic disorders is a tripartite model initially introduced by Lang (1968). In this model one is interested in assessing behavioral responses in three separate response modes which may or may not be highly intercorrelated. The response modes are, of course, cognitive, physiologic, and motoric.

COGNITIVE AND SELF-REPORT ASPECTS
OF ASSESSMENT

In this response mode are included not only material related to thoughts, images, attitudes, and affective statements, but also the self-report of symptoms and the patient's narrative of symptoms. A better subtitle might be "Self-Report Measures," rather than strictly cognitive ones. Thus the self-report measures include both the patient's report of cognitive and affective aspects of his disorder as well as his narrative account of motoric behavior associated with the disorder or with symptoms. The latter can, or course, be at variance with that which is observed with staged behavioral situations or in actual sampling of behavior, as will be noted later.

HISTORY

First and foremost in this area, it is necessary to obtain a good history of the patient's symptoms and disorders as well as a clear description of the phenomenology associated with the disorder. As one begins to collect this history, or narrative material, an important distinction emerges between two general classes of psychophysiologic disorders: those which are primarily episodic and are accompanied by acute symptoms which cause the patient some degree of distress, and those disorders which are more relatively chronic and are not especially noticeable to the patient.

A prime example of the episodic kind of disorder would be headache, especially migraine headache. In this instance the patient probably experiences the disorder and accompanying distress for a matter of hours to days with some frequency. There are also periods of time—days, weeks, or months—between episodes of the disorder.

The prime disorder in the latter category is essential hypertension, which has been popularly labeled "the silent killer." This label refers to the fact that patients are typically unaware of elevated blood pressure because of a lack of symptoms; however, these blood-pressure elevations, if untreated over long periods of time, can lead to major cardiovascular morbidity or mortality. Other disorders of a more chronic, nonepisodic nature include rheumatoid arthritis, cardiac arrhythmias, and some chronic pain disorders. With some forms of chronic pain and with rheumatoid arthritis, the patient does become aware of the disease because of pain and distress associated with movement. However, they are somewhat like hypertension in that these disorders tend to be present all of the time rather than being episodic.

In taking the patient's narrative history of the disorder, there are several general points one would like to cover: the age of onset and circumstances surrounding onset of the disorder, previous forms of treatment and their relative success, the circumstances surrounding the onset of an episode of the disorder, what happens at the subjective or experiential level during an attack of the disorder, the time parameters involved, and, *very importantly*, the environmental response to the patient's disorder. Also, with some disorders one is interested in the family history of the disorder. Certain psychophysiologic disorders seem to run in families or to present some evidence for genetic loading. For instance, both hypertension and vascular headaches tend to be of this type. While this information may not be of direct use in treatment planning, it is of assistance in confirming diagnosis.

Although the reasons for many of the preceding would be obvious to the experienced behavioral clinician, I will go into some detail on the foregoing list, illustrating the points with headache. The two chief points one would hope the narrative would provide are (1) a detailed description of the circumstances immediately preceding the onset of the symptomatic phase of the disorder and (2) the patient's subjective experience or phenomenology associated with the disorder. The reason for the first is fairly obvious: one is interested in learning if the onset of the disorder is related temporally with any particular environmental events. Typically, the patient will have attempted his or her own naive analysis of what leads to what, or what stimulus factors are involved in the onset of the disorder. However, this may not have been done in a very systematic fashion.

For example, I saw a 35-year-old female patient who initially complained of having chronic headaches almost every day. Further detailed questioning revealed that the headaches were present Monday through Friday and occasionally on weekends. It turned out that one could begin to make a case for her headaches being related to conflicts associated with her job. This particular simple functional analysis based on temporal contiguity had never occurred to the patient, despite the fact that she was an intelligent, well-educated nursing instructor.

Thus, one has to ask repeatedly what was going on immediately preceding the onset of the symptoms, and what had been going on the day or a few days preceding them. For some disorders, such as tension headaches, the onset of symptoms tends to follow very close in time to particularly stressful events. For other forms of disorders, including vascular headaches, the onset of the symptoms tends to be somewhat removed from the stressful situation. One upper-level male mental-health administrator who suffered from migraine headaches and who we saw, had come to recognize that the day following critical periods and situations involving interpersonal confrontation, he could expect a migraine headache.

One of the greatest aids to this type of functional analysis is the systematic diary which one can have patients keep. My own experience with numerous disorders has shown that having patients keep a small diary, typically in a 3 × 5 spiral notebook from which the pages are easily removed, can prove very helpful. (I use the same format in private practice and in clinical research projects.) With headaches, my practice has been to ask patients to rate headache intensity on a simple six-point scale four times a day, roughly at breakfast, lunch, dinner, and bedtime (Blanchard, Theobald, Williamson, Silver, & Brown, 1978). I also typically ask patients to record what kinds of medications they take. When attempting a more detailed functional analysis, I will also ask the patient to indicate what seemed to have been going on when the headache started and what was done about it. Only when the patient keeps detailed, day-by-day records does this material become especially useful. When the patient tries to recall the events of the whole preceding week, the events often tend to blend into each other. The diary thus helps to serve as a memory aid to the patient, and provides the clinician with the raw material for the behavioral analysis.

In taking the detailed history of the headache, or any other psychophysiologic disorder, one should include a careful description of the patient's phenomenology, that is, his or her description of what the headache is like at the experiential level. Additionally, the clinician is interested in the background history of the disorder, including such factors as age of patient and circumstances surrounding onset, and especially details of the circumstances surrounding diminution of the problem or exacerbation of symptoms.

This detailed history or narrative from the patient, in combination with the systematic self-report from the headache diary or some other form of diary, serves two purposes: first, it helps one to arrive at an appropriate diagnosis, and secondly, it helps one to make a functional analysis of the disorder.

Some behaviorists have been rather opposed to the whole notion of diagnosis, since it is an integral part of that terrible creature, the medical model. However, *diagnosis* and *differential diagnosis* have a place in the treatment of psychophysiologic disorders, and probably in the treatment of other disorders, if differential diagnosis leads to differential prognosis and/or differential treatment plans (Goodwin & Guze, 1979). In the case of headache, the two most common types of headache are tension or muscle-contraction or psychogenic headaches and vascular or migraine headaches. These typically can be distinguished both on the basis of the patient's narrative and description of phenomenology and from the diary.

For example, the muscle-contraction headache is typically described as dull, aching pain which starts in the back of the neck or the occipital region of the head, spreads forward bilaterally, and is experienced as a cap or band or a dull, aching tightness over the whole head. The diary will typically reveal, for the chronic tension headache sufferer, that headaches are present almost every day and that they may start at a reasonably regular time of the day and progress to somewhat higher levels during the day.

By way of contrast, the migraine headache will be described as an intense, throbbing, burning pain, usually on one side of the head and located typically inside the head behind the eye. During later stages it may spread to be bilateral and the patient may not be able to discriminate one side as being worse than the other. Migraine headache is typically episodic; therefore one should expect in the headache diary days for which headache ratings would be zero or the patient would be headache-free. Migraine headaches are typically subdivided into two groups, classical and common. In the classical migraine headache there is a definite prodromal phase which lasts several minutes and in which there are visual disturbances in the form of jagged lines or spots of lights or the like. In common migraine this prodromal phase although present physiologically, does not have a phenomenological component. Other kinds of headaches which are distinguishable by history include cluster headaches, which seem to be a form of vascular headache, but for which the patient will be headache-free, or relatively headache-free, for weeks or months. This headache-free phase is then followed by a period of days to weeks during which there will be one or more relatively brief, very intense headaches. These headaches will last for as little as a few minutes to up to an hour or so. The headaches thus occur in a cluster; hence the name.

One of the reasons for engaging in this type of diagnostic exercise is that headache is also a common concomitant of other disorders. In some instances headache is a symptom of a very severe medical disorder such as a space-occupying tumor in the cranium, subdural hematoma, or even impending stroke. The nonphysician behaviorist is thus well advised to try to be able to recognize these problems and refer the patient *immediately* to the physician. This also highlights one of the reasons for the recommendation to work closely with the physician in treating psychophysiologic disorders.

As to the justification for differential diagnosis of headaches, there are, at least within one common behavioral modality, *biofeedback,* differential treatments for different kinds of headaches. The accepted form of biofeedback treatment for muscle-contraction or tension headaches if frontal EMG biofeedback, whereas the accepted form of treatment for vascular headaches is some form of temperature biofeedback in which the patient is taught to generate a hand-warming response. Other behavioral forms of treatment, such as training in progressive relaxation, seem equally effective for both kinds of headaches. Thus there is, from the point of view of this latter treatment procedure, no need to differentiate one kind of headache from the other.

Pain and subjective discomfort are common symptoms in many psychophysiologic disorders. However, this particular symptom, pain, can be one of the most difficult to assess. Pain is entirely a subjective experience. Thus one must rely upon the patient's self-report of pain as to its presence or absence and its degree in order to know something about it. In many ways it is best to conceptualize this problem as pain-complaining behavior rather than as pain.

Another problem presented by pain is a semantic trap which our language system sets for us. We use the same kinds of words to describe our response to tissue damage such as mashing one's finger with a hammer or burning the skin with a match (for both of these we would say it hurts, or, perhaps, it hurts very much!). Likewise, we use expressions such as it hurts or it is painful, to describe the subjective experience of the death of a loved one, being in an embarrassing situation (a typical description is that it hurts). Thus we tend to use the same descriptors for both a situation in which there is real or impending tissue damage and in a situation where there is no tissue damage but much distress. Because of this, until recently there was much debate as to whether, in a particular patient, the pain was *real* or not. One way out of this problem is to disregard the issue of whether pain is real or not, by which was typically meant: Is there some form of tissue damage or something impending upon the central nervous system receptors?, and to proceed to the notion of pain-complaining behavior.

The work of Fordyce, Bonica, and their colleagues has shown that much pain-complaining behavior is under the control of environmental response to this behavior; in other words, that there is a large operant component in chronic pain-complaining behavior. One needs to keep this in mind in dealing with the complaints of pain or distress in the patient with psychophysiologic disorder such as headaches. It may well be that the complaint of headache or headache pain is as much under the control of environmental events — that is, it is an operant — as it is under the control of physiological events within the individual. For example, recent work by Epstein and Abel (1977) and by Philips (1977, 1978) has shown a marked lack of correlation between the supposed physiological substrate of tension-headache pain — sustained contraction of the muscles of the face and scalp — and the report of pain. In some individuals these two were highly correlated. However, in other individuals there was no correlation or even an inverse correlation. Methods for assessing this operant aspect of pain complaining, in headaches and in other psychophysiologic disorders, will be discussed in a later section on motoric responses. At this point it suffices to say that one should be very aware of this aspect of assessment in psychophysiologic disorders.

In other psychophysiologic disorders such as Raynaud's disease, and various GI disorders such as gastritis or colitis, pain is a typically reported symptom. Thus one can use the systematic self-report diary to keep track of pain-complaining behavior in these disorders.

The issue of pain and environmental responses to pain complaining, brings up another important aspect of the assessment of psychophysiologic disorders, the issue which has historically been called "secondary gains" and which refers to the environmental reinforcement of sick role and complaining behavior. It is very important to assess this within psychophysiologic disorders. The method of assessment, of necessity, is primarily through the patient's self-report, either in a narrative or from a systematic diary. A clinician is interested in such issues as what happens when the person has an episode of the disorder: What is the response of significant others? Can the significant others tell that the patient is experiencing an episode and is in distress? How can they tell? What happens? For example, does the chronic headache patient avoid unpleasant social situations, avoid household duties, become eligible for sick leave? All of these environmental responses may play some role, as reinforcers, in maintaining the pain-complaining behavior.

Returning to our notion that assessment is determined by treatment, and to our distinction between palliative and preventive treatments, one needs to decide among various treatment programs. If the treatment to be given to the headache is to be palliative, then either some form of relaxation training or biofeedback training is probably indicated. Even within forms of relaxation training, however, Davidson and Schwartz (1976) have indicated that, depending upon the presenting picture of the client, there are varients of relaxation training that one might want to choose. Thus for patients with more cognitive, ruminative features to their distress, Davidson and Schwartz recommend a meditative form of relaxation, such as Benson's (1975) regular elicitation of relaxation response; when there is more of a physiological aspect to the disorder, they recommend something like progressive relaxation (Jacobson, 1976).

In terms of the preventive form of treatment, one needs to identify psychosocial situations which could be leading to the headache. Pioneering work in this direction has been provided by Holroyd and Andrasik (1978) and Holroyd, Andrasick, and Westbook (1977), with a cognitive approach to tension headaches. This approach included helping individuals identify situations in which they felt an impending sense of tension, identifying their own self-statements or cognitions in the fashion of Meichenbaum and Ellis, and applying preventive or prophylactic techniques such as cognitive preevaluation and/or brief forms of relaxation to help with these situations.

Another possible aspect of preventive treatment, which can be identified through either interview or self-report measure, is difficulties in interpersonal situations, which typically go under the label of assertiveness deficits. It has been shown by Brooks and Richardson (1980) that patients with peptic ulcer disease frequently have difficulties in interpersonal conflict situations and are helped by assertiveness training. Moreoever, our overall model of psychophysiologic disorders would point to conflicts, especially interpersonal conflicts, as an immediately precipitating event for physiological arousal and symptom formation. In order to assess whether interpersonal conflicts and/or interpersonal style in such areas as assertiveness are major components of the psychophysiologic disorder, an initial screening can be obtained using any of the assertiveness inventories. Our own work with headaches has shown that there are a subset of headache patients who report themselves as underassertive on the Rathus Assertiveness Scale (Rathus, 1973). The treatment implications of this finding, consistent with Brooks and Richardson's (1980) finding with ulcer patients, are that a more thorough assessment of interpersonal competence or social skills is needed.

An assessment of social skills could take many forms, ranging from something as simple as a self-report inventory to elaborate videotaped role-played situations such as those described by Eisler, Hersen, Miller, and Blanchard (1975). In the latter, one is concerned with the specifics of the interpersonal deficit. The specifics and the specific types of situations which lead to difficulty can then be identified and treated through a standard social-skills training program.

Although interpersonal conflicts are frequently found in the individual with psychophysiologic disorders, this is not always the case. For example, patients with Raynaud's disease almost invariably suffer blanching of the fingertips and the pain of the vasospastic episode from contact with cold objects. It may also be the case, however, that they will suffer the same blanching and vasospastic pain in certain interpersonal situations. In one Raynaud's patient whom I treated reasonably successfully with temperature biofeedback training, keeping a diary helped this patient to identify situations in which vasospastic episodes occurred. We found that they were related to intensely competitive situations such as playing tennis, as well as to interpersonal conflict situations with a supervisor and to the patient's father. The temperature biofeedback training was useful in helping this patient to reduce the overall frequency of Raynaud's attacks. However, additional counseling, including some social-skills training, was needed to help the patient identify more adaptive ways of dealing with the interpersonal conflict situations. In the latter instance, then, the focus of treatment moved from the palliative approach to a more preventive approach by helping the patient to find more adaptive ways of dealing with the conflict situations, thus preventing the occurrence of the Raynaud's episode rather than relying upon a method of palliating the symptomatic response once it had occurred.

In taking a history from a patient with psychophysiologic disorders, I have found it useful to inquire about potential problems within a number of areas. Thus I routinely inquire, if the patient is married or involved in some type of intimate relationship, about any difficulties in this relationship. I also inquire about difficulties with other family members and with supervisors. The reason for these inquiries is that a number of patients have not identified these situations as stressful or tension-producing or as being related to their symptom, even when they are. Others, for whatever reason, seem reluctant to bring up these issues when they are presenting for treatment of a specific psychophysiologic problem. Thus good clinical practice would seem to dictate screening the common areas of interpersonal conflict to see if there are problems in these areas and if they are at all related to the psychophysiologic disorder.

PHYSIOLOGIC ASPECTS OF ASSESSMENT

Although one might expect that physiologic aspects of assessment would play a major role in the behavioral assessment of psychophysiologic disorders, such is not quite the case. Even though there is a moderate and growing literature on the use of physiologic assessment in these disorders, for the most part, as noted above, systematic self-report has been the primary assessment vehicle.

There are three general ways in which physiologic measures have been used as part of a behavioral assessment package in the treatment of psychophysiologic disorders: (1) It has been fairly routine to obtain basal, or resting, levels of a variety of physiologic responses from psychophysiologic patients before and after treatment, or even as a matter of ongoing treatment. The psychophysiologic responses which have typically been measured include as heart rate, blood pressure, peripheral temperature, muscle-tension level is measured by the EMG, and so on. (2) The assessment of the ability of the patient to exercise instructional control or, in the language of Blanchard and Epstein (1978), self-control, of the physiologic response in the absence of any type of aid such as biofeedback has also been frequently reported. (3) A third way in which physiologic measures have been used in this assessment scheme has been to monitor the patient's physiologic response to various kinds of stressors. This seems a very promising avenue of research but has received only limited attention thus far.

Basal levels of physiologic responses may constitute the primary measure in certain psychophysiologic disorders for either defining the individual as "disordered" or for assessing treatment progress in disorders such as essential hypertension. Thus the measurement of blood pressure at intervals throughout the baseline and treatment may be the primary indication of treatment effectiveness. Certainly this is the physician's standard method of assessment in the management of essential hypertension. For many other psychophysiologic disorders, other kinds of basal physiologic measures may be taken, such as fingertip temperature in patients with Raynaud's disease.

The usefulness of basal physiologic measures is illustrated in a case report of the treatment of Raynaud's disease by Blanchard and

Haynes (1975). In this study, the primary patient datum reported was the ability of the patient to show in-session changes in fingertip temperature. However, during each session an in-session basal recording of temperature was made. Over the course of treatment these basal temperatures, obtained prior to the biofeedback training, showed a significant shift from before treatment to after treatment, indicating an increase in basal, or resting, hand temperature which was maintained throughout the follow-up. This physiologic change helped confirm the patient's self-report as noted in the study.

Returning to our detailed assessment of headaches, we routinely monitor basal response levels for muscle activity of the frontalis and of the forearm flexor muscle. We also measure peripheral fingertip temperature of all headache patients, seeking to learn if the basal temperature of migranous patients is lower. We also monitor basal levels of vasomotor activity for the temporal artery, following the leads of Price and Tursky (1976). Other workers in the headache field have monitored not only frontalis muscle activity but also muscle activity in other head and neck groups such as the temporalis and the trapezius (Philips, 1977), and have found greater deviations from normal at these sites than at the frontal monitoring site.

If the treatment to be used for a psychophysiologic disorder involves biofeedback, it becomes an easy matter to obtain ongoing physiologic response measures as a part of treatment. We routinely use a four-part measurement scheme in our biofeedback treatment sessions. This includes, after an adequate adaptation period, a basal recording phase of three to five minutes which can be conceived of as an in-session baseline. During this time the patient is typically asked to relax. This provides the ongoing measure of basal physiological response described above. Next we routinely include an initial self-control phase. In this phase we ask the patient to try to emit the physiologic response of interest before the biofeedback training phase in order for us to determine how well the patient is acquiring the ability to make the change in the absence of feedback. (This provides ongoing data for the second point mentioned above.) The difference between the in-session baseline and the first self-control phase provides a ready index of this aspect of treatment.

We then provide the biofeedback treatment and obtain measures of physiologic response during that segment of the session. We typically close the session with another self-control phase at the end of biofeedback treatment to see how well the patient can continue to control the response once the feedback has been discontinued. The ability to continue to maintain the response in the absence of feedback, even for this brief five-minute period, again provides evidence that the patient is learning a degree of control of his or her physiology which can be carried over into the natural environment.

To be a bit redundant, if the behavioral-treatment approach is to be through biofeedback, then one certainly must be interested in being able to determine if there has been a change in the physiologic response as a result of treatment. Many psychophysiologic disorders, especially headaches, present primarily as a self-report phenomenon. Showing that there has been a basal physiologic change which accompanies change in report of pain provides more presumptive evidence that the effect is due to the physiologic change rather than merely to a change in self-report responding.

This point, as well as the utility of the four-part session described above, was illustrated in a case report of causalgia, a form of chronic pain, treated with temperature biofeedback by Blanchard (1979). The patient had two distinctly different pain sites, the arm which had the causalgia, and pain in the back. The temperature biofeedback was specifically designed to help the pain in the arm. Over a series of treatment sessions, as the patient learned control of the hand-warming response and began to practice it regularly, the report of pain in the arm decreased. This decrease was coincident with the patient's achieving some degree of self-control of his hand-warming response as shown in basal recordings and in self-control recordings of temperature. The self-report of pain in the back was not particularly affected. The concordant change in arm-pain complaint and physiologic response and the absence of a correlated change in another type of pain complaining (back) provided evidence that the changes were specific to the particular treatment rather than a generalized change in response set.

For headache patients, particularly those suffering from tension headaches, the current picture is quite mixed in regard to the role of muscle tension, particularly frontalis tension, in headaches. For example, Epstein and Abel (1977) found an almost total lack of correspondence between patients' self-report of head pain during treatment sessions, and from an ongoing headache diary, with muscle-tension levels. For approximately one-third of their patients there was very good correspondence; however, for the other two-thirds there was either no correspondence and almost an inverse relation. This report, along with that of Philips (1977) began to cast doubt on the role of muscle-tension control in the EMG biofeedback treatment of tension headaches.

To sum up, if one is interested in teaching self-control or self-regulation of a physiologic response, which is the essence of most biofeedback treatments, then to make strong causal statements about the acquisition of this ability, one should assess the ability of the patient to control the response prior to the training itself and then in an ongoing manner throughout treatment. Finding an increase in the ability to control the response for which training was given becomes corroborating evidence that the physiologic training was responsible for improvement. In our assessment of headache patients we routinely assess their ability to warm their hands and to relax their foreheads prior to any particular treatment. It would also be of interest to include similar psychophysiologic measurements of basal level and self-control level for other forms of behavioral treatment of headaches and other kinds of responses.

As mentioned above, the third use of assessment of physiologic responses involves measuring the response of the individual patient to specific forms of stress. One postulate of my model of psychophysiologic disorders, and a consistent opinion in this sphere (Cohen, Rickles, & McArthur, 1978), is that the patient tends to be overresponsive in the organ system, or response system, which becomes symptomatic. One way of assessing the validity of this postulate would be to measure the response under basal, or resting, conditions and under stress conditions. This can be done fairly easily in the laboratory.

The practical values of measuring physiologic response to standard stressors are twofold: (1) to use changes in stress responsivity as an index of change and (2) to determine what response system should be targeted for treatment. The first use of stress responsivity has been very well illustrated by Patel (1975), in treating hypertensive patients with a combination of biofeedback and relaxation training. Both treated and untreated groups of patients were exposed to the cold pressor test before and after treatment; furthermore, both blood-pressure acceleration and recovery time for return to basal levels were measured. After treatment it was found that the treated patients were much less responsive to this physiologic stressor in terms of both reduced blood pressure acceleration and more rapid return to basal conditions.

Surwit, Pilon, and Fenton (1978) have also used this form of assessment. In a study of treatment of Raynaud's disease they included response to a cold challenge as a pre-post assessment for such patients. Interestingly, those patients successfully treated showed less decrease in hand temperature and more ability to maintain a stable basal temperature in the cold challenge as a result of treatment.

In our headache research we routinely measure psychophysiologic responses under three different kinds of stress conditions: mental arithmetic—which proves to be a mild stressor for many subjects—a physiologic stressor—in our case, the cold pressor test—and then with an imagined stressor. A fairly routine assessment for borderline hypertension has been the cold pressor test. In this test, in which the patient sticks a hand or foot in very cold water, typically ice water, one finds among borderline hypertensive of potential hypertensive patients a much greater pressor response, or increase in blood pressure, than in the general population.

Although physiologic response to imagined stressors has not been widely utilized in the behavioral assessment of psychophysiologic disorders, it seems to have some promise. Vaughn, Pall, and Haynes (1977) have reported a higher level of frontal EMG responding among patients with chronic tension headaches than a group of controls. Moreover, Price and Tursky (1976) have reported a higher degree of temporal artery vasomotor responding among patients with migraine headaches than among the matched controls.

Another example of the use of physiologic responding to imagined stressors is provided by a case treated by Blanchard and Abel (1976). The patient, a woman who suffered from episodic tachycardia, showed a specific acceleration of cardiac rate to specific imagined scenes. The progress of the biofeedback treatment was assessed through measuring change in heart rate from basal, or resting, levels to imagined levels before and after treatment. The successful treatment was documented by the ability of the patient to control heart rate when confronted by the stressful imagery at the end of treatment. A similar scheme would seem plausible for other kinds of psychophysiologic disorders.

One aspect of the physiologic assessment of psychophysiologic disorders which has not yet been widely used to date, is the possible prediction, from psychophysiologic measures, of potential response to various behavioral treatments. It is tempting to speculate that if the person had numerous responses monitored, including those of particular interest or involvement in the psychophysiologic disorder under basal, self-control, and stressful conditions prior to treatment, the degree of responsivity of various response systems could provide a clue to an appropriate treatment strategy. Certainly increased responsivity to stressors could provide confirmatory evidence of this patient's self-report. Moreover, there are those (Budzynski, Stoyva, Adler, & Mullaney, 1973) who believe that the frontal EMG biofeedback treatment for tension headache is only appropriate when the patient shows a high basal level of muscle tension. The low correlations found by some between change in EMG and self-report of headache pain may result from using patients who present with low basal levels of EMG. (However, Epstein and Abel [1977] also found this lack of correlation among a group of patients selected to have high resting levels of EMG.)

Measuring physiologic responses under resting conditions and in response to stress would certainly seem consistent with our model of psychophysiologic disorders. Such assessment would allow one to determine easily whether an overall palliative form of treatment in terms of lowered physiologic arousal in a number of systems seemed appropriate of whether palliation within a particular response system seemed more appropriate. Finally, the regular monitoring of physiologic responsivity to stress throughout treatment could serve as confirmatory evidence of systematic self-report of improved control in stressful situations: the "faking" of this kind of response is more difficult than that of self-report.

One other aspect of the physiologic monitoring which should be noted is that with the proliferation of biofeedback training equipment, it becomes possible to use this device as a monitor, for "feedback" to the clinician, of patients' physiologic responses. Earlier, the routine inclusion of a basal monitoring period within the biofeedback treatment session was recommended. Thus the clinician with biofeedback equipment as part of his or her armentarium has the ability to monitor these responses.

Along this line, Burish and Horn (1979) have recently reported some interesting findings. Using biofeedback equipment as monitors, they have shown that forehead EMG is not a particularly responsive overall measure to threat or anxiety arousal, while fingertip temperature is. In a series of two studies they found that fingertip temperature showed a drop under a threat of physical harm and under threat of social evaluative, whereas frontal EMG was not different from basal levels within these conditions; moreover, it did not differ between the threatened groups and the controls. This would lead one to conclude that fingertip temperature, or peripheral vascular response, might be more indicative of emotional response than frontal EMG.

It is also possible to use biofeedback equipment to monitor physiologic response during an interview. This has been reported by Toomin and Toomin (1975), using skin resistance level and skin resistance response. It has long been known that some patients will overtly deny the emotional content of material but will show heightened physiologic responses to it. This is, of course, the whole basis of the lie detector, or deception detection, enterprise. For the cooperative patient, the increased physiologic responding, as shown by biofeedback equipment, could make it easier for the clinician to identify potential conflict areas and make it a more public or less readily deniable event for the patient. The efficacy of these ideas has yet to be explored in a systematic fashion, however.

It is possible, of course, to obtain measures of physiologic responses while the patient is in his or her natural environment in order to check on self-report. Although this involves a fairly elaborate technology, it is available and has been used. There is equipment available to monitor blood pressure and cardiac rate in the natural environment. These responses can be automatically monitored and recorded on a small tape recorder which the patient carries. Moreover, through the use of liquid crystals, it becomes possible for patients to monitor their own fingertip temperature in their natural environment. We have used this procedure with Raynaud's patients to help them more clearly identify situations in which they were beginning to experience vasospasm and hand cooling. A clever use of *in vivo* physiologic monitoring has been described by Rugh for patients with bruxism and TMJ problems (Rugh & Solberg, 1974). A small EMG biofeedback device was attached to facial musculature, with feedback provided through an earphone. The patient was then able to monitor more carefully his level of jaw clenching and facial-muscle tensing in his natural environment.

In these applications, the assessment and treatment can tend to blend as the patient becomes more aware of arousing environmental events and begins to take steps to alter them. This blend can work both ways, as mentioned above, in that biofeedback treatment equipment used for treatment can also become an assessment device for the practicing clinician to record basal levels and self-control levels on an ongoing basis. This particular policy is recommended.

In conclusion, one can see that physiologic responses are beginning to play an increasingly important role in the assessment and treatment of psychophysiologic disorders.

ASSESSMENT OF MOTORIC RESPONSES

Assessment of motor behavior typically plays a very small role in the overall behavioral assessment of psychophysiologic disorders. This is in contrast to other kinds of disorders described in this volume. Moreover, the assessment of motor behavior is, for the most part, second-hand, in that it relies primarily upon the patient's self-report and secondarily upon information from the patient's diary, which is also a form of self-report. The reason for the small role is that motor behaviors typically play a small part in psychophysiologic disorders.

The chief motor behavior assessed in headaches is analgesic medication consumption. This information is routinely recorded in the headache diary. Coyne, Sargent, Segerson, and Obourn (1976) have developed an ordinal scale for scaling relative potencies of a wide variety of analgesic drugs. With this scale it is possible to construct a medication index in which potency of drugs times dosage yields a medication score. This score tends to be sensitive to improvement as shown in studies by Blanchard *et al.* (1978) and others.

A similar use of systematic self-report of medication consumption has been found to be a useful measure in the treatment of ulcer disease by Brooks and Richardson (1980). In this instance, consumption of antacid, measured by the number of empty medication bottles returned, was used as an ongoing measure of outcome. In fact, in the general area of medication compliance, a standard assessment technique has been the "pill count" (Sackett & Haynes, 1977). In this procedure, patients are asked to bring the container of their medication with them at each periodic visit. Knowing the number of pills or tablets dispensed, it is possible, through counting the remaining number, to obtain a gross indication of how well patients have complied with the regimen. This measure is, of course, open to much manipulation and faking by the patient: the patient can throw away pills or remove pills from the bottle in order to appear compliant; also, there is no record from the periodic pill count of how well the patient has adhered on a day-to-day basis. In a study of how mothers complied in dispensing medication to their children with otitis media (middle-ear infection), we found that the amount of medication dispensed could vary by as much as 100% in terms of the mothers' measuring of liquid medication for their children.

In a recent study of the psychological treatment of patients suffering from rheumatoid arthritis, Achterberg, McGraw, and Lawlis (1979) introduced another behavioral assessment procedure: a standard range-of-motion test. It proved sensitive to improvement from pretreatment to posttreatment.

Another kind of information which typically comes from systematic self-report and has been found useful in assessing the progress of chronic pain patients, is a report of activities and a report of "up" versus "down" time. The patient can be asked to record on an hourly basis what he or she is doing, and inferences can be drawn from this. Moreover, the patient can be asked to record lengths of time in which he or she is sitting or lying in order to rest. It has been found by Fordyce (1976) that "up time" versus "down time" tends to increase with overall clinical improvement.

Thus the assessment of motoric behavior, though less well advanced than systematic self-report in psychophysiologic disorders, plays a part in assessment. Its use will probably require more ingenuity by the individual clinician because of the present lack in the literature.

Two other points should be considered in discussing assessment of motoric responses in psychophysiologic disorders: (1) In the diary one can also ask the patient to systematically record activities which are avoided or foregone. This can give some indication of the response cost associated with episodes of the psychophysiologic disorder. Again, this is a self-report measure, but of motor behavior rather than cognitive or affective behavior. (2) A second type of motor behavior which could come either from a systematic questioning or from self-report are periodic visits to physicians and days hospitalized. These particular motor behaviors become especially important because of the financial cost to the patient and to society. Brooks and Richardson (1980) have showed this type of measure to be sensitive to a behavioral treatment program over a three-year follow-up of ulcer patients.

It is possible to try to obtain corroborating evidence from some of the self-reporting of motor behavior in a patient's diary. Thus the spouse or a significant other or family member can be asked also to keep a diary of "up time" versus "down time" for the chronic-pain patient. This has been used by Fordyce (1976). It is also possible to use systematic observation by another to time-sample the patient's activities and to monitor medication. One would probably resort to this only when the patient's self-report did not seem consistent with other clinical observations. It is also fraught with all of the difficulties in obtaining corroborating evidence from others found in the smoking literature and elsewhere.

Future Directions

The field of the behavioral treatment of psychophysiologic disorders is fairly young; approximately 90% of the published research has appeared since 1970. An obvious implication of this fact is that formal work on the behavioral assessment of psychophysiologic disorders is even younger. To the best of my knowledge, this chapter represents the first attempt to deal with the topic systematically.

I have attempted to outline an assessment scheme for psychophysiologic disorders and also to survey actual procedures. The assessment model, of course, is not new but rather has been the mainstay of behavioral assessment.

I expect to see the assessment aspects of the behavioral approach to psychophysiologic disorders grow hand in hand with the treatment aspects. One obvious direction of growth will be the adoption, and probably subsequent improvement, of assessment procedures used in traditional medical approaches. The use by Achterberg *et al.* (1979) of range-of-motion data in their study of arthritics is an example. I would also expect those operating within a behavioral approach to contribute new assessment methodology which will be integrated into standard medical assessment, especially as the impact of the behavioral medicine movement is felt.

Two areas of future research and development direction stand out: the first is the area of *prediction*. In many psychophysiologic disorders, one finds specific behavioral treatments effective with between 30% and 80% of a sample. For example, in the treatment of migraine headache, relaxation training leads to about 50% improvement, while temperature biofeedback results in about 55% improvement (Blanchard & Ahles, 1979b). There is thus a great need to be able to predict, on an a priori basis, who is a good candidate for a particular behavioral treatment and who is not. Certainly the treatment response variance is there. To make such prediction, one will need a large number of patients who are all treated in the same way. One will also need a wide-ranging predictor battery. Then, using strictly empirical procedures, one could develop a statistical prediction scheme.

The battery for this type of work would probably include all of the varieties of assessment information which have been described in this chapter, and possibly more. We might be forced back to some of the more traditional psychological assessment devices, such as the MMPI, and also to examine biochemical and physiologic data obtained by the physician. Only future research will tell.

The second aspect also involves prediction but is related to the prediction and ongoing assessment of drug–behavior interactions. I suspect that we will gradually see a marriage of therapies in which the psychophysiologic disorder is treated by a combination of behavior-change procedures and drugs. For example, one might attempt to optimize (at the low end) the dosage of antihypertensive medication by combining it with relaxation training and diet modification. An optimal drug dose might, in such combination therapy, be much lower, with fewer side effects.

The field of the interaction of behavioral treatment and drug treatment is new, but clearly seems a direction of the future. Behavioral assessment in combination with standard medical assessment will probably play a vital role in this marriage.

ACKNOWLEDGMENT

Preparation of this manuscript was supported in part by Grant NS-15235-01 from the National Institute of Neurological and Communicative Disorders and Stroke.

References

Achterberg, J., McGraw, P., & Lawlis, G. F. *Rheumatoid arthritis: A study of relaxation and temperature biofeedback training as adjunctive therapy.* Unpublished manuscript, Department of Physical Medicine and Rehabilitation, University of Texas Health Sciences Center at Dallas, 1979.

Alexander, F. *Psychosomatic medicine.* New York: W. W. Norton, 1950.

Benson, H. *The relaxation response.* New York: William Morrow, 1975.

Blanchard, E. B. A case study of the use of temperature biofeedback in the treatment of chronic pain due to causalgia. *Biofeedback and Self-Regulation*, 1979, *4*, 183-188.

Blanchard, E. B., & Abel, G. G. An experimental case study of the biofeedback treatment of a rape-induced psychophysiological cardiovasular disorder. *Behavior Therapy*, 1976, *7*, 113-119.

Blanchard, E. B., & Ahles, T. A. Behavioral treatment of psychophysical disorders. *Behavior Modification*, 1979, *3*, 518-549.(a)

Blanchard, E. B., & Ahles, T. A. *The relaxation factor in migraine treatment.* Paper presented at a symposium, Biological Basis for Pharmacological and Biofeedback Treatment of Migraine, Texas Research Institute of Mental Sciences, Houston, December 1979.(b)

Blanchard, E. B., Ahles, T. A., & Shaw, E. R. Behavioral treatment of headaches. In M. Hersen, R. M. Eisler, & P. M. Miller (Eds.), *Progress in behavior modification* (Vol. 8). New York: Academic Press, 1979.

Blanchard, E. B., & Epstein, L. H. *A biofeedback primer.* Reading, MA: Addison-Wesley, 1978.

Blanchard, E. B., & Haynes, M. R. Biofeedback treatment of a case of Raynaud's disease. *Journal of Behavior Therapy and Experimental Psychiatry*, 1975, *6*, 230-234.

Blanchard, E. B., & Hersen, M. Behavioral treatment of hysterical neurosis: Symptom substitution and symptom return reconsidered. *Psychiatry*, 1976, *39*, 118-129.

Blanchard, E. B., & Miller, S. T. Psychological treatment of cardiovascular disease. *Archives of General Psychiatry*, 1977, *34*, 1402-1413.

Blanchard, E. B., Theobald, D. E., Williamson, D. A., Silver, B. V., & Brown, D. A. Temperature biofeedback in the treatment of migraine headaches. *Archives of General Psychiatry*, 1978, *35*, 581-588.

Brooks, G. R., & Richardson, F. C. Emotional skills training: A treatment program for duodenal ulcer. *Behavior Therapy*, 1980, *11*.

Budzynski, T. H., Stoyva, J. M., Adler, C. S., & Mullaney, D. J. EMG biofeedback and tension headache: A controlled outcome study. *Psychosomatic Medicine*, 1973, *6*, 509-514.

Burish, T. G., & Horn, P. W. An evaluation of frontal EMG as an index of general arousal. *Behavior Therapy*, 1979, *10*, 137-147.

Cohen, M. J., Rickles, W. H., & McArthur, D. L. Evidence for physiological response stereotypy in migraine headache. *Psychosomatic Medicine*, 1978, *40*, 344-354.

Coyne, L., Sargent, J., Segerson, J., & Obourn, R. Relative potency scale for analgesic drugs: Use of psychophysical procedures with clinical judgments.. *Headache*, 1976, *16*, 70-71

Davidson, R. J., & Schwartz, G. E. The psychobiology of relaxation and related states: A multi-process theory. In D. J. Mostofsky (Ed.), *Behavior control in modification of physiological activity*. New York: Prentice-Hall, 1976.

Diagnostic and statistical manual of mental disorders (2nd ed.). Washington, D.C.: American Psychiatric Association, 1968.

Diagnostic and statistical manual of mental disorders (3rd ed.) (draft). Washington, D.C.: American Psychiatric Association, 1978.

Eisler, R. M., Hersen, M., Miller, P. M., & Blanchard, E. B. Situational determinants of assertive behavior. *Journal of Consulting and Clinical Psychology*, 1975, *43*, 330-340.

Epstein, L. H., & Abel, G. G. An analysis of biofeedback training effects for tension headache patients. *Behavior Therapy*, 1977, *8*, 37-47.

Fordyce, W. *Behavioral methods for chronic pain and illness.* St. Louis: Mosby, 1976.

Goodwin, D. W., & Guze, S. B. *Psychiatric diagnosis* (2nd ed.). New York: Oxford University Press, 1979.

Holmes, T. H., & Rahe, R. H. The social readjustment rating scale. *Journal of Psychosomatic Research,* 1967, *11,* 213.

Holroyd, K. A., & Andrasik, F. Coping and the self-control of chronic tension headache. *Journal of Consulting and Clinical Psychology,* 1978, *46,* 1036–1045.

Holroyd, K. A., Andrasik, F., & Westbrook, T. Cognitive control of tension headache. *Cognitive Therapy and Research,* 1977, *1,* 121–133.

Jacobson, E. *You must relax* (5th ed.). New York: McGraw-Hill, 1976.

Lang, P. J. Fear reduction and fear behavior: Problems in treating a construct. In J. M. Shlien (Ed.), *Research in psychotherapy* (Vol. 3). Washington, D.C.: American Psychological Association, 1968.

Lipowski, Z. J. Psychosomatic medicine in the seventies: An overview. *American Journal of Psychiatry,* 1977, *134,* 233–244.

Patel, C. H. Yoga and biofeedback in the management of "stress" in hypertensive patients. *Clinical Science and Molecular Medicine,* 1975, *48,* 171–174.

Philips, C. The modification of tension headache pain using EMG biofeedback. *Behaviour Research and Therapy,* 1977, *15,* 119–129.

Philips, C. Tension headache: Theoretical problems. *Behaviour Research and Therapy,* 1978, *16,* 249–261.

Price, K. P., & Tursky, B. Vascular reactivity of migraineurs and non-migraineurs: A comparison of responses to self-control procedures. *Headache,* 1976, *16,* 210–217.

Rahe, R. H., Floistad, I., Bergen, T., Ringdal, R., Gerhardt, R., Gunderson, R. J., & Arthur, R. J. A model of life changes and illness research. *Archives of General Psychiatry,* 1974, *31,* 172–180.

Rathus, S. A. A 30-item schedule for assessing assertive behavior. *Behavior Therapy,* 1973, *4,* 398–406.

Rugh, J. D., & Solberg, W. K. The identification of stressful stimuli in natural environments using a portable biofeedback unit. Proceedings of the Biofeedback Research Society, fifth annual meeting, Colorado Springs, 1974.

Sackett, D. L., & Haynes, R. B. (Eds.). *Compiance with therapeutic regimens.* Baltimore: Johns Hopkins University Press, 1977.

Schwab, J. J., Fennell, E. B., & Warheit, G. T. The epidemiology of psychosomatic disorders. *Psychosomatics,* 1974, *15,* 88–93.

Surwit, R. S., Pilon, R. N., & Fenton, C. H. Behavioral treatment of Raynaud's disease. *Journal of Behavioral Medicine,* 1978, *1,* 323–336.

Toomin, M. K., & Toomin, H. GSR biofeedback in psychotherapy: Some clinical observations. *Psychotherapy: Theory, Research and Practice,* 1975, *12,* 33–38.

Vaughn, R., Pall, M. L., & Haynes, S. N. Frontalis EMG response to stress in subjects with frequent muscle-contraction headaches. *Headache,* 1977, *16,* 313–317.

Weiner, H. *Psychobiology and human disease.* New York: Elsevier, 1977.

CHAPTER

9

Assessment of Alcohol Abuse

PETER M. MILLER

Substance Abuse

The abuse of alcohol and drugs represents a widespread social and health problem throughout the United States. Alcohol is by far the most abused drug in our society. Approximately 90 million Americans drink alcohol, with nine million considered to be alcoholics (Department of Health, Education, and Welfare, 1978). Abuse is generally defined as regular, excessive use of a chemical substance that significantly interferes with optimum social, marital, occupational, emotional, or health functioning (Miller & Eisler, 1977). While this chapter will focus primarily on the abusive use of alcohol, the general principles of assessment can be applied to any addictive habit pattern.

Behavioral assessment of substance abuse is an essential element of treatment and research on addictions. Adequate objective assessment is necessary for several reasons. Clinically, behavioral assessment provides a baseline from which treatment goals and techniques can be planned. Assessment of quantity/frequency patterns of use together with social, marital, occupational, and physiologic functioning provides the clinician with a total picture of the patient's prob-

Peter M. Miller. Sea Pines Behavioral Institute, Sea Pines Plantation, Hilton Head Island, South Carolina.

lem. In addition, behavioral assessment provides an objective means of evaluating the effectiveness of treatment programs. Techniques of behavioral assessment of drinking behaviors also have proved invaluable in behavioral alcoholism research. Such procedures allow an investigator to study the relationship between drinking and a whole host of specific social, psychological and physiologic variables. For example, Marlatt, Demming, and Reid (1973) examined the concept of "loss of control" by means of a novel taste-test measure of drinking. This term refers to the theoretical notion that once an alcoholic consumes even a small amount of alcohol, he will automatically lose all control and continue to drink to excess. The assumption is that this phenomenon is somehow physiologically related to the "disease" of alcoholism. In order to study loss of control in a controlled laboratory environment, Marlatt *et al.* (1973) developed a taste-rating task. Subjects were presented with several beverages and asked to rate their tastes on various dimensions. The assessment of drinking was surreptitious since subjects were unaware that the total amount of beverage consumed was being measured. Half of the subjects were led to believe that the beverages contained alcohol while the other half were told that the drinks were nonalcoholic. Half of the subjects in each instructional condition were given alcoholic beverages and half were provided with nonalcoholic beverages. The results demonstrated that the amount of alcohol consumed was significantly related to the instructional set. That is, if subjects thought they were drinking alcohol, they consumed more beverage, whether or not they were actually drinking alcohol. Thus, alcohol itself did not trigger loss of control. The authors discussed these findings in terms of the importance of cognitive variables in determining loss-of-control drinking. The taste-test assessment provided a simple and objective means of measuring drinking behavior in a laboratory setting. Such assessment procedures have provided the mechanism for a more detailed analysis of several major theoretical notions regarding alcohol use and abuse.

Framework for Alcohol Assessment

Behavioral assessment must be considered within the total framework of current knowledge regarding the etiology of alcoholism. That is, *what* to measure must be determined, based on those factors that are most relevant to the development and maintenance of alcohol abuse.

Miller and Eisler (1977) stress the necessity of differentiating between precipitating and maintaining etiological factors in reference to both assessment and treatment. They give the example of a middle-aged housewife who is experiencing marital difficulties and begins to drink to relieve tension and worry. She and her husband obtain a divorce and her drinking increases. Drinking is now generalized and occurs in response to any stressful emotional experience. Being intoxicated relieves anxiety and enables her to escape from stressful circumstances. Once drinking increases to a daily frequency, early morning drinking is reinforced by escape or avoidance of the agitation and hangover resulting from the previous evening's drinking. Daily excessive drinking begins to change her life-style so that she associates exclusively with other women who drink to excess. Her "drinking buddies" become a closely knit group serving to encourage and reinforce alcohol abuse. At this point in time the original precipitating factor involved in her excessive drinking—namely, tension resulting from marital problems—is no longer present. Assessing her level of anxiety in relation to close emotional encounters would hardly provide an accurate evaluation of her drinking problem. This is not to say that interpersonal anxiety is totally irrelevant. It is simply low on the list of current factors influencing drinking. An assessment of peer approval, encouragement, and recognition—that is, maintaining factors—must be included.

Assessment of maintaining factors is based on a functional relationship between (1) drinking behavior (2) stimulus-control variables, and (3) outcome variables. Within a social learning framework, abusive drinking is a function of the relationship among these factors at any point in time. A detailed assessment of antecedent events, cognitive expectations, and consequent events can lead to an understanding of the mechanisms controlling drinking behavior.

Stimulus-control variables are antecedent cues or "triggers" in the environment that set the occasion for excessive drinking. One of the most basic antecedent influences is situational in nature. That is, beer advertisements, the sight of the local neighborhood bar, or being exposed to someone consuming a favorite alcoholic beverage can trigger a drinking episode. Social influences can also precipitate alcohol consumption. These include social pressure from friends to have "one more for the road," a critical comment from an employer, or a sarcastic remark regarding drinking from a spouse. Drinking in relation to these social stimuli seems to be partially a function of the alcoholic's inability to deal directly and assertively with others (Miller & Eisler, 1977).

Social influences can be more subtle. Several investigators (Cutler & Storm, 1975; Rosenbluth, Nathan, & Lawson, 1978) have reported that in bar settings, drinkers in groups consume more alcohol than drinkers who are alone or with one other person. These social influences appear to be different for women than men (Rosenbluth *et al.*, 1978). Men tend to drink more alcohol and drink at a faster rate when with other men than when with women. Women, however, drink more in the company of men than when they are with women. This social modeling effect has been noted by several investigators. Caudill and Marlatt (1975), for example, studied the effects of social influences on a group of heavily drinking college students. Subjects were divided into three modeling conditions: high-consumption model, low-consumption model, and a no-model control condition. In addition, half of the students in each group were exposed to an argumentative social interaction with the model prior to the drinking task. The other half interacted with a warm, friendly model. All subjects participated in a taste-rating task in which they were requested to rate the taste of three types of wine. In the high-consumption modeling condition, subjects performed the drinking task in the presence of a confederate subject who drank the equivalent of a full bottle of wine in 15 minutes. In the low consumption modeling condition, the model limited his drinking to 100 ml in fifteen minutes. Subjects exposed to the high-consumption model drank significantly more wine than subjects exposed to the low-consumption or no-model condition. The prior argumentative or warm social interaction did not affect consumption.

Emotional factors as antecedents to drinking are not clear-cut. Early behavioral formulations of alcoholism stressed the importance of anxiety as a cue for abusive drinking. This "tension-reduction hypothesis" was based primarily on animal experimentation and anecdotal evidence from human experience. After an extensive review of the literature in this area, Cappel and Herman (1972) concluded that evidence to support the tension-reduction hypothesis is lacking and that this notion does not offer a valid explanation of abusive drinking patterns. In fact, Nathan and O'Brien (1971) found alcoholics to be *more* anxious, depressed, and pathological after drinking. More recent studies investigating the relationship between emotional arousal and alcohol consumption have been contradictory. Higgins and Marlatt (1975) found no relationship between anxiety arousal and drinking, while Miller, Hersen, Eisler, and Hilsman (1974) found a significant one. One reason for contradictions appears to be related to the complex nature of stress and factors associated with it. Anxiety in relation to alcohol seems related to such variables as characteristics of the individual, type of stress (e.g., interpersonal or environmental), and the context in which stress occurs (Allman, Taylor, & Nathan, 1972).

Correlations between other mood states such as depression, anger, boredom, and restlessness have been reported, although the causative influence of mood states is unclear (Miller, 1979). For example, depression could be either a cause or an effect of excessive drinking. From an assessment standpoint, Miller (1976) suggests that it is more productive to evaluate the nature of specific social–emotional situations preceding excessive drinking than to examine anxiety as a general trait.

Cognitive factors are not only important in triggering alcohol abuse in their own right but also interact with other antecedents to determine their influence. For example, the effects of mood on drinking and vice versa seem primarily due to expectancy factors as opposed to the actual content of the beverage. For example, Wilson and Abrams (1977) examined the effects of alcohol on social anxiety, physiologic arousal, and expectancy factors. Social drinkers were given either vodka and tonic or tonic alone. Half of the subjects in each group were told they were receiving alcohol and half were told they were receiving tonic alone. The results indicated that subjects who *believed* they had consumed alcohol, whether or not they actually had consumed an alcoholic drink, showed less anxiety in response to an anxiety-provoking social situation than those who believed they drank only tonic. Expectancies not only affected self-reports of anxiety but also a physiologic measure of arousal (heart rate).

As mentioned earlier, another characteristic in which cognitive factors influence drinking is via what is known as the loss-of-control phenomenon. Marlatt *et al.* (1973) have demonstrated that continued alcohol consumption beyond the first drink is a function of an individual's expectations and beliefs, and *not* whether he has consumed an alcoholic or nonalcoholic beverage. Thus, the important aspect of this phenomenon involves whether or not the drinker *believes* that he has no control over his drinking.

Belief in loss of control can serve to foster and maintain abusive drinking patterns. Caddy, Goldman, and Huebner (1976) found that heavily drinking college students were more likely to believe that alcoholism is an inherited disease outside of an individual's control than were light or moderate drinkers. He also found that alcoholics were more likely to believe this idea than either social drinkers or abstinent individuals. Similarly, Sobell, Sobell, and Christelman (1972) found that as many as 67% of alcoholics believe that if they have one drink, they will continue drinking to the point of intoxication.

Another cognitive influence on drinking is related to positive expected consequences of excessive drinking. For example, Lang, Goeckner, Adesso, and Marlatt (1975) investigated the effects of expectancy on aggressive behavior after drinking. Clinically, many alcoholics ascribe their uninhibited expression of emotions after drinking to the physiologic effects of alcohol. Lang *et al.* (1975) indicated that the consumption of alcohol per se had no significant influence on aggressive behavior. However, if the subjects believed they had been consuming alcohol, even if they had not, they behaved in a more aggressive manner. In a similar study, Wilson and Lawson (1976) demonstrated the same phenomenon with sexual behavior and alcohol use. They studied male social drinkers, using a balanced placebo design. Some subjects were led to believe they had consumed alcohol while others were not. False breathalyzer feedback was provided to some subjects to enhance the credibility of the expectancy manipulation. Sexual response to erotic films was assessed via changes in penile tumescence as measured by a strain gauge apparatus. Results indicated that alcohol itself had no effect on sexual arousal. As with other studies on alcohol and expectancy, subjects who believed they had consumed alcohol showed a more significant sexual response than those who believed they were consuming a nonalcoholic beverage.

It is interesting to note that expectancy factors seem to play less of a role in the relationship between alcohol and sexual behavior in females. Wilson and Lawson (1978) found decreases in physiologically measured sexual arousal in women as a function of alcohol intake. These decreases were directly related to dose rather than cognitive factors. Self-reports of sexual arousal, however, *increased* after alcohol consumption and were related to expectancy factors.

General attitudes toward alcohol appear related to an individual's drinking pattern. Cahalan (1970) has found that the extent of drinking varies with age, sex, religion, socioeconomic status, education, occupation, residence, and ethnic background. The amount an individual drinks appears related to the beliefs he or she holds about alcohol, which are provided via these demographic influences. For example, the small number of problem drinkers in the Jewish popuation seems linked to their belief that alcohol usage is part of an institutional set of behaviors strongly related to religion and culture. Attitudinal expectations of drinking excessively or under circumstances outside of prescribed family and religious ones involve negative consequences such as social censure and criticism.

Cahalan (1970) also found that individuals who express more favorable attitudes toward drinking tend to be heavier drinkers than those who express neutral or more negative attitudes. Abstainers and light drinkers are less likely to exaggerate the positive effects of alcohol. Cahalan also found that attitudes, beliefs, and expectations are the strongest predictors of drinking behavior. Although it is not possible to make causal assumption based on attitudinal–behavioral correlations, favorable attitudes toward drinking were found to precede alcohol-related problems more often than these problems preceded a favorable attitude.

In addition to expectancies, Miller (1979) has discussed the influence of specific self-defeating thoughts on alcohol use and abuse. Clinically, thoughts such as the following appear to precipitate excessive drinking:

"Why should I have to quit drinking? It's not fair!"

"I have too many problems to quit. I'm tense and depressed. It wouldn't be good for me to quit."

"If it weren't for my job, I'd quit drinking tomorrow. I have to drink with my customers or I'd lose some of my accounts."

Unfortunately, very little controlled experimentation of even systematic clinical evaluations are available in this area. In the area of excessive eating, Mahoney and Mahoney (1976) have reported that changes in perfectionistic standards (e.g., "I'll never eat another piece of bread for the rest of my life"), negative beliefs, and self-defeating private monologues were extremely important in determining 12-month success in a behavioral weight-control program. More detailed attention to such cognitive influences in the field of alcoholism is warranted. Unfortunately, few assessment instruments have been developed to assess all of these cognitive antecedents. At present, the clinician must rely primarily on self-monitoring data for this information. This technique is described later in this chapter.

Thus, behavioral assessment should be multimodal and aim at the following target areas: (1) consummatory behavior, (2) physiologic monitoring and health, (3) social–psychological functioning, (4) motivation, (5) life problems correlated with abuse, and (6) specific therapeutic procedures employed by the patient. The following description of methods used to assess these areas is meant to provide an overview of a range of possible techniques. Neither the clinician nor the researcher would use all of these procedures since one must consider practical issues of time, patient compliance, and overall cost effectiveness. However, each of the seven major areas should be assessed even at some minimal level.

Consummatory Behavior

Several methods of evaluating alcohol or drug abuse per se are available. Several analogue procedures have been developed, although these are currently used more for research rather than clinical assessment and evaluation. Self-monitoring and direct observation of drinking by relatives and friends are the most prevalent clinical procedures.

ANALOGUE MEASURES

Analogue measures include operant systems, taste-rating tasks, and simulated-environment methods. Each of these procedures was originally developed to provide a more objective way of studying the elements of drinking behavior and consumption and antecedent and consequent events.

In an operant assessment system, alcohol is made contingent on a simple motor response such as lever pressing. Number or patterning of responses is a quantitative index of the reinforcement values of alcohol. For example, Nathan and O'Brien (1971) used an operant assessment procedure to study alcohol consumption and social behavior among inpatient chronic alcoholics. Their patients earned points for their lever pressing which were exchangeable for either alcohol or opportunity for social interaction. The assessment method provided a quantitative means of comparing the relative reinforcement value of alcohol versus social isolation. An operant system would allow for the comparison of the personal value of a number of reinforcers such as alcohol versus cigarettes or alcohol versus marijuana.

Data from operant assessment tasks may also be predictive of response to treatment. Miller, Hersen, Eisler, and Elkin (1974) assessed alcoholics prior to treatment on an operant assessment procedure. Patients received three 10 minute sessions during which lever pressing was reinforced with alcohol. Relationships between number of lever presses and later clinical outcome in a behavioral treatment program were analyzed. Patients who responded poorly to treatment had a mean number of responses of 2116, while the mean for the successes was only 1176. Thus, a higher operant rate was indicative of poor treatment prognosis.

The taste-rating task is an analogue drinking measure that is a more surreptitious measure of alcohol consumption (Marlatt et al., 1973; Miller & Hersen, 1972). During this assessment, patients are provided with several alcoholic and nonalcoholic beverages. They are provided with a rating sheet and asked to rate the tastes of each beverage on several dimensions (e.g., weak, strong). After a specified period of time (usually 10 to 15 minutes), the task is completed. After the patient leaves the room the exact amount of alcoholic versus nonalcoholic beverage consumed is calculated. This taste test has been used in basic behavioral research (Marlatt et al., 1973) and as part of an assessment of therapeutic effectiveness. For example, Miller, Hersen, Eisler, and Hemphill (1973) used a taste-rating task to evaluate the effects of electrical aversion conditioning with 30 chronic alcoholics. Aversion therapy was administered over a ten-day period with a total of 500 conditioning trials. A pseudoconditioning control group received the same procedure, except that mild shocks that were barely perceptible were substituted for aversive shocks. A third group of patients received insight-oriented group psychotherapy. All patients' drinking was assessed before and after treatment via a taste test. On the basis of reduction in total amount of alcohol consumed during this task, no significant differences were found among the three groups. Approximately one-third of patients in each of the groups decreased their drinking by more than 50%. In this study the taste test provided a quantitative measure of drinking behavior in the treatment setting itself. Certainly if drinking is not reduced immediately subsequent to treatment, longer-term clinical effects could not be expected. In fact, one of the advantages of analogue measures is that they allow the clinician to evaluate treatment easily and quickly so that other therapeutic strategies can be applied if necessary. Otherwise, the clinician must wait days or weeks to determine if drinking in the natural environment has decreased.

A final analogue method for assessing drinking consists of simulated environments. Essentially, the patient's typical drinking environment is reproduced in the treatment setting. Direct observations of drinking patterns can then be obtained. Typical settings include bars, living rooms, and party situations. Schaefer, Sobell, and Mills (1971) and Mills, Sobell, and Schaefer (1971) converted a hospital dayroom into a cocktail lounge complete with padded bar, dimmed lighting, and bartender. Patients were allowed access to this setting at specified times and observers recorded (1) number of drinks ordered, (2) types of drinks ordered, (3) size of sips, and (4) pace of drinking. Miller, Becker, Foy, and Wooten (1976) used a living-room setting since their patients were from rural southern areas and reported drinking mostly at home. These settings can be monitored via closed-circuit television to provide detailed analyses of drinking patterns. In addition to evaluating treatment effectiveness with this method, it is also useful in analyzing specific factors influencing drinking behavior. For example, Foy and Simon (1978) evaluated the drinking behavior of 30 chronic alcoholics in a simulated living-room setting. Patients' preferred beverages were made available and they were instructed to drink as they usually do in the natural environment. All drinking sessions were videotaped. During half of the assessments session, patients were alone, and during half they drank with two other alcoholics. This assessment procedure allowed a detailed analysis of number of sips, sip magnitude, intersip interval, and amount of alcohol consumed as a function of social context. Results indicated that these alcoholics subjects drank in a similar manner whether they were alone or with others. It may be, however, that social drinkers respond differently in this regard. Indeed, when observed in a barroom setting, young social drinkers drink more alcohol in groups than when alone (Rosenbluth, Nathan, & Lawson, 1978). In any event, simulated environments can be used as a valuable adjunct to the total clinical assessment process.

SELF-MONITORING

Probably the most practical method of assessing drinking behavior is simply to ask the patient to report on his or her drinking in a systematic fashion. Self-monitoring forms such as the Alcohol Intake Sheet developed by Sobell and Sobell (1973) provide a vehicle for such assessment. This form represents essentially a drinking diary, and provides space for such entries as date, specific type of alcohol consumed, time of day, and place where drink was consumed. Patients keep a continuous daily record of drinking prior to, during, and after treatment. Various other categories can be added, such as thoughts and feelings associated with drinking. In addition to providing assessment data per se, Sobell and Sobell (1973) note that this technique also helps to make the alcoholic aware of his or her drinking patterns and promotes discussion of situations, thoughts, and feelings associated with drinking.

The reliability and validity of these self-monitoring records must be assessed when possible. Monitoring of the patient's drinking behavior by friends and relatives is one method of assessing the accuracy of self-reports. These informants, however, must be carefully selected to insure objective reporting. An overly emotional spouse can not only provide invalid reports of his or her partner's drinking, but his or her observations may serve as antecedents for drinking episodes.

It is interesting to note that Maisto, Sobell, and Sobell (1979) found that alcoholics' self-reports and collateral reports of their drinking were highly correlated. The correlation was highest when patients were mostly abstinent or mostly intoxicated, and lowest when drinking was more limited. When differences in reports did occur, patients reported fewer "drunk" days and hospitalizations, and jail days than did relatives or friends. Generally these researchers found that alcoholics provide fairly reliable reports of their drinking, and that gathering data from collateral informants is an effective method of corroborating self-reports.

In addition to specific day-to-day drinking data, drinking inventories can provide a self-report means of obtaining an overall picture of the patient's drinking pattern. Marlatt's (1977) Drinking Profile is a detailed questionnaire emphasizing a functional analysis of the antecedents and consequences of drinking behavior. Questions relate to early development of drinking patterns, current drinking habits, factors associated with drinking, drinking locations, attitudes and expectations regarding alcohol use, reasons for drinking, effects of drinking, motivation to change, and treatment-outcome expectancies. The combination of this profile with self-monitoring data and information from relatives can provide a great deal of clinically relevant assessment information.

Physiologic Monitoring and Health

Physiologic measures correlated with drinking behavior provide an objective means of assessing drinking patterns. Analysis of blood/alcohol concentration is the most direct method of this type. In fact, blood/alcohol concentration is probably a better index of overall impairment than number of drinks consumed. This is particularly true for females, whose response to alcohol varies considerably as a function of phase of menstrual cycle (Jones & Jones, 1976). Blood/alcohol concentration can be obtained via direct blood samples or by means of a breathalyzer. These latter devices are more practical and correlate highly (.95) with blood tests (Dubowski, 1975). The simple portable screening devices are less accurate, however.

Breathalyzers have been used to provide pretreatment baseline information on drinking and to assess treatment effectiveness. For example, Miller (1975) used random breath tests to evaluate the effectiveness of a behavioral intervention program for chronic Skid Row alcoholics. Twenty alcoholics served as subjects, with ten receiving behavioral intervention and ten serving as the control group. The behavioral intervention was implemented by social service agencies and missions located in the deteriorated downtown area of the city. The behavioral intervention group received the services of these agencies (clothing, shelter, food, cigarettes, job consulting) on a contingent basis. That is, goods and services were provided only if blood/alcohol concentrations remained very low. Evidence of intoxication on any breath test resulted in a five-day suspension of eligibility for services. The control group received services on the usual noncontingent basis offered by these agencies. In this study, the breathalyzer assessments not only assisted in the analysis of the results but also was an integral part of the contingency management procedure. In fact, with this behavioral treatment method, an objective, reliable assessment technique on which to base contingencies is crucial. In the present study the breathalyzer assessment indicated the superiority of the behavioral intervention with blood/alcohol concentrations decreasing from .05% before treatment to .002% after treatment.

Breath analyses have also been used to assess an individual's ability to estimate his or her own blood/alcohol level. This ability appears to be important in developing controlled, responsible drinking skills (Nathan, 1978). Further, this ability is lacking in alcoholics and its assessment may provide a method of screening alcoholic individuals (Lansky, Nathan, & Lawson, 1978). To assess this ability, patients are requested to estimate their blood/alcohol level periodically while they are consuming fixed amounts of alcohol. Patients are instructed to focus on specific emotional and physiologic experiences (e.g., feelings of warmth, relaxation, numbness, tingling sensations) associated with specific blood/alcohol levels. Breath tests provide a means of feedback on accuracy of estimates and a method of evaluating the patients in learning this skill.

Other physiologic–health factors correlated with alcohol abuse can also be assessed. For example, liver-function studies given prior to treatment and at follow-up sessions can assist in the overall assessment and corroborate self-reports of drinking.

Social–Emotional Functioning

Behavioral assessment of social–emotional responses has focused on the following techniques: (1) self- and others' reports, (2) behavioral inventories, and (3) videotaped interactions.

SELF- AND OTHERS' REPORTS

Specific methods of self-monitoring various behavior patterns have been described in detail (Ciminero, Nelson, & Lipinski, 1977). Basically, monitoring social–emotional patterns is similar to monitoring drinking behavior. Miller and Mastria (1977) have discussed the utility of instructing patients to maintain "behavioral diaries" of social behaviors. Patients record number and types of social interactions, duration of each interaction, interpersonal problems, and responses to interpersonal problems. Monitoring might focus on work, family interactions, or friendships. Emphasis is placed on situations that trigger cravings to drink or trigger drinking episodes.

As with drinking behavior, reliability checks by friends or relatives provide a method of corroborating self-report data. These observations can be in the form of "diaries" or on a weekly or monthly basis with the aid of a social-interaction rating scale such as the Katz Adjustment Scale (Katz & Lyerly, 1963).

Self-monitoring must be simplified and limited to a few discrete problem areas, or patients will have difficulty in providing the data. Azrin (1976) has used global, discrete categories such as time spent away from home to ease the burden of self-monitoring for alcoholics and their spouses.

INVENTORIES

Behavioral inventories used with alcoholics have focused on the assessment of assertiveness, marital interactions, and emotional functioning.

Several inventories are available for the assessment of assertiveness, although the one developed by Gambrill and Richey (1975) has several advantages. This inventory consists of 40 specific behaviors (e.g., resist sales pressure, request the return of a borrowed item, compliment a friend). The scale provides information on (1) the patient's degree of discomfort in dealing with each situation, (2) the probability of his or her engaging in that behavior, and (3) specific situations that the client acknowledges as problems. In addition, the scale measures both negative assertiveness (i.e., the expression of anger, disagreement, criticism) and positive assertiveness (the expression of affectional or complimentary remarks). Such inventories are easily administered and can provide valuable information for the establishment of treatment goals.

Although several marital inventories are available (Weiss & Margolin, 1977), Azrin, Naster, and Jones (1973) have developed a simple qustionnaire known as the Marital Happiness Scale. This scale contains ten separate marital areas, including (1) household responsibilities, (2) child rearing, (3) social activities, (4) money, (5) communication, (6) sex, (7) occupational or academic progress, (8) personal independence, (9) spouse independence, and (10) general happiness. Patients rate themselves on each dimension on a ten-point scale.

VIDEOTAPED RATINGS AND BEHAVIOR

Behavioral assessment using ratings of videotaped samples of behavior has been used extensively, particularly when social-skills training and behavioral marital counseling are part of the treatment regime. Such assessment provides a baseline from which to judge the extent of the social interactional deficits. Miller (1976) also notes that this provides corroboration of self-report data on social behavior. The necessity for videotaped behavioral samples was illustrated in a study by Miller and Eisler (1977). The assertiveness of alcoholic and nonalcoholic psychiatric patients was assessed by a self-report questionnaire and by behavioral ratings of videotaped responses to role-played interpersonal encounters. Both positive and negative assertiveness was assessed. On the self-report measure, alcoholics rated themselves as being significantly more assertive than nonalcoholics. Generally they rated themselves as very assertive individuals. However, both alcoholics and nonalcoholics were lacking in assertive skills based on the behavioral ratings. This discrepancy between self-reports and actual behavior was particularly evident when assessing negative assertiveness. Thus, simply using self-monitoring or self-reports on questionnaires may provide inaccurate information, and possibly suggest a faulty treatment plan.

Behavioral assessment using videotaping is relatively simple and has been described in detail elsewhere (Hersen & Bellack, 1977). Basically, a sample of the patient's interpersonal behavior is videotaped and then rated on specific dimensions. Samples can be structured or unstructured. Assertive behavior samples are structured in such a way that specific scenes are presented and the patient role-plays his or her responses with one of the treatment or research staff members. A study by Foy, Miller, Eisler, and O'Toole (1976) provides an example of this approach. Patients included three chronic alcoholics who had difficulty dealing with social pressure to take a drink. Inability to refuse drinks when pressured, frequently precipitated drinking episodes. As part of the initial behavioral assessment, patients were requested to role-play scenes in which two treatment staff members (acting as "drinking buddies") attempted to talk him or her into having a drink. Each scene was described with the "pushers" then using various arguments to tempt the patient. An example of such a scene follows: "You are driving home from work with a friend. You've both had a stressful day. As you pass the local tavern he says, 'Hey, George, let's stop in here for a couple of quick beers!' " Social pressure included such statements as, "Come on, one beer won't hurt you"; "What kind of a man are you!" "We've had a rough day. We deserve it. Besides it'll calm you down."

Patients' responses were videotaped and rated on the following dimensions; (1) eye contact, (2) affect, (3) requesting a change in the other person's behavior (e.g., "You could help me out a lot by never offering me a drink again"), (4) offering an alternative (e.g., "No, I don't want a beer but I'd love a cup of coffee"), and (5) changing the subject. Treatment consisted of assertiveness training using behavioral rehearsal, instructions, feedback, and videotaped modeling of appropriate responses. Ratings of videotaped responses provided a daily assessment of the progress of training. This assessment was also used at follow-up to corroborate reports that these drink-refusal skills had been maintained over time.

Videotaped behavioral assessment of marital behaviors in alcoholics often involves a more unstructured behavioral sample. Alcoholics and their spouses can be videotaped while freely interacting in a simulated living room environment. Behavior can be rated on such dimensions as speech duration, eye contact, references to drinking, nagging, or positive affectional statements (Eisler, Miller, Hersen, & Alford, 1974). This technique has been used frequently in descriptive experimental analyses of alcoholics' marital interactions. Hersen, Miller, and Eisler (1973) evaluated the behavioral interactions of four alcoholics and their wives, using a videotaped assessment system. Couples were monitored via a closed-circuit television system for 24 minutes. During the first and third six-minute intervals, couples were requested to discuss any topic of their choosing, while during the second and fourth intervals, they were to discuss the husband's alcohol problem. Subsequent to these interactions, two observers independently rated each six-minute behavioral sample of the dimension of (1) duration of looking and (2) duration of speech. Mean percentage of agreement between raters ranged from 95% to 100%. These high levels of agreement are typical of these assessments, particularly when raters are well trained and behavior being rated is simple and discrete. Results indicated that wives looked more at their husbands than husbands looked at their wives during all phases of the study. Wives' looking increased dramatically when the husband's drinking behavior was being discussed. Speech duration remained constant throughout all phases. The investigators theorized that the wives' differential attention through eye contact may be reinforcing alcohol-related speech patterns and extinguishing more appropriate, productive conversation.

In a therapeutic setting, videotaped assessments can provide a means of giving feedback to patients on the specifics of their marital interactions. For example, Miller (1978) used such assessments to increase awareness of verbal and nonverbal reinforcers in marital counseling with an alcoholic and his wife. In the same study, home videotape recordings were also used to assess interaction in a naturalistic setting. The alcoholic and his spouse were instructed, on two separate occasions, to record mealtime interaction at home. These tapes were rated for number of interruptions, number of positive comments, and number of requests for the partner to change his or her behavior. Ratings indicated that the husband spoke little during the tapings. The wife, however, not only dominated the conversation but interrupted her husband 30 times in a 40-minute taped session.

Although these assessment procedures seem a bit artificial, patients adjust well to them and, with proper instruction and explanation, are very cooperative. An initial five- to ten-minute warm-up period is often necessary to accustom patients to the equipment and environment.

Motivational Behaviors

Motivation is a ubiquitous term that is used extensively in reference to alcoholics and their treatment. Few clinicians or researchers have discussed the assessment of this factor, especially within a behavioral framework. One aspect of motivation might involve the patients' expectations regarding the likelihood of their success in treatment. As such, Marlatt's (1977) Drinking Profile, which was described earlier, provides for an assessment of these expectancies. The patient is simply requested to estimate his or her chances of a successful treatment outcome on a ten-point scale, with "1" being little or no chance and "10" being an excellent chance. While this procedure is rather simplistic, it can provide a means of evaluating changes in "motivation" over time. Investigations regarding the predictive value of this procedure are needed.

In addition, motivation refers to a set of behaviors that either increase or decrease the probability of a successful treatment outcome. For example, motivation might consist of (1) frequency of treatment-directed or change-directed statements (e.g. "I want to stop drinking" as opposed to "I'm not sure if I want to stop drinking"), (2) frequency of admissions regarding the extent of drinking problems, (3) frequency of treatment sessions attended, and (4) frequency of compliance with therapeutic instructions (e.g., "I would like you to keep a written record of your drinking behavior"). In regard to the final behavior, Pomerleau, Adkins, and Pertschuk (1978) found that compliance with instructions to keep written records of cigarette consumption was highly related to success in a smoking clinic. Thus, motivation is a general summary term which, when broken down into its component parts, can be readily assessed within a behavioral framework.

Life Problems Associated with Drinking

Chronic abusive drinking is correlated with other life-problem behaviors related to employment, school, or the criminal justice system. Such factors as conflict with the law and job instability have been related to heavy drinking (McCance & McCance, 1969) at treatment follow-up. Voegtlin and Broz (1949) found that 71% of alcoholic patients with a stable work record remained abstinent after alcoholic treatment, while only 21% of unemployed patients were abstinent. By assessing behaviors in these areas the clinician or researcher can obtain an indirect index of drinking behavior. The assumption is that it is unlikely that an individual can drink excessively and avoid life problems of this nature.

These problems can be assessed by obtaining information on number of arrests or hospitalizations for alcohol-related reasons. Some investigators have assessed number of days in a hospital or jail within a specified period of time (usually 6 or 12 months). This information can be obtained by the patient, his or her relatives, or local hospitals and law-enforcement agencies. The latter approach, of course, involves obtaining the patient's full written consent and permission.

Employment status in terms of type of job, number of job changes, number of days worked, number of days late for work, and work performance can be assessed via self-reports from patients or periodic reports from employers. To corroborate self-report data, paycheck stubs provide an objective means of assessing job stability.

Cahalan (1970) reports the use of an alcohol problems questionnaire which assesses a number of problem areas. This instrument covers the following categories: (1) frequent intoxication, (2) binge drinking, (3) symptomatic drinking, (4) physiologic dependence, (5) problems with spouse or relatives, (6) problems with neighbors or friends, (7) job problems, (8) problems with the law, police, or accidents, (9) health, (10) financial problems, and (11) belligerence associated with drinking.

Sobell, Maisto, Sobell, and Cooper (1979) found that alcoholics' reports of alcohol-related incarcerations and their drinking-problem histories were highly reliable even when they were reporting on incidents over the previous twelve months.

Specific Therapeutic Procedures Used by Patients

An essential area of assessment after treatment is completed involves the evaluation of the patient's use of therapeutic modalities. Unfortunately, such an analysis has been lacking in the alcoholism treatment literature. Even behavioral clinicians who pride themselves on detailed evaluation of results have disregarded this aspect of assessment. This assessment is important in order to determine if success is associated with the actual use of therapeutic procedures. Clinicians frequently assume that a patient's success after going through an alcoholism program is indeed due to the treatment procedures used in that program. This assumption may be a faulty one. For example, let us suppose that after learning methods of relaxation and stress management, a patient successfully remained abstinent for twelve months. It would be tempting to attribute this change in drinking to the stress-management training. If, however, the patient reported that he or she never used any of the stress techniques learned, we would not be able to attribute that success to our therapeutic procedures. Seldom do clinicians assess this area. In fact, most emphasis is placed on factors precipitating failure—that is, drinking episodes—rather than on episodes of self-control.

Another related factor that must be assessed is the number and types of treatment programs to which the patient is exposed. If, during follow-up after a behavioral treatment program, a successful patient attends Alcoholics Anonymous meetings on a weekly basis, his or her success could be due to the behavioral treatment, AA, or a combination of both. On the other hand, if the clinician fails to assess participation in other treatment programs, he or she may falsely attribute success to his or her treatment alone. That treatment may, indeed, be the effective ingredient in success, but controlled experimentation would be needed to evaluate that possibility.

A framework for assessing alcoholic patients' use of therapeutic procedures is found in the obesity literature. Recently, the evaluation of behavior-modification weight-control programs has included an analysis of patients' use of habit-change techniques. In spite of the vast number of studies extolling the virtues of behavior modification in the treatment of obesity, several investigators have found no relationship between the actual implementation of behavioral techniques and weight loss (Bellack, Rozensky, & Schwartz, 1974; Brownell, Heckerman, Westlake, Hayes, & Monti, 1978; Miller & Simms, 1979; Stalones, Johnson, & Christ, 1978). To be more specific, the behavioral techniques that were not related to outcome were stimulus-control procedures (e.g., keeping a daily written record of eating; breaking associations between eating and non-food-related activities). It is interesting to note that such procedures have been considered to be the backbone of behavioral weight-control treatments (Stuart & Davis, 1972). Brownell and Stunkard (1978) concluded that weight loss in behavioral programs may be a function of factors other than those prescribed in treatment. Indeed, recent reports indicate that the most relevant variables involved in behavior change were not even being assessed. For example, Stalones, Johnson, and Christ (1978) found a significant relationship between regularly scheduled aerobic exercise and weight loss at one-year follow-up contacts. Exercise and physical activity are seldom assessed in behavioral weight-control or alcoholism programs. Such activities are generally dismissed by clinicians as being much too simplistic to be related to changes in addictive habit patterns. In spit of this fact, Gary and Guthrie (1972) reported improvements in alcoholics' self-esteem, anxiety, sleeping patterns, and cardiovascular condition as a function of a daily physical fitness program in which patients jogged one mile per day. In addition, an annual Alcoholics Olympics is held each year in California to promote running as a method of maintaining sobriety.

Studies (Brownell et al., 1978; Mahoney & Mahoney, 1976) have also indicated that social support by family members is positively related to weight-loss maintenance. Family and peer support must be evaluated in detail rather than simply assessing its presence or absence. For example, Miller and Sims (1979) assessed patients' use of social skills designed to obtain optimum support from their family members. Patients were asked about the frequency of occasions on which they refused offers of alcohol or food and in which they instructed family and friends on ways of being more supportive.

Patients should be routinely evaluated as to their frequency and extent of use of specific behavioral procedures. Thus, how often and under what circumstances does the client practice relaxation training, self-management skills, or self-reinforcement? This type of assessment would provide valuable information on the nature of treatment programs and is especially needed at this stage in our knowledge about alcohol-abuse treatment.

Special Assessment Problems with Female Drinkers

Recent research on female drinkers by Jones and Jones (1976) has shed light on important areas of assessment needed when dealing with female social drinkers or female alcoholics. Overall, female drinkers reach higher peak blood/alcohol levels than males even when weight differences are taken into account. Jones, Jones, and Paredes (in press) administered .66 ml of 190-proof ethanol per kg of body weight to 22 women and 11 men. The women reached a mean peak blood/alcohol level of .072%, while the mean level for men was .059%. It was evident that the women became more intoxicated than men on a similar alcohol dose adjusted for weight. This finding has important implications in terms of evaluating self-monitored drinking patterns. That is, a female's reports of frequency and quantity of drinking must be evaluated, in terms of severity, as a function of gender. Thus, less absolute amount of alcohol consumed by a female as compared to a male would not necessarily indicate less of a drinking problem. In addition, clinicians accustomed to treating male patients must be careful when corroborating females' self-reports of drinking by means of breath tests or blood tests. A blood/alcohol level higher than *expected* based on drinking data provided by the patient may not indicate an invalid self-report. It may simply reflect the female's higher level of responsiveness to a particular dose of alcohol.

Assessment becomes even more complex when one examines the relationship between blood/alcohol level and the menstrual cycle. Jones and Jones (1976) examined this relationship with young female social drinkers aged 21 to 35 years. The women were scheduled for drinking sessions during different times of their menstrual cycles. Sessions were conducted during three phases: (1) *menstrual* (defined as the first day of menstrual flow), (2) *intermenstrual* (defined as the middle of the menstrual cycle—about day 14), and (3) *premenstrual* (the day preceding the beginning of the next menstrual cycle—about day 28). Mean amount of ethanol provided was 41.5 ml (given at a dose of .66 ml/kg body weight), which is equivalent to approximately three ounces of 100-proof liquor. The highest peak blood/alcohol level was reached during the *premenstrual* time. The lowest level occurred during the *menstrual* time, although it was still higher than the level for males. Peak blood/alcohol levels for individual women varied significantly, from .04% to .10%, throughout the menstrual cycle. Thus, the clinician and researcher must assess phase of menstrual cycle to evaluate self-monitored drinking data and/or breathalyzer data for female drinkers.

These findings are particularly relevant for research and treatment involving blood/alcohol discrimination training. This training was originally developed by Lovibond and Caddy (1970) as a means of teaching drinkers to become aware of the intoxicating effects of alcohol and to control and moderate their drinking. A fixed amount of alcohol is provided to the patient, who is asked to estimate his or her blood/alcohol level after a 20 to 30 minute time interval. Bodily sensations (e.g., warmth, numbness, tingling) associated with various blood/alcohol levels are discussed to help patients estimate accurately. A breath analysis is conducted to determine the patient's exact blood/alcohol concentration. The results of the breath test are provided to patients and reasons for discrepancies are discussed.

Lansky, Nathan, and Lawson (1978) found that while moderate social drinkers could learn this estimation ability with little difficulty, alcoholics are unable to learn accurately to discriminate blood/alcohol levels based on internal sensations. These investigators hypothesized that one possible reason for this deficit is related to frequent changes in tolerance level (owing to periods of heavy drinking followed by periods of "drying out"). Thus, alcoholics lack a stable reference point from which to judge blood/alcohol level. Because of changes in response to alcohol as a function of menstrual cycle, women also lack a stable reference point. Thus, females may demonstrate deficits in blood/alcohol level discrimination skills similar to those of alcoholics. In addition, female drinkers may react differently to estimation training depending on when that training occurs in their menstrual cycles. These issues are becoming especially important with the increasing emphasis on research and treatment of female alcoholics.

One final variable that should be assessed is the use of oral contraceptives. Jones and Jones (1976) found that while oral contraceptives had little influence on peak blood/alcohol level, they drastically altered alcohol metabolism. Oral contraceptives tended to slow down the metabolism of alcohol. Thus, women taking birth-control pills would remain intoxicated longer than women not taking contraceptives. However, they also found that women taking oral contraceptives tend to drink less alcohol than other women, possibly in an attempt to compensate for the longer effects of alcohol in the body.

Since the affects of menstrual cycle and contraceptives on physiologic reactions to alcohol may depend, at least in part, on estrogen levels, the assessment of a woman's drinking should take any factor into account that might influence hormone level. Such factors might include hysterectomy, estrogen supplements during menopause, and type of oral contraceptives used. Assessment of these influences should be routinely accomplished with female social drinkers and alcoholics.

Implications for Treatment

From a purely clinical standpoint, some of these assessment procedures have more implications for treatment than others. For example, the most essential target of measurement is drinking behavior itself. The self-monitoring records of the alcoholic provide valuable information on situations and internal sensations that trigger excessive drinking. Without these data the clinician would have difficulty in accurately developing treatment goals and planning appropriate treatment strategies to accomplish these goals. While physiologic monitoring via breath tests or laboratory tests are useful in corroborating self-reports to determine if the goals of intervention are valid, most clinicians are not likely to use such procedures. These techniques can be time-consuming, expensive, and, in some settings, impractical. They are, however, extremely important in treatment research evaluation to insure reliability and validity of results. Verbal and/or written reports from relatives, employers, and close friends are often sufficient to verify the alcoholic's reports in a clinical setting.

Measures of social–psychological functioning are especially useful since deficits in interpersonal functioning frequently are correlated with alcohol abuse. While such deficits (e.g., marital discord) can be the *result* of chronic excessive drinking, they often serve to precipitate episodes of alcohol consumption. Thus, measurement of assertiveness or marital interaction skills is also necessary in order to establish treatment goals.

The assessment of life problems correlated with abuse is not as essential for treatment planning and implementation as, for example, the assessment of consumatory behavior. The number of drunken-driving arrests or the amount of financial indebtedness is not extremely relevant for treatment. However, such measurements would have more important implications for follow-up evaluation since success is highly correlated with these life-problem measures.

The following case will serve to highlight the use of those measures which have more implications for treatment than the others. John T. is a 47-year-old alcoholic who is married, with three children. He is employed as an accountant by the city of Detroit. John is a rather mild-mannered individual who has increased his drinking gradually over the past few years. He now consumes approximately one pint of bourbon per day. His excessive drinking has caused problems for him at work and at home. He frequently misses work owing to "sickness," and has made two significant errors in the city's payroll accounts in the last month. His wife has been extremely upset over his drinking and her pleas for him to discontinue only serve to make him defensive and hostile. Finally, John's employer persuades him to seek help at a local alcoholism treatment agency.

At the initial visit the alcoholism counselor provides John with index-sized forms on which to self-monitor his drinking behavior on a daily basis. The first day of John's monitoring is presented in Table 1. John's wife is also asked to monitor his drinking. Her records indicate only the 6:00 PM to 7:30 PM drinking and her suspicion that he drinks before bedtime. From these records the counselor determines that much of John's drinking occurs during the morning and evening hours, often in response to tension or feelings of anger. He drinks mostly alone. He rarely drinks when he is actively engaged in an interesting activity or hobby (e.g., woodworking). Since much of John's drinking occurs in the early morning hours to avoid withdrawal symptoms and since he had difficulty stopping voluntarily, the counselor suggests that John be admitted to the treatments center's detoxification unit. After he is fully detoxicated, John is asked to continue to monitor any drinking episodes or cravings to drink. His wife is instructed to keep her records of any drinking that occurs. In addition, John is requested to submit to a breath test prior to his twice-weekly treatment sessions at the clinic. Continued monitoring of drinking allows the counselor to assess progress and to determine changes in circumstances precipitating John's cravings or drinking.

Since drinking occurs frequently in response to feelings of anger,

Table 1
John's Self-Monitoring Forms

Date	Amount and type consumed	Time	Place	Circumstance	Mood or thoughts
8-14-79	6 oz. bourbon	10:00 AM	Office (at work)	Doing budget	Restless, agitated
8-14-79	10 oz. bourbon and water	1:00 PM	Local bar	Lunch hour	Slightly depressed; angry at boss
8-14-79	8 oz. bourbon	6:00 PM 7:30 PM	Home	Reading news-paper in family room	Angry at wife
8-14-79	5 oz. bourbon	11:00 PM	Home	Alone in garage (bottle hidden in trunk of car)	Restless, tense. "I need a drink so that I can get some sleep."

the counselor administers the Gambrill–Richey Assertiveness Inventory. This inventory indicates that John has a great deal of difficulty in being appropriately assertive. For example, John cannot express feelings of annoyance at his boss, wife, or children. The counselor also role-plays several situations from John's life that require assertiveness. For example, the boss criticizes John unfairly for an error that was someone else's fault:

> BOSS [counselor]: John, how can you be so stupid? This error is inexcusable.
> JOHN: . . .

By observing John's verbal and nonverbal behavior in these role-played scenes, the counselor can assess his typical ways of handling annoyance and anger and corroborate John's responses on the assertiveness inventory. These assessment tools enable the counselor to pinpoint specific interactions that require behavior changes.

In summary, the counselor used the following assessment techniques: (1) self-monitoring, (2) monitoring by John's wife, (b) breath testing for blood/alcohol level, (4) an assertiveness inventory, and (5) direct observations via role playing. These assessment tools enabled the counselor to determine that detoxification, assertiveness training, and relaxation training were essential therapeutic techniques in the beginning of treatment. Continuous assessment throughout treatment helps to evaluate the efficacy of treatment strategies with individual clients.

Conclusion

The field of assessment of substance abuse has made great strides in the past ten years. The alcohol- and drug-abuse literature is becoming increasingly characterized by uniformity and objectivity of assessment procedures. In addition, assessment and evaluation have become essential elements of substance-abuse treatment and research. In the past, much emphasis was on an initial diagnosis combined with periodic, subjective reports of progress by patients. Such limited assessment procedures are no longer acceptable.

While substance-abuse assessment is much improved from a historical perspective, important needs are still apparent. For example, the essential role of cognitions and expectancies in substance abuse was discussed earlier in this chapter. Unfortunately, few standard measures of these influences have been developed. More research is needed on a more reliable systematic and objective measure of specific expectations regarding the use of alcohol and its consequences. Similarly, the concept of the "motivation" for treatment as it relates to attitudes and expectancies must be more fully evaluated. Clinicians, particularly behavioral ones, have skirted the entire issue of motivation. Rather than attempting to define and measure motivation, clinicians often use the term to explain away treatment failures (e.g., "He was poorly motivated"). Certainly, there are precedents for the objective assessment of this aspect of treatment in the general and abnormal psychology literature.

Development of new assessment procedures has frequently been hampered by the isolationist attitude of substance-abuse clinicians and researchers. That is, alcoholism clinicians are often unaware of the latest developments in the fields of obesity or smoking even though the behaviors to be evaluated are similar. In addition, similar problems of assessment, such as practicality of the instrument or issues of reliability and validity, are encountered with all addictive behaviors. A growing trend, however, is apparent in which substance-abuse workers are pooling their efforts and examining the assessment and treatment of addictions as a whole. Several new trends in psychology such as the growth of the fields of behavioral medicine and health psychology have helped to foster this approach.

References

Allman, L. R., Taylor, H. A., & Nathan, P. E. Group drinking during stress: Effects of drinking behavior, affect, and psychopathology. *American Journal of Psychiatry*, 1972, *129*, 669-678.

Azrin, N. H. Improvements in the community reinforcement approach to alcoholism. *Behaviour Research and Therapy*, 1976, *14*, 339-348.

Azrin, N. H., Naster, B. J., & Jones, R. Reciprocity counseling: a rapid-learning-based procedure for marital counseling. *Behaviour Research and Therapy*, 1973, *11*, 365-382.

Bellack, A. S., Rozensky, R., & Schwartz, J. A comparison of two forms of self-monitoring in a behavioral weight reduction program. *Behavior Therapy*, 1974, *5*, 523-530.

Brownell, K. D., Heckerman, C. L., Westlake, R. J., Hayes, S. C., & Monti, P. M. The effect of couples training and partner cooperativeness in the behavioral treatment of obesity. *Behaviour Research and Therapy*, 1978, *16*, 323-333.

Brownell, K. D., & Stunkard, A. J. The behavioral treatment of obesity in children. *American Journal of Children's Disease*, 1978, *132*, 403-412.

Caddy, G. R., Goldman, R. D., & Huebner, R. Group differences in attitudes toward alcoholism. *Addictive Behaviors*, 1976, *1*, 281-286.

Cahalan, D. *Problem drinkers*. San Francisco: Jossey-Bass, 1970.

Cappell, H., & Herman, C. P. Alcohol and tension reduction: A review. *Quarterly Journal of Alcohol*, 1972, *33*, 33-64.

Caudill, B. D., & Marlatt, G. A. Modeling influences in social drinking: An experimental analogue. *Journal of Consulting and Clinical Psychology*, 1975, *43*, 405-415.

Ciminero, A. R., Nelson, R. O., & Lipinski, D. P. Self-monitoring procedures. In A. R. Ciminero, K. S. Calhoun, & H. E. Adams (Eds.), *Handbook of behavioral assessment*. New York: John Wiley & Sons, 1977.

Cutler, R. E., & Storm, T. Observational study of alcohol consumption in natural settings: The Vancouver beer parlour. *Journal of Studies on Alcohol*, 1975, *36*, 1173-1183.

Department of Health, Education, and Welfare. *Alcohol and health*. Washington, D.C.: U. S. Government Printing Office, 1978.

Dubowski, K. M. Studies in breath alcohol analysis: Biological factors. *Zeitschrift fuer Rechtsmedizin*, 1975, *76*, 93-117.

Eisler, R. M., Miller, P. M., Hersen, M., & Alford, H. Effects of assertive training on marital interaction. *Archives of General Psychiatry*, 1974, *30*, 643-649.

Foy, D. W., Miller, P. M., Eisler, R. M., & O'Toole, D. H. Social skills training to teach alcoholics to refuse drinks effectively. *Journal of Studies on Alcohol*, 1976, *37*, 1340-1345.

Foy, D. W., & Simon, S. J. Alcoholic drinking typography as a function of solitary versus social context. *Addictive Behaviors*, 1978, *3*, 39-41.

Gambrill, E. D., & Richey, C. A. An assertion inventory for use in assessment and research. *Behavior Therapy*, 1975, *6*, 550-561.

Gary, V., & Guthrie, D. The effect of jogging on physical fitness and self-concept in hospitalized alcoholics. *Quarterly Journal of Studies on Alcohol*, 1972, *33*, 1073-1078.

Hersen, M., & Bellack, A. S. Assessment of social skills. In A. R. Ciminero, K. S. Calhoun, & H. E. Adams (Eds.), *Handbook of behavioral assessment*. New York: John Wiley & Sons, 1977.

Hersen, M., Miller, P. M., & Eisler, R. M. Interactions between alcoholics and their wives: A descriptive analysis of verbal and nonverbal behavior. *Quarterly Journal of Studies on Alcohol*, 1973, *34*, 516–520.

Higgins, R. L., & Marlatt, G. A. Fear of interpersonal evaluation as a determinant of alcohol consumption in male social drinkers. *Journal of Abnormal Psychology*, 1975, *84*, 644–651.

Jones, B. M., & Jones, M. K. Women and alcohol: Intoxication, metabolism, and menstrual cycle. In M. Greenblatt & M. A. Schuckit (Eds.), *Alcoholism problems in women and children*. New York: Grune & Stratton, 1976.

Jones, B. M., Jones, M. K., & Paredes, A. Oral contraceptives and ethanol metabolism. *Review of Clinical Investigations*, in press.

Katz, M. M., & Lyerly, S. B. Methods for measuring adjustment behavior in the community: 1. Rationale, description, discrimination, validity, and scale development. *Psychological Reports*, 1963, *13*, 503–535.

Lang, A. R., Goeckner, D. J., Adesso, V. J., & Marlatt, G. A. Effects of alcohol on aggression in male social drinkers. *Journal of Abnormal Psychology*, 1975, *84*, 508–518.

Lansky, D., Nathan, P. E., & Lawson, D. Blood alcohol level discrimination by alcoholics: The role of internal and external cues. *Journal of Consulting and Clinical Psychology*, 1978, *46*(5), 953–960.

Lovibond, S. H., & Caddy, G. Discriminated aversive control in the moderation of alcoholics' drinking behavior. *Behavior Therapy*, 1970, *1*, 550–561.

Mahoney, M. J., & Mahoney, K. Treatment of obesity: A clinical exploration. In B. J. Williams, S. Martin, & J. P. Foreyt (Eds.), *Obesity: Behavioral approaches to dietary management*. New York: Brunner/Mazel, 1976.

Maisto, S. A., Sobell, L. C., & Sobell, M. B. Comparison of alcoholics' self-reports of drinking behavior with reports of collateral informants. *Journal of Consulting and Clinical Psychology*, 1979, *47*, 106–112.

Marlatt, G. A. The drinking profile: A questionnaire for the behavioral assessment of alcoholism. In E. J. Mash & L. G. Terdal (Eds.), *Behavior therapy assessment: Diagnosis and evaluation*. New York: Springer Publishing Co., 1977.

Marlatt, G. A., Demming, B., & Reid, J. B. Loss of control drinking in alcoholics: An experimental analogue. *Journal of Abnormal Psychology*, 1973, *81*, 133–241.

McCance, C., & McCance, P. F. Alcoholism in Northeast Scotland: Its treatment and outcome. *British Journal of Psychiatry*, 1969, *115*, 189–198.

Miller, P. M., A behavioral intervention program for chronic public drunkenness offenders. *Archives of General Psychiatry*, 1975, *32*, 915–922.

Miller, P. M. *Behavioral treatment of alcoholism*. New York: Pergamon Press, 1976.

Miller, P. M. Alternative skills training in alcoholism treatment. In P. E. Nathan, G. A. Marlatt, & T. Lorberg (Eds.), *Alcoholism: New directions in behavioral research and treatment*. New York: Plenum Publishing Corp., 1978.

Miller, P. M. *Personal habit control*. New York: Simon & Schuster, 1979.

Miller, P. M., Becker, J. V., Foy, D. W., & Wooten, L. S. Instructional control of components of alcohol drinking behavior. *Behavior Therapy*, 1976, *1*, 471–480.

Miller, P. M., & Eisler, R. M. Assertive behavior of alcoholics: A descriptive analysis. *Behavior Therapy*, 1977, *8*, 146–149.

Miller, P. M., & Hersen, M. Quantitative changes in alcohol consumption as a function of electrical aversive conditioning. *Journal of Clinical Psychology*, 1972, *28*, 590–593.

Miller, P. M., Hersen, M., Eisler, R. M., & Elkin, T. E. A retrospective analysis of alcohol consumption on laboratory tasks as related to therapeutic outcome. *Behaviour Research and Therapy*, 1974, *12*, 73-76.

Miller, P. M., Hersen, M., Eisler, R. M., & Hemphill, D. P. Electrical aversion therapy with alcoholics: An analogue study. *Behaviour Research and Therapy*, 1973, *11*, 491-497.

Miller, P. M., Hersen, M., Eisler, R. M., & Hilsman, G. Effects of social stress on operant drinking of alcoholics and social drinkers. *Behaviour Research and Therapy*, 1974, *12*, 67-72.

Miller, P. M., & Mastria, M. A. *Alternatives to alcohol abuse*. Champaign, IL: Research Press, 1977.

Miller, P. M., & Simms, K. *A component analysis of a comprehensive behavioral weight control program*. Unpublished manuscript, Hilton Head Hospital, 1979.

Mills, K. C., Sobell, M. B., & Schaeffer, K. C. Training social drinking as an alternative to abstinence for alcoholics. *Behavior Therapy*, 1971, *2*, 18-27.

Nathan, P. E. Studies in blood alcohol level discrimination. In P. E. Nathan, G. A. Marlatt, & T. Loberg (Eds.), *Alcoholism: New direction in behavioral research and treatment*, New York: Plenum Publishing Corp., 1978.

Nathan, P. E., & O'Brien, J. S. An experimental analysis of the behavior of alcoholics and nonalcoholics during prolonged experimental drinking. *Behavior Therapy*, 1971, *2*, 419-430.

Pomerleau, O., Adkins, D., & Pertschuk, M. Predictors of outcome and recidivism in smoking cessation treatment. *Addictive Behaviors*, 1978, *3*, 65-70.

Rosenbluth, J., Nathan, P. E., & Lawson, D. M. Environmental influences on drinking by college students in a college pub: Behavioral observations in the natural setting. *Addictive Behaviors*, 1978, *3*(2), 117-122.

Schaeffer, H. H., Sobell, M. B., & Mills, K. C. Baseline drinking behaviors in alcoholics and social drinkers: Kinds of sips and sip magnitude. *Behaviour Research and Therapy*, 1971, *9*, 23-27.

Sobell, L. C., Maisto, S. A., Sobell, M. B., & Cooper, A. M. Reliability of alcohol abusers' self-reports of drinking behavior. *Behaviour Research and Therapy*, 1979, *17*, 157-160.

Sobell, L. C., & Sobell, M. B. A self-feedback technique to monitor drinking behavior in alcoholics. *Behaviour Research and Therapy*, 1973, *11*, 237-238.

Sobell, L. C., Sobell, M. B., & Christelman, W. C. The myth of "one drink." *Behaviour Research and Therapy*, 1972, *10*, 119-123.

Stalones, P. M., Johnson, W. G., & Christ, M. Behavior modification for obesity: The evaluation of exercise, contingency management, and program adherence. *Journal of Consulting and Clinical Psychology*, 1978, *46*, 463-469.

Stuart, R. B., & Davis, B. *Slim chance in a fat world: Behavioral control of obesity*. Champaign, IL: Research Press, 1972.

Voegtlin, W. L., & Broz, W. R. The conditioned reflect treatment of chronic alcoholism: X. An analysis of 3,125 admissions over a period of ten and a half years. *Annals of Internal Medicine*, 1949, *30*, 580-597.

Weiss, R. L., & Margolin, G. Assessment of marital conflict and accord. In A. R. Ciminero, K. S. Calhoun, & H. E. Adams (Eds.), *Handbook of behavioral assessment*. New York: John Wiley & Sons, 1977.

Wilson, G. T., & Abrams, D. Effects of alcohol on social anxiety and physiological arousal: Cognitive versus pharmacological process. *Cognitive Therapy and Research*, 1977, *1*, 195-210.

Wilson, G. T., & Lawson, D. M. Expectancies, alcohol, and sexual arousal in male social drinkers. *Journal of Abnormal Psychology*, 1976, *85*, 587-594.

Wilson, G. T., & Lawson, D. M. Expectancies, alcohol, and sexual arousal in women. *Journal of Abnormal Psychology*, 1978, *87*, 358-367.

Assessment of Sexual Behavior

JOHN P. WINCZE
JAMES D. LANGE

Introduction

Scientific writings on the assessment of sexual behavior are a relatively recent development, and only within the last five years have books and review articles appeared in this area (Abel, 1976; Barlow, 1977; Caird & Wincze, 1977; Hoon, 1978). Much of this current interest in assessment is a spillover from the major interest in the whole area of human sexuality generated in large part by the work of Masters and Johnson (1966, 1970). Following the publication of their two books, a generation of sex therapy and sex research began. Sex clinics emerged throughout the United States and Europe, and many researchers turned their attention to ferreting out answers to some of the more complex questions concerning sexual behavior. A renewed legitimacy was given to this area, which has since yielded hundreds of research papers, scientific journal articles, and books.

Initially, researchers chose to use rather global descriptive measures of sexual behavior, such as intercourse frequency, but as work in the field advanced and became more sensitive to the complexity of

John P. Wincze. Psychology Service, Veterans Administration Medical Center, and Department of Psychiatry and Human Behavior, Brown University, Providence, Rhode Island.
James D. Lange. Psychology Service, Veterans Administration Medical Center, Providence, Rhode Island.

the problems involved, more molecular studies of sexual behavior were required. In addition, a number of psychologists began to participate actively in sex research in medical settings in collaboration with cardiovascular surgeons, urologists, gynecologists, and obstetricians. These collaborative relationships have brought about an increased focus on psychophysiologic aspects of sexual response, and some of the most exciting advances in assessment today are being made in this area.

Although contemporary sex therapists and researchers are enjoying considerably more freedom than Alfred Kinsey did, there still exist some problems (Wincze, 1977). Passing research proposals through hospital and university ethics committees can be a major obstacle. A multidisciplinary ethics committee will often approve extremely invasive surgical and medical research proposals without raising an eyebrow, but may instantly become a group of prosecuting attorneys when a research proposal including the word "sex" is reviewed. It may be that such committees have often diluted or rejected sex research proposals because of members' discomfort with sex research in general. Exhaustive lobbying and careful presentation of research goals is usually required when proposing sex research to human-research committees.

In spite of these problems and the related problem of obtaining grants for sex research, much has been achieved and the prospects for the future are promising. Advancements in computer programming and hardware technology and in development of new methodology for recording physiologic response signals have contributed greatly to our assessment sophistication (Hoon, 1978). We can now examine muscle potential and vascular dynamics from any single site or from multiple sites on the body and instantly analyze the physiologic changes which may occur during sexual arousal or sexual anxiety. Such capability is leading to an increased understanding of the neurology and hemodynamics of the sexual-arousal process and is also leading to greatly improved treatment and assessment procedures.

Model of Sexual Distress

Although the contributions of Masters and Johnson to our understanding of human sexuality and to our treatment of sexual problems has loomed large, all too often their conceptualization of sexual function and dysfunction has been overly simplified by others. Sexual problems are often classified into discrete categories (e.g., impotency), and package-like treatment is offered. While Masters and Johnson recognized the complexity of sexual functioning, many sex therapists did not. The frequent offering of one-weekend-only training clinics for sex therapists with promises of appearances by Masters and Johnson may be gimmicky showmanship as often as serious clinical training. Such seemingly effortless learning experiences cannot help but lead many into conceptualizing sexual problems into simplistic categories.

Assessment emanating from a simplistic model often looks at sexual behavior in a binary fashion: it is sexually healthy or sexually dysfunctional. As has been pointed out elsewhere, a much more complex model is required to adequately explain sexual behavior (Barlow & Wincze, 1980; Wincze, 1980). A model of sexual behavior should be conceptualized in a continuum. Such a model deemphasizes simplistic categorizing of problems and encourages a functional behavioral analysis specific to the individual's difficulties. A Functional Behavioral Analysis Model applied to nondeviant sexual behavior, developed by Wincze (1980), is presented in Figure 1. This model emphasizes a problem-oriented approach (Fowler & Longabaugh, 1975) to sexual behavior and links assessment and treatment. A functional behavioral model which includes deviant sexual behavior has been presented by Barlow (1977). The latter model breaks down sexual behavior into three major categories: (1) sexual arousal problems, (2) heterosocial skill problems, and (3) gender-identity problems.

In both of these models, the key is a comprehensive, individualistic problem-oriented categorization of sexual behaviors. The models reflect and accommodate the complexity of the real world with all its intensities and variations. Since each case is viewed as unique, this comprehensive assessment allows for the development of therapeutic tactics most effective for each client. Additionally, components of these models are viewed independently of each other; that is to say, modifying one component does not necessarily produce changes in another. For example, a women's sexual anxiety will not concomitantly increase a women's orgasmic ability, which will most likely have to be a concurrent, but separate, focus of therapy (Caird & Wincze, 1977; Wincze & Caird, 1976). Similarly, therapy aimed at suppressing a pedophiliac's deviant arousal will not necessarily increase his heterosocial skills.

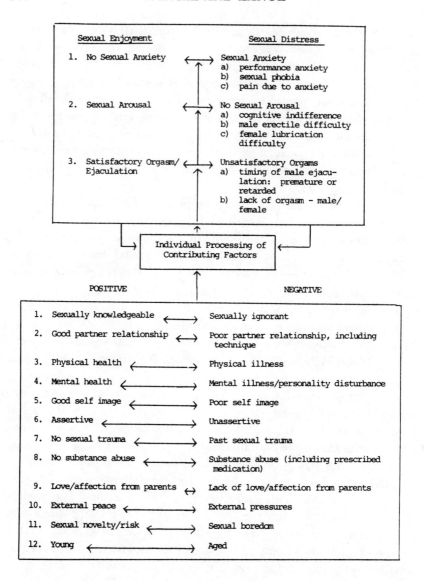

Figure 1

A behavioral model illustrating various categories of sexual distress and enjoyment. Important factors which may contribute to sexual enjoyment or distress are listed in the bottom half of the figure. The two-way arrows indicate that each category of sexual behavior and each contributing factor may be viewed on a continuum. The single-direction arrows indicate that contributing factors are processed on a cognitive level by an individual and, subsequently, affect that person's sexual behavior in a positive or negative direction.

In summary, the models for nondeviant (Wincze, 1980) and deviant (Barlow, 1977) sexual behavior are similar in their basic structure in the following three ways:

1. Sexual problems are categorized independently and on a continuum.
2. The individual's processing of contributing factors determines the manifestation of the problem(s).
3. Contributing factors to the sexual problems are also viewed on a continuum and may or may not be a focus of therapy.

Through these models, a therapist can review assessment data with a client and make a joint decision as to whether or not treatment should be pursued, and if so, what types of problems should be brought into focus. As Barlow and Wincze (1980) point out, one role of the therapist is to act as a consultant to help achieve goals set by the client.

What Should Be Assessed?

The models for nondeviant and deviant sexual behavior specify the areas of sexual concern. For nondeviant sexual behavior, this primarily includes anxiety, arousal, and orgasmic problems; while for deviant sexual behavior, this primarily includes arousal-object, social-skills, and gender-identity problems. Theoretically, all potential problem areas should be assessed for every client regardless of whether it is a deviant or nondeviant sexual problem.

These areas of concern are somewhat different from the DSM-III (1980) categories listed under psychosexual disorders. DSM-III for nondeviant sexual disorders (Psychosexual Dysfunctions) borrows heavily from the work of Masters and Johnson (1966, 1970) for its descriptive categories. The sexual response cycle is divided into the four phases outlined by Masters and Johnson as follows: (1) appetitive, (2) excitement, (3) orgasm, and (4) resolution. These categories are very similar to those presented in Figure 1 and take into account the sometimes observed independence of cognitive arousal (appetitive) and physiologic arousal (excitement) problems. One marked difference between the DSM-III classification and a functional behavioral analysis model of sexual problems is that the latter includes a separate category for sexual anxiety. DSM-III includes anxiety in psychosexual dysfunctions only as an associated feature and not as a major focal area of sexual problems. The decision to include sexual anxiety in the functional behavioral analysis model was based on the frequent clinical observation that significant anxiety was often present in cases of sexual dysfunction for both men and women. Sexual anxiety, however, may or may not disrupt any or all of the four response cycle phases implied in the psychosexual disorders listed in DSM-III.

One additional difference between DSM-III and a functional behavioral analysis model of nondeviant sexual behavior is the penchant of DSM-III to classify or not to classify a disorder. For example, DSM-III states: "If there is inadequate sexual stimulation, either in focus, intensity or duration, the diagnosis of Psychosexual Dysfunction involving excitement or orgasm is not made" (p. 278). Furthermore, in making a judgment to classify or not to classify, great reliance is placed on the clinician's ability to determine what a normal sexual excitement phase should be and whether sexual activity is adequately focused, adequately intense, or of adequate duration. This implies that sufficient knowledge and understanding of human sexuality exist to determine what constitutes a disorder and what does not. The functional behavioral analytic model, on the other hand, does not attempt to determine whether a person's behavior should be classified as a disorder or not; rather, this model advocates an accurate description of the behavior and encourages therapist and client to jointly decide if there is sufficient concern to warrant therapy.

It appears that DSM-III has accepted the work of Masters and Johnson (1966, 1970) as the last word in understanding sexual mores and physiologic and psychological aspects of human sexual response. Our actual understanding of the psychophysiology of sexual response continues to advance as more sophisticated assessment procedures are developed, but unfortunately, we are not as advanced as DSM-III presumes.

There are other problems with DSM-III. For example, DSM-III hedges on the old controversy of vaginal versus clitoral orgasm. While recognizing that women can experience only clitoral orgasm through direct stimulation and still be considered normal, DSM-III leaves some Freudian closet doors open by suggesting that exclusive reliance on manual clitoral stimulation to achieve orgasm may be pathologic.

Classification of certain variations of nondeviant sexual behaviors as pathologic or dysfunctional may represent one of the more glaring examples of DSM-III's shortcomings. A recent paper by Frank, Anderson, and Rubenstein (1978) points out that up to 75% of the couples who rate their marriages and sex lives as successful, experience sexual behaviors which could be classified by DSM-III as dysfunctional or pathologic. Although worded very carefully, DSM-III still exhibits evidence of pre-Kinsey thinking.

The DSM-III classification of deviant sexual behaviors also differs somewhat from the functional behavioral analysis model of deviant behavior. In the latter model, heterosexual and heterosocial skills are of major concern in assessing deviancy. While recognized as independent categories of behavior, sexual and social skills are so often areas of deficit in individuals expressing deviant sexual preference that they are routinely included in a behavioral assessment and therapy program. DSM-III does not place the same emphasis on this area. For some disorders, DSM-III alludes to social adjustment problems, but does not focus on heterosocial deficits.

The DSM-III categories under the heading "paraphilias" are widely accepted as reasonable classifications since in many cases these behaviors are legally defined as well. The concern of what behaviors should be assessed, which was raised in reference to "dysfunctions," is not of concern here because of the widespread agreement of classification categories related to sexual deviancy. The functional behavioral model, however, places more emphasis on individual descriptive categories as opposed to the more global categorization of types of disorders by DSM-III. The deficits in DSM-III as related to sexual "dysfunctions" are serious enough to be misleading in some cases. For the reasons pointed out above, the functional behavioral analysis offers a more accurate and useful approach to conceptualizing distressing sexual problems of a nondeviant nature. For deviant sexual behaviors, however, DSM-III offers a very sensible first step in categorization. The functional behavioral model may follow in some cases in order to add information about a person's nondeviant sexual behavior which also may need therapeutic attention.

Assessment Strategies: An Overview

A number of recent discussions have appeared related to the assessment of sexual behavior (Barlow, 1977; Barlow & Wincze, 1980; Caird & Wincze, 1977; Hoon, 1978; Wincze, 1980). Assessment is usually approached through three strategies: (1) self-report by interview and paper-and-pencil questionnaire, (2) behavioral observation, and (3) physiologic recordings. Use of these strategies, singularly and in combination, assists in identifying specific areas of concern, analyzing the topography of problem behaviors, and analyzing the environment in which the problem behavior occurs. Specific mechanics of the various sexual-assessment strategies have been reviewed elsewhere (Barlow & Wincze, 1980; Hoon, 1978; Wincze, 1980). This chapter will concentrate on new advances in assessment and make general comments about sexual assessment.

ASSESSMENT BY SELF-REPORT: INTERVIEW AND QUESTIONNAIRES

Assessment of sexual behavior was founded on interview and questionnaire approaches. Kinsey and his colleagues (Kinsey, Pomeroy, & Martin, 1948; Kinsey, Pomeroy, Martin, & Gebhard, 1953) outlined very carefully procedures for obtaining sexual information and attempted to objectify and standardize their approach as much as possible. Kinsey has been criticized, however, for obtaining information in this way. It has been argued that volunteers for sex research constitute a small group which is atypically sexually permissive (Maslow & Sakoda, 1952). Specifically, Maslow and Sakoda wrote: "The bias introduced into a sex study by the use of volunteers is, in general, in the direction of inflating the percentage reporting unconventional or disapproved sexual behavior—such as masturbation, oral sexuality, petting to climax, premarital and extramarital intercourse, etc." (p. 261).

A number of researchers have attempted to answer these criticisms. In general, it is agreed that volunteers for sex research studies are not different on any personality traits from nonvolunteers, and like volunteers for other types of research projects, sex research volunteers tend to be more liberal (Barker & Perlman, 1975; Koats & Davis, 1971). Undry and Morris (1967) have also presented evidence that sexual information obtained through an interview is valid.

Methods of approaching sexual interviews (Caird & Wincze, 1977; Green, 1975) and questionnaire methods of sexual assessment (Hoon, 1978) have been reviewed elsewhere, and the interested reader is invited to go directly to those sources for more detailed information. One recent development in the area of self-report assessment which allows a more molecular study of problems is the use of a continuous self-monitoring procedure during erotic arousal experiences (Wincze, Hoon, & Hoon, 1977). The validity and reliability of this procedure requires considerably more investigation, but at this time it appears to be a valuable research and clinical-assessment tool. It offers the opportunity for correlational analyses of physiologic and cognitive arousal processes, which can further our understanding of sexual problems.

In addition to the interview, a number of widely used questionnaires are available to the therapist to help determine the client's exact problem and his or her resources. The SCL-90 (Derogatis, Rickles, & Rock, 1976) can help provide an estimate of the individual's psychiatric state. The Locke–Wallace Inventory (Locke & Wallace, 1959) is useful in establishing the degree of marital discord or harmony between the client and his or her sexual partner. Questionnaires provide useful information for the therapist, but should be presented to the client only after a therapeutic relationship has been established and after he or she has understood that they are a necessary part of the treatment plan. Many people have a low tolerance for questionnaires and may wonder whether they are seeing the therapist to get help or to fill out questionnaires.

Over the past few years, a number of inventories have been developed to assess parameters of sexual problems. The therapist may wish to know if the problem is one of sexual anxiety, an absence of sexual arousal, or perhaps some difficulty with the sexual interchanges between the client and his or her partner. One assessment of sexual anxiety or arousal can be made through a card-sort method in which individual sexual situations or activities are placed on small cards and the client sorts these into different categories, evaluating each sexual behavior for the degree of sexual arousal or sexual anxiety it causes him or her (Barlow, Leitenberg, & Agras, 1969). A paper-and-pencil measure of sexual anxiety frequently used is a variation of the Bentler Heterosexual Behavior Hierarchy (Bentler, 1968). This inventory lists 25 sexual behaviors in which the subject indicates whether or not he or she has participated. This same list may be used to ask subjects to indicate the degree of anxiety each behavior may cause. Although sexual anxiety is frequently a factor in a sexual problem, the absence or very low level of sexual arousal can present equal difficulties. An inventory for the assessment of female sexual arousal has been developed by Hoon, Hoon, and Wincze (1976), and provides an assessment of the level of subjective sexual arousal in the female. Application of this instrument to male problems is currently under investigation. LoPiccolo and Steger (1974) have developed an inventory for use with heterosexual couples which assesses the degree of sexual adjustment and sexual satisfaction of the couple. The Sexual Interaction Inventory has diagnostic utility in that it may indicate what aspects of a couple's sexual relationship are problematic; it can also be used as a measure of treatment outcome.

The use of these paper-and-pencil questionnaires is primarily a clinical decision made by the therapist, who may pick and choose among them, depending upon data in the initial contact with the client.

One assessment device which has been found to be useful throughout the course of therapy is the Sexual Behavior Checklist, devised by Lange and described by Caird and Wincze (1977). This is simply a paper-and-pencil checklist which contains 10 or so sexual behaviors. The client rates frequency of occurrence weekly and evaluates the sexual anxiety of arousal experienced. From this information, as well as from other assessment procedures, the therapist can initially describe and plan a treatment program, and later evaluate that program.

SELF-REPORT ASSESSMENT
BY CONTINUOUS MEASUREMENT

The use of continuous monitoring methods of subjective arousal referred to above is a recent development. In this procedure, individuals continuously rate their feelings of arousal by moving a lever along a calibrated scale. The lever is mounted on a potentiometer, which in turn is connected directly to a polygraph. This system allows the "side-by-side" comparison of physiologic and subjective responding on a polygraph stripchart or a computer printout.

The continuous monitoring method for assessing subjective states of sexual arousal has recently undergone further investigation. Wincze, Hoon, and Hoon (1977) pointed out in their original study that continuous monitoring of subjective states allows better evaluation of (1) the precise relationship between cognitive and physiologic processes throughout a stimulus interval, (2) early reports of subjective arousal during a stimulus presentation, and (3) determination of individual differences in arousal patterns. A study by Geer and Fuhr (1976), however, pointed out that distraction of cognitive processes could interfere with sexual arousal. The implications of the Geer and Fuhr study could be extended to the question of the validity of the continuous monitoring method, since concentration on sexual arousal via a monitoring task may have a distracting effect.

Wincze, Venditti, Barlow, and Mavissakalian (1980) directly tested the distracting effects of continuous monitoring of subjective arousal. The results of their research, in which six men and eight women were used as their own controls, suggests that for women, there was no interference in the magnitude of physiologic arousal during continuous monitoring of subjective arousal. Men, on the other hand, did experience some decrease in their erectile response during periods in which they continuously monitored their sexual arousal. Wincze *et al.* (1980) speculated that since women lack obvious physiologic feedback mechanisms, they are more accustomed to judging their arousal on the basis of a subjective feeling. Consequently, a subjective monitoring task caused little interference with sexual arousal.

Men, on the other hand, tend to use their erectile response to judge their arousal state. Apparently, the addition of a further monitoring task tended to interfere somewhat with the magnitude of the erectile response. Additional research with the continuous monitoring procedure is currently in progress. Wincze, Barlow, Qualls, and Steinman (1979) have completed a study which examined the validity and reliability of the continuous subjective monitoring procedure. They found this procedure has discriminate and convergent validity and is reliable over time. Heterosexual males tend to have higher correlations than heterosexual females between physiologic indices of arousal and the continuous subjective monitoring. In addition, it appears that the continuous monitoring procedure correlates highly with other self-report measures of subjective sexual arousal.

ASSESSMENT BY DIRECT OBSERVATION OF BEHAVIOR

Use of direct observation of sexual behavior as an assessment strategy has not been widespread. There are several paper-and-pencil scales available, as reported above, which ask clients to record sexual behavior (Lange, 1974; LoPiccolo & Steger, 1974), but these scales are another variation of self-report. Most clinicians and researchers are reluctant to observe couples directly engaging in sexual behavior. Such direct observation would most likely be considered unethical and place the clinician or researcher under suspicion. Only Masters and Johnson have been able to muster the necessary scientific clout to investigate actual sexual behavior systematically in the research laboratory. Based on their observations, they have been able to describe the normal sexual response cycle in males and females. They have not systematically observed and reported the sexual behavior of sexually dysfunctional couples. Their information about sexual inadequacy has come from their interviews of hundreds of sexually distressed couples.

Some clinicians have reported the use of sexual surrogates for therapy purposes. The use of sexual surrogates for the purpose of behavioral assessment has not been reported and would be a somewhat questionable practice. At least one clinician has reported to us that he asks couples who are sexually distressed to stimulate sexual activity in his office while the couple is fully clothed. He claims this procedure helps in his assessment of the problem by readily disclosing problem approaches to sexual behavior. Such a procedure may also be questionable and of limited value.

ASSESSMENT BY PHYSIOLOGIC RECORDINGS

The work of Masters and Johnson (1966, 1970) was a breakthrough in the development of more objective procedures for assessing human sexual response. Although electromechanical devices for the objective recording of male sexual arousal have existed for over 50 years (Mountjoy, 1974), Masters and Johnson served as catalysts for the refinement of objective (behavioral and physiologic) measures of sexual response. Masters and Johnson relied mainly on visual observation of actual sexual behavior and observation of physical changes during sexual arousal for their data. For example, they observed color changes in the vaginal barrel and nipple changes during sexual arousal. They obtained much of their data on vaginal response through an optical system employing clear-plastic artifical phalli during simulated coitus. They did not have available to them any of the modern photoplethysmographic equipment which can measure the degree of vaginal vasocongestive changes more accurately.

It is surprising that Masters and Johnson did not take advantage of any of the electromechanical devices available for measuring penile changes and relied only on visual observation for information about male sexual response. Apparently, the only physiologic recordings were heart rate and blood pressure, since even muscle tension was recorded by visual observation.

Although Masters and Johnson seem to have been reluctant to

explore physiologic measures of sexual arousal, those who have followed them have not. The use of sophisticated physiologic recording procedures for measuring both male and female sexual response has increased dramatically since 1974. The reliability and validity of physiologic recordings of genital responding have been explored (Hoon, Wincze, & Hoon, 1976) and new measurement procedures have been developed (Henson, 1978). Research in this area is increasing at a fast pace, taking advantage of new computer technology (Hoon, 1978) and new physiologic recording procedures. These efforts will lead to our most complete understanding of the sexual response cycle.

PROCEDURES FOR THE PHYSIOLOGIC ASSESSMENT OF FEMALE AROUSAL

Details of our current state of knowledge in assessing female sexual arousal by physiologic procedures has been recently covered in a comprehensive review by Hoon (1978). The most valid and reliable physiologic procedures for measuring female sexual response are the photoplethysmography method (Sintchak & Geer, 1975; Hoon, Wincze, & Hoon, 1976) and the thermistor method (Henson, 1978). In the photoplethysmography, a clear-plastic sterilized probe is inserted by the female into her vagina. The probe contains a light source and a photodetector cell which is capable of measuring extremely small changes in light fluctuation. As a woman becomes sexually aroused, vasocongestion occurs in her vaginal barrel. Light reflectance is decreased during vasocongestion as more light is absorbed by the darker red coloring, and thus measurable changes are received by the photodetector cell and transmitted to a physiologic recording device.

In the thermistor method, a temperature-sensitive thermistor probe is attached to the labia majora of the female. As sexual arousal occurs, vasocongestion of the labia majora occurs, increasing the temperature of the surrounding tissue on the skin surface. Again, changes are transmitted to a physiologic recording device.

PROCEDURES FOR THE PHYSIOLOGIC ASSESSMENT OF MALE AROUSAL

The assessment of male sexual arousal by direct measurement of changes in penile diameter or volume in response to erotic stimuli is now widely accepted as one of the most valid assessment techniques available. The review by Zuckerman (1971) and further elaboration by Barlow (1977) make clear the utility of these measurement devices.

Tumescence and detumescence of the penis are vascular events under the control of the autonomic nervous system (Newman, Northup, & Devlin, 1964; Weiss, 1972). The physiology of male erection has been described in detail by Masters and Johnson (1966), and the exact mechanism of parasympathetic and sympathetic nervous system interplay resulting in erection has been hypothesized in more detail by Newman *et al.* (1964) and Weiss (1972).

The use of the objective assessment techniques can be modified, depending on the needs of the individual client, but typically have the same general format. In a private setting, one of the transducers for measurement of penile changes, for example a Barlow-type strain gauge (Barlow, Becker, Leitenberg, & Agras, 1970), is attached to the midshaft of the client's penis. Following this, the subject may view a series of videotapes or listen to audiotapes which depict a variety of sexual activities. As the client watches or listens, changes in tumescence or detumescence are recorded concurrently and provide a direct physiologic measure of male sexual arousal.

NEW DIRECTIONS FOR PHYSIOLOGIC ASSESSMENT

In our own laboratory, we are adapting procedures used by cardiovascular surgeons to investigate vascular changes during the sexual arousal cycle. One very promising instrument is the directional doppler, which uses ultrasound to determine flow rates in arteries and veins. The doppler has been successfully used for over ten years as a means of diagnosing vascular disease. This noninvasive diagnostic procedure can be applied to any vein or artery on the body surface. The doppler transducer houses a transmission crystal which emits an ultrasonic pulse and a receiver crystal which captures the returning sound wave. Since the emitted sound wave is of known constant frequency, differences in the returning sound wave frequency are the result of changes in the flow rate of blood in an artery or vein. Cardiovascular surgeons are interested in the topography of the ultrasonic wave form which can be diagnostic of certain vascular disease processes. The patency and compliance of the vascular system can be determined by ultrasonic procedures. For our purposes, flow rate changes can be determined during the sexual arousal cycle. Because the doppler technique is noninvasive, extremely sensitive, and applicable to any body surface, we see it as an extremely valuable addition to our research armamentarium. We have observed changes in flow rate in both males and females, using genital placements of the doppler. Currently, we are systematically exploring nongenital sites which may also demonstrate flow-rate changes and may lead to a complete mapping of the vascular system during the sexual arousal cycle. In addition to providing important information about the process of sexual arousal, a mapping of vascular activity may be important for assessment in males and females where genital measures are useless (erectile failure) or disturbing (dyspareunia in women).

The physiologic assessment of sexual arousal may have important implications for similar assessment of other emotional states. The search for specific physiologic indices of certain emotional states (e.g., anxiety) has a long and somewhat frustrating history. No single physiologic marker has been reliably and validly related to a definable emotional state. Measures of genital changes, however, have been more reliably and validly related to sexual arousal states than to other emotional states (Hoon, Wincze, & Hoon, 1976).

Because sexual arousal states can be reliably and validly assessed, scientists have been able to use sex research as a model for answering basic psychophysiology questions. For example, the relationship between subjective and physiologic states can be measured and correlational analyses can be computed. A comparable analysis with other emotional states, such as anxiety, has been difficult because there are no clear physiologic markers of anxiety.

HORMONAL ASSESSMENT

An exciting new area of assessment of sexual behavior and disorders is now beginning to expand, namely, the study of how "sexual" hormones interface with sexual behavior.

Within the past ten years, there have been several attempts to evaluate testosterone levels of impotent males, on the assumption that they might be deficient in testosterone and with a view toward cure by hormonal replacement. These studies have had mixed results, and in some ways this is not unexpected.

The relationship between testosterone and sexual behavior, and indeed, testosterone and other behaviors, is highly complex. It is not too surprising, therefore, that previous attempts to relate the levels of testosterone, which before 1970 were assayed by a somewhat unreliable method, to sexual behavior, usually measured by self-reported sexual activity or interest, did not yield useful information.

The development of a very reliable testosterone assay in the early 1970s, and the parallel development of an accurate measure of penile tumescence, the strain gauge, allowed for the investigation of relationships between hormones and sexual behavior. Recent research on sexual arousal patterns in healthy males by Lange, Brown, Wincze, and Zwick (1979) has made the first finding of a relationship between testosterone levels and an objective measure of an individual's sexual response. These authors found that the level of testosterone was significantly and negatively correlated with the latency to erection. That is, the lower an individual's testosterone, the more time it takes him to become erect. This suggests that males with lower testosterone levels may have a higher threshold of sexual arousal, which may be a factor in the development of erectile dysfunction in some males.

Pending further research, this finding may have utility in the assessment of male sexual problems. Assay of an individual's testosterone level, in conjunction with the assessment of tumescence changes, may lead to the identification of a subgroup of males who would benefit from administration of exogenous testosterone, and who characteristically have arousal patterns different from other males. This may also be an approach to the physiologic assessment and treatment of the organic versus psychogenic problem of impotence. This in turn would lead to a specific treatment program for such individuals, and would open the door to more research in the important area of endocrine–behavior relationships.

Clinical Assessment of Female and Male Sexual Problems

The overview of assessment strategy touched on the basic technology at hand for conducting assessments of sexual behavior. In the next section, we discuss in more detail the specific assessment strategies when conducting therapy or research.

The assessment procedure for female and male clinical sexual problems relies mainly on interview and questionnaire procedures. Caird and Wincze (1977) have outlined a strategy for assessing clinical sexual problems in a therapy program which follows a behavioral model. Clinical assessment may be divided into two phases: (1)

initial assessment for the determination of the problem, and (2) ongoing assessment for determination of progress or deterioration.

The initial assessment by interview is very individualistic, although many clinicians follow the suggestions made by Masters and Johnson (1970) for conducting intake interviews. In our own procedure, we interview sexual partners separately at first to insure that each person communicates honestly and freely without fear of hurting or angering his or her partner. Following separate interviews, a third interview is held, in which we outline for the couple the major areas of concern. In addition, the third interview serves as an assessment of how much and how well the couple has communicated to each other information about the separate interviews. Couples with communication difficulties often have not shared any information or have given each other distorted reports of their sessions.

The interview format is very closely linked to the model of sexual distress presented in Figure 1. Many nonsexual areas (contributing factors) are explored along with the sexual areas. Since the interview may be the most valuable source of information, it is important that it be conducted with the utmost clinical skill. In addition to the content areas of the interview, which should cover the areas outlined in the model, the interview may be facilitated by the following considerations:

1. *The interviewer should assume that the client has never discussed sexual issues before and that it is very difficult for him or her to do so.* Bold questions about sexual behavior without first building a rapport may shock a timid client and inhibit responding. We always begin our interviews with nonthreatening questions about the client's background—for instance, "How old are you?" "How long have you been married?"—and then move chronologically to the client's social and sexual history. It is better to err in the direction of caution than to overwhelm a client with pointed sexual questioning.

If a client does appear to be having some difficulty in answering sexually related questions (once the topic is approached), then we attempt to paraphrase the client's response in mutually understandable terms. We also may make a statement to the client acknowledging his or her difficulty. For example:

THERAPIST: Mrs. M., would you please tell me what sex was like at the beginning of your marriage.
CLIENT: Well, uh, it was okay, I guess. (*Client blushes and stammers.*)

THERAPIST: Mrs. M., I want you to know that many people find it very difficult to talk about sex and I wonder if this subject is something you have talked about much with other people?

CLIENT: No, I'm not used to it.

THERAPIST: Well, I hope this isn't too difficult for you. When you said that sex was okay at the beginning of your marriage, did you mean that there were no problems at all and you were perfectly happy, or did you mean that there were some problems but not serious ones?

This is an example of how a therapist might facilitate communication with an inhibited client. The exact content and strategy of the interview would naturally depend on the therapist's judgment of the client's capabilities.

2. *The interviewer should assume that the client has little sexual knowledge and does not understand technical or medical terms describing sexuality.* Approximately 25% of the clients we see have never had discussions about sex and many of them are unfamiliar with sexually related terms. For example, words like clitoris, ejaculation, and orgasm are either misunderstood, mispronounced, or totally unknown. In conducting an interview, we attempt to judge the client's sexual understanding and adjust our vocabulary level to theirs. Often we use their terms along with our own in order to assure that we have a mutual understanding. We feel it is better to err in the direction of breaking down sexual concepts too simply than to err in the direction of confusing a client with medical terminology.

3. *The interviewer should be accepting of all sexual behavior and convey this attitude to the client.* If the interviewer shows surprise, shock, or embarrassment, then the client may be greatly inhibited in his or her responses. We have had clients who reported that they attempted to tell their physician about their sexual problem, but stopped when the physician became embarrassed.

4. *The interviewer should attempt to get as detailed a description as possible of the client's problem.* Clients most often report their sexual problems in very global, nonspecific terms. For example, a male client may state, "I can't get it up anymore." Accepting this information without further questioning may lead to a very incomplete assessment. Male clients will often describe themselves as impotent even though they are experiencing erections on some occasions. It is important for the therapist to inquire about degree of erection, circumstance during which erections occur, masturbation experience,

and nighttime and morning erections. It is very common for a male patient to be referred by a physician with the diagnosis of impotence. Careful interviewing following the behavioral model will often reveal that the erectile difficulties are situational and not general or that the difficulties are largely psychological and not organic.

The four suggestions listed above are necessary to maximize the amount of information that can be obtained through a clinical interview when assessing sexual problems.

Our interview assessment is usually augmented with a number of questionnaires which are distributed to the clients on the first meeting. The questionnaires we most frequently use are (1) a general history and background questionnaire (2) the Azrin Marital Happiness Scale (Azrin, Naster, & Jones, 1973), (3) the Sexual Arousal Inventory (Hoon, Wincze, & Hoon, 1976), (4) the Beck Depression Scale (Beck, 1967), (5) an assertiveness scale, and (6) the Bentler Sexual Experience Scale (Bentler, 1968). This range of questionnaires generally provides a broad sampling of behavior which may cue different strengths and weaknesses in an individual or a couple. Additional scales and psychological testing may be used depending on the individual's response to the initial assessment.

Assessment of the ongoing thearpy progress can be achieved by interview and questionnaire methods. We have found the use of the card sort and the Lange behavioral checklist (Caird & Wincze, 1977) to be particularly useful and sensitive measures of ongoing progress in the area of sexual behaviors.

The card sort is used for men or women who are experiencing anxiety associated with sexual behavior. Separate descriptive scenes of various degrees of sexual intimacy are typed on 3×5 index cards and clients are asked to sort the cards into categories representing different degrees of anxiety (usually on a five-point scale). The card sort can be used as a generalization measure of an anxiety-reduction program. The client can be asked to sort the cards at each session so that an ongoing record of anxiety reaction to specific sexual scenes is established. The instructions for the card sort can also be oriented toward a measure of sexual arousal rather than anxiety. This can be used for ongoing assessment of both deviant and nondeviant sexual problems.

The Lange behavioral checklist simply asks a client to check off on a sheet of paper the sexual behaviors which occurred during the past week and the amount of anxiety or arousal associated with the

behaviors. This checklist has been used successfully with couples undergoing a sex therapy program. Since couples fill out the checklist
independently, this offers a check on the agreement between the
couple.

Both of these assessment procedures provide an expeditious
method of monitoring sexual behaviors and attitudes. These specific
types of ongoing assessment tools are important supplements to the
usual more global ratings clinicians use. Global judgments such as
"much improved," "somewhat improved," "no change," or "somewhat worse" are limited in conveying important information.

In addition, the use of specific assessment tools such as those
mentioned above help to bypass some of the methodological problems
of self-report measures. Since self-reported clients' ratings are critical
data, it is important to control for the demand characteristics in therapy in obtaining this data. While specific scales do not entirely
eliminate demand characteristics, they certainly reduce this problem
(Hoon, 1978). Hoon (1978) has discussed the use of other self-report
measures which are commonly used in sexual behavior assessment.
Two of the best self-report paper-and-pencil assessment inventories
are the Sexual Arousal Inventory (Hoon, Hoon, & Wincze, 1976) and
the Sexual Interaction Inventory (LoPiccolo & Steger, 1974). Both of
these instruments are valuable for ongoing assessment since they provide guidelines for specific sexual problems.

A comprehensive assessment for clinical purposes of both male
and female sexual problems is tied very closely to the model outlined
in Figure 1. In a clinical setting, this information leads to the formulation of a treatment plan aimed at the sexual difficulty itself, the
contributing factors, or some combination of these.

ASSESSMENT OF THE NEED FOR
PENILE IMPLANT SURGERY

The procedures outlined above are general guidelines for a clinical screening of deviant and nondeviant sexual problems. A more
specific assessment procedure is necessary for some very specialized
problems, such as male erectile failure when penile implant surgery is
being considered. Since 1952, penile prosthesis operations have been
performed in cases of male erectile failure associated with organic
factors. Over the years, the surgical procedures have been refined,
and what used to be a relatively rare operation has become more

commonplace today (Sotile, 1979). One of the most widely used procedures was developed by Small, Carrion, and Gordon (1975). The Small–Carrion penile prosthesis consists of two semirigid silicone rods implanted in each corpus cavernosa. The rods are flexible, and once implanted, the penis is held in a permanently erect state.

Another major type of penile implant device is a hydrolic one developed by Scott, Bradley, and Timm (1973). This device consists of inflatable cylinders placed inside each corpus cavernosum and connected to a pumping mechanism inserted in the scrotal pouch and a fluid reservoir placed in the abdominal wall. The advantage and disadvantages of each procedure have been recently reviewed (Sotile, 1979). Because of the possibility of medical complications and potential for psychological distress associated with the operation, a thorough assessment procedure must be followed whenever such an operation is considered. The possibility of surgical "cure" of erectile failure is very seductive, and many impotent men would readily agree to the operation if their physician suggested it. Unfortunately, there is a potential for extreme distress, and the assessment procedure must not be guided and possibly misled by a patient's enthusiasm. Our assessment procedure for potential implant operations utilizes in-depth interviews with the male and his sexual partner, paper-and-pencil questionnaires, psychological testing, and physiologic examination such as we outlined earlier. In some clinics, nocturnal penile recordings are used to examine erection response during sleep.

There are a number of very specific concerns which the assessment procedure should address before a decision to operate is made.

1. *Psychological stability of the patient.* We typically use the MMPI as an adjunct to our interview. Any signs of disturbance must be weighed in light of the impact the operation may have on the individual's life. Signs of disturbance in any areas of psychological functioning may raise a question of the client's suitability for the operation.

2. *The presence of a strong and active sex drive.* Clients who have not attempted sexual contact for a long time or who have not exposed themselves to erotic cues may not function adequately following the operation. Males with erectile-failure problems who continue very active sexual lives in spite of the lack of intercourse are viewed as more favorable candidates. In addition to the assessment interview, sex drive is gauged by the responses to specific arousal inventories and subjective responses to viewing erotic videotapes. Clients who have been

living lives of sexual abstinence and have systematically avoided erotic cues most likely are not ready for an implant operation. Sex therapy techniques such as pleasuring and fantasy enrichment are generally necessary steps to be taken before surgical intervention is considered.

3. *Unrealistic expectations must be detected.* If a client did not have a very active or satisfying sexual life before experiencing erectile failure, then it is unlikely that a prosthesis device will help him. The client and his sex partner must be carefully interviewed and thoroughly questioned about their previous sexual experiences and their expected sexual experiences following the operation. In addition, they should be made aware of all of the pros and cons of the prosthetic devices. Discussions with patients who have undergone the operation may be helpful to patients considering the operation. Such a thorough assessment can reveal any unreasonable expectations a client might have and place the operation into a more realistic perspective.

4. *The stability of the patient's relationship with his sexual partner.* In cases where sexual activity has been associated with failure, anxiety, and withdawal, there is great potential for partner dissatisfaction. In addition, there are cases in which a sexual partner may have adjusted to the lack of sexual activity in a relationship. With a return of functioning erection, there may be increased anxieties and distress on the partner's part. A thorough interview with the partner is necessary to evaluate this potential.

Attention to the above concerns is necessary for a thorough assessment of the client considering a penile implant operation.

CASE HISTORY

The following case illustrates a comprehensive assessment procedure utilizing many of the assessment strategies outlined above.

Mr. F. was a 42-year-old veteran who had been suffering from multiple sclerosis for 10 years. During the initial interview, Mr. F. reported that he had experienced a gradual loss of his erectile capacity over the past five years and currently was totally impotent. He was referred by a urologist for assessment regarding an implant operation. Mr. F. was very open and comfortable in discussing his sexual difficulties and was very articulate. An interview with Mr. F. and with

Mrs. F. revealed only medical problems as major contributors to the sexual problem. Mrs. F. was also very articulate and did not harbor any unrealistic expectations related to the implant operation. The couple's marriage seemed very strong and their sexual relationship had been excellent before erectile difficulties occurred. Although the couple had continued participating in sexual activity in spite of erectile failure, they wished to enrich their relationship more by again including intercourse as part of their sexual activity.

Following the in-depth interviews, readings were provided related to the pros and cons of implant operation. In addition, an interview with a patient who had undergone such an operation was arranged. The Background Questionnaire, Marital Happiness Scale, Sexual Arousal Inventory, and the Bentler Sexual Behavior Scale were given to Mr. and Mrs. F. to complete. After the couple had completed the questionnaires and discussed the operation with a former implant patient, additional assessment sessions were scheduled. Mr. F. was asked to complete a MMPI, Willoughby Scale, and Beck Depression Scale. In addition, a physiologic assessment session was conducted in order to obtain additional information about his physiologic and subjective sexual response to erotic stimuli.

The interviews, questionnaires, and psychological testing portrayed Mr. F. as a very intelligent, well-informed, and stable individual. He did not appear to have any sexual attitudes which were restrictive or potentially harmful and he had a very stable marital relationship. The interview, questionnaires, and subjective monitoring during erotic tapes indicated that Mr. F. had very strong heterosexually oriented sexual desires. He showed no degree of penile tumescence during the physiologic assessment.

All of the assessment information led to the recommendation for implant surgery. There was overwhelming convergence in the components of the assessment package which supported this decision. Mr. F. underwent the operation, and at a six-month follow-up, reported complete satisfaction and no apparent difficulties.

This case illustrates the procedure for the clinical assessment of a sexual problem. Although the assessment material in this case converged to support the clinical decision, not all cases yield such straightforward information. If psychological problems or other problem areas were revealed, then intervention would have proceeded along other lines.

Research Assessment of Female and Male Sexual Behavior

It is important to distinguish between research assessment and clinical assessment. For example, a research assessment of female sexual behavior is more likely to use physiologic information. In a research assessment, Wincze, Hoon, and Hoon (1976) have found physiologic response differences (vaginal vasocongestion) between women complaining of sexual difficulties and women with no sexual difficulties, but such information is of little value to a clinical treatment program. It is not known, for example, if sexually distressed women have a lower physiologic response to erotic stimuli because they have innate physiologic differences or because they just do not feel as sexually aroused. There are probably a dozen or more explanations which are equally plausible. The point is that for the most part, we just do not understand enough about physiologic arousal processes in females to translate a physiologic assessment into useful clinical information.

In the assessment of gender-identity problems, however, we are beginning to make some headway. Measurement of the vaginal vasocongestive response is proving useful in assessing the pattern of arousal in presurgical transsexual women. As more data are gathered from this population of women, as well as from lesbian and heterosexual women, patterns of physiologic response will emerge which may be valuable in distinguishing these populations. Such information will help formulate treatment programs by assisting the therapist and client in identifying stimuli which evoke sexual response and matching this response "pattern" to known population responses. For example, a woman who is unsure as to whether she is lesbian or transsexual may demonstrate a physiologic pattern more closely associated with one population or another. This information will be used along with other assessment information to formulate the final treatment program. It should be noted that the use of physiologic assessment information for the treatment of gender-identity problems in women is very much in the experimental stage, although much more work is anticipated in this very promising area over the next few years.

The greatest value of physiologic assessment in women at this time is for research purposes. Exploring the process of sexual arousal, the hemodynamics of sexual arousal, the relationship between cognitive and physiologic processes, and the relationship between various emotional states and sexual arousal are all current research interests. These research interests have been fueled by the notable lack of adequate physiologic information about female sexual response and by the blossoming technical information that has emerged within the last seven years as a spillover from the space race.

As is the case with females, research assessment of males' sexual problems is likely to be more physiologic than psychological in nature. However, the research assessment for males currently overlaps to a large degree with clinical assessment, although this was not always the case. The overlap is largely due to the relatively longer developmental period of the methodology and technology involved in measuring male sexual behavior, which began 10 or 15 years in advance of the assessment of female sexual behavior. There are no doubt many reasons for this discrepancy between male and female assessment, including the somewhat greater technological sophistication required for female assessment and, less palatably, sexism.

In any event, what were the research frontiers for male sexual problems are now clinical territories, and previously experimental devices such as the strain gauge are now in routine use in psychiatric settings. Formerly experimental biofeedback programs using strain gauges are now used in the treatment of impotence, and methodology developed for the assessment and treatment of pedophiles is often used with forensic patients. These examples are worth citing, because there is occasionally a tendency to forget that clinical procedures have their roots in basic research and that such research is necessary if we are to completely understand and eventually treat male sexual problems.

Research in the assessment of male sexual problems has been involved with questions similar to those with females, although the relatively greater development of male assessment has allowed researchers to begin exploring new directions and interfacing with other disciplines studying human behavior. For example, clarification of the relationships between hormonal variables and sexual behavior is now several steps closer than it was, although its elucidation is still far from complete. This type of research will no doubt begin soon with female sexual behavior, once researchers further clarify essential processes of female sexuality.

Summary

This chapter has reviewed the area of assessment of sexual arousal in men and women. Since there are some recent reviews within this area (Barlow & Wincze, 1980; Hoon, 1978), we have attempted to concentrate on those areas of assessment that have not been adequately covered elsewhere. This chapter points out that assessment for applied clinical purposes is often very different from assessment for research purposes. As our sophistication grows in the use of physiologic information and computer programming, we hope to translate our research assessment procedures into useful diagnostic tools. This translation has occurred more completely to date with male assessment than with female assessment.

References

Abel, G. G. *The assessment of rapists.* Paper presented at Butler Hospital Fall Grand Rounds, October 1976.

Azrin, N. H., Naster, B. J., & Jones, R. Reciprocity counseling: A rapid learning-based procedure for marital counseling. *Behaviour Research and Therapy,* 1973, *11,* 356–382.

Barker, W. J., & Perlman, D. Volunteer bias and personality traits in sexual standards research. *Archives of Sexual Behavior,* 1975, *4,* 161.

Barlow, D. H. Assessment of sexual behavior. In A. R. Ciminero, H. Adams, & K. Calhoun (Eds.), *Handbook of behavioral assessment,* New York: John Wiley & Sons, 1977.

Barlow, D., Becker, R., Leitenberg, H., & Agras, W. S. A mechanical strain gauge for recording penile circumference change. *Journal of Applied Behavior Analysis,* 1970, *3,* 73–76.

Barlow, D., Leitenberg, H., & Agras, W. S. The experimental control of sexual deviation through the manipulation of the noxious scene in covert sensitization. *Journal of Abnormal Psychology,* 1969, *74,* 596–601.

Barlow, D. H., & Wincze, J. P. Treatment of sexual deviations. In S. R. Leiblum & L. A. Pervin (Eds.), *Principles and practice of sex therapy.* New York: Guilford Press, 1980.

Beck, A. T. *Depression: Clinical, experimental, and theoretical aspects.* New York: Harper & Row, 1967.

Bentler, P. Heterosexual behavior assessment. I. Males. II. Females. *Behaviour Research and Therapy,* 1968, *6,* 21–25.

Caird, W. K., & Wincze, J. P. *Sex therapy: A behavioral approach.* Hagerstown: Harper & Row, 1977.

Derogatis, L. R., Rickles, K., & Rock, A. F. The SCL-90 and the MMPI: A step in the validation of a new self-report scale. *British Journal of Psychiatry,* 1976, *128,* 280–289.

Diagnostic and statistical manual of mental disorders (3rd ed.) Washington, D.C.: American Psychiatric Association, 1980.

Ferster, C. B. Classification of behavioral pathology. In L. Krasner & L. D. Ullmann (Eds.), *Research in behavior modification.* New York: Holt, Rinehart, & Winston, 1965.

Fowler, R., & Longabaugh, R. The problem-oriented record problem definition. *Archives of General Psychiatry,* 1975, *32,* 831–834.

Frank, E., Anderson, C., & Rubenstein, D. Frequency of sexual dysfunction in "normal" couples. *New England Journal of Medicine,* 1978, *249,* 111–115.

Geer, J., & Fuhr, R. Cognitive factors in sexual arousal: The role of distraction. *Journal of Consulting and Clinical Psychology*, 1976, *44*, 238–243.

Green, R. *Human sexuality: A health practitioner's text*. Baltimore: Williams & Wilkins, 1975.

Henson, D. *Analysis of three concurrent measures of female sexual arousal*. Paper presented at the American Psychological Association Convention, Toronto, 1978.

Hoon, P. *Photoplethysmography findings during sleep in women*. Paper presented at Fourth Annual Southeastern Regional Conference of the American Association of Sex Educators, Counselors, and Therapists, Charleston, 1978.

Hoon, E., Hoon, P., & Wincze, J. The SAI: An inventory for the measurement of female sexual arousal. *Archives of Sexual Behavior*, 1976, *5*, 208–215.

Hoon, P., Wincze, J., & Hoon, E. Physiological assessment of sexual arousal in women. *Psychophysiology*, 1976, *13*, 196–208.

Kanfer, F., & Saslow, G. Behavioral diagnosis. In C. M. Franks (Ed.), *Behavior therapy: Appraisal and status*. New York: McGraw-Hill, 1969.

Kinsey, A. C., Pomeroy, W. B., & Martin, C. E. *Sexual behavior in the human male*. Philadelphia: W. B. Saunders, 1948.

Kinsey, A. C., Pomeroy, W. B., Martin, C. E., & Gebhard, P. H. *Sexual behavior in the human female*. Philadelphia: W. B. Saunders, 1953.

Koats, G. R., & Davis, K. Effects of volunteer biases in studies of sexual behavior and attitudes. *Journal of Sex Research*, 1971, *7*, 26–34.

Lange, J. D. *Behavioral research and video desensitization: An experimental investigation of their efficacy in treatment of couples with sexual dysfunction*. Unpublished master's thesis, Dalhousie University, Halifax, Nova Scotia, 1974.

Lange, J., Brown, W., Wincze, J., & Zwick, W. *Serum testosterone concentration and penile tumescence changes in men*. Paper presented at the annual meeting of the American Psychosomatic Society, Dallas, 1979.

Locke, J. J., & Wallace, K. M. Short-term marital adjustment and prediction tests: Their reliability and validity. *Journal of Marriage and Family Living*, 1959, *21*, 251–255.

LoPiccolo, J., & Steger, J. C. The sexual interaction inventory: a new instrument for assessment of sexual dysfunction. *Archives of Sexual Behavior*, 1974, *3*, 585–595.

Maslow, A., & Sakoda, J. Volunteer error in the Kinsey study. *Journal of Abnormal Psychology*, 1952, *47*, 259–267.

Masters, W. H., & Johnson, V. E. *Human sexual response*. Boston: Little, Brown, 1966.

Masters, W. H., & Johnson, V. E. *Human sexual inadequacy*. Boston: Little, Brown, 1970.

Mountjoy, P. Some early attempts to modify penile erection in horse and human: A historical analysis. *The Psychological Record*, 1974, *24*, 291–308.

Newman, H. F., Northup, J. D., & Devlin, J. Mechanism of human penile erection. *Investigative Urology*, 1964, *1*, 350–353.

Scott, F. B., Bradley, W. E., & Timm, G. W. Management of erectile impotence: Use of implantable, inflatable prosthesis. *Urology*, 1973, *2*, 80–82.

Sintchak, G., & Geer, J. A vaginal plethysmograph system. *Psychophysiology*, 1975, *12*, 113–115.

Sotile, W. The penile prosthesis: A review. *Journal of Sexual and Marital Therapy*, 1979, *5*, 90–102.

Small, M. P., Carrion, H. M., & Gordon, J. A. Small-Carrion penile prosthesis. *Urology*, 1975, *5*, 479.

Story, N. L. Sexual dysfunction resulting from drug side effects. *Journal of Sex Research*, 1974, *10*, 132-149.

Undry, J. R., & Morris, N. M. A method for validation of reported sexual data. *Journal of Marriage and the Family*, 1967, *5*, 442-446.

Weiss, H. D. The physiology of human penile erection. *Annals of Internal Medicine*, 1972, 793-799.

Wincze, J. P. Selected review of current books on sexuality and sex therapy. *International Journal of Family Counseling*, 1977, *5*, 86-88.

Wincze, J. P. Sexual dysfunction. In S. Turner, K. Calhoun, & H. Adams (Eds.), *Handbook of clinical behavior therapy*. New York: John Wiley & Sons, 1980.

Wincze, J., Barlow, D., Qualls, B., & Steinman, D. *Continuous subjective and physiological measurement of sexual arousal.* Paper presented at the American Association of Sex Educators, Counselors, and Therapists, Charleston, October 1979.

Wincze, J., & Caird, W. The effects of systematic desensitization and video desensitization in the treatment of essential sexual dysfunction in women. *Behavior Therapy*, 1976, *7*, 155-166.

Wincze, J. P., Hoon, P., & Hoon, E. A comparison of the physiological responsivity of normal and sexually dysfunctional women during exposure to erotic stimulus. *Journal of Psychosomatic Research*, 1976, *20*, 44-50.

Wincze, J. P., Hoon, P., & Hoon, E. Sexual arousal in women: A comparison of cognitive and physiological responses by continuous measurement. *Archives of Sexual Behavior*, 1977, *6*, 230-245.

Wincze, J. P., Venditti, B., Barlow, D., & Mavissakalian, M. The effects of a subjective monitoring task on the physiological measure of genital response to erotic stimulation. *Archives of Sexual Behavior*, 1980, *9*, 240-255.

Zuckerman, M. Physiological measures of sexual arousal in the human. *Psychological Bulletin*, 1971 *75*, 347-356.

11

Assessment of Eating Disorders

KELLY D. BROWNELL

Introduction

Any therapeutic procedure is only as strong as the assessment used to evaluate its efficacy. In his essay "The Genealogy of Etiquette," H. L. Mencken (1919) underscored this point by questioning the contribution of psychology:

> Barring sociology . . . psychology is the youngest of the sciences, and hence chiefly guesswork, empiricism, hocus-pocus, and poppycock. On the one hand, there are still enormous gaps in its data, so that the determination of its simplest principles remains difficult, not to say impossible; and, on the other hand, the very hollowness and nebulosity of it, particularly around its edges, encourages a horde of quacks to invade it, sophisticate it, and make nonsense of it. Worse, this state of affairs tends to such confusion of effort and direction that the quack and honest inquirer are often found in the same man. [Psychology] . . . is still unable to differentiate accurately between the true and the false, or to give us any effective protection against the fallacies, superstitions, crazes, and hysterias which rage in the world. (p. 56)

Mencken's qualms reflected a lack of regard for the psychologist's ability to assess human behavior. In the absence of valid measurement, there was little way to distinguish between science and quackery.

Kelly D. Brownell. Department of Psychiatry, University of Pennsylvania School of Medicine, Philadelphia, Pennsylvania.

Great strides in the technology of modifying behavior have been made since Mencken issued his pessimistic verdict, yet the assessment of behavior has concerned the scientific community only recently.

Research on psychotherapy has become increasingly sophisticated, and the days of faith in uncontrolled case studies and anecdotal reports have passed. The result has been much-needed improvement in studying behavior change, and a growing demand for researchers to provide valid and reliable measurement of socially relevant behaviors.

In large part, the treatment of any disorder will depend on the results of assessment. A comprehensive assessment of behavior will often lead to the application of established techniques to specific problems (Barlow, 1977; Bergin & Strupp, 1972). Therefore, the absence of adequate assessment would make the selection of appropriate intervention techniques more difficult. Oddly, our ability to measure behavior lags far behind our ability to modify behavior. The historical development of this phenomenon can be seen by tracing the evolution of behavior therapy.

The earliest writings on behavior therapy and applied behavior analysis focused on methods of altering rather than of assessing behavior (Eysenck, 1959; Lazarus, 1958; Wolpe, 1954, 1958). The results of treatment were so impressive in many cases that there appeared to be little need for rigorous measurement. More recently, however, it has been recognized that the conceptual and methodological foundations of therapy rest on the nature of assessment (Cone & Hawkins, 1977). This is particularly true in the area of eating disorders, where techniques are plentiful but measurement is scarce (Foreyt & Goodrick, 1980).

Assessment and Treatment of Eating Disorders

There has been a remarkable increase in research on eating disorders within the past 15 years. Over 100 controlled studies on the behavioral treatment of obesity have appeared since Stuart's (1967) pioneering report. The interest in behavior therapy for obesity has not been confined to the academic community. In the United States alone, more than one million people each week receive treatment for obesity under the auspices of self-help and commercial weight-loss groups, and behavioral procedures have been instituted by most of these programs (Stunkard & Brownell, 1979). Behavioral techniques have been introduced systematically into Weight Watchers, the largest of these organizations (Stuart, 1977). Self-help books for the dieter have appeared over the past several years (Jeffrey & Katz, 1977; Jordan, Levitz, & Kimbrell, 1976; Mahoney & Mahoney, 1976; Stuart, 1978). This burgeoning of treatment programs occurred well in advance of careful assessment of the behaviors we are attempting to modify, and with little knowledge of the medical and psychological hazards of dieting (Brownell, 1978; Stunkard & Rush, 1974; Wooley, Wooley, & Dyrenforth, 1979). Why has this occurred?

In a paper on treatment-outcome research on obesity, Wilson (1978) described the influences on the research and writing behaviors of scientists. First, there has been major growth of research on therapy in general and behavior therapy in particular. Second, obesity offers a convenient and definitive measure of treatment outcome: weight change. In contrast to the difficulties in measuring depression, anxiety, adjustment, and so forth, subjects in obesity studies need merely step on a scale to provide an index of treatment efficacy. Third, a population for study is readily available. Because 15–25% of the adult American population is overweight (Build and Blood Pressure Study, 1959; Kannel & Gordon, 1974; Metropolitan Life Insurance Company, 1960), and relatively few reduce to ideal weight, clinics and treatment programs are typically deluged with applicants. Fourth, the convenient measure of treatment outcome in obesity led to the choice of this problem as a proving ground for behavioral self-control procedures.

The popularity of research on obesity has been useful because behavioral procedures have been tested in a wide variety of settings, and there now is a generally used "package" of techniques to be applied to the problem. Yet the eating disorders have serious physiologic as well as emotional sequelae. This makes careful assessment critical in designing and evaluating any treatment program.

Articles on assessment of the eating disorders have begun to appear, yet they are scattered among the literature of medicine, psychology, psychiatry, biology, and nutrition. There have been few attempts to coordinate the findings into a comprehensive assessment program (Bray, 1976). This leads to incomplete treatment programs when researchers in one discipline are unaware of findings from other disciplines.

Two eating disorders will be discussed in this chapter: obesity and anorexia nervosa. These are the two most commonly studied eating disorders and provide fertile ground for the development of assessment procedures (Stunkard, 1972). Obesity, probably because of its prevalence, has been studied more frequently than anorexia. Because findings from studies on obesity are often useful in the study of anorexia, obesity will be discussed first and in most detail, followed by findings from studies on anorexia.

Assessment of eating disorders can be divided into six areas, each of which will be discussed separately in this chapter. The first section deals with defining and measuring the extent of the problem, a task that seems deceptively simple. Second, the biological and genetic determinants will be discussed in light of possible implications for treatment. Third, the behavioral determinants will be covered. As will be seen, this area has been the most fruitful in terms of behavioral assessment. Fourth, the assessment of activity and exercise will be discussed. This area is often overlooked in the study of eating disorders. Fifth, the assessment of independent variables will be emphasized to highlight the importance of strict evaluation of treatment procedures. Finally, the evaluation of treatment outcome will be discussed. It will be shown that evaluation of therapies for obesity or anorexia nervosa are more complex than simply determining weight change.

Obesity

Obesity is the number-one nutritional problem in the United States (U.S. Senate, 1977). Thirty percent of men and 40% of women aged 40 to 49 are at least 20% overweight (Metropolitan Life Insurance Company, 1960). The prevalence is even higher with advancing age (Build and Blood Pressure Study, 1959), with decreasing socioeconomic status (Goldblatt, Moore, & Stunkard, 1965), and in a variety of ethnic groups (Stunkard, 1975). Furthermore, the prevalence of obesity is increasing (Van Itallie, 1977). The public holds strongly to several beliefs about obesity: (1) obesity is so prevalent because people are lazy and food is abundant, (2) obesity in an individual is simply due to gluttonous overindulgence, and (3) weight loss is a simple task, and failure in this regard is due to lack of willpower and self-esteem. Contrary to this simplistic view, obesity is a complex phenomenon with genetic, biological, psychological, and environmental origins

(Bray, 1976; Stunkard, 1978; Van Itallie, 1977; Wooley *et al.*, 1979). This diversity in origin and treatment makes the issue of assessment particularly important for defining the type of obesity, the controlling variables, the effects on the environment and the physiology of the person, and the ramifications of weight change.

DEFINING AND MEASURING OBESITY

At first glance, defining obesity would not seem difficult. In most cases, these people viewed as obese would be considered so by any standard. Yet a precise definition of obesity is very important, both for studying prevalence and for determining those for whom weight reduction is appropriate.

The most commonly used criterion for obesity is body weight. If a person's weight exceeds some standard, usually life-insurance-company statistics, then that person is labeled obese. For a person to exceed body weight standards is justification for the label "overweight." However, obesity is a measure of body fat, not body weight. This distinction is important. In many cases, body weight and body fat are correlated, but there are notable exceptions. Some athletes, for example, will have greater body weight but lower body fat than more sedentary persons. Measures of body weight are easy to obtain with a reliable and accurate scale. Measures of body fat are more difficult to obtain and interpret.

MEASURING BODY FAT

The only direct method for measuring body fat is to analyze carcass composition; this has been performed on the cadavers of only eight adults in the past 50 years (Bray, 1976). Indirect methods are most frequently used. Bray (1976) provides a detailed description of each method and an exhaustive list of references in each area. The various methods will be briefly outlined in this chapter.

Simple Rules. A number of simple equations and tests have been devised for measuring body fat. Each has some validity for making gross judgments about individuals, but lacks the specificity for careful research.

1. *Height–weight subtraction.* For a height of 60 inches (150 cm), 100 pounds (45 kg) is the desired weight for a woman and 106 pounds (48 kg) is the desirable weight for a man. To calculate desir-

able weights at other heights, add 5 pounds (2.3 kg) for women and 6 pounds (2.7 kg) for men for every inch (2.5 cm) above this height.

2. *Broca index.* Using metric measures, subtract 100 from the height in centimeters. If the body weight (in kg) exceeds height in centimeters minus 100, then the person is overweight.

3. *Magic 36.* Subtract the waist dimension in inches from height in inches. If the remainder is less than 36, the individual is probably obese.

4. *Ruler test.* With an individual supine, if a ruler placed along the sternum slopes upward toward the umbilicus and touches the skin on the abdomen, the person is obese.

5. *Belt test.* If a belt adjusted to fit tightly around the rib cage cannot be lowered easily down over the abdomen, the person is obese.

6. *Eyeball test.* This is the most common measurement and follows this simple rule. If a person looks fat, he or she *is* fat (Mayer, 1968).

Anthropometric Measures. Bray (1976) and Sims (1977) have described the most useful anthropometric indices of overweight and obesity.

1. *Height–weight tables.* In research, the most widely used measure of excess weight has been the distribution of weights at given heights. The Metropolitan Life Insurance Company (1960) has prepared a table of weight distributions based on the Build and Blood Pressure Study (1959). Frequently, the "ideal" weights listed in the table are mistakenly thought to be average weights or the weights physicians feel are best. Actually, the figures represent the weights at which mortality was lowest. The standards have many limitations: the selection of subjects was biased (only insured persons were measured), the subjects were classified arbitrarily for body-frame size, and all were weighed in shoes and clothes (Sims, 1977).

Height and weight measures have been used in various combinations as indices of obesity. The three ratios most commonly used are weight/height, weight/(height)^2 (the body-mass index), and height/$\sqrt[3]{\text{weight}}$ (the ponderal index). Several authors claim that height/weight is the best measure for women, whereas the body-mass index is best for men (Benn, 1971; Florey, 1970). One study compared these measures with the more direct measurements of density and skinfold thickness, and found the body-mass index to be most valid (Keys, Fidanza, Karvonen, Kimura, & Taylor, 1972). It would appear that height/weight and the body-mass index are the best measures, although an additional measure of fatness such as skinfold thickness is valuable (Bray, 1976).

2. *Skinfold thickness.* Because the thickness of skin from site to site is known, and most of the distance between a fold of skin is body fat, total body fat can be estimated by measuring skinfold thickness from several sites. This method is considered valid by many researchers (Bray, 1976; Franzini & Grimes, 1976; Sims, 1977). There are, however, some limitations. Observers must be very experienced in the use of skinfold calipers, or reliability is unacceptably low (Durnin, Armstrong, & Womersley, 1973). Obesity standards for skinfolds have been developed by Seltzer and Mayer (1965), using the triceps site, and by Durnin and Womersley (1974), using the sum of skinfolds obtained from the triceps, biceps, subscapular, and suprailiac sites. Bray (1976) has encouraged the use of at least two sites when measuring skinfolds.

3. *Body circumferences and diameters.* Behnke and Wilmore (1974) have devised complicated formulas for estimating body fat from measurements of distances around the neck, chest, waist, hips, and thighs, and the diameters or distances between the shoulders or hips. Measurements of this nature tend to be more reliable than skinfolds and are as accurate for obese as for lean subjects (Bray, 1976). This measure is, therefore, quite useful if the sophisticated analyses can be undertaken.

4. *Somatyping.* Sheldon (1954) used pictures of individuals to classify people as endomorphic, mesomorphic, or ectomorphic. These estimations are relatively crude and require extensive training for reliability, but can be useful for making rapid judgments of weight in studies where subjects are not aware of being observed (Brownell, Stunkard, & Albaum, 1978).

5. *Density.* A submerged object displaces its own weight in water. Fat estimates can be obtained by submerging the body in water, then calculating body fat by the use of equations taking into account the average density of fat and nonfat body constituents (Pierson & Lin, 1972). This method, known as hydrostatic weighing, is valid except in cases where body fat distribution is unusual, as with athletes (Bray, 1976). Its use is also limited because sensitive equipment is necessary.

6. *Other methods.* A variety of more sophisticated and costly methods exist for determining body fat, including dilutional tech-

niques, determination of total body water, determination of body potassium, the use of fat-soluble chemicals, ultrasound techniques, and the use of soft X rays. Bray (1976) gives detailed descriptions of these procedures.

To summarize the findings from various measurements of body fat and overweight, the simplest method of determining overweight is to use the Metropolitan Life Insurance Company tables (1960) or a revised version of the same tables developed at the 1977 Fogarty conference (Sims, 1977). This method is criticized by some because body weight rather than body fat is measured (LeBow, 1977; Wilson, 1978). However, weight reduction is prescribed primarily because of the relationship between excess *weight* and health disorders, most notably coronary heart disease (Dyer, Stamler, Berkson, & Lindberg, 1975; Kannel & Gordon, 1977). Similarly, the mortality rates from the Metropolitan Life tables are based on body weights. The relationship between body *fat* and heart disease is probably as strong, if not stronger, because obesity may contribute to heart disease through the development of hyperlipidemia, but this is not as well documented. Therefore, using the height–weight tables may be the most reasonable approach. This information could then be supplemented by the skinfold measure of body fat.

DETERMINANTS OF OBESITY: ASSESSING GENETIC AND BIOLOGICAL FACTORS

The enormous popularity and relative success of behavioral treatments for obesity have reinforced several of the principles upon which these treatments are based: (1) obesity is a function of overconsumption, (2) overconsumption results from learned eating behaviors, and (3) the environment exerts control over ingestion by confronting the obese with cues that serve as discriminative stimuli for eating. Each of these assumptions has been flatly contradicted by well-controlled research. Obese persons do not necessarily eat more than lean persons (Garrow, 1974; Wooley et al., 1979), there does not seem to be an obese eating style (Stunkard & Kaplan, 1977), and the environmental control of eating has only mixed support (Rodin, 1978). These findings point to the important contributions of biology and genetics to obesity. Only recently has this been acknowledge in the behavioral literature (Wooley et al., 1979).

Significant advances are being made in the study of the biological and genetic factors that influence weight regulation. Thus far, however, the findings have not directly related to treatment, so that the assessment of biological and genetic factors does not lead to specific treatment strategies. For this reason, these areas will only be discussed briefly in this chapter. It *is* important that these factors be considered, because the time when treatment is tailored to biology is probably not far in the future.

GENETICS

Genetic factors may be important etiological factors in obesity for both animals and humans. Obesity can be genetically transmitted in experimental animals (Bray & York, 1971). The genetic contribution to obesity in humans has been demonstrated in several ways. First, obesity can be familial: if a child has one overweight parent, there is a 40% chance that that child will be overweight; if both parents are obese, the chances increase to 80% (cf. Bray, 1976). This tendency could result from environmental as well as genetic influences. Results of studies of twins and adopted children are mixed, with some studies finding no genetic contribution (Garn, 1976; Garn & Bailey, 1976) and others finding a substantial contribution (Biron, Mongeau, & Bertrand, 1977; Shields, 1962). Stunkard and his colleagues are now conducting an ambitious study of this question, but the final answer is not yet available. Presently, it can be concluded that genetic factors are clearly related to obesity, but that even in susceptible persons, environmental factors may override genetic ones (Bray, 1976). Genetic factors may create a biological setting for some persons in which obesity is the most favorable state (Keesey, 1978). If so, weight reduction from this optimal obese state could have untoward metabolic consequences. Assessment of genetic factors may be crucial in determining the most suitable body weight.

BIOLOGY

The biology of obesity and its interactions with physiology and metabolism are enormously complex. Thorough coverage of this area is far beyond the scope and purpose of this chapter, and this information appears elsewhere (Bray, 1976). There are, however, two important topics that will be presented here: the set-point theory of weight regulation, and adipose cellularity theory (fat-cell theory). Both topics have implications for assessment and will be critical in our understanding of the development and treatment of obesity.

Set-Point Theory. Keesey (1978) has noted that complex organisms maintain remarkable stability in their internal environment. For each physiologic system, there could be a set-point regulator that controls input and output to maintain regulatory balance. There is mounting evidence that humans have such a set point for body weight and that, in the presence of weight changes, physiologic and metabolic changes occur to defend the suitable body weight (Nisbett, 1972). In the framework of this theory, suitable body weight is determined by many factors, most notably genetics, prenatal conditions, early feeding experiences, and hypothalamic development (Bray, 1976). The set point may vary among individuals, so that for some, the obese state may be most suitable. The remarkable failure of most obese persons to maintain weight loss (Stunkard & McLaren-Hume, 1959) may be a reflection of the tenacity to which the body adheres to a certain weight, even in the face of immense social pressure to reduce.

A number of studies have demonstrated that laboratory animals will adjust food intake and activity to compensate for changes in body weight produced by forced feeding or food restriction (Adolph, 1947; Brooks & Lambert, 1946). Lesions of the lateral hypothalamus and the ventromedial hypothalamus respectively will cause hypophagia and hyperphagia in animals; these changes are accompanied by reliable changes in body weight. These animals will subsequently defend a new body weight as if a new set point had been established (Hoebel & Teitelbaum, 1966; Mitchel & Keesey, 1977). Humans also tend to regulate body weight around a defined point in the face of experimental starvation (Keys, Brozek, Henschel, Mickelson, & Taylor, 1950) or excessive feeding (Sims & Horton, 1968). Wirtshafter and Davis (1977) have proposed an alternate model for this phenomenon that does not include a hypothesized set point. Nevertheless, a set-point does seem to exist even though its controlling mechanisms are not understood clearly (Keesey, 1978).

If, in the attempt to attain society's "ideal" weight, a person reduces to a point below his or her biological set point, the body may react with internal pressures to increase ingestion or decrease energy expenditure. This pressure may have physiologic and emotional manifestations (Keesey, 1978; Wooley et al., 1979).

Assessment of the obese should include a detailed weight history.

If past efforts at weight reduction and periods of weight gain eventually lead to a consistent body weight, a set-point regulatory mechanism may be operating. At present, the set point cannot be determined for individuals. But with increasing sophistication of research in this area, the set point may become an important factor in determining appropriate treatment methods.

Adipose Cellularity. Adipose tissue mass is fundamental in determining body weight (Sjöström, 1978). Changes in the adipose depot can influence body weight by cellular multiplication (hyperplasia) and by cellular enlargement (hypertrophy) (Björntörp & Sjöström, 1971; Bray, 1970; Hirsch & Knittle, 1970). In adults with juvenile-onset obesity (prior to age 12), fat cell *size* typically does not differ from that of normal-weight adults, whereas fat cell *number* can be increased as much as fivefold (Hirsch & Knittle, 1970). Persons with adult-onset obesity are likely to have a normal number of adipocytes but an enlarged cell size (Hirsch & Knittle, 1970; Salans, Horton, & Sims, 1971). It was, therefore, thought that weight gain during adulthood was the result of hypertrophy and, conversely, weight reduction reflected a decrease in cell size, not number (Hirsch & Knittle, 1970).

Weight loss in a hyperplastic individual could theoretically lead to lipid-depleted adipose cells if body weight were lowered while fat-cell number remained constant. The body would respond as if in a state of semistarvation, to replenish the large number of adipose cells with essential constituents. The implication is that those with juvenile-onset obesity would resist weight reduction to maintain an elevated body weight, supposedly because of the association and hypercellularity (Grinker, 1973).

Several studies have evaluated the association between age at onset of obesity and weight loss. There is strong evidence that age at onset does not predict response to treatment or general success at weight reduction (Ashwell, 1975; Brownell, Heckerman, & Westlake, 1979; Brownell, Heckerman, Westlake, Hayes, & Monti, 1978; Ferguson, 1976; Mahoney, Rogers, Straw, & Mahoney, in press). One study even found that persons with juvenile-onset obesity lost more weight than their adult-onset counterparts (Jeffery, Wing, & Stunkard, 1978).

The lack of a relationship between age at onset and success at weight reduction does not rule out the possibility of a relationship between cellularity and weight reduction. Age at onset may not relate strongly enough to cellularity, thus making age at onset a poor predictor (Grinker, 1973; Hirsch & Knittle, 1970). In the most recent review on this subject, Sjöström (1978) concluded that formation of fat cells *can* occur after adolescence. The next logical step would be to measure adipose cellularity in persons losing weight.

Björntörp and his colleagues obtained remarkable results by studying hyperplastic and hypertrophic obese women on a weight-reduction regimen (Björntörp, Carlgren, Isaksson, Krotkiewski, Larsson, & Sjöström, 1975). At the point where each subject stopped losing weight, fat-cell size and number were determined. At this point, fat-cell size for hyperplastic and hypertrophic subjects had reached the size of fat cells of controls, but fat-cell number remained unchanged (Figure 1). Thus, the hypertrophic subjects had a normal

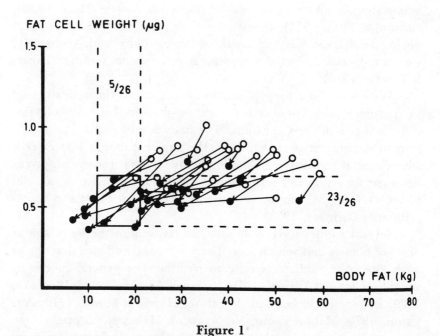

Figure 1

Body fat and average fat-cell size in obese women (open symbols). Changes after failure to reduce in body weight on an energy-reduced diet (arrows and filled symbols). Rectangle denotes mean ± SD of values of controls. Values are corrected for age effects on body fat and cell size. Note the consistent fat-cell weight at which patients failed to decrease body weight. Reprinted by permission from Björntörp *et al.* (1975).

amount of body fat; the hyperplastic subjects remained obese. This suggests that fat-cell number may predict response to treatment and that weight loss in the hyperplastic obese may cease before "ideal" body weight is attained.

Further research is necessary to define the exact relationship between cellularity and weight change. It is potentially a most important association, and at some point may yield guidelines to specify treatments for individuals. Assessment of adipose cellularity may become routine in obesity treatment programs. Unfortunately, determination of fat-cell number and size can be both complicated and costly. Total body fat can be measured with relative ease, as mentioned earlier. Fat-cell determinations are more difficult, and require fat-cell biopsy, microscopic examination, and statistical conversion for standard use (Bray, 1976; Sjöström, 1978). Therefore, this may be a measure of the future.

DETERMINANTS OF OBESITY: EVALUATING EATING BEHAVIOR

Programs based on behavioral principles have been the most effective in treating obesity (Stunkard & Brownell, 1979; Stunkard & Mahoney, 1976; Wilson, 1978). Most of the programs have focused on changing eating behaviors (Ferster, Nurnberger, & Levitt, 1962; Stuart, 1967; Stuart & Davis, 1972). Inherent in this approach is the assumption that the obese display a distinct eating style and that the alteration of this style would produce weight loss (Mahoney, 1975a). Oddly, the efficacy of behavioral treatments was the cause, rather than the result, studies on eating behavior.

Mahoney (1978) described several basic assumptions made by behavioral researchers in the enthusiastic attempt to treat this difficult problem.

1. Obesity is a learned disorder that can be remedied by applying the principles of learning.
2. Obesity is simply a matter of excessive energy intake.
3. The obese overeat.
4. Obese persons are more sensitive than the nonobese to food stimuli.
5. Obese and nonobese persons have different eating styles.
6. Training an obese person to respond like a nonobese person will result in weight loss.

7. Psychological factors do not need to be considered in understanding and treating obesity.

8. Biological and metabolic factors are responsible for only rare cases of obesity.

Most of these assumptions are subject to direct testing, yet only within the past several years have attempts been made to systematically evaluate eating behavior. This is strange, considering that the relationship between eating and body weight is hardly equivocal. Assessment of eating behavior is a crucial issue in studying obesity, and there are four important variables to consider: eating style, responsiveness to food stimuli, food choice, and food preference.

EATING STYLE

Ferster *et al.* (1962) described an "obese eating style" but did not present data to support the existence of such a style. The obese were said to eat more rapidly than normal-weight persons by taking larger and more frequent bites. As Stunkard and Kaplan (1977) have pointed out, it was further assumed that this eating style was instrumental in the pathogenesis of obesity. Accordingly, treatments for the obese generally included techniques aimed at slowing the rate of eating (Stuart & Davis, 1972). These procedures, such as putting down the fork between bites, became the hallmark of behavioral treatments before direct observations of eating behaviors were made (Mahoney, 1975a, 1975b). It is possible, of course, that techniques designed to alter eating style will promote weight loss, even if the obese and nonobese do not differ in eating styles (Stunkard & Brownell, 1979). Even recent programs incorporate eating-style change (Brownell & Stunkard, 1978a; Mahoney & Mahoney, 1976; Stuart, 1978). The role of these techniques in weight-reduction programs will be discussed in the section on assessment of independent variables, but assessment of eating style is important in the understanding of obesity.

For the purposes of this chapter, the methods of studying eating behaviors are as important as the findings from the studies. Therefore, this section and those following will be organized according to the approach of the measurement. For the assessment of eating style, measurement falls into three categories: laboratory measurement of artificial eating situations (eating machines), laboratory observations of normal eating behaviors, and naturalistic observations.

Laboratory Measurement of Feeding. Food dispensers, or eating machines, have been used to evaluate eating patterns in both obese and nonobese humans (Campbell, Hashim, & Van Itallie, 1971; Jordan, Wieland, Zebley, Stellar, & Stunkard, 1966; Walike, Jordan, & Stellar, 1969). Food dispensers have been particularly useful in studying manipulations of oral and gastric preloading (Walike *et al.,* 1969) and the caloric density of meals (Campbell *et al.,* 1971). A variation of this approach has been to supply subjects with liquid meals (Wooley, 1971; Wooley, Wooley, & Dunham, 1972). These methods are useful because the nutritional constitution of meals can be disguised, and subjects do not have the visual cues necessary to measure the amount consumed. A recent innovation in this area has been the use of a feeding machine to give specific feedback to gastric-bypass patients during feeding retraining (Halmi, Stunkard, & Mason, 1980).

There are two eating machines that have been useful in laboratory studies of food consumption. With the machine designed by Jordan *et al.* (1966), subjects ingest liquid meals through a plastic or glass straw attached to a food reservoir (Figure 2). The reservoir can be hidden from the subject or in the subject's view to allow a visual display of food ingestion. The device is convenient because subjects can engage in activities other than eating, if they wish (for example, reading a book). This approach has the disadvantage of using only liquid meals, and there may be differences in the way subjects ingest liquid and solid foods. Kissileff, Klingsberg, and Van Itallie (1980) have developed a Universal Eating Monitor for the study of eating behavior in the laboratory. Subjects are seated at a table and eat from dishes placed on a false platform that is actually a very sensitive scale (Figure 3). The platform is covered with a tablecloth so subjects are not aware that the amount of food they eat is being monitored continuously by a recorder attached to the scale. The monitor can be used to measure intake of solid or liquid meals and is extremely accurate. Its cost and the fact that it must be used in the laboratory prevent routine use in research.

Food dispensers and eating machines will undoubtedly play an increasingly important role in the study of eating style. This type of measurement has not been developed to the point where it can be used for diagnostic purposes or to devise treatment strategies, but this may be possible in the near future. The laboratory is an ideal place to

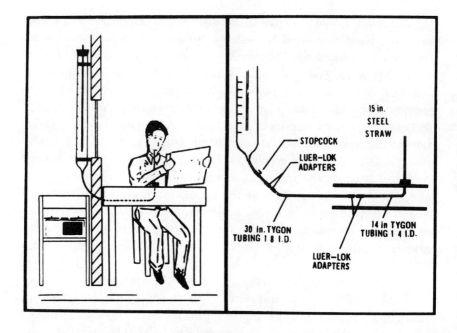

Figure 2
The feeding machine used to assess eating patterns in the laboratory. The food reservoir is hidden from view in this instance but can be placed in view of the subject to provide feedback. Reprinted by permission from Jordan *et al.* (1966).

control the eating situation, yet the artificiality may influence the very behaviors being evaluated. This has led to the laboratory study of more conventional methods of ingestion.

Laboratory Measurement of Conventional Eating Practices. Some researchers have attempted to simulate natural eating conditions in the laboratory. Mahoney (1975b), for example, assessed eating style in obese and nonobese humans by providing a standardized laboratory meal consisting of a roast beef sandwich, an apple turnover, and a drink. Subjects were observed via a closed-circuit television and were scored for meal duration and bites per minute. Schachter and his colleagues have used similar procedures to measure the amount eaten in response to manipulations of the environment (Goldman, Jaffe, & Schachter, 1968; Schachter & Gross, 1968; Schachter & Rodin, 1974). These studies typically involve disguising the nature of the study and then allowing subjects free access to "normal" foods such as peanuts and sandwiches. Reviews of this method of studying eating behavior have been written by Rodin (1977, 1978) and Schachter and Rodin (1974).

It has been assumed that allowing subjects access to conventional foods is preferable to the artificiality of a feeding machine. However, the behavior under study (eating patterns) can be influenced by seemingly trivial alterations in the way conventional foods are presented. Nisbett (1968a), for example, found that the number of sandwiches presented to subjects influenced the number eaten. Also, eating behavior in the laboratory, either with feeding machines or conventional foods, has never been tested to determine how closely it approximates eating in natural settings. Therefore, the laboratory is a

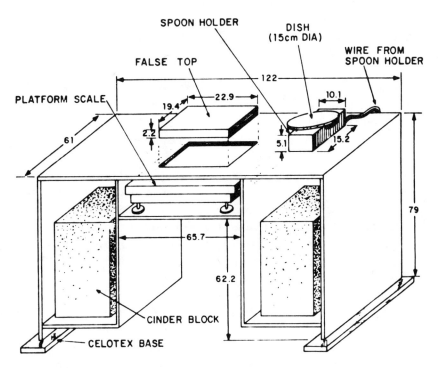

Figure 3

The Universal Eating Monitor for measuring eating behavior in the laboratory. Food is placed in a dish on the false top and then weighed continuously by the platform scale. The spoon holder records the amount of time the spoon is in place on the table. Reprinted by permission from Kissileff *et al.* (1980).

promising site for the study of eating styles, but validity studies are necessary and the influence of the nature of the setting must be evaluated.

Naturalistic Observations. To escape the confines of the laboratory, researchers have recently studied humans in their homes and in restaurants. This movement was born from the desire to settle the question of an obese eating style (Mahoney, 1975b; Stunkard & Kaplan, 1977). These studies have allowed comparisons of obese and nonobese subjects for the rate of eating, the number of bites, meal duration, meal size, meal composition, food choice, and so forth. The methods for studying eating style have improved greatly in the past several years, and there is much evidence bearing on the eating style of the obese.

The majority of naturalistic studies have been conducted in fast-food restaurants or cafeterias (Coll, Meyers, & Stunkard, 1979; Dodd, Birky, & Stalling, 1976; Gates, Hueneman, & Brand, 1975; Gaul, Craighead, & Mahoney, 1975; Krassner, Brownell, & Stunkard, 1979; Mahoney, 1975b; Marston, London, Cooper, & Cohen, 1975). These studies have found that the obese and nonobese cannot be distinguished on the basis of eating style, and that the eating site exerts a much greater influence on eating than does body weight. Support for this notion comes from an elaborate study by Meyers, Coll, and Stunkard (1977) of 5041 food choices in five eating sites: a fast-food hamburger and chicken shop, an ice cream shop, a cafeteria regular service counter, a cafeteria fast-service counter, and a race track. There were no differences among obese and nonobese subjects for rate of eating, amount of food chosen, or duration of the meal. It does appear, however, that the obese may seek out eating situations such as smorgasbords where increased intake is the rule (Stunkard & Mazer, 1978).

The methods used in these studies are noteworthy. Subjects are typically observed without their knowledge and are rated for the amount of food chosen, duration of the meal, number of mouthfuls, number of chews and sips, and the amount of food left over (Gaul *et al.*, 1975; Stunkard & Kaplan, 1977). These observations are made using a time-sampling technique which allows for calculation of specific eating behaviors per unit time. Sophisticated analyses have been developed to form a model of eating topography (Stunkard, Coll, Lundquist, & Meyers, in press). Blundell (1980) has shown that the number of calories per minute is the most sensitive measure of changes produced by appetite-suppressing medications and other interventions. Naturalistic measurement of eating behaviors may be more useful in evaluating treatment-produced changes in obese persons than in distinguishing the obese from the nonobese. If specific behaviors (for example, calories consumed per minute) are associated with weight change, then treatment can be designed accordingly.

Interestingly, very little observation of eating practices in the home has been done. Self-monitoring of food intake has been used as much as a reactive tool as a measurement device, and there is some evidence that self-monitoring records may not be accurate (Brownell et al., 1978). Coates (1977) developed the Eating Analysis and Treatment Schedule (EATS) to be used in the home. The EATS is scored by nonparticipant observers in the homes of overweight subjects. Before a meal, various locations in the home are scored for the presence of specific foods, and the meal preparation is scored for the type of food that was prepared and how it was served. During the meal the subjects are observed for bites, chews, and the other eating behaviors mentioned above. The EATS is a promising measure, and takes into account the situation as well as the actual eating behavior.

Waxman and Stunkard (1979) have used the technology developed in naturalistic settings to measure eating and activity patterns of young children in the home. The same children were rated for the same behaviors in the school, and in some cases, differences emerged for the same child across settings. Because much of a person's eating may be done in the home, and because the situational control over eating is well documented, measurement in the home is increasingly important.

ENVIRONMENTAL CONTROL OF EATING

In 1964, Stunkard and Koch reported findings that spurred more than 10 years of research into the internal and external events that influence eating. In this study, high correlations between gastric contractions and reported hunger were found for normal-weight subjects but not for obese subjects. Subsequent reports indicate that gastric motility is not a useful measure of hunger (Janowitz, 1967; Stunkard & Fox, 1971), but the implication of the original study— that the obese and nonobese differ in response to food cues—has had a strong impact on research on obesity. Schachter (1968) used the Stunkard and Koch (1964) findings to argue that obese persons are

more responsive to external eating cues than thin persons. Several in-
genious experiments were then performed that supported this notion
(Rodin & Slochower, 1976; Schachter, Goldman, & Gordon, 1968;
Schachter & Gross, 1968; Schachter & Rodin, 1974). This heightened
external responsiveness has been proposed as an etiological factor in
obesity (Schachter & Rodin, 1974).

There has been great dispute recently about the externality hypothesis. It is now clear that there are two *independent* phenomena to
study: the sensitivity of the obese to external cues, and the insensitiv-
ity of the obese to internal signals of hunger. The implications for assessment and treatment are far-reaching. If the obese could profit
from increased sensitivity to internal hunger signals, assessment of
hunger would be of great importance. Hunger is a complex physiologic process that has been difficult to define, measure, and study. A
detailed analysis of this area of research is given in a recent book edited by Booth (1978). Wooley *et al.* (1979) have also reviewed the studies on the relation between hunger and obesity. At present, assessing
hunger for clinical purposes is best accomplished with a simple (but
crude) self-report (Monello & Mayer, 1967). More sophisticated
measures include assessment of salivary secretion (Grill, 1979; Wooley
& Wooley, 1973) and other physiologic processes (Booth, 1978).

Measuring external control over eating is much easier. The technology for doing so will be discussed briefly, as will restrained eating,
a new development in the field. Studies on external responsiveness
note the presence of the phenomenon, and studies on restrained eating attempt to explain it.

External Cues. Many external factors may influence eating.
These include time, sight of food, environmental factors, and the
taste of food (Rodin, 1978). The sensitivity of the obese to these factors has been measured primarily in sociopsychological laboratory research. The results from these studies are informative and suggest
that obese and nonobese persons may differ in their response to food
cues in some situations. Assessing cue sensitivity in clinical situations
is more complex, and little research has been devoted to this problem.

Studies of naturally occurring and artificial manipulations of
time suggest that the obese are more responsive to this cue than the
nonobese. Obese subjects have shown greater changes in eating in response to the time they *thought* had passed while they were engaged
in various tasks (Rodin, 1975). Schachter and Gross (1968) noted that

east-west travel creates a situation in which scheduled eating times at the point of departure differ from those at the point of arrival, thus providing a test of whether the obese are more responsive to the body's need for energy or to the scheduled eating times at the location. Accordingly, Goldman *et al.* (1968) studied Air France personnel and found a consistent relationship between the degree of overweight and the difficulty adjusting to differences in physiologic state and local meal times.

Nisbett (1968b) studied the prominence of visual food cues by allowing obese and nonobese subjects access to an unlimited number of sandwiches while manipulating the number of sandwiches in sight. Obese subjects ate almost one sandwich more when three were in sight than when one was in sight; nonobese subjects did not differ in the two situations. Ross (1974) found that obese persons ate twice as much when cashews were brightly lighted than when they were dimly lighted. Obese subjects actually ate less than normal-weight subjects when the cashews were dimly lighted.

Stimulus control procedures form the foundation of behavioral treatment programs and are predicated on the notion that the obese will profit from avoiding environmental eating cues. The cues mentioned previously, time and sight of food, are important, but there are other hypothesized cues. These include location, other people present, activities (for example, watching televison, reading the morning paper). Supposedly, repeated pairings of eating with these cues could lead the cues to become discriminative stimuli that could provoke eating. For four reasons this notion is unsupported: (1) there have been no direct tests that demonstrate a conditioned association between food cues and eating; (2) no studies have shown that the obese are particularly sensitive to these specific cues; (3) there is no indication that such an association, if it does exist, is an etiologic factor in obesity; and (4) there is no evidence that decreasing the salience of these cues will lead to weight change. Research may prove any of these factors to be true, but at present only the success of behavioral treatments can be used to infer the importance of these cues. The only direct attempts to assess the importance of these factors have shown no relationship between cue change and weight change (Brownell *et al.*, 1978; Stalonas, Johnson, & Christ, 1978).

Taste would seem to be the most important external determinant of eating behavior (Rodin, 1978). Palatability influences food intake in persons in all weight categories (Young, 1967), although manipulations of palatability seem to influence the obese more than the nonobese. Several studies have shown that obese subjects eat significantly more of highly palatable foods than nonobese subjects, and eat significantly less of low palatability foods (Decke, 1971; Nisbett, 1968b; Price & Grinker, 1973; Rodin, 1975). Wooley and Wooley (1975) have noted that many of these studies on palatability have not been replicated. The relationship between hunger, palatability, and eating is very complex, and adequate measurement of the critical factors is only now being developed (Wooley et al., 1979).

It is possible that overweight people show greater responsiveness to food stimuli than do thin people. It is more likely, however, that most people are responsive to food cues, and that some people in all weight classifications are extraordinarily sensitive (Rodin, 1978). The issue is complicated further by findings that animals can show heightened responsiveness to food cues, that obese animals can differ in this regard from normal-weight animals, and that heightened responsiveness may have physiologic consequences which can influence subsequent sensitivity to food cues (Powley, 1977; Schachter & Rodin, 1974). Most likely, there is a subgroup of the obese population that displays this heightened sensitivity, which may or may not contribute to their obesity: modification of this sensitivity may or may not contribute to weight change. It is important to evaluate the relationship between behavior change and weight change, an issue that will be discussed later. Assessing external responsiveness is an important factor in this measurement.

Measures of responsiveness to external cues need to be developed and perfected. The laboratory measures are useful for determining differences among populations, but are not useful clinically. In most behavioral programs, participants are asked to complete a detailed self-monitoring record that includes information on the times, places, activities, and feelings associated with eating (Brownell & Stunkard, 1978a; Stuart & Davis, 1972). From this, a therapist can formulate a clinical impression about the situations associated with eating, but this type of measurement has never been validated and is likely to be a crude method for assessing external responsiveness. The Mahoney Master Questionnaire (Wollersheim, 1970) can be useful in assessing external responsiveness. A great deal of work is currently being done on the Mahoney Master Questionnaire, and this may prove to be a valuable tool for measuring a number of factors associated with weight change.

Restrained Eating. As mentioned in the section on biological determinants of obesity, there is a hypothesized set point — a weight that the body is "set" to defend (Nisbett, 1972). The set point may be determined by the number of adipocytes or other factors (Hirsch & Knittle, 1970). When a person, obese or nonobese, suppresses weight to a level under that set point, physiologic and psychological changes may occur that promote increased eating in order to increase weight. Nisbett (1972) proposed that deviation from the set point, rather than weight per se, would determine sensitivity to food cues.

Herman and Mack (1975) used Nisbett's theory to propose that persons below their set point are "restrained eaters": by definition they must restrain their eating to avoid moving toward their natural weight. This restraint, or resistance to physiologic signals to gain weight, would be manifested by attempts at dieting. Under the guise of a taste test, Herman and Mack (1975) administered a restraint scale to subjects who were then given zero, one, or two milkshakes before having free access to ice cream. Unrestrained eaters, those not dieting, showed a consistent decrease in eating in response to the size of the preload, whereas restrained eaters consumed *more* as the size of the preload increased. Polivy (1976) then manipulated the perceived size of the preload and found that restrained eaters who thought they had a large preload consumed more than those believing they had received a small preload. Other subsequent studies had similar results (see Herman, 1978, for a review of the area).

This finding that restrained eaters (dieters) would increase consumption after a large preload is counterintuitive because these people have the greatest desire to limit intake. Herman and his colleagues suggested that ingestion of the large preload was inconsistent with short-term dieting, thus creating disinhibition for later eating (Herman, 1978; Herman & Polivy, 1975; Spencer & Fremouw, 1979). Such a restrained eater might think, "I've already blown my diet for the day with all this food, so I may as well eat all I want now." As a result of many studies, Herman (1978) has presented a reviewed Restraint Scale (Figure 4). Stunkard and Messick (1979) have devised a Restraint in Eating Questionnaire which contains approximately 60 items. Psychometric testing shows that this questionnaire is valid, reliable, and predictive.

Restrained eating is a measurable and useful construct. Unlike most characteristics associated with dieting, restraint can be assessed and related to problems that may be related to difficulties with diet-

1. How often are you dieting? Never; rarely; sometimes; often; always.
    (Scored 0-4)

2. What is the maximum amount of weight (in pounds) that you have ever lost
    in one month? 0-4; 5-9; 10-14; 15-19; 20+. (Scored 0-4)

3. What is your maximum weight gain within a week? 0-1; 1.1-2; 2.1-3;
    3.1-5; 5.1+. (Scored 0-4)

4. In a typical week, how much does your weight fluctuate? 0-1; 1.1-2;
    2.1-3; 3.1-5; 5.1+. (Scored 0-4)

5. Would a weight fluctuation of 5 pounds affect the way you live your life?
    Not at all; slightly; moderately; very much. (Scored 0-3)

6. Do you eat sensibly in front of others and splurge alone? Never; rarely;
    often; always. (Scored 0-3)

7. Do you give too much time and thought to food? Never; rarely; often;
    always. (Scored 0-3)

8. Do you have feelings of guilt after overeating? Never; rarely; often;
    always. (Scored 0-3)

9. How conscious are you of what you are eating? Not at all; slightly;
    moderately; extremely. (Scored 0-3)

10. How many pounds over your desired weight were you at your maximum weight?
    0-1; 1-5; 6-10; 11-20; 21+. (Scored 0-4)

Figure 4

A scale to measure restraint in eating. Reprinted by permission from Herman (1978).

ing (for example, hyperemotionality, external responsiveness). Information from restrained-eating scales may yield accurate information which can be used to prescribe treatment strategies.

FOOD CHOICE

The type and amount of food chosen by obese persons is a factor of obvious importance, yet only within the past several years has there been research on this issue. Little was known about the food-choice patterns of obese persons, or whether obese and nonobese persons differ in this regard. Information about the food consumption of obese and normal-weight persons has come from two different sources: nutritional surveys and metabolic studies (Coll *et al.*, 1979). Nutritional surveys show that the obese eat no more than the nonobese (cf. Wooley *et al.*, 1979), whereas metabolic studies show that the obese eat much more (cf. Bray, 1976). Why this confusing picture, and what is the resolution of this question?

Coll *et al.* (1979) studied more than 5000 food choices at nine eating sites. Body weight had no effect on food choice in eight of the nine sites; only at the site serving food with the highest caloric content did the obese eat somewhat more. Wooley *et al.* (1979) and Garrow (1974) have completed exhaustive reviews of the literature, and suggest that there is no difference in food intake between obese and nonobese persons. It is possible, of course, that excessive consumption in the obese is under strict situational control. There are two possible implications of this. First, the obese may overeat when alone, whereas in public places or with others their eating behavior is controlled to approximate "normal" practices. Second, the obese may seek out eating sites where excessive ingestion is encouraged. Coll *et al.* (1979) concluded from their study of food choices that location is the most powerful determinant of consumption, and Stunkard and Mazer (1978) found that obese persons were overrepresented at a smorgasbord.

Unfortunately, these studies have not focused on the types of food chosen by obese persons. The nutritional composition of food choices could effect total caloric ingestion, subsequent hunger, and lipogenesis. Studies of this nature are necessary, yet potentially suffer from the same problems as studies of the amount of food chosen: eating may be under situational control. A description of the means of assessment in this area will indicate the narrow range of situations in which the obese have been observed.

Naturalistic observations of food choice have commonly been done by unobtrusive observers in public locations such as fast-food restaurants. Observers may have scoring sheets which indicate the weight status and categories of food choices for the subjects. Reliability for weight status can be good with this type of measurement, particularly if subjects are placed in a small number of categories (for example, if a dichotomy is made between obese and nonobese). Food choice may be difficult to quantify if serving sizes are not constant, but this can be overcome to some extent by weighing foods prior to serving and then again at the end of a meal (Meyers *et al.*, 1977). Laboratory studies are useful, yet food choice is limited and the artificial environment could influence the behavior being studied.

Nutrition surveys are typically used as self-reports of dietary recall (Johnson, Burke, & Mayer, 1956). These studies usually show that the obese eat no more than the nonobese and that reported food intake is not associated with physiologic factors such as serum cholesterol. The validity of these measurements has been evaluated in only one study, and the accuracy of self-monitoring was poor (Dwyer & Mayer, 1969). Brownell *et al.* (1978) found that self-reported caloric intake was not correlated with weight change, even though daily records were kept and the correlations were calculated over a 10-week period. This suggests that records of food consumption may not be accurate.

In clinical practice, food choice is best measured by self-report. The accuracy can probably be improved by having a convenient monitoring form, instructing subjects to monitor immediately after consumption reinforcing record keeping, and having checks (perhaps from family members) on the accuracy. Other methods are also available for improving the accuracy of self-monitoring (Mahoney, 1977; Nelson, 1977). Obtaining reports from family members may be useful because they would have more direct access to the dieter's food choices, but in some cases even the family is unaware of the eating of the obese person because much is done privately. Unfortunately, these methods for assessing food choice are untested, but seem to be the best available currently.

Some studies have inferred food consumption from food choice; if obese people choose the same amount of food as nonobese persons, it is assumed that caloric consumption is also the same. This is based on the assumption that all people eat everything they choose, or at least that the obese and nonobese do not differ in this respect. Several studies have shown that the obese are more likely than the nonobese to finish the food they choose (Dodd *et al.*, 1976; Krassner *et al.*, 1979, Marston *et al.*, 1975). Therefore, measures of food intake must take into account food chosen and food left over.

FOOD PREFERENCE

Food preference may be one of the most important factors to evaluate in the treatment of obesity. If the obese prefer foods that contribute to excess weight, modifying food preferences could facilitate weight reduction. There is evidence that food preferences can be changed by reinforcing modifications in food choice (Epstein, Masek, & Marshall, 1978; Herbert-Jackson & Risley, 1977; Madsen, Madsen, & Thompson, 1974). A great deal of work has been done on the development of food preferences in animals and humans. It appears that food preference can be influenced by biological/genetic factors, cultural background, food availability, family environment, and by powerful learning experiences. The complexity of this matter becomes more evident as anthropological, biological, sociological, psychological, and nutritional research is devoted to this subject. Not surprisingly, measurement of food preference is not well developed.

In animals, food preference can be determined merely by allowing the animal access to a variety of foods. In humans, such is not the case, and food preference must be inferred from food choice. This inference may be problematic. If obese persons are being observed choosing food in a public restaurant, for example, the food chosen may vary as a function of whether the obese person is alone or with other people.

One method for assessing food preference is the salivary measure developed by Wooley and Wooley (1973). This procedure involves placing three one-and-one-half-inch dental rolls in the mouth, one sublingually and two buccally bilaterally. Subjects are exposed to food and are asked to imagine eating it. The dental rolls are then weighed to measure the degree of salivation in response to exposure to the food. Another salivary measure, which dates back to Pavlov, involves placing a small suction-type cup over the parotid gland in the mouth. Recent studies show that this approach may be more accurate than the dental roll procedure and that the results may be more valid (Grill, 1979).

This area may be one of the most important for research on assessment. Food preferences and food availability may underlie changes in weight, or may be crucial to the modification of weight. These possibilities are largely unexplored. This is due in part to the lack of emphasis on these factors, but also to the lack of adequate measurement. The modification of food preferences may be especially important for children during periods when food preferences are acquired.

DETERMINANTS OF OBESITY:
EVALUATING PHYSICAL ACTIVITY

The word "obesity" is derived from *ob* (over), and *edere* (to eat). This age-old bias, that obesity is solely a function of excessive ingestion, still lingers today. Nearly every treatment program for obesity has focused primarily on food intake, and little emphasis has been placed on energy expenditure. There is a tendency to infer cause from this bias in treatment, a phenomenon that perpetuates the notion that a person becomes obese because of poor restraint and extraordinary consumption. Surprisingly little is known about the relative contribution of eating and exercise patterns in the obese. Exercise physiologists have developed sophisticated measures of activity, but use of these measures in clinical practice has lagged far behind. Much of the important work in this area has been done with children.

In 1940, Bruch reported that obese children eat more and exercise less than thin children. Subsequent studies indicated that obese children consume no more than nonobese children, but the obese children were still found to be less active (Bullen, Reed, & Mayer, 1964; Cahn, 1968; Johnson *et al.*, 1956; Maxfield & Konishi, 1966; Stephanic, Heald, & Mayer, 1959). Data from the studies by Mayer and colleagues have led to the speculation that inactivity is implicated in obesity but that overeating is not (Mann, 1974; Mayer, 1968; Wooley *et al.*, 1979). Yet with the exception of the study by Bullen *et al.* (1964), information on food consumption and activity had been gathered from self-reports by the children or from recordings by the parents. In addition, other studies that employed more objective measures of exercise (pedometers and continuous heart-rate monitoring) found few differences in activity between obese and nonobese children (Bradfield, Paulos, & Grossman, 1971; Stunkard & Pestka, 1962; Wilkinson, Parklin, Pearloom, Strang, & Sykes, 1977). This confusing picture can only be cleared by the intensive assessment that the following study typifies.

Waxman and Stunkard (1979) conducted an intensive evaluation of eating and activity in children and have made an important advance in the study of these behaviors. Caloric intake and energy expenditure of children in four families were assessed by nonparticipant observers during family dinners, school lunches, play inside and outside of the home, and play at school recess. Each family had one obese and a nonobese brother less than two years apart in age. The nonobese brother served as a control for the obese boy for activity inside and outside the home and for family dinners, whereas a nonobese peer served as the control for school lunches and school recess. Oxygen consumption levels for various activities were measured for the obese boys and the controls in the laboratory to calculate caloric expenditure from the observed activities.

The results showed that obese boys consumed more calories than did their nonobese brothers at home, and far more calories than their nonobese peers at school. The obese boys also ate faster than their controls at home and at school. The assessment of exercise showed that the obese boys were far less active than their brothers inside the home, slightly less active outside the home, and as active as their nonobese peers at school. However, since the obese boys weighed more, they expended more calories than did their thin controls for the same activity. The activities were converted to caloric expenditure, using oxygen-consumption information from the laboratory. The obese boys were then found to expend as many calories through exercise as their brothers in the home; and outside the home and in school, the obese boys expended *more* calories.

This study needs to be replicated with girls, and with adults of both sexes. The technology for measuring eating and exercise in the natural environment may be useful for further study in this area. The fact that the relative caloric expenditure for the obese and nonobese boys could only be determined accurately after physiologic measurement of oxygen consumption suggests that self-report and observational measures be construed as gross indicators of energy expenditure.

ACTIVITY, FOOD INTAKE, AND BODY WEIGHT

Body weight is a simple function of energy consumed versus energy expended. This elementary energy balance model oversimplifies a very complex network of physiologic processes (Bray, 1976). Actually, only a portion of the body's energy expenditure can be attributed to obvious physical activity. Basal metabolism, the total of the minimal activity of all body tissue under steady-state conditions, accounts for a great deal of the body's energy needs. The basal metabolic rate (BMR) is influenced by body weight, sex, age, climate, drugs, hormones, the specific dynamic action of food, and physical activity (Bray, 1976). The BMR varies widely among individuals. There is some truth to the widely disputed claim of some obese persons that they eat very little and still maintain a high body weight (Durnin, Blake, & Brockway, 1957; Rose & Williams, 1961). These people could be victims of very efficient metabolic systems; that is, energy consumed is converted to body tissue with little waste in the process. In addition, metabolic rate can change within the same person over time. Bray (1969) studied six obese patients on an intake of 450 calories per day, after having intakes of 3500 calories per day for one week. As Figure 5 illustrates, body weight decreased with the lowered intake, and BMR (oxygen consumption) also decreased. At this point, the body was more efficient than before the change in body weight.

It appears that measuring overt activity is only part of the challenge in assessing the energy-expenditure portion of the energy-balance equation. The information presented above documents the complexity of energy expenditure. It is unclear to what extent measuring physical activity reflects total energy expenditure. This measurement is, however, important for clinical purposes in a program where an increase in activity is important. What measures of activity are there?

DIRECT MEASUREMENT OF ENERGY EXPENDITURE

Direct Calorimetry. The only known method for measuring total energy expenditure is by direct calorimetry. Total heat loss from the body is measured by placing the organism in a chamber that will measure all the heat released from the body in the form of thermal energy, radiant energy, energy from vaporization of water from the lungs, the production of carbon dioxide, and the uptake of oxygen (Bray, 1976). This method has been used with animals (Blaxter, 1971) and in only a few instances with humans (Atwater & Benedict, 1905). The use of this procedure is of course limited by practical concerns.

INDIRECT MEASUREMENT OF ENERGY EXPENDITURE

Indirect Calorimetry. Total energy expenditure can be estimated by measuring carbon dioxide production, oxygen uptake, and nitrogen excretion. Known values for carbohydrate and fat oxidation are then used to calculate metabolic rate (Astrand & Rodahl, 1970; Durnin & Brockway, 1959). Also, total energy expended can be estimated from vaporization from the lungs (Johnston & Newburgh,

ENERGY EXPENDITURE

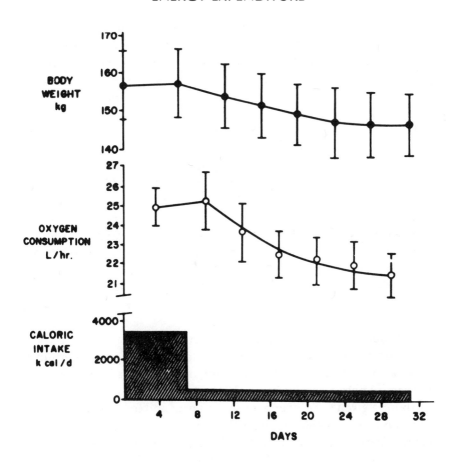

Figure 5

Effect of caloric restriction on oxygen consumption of six obese patients. After one week on a diet of 3500 kcal/day, caloric intake was reduced to 450 kcal/day. Body weight declined but the drop in oxygen uptake was proportionally faster, representing a fall of 15% by the end of two weeks. Reprinted by permission from Bray (1969).

1942) and from heart rate (Bradfield, 1971; Mayfield, 1971). These methods are also somewhat complicated to use, so most clinical researchers have measured exercise rather than energy expenditure.

MEASUREMENT OF EXERCISE

The exact relationship between exercise and energy expenditure is unclear, yet many researchers equate the two. In clinical use, measures of activity are probably the best way to estimate energy expenditure, and the measures discussed below are the most commonly used.

Self-Report. As mentioned earlier, the early studies of exercise used self-report (Johnson *et al.*, 1956; Stephanic *et al.*, 1959). More recent studies of the modification of activity patterns and of the epidemiology of heart disease have used continuous self-recording of activity (Epstein, Thompson, & Wing, in press) or retrospective questionnaires on exercise habits (Paffenbarger & Hale, 1975). Neither of these measures has been tested against more objective measures to assess validity, although the study by Epstein *et al.* (in press) indicates that self-report may be valid. This type of measurement is probably the easiest to use and offers the advantage of giving some indication of what a person is doing outside the laboratory setting. It is likely that self-monitoring of activity could be improved by the guidelines presented in research on self-monitoring of other target behaviors (Mahoney, 1977; Nelson, 1977).

Laboratory Regimens. Physical activity can be controlled and therefore measured by having subjects take part in a predetermined program in the laboratory. This is the method most frequently used in exercise physiology studies. Subjects run, walk, swim, cycle, and so forth for a given time, over a given distance, and for a given intensity, and then the physiologic effects of the activity are measured. This control is useful because it standardizes the amount of exercise across subjects, but metabolic differences among individuals make this an imprecise measure of energy expenditure.

Prescribed Activity Programs. Subjects may be instructed to exercise a given amount outside the laboratory. This is a less costly method of measurement, but some subjects may exercise more or less than the prescribed amount, thus complicating interpretation of the results.

Pedometers. A pedometer is about the size of a pocket watch. A delicately balanced arm is displaced by slight movement in the vertical plane. These displacements turn a series of gears. When the pedometer is worn from the waist, walking transmits an impulse to the balance arm. The pedometer can be calibrated for the length of stride to convert impulses to distances. Pedometers are quite useful in research on obesity (Stunkard, 1960) and in clinical practice (Ferguson, 1975). However, the instruments have some error in measurement, are easily broken, and may be too sensitive to extraneous movement. Pedometers are relatively unobtrusive and offer a good general measure of activity. Electronic pedometers are now being developed and will probably be more accurate.

Heart Rate. Changes in heart rate offer some indication of physical activity. Cardiologists use a portable heart-rate monitor for many patients with heart disease. Some machines even provide a continuous electrocardiogram. The monitor can be carried in a pocket or in a small holster and the impulses are recorded on a tape that can be analyzed later. If this were combined with a pedometer reading, a somewhat unbiased report of physical activity could be obtained.

Observation in the Natural Environment. All the measures listed above may have reactive effects on the very activity being measured. In addition, little is known about exercise patterns in the natural environment. Bullen *et al.* (1964) used motion picture sampling to test the activity of girls in a summer camp. The girls were taped at various activities (for example, during volleyball). The tapes were then rated for the amount of activity displayed during a certain time interval. This could also be reactive, but is one means of measuring activity in a natural setting.

Another way of measuring activity is to evaluate routine exercise in natural settings. In two studies this was done by measuring the choice between stairs and escalators in locations where the two were adjacent (Brownell, Stunkard, & Albaum, in press; Meyers, Stunkard, Coll, & Cooke, 1980). In the Brownell *et al.* (in press) study, more than 40,000 persons were observed by inconspicuously located observers in a shopping mall, a train station, and a bus terminal. The observation procedures were reliable and provided information about activity choice in the natural environment.

ASSESSING INDEPENDENT VARIABLES

One major problem in evaluating treatment strategies has been the lack of measurement of independent variables. In most cases, behavior change (adherence to the program guidelines) is inferred from weight change. When patients lost weight after completing a diet program of any sort, it is often assumed that the program caused the change, and that the specific techniques of the program were responsible for the change. If a group of patients are put on a ketogenic diet and lose weight, it is assumed that the patients actually used the diet and that the diet made them lose weight. Mahoney (1975a) has noted the same tendency among behavioral researchers to infer behavior change from weight change. Brownell and Stunkard (1978b) raised a troubling question in a review of behavioral treatment studies: "Does the weight loss in behavioral programs result from the specific changes prescribed by the programs?" Few studies have addressed this issue.

At first glance, the answer to this question seems obvious. Behavioral treatments have consistently produced greater weight loss than a variety of nonbehavioral treatments. Both Wollersheim (1970) and Hagen (1974) found significant correlations between weight change and behavior change assessed by an Eating Patterns Questionnaire. Mahoney (1974) reported a significant correlation between weight loss and behavior change scores from an Eating Habits Booklet. Why doubt that the programs produce the prescribed behavior change and that the change leads to weight loss?

These studies were all based on self-report of habit change, and the Eating Patterns Questionnaire is a post hoc inventory of a variety of eating behaviors. Studies with more detailed measures have led to surprising results. Jeffery *et al.* (1978) analyzed daily eating-behavior records kept by 31 patients during the first and fifth weeks of treatment and quantified changes in the nine behaviors that were the object of the program. None of the correlations between behavior and weight was statistically significant. Bellack, Rozensky, and Schwartz (1974) had subjects rate compliance with program guidelines and found no relationship with weight loss. Epstein and Martin (1977) had 12 patients self-monitor food intake and exercise habits and concluded that compliance was too low to allow learning of the prescribed procedures.

Brownell *et al.* (1978) carried out a more extensive analysis of behavior records from 29 subjects for each day of a 10-week program. Behavior changes were not correlated with weight changes during treatment or at a six-month follow-up. For nine subjects, these records were supplemented by spouses' records of the subjects' behavior.

Again, there was no correlation between weight loss and behavior, this time as measured by the spouses. In a similar analysis, Stalonas *et al.* (1978) collected daily records from 44 subjects and correlated 10 categories of behaviors with weight change. Nine of the 10 categories and an overall compliance score did not correlate with weight loss.

One study did find a correlation between weight change and a combined score of food choice and exercise (Öst & Götestam, 1976). However, the behavioral measures were not clearly defined and it is not clear how this study differed from others. Jeffery and Wing (1979) found that a self-reported measure of caloric intake correlated with weight loss; a self-report of exercise did not. No measure of behavior was reported.

These findings have implications for behavioral weight-control programs. The most extensive studies have found no relationship between behavior change and weight change (Brownell *et al.*, 1978; Stalonas *et al.*, 1978). This result does not mean that such a relationship does not exist, but it does suggest that the relationship does not necessarily exist. The relationship between adherence and weight change is even less clearly understood with nonbehavioral programs, for only the behavioral researchers have addressed the issue.

. Assessment of independent variables is the cornerstone of program evaluation. Without this assessment, the action of specific treatments can only be inferred from outcome, a step that is unacceptable. Eating and activity behaviors can be measured according to the guidelines provided in earlier sections of this chapter. It is important for researchers and clinicians alike to pay careful attention to adherence to program prescriptions.

ASSESSMENT OF TREATMENT OUTCOME

There are a number of methods for determining changes in body weight and body fat (Bray, 1976). After an adequate measure has been selected, there are many ways of presenting and evaluating treatment data. Wilson (1978) has presented these methods and has outlined the shortcomings of each. As mentioned earlier, the most fruitful method of measuring treatment outcome is to use a combination of body-weight change and change in body fat (skinfold thickness). The means of dealing with body-weight data are outlined below.

ABSOLUTE WEIGHT CHANGE

Weight-change data are most commonly presented in terms of the absolute weight change (the number of pounds lost or gained). This can be misleading; a 30-pound weight loss in a 300-pound person may be quite different from a 30-pound loss in a 120-pound person. Despite its problems, this method of presentation should be used in reports of treatment outcome so comparisons can be made with previous studies. This method is useful but not sufficient.

CHANGE IN PERCENTAGE OVERWEIGHT

Percentage overweight is determined from ideal weights, typically the Metropolitan Life Insurance Company tables (1960). The percentage is calculated by subtracting ideal weight from actual weight, then dividing by ideal weight. This measure is some improvement over absolute body weight because it takes into account a person's body size (from which ideal weight is determined). In essence, this measure indicates *how* overweight a person is, given a specific sex, height, and body-frame size.

CATEGORICAL WEIGHT LOSS

Some studies have reported the percentage of the subjects who lose a specified amount of weight, say 20, 30, or 40 pounds. As with absolute weight change, this information is useful for comparison with older studies in which data were presented in the same fashion. However, this measure does not account for differences in body size or in initial weight. Because initial weight is positively correlated with weight change (Brownell *et al.*, 1978; Murray, 1975), the percentage of subjects losing predetermined amounts of weight can be influenced by factors other than a treatment intervention.

WEIGHT-REDUCTION QUOTIENT

Feinstein (1959) proposed a weight-reduction quotient as a measure of treatment outcome. The quotient is a function of the percentage of surplus weight lost times the relative initial overweight:

$$\text{Weight-reduction quotient} = \frac{\text{Pounds lost}}{\text{Pounds overweight}} \times \frac{\text{Initial weight}}{\text{Ideal weight}} \times 100$$

The reduction quotient accounts for height, degree overweight, weight-reduction goals, and the number of pounds lost, and is probably the best means of presenting treatment outcome data (Wilson, 1978). The weight-reduction quotient and change in absolute weight are a useful means of evaluating data and comparing them to those from previous studies.

Assessment of treatment outcome must also include an analysis of the dropout rate. Attrition is a major problem in weight-control programs, particularly in commercial self-help groups (Stunkard & Brownell, 1979). If the least successful patients discontinue treatment, the results based on weight losses for the survivors will be biased. One of the strongest virtues of some programs is the capacity to keep patients in treatment (Stunkard, 1975). Information on attrition should be reported routinely in treatment-outcome studies.

OBESITY: A COMPREHENSIVE ASSESSMENT PLAN

Obesity is a complex disorder with a number of possible causes and with many diverse medical and psychological consequences. The development of a comprehensive framework for assessment is necessary to define treatment goals, to fully evaluate a patient's functioning in all areas, and to test the effectiveness of treatment procedures. In the absence of such a framework, some important areas may be overlooked. Table 1 presents a comprehensive treatment plan for assessment in each of the primary areas to be considered in the evaluation and treatment of obesity. In several areas, valid, reliable, and inexpensive measures have not been developed. Therefore, the "preferred measures" in some instances may be the best available, but may not be very good. The lack of useful measures results in part from the fact that interest in assessment is reasonable new, and from the fact that measuring some facets of obesity is quite difficult. Assessment is important for physiology, eating behavior, activity, and treatment outcome. The most impressive assessment program available is the one by Mahoney et al. (in press). This program may become the standard by which other programs are judged. There are, however, more complete guidelines in several of the areas to be assessed. The comprehensive assessment plan is outlined below and appears in Table 1.

Many physiologic processes may be related to obesity, either as its cause or its consequence. Careful medical screening is important to evaluate the possibility of biological origins of overweight, medical

Table 1

Comprehensive Assessment Plan for Obesity and Its Treatment

Target	Methods	Advantages	Disadvantages	Preferred method(s)
		Physiology		
Adipose cellularity (size)	Microscopic assessment	Economy, simplicity	Measurement error	Microscopic measurement or electronic count
	Optical measurement of collagenase-treated tissue	Economy, simplicity	Measurement error	
	Electronic count of osmium-fixed cells	Many cells are counted, small error	Cost, toxicity risk, exclusion of small cells	
Adipose cellularity	Calculation from average cell size and total body fat (no direct methods available)	Simplicity	Multiplication of measurement error	Calculation from average cell size determined from four areas
Physical status Endocrine Hypothalamic Cardiopulmonary Orthopedic Genetic Weight history Family history	Standard physiologic assessment	Specific to method	Specific to method	Algorithm by Bray et al. (1976)

Body fat	Carcass composition	Less error, direct measurement	Cost, difficulty	Body-mass index plus skinfold thickness
	Height–weight subtraction	Simplicity, economy		
	Broca index	Simplicity, economy	Calculation error, measurement error	
	Magic 36	Simplicity, economy	?Relation to body fat	
	Ruler test	Simplicity, economy		
	Eyeball test	Simplicity, economy	Large error	
	Height–weight tables	Simplicity, economy	?Relation to body fat	
	Weight/height	Simplicity, economy	?Relation to body fat	
	Body-mass index	Simplicity, economy	Poor reliability	
	Skinfold thickness	Economy, validity	Sophisticated analyses	
	Body circumference	Economy, validity	?Relation to body fat	
	Somatyping	Economy	Cost	
	Hydrostatic weighing	Accuracy		
Body weight	Weighing on scale	Accuracy	None	Weighing, self-report
	Self-report	Accuracy	Subject to distortion	
	Naturalistic observation	Nonobtrusive, economy	?Reliability, validity	

(continued)

Table 1 (continued)

Target	Methods	Advantages	Disadvantages	Preferred method(s)
		Eating behaviors		
Eating style	Eating machines	Accurate, disguise amount, can vary amount	Artificial situation, reactivity	Universal Eating Monitor for laboratory, Mahoney Master Questionnaire for self-report, Eating Analysis and Treatment Schedule for naturalistic observations
	Universal Eating Monitor	Accurate, disguise amount and caloric density, can vary amount	Cost, artificial situation, reactivity	
	Laboratory observation	Economy, reliability, can vary amount	Artificial situation, reactivity	
	Naturalistic observation (restaurants)	Nonobtrusive, economy	?Reliability and generalizability, cannot track individuals	
	Naturalistic observation (home)	Non-self-report measure of important target	?Reactivity, misses "private" eating	
	Eating Patterns Questionnaire	Economy	Never validated	
	Mahoney Master Questionnaire	Economy, comprehensiveness, psychometric evaluation	Validity untested, potential distortion	

368

	Eating Analysis and Treatment Schedule Self-report	Economy, measures many aspects of eating	Validity untested, reactivity	
	Self-report	Transportable, economy	Validity untested, potential distortion	
Food choice	Nutrition surveys, self-report	Economy, retrospective evaluation possible	?Accuracy of recall, potential distortion	
	Laboratory observation	Economy, reliability	Limited range of foods, artificial situation, reactivity	
	Naturalistic observation	Non self-report measure in natural setting	?Reliability and generalizability	
Food preference	Self-report surveys	Economy, simplicity	Potential distortion	Self-report
	Salivary measures	Accuracy, not subject to distortion	? of inference to preference, some measures are costly	
Hunger	Self-report	Economy	Potential distortion, gross measurements	
	Salivary measures	Accuracy, not subject to distortion	Cost, obtrusiveness	Salivary measures or self-report

(continued)

Table 1 (*continued*)

Target	Methods	Advantages	Disadvantages	Preferred method(s)
		Eating behaviors		
Environment responsivity	Food choice	Measurable in natural settings	? of inference to hunger	
	Ad libitum food after manipulation of cue salience	Can alter cue salience and study in laboratory	Inference from independent variable reactivity, artificial situation	Mahoney Master Questionnaire
	Mahoney Master Questionnaire	Economy, psychometric evaluation	Validity untested, potential distortion	
	Eating Patterns Questionnaire	Economy	Never validated	
Restrained eating	Herman Scale	Economy, brevity, general use	Validity untested, potential distortion	Herman Questionnaire
	Stunkard Scale	Economy, psychometric evaluation	Further evaluation of validity needed, potential distortion	Stunkard Questionnaire
		Physical activity		
Total energy expenditure (direct measurement)	Direct calorimetry (heat loss from controlled chamber)	Direct and total measure, no error, control of environment	Cost, not practical for humans	Direct calorimetry

Total energy expenditure (indirect measurement)	Metabolic rate calculated from oxidation values	Somewhat precise	Error in measurement, cost, obtrusiveness	Heart rate
	Water vaporization from lungs	Good correlation with total energy expenditure	Error in measurement, cost, obtrusiveness	
	Heart rate	Accuracy	Cost, obtrusiveness, subject to extraneous influence	
Programmed exercise	Self-report	Economy, continuous measure, simplicity	?Validity and reactivity, possible distortion and error in measurement	Pedometer for measure of magnitude, direct observation and heart-rate recording for intensity
	Direct observation	Validity and low measurement error	?Reactivity, cost, obtrusiveness	
	Motion picture sampling	Reliability, possibly high validity	?Reactivity, cost, obtrusiveness	
	Pedometer	Economy, simplicity, fairly high accuracy	Mechanical malfunction, ?reactivity, cannot measure intensity	

(continued)

Table 1 (continued)

Target	Methods	Advantages	Disadvantages	Preferred method(s)
		Physical activity		
	Heart-rate recording	Accuracy	Cost, obtrusiveness, subject to extraneous influences	
Routine exercise	Self-report	Economy, continuous measure, simplicity	?Validity and reactivity, possible distortion and error in measurement	Pedometer
	Naturalistic observation	Economy, nonobtrusive	Difficult to track individuals, ?generalizability	
	Pedometer	Economy, simplicity, fairly high accuracy	Mechanical malfunction, ?reactivity	
	Heart-rate recording	Accuracy	Cost, obtrusiveness, subject to extraneous influences	
		Psychological and social adjustment		
Psychological functioning	Self-report	Economy, allows questioning	Potential distortion	Beck Depression Inventory, Mahoney Master Questionnaire, SCL-90, self-report, report from others

	Measure	Advantages	Disadvantages
	Reports from family or friend	Allows view of "real world" behavior, economy	Accuracy and potential distortion
	Beck Depression Inventory	Economy, validated, easy to administer frequently	Measures only depression, potential distortion
	Symptom Checklist (SCL-90)	Economy, measures several areas of functioning, validated	Potential distortion
	MMPI	Validated psychometric evaluation, general use	Potential distortion, somewhat difficult to score
	Mahoney Master Questionnaire	Measures psychological responses specific to obesity, measures cognitive behavior, psychometric evaluation	Validity untested, potential distortion
Social functioning	Self-report	Economy, allows questioning	Potential distortion
	Marital Adjustment Test, self-report, report from others		

(continued)

Table 1 *(continued)*

Target	Methods	Advantages	Disadvantages	Preferred method(s)
		Psychological and social adjustment		
	Reports from family or friend	Allows view of "real world" behavior, economy	Accuracy and potential distortion	
	Locke–Wallace Marital Adjustment Test	Validated, economy, simplicity, interpretability, can be completed by partner	Potential distortion, measures only one facet of adjustment	
	Other adjustment inventories	Economy, simplicity	Potential distortion, ?validity	
		Independent variables (adherence)		
Dietary change	Self-report	Economy, simplicity	?Reactivity, potential distortion, error in measurement	Self-report with collaboration from others
	Reports from family or friend	Substantiates self-report, economy	Error in measurement, potential distortion	
	Nutrition survey	Economy, simplicity	Potential distortion, error in measurement	

374

	Advantages	Disadvantages	
Prescribed behaviors			
Blood or urine analysis	Accuracy	Cost, obtrusiveness, subject to extraneous influences	Self-report with collaboration from others
Self-report	Economy, simplicity	?Reactivity, potential distortion, error in measurement	
Reports from family or friend	Substantiates self-report, economy	Error in measurement, potential distortion	
Mahoney Master Questionnaire	Economy, psychometric evaluation	Validity untested, potential distortion	
Treatment outcome			
Weight change			
Absolute weight change	Simplicity, economy, accuracy, general use	Ignores body fat, body size	Weight-reduction quotient, absolute weight change
Change in percentage overweight	Simplicity, economy, accuracy, accounts for ideal weight	?Norms, ignores body fat	
Categorical weight loss	Economy, general use, accuracy	Ignores body fat, body size, sex, and variability	

(continued)

375

Table 1 (*continued*)

Target	Methods	Advantages	Disadvantages	Preferred method(s)
		Treatment outcome		
	Weight-reduction quotient	Economy, accuracy, accounts for ideal body weight and surplus weight, increasing general use	Ignores body fat	
Medical change				
Blood pressure	Pressure cuff	Economy, general use	Some measurement error	Medical practices in use
Plasma lipids	Lipid analysis	Accuracy	Cost, obtrusiveness	
Glucose tolerance	Tolerance test	Accuracy	Cost, obtrusiveness	
Cardiac efficiency	Stress test	Accuracy	Cost, obtrusiveness	

376

complications secondary to overweight, and contraindications for losing weight. The very importance of obesity lies in its association with medical (and psychological) disorders. There is a tendency to attribute obesity to psychological characteristics (lack of willpower) if gross disease or endocrine malfunction are not present. This attribution neglects the complexity of this disorder and suggests a treatment approach that may be of little use.

Bray, Jordan, and Sims (1976) have developed a flow chart for evaluating obesity (Figure 6). This scheme was developed at the 1973

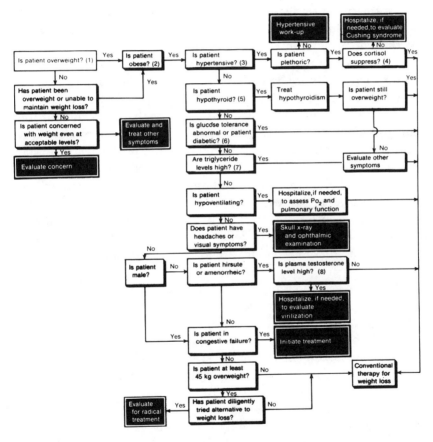

Figure 6

A flow chart for evaluating the medical status of the obese patient. Reprinted by permission from Bray *et al.* (1976). Copyright 1976, American Medical Association.

Fogarty International Conference on Obesity and is the most comprehensive plan for assessing the medical implications of obesity. The scheme takes into account causes, anatomic diagnosis, and contributory factors. The paper by Bray et al. (1976) is also useful because it provides normal and abnormal values for tests in each area. The evaluating physician can then determine whether symptoms other than the excess of weight require treatment. This scheme can also be used by clinicians to determine whether their patients have been adequately evaluated.

Unfortunately, a comprehensive medical screening such as the one recommended by Bray et al. (1976) is not likely to be undertaken in most treatment settings. Many research programs require a "physician's consent form" to be completed by the patient's family doctor, but there is no guarantee that the appropriate tests will be done. Other programs require no medical screening. In these cases, the Stanford Eating Disorders Questionnaire may be useful (Agras, Ferguson, Greaves, Qualls, Rand, Ruby, Stunkard, Taylor, Werne, & Wright, 1976). This self-report inventory gathers information on demographic factors, weight history, psychological and social functioning, and medical history. The medical and psychiatric information can identify some patients in need of referral. Also, Agras et al. (1976) have reported that the questionnaire may be useful as a screening device; a large percentage of their patients who completed the form remained in treatment. This questionnaire is extremely useful in clinical settings because it yields information in several important areas. Its primary shortcomings are its length and its untested validity.

Weight reduction is prescribed for the obese because of its association with medical disorders, particularly cardiovascular disease. Body weight or body fat are the targets of treatment only because of their hypothesized relationship to these disorders. Surprisingly few studies have assessed changes in the critical physiologic processes (for example, blood pressure, serum lipid levels, cardiac efficiency). It is only with evidence of this nature that we will know the extent to which weight reduction is actually accomplishing its purpose. In several studies this has been accomplished nicely.

Craighead, Stunkard, and O'Brien (1978) followed 150 obese persons for up to one year after completion of a behavioral treatment program. The patients had clinically significant weight losses (average of approximately 25 pounds after treatment). Blood pressures were taken each week of the program. Many of the hypertensive patients became normotensive and were able to discontinue antihypertensive medication. Hypertensive patients are frequently prescribed weight-loss regimens to reduce carviovascular risk, so this type of evaluation is important. Foreyt, Scott, Mitchell, and Gotto (1979) presented a model for evaluating plasma lipid changes after a behavioral program, although this program was not specifically for obese people. Brownell and Stunkard (1979) found beneficial serum lipid changes (including high-density lipoprotein cholesterol) in response to weight loss, and suggested that these changes may be one of the primary medical benefits of weight reduction.

The comprehensive study by Mahoney *et al.* (in press) includes evaluation of several of these cardiovascular risk factors and of several psychological measures. Again, the Mahoney program is the one that best exemplifies a complete assessment package. Studies of exercise physiology have also included complete assessment of the physiologic effects of weight loss (e.g., Lewis, Haskell, Wood, Manoogian, Bailey, & Pereira, 1976). These studies provide useful information for clinicians and researchers desiring to evaluate the physiologic impact of their treatments.

Because dieting carries a high risk of psychological disturbance, it is important to assess a patient's psychological and social functioning (Stunkard, 1976; Stunkard & Rush, 1974). One of the hallmarks of behavior therapy for obesity has been the reduction of untoward emotional reactions suffered by dieters (Stunkard, 1975). Again, few studies have assessed this factor, and they focused on psychological functioning as a predictor of weight loss. The most important psychological factors to evaluate are discussed by Stunkard and his colleagues (Mills & Stunkard, 1976; Stunkard, 1975; Stunkard & Rush, 1974). In two programs there has been extensive testing of psychological functioning. Mahoney *et al.* (in press) have carefully measured psychological and cognitive adjustment, and Craighead *et al.* (1978) obtained useful data by administering the Beck Depression Inventory (Beck, Ward, Mendelson, Mock, & Erbaugh, 1961) and a Symptom Checklist (SCL-90) (Lipman, Covi, & Shapiro, 1979). Social adjustment is typically measured by self-report (if measured at all). In our work with spouse training, we routinely administer the Locke-Wallace Marital Adjustment Test (Locke & Wallace, 1959) to assess changes in the marital relationship.

Even though behavioral treatments are designed to alter eating behaviors (cf. Foreyt, 1977), relatively little research has been devoted to developing accurate measures of these behaviors. As a result, the behaviors have been measured only rarely and there is some question about whether behavior change and weight change are even related (Brownell & Stunkard, 1978b; Mahoney, 1975a). Studies of obese and normal-weight people in the natural environment have taught us a great deal about the way they eat (cf. Stunkard & Kaplan, 1977). These studies have spurred other attempts to evaluate eating behavior, and systematic evaluation will, it is hoped, become the rule rather than the exception.

In this chapter, "eating behavior" refers not only to the topographical components of food consumption but to the hypothesized cognitive processes that govern food selection (such as food preference and restraint in eating). There are numerous methods of assessing behaviors in each area (Table 1). For measuring the topography of eating (rate, portions, and so forth), naturalistic observations are probably most valid, although this has never been tested. These observations can be made without the knowledge of the subject if made in public places such as restaurants, but this does not allow repeated measurements of individuals. The observations can be made in the home but subjects may alter their behavior because they are being observed. These measures are also problematic because there is no way to evaluate "private eating," a potentially important concern for the obese. The validity of self-report has not been evaluated rigorously, but it may be a useful procedure for those situations in which subjects cannot be observed.

It is also important to measure food choice, food preference, hunger, external responsiveness, and restrained eating. These may not all be influential for all patients, but without adequate measurement there is no way of determining which areas are important for a given patient. The methods for measuring these factors (Table 1) have not been refined, with the exception of questionnaires for assessing restrained eating. In fact, in three of the five areas no measures have been proven more accurate than self-report. Of the different facets of obesity, we know the least about the assessment of eating behavior.

Physical activity is often ignored in programs for weight reduction, and it is not surprising that methods for assessment in this area are not very advanced. This area will probably become a focus for major research efforts because of the relationship between physical inactivity, obesity, and coronary heart disease. Total energy expenditure can be measured only by determining total heat loss from the body. This measure requires direct or indirect calorimetry; both are costly and difficult. Estimated energy expenditure can be made from assessing the degree of physical activity. Physical activity can be divided into two categories: programmed exercise (regular and usually strenuous exercise) and routine exercise (activity during day-to-day activities). Programmed exercise has been measured with great accuracy by exercise physiologists, using treadmills to calculate oxygen uptake at various workloads. An exercise regimen of jogging, swimming, and so forth can be measured by direct observation, self-report, a heart-rate monitor, and at times with a pedometer (Table 1). The heart-rate monitor is the most precise measure of exertion but also the most costly. Pedometers, self-report, and observation are the measures most suited for clinical practice and clinical research.

For the obese, routine exercise is most likely to play a prominent role. Programmed exercise for the obese is difficult, painful, and, in many cases, impossible. Adherence is likely to be greatest if prescribed exercises are attainable. Behavioral progams encourage modest changes in activity such as using stairs in lieu of elevators and escalators, parking some distance from a destination, and disembarking from a bus several stops early (Brownell, 1979; Mahoney & Mahoney, 1976). The measures mentioned above are also useful for routine activity. Pedometers may be the most useful measure in this case.

Assessing the independent variables (adherence to the treatment regimen) is a critical component of evaluating treatment efficacy. It cannot be assumed that a patient losing weight in a given program did so because of adherence to specific program guidelines. Dietary change, behavior change, and activity change are the most important targets to consider. In some cases, self-report, with substantiation from other sources if possible, is the best means of assessment. These are presented in Table 1.

Finally, treatment outcome must be assessed with great care (Wilson, 1978). Treatment outcome refers not only to a change in weight and body fat but to collateral changes in psychological and social adjustment and to changes in physical health. Body-weight data can be presented in many ways (Table 1). The weight-reduction quotient (Feinstein, 1959) is the most meaningful measure, but changes in absolute body weight should be presented also, to allow comparison with previous studies. Body fat can be most easily measured with skinfold calipers, but intensive training is necessary for this method to be reliable. As mentioned earlier, the physiologic and psychological changes are important to measure because, after all, why are people to lose weight? The physiologic processes most germane to weight reduction are blood pressure, plasma lipid concentrations, glucose tolerance, and cardiac functioning. The psychological processes to consider are depression, anxiety, irritability, preoccupation with food, body image, and interpersonal adjustment.

Anorexia Nervosa

Few illnesses generate as much confusion as anorexia nervosa. It involves behaviors aimed at losing weight — not an uncommon practice in today's world. But these behaviors are carried to extremes, to the point where the sustenance of life (food intake) is threatened. Anorexia nervosa is one of the few psychiatric illnesses that may be unremitting until death (Halmi, 1980). As with obesity, assessment of anorexia nervosa has lagged behind advances in treatment. In part, this is due to a general lack of emphasis on the assessment of all psychological disorders (Cone & Hawkins, 1977). Also, clinical improvement seems deceptively easy to measure: a patient need merely to gain weight. This simple notion has given way to a view of this disease as a complex series of psychological and physiologic processes (Bruch, 1966; Crisp, 1965; Halmi, 1978).

CHARACTERISTICS

DEFINITIONS AND DIAGNOSIS

The first reported clinical description of "nervous atrophy" was made by Richard Morton in 1689 (Morton, 1720). William Gull (1868) gave the illness its current name, but several important transition periods occurred during the intervening years. Huchard followed with the term "anorexia mentale," the term still used in France. In 1914 Simmonds noted an emaciated woman with a destroyed pituitary gland, and for the following 45 years anorexia nervosa was often incorrectly diagnosed as Simmonds disease.

More recent diagnostic criteria have included oral–sadistic

wishes, 25-pound weight loss due to any psychiatric condition (Bliss & Branch, 1960), drive disturbance (Thoma, 1963), struggle for a sense of effectiveness (Bruch, 1962), aversiveness of eating (King, 1963), impaired hypothalamic functioning (Russell, 1969), and weight phobia (Crisp, 1965). Halmi (1980) has presented the evidence justifying the diagnosis for anorexia nervosa set forth in the third edition of the American Psychiatric Association's *Diagnostic and Statistical Manual of Psychiatric Disorders* (DSM-III, 1980) (Table 2). These criteria are the most up-to-date, and the diagnosis should not be made unless these factors are present. This diagnosis is sometimes difficult to ascertain because patients are often secretive and deny their symptoms (Halmi, 1980).

CLINICAL FEATURES

A detailed account of the features of anorexia nervosa has been presented by Halmi (1980), and will be discussed only briefly. The features most commonly associated with anorexia nervosa are categorized in Table 3.

Anorexia nervosa occurs between the ages of 10 and 30. Approximately 85% of all cases occur between 13 and 20 years of age, with the age of maximum frequency being 17 to 18. Females comprise

Table 2
Diagnostic Criteria for Anorexia Nervosa[a]

1. Refusal to maintain body weight over a minimal normal weight for age and height.
2. Weight loss of at least 25% of original weight, or if under 18 years of age, weight loss from original body weight plus projected weight gain expected on pediatric growth charts may be combined to comprise the 25%.
3. Disturbance of body image with inability to accurately perceive body size.
4. Intense fear of becoming obese. This fear does not diminish as weight loss progresses.
5. No known medical illness that would account for loss.
6. Amenorrhea (in females).

[a]Adapted with permission from DSM-III (1980).

Table 3
Factors Found to Be Associated with Anorexia Nervosa[a, b]

Predisposing factors

Death of close relative or friend	Sexual conflicts
Illness	Failure at school or work

Behavioral factors

Refusal to eat with others	Denial of characteristic behaviors
Eating binges	Hiding of food
Self-induced vomiting	Overestimation of body size
Large decrease in high-fat and	Obsessive–compulsive behavior
high-carbohydrate foods	Suicide attempts
Ritualistic exercising	Somatic complaints
Compulsive stealing	Low sexual interest

Psychological/social factors

Unrealistic fear of failure	Depression
Preoccupation with food	Anxiety
Distorted body image	Delayed psychosexual development
Intense fear of weight gain	

Physiologic factors

Turner syndrome	Low serum triiodothyronine (T3)
Amenorrhea	levels
Hypothermia	Slightly elevated serum reverse T3
Edema	levels
Bradycardia	Elevated growth hormone levels
Hypotension	Low erythrocyte sedimentation
Lanugo	Electrocardiographic abnormalities
Leukopenia	Regressed luteinizing hormone
Lymphocytosis	secretion
Hypocarotenemia	Impaired water diuresis
	Low estrogen levels

[a]Adapted with permission from Halmi (1980).
[b]These symptoms are not found in all cases.

95% of the cases. Most patients are preoccupied with food and often show an inspired drive to collect recipes and to prepare elaborate meals for others. Appetite loss is rare until late in the illness and many patients have eating binges owing to lack of control over food intake. The binges usually occur privately and often at night; they are sometimes followed by self-induced vomiting. Body weight is controlled by severe restriction of food intake (particularly high-carbohydrate and high-fat foods), ritualistic exercising, and even by abuse of laxatives and diuretics.

Anorectic patients often carry food with them or hide food around the house, yet may dispose of food in their napkins or hide it in their pockets when they eat with others. A number of studies have found that these patients overestimate the width of various body parts (Casper, Halmi, Goldberg, Eckert, & Davis, 1979; Crisp & Kalucy, 1974; Garner, Garfinkel, Stancer, & Moldofsky, 1976; Slade & Russell, 1973). However, the same is true of normal-weight age-matched females. An intense fear of gaining weight and becoming obese is the predominant psychological disturbance. Others include obsessive–compulsive behavior, anxiety, somatic complaints, poor sexual adjustment, and depression (crying spells, sleep disturbance, suicide attempts).

The most prominent physical symptom is amenorrhea. In about one-third of patients, amenorrhea occurs before significant weight loss. This apparent hormonal disturbance has prompted a number of studies on the hypothalamic–pituitary–ovarian axis (see Halmi, 1978, for a review of this area). Hypothermia occurs with profound weight loss as may edema, bradycardia, hypotension, and lanugo (Table 3).

PREVALENCE AND PROGNOSIS

In the only incidence study of anorexia nervosa in the United States, an average incidence of .37 cases per 100,000 population per year was reported in Monroe County in upper New York State between 1960 and 1969 (Kendall, Hall, Harley, & Babigian, 1973). The incidence per 100,000 population per year has been reported as 1.6 in Scotland (Kendall *et al.*, 1973) and .45 in Sweden (Theander, 1970). In the high-risk group of females aged 12 to 18, the prevalence of anorexia nervosa may be as high as 1 in 200 (Crisp, Palmer, & Kalucy, 1976). Also, sisters of anorectic patients are at greater-than-expected risk to develop the disease, and the parents of these patients have a greater prevalence of the disease (Kalucy, Crisp, & Harding, 1977; Theander, 1970).

The course of anorexia nervosa is highly variable and ranges from spontaneous recovery without treatment, recovery after one of several treatments, and fluctuating weight gains and relapses, to gradual deterioration resulting in death due to starvation (Halmi, 1980). Studies following diagnoses cases four years or longer have shown mortality rates between 5% and 21.5% (Dally & Sargant, 1960; Halmi, Brodland, & Rigas, 1975; Kay & Leigh, 1954; Morgan

& Russell, 1975; Seidensticker & Tzagournis, 1968; Theander, 1970). Short-term response to almost all hospital treatment programs is good, but studies are difficult to compare because of different measures of success (Halmi, 1980). In one follow-up study of anorexia patients, one-third were obese at their last follow-up evaluation (Halmi, Brodland, & Loney, 1973).

Because outcome has been assessed in various studies with different methods, prognostic factors have been inconsistently related to improvement. The most reliable indicators of good outcome are early age at onset (Frazier, 1965; Halmi et al., 1973; 1975; Rowland, 1970), and no prior hospitalizations (Halmi, Goldberg, Casper, Eckert, & Davis, 1979). Poor outcome has been related to late onset of the illness and the number of previous hospitalizations (Halmi et al., 1975; Morgan & Russell, 1975; Theander, 1970). Other variables have predicted response to treatment in some studies but not in others (cf. Halmi, 1980).

ASSESSMENT IN ANOREXIA NERVOSA

Until recently, assessment has not been considered important in the treatment of anorexia nervosa. Weight gain was the variable of concern, especially in cases where a patient's life was in danger from starvation. It is now being acknowledged that anorexia nervosa is a multifaceted disorder and that assessment of its origins and its associated factors is important (Halmi, 1980; Stunkard, 1972).

Several of the areas to be discussed in this section overlap with assessment of the various aspects of obesity. For example, psychological evaluation of the obese patient and the anorectic patient may be similar if depression is the target. The reader should refer to earlier sections of this chapter and to Table 1 to find the assessment approaches that may be helpful for anorexia nervosa. What follows is a description of new areas which have not been mentioned previously and which are specific to anorexia nervosa.

PHYSIOLOGIC EVALUATION

Change in Body Weight. Declining body weight is the primary signal that identifies the anorectic patient. In contrast to obesity, where body fat is important, absolute body weight and weight gain are the critical factors in anorexia nervosa. Body weight can be measured simply with an accurate scale. It may be helpful to use a scale with small gradations in weight (.1 to .25 pound) if changes in weight are used as criteria for reinforcement.

General Medical Assessment. Table 3 presents the possible medical consequences of anorexia nervosa. Serious physiologic problems are often associated with this disorder, and careful assessment before and during treatment is necessary to ensure the safety of the patient. Several studies have carried out this careful assessment and may be used as models for physiologic evaluation. Garfinkel, Kline, and Stancer (1973) have described the important laboratory tests administered to their patients in a study of five anorectic females. Hypothalamic and pituitary function and its assessment is described in another study by the same group (Garfinkel, Brown, Stancer, & Moldofsky, 1975). Halmi (1978) has reviewed the literature on the metabolic concomitants of anorexia nervosa and has presented the factors most likely to influence the course of the disease. Finally, a comprehensive view of the physiologic processes associated with anorexia nervosa is in the recent chapter by Halmi (1980).

ASSESSMENT OF EATING BEHAVIOR

Very little work has been done on assessing eating behaviors in anorexia nervosa, unlike obesity. Undoubtedly this is due to the presumed causes of the two disorders. In obesity, learned eating habits were thought to contribute to the problem, and therapy was therefore aimed at structuring new patterns of intake. Anorexia nervosa has been considered a result of impaired psychological development or disturbed family interactions. Therapy was aimed at solving these problems and producing weight gain. The topography of eating, hunger, and the constitution of the diet were not considered important; therefore, few assessment devices specific to anorexia nervosa have been developed, and much of what is known must be adapted from research on obesity.

Eating Topography. The rate of eating, the number of calories consumed per unit time, the size of mouthfuls, and so forth may be important in anorexia nervosa. If these factors are not of etiologic significance, they may be important targets for a program ultimately aimed at weight gain. Unfortunately, much of the anorectic patient's characteristic eating behavior occurs in private. Naturalistic observations are not possible, and observations of eating in the laboratory

would be unlikely to yield valid information on eating patterns because of the situational control over the important targets (binging,
vomiting, and so forth). The only option would be to hospitalize a
small number of patients and maintain continual observation of all
aspects of eating.

The most practical means of assessing eating topography is by
self-report. Garfinkel, Moldofsky, and Garner (1977) have developed
a global self-report measure for anorexia nervosa that includes questions on food fadishness, vomiting, bulimic episodes, and laxative
abuse. This is not a continuous measure and has not been validated.
Self-monitoring records similar to those completed by obese patients
may be of some use for anorectic patients. Diet diaries can be a continuous measure, and otherwise private events can be recorded. The
accuracy of self-monitoring can be increased with methods mentioned
earlier in this chapter. However, the tendency for anorectic persons to
deny their behavior may make it difficult to obtain accurate records.
The patient's records can be checked against accounts from family
members and friends, but these people may not be able to view the
patient's behavior.

Hunger and Satiety. The reduced food intake of persons with
anorexia nervosa could be viewed as a disturbance of hunger signals:
these patients may not be hungry. However, there have been reports
that anorectic persons are preoccupied with food and that appetite
loss is uncommon until the late stages of the disorder (Halmi, 1980).
It is also plausible that satiety is the important mechanism and that
anorectic patients experience hunger normally but satiety signals terminate eating prematurely. Garfinkel (1974) has studied this theory
by evaluating perceptions of hunger and satiety in 11 anorectic patients and 11 matched controls. He found that anorectic patients
perceived hunger in a manner similar to controls but were more preoccupied with thoughts of food, had a *stronger* urge to eat, and were
more anxious when hungry. However, the controls experienced satiety as a fullness in the stomach, whereas the anorectic patients experienced satiety without gastric sensations or as a bloated feeling alternating with no sensations. These findings suggest that measurement
of hunger and satiety may be important in studying anorexia nervosa
and may become an important part of the clinical treatment of these
patients.

Hunger and satiety can be measured simply by asking people
how hungry they feel or how full they feel during various stages of a

meal. Because no physiologic indices of hunger and satiety have been defined, it has been impossible to validate other less objective measures such as self-report. In the section on obesity, salivary measures were mentioned for assessing hunger and satiety. Again, these have not been validated and are somewhat difficult to use. Food choice and meal size can be influenced by a number of factors other than physiologic state and are probably imprecise measures.

Monello and Mayer (1967) developed a Hunger–Satiety Questionnaire, a structured self-rating instrument which can be used for anorectic patients. Garfinkel (1974) made slight modifications in this questionnaire for his study on perceptions of hunger and satiety in anorexia nervosa (Figure 7). As with other measures, this has not been validated but is a useful device for assessing hunger, satiety, and their correlates.

Constitution of the Diet. Since anorectic patients jeopardize their health by underconsumption, the constitution of the diet during restriction and during refeeding is important to assess. Proper nutritional management in general can be accomplished according to the guidelines outline by Whitney and Hamilton (1977), but special dietary measures may be indicated after profound weight loss (Halmi, 1980). Assessment of diet in nonhospitalized patients is difficult and the best measure may be self-report. Again, anorectic patients tend to deny their unusual dietary patterns, and validity checks from others in the environment may be useful only to the extent that food intake is observable. A detailed self-monitoring form may be the most practical measure, even considering its shortcomings.

PHYSICAL ACTIVITY

Anorectic patients are characterized by excessive and ritualized exercising — commonly, jogging, walking, or cycling. This desire for activity is so strong that several programs have used access to physical activities to contingently reinforce weight gain (Agras, Barlow, Chapin, Abel, & Leitenberg, 1974; Garfinkel *et al.*, 1973). Because the amount of exercise done by anorectic patients is extraordinary, the caloric expenditure can be substantial. Also, the metabolic consequences of exercise may contribute to weight loss. It is therefore important to accurately assess physical activity. Assessment can be carried out in the same fashion as that outlined in the section on obesity (see Table 1).

HUNGER

This questionnaire is about hunger. For each heading circle as many of the answers as are
appropriate to how you feel now. You may leave a section out or answer more than once. At
the end add any general comments about your usual feelings of hunger.

I.   Gastric sensations: II.   Mouth and throat sensations:

        1. feeling of emptiness   1. emptiness
        2. rumbling   2. dryness
        3. ache   3. salivation
        4. pain   4. unpleasant taste or sensation
        5. tenseness   5. pleasant
        6. nausea   6. tightness
        7. no gastric sensations to pro-
           vide information for hunger

III. Cerebral sensations: IV.   General overall sensations:

        1. headache   1. weakness
        2. dizziness   2. tiredness
        3. faintness   3. restlessness
        4. spots before the eyes   4. cold
        5. ringing in ears   5. warmth
                                                           6. muscular spasms

V.   Mood when hungry: VI.   Urge to eat:

        1. nervous   1. no urge to eat
        2. irritable   2. mild-would eat if food were
        3. tense   available but can wait comfort-
        4. depressed   ably
        5. apathetic   3. fairly strong - want to eat soon,
        6. cheerful   waiting is fairly uncomfortable
        7. excited   4. so strong you want to eat now,
        8. calm   waiting is very uncomfortable
        9. relaxed
       10. contented

VII. Preoccupation with thoughts of food: VIII. Time of day or night when hungriest:

        1. not at all-no thoughts of food
        2. mild-only occasional thoughts
           of food
        3. moderate-many thoughts of food
           but can concentrate on other   IX.   Other comments about hunger:
           things
        4. very preoccupied-most of
           thoughts are of food and it is
           difficult to concentrate on
           other things

Figure 7

Hunger–satiety questionnaire developed by Monello and Mayer and modified
by Garfinkel. Reprinted by permission from Garfinkel (1974).

SATIETY

This questionnaire is about fullness. For each heading circle as many answers as are appropriate to how you've felt since completing the meal. You may leave a section out or answer more than once. At the end add any general comments about your feelings of fullness.

I. One most important reason for stopping eating:

1. no more food available
2. eat until feeling of satisfaction
3. "diet-limit" set for figure or health

II. Gastric sensation at end of eating:

1. full stomach
2. distended
3. bloated
4. nausea
5. ache
6. pain
7. feeling of emptiness
8. no stomach sensations to provide information for stopping

III. Cerebral sensations at end of eating:

1. headache
2. dizziness
3. faintness
4. spots before the eyes
5. ringing in ears

IV. General overall sensations at end of eating:

1. weakness
2. tiredness
3. restlessness
4. cold
5. warmth
6. muscular spasms

V. Mood at end of eating:

1. nervous
2. irritable
3. tense
4. depressed
5. apathetic
6. cheerful
7. excited
8. calm
9. relaxed
10. contented

VI. Urge to eat at end of eating:

1. no urge to eat
2. mild-would eat if food were available
3. moderate-want to eat again soon, waiting is fairly uncomfortable
4. strong-want to eat again now, waiting is very uncomfortable

VII. Preoccupation with thoughts of food:

1. not at all-no thoughts of food
2. mild-only occasional thoughts of food
3. moderate-many thoughts of food but can concentrate on other things
4. very preoccupied-most of thoughts are of food and it is difficult to concentrate on other things

VIII. Willpower required to stop eating:

1. none-stopping is an abrupt process
2. none-stopping a gradual process
3. some-willpower required since the urge to eat is still present
4. considerable willpower is required

IX. Other comments about feeling full:

Psychological/Social Functioning

Psychological and social problems can be associated with anorexia nervosa (Halmi, 1980). These may be the cause and/or the consequence of the disorder, and are crucial in an overall assessment plan. The most serious of these is depression and the possibility of suicide attempts. Psychometric evaluation of depression, anxiety, and the other factors outlined by Halmi (1980) was described earlier in this chapter in the section on psychological factors in obesity. The Beck Depression Inventory (Beck *et al.*, 1961) and the Hopkins Symptom Checklist (SCL-90) (Lipman *et al.*, 1979) may be the most useful measures, although some researchers have used the MMPI, the Rotter Locus of Control Scale (Rotter, 1966), and the Eysenck Personality Inventory (Eysenck & Eysenck, 1968).

The role of the family has also been suggested as a major factor in anorexia nervosa (Leibman, Minuchin, & Baker, 1974), and even though their findings are from uncontrolled research, these authors have reported positive results from treatment techniques aimed at involving the family. Family interactions can be viewed and rated in the context of the psychotherapeutic interview or can be observed in the home. Unfortunately, no useful scales have been developed for assessment in this area.

Body Image. This refers to a person's mental image of his or her body and the feelings and attitudes about the body. Body-image distortion and body-image disparagement are present in many obese people and most anorectic patients. In the study of anorexia nervosa, body image has received more attention that actual eating behavior or hunger.

The simplest method of assessing body image has been to have patients draw an image of their body (Gottesfeld, 1962; Nathan & Pisula, 1970). Stunkard and Mendelson (1967) had patients rate their images in a mirror. Other devices have included calipers to estimate the size of body parts (Slade & Russell, 1973), and a distorting mirror (Shipman & Sohlkah, 1967). Glucksman and Hirsch (1969) used a distorting photograph apparatus to measure body image. Photographs of a patient can be distorted to look heavier or lighter and patients can choose the fitting they feel most closely approximates their body size. This assessment device allows comparison of perceived body image with actual body size, and has been used in several recent studies (Garner & Garfinkel, 1977; Garner *et al.*, 1976).

A COMPREHENSIVE ASSESSMENT PLAN

The areas listed above are the most important to assess in the treatment of anorexia nervosa. Weight gain is, of course, the first concern in treatment if the patient is in ill health, but assessment in these other areas must be undertaken to develop a comprehensive treatment plan. As with any disorder, assessment in anorexia nervosa is the foundation for evaluating treatment strategies. It is now known that weight gain is typical for anorectics during an inpatient treatment program (Halmi, 1980). In some cases, weight gain is used in an operant fashion by the patient to gain release from the hospital (Agras *et al.*, 1974). This does not mean that weight gains are maintained or that psychological functioning improves.

In the assessment of eating behavior and exercise, the majority of what we know comes from work with obese persons. Many of the assessment devices developed for assessment in obesity are relevant for the study of anorexia nervosa. These are summarized in Table 1. Garfinkel *et al.* (1977) have proposed guidelines for a global measure of improvement in anorexia nervosa, yet their guidelines cover only a portion of the important areas for assessment. A comprehensive plan similar to the one outlined for obesity in this chapter may be useful in solving some of the problems associated with anorexia nervosa.

Summary

This chapter has explored assessment methods for the two most prevalent eating disorders: obesity and anorexia nervosa. The tendency in the past has been to focus treatment, and therefore assessment, on changes in weight. The criteria for clinical improvement, a decrease in body weight for the obese patient and an increase for the anorectic patient, have changed an assessment has become more sophisticated. It is increasingly evident that obesity and anorexia nervosa are complex disorders with multiple determinants and with interdependent systems of physiologic and psychological processes.

The comprehensive assessment scheme developed in this chapter is intended to provide a model for assessment as well as to catalog the available measurement procedures. It is my hope that this conceptual scheme will be useful for both clinical and research endeavors in the treatment of eating disorders. In clinical practice, assessment in each of the areas mentioned in this chapter may help determine the natural history of the disorder, its contributing factors, the most relevant treatment procedures, and the efficacy of specific interventions. Assessment within this scheme may be useful for the study of the etiology of eating disorders, the physiologic and psychological ramifications of changes in body weight and body fat, the relationship between eating and exercise patterns, and the comparative effectiveness of experimental treatment approaches. There are obvious gaps in our ability to assess the behavior of obese and anorectic patients. Advances in assessment will be helpful in our understanding of the development and the treatment of these disorders.

ACKNOWLEDGMENT

Research for this chapter was supported in part by Grant HL22345 from the National Heart, Lung, and Blood Institute.

References

Adolph, E. F. Urges to eat and drink in rats. *American Journal of Physiology*, 1947, *151*, 110-125.

Agras, W. S., Barlow, D. H., Chapin, H. N., Abel, G. G., & Leitenberg, H. Behavior modification of anorexia nervosa. *Archives of General Psychiatry*, 1974, *30*, 279-286.

Agras, W. S., Ferguson, J. M., Greaves, C., Qualls, B., Rand, C. S. W., Ruby, J., Stunkard, A. J., Taylor, C. B., Werne, J., & Wright, C. A clinical and research questionnaire for obese patients. In B. J. Williams, S. Martin, & J. P. Foreyt (Eds.), *Obesity: Behavioral approaches to dietary management*. New York: Brunner/Mazel, 1976.

Ashwell, M. The relationship of the age of onset of obesity to the success of its treatment in the adult. *British Medical Journal*, 1975, *34*, 201-204.

Astrand, P. O., & Rodahl, K. *Textbook of work physiology*. New York: McGraw-Hill, 1970.

Atwater, W. P., & Benedict, F. G. *A respiration calorimeter with appliances for the direct determination of oxygen*. Washington, D.C.: Carnegie Institution of Washington, Publ. 42, 1905.

Barlow, D. H. Assessment of sexual behavior. In A. R. Ciminero, K. S. Calhoun, & H. E. Adams (Eds.), *Handbook of behavioral assessment*. New York: John Wiley & Sons, 1977.

Beck, A. T., Ward, C. H., Mendelson, M., Mock, J., & Erbaugh, J. An inventory for measuring depression. *Archives of General Psychiatry*, 1961, *4*, 561-571.

Behnke, A. R., & Wilmore, J. H. *Evaluation and regulation of body build and composition*. Englewood Cliffs, NJ: Prentice-Hall, 1974.

Bellack, A. S., Rozensky, R., & Schwartz, J. A comparison of two forms of self-monitoring in a behavioral weight reduction program. *Behavior Therapy*, 1974, *5*, 523-530.

Benn, R. T. Some mathematical properties of weight-for-height indices used as measures of adiposity. *British Journal of Preventive Social Medicine*, 1971, *25*, 42-50.

Bergin, A., & Strupp, H. *Changing frontiers in the science of psychotherapy.* Chicago: Aldine Atherton, 1972.

Biron, P., Mongeau, J. G., & Bertrand, D. Familial resemblance of body weight and weight/height in 374 homes with adopted children. *Journal of Pediatrics*, 1977, *91*, 555-558.

Björntörp, P., Carlgren, G., Isaksson, B., Krotkiewski, M., Larsson, B., & Sjöström, L. Effect of an energy-reduced dietary regimen in relation to adipose tissue cellularity in obese women. *American Journal of Clinical Nutrition*, 1975, *28*, 445-452.

Björntörp, P., & Sjöström, L. Number and size of adipose tissue fat cells in relation to metabolism in human obesity. *Metabolism*, 1971, *20*, 703-713.

Blaxter, K. L. Methods of measuring the energy metabolism of animals and interpretation of results obtained. *Federation Proceedings*, 1971, *30*, 1436-1443.

Bliss, E. L., & Branch, C. H. *Anorexia nervosa: Its history, psychology, and biology.* New York: Harper & Row, 1960.

Blundell, J. Pharmacologic adjustment of the mechanisms underlying feeding and obesity. In A. J. Stunkard (Ed.), *Obesity.* Philadelphia: Saunders, 1980.

Booth, D. A. (Ed.). *Hunger models: Computable theory of feeding control.* New York: Academic Press, 1978.

Bradfield, R. B. A technique for determination of usual daily energy expenditure in the field. *American Journal of Clinical Nutrition*, 1971, *24*, 1148-1154.

Bradfield, R., Paulos, J., & Grossman, H. Energy expenditure and heart rate of obese high school girls. *American Journal of Clinical Nutrition*, 1971, *24*, 1482-1486.

Bray, G. A. Effect of caloric restriction on energy expenditure in obese patients. *Lancet*, 1969, *2*, 397-398.

Bray, G. A. Measurement of subcutaneous fat cells from obese patients. *Annals of Internal Medicine*, 1970, *73*, 565-569.

Bray, G. A. *The obese patient.* Philadelphia: Saunders, 1976.

Bray, G. A., Jordon, H. A., & Sims, E. A. H. Evaluation of the obese patient, *Journal of the American Medical Association*, 1976, *235*, 1487-1491.

Bray, G. A., & York, D. A. Genetically transmitted obesity in rodents. *Physiological Review*, 1971, *51*, 598-646.

Brooks, C. McC., & Lambert, E. F. A study of the effect of limitation of food intake and the method of feeding on the rate of weight gain during hypothalamic obesity in the albino rat. *American Journal of Physiology*, 1946, *147*, 695-707.

Brownell, K. D. *The psychological and medical sequelae of nonprescription weight reduction programs.* Paper presented at the Annual Meeting of the American Psychological Association, Toronto, August 1978.

Brownell, K. D. *Behavior therapy for weight control: A treatment manual.* Unpublished manuscript, University of Pennsylvania, 1979.

Brownell, K. D., Heckerman, C. L., & Westlake, R. J. The behavioral control of obesity. A descriptive analysis of a large-scale program. *Journal of Clinical Psychology*, 1979, *35*, 864-869.

Brownell, K. D., Heckerman, C. L., & Westlake, R. J., Hayes, S. C., & Monti, P. M. The effect of couples training and partner cooperativeness in the behavioral treatment of obesity. *Behaviour Research and Therapy*, 1978, *16*, 323-333.

Brownell, K. D., & Stunkard, A. J. Behavioral treatment of obesity in children. *American Journal of Diseases of Children*, 1978, *132*, 403-412.(a)

Brownell, K. D., & Stunkard, A. J. Behavior therapy and behavior change: Uncertainties in programs for weight control. *Behaviour Research and Therapy*, 1978, *16*, 301.(b)

Brownell, K. D., & Stunkard, A. J. *Changes in plasma levels of high density lipoprotein cholesterol and other lipids in response to weight reduction.* Unpublished manuscript, University of Pennsylvania, 1979.

Brownell, K. D., Stunkard, A. J., & Albaum, J. M. Evaluation and modification of activity patterns in the natural environment. *American Journal of Psychiatry*, in press.

Bruch, H. Obesity in childhood, IV. Energy expenditure of obese children. *American Journal of Diseases of Children*, 1940, *60*, 1082-1109.

Bruch, H. Perceptual and conceptual disturbances in anorexia nervosa. *Psychosomatic Medicine*, 1962, *24*, 287-194.

Bruch, H. Anorexia nervosa and its differential diagnosis. *Journal of Nervous and Mental Disease*, 1966, *141*, 555-566.

Build and Blood Pressure Study. Chicago: Society of Actuaries, 1959.

Bullen, B. A., Reed, R. B., & Mayer, J. Physical activity of obese and nonobese adolescent girls, appraised by motion picture sampling. *American Journal of Clinical Nutrition*, 1964, *14*, 211-223.

Cahn, A. Growth and caloric intake of heavy and tall children. *Journal of the American Dietetic Association*, 1968, *53*, 476-480.

Campbell, R. G., Hashim, S. A., & Van Itallie, T. B. Studies of food intake regulation in man: Responses to variations in nutritive density in lean and obese subjects. *New England Journal of Medicine*, 1971, *285*, 1402-1406.

Casper, R. C., Halmi, K. A., Goldberg, S. C., Eckert, E. D., & Davis, J. M. Disturbances in body image estimation as related to other characteristics and outcome in anorexia nervosa. *British Journal of Psychiatry*, 1979, *134*, 60-66.

Coats, T. J. *The efficacy of a multicomponent self-control program in modifying the eating habits and weight of three obese adolescents.* Unpublished doctoral dissertation, Stanford University, 1977.

Coll, M., Meyers, A., & Stunkard, A. J. Obesity and food choices in public places. *Archives of General Psychiatry*, 1979, *36*, 795-797.

Cone, J. D., & Hawkins, R. P. (Eds.). *Behavioral assessment: New directions in clinical psychology.* New York: Brunner/Mazel, 1977.

Craighead, L. W., Stunkard, A. J., & O'Brien, R. *New treatment for obesity.* Paper presented at the Annual Meeting of the American Psychological Association, Toronto, August 1978.

Crisp, A. J. Clinical and therapeutic aspects of anorexia nervosa: A study of 30 cases. *Journal of Psychosomatic Research*, 1965, *9*, 67-78.

Crisp, A. J., & Kalucy, R. S. Aspects of perceptual disorder in anorexia nervosa. *British Journal of Medical Psychology*, 1974, *47*, 349-361.

Crisp, A. J., Palmer, R. L., & Kalucy, R. S. How common is anorexia nervosa? A prevalence study. *British Journal of Psychiatry*, 1976, *128*, 549-554.

Dally, P. J., & Sargant, W. A new treatment of anorexia nervosa. *British Medical Journal*, 1960, *1*, 1770-1773.

Decke, E. Effects of taste on the eating behavior of obese and normal persons. In S. Schachter (Ed.), *Emotion, obesity, and crime.* New York: Academic Press, 1971.

Diagnostic and statistical manual of mental disorders (3rd ed.). Washington, D.C.: American Psychiatric Association, 1980.

Dodd, D. K., Birky, H. J., & Stalling, R. B. Eating behavior of obese and nonobese females in a natural setting. *Addictive Behaviors*, 1976, *1*, 321-325.

Durnin, J. V. G. A., Armstrong, W. H., & Womersley, J. An experimental study on the variability of measurement of skinfold thickness by three observers on 23 young women and 27 young men. *Human Biology*, 1973, *45*, 281-292.

Durnin, J. V. G. A., Blake, E. C., & Brockway, J. M. The energy expenditure and food intake of middle-aged Glasgow housewives and their adult daughters. *British Journal of Nutrition*, 1957, *11*, 85-93.

Durnin, J. V. G. A., & Brockway, J. M. Determination of the total daily energy expenditures in man by indirect calorimetry: Assessment of the accuracy of a modern technique. *British Journal of Nutrition*, 1959, *13*, 41-53.

Durin, J. V. G. A., & Womersley, J. Body fat assessed from total body density and its estimation from skinfold thickness: Measurements on 481 men and women aged from 16 to 72 years. *British Journal of Nutrition*, 1974, *32*, 77-97.

Dwyer, J. T., & Mayer, J. Biases in counting calories. *Journal of the American Dietetic Association*, 1969, *54*, 305-307.

Dyer, A. R., Stamler, J., Berkson, D. M., & Lindberg, H. A. Relationship of relative weight and body mass index to 14-year mortality in the Chicago Peoples Gas Company Study. *Journal of Chronic Disease*, 1975, *28*, 109-123.

Epstein, L. H., & Martin, J. E. Compliance and side effects of weight regulation groups. *Behavior Modification*, 1977, *1*, 551-558.

Epstein, L. H., Masek, B. J., & Marshall, W. R. A nutritionally based school program for control of eating in obese children. *Behavior Therapy*, 1978, *9*, 766-778.

Epstein, L. H., Thompson, J. K., & Wing, R. R. The effects of contract and lottery procedures on attendance and fitness in aerobics exercise. *Behavior Modification*, in press.

Eysenck, H. J. Learning theory and behaviour therapy. *Journal of Mental Science*, 1959, *105*, 61-75.

Eysenck, H., & Eysenck, S. *Eysenck Personality Inventory* (manual). San Diego: Educational and Industrial Testing Service, 1968.

Feinstein, A. R. The measurement of success in weight reduction: An analysis of methods and new index. *Journal of Chronic Disease*, 1959, *10*, 439-456.

Ferguson, J. M. *Learning to eat: Behavior modification for weight control*. Palo Alto: Bull, 1975.

Ferguson, J. M. A clinical program for the behavioral control of obesity. In B. J. Williams, S. Martin, & J. P. Foreyt (Eds.), *Obesity: Behavioral approaches to dietary management*. New York: Brunner/Mazel, 1976.

Ferster, C. B., Nurnberger, J. I., & Levitt, E. B. The control of eating. *Journal of Mathetics*, 1962, *1*, 87-109.

Florey, C. V. The use and interpretation of the ponderal index and other weight-height ratios in epidemiological studies. *Journal of Chronic Disease*, 1970, *23*, 93-103.

Foreyt, J. P. (Ed.). *Behavioral treatments of obesity*. New York: Pergamon Press, 1977.

Foreyt, J. P., & Goodrick, G. K. Assessment of childhood obesity. In E. Mash & L. Terdal (Eds.), *Behavioral assessment of childhood disorders*. New York: Guilford Press, 1980.

Foreyt, J. P., Scott, L. W., Mitchell, R. E., & Gotto, A. M. Plasma lipid changes in the normal population following behavioral treatment. *Journal of Consulting and Clinical Psychology*, 1979, *47*, 440-452.

Franzini, L. R., & Grimes, W. B. Skinfold measures as the criterion of change in weight control studies. *Behavior Therapy*, 1976, *7*, 256-260.

Frazier, S. H. Anorexia nervosa. *Diseases of the Nervous System,* 1965, *26,* 155–166.

Garfinkel, P. E. Perception of hunger and satiety in anorexia nervosa. *Psychological Medicine,* 1974, *4,* 309–315.

Garfinkel, P. E., Brown, G. M., Stancer, H. C., & Moldofsky, H. Hypothalamic-pituitary function in anorexia nervosa. *Archives of General Psychiatry,* 1975, *32,* 739–744.

Garfinkel, P. E., Kline, S. A., & Stancer, H. C. Treatment of anorexia nervosa using operant conditioning techniques. *Journal of Nervous and Mental Disease,* 1973, *157,* 428–433.

Garfinkel, P. E., Moldofsky, H., & Garner, D. M. The outcome of anorexia nervosa: Significance of clinical features, body image and behaviour modification. In R. A. Vigersky (Ed.), *Anorexia nervosa.* New York: Raven Press, 1977.

Garn, S. M. The origins of obesity. *American Journal of Diseases of Children,* 1976, *130,* 465–467.

Garn, S. M., & Bailey, G. M. Fatness similarities in adopted pairs. *American Journal of Clinical Nutrition,* 1976, *29,* 1067–1068.

Garner, D. M., & Garfinkel, P. E. Measurement of body image in anorexia nervosa. In R. A. Vigersky (Ed.), *Anorexia nervosa.* New York: Raven Press, 1977.

Garner, D. M., Garfinkel, P. E., Stancer, H. C., & Moldofsky, H. Body image disturbances in anorexia nervosa and obesity. *Psychosomatic Medicine,* 1976, *38,* 327–336.

Garrow, J. *Energy balance and obesity in man.* New York: Elsevier, 1974.

Gates, J. C., Huenemann, R. L., & Brand, R. J. Food choices of obese and non-obese persons. *Journal of the American Dietetic Association,* 1975, *67,* 339–343.

Gaul, D. J., Craighead, W. E., & Mahoney, M. J. Relationship betwen eating rates and obesity. *Journal of Consulting and Clinical Psychology,* 1975, *43,* 123–125.

Glucksman, M. L., & Hirsch, J. The response of obese patients to weight reduction: III. The perception of body size. *Psychosomatic Medicine,* 1969, *31,* 1–7.

Goldblatt, P. B., Moore, M. E., & Stunkard, A. J. Social factors in obesity. *Journal of the American Medical Association,* 1965, *192,* 1039–1044.

Goldman, D., Jaffe, M., & Schachter, S. Yom Kippur, Air France, dormitory food, and eating behavior of obese and normal persons. *Journal of Personality and Social Psychology,* 1968, *10,* 117–123.

Gottesfeld, H. Body and self-cathesis of super-obese patients. *Journal of Psychosomatic Research,* 1962, *6,* 177–183.

Grill, H. *A method for measuring salivary secretion.* Unpublished manuscript, University of Pennsylvania, 1979.

Grinker, J. Behavioral and metabolic consequences of weight reduction. *Journal of the American Dietetic Association,* 1973, *62,* 30–34.

Gull, W. W. The address on medicine. *Lancet,* 1868, *2,* 171–176.

Hagen, R. L. Group therapy versus bibliotherapy in weight reduction. *Behavior Therapy,* 1974, *5,* 222–234.

Halmi, K. A. Anorexia nervosa: Recent investigations. *Annual Review of Medicine,* 1978, *29,* 137–148.

Halmi, K. A. Anorexia nervosa. In A. M. Freedman, H. I. Kaplan, & B. J. Saddock (Eds.), *Comprehensive textbook of psychiatry* (Vol. 3). Baltimore: Williams & Wilkins, 1980.

Halmi, K. A., Brodland, G., & Loney, J. Prognosis in anorexia nervosa. *Annals of Internal Medicine,* 1973, *78,* 907–909.

Halmi, K. A., Brodland, G., & Rigas, C. A follow-up study of 79 patients with anorexia nervosa: An evaluation of prognostic factors and diagnostic criteria. *Life History Research in Psychopathology*, 1975, *4*, 290-301.

Halmi, K. A., Goldberg, S. C., Casper, R. C., Eckert, E. D., & Davis, J. M. Pretreatment predictors of outcome in anorexia nervosa. *British Journal of Psychiatry*, 1979, *134*, 71-78.

Halmi, K. A., Stunkard, A. J., & Mason, E. A. Emotional responses to weight reduction by three methods: Gastric bypass, jejunoileal bypass, diet. *American Journal of Clinical Nutrition*, 1980, *33*, 446-451.

Herbert-Jackson, E., & Risley, T. R. Behavioral nutrition: Consumption of foods of the future by toddlers. *Journal of Applied Behavior Analysis*, 1977, *10*, 407-414.

Herman, C. P. Restrained eating. *Psychiatric Clinics of North America*, 1978, *1*, 593-607.

Herman, C. P., & Mack, D. Restrained and unrestrained eating. *Journal of Personality*, 1975, *43*, 647-660.

Herman, C. P., & Polivy, J. Anxiety, restraint and eating behavior. *Journal of Abnormal Psychology*, 1975, *84*, 666-672.

Hirsch, J., & Knittle, J. L. Cellularity of obese and nonobese human adipose tissue. *Federation Proceedings*, 1970, *29*, 1516-1521.

Hoebel, B. G., & Teitelbaum, P. Weight reduction in normal and hypothalamic hyperphagic rats. *Journal of Comparative and Physiological Psychology*, 1966, *61*, 189-193.

Janowitz, H. D. Role of the gastrointestinal tract in the regulation of food intake. In C. F. Code (Ed.), *Handbook of physiology. I: Alimentary canal.* Washington, D.C.: Physiological Society, 1967.

Jeffery, R. W., & Wing, R. R. Frequency of therapist contact in the treatment of obesity. *Behavior Therapy*, 1979, *10*, 186-192.

Jeffery, R. W., Wing, R. R., & Stunkard, A. J. Behavioral treatment of obesity: The state of the art in 1976. *Behavior Therapy*, 1978, *9*, 189-199.

Jeffrey, D. B., & Katz, R. C. *Take it off and keep it off: A behavioral program for weight loss and health living.* Englewood Cliffs, NJ: Prentice-Hall, 1977.

Johnson, M. L., Burke, B. J., & Mayer, J. Relative importance of inactivity and overeating in the energy balance of obese high school girls. *American Journal of Clinical Nutrition*, 1956, *4*, 37-44.

Johnston, M. W., & Newburgh, L. H. Calculation of heat production from insensible loss of weight. *Journal of Clinical Investigation*, 1942, *21*, 357-363.

Jordan, H. A., Levitz, L. S., & Kimbrell, G. M. *Eating is okay: A radical approach to weight loss, the behavioral control diet.* New York: Rawson, 1976.

Jordan, H. A., Wieland, W. F., Zebley, S. P., Stellar, E., & Stunkard, A. J. Direct measurement of food intake in man: A method for the objective study of eating behavior in man. *Psychosomatic Medicine*, 1966, *28*, 836-842.

Kalucy, R. S., Crisp, A. H., & Harding, B. A study of 56 families with anorexia nervosa. *British Journal of Medical Psychology*, 1977, *50*, 381-395.

Kannel, W. B., & Gordon, T. Obesity and cardiovascular disease: The Framingham study. In W. L. Burland, J. Yudkin, & P. Samuel (Eds.), *Obesity: Proceedings of a Servier Research Institute on Obesity.* Edinburgh: Churchill Livingstone, 1974.

Kannel, W. B., & Gordon, T. *Risks and hazards of obesity.* Paper presented at the Fogarty Conference on Obesity, Washington, D.C., 1977.

Kay, D. W. K., & Leigh, D. The natural history, treatment, and prognosis of anorexia nervosa, based on a study of 38 patients. *Journal of Mental Science*, 1954, *100*, 411-430.

Keesey, R. E. Set-points and body weight regulation. *Psychiatric Clinics of North America*, 1978, *1*, 523-544.

Kendall, R. E., Hall, D. J., Harley, A., & Babigian, H. M. The epidemiology of anorexia nervosa. *Psychological Medicine*, 1973, *3*, 200-213.

Keys, A., Brozek, J., Henschel, A., Mickelson, O., & Taylor, H. L. *The biology of human starvation* (Vols. 1 & 2). Minneapolis: University of Minnesota Press, 1950.

Keys, A., Fidanza, F., Karvonen, M. J., Kimura, N., & Taylor, H. L. Indices of relative weight and obesity. *Journal of Chronic Disease*, 1972, *25*, 329-343.

King, A. Primary and secondary anorexia nervosa syndrome. *British Journal of Psychiatry*, 1963, *109*, 470-479.

Kissileff, H., Klingsberg, H. R., & Van Itallie, T. B. A universal eating monitor for measuring solid-liquid consumption in man. *American Journal of Physiology*, 1980, *238*, 14-22.

Krassner, H. A., Brownell, K. D., & Stunkard, A. J. Cleaning the plate: Food left over by overweight and normal weight persons. *Behaviour Research and Therapy*, 1979, *17*, 155-156.

Lazarus, A. A. New methods in psychotherapy: A case study. *South African Medical Journal*, 1958, *32*, 660-664.

LeBow, M. Can lighter become thinner? *Addictive Behaviors*, 1977, *2*, 87-94.

Leibman, R., Minuchen, S., & Baker, L. An integrated treatment program for anorexia nervosa. *American Journal of Psychiatry*, 1974, *131*, 432-436.

Lewis, S., Haskell, W. L., Wood, P. D., Manoogian, N., Bailey, J. E., & Pereira, M. Effects of physical activity on weight reduction in obese middle-aged women. *American Journal of Clinical Nutrition*, 1976, *29*, 151-156.

Lipman, R. S., Covi, L., & Shapiro, A. The Hopkins Symptom Checklist: Factors derived from the HSCL-90. *Journal of Affective Disorders*, 1979, *1*, 9-24.

Locke, H. J., & Wallace, K. M. Short marital adjustment and prediction tests: Their reliability and validity. *Marriage and Family Living*, 1959, *21*, 251-225.

Madsen, C. H., Madsen, C. K., & Thompson, F. Increasing rural Head Start children's consumption of middle-class meals. *Journal of Applied Behavior Analysis*, 1974, *7*, 257-262.

Mahoney, B. K., Rogers, T., Straw, M. K., & Mahoney, M. J. *Human obesity: Assessment and treatment*. Englewood Cliffs, NJ: Prentice-Hall, in press.

Mahoney, M. J. Self-reward and self-monitoring techniques for weight control. *Behavior Therapy*, 1974, *5*, 48-57.

Mahoney, M. J. Fat fiction. *Behavior Therapy*, 1975, *6*, 416-418.(a)

Mahoney, M. J. The obese eating style: Bites, beliefs, and behavior modification. *Addictive Behaviors*, 1975, *1*, 47-53.(b)

Mahoney, M. J. Some applied issues in self-monitoring. In J. P. Cone & R. P. Hawkins (Eds.), *Behavioral assessment: New directions in clinical psychology*. New York: Brunner/Mazel, 1977.

Mahoney, M. J. Behavior modification in the treatment of obesity. *Psychiatric Clinics of North America*, 1978, *1*, 651-660.

Mahoney, M. J., & Mahoney, K. *Permanent weight control: A total solution to the dieter's dilemma*. New York: W. W. Norton, 1976.

Mann, G. V. The influence of obesity on health. *New England Journal of Medicine*, 1974, *291*, 178-185, 226-232.

Marston, A. R., London, P., Cooper, L. M., & Cohen, N. *In vivo* observation of the eating behavior of obese and nonobese subjects. In A. Howard (Ed.), *Recent advances in obesity research.* London: Newman, 1975.

Maxfield, E., & Konishi, F. Patterns of food intake and physical activity in obesity. *Journal of the American Dietetic Association,* 1966, *49,* 406-408.

Mayer, J. *Overweight: Causes, cost, and control.* Englewood Cliffs, NJ: Prentice-Hall, 1968.

Mayfield, M. E. The indirect measurement of energy expenditure in industrial situations. *American Journal of Clinical Nutrition,* 1971, *24,* 1126-1138.

Mencken, H. L. The genealogy of etiquette. In J. T. Farrell (Ed.), *H. L. Mencken: Prejudices, a selection.* New York: Vintage, 1919.

Metropolitan Life Insurance Company. Frequency of overweight and underweight. *Statistical Bulletin,* 1960, *41,* 4-7.

Meyers, A., Coll, M., & Stunkard, A. J. *Eating in public places: There is no "obese eating style."* Paper presented at the annual meeting of the American Psychological Association, San Francisco, August 1977.

Meyers, A. W., Stunkard, A. J., Coll, M., & Cooke, C. Obesity and activity choice. *Behavior Modification,* 1980, *4,* 355-360.

Mills, M. J., & Stunkard, A. J. Behavioral changes following surgery for obesity. *American Journal of Psychiatry,* 1976, *133,* 527-531.

Mitchel, J. S., & Keesey, R. E. Defense of a lowered weight maintenance level by lateral hypothalamically lesioned rats: Evidence from a restriction-refeeding regimen. *Physiology and Behavior,* 1977, *18,* 1121-1125.

Monelio, L. F., & Mayer, J. Hunger and satiety sensations in men, women, boys and girls. *American Journal of Clinical Nutrition,* 1967, *20,* 253-261.

Morgan, H. G., & Russell, G. F. M. Value of family background in clinical features as predictors of long-term outcome in anorexia nervosa: Four-year follow-up study of 41 patients. *Psychological Medicine,* 1975, *5,* 355-371.

Morton, R. *Phthisiologia—Or a treatise of consumption.* London: Smith, 1720.

Murray, D. C. Treatment of overweight: Relationship between initial weight and weight change during behavior therapy of overweight individuals: Analysis of data from previous studies. *Psychological Reports,* 1975, *37,* 243-248.

Nathan, S., & Pisula, D. Psychological observations of obese adolescents during starvation treatment. *Journal of Child Psychiatry,* 1970, *9,* 722-740.

Nelson, R. O. Methodological issues in assessment via self-monitoring. In J. P. Cone & R. P. Hawkins (Eds.), *Behavioral assessment: New directions in clinical psychology.* New York: Brunner/Mazel, 1977.

Nisbett, R. E. Determinants of food intake in human obesity. *Science,* 1968, *159,* 1254-1255.(a)

Nisbett, R. E. Taste, deprivation and weight determinants of eating behavior. *Journal of Personality and Social Psychology,* 1968, *10,* 107-116.(b)

Nisbett, R. E. Hunger, obesity, and the ventromedial hypothalamus. *Psychological Review,* 1972, *79,* 433-453.

Öst, L., & Götestam, K. G. Behavioral and pharmacological treatments for obesity: An experimental comparison. *Addictive Behaviors,* 1976, *1,* 331-338.

Paffenbarger, R. S., & Hale, W. E. Work activity and coronary heart mortality. *New England Journal of Medicine,* 1975, *292,* 545-550.

Pierson, R. N., & Jr., & Lin, D. H. Measurement of body compartments in children: Whole body counting and other methods. *Seminars in Nuclear Medicine,* 1972, *2,* 373-382.

Polivy, J. Perception of calories and regulation of intake in restrained and unrestrained subject. *Addictive Behaviors,* 1976, *1,* 237-243.

Powley, T. The ventromedial hypothalamic syndrome, satiety, and a cephalic phase hypothesis. *Psychological Review*, 1977, *84*, 89–96.

Price, J. M., & Grinker, J. Effects of degree of obesity, food deprivation and palatability on eating behavior of humans. *Journal of Comparative and Physiological Psychology*, 1973, *85*, 265–271.

Rodin, J. The effects of obesity and set-point on taste responsiveness and intake in humans. *Journal of Comparative and Physiological Psychology*, 1975, *89*, 1003–1009.

Rodin, J. Research on eating behavior and obesity: Where does it fit in personality and social psychology? *Personality and Social Psychology Bulletin*, 1977, *3*, 333–355.

Rodin, J. Environmental factors in obesity. *Psychiatric Clinics of North America*, 1978, *1*, 581–592.

Rodin, J., & Slochower, J. Externality in the nonobese: The effects of environmental responsiveness on weight. *Journal of Personality and Social Psychology*, 1976, *29*, 557–565.

Rose, G. A., & Williams, R. T. Metabolic studies on large and small eaters. *British Journal of Nutrition*, 1961, *15*, 1–9.

Ross, L. Effects of manipulating the salience of food upon consumption by obese and normal eaters. In S. Schachter & J. Rodin (Eds.), *Obese humans and rats*. Washington, D. C.: Erlbaum/Halsted, 1974.

Rotter, J. Generalized expectations for internal versus external control of reinforcement. *Psychological Monographs*, 1966, *80*, 1–28.

Rowland, C. V. Anorexia nervosa: A survey of the literature and review of 30 cases. *International Psychiatry Clinics*, 1970, *7*, 37–137.

Russell, G. F. M. Metabolic, endocrine, and psychiatric aspects of anorexia nervosa. *Scientific Basis of Medicine*, 1969, *236*, 84–93.

Salans, L. B., Horton, E. S., & Sims, E. A. H. Experimental obesity in man: Cellular character of the adipose tissue. *Journal of Clinical Investigation*, 1971, *50*, 1005–1011.

Schachter, S. Obesity and eating. *Science*, 1968, *161*, 751–756.

Schachter, S., Goldman, R., & Gordon, A. Effects of fear, food deprivation and obesity on eating. *Journal of Personality and Social Psychology*, 1968, *10*, 91–97.

Schachter, S., & Gross, L. Manipulated time and eating behavior. *Journal of Personality and Social Psychology*, 1968, *10*, 98–106.

Schachter, S., & Rodin, J. (Eds.). *Obese humans and rats*. Washington, D.C.: Erlbaum/Halsted, 1974.

Seidensticker, J. F., & Tzagournis, M. Anorexia nervosa — clinical features and long-term follow-up. *Journal of Chronic Disease*, 1968, *21*, 361–367.

Seltzer, C. C., & Mayer, J. A simple criterion of obesity. *Postgraduate Medicine*, 1965, *38*, 101–107.

Sheldon, W. H. *Atlas of men*. New York: Harper & Brothers, 1954.

Shields, J. *Monozygotic twins brought up apart and brought up together*. London: Oxford University Press, 1962.

Shipman, W., & Sohlkah, N. Body distortion in obese women. *Psychosomatic Medicine*, 1967, *29*, 540.

Sims, E. A. H. *The types of obesity: Definitions, criteria, and prevalence*. Paper presented at the Fogarty Conference on Obesity, Washington, D.C., October 1977.

Sims, E. A. H., & Horton, E. S. Endocrine and metabolic adaptation to obesity and starvation. *American Journal of Clinical Nutrition*, 1968, 21, 1455–1470.

Sjöström, L. The contribution of fat cells to the determination on body weight. *Psychiatric Clinics of North America*, 1978, *1*, 493, 522.

Slade, P. D., & Russell, G. F. M. Awareness of body dimension in anorexia nervosa: Cross-sectional and longitudinal studies. *Psychological Medicine*, 1973, *3*, 188–199.

Spencer, J. A., & Fremouw, W. J. *Binge eating as a function of restraint and weight classification.* Unpublished manuscript, West Virginia University, 1979.

Stalonas, P. M., Johnson, W. G., & Christ, M. Behavior modification for obesity: The evaluation of exercise, contingency management, and program adherence. *Journal of Consulting and Clinical Psychology*, 1978, *46*, 463–469.

Stephanic, P. A., Heald, F. P., & Mayer, J. Caloric intake in relation to energy output of obese and nonobese adolescent boys. *American Journal of Clinical Nutrition*, 1959, *7*, 55–62.

Stuart, R. B. Behavioral control of overeating. *Behaviour Research and Therapy*, 1967, *5*, 357–365.

Stuart, R. B. Self-help for self-management. In R. B. Stuart (Ed.), *Behavioral self-management.* New York: Brunner/Mazel, 1977.

Stuart, R. B. *Act thin, stay thin.* New York: W. W. Norton, 1978.

Stuart, R. B., & Davis, B. *Slim chance in a fat world: Behavioral control of obesity.* Champaign, IL: Research Press, 1972.

Stunkard, A. J. A method of studying physical activity in man. *American Journal of Clinical Nutrition*, 1960, *8*, 595–601.

Stunkard, A. J. New therapies for the eating disorders. *Archives of General Psychiatry*, 1972, *26*, 391–398.

Stunkard, A. J. From explanation to action in psychosomatic medicine: The case of obesity. *Psychosomatic Medicine*, 1975, *37*, 195–236.

Stunkard, A. J. *The pain of obesity.* Palo Alto: Bull, 1976.

Stunkard, A. J. Basic mechanisms which regulate body weight: New perspectives. *Psychiatric Clinics of North America*, 1978, *1*, 461–472.

Stunkard, A. J., & Brownell, K. D. Behavior therapy and self-help programs for obesity. In J. F. Munro (Ed.), *The treatment of obesity.* London: MTP Press, 1979.

Stunkard, A. J., Coll, M., Lundquist, S., & Meyer, A. Obesity and eating style. *Archives of General Psychiatry*, in press.

Stunkard, A. J., & Fox, S. The relationship of gastric motility and hunger: A summary of the evidence. *Psychosomatic Medicine*, 1971, *33*, 123–134.

Stunkard, A. J., Kaplan, D. Eating in public places: A review of reports on direct observation of eating behavior. *International Journal of Obesity*, 1977, *1*, 89–101.

Stunkard, A. J., & Koch, C. The interpretation of gastric mobility: Apparent bias in the reports of hunger by obese persons. *Archives of General Psychiatry*, 1964, *11*, 74–82.

Stunkard, A. J., & Mahoney, M. J. Behavioral treatment of eating disorders. In H. Leitenberg (Ed.), *The handbook of behavior modification.* Englewood Cliffs, NJ: Prentice-Hall, 1976.

Stunkard, A. J., & Mazer, A. Smorgasbord and obesity. *Psychosomatic Medicine*, 1978, *40*, 173–175.

Stunkard, A. J., & McLaren-Hume, M. The results of treatment for obesity. *Archives of Internal Medicine*, 1959, *103*, 79–85.

Stunkard, A. J., & Mendelson, M. Obesity and body image: I. Characteristics of disturbances in the body image of some obese persons. *American Journal of Psychiatry*, 1967, *123*, 1296–1300.

Stunkard, A. J., & Messick, S. *A new scale to assess restrained eating.* Unpublished manuscript, University of Pennsylvania, 1979.

Stunkard, A. J., & Pestka, J. The physical activity of obese girls. *American Journal of Diseases of Children,* 1962, *103,* 812-817.

Stunkard, A. J., & Rush, A. J. Dieting and depression reexamined: A critical review of reports of untoward responses during weight reduction for obesity. *Annals of Internal Medicine,* 1974, *81,* 526-533.

Theander, S. Anorexia nervosa. *Acta Psychiatrica Scandinavica,* 1970, *214,* 1-194.

Thoma, H. Some psychoanalytic observations on anorexia nervosa. *British Journal of Medical Psychology,* 1963, *36,* 239-248.

United States Senate Select Subcommittee on Nutrition and Human Needs. Proceedings from hearings. Washington, D. C.: U.S. Government Printing Office, 1977.

Van Itallie, T. Testimony before Senate Select Committee on Nutrition and Human Needs. Washington, D.C.: U.S. Government Printing Office, 1977.

Walike, B. C., Jordan, H. A., & Stellar, E. Preloading and the regulation of food intake in man. *Journal of Comparative and Physiological Psychology,* 1969, *68,* 327-332.

Waxman, M., & Stunkard, A. J. *Caloric intake and expenditure of obese children.* Unpublished manuscript, University of Pennsylvania, 1979.

Whitney, E. N., & Hamilton, E. M. N. *Understanding nutrition.* St. Paul: West, 1977.

Wilkinson, P., Parklin, J., Pearloom, G., Strang, H., & Sykes, P. Energy intake and physical activity in obese children. *British Medical Journal,* 1977, *1,* 756.

Wilson, G. T. Methodological considerations in treatment outcome research on obesity. *Journal of Consulting and Clinical Psychology,* 1978, *46,* 687-702.

Wirtshafter, D., & Davis, J. D. Set-points, settling points, and the control of body weight. *Physiology and Behavior,* 1977, *19,* 75-78.

Wollersheim, J. P. Effectiveness of group therapy based on learning principles in the treatment of overweight women. *Journal of Abnormal Psychology,* 1970, *76,* 462-474.

Wolpe, J. Reciprocal inhibition as the main basis of psychotherapeutic effects. *Archives of Neurology and Psychiatry,* 1954, *72,* 205-226.

Wolpe, J. *Psychotherapy by reciprocal inhibition.* Stanford: Stanford University Press, 1958.

Wooley, O. W. Long-term food regulation in the obese and nonobese. *Psychosomatic Medicine,* 1971, *33,* 436-444.

Wooley, O., & Wooley, S. C. The experimental psychology of obesity. In T. Silverstone & J. Fincham (Eds.), *Obesity: Pathogenesis and management.* Lancaster, England: Medical and Technical Publishing Co., 1975.

Wooley, O. W., Wooley, S. C., & Dunham, R. B. Can calories be perceived and do they affect hunger in obese and nonobese humans? *Journal of Comparative Physiological Psychology,* 1972, *80,* 250-258.

Wooley, S. C., & Wooley, O. W. Salivation to the sight and thought of food: A new measure of appetite. *Psychosomatic Medicine,* 1973, *35,* 136-142.

Wooley, S. C., Wooley, O. W., & Dyrenforth, S. R. Theoretical, practical, and social issues in behavioral treatments of obesity. *Journal of Applied Behavior Analysis,* 1979, *12,* 3-26.

Young, P. T. Palatability: The hedonic response to foodstuffs. *Handbook of Physiology,* 1967, *1,* 353-366.

12

Assessment of Social Inadequacy

JAMES P. CURRAN
HAROLD W. WESSBERG

Introduction

Although numerous theories of psychopathology ranging from neo-Freudian (Sullivan, 1954) to operant-learning paradigms (Homans, 1961) have stressed the importance of social competency to mental health, until recently a direct and systematic approach to the treatment of social incompetency has not been undertaken (Hersen & Bellack, 1976). Empirical data support the importance of social competency to mental health. The work of Zigler and Phillips (1961) suggested that premorbid level of social functioning was a good predictor of posthospital adjustment. Lentz, Paul, and Calhoun (1971) demonstrated that level of social functioning was related to discharge from the hospital and to recidivism rate. Increasingly greater numbers of researchers (Argyle & Kendon, 1967; Gladwin, 1967; Libet & Lewinsohn, 1973; Sylph, Ross, & Kedward, 1978) have stressed social-skill deficits as a basis for the major forms of psychopathology. It also appears that social-skill deficits are not only associated with major forms of psychopathology, but to numerous other dysfunctional behaviors such as sexual problems (Barlow, 1973), alcohol abuse (Kraft, 1971; Miller, Hersen, Eisler, & Hilsman, 1974), drug addiction (Callner &

James P. Curran and Harold W. Wessberg. Brown University Medical School and Veterans Administration Medical Center, Providence, Rhode Island.

Ross, 1976), heterosexual social anxiety (Curran, 1977), and marital dysfunctioning (Eisler, Miller, Hersen, & Alford, 1974).

In the last decade, social-skills training has been established as a viable approach to increasing the social functioning of socially inadequate patients suffering from a wide variety of psychological disorders (Hersen & Bellack, 1976). Goldsmith and McFall (1975, p. 51) described social-skills training as

> a general therapy approach aimed at increasing performance competence in critical life situations. In contrast to the therapies aimed primarily at the elimination of maladaptive behaviors, skills training emphasizes the positive educational aspects of treatment. It assumes that each individual always does the best he can, given his physical limitations and unique learning history in every situation. Thus, when an individual's best effort is judged to be maladaptive, this indicates the presence of a situation-specific skill deficit in the individual's repertoire. . . . Whatever the origin of this deficit (e.g., lack of experience, faulty learning, biological dysfunction), it often may be overcome or partially compensated through appropriate training in more skillful response alternatives.

Phillips (1978) perceives social-skills training not just as another treatment approach, but as an alternative model to the traditional medical model of psychopathology. For Phillips, psychopathology results from an organism's inability to solve problems, to resolve conflicts, and to reach goals. The organism's lack of requisite skills results in less adaptive, and in some cases maladaptive, strategies. Negative emotional states (e.g., anxiety) and maladaptive cognition occur in lieu of social solutions to problems. It is Phillips's opinion that the social-skills model obviates the need for traditional diagnosis, classification, and nosological groupings and requires, instead, a thorough analysis of behavioral situations. Phillips (1978, p. xvii) states: "The viewpoint proffered here posits the lack of social skills as the essential behavioral deficit, owing to conflictual person–environmental conditions and sets out to promote change through better understanding of, and alterations in, the environmental contingencies regulating behavior."

Regardless of whether social-skills training is viewed as a treatment strategy or as a model for psychopathology and treatment, there is a need to develop reliable and valid assessment instruments to measure social skills. Several recent reviews (Curran, 1979; Curran & Mariotto, in press; Hersen & Bellack, 1977) have concluded that social-skills assessment is at a very primitive level, with no one instrument adequately validated. In this chapter, we do not offer a resolution to the problems associated with the assessment of social skills because of the years of empirical research that are required. What we do propose is a classificatory scheme wherein various assessment strategies can be ordered and their advantages and disadvantages examined. Before presenting this classificatory scheme, it is pertinent to (1) examine some theoretical–definitional issues involved in the assessment of social skills, (2) review various theories regarding the etiology and maintenance of social-skills deficits, and (3) present data regarding incidence rate of social skills deficits as well as to examine their multifaceted nature.

Theoretical–Definitional Issues

In this section, we do not intend to present a definition of social inadequacy because it is beyond the scope of the chapter and beyond the present state of knowledge in the field. We would, however, like to briefly mention some theoretical–definitional issues which we feel are particularly germane to the assessment of social skills. For a more detailed exposition of some of these issues, the interested reader is referred to Curran (1979) and Curran and Mariotto (in press).

First of all, we wish to remind the reader that the constructs of social inadequacy, social competence, social skills, and so on, are mega-constructs. These mega-constructs are useful for relating a variety of superficially dissimilar response classes under a single organizational principle. While there is some utility in the use of mega-constructs, there are also some inherent problems. For example, Curran (1979) has noted that investigators should proceed with caution in their use of these mega-constructs and not make the same mistake that trait theorists did when they regarded their constructs as invariant dispositional units. The response classes subsumed under the mega-construct of social skills are not causal variables but response capabilities whose probabilities of occurrences in criterion situations are determined by environmental and person variables and the interaction between these sets of variables. Neither behavioral consistency nor cross-situational generality should be expected, but both should be determined on empirical grounds.

Definitions of the mega-constructs such as social skills and social inadequacy generally employ the resulting consequences of the behaviors in question as a major criterion. For example, Libet and Lewinsohn (1973, p. 311) define social skills as "the complex ability to maximize the rate of positive reinforcement and to minimize the strength of punishment from others." While, in the abstract, a response–consequence definition makes sense, it is an impossible criterion to use with precision in our assessment paradigms. A response–consequence definition assumes that we know what is reinforcing and what is punishing for a particular individual and that we are able to correctly identify not only the short-term but also the long-term consequences of a response. In practice, when conducting social-skills training or assessing the adequacy of a response, we are making a judgment that these behaviors are *generally* regarded an appropriate (for this situation, for someone with these particular characteristics, and so on) and *generally* result in favorable consequences (given the situation, reinforcing agents involved, and the like).

Different situations have different requisite behaviors. The response classes needed for a successful delivery of a speech are considerably different from those response classes necessary for the continuance of an intimate relationship. Cultural and subgroup differences exist regarding the judgment of the appropriateness of any social behaviors. In addition, characteristics of the subjects also interact with the inferential judgment of the observers in their evaluation of the appropriateness of a response. For example, in a study by Bryant, Trower, Yardley, Urbieta, and Letemendia (1976), sex of the subjects appeared to affect judges' evaluation of the social adequacy of the subjects. Subjects in the Bryant *et al.* (1976) study were psychiatric outpatients who participated in a simulated social situation. Judges rated the subjects' performances in the simulated social interaction for a variety of specific measures such as voice volume and facial expression, and also on a number of bipolar adjectives, such as assertive–nonassertive, warm–cold, and so forth. There were no differences between the male and female subjects on any of the specific behaviors or on any of the rated adjectives. Yet on a global measure of social adequacy, 46% of the males were judged to be socially inadequate while only 16% of the women were judged to be inadequate. In other words, although the judges felt that there were no differences with respect to specific behaviors rated between males and females, a disproportionate number of males were evaluated as being socially inadequate. Either the specific behaviors which were rated from the simulated situations were not particularly relevant to the judges in making their overall judgment of adequacy, or a double standard exists with respect to men and women. In another study, Rose and Tryon (1979) found that both male and female judges gave more aggressive ratings to the behavior of female actors than to male actors, even though the male and female actors had been programmed to perform in a largely similar manner.

Another theoretical–definitional issue that needs to be addressed in the assessment of social competency is the size of the behavioral unit to be measured. The unit of measurement for assessing social skills has varied from large molar units such as global ratings of social skills to more molecular units such as duration of eye contact. Behaviorally oriented assessors have generally preferred molecular units because they can be operationalized with greater precision, and consequently require fewer inferences on the part of the observers. However, as Wiggins (1973, p. 325) noted, "The relationship between unit size and criterion relevance cannot be stated dogmatically. Narrowly defined behavioral attributes run the risk of a high degree of specificity which may preclude the possibility of generalizability to criterion behaviors. On the other hand, units that are too global in nature may yield only vacuous statements that are true of everyone or of no one." We regard the molecular- versus molar-unit question as somewhat of an artificial controversy. Rather than viewing unit size as a dichotomy, unit size can be seen as a gradient. We prefer a hierarchical multiple-level approach to the assessment of social skills. The choice of unit size within these multiple levels is dependent upon the assessment questions asked and the empirical relationships established. The "proper" units of observation are those which have been empirically determined as possessing the highest degree of criterion relevance, and these units may vary depending upon various assessment questions.

Lastly, with respect to our theoretical–definitional concerns, we would like to address our choice of words for the title of this chapter. We chose "Assessment of Social Inadequacy" because we felt it was most consistent with the title of this book, *Behavioral Assessment of Adult Disorders.* However, we wish to remind the reader that the goal of social-skills training as stated by Goldsmith and McFall (1975, p. 51) is "increasing performance competence in critical life situations." The assessment of social inadequacy is quite a different phenomenon from the assessment of social competency. It may very well be easier to assess what not to do (incompetency) than to assess what to do (competency) in critical life situations. Furthermore, within our social-skills training programs, there appear to be differential emphases with respect to the levels of requisite behaviors that are taught, ranging from minimal requisite behaviors within certain populations (e.g., psychiatric patients) to more optimal, higher-order behaviors in other populations. The response classes and processes involved in inadequate social performance, adequate minimal social performance, and adequate optimal social performance may differ; consequently, our assessment and treatment paradigms might also have to differ, depending upon the type and level of behavior in question.

Although we have only briefly mentioned some of the major theoretical–definitional issues involved in the assessment of social skills, it is not because they are unimportant. On the contrary, we need to be extremely cognizant of these issues if we are to improve our assessment of social skills. An equally important consideration for the assessment of social skills is the understanding of etiologic and maintaining factors of inadequate social performance.

Etiologic and Maintaining Factors of Inadequate Social Performance

The authors regard social skills as response capabilities inferred from performance. The probability of occurrence of any skill in any criterion situation is determined by environmental factors, person variables, and the interaction between environmental factors and person variables. Unfortunately, because performance is affected by so many other variables in addition to response capabilities, it is difficult to assess the nature of the deficient performance.

Inadequate social performance may be due to an actual skills deficit. The individual may never have learned the appropriate behavior, and consequently is incapable of behaving appropriately in the criterion situations. A variant of the deficiency hypothesis is that at one time the individual may have possessed the requisite skills, but these behaviors are no longer readily available because of some sort of deterioration process such as that often found in chronically institutionalized psychiatric patients. Inadequate social performance may also result if an individual has learned socially inappropriate responses to the criterion situations. If these inappropriate responses have a high probability of occurrence because of previous learning, then even if the individual does possess the requisite skills for the criterion situation, inappropriate responses may supercede the more appropriate skills and the individual's performance is judged as inadequate and/or inappropriate.

Various interference mechanisms may also be responsible for inadequate social performance because they inhibit and/or disrupt the effective application of the individual's response capabilities. Numerous emotional cognitive, and motivational factors may all interfere with adequate social performance. For example, an individual may possess the requisite skills in a situation, but as a result of a classical conditioning process, may be so anxious in the criterion situation that his or her performance is compromised. Trower, Yardley, Bryant, and Shaw (1978) also make a distinction between a skills-deficit and an interference interpretation of inadequate social performance. They have labeled this distinction as primary versus secondary social failure. They define primary social failure as the result of faulty socialization or lack of social experience. Secondary social failure is attributed to other kinds of psychopathology resulting from biological, cognitive, or dynamic disturbances. Trower et al. (1978, p. 42) further state that the difference between primary and secondary social failure is

> comparable by analogy to the distinction in linguistics between competence and performance, competence in the present instance referring to central cognitive processes and knowledge such as decision-making capability and skill repertoire, and performance the production of skilled behavior. Primary failure refers to the loss of or failure to acquire competence, while secondary failure refers to the disruption or inhibition of performance, with competence intact.

Figure 1 contains a model illustrating some of the factors which need to be assessed in the measurement of social inadequacy. While this model is greatly simplified for presentation and does not include all potential factors, we find it a heuristic conceptual device for the assessment of social skills. Individuals in Cell A have adequate skills for the criterion situation, and their performance is not interfered with by emotional, motivational, or cognitive factors. Individuals in Cell B also possess an adequate behavioral repertoire, but their performance is so interfered with by emotional, motivational, or cognitive factors that their performance is judged as inadequate. Using

Social Skills Repertoire

		Adequate	Inadequate
	Absent	Cell A Adequate Skills/ No Interference	Cell C Inadequate Skills/ No Interference
	Present	Cell B Adequate Skills/ Interference	Cell D Inadequate Skills/ Interference

Interference Mechanisms

Figure 1
Mini-model of social-skills performance.

the terminology proposed by Trower *et al.* (1978), individuals in Cell B would be regarded as secondary social failures. Emotional states such as anxiety or depression can severely interfere with 'social-skills performance. If an individual is not motivated to do well in a criterion situation, then poor performance may be more a function of disinterest than of a lack of requisite behaviors. Cognitive factors such as misperception of social cues, unrealistic expectations regarding criterion behaviors, and soon can result in inadequate performance even though the individual possesses an adequate behavioral repertoire.

Individuals in Cells C and D can be characterized as primary social failures because they do not possess the response capabilities required in the criterion situations. The inadequate performance of individuals in Cell C is not due to any interference mechanism, but to a lack of requisite skills. These individuals are neither particularly anxious nor depressed. Although we have no empirical data to support this contention, it is our belief that the majority of individuals who are judged as unskilled because of their high rate of obnoxious behaviors fall into Cell C. Individuals in Cell D also lack an adequate behavioral repertoire and, in addition, experience adverse emotional, motivational, and cognitive states. For individuals in Cell D, these adverse states are the results of their skills deficits rather than the cause of their poor social performance. For example, inadequate repertoires can lead to poor social performance, which may result in aversive consequences, which may, in turn, elicit anxiety. Paul and Bernstein (1973) have labeled the anxiety experience due to inadequate social performance as reactive anxiety. Inadequate performance can lead to failure to secure reinforcement, which may, in turn, lead to depression. Perhaps the most difficult determination in assessing social inadequacy is differentiating individuals in Cell B from those in Cell D. Individuals in both of these cells are performing inadequately in social situations and their performance is accompanied by adverse emotional states. In Cell B, the emotional states appear to be primarily responsible for the poor performance, while in Cell D, emotional states are the result of the poor performance.

We mentioned previously Phillips's (1978) social-skills model of psychopathology. In Phillips's model, adverse cognitive and emotional states would be viewed as the result of a lack of social skills, that is, the individual's inability to cope with problematic situations. For example, classifically conditioned anxiety, which we view as possibly occurring even in the presence of requisite skills for the criterion situation, would be viewed by Phillips as the result of inadequate skills to handling the conditioning process. We feel that Phillips too broadly interprets the role of social skills and his interpretation is so inclusive that it is equated with all of human behavior, and consequently becomes a meaningless term. Trower *et al.* (1978) and Liberman, Vaughn, Aitchison, and Falloon (1977) also present models of social skills which we feel are too inclusive. Both sets of investigators have included perceptual and cognitive processing factors as well as motoric responses in their definition of social skills. They stress the point that inadequate behavioral performances may not be due to a lack of necessary motoric responses, but rather to perceptual or cognitive processing factors. Some perceptual and cognitive processing factors which they list as potential variables in inadequate social performance are: low level of discrimination, inaccurate stereotypes, faulty attribution, failure to consider alternatives, failure to acquire the right knowledge for making decisions, and failure to discriminate appropriate and effective actions from ineffective ones. While agreeing with these investigators that these factors may interfere with social performance, we prefer not to regard these factors as social skills per se. We prefer to limit our definition of social skills to observable motoric responses for fear that the term "social skills" will become too inclusive and perhaps meaningless.

Since we are speaking of etiology, we would like to digress briefly and state that what little evidence we have would seem to indicate that social-skills difficulties may be evident quite early in life. Trower, Bryant, and Argyle (1978, p. 55) state that "inadequate patients reported having significantly more difficulties in mixing with others and in dating the opposite sex in adolescence, and were judged by the clinic psychiatrists to have had social difficulties long before their illness." Gottman (1977, p. 513) notes that "there are data to suggest that children who are rejected or not accepted by their peers are at risk and that sociometric measures are predictive of later social functioning." Gottman, Gonso, and Rasmussen (1975) have indicated that early sociometric ratings are associated with a host of later problematic behaviors ranging from delinquency to schizophrenia.

As previously mentioned, Figure 1 has been greatly oversimplified for presentation. Once a determination of an actual skill deficit has been made, it is imperative to complete a thorough functional analysis of the individual vis-à-vis the criterion situation. An analysis of all of the micro-units required in the situation as well as the sequence and timing of these micro-units must be examined. If it has been determined that the poor social performance is due to interference mechanisms, then the exact nature of these interference mechanisms must be explored thoroughly. The determination of which factors are responsible for inadequate social performance is extremely difficult and complex. No one assessment procedure is capable of yielding information pertinent to all factors that may effect skills performance. In discussing our conceptual model for social-skills assessment strategies later in this chapter, we will try to indicate the relative merits and liabilities of each of these assessment strategies in relation to the relevant factors that need to be assessed. In the next section of this chapter, we will examine the incidence of social-skills deficits in psychiatric patients and explore its multifaceted nature.

Incidence and Multifaceted Nature of Social-Skills Deficits

Two recent surveys (Bryant *et al.*, 1976; Curran, Miller, Zwick, Monti, & Stout, 1980) with psychiatric patients provide us with an estimate of the incidence of social inadequacy in a patient population and some descriptive characteristics of those patients so labeled. Subjects in the Bryant *et al.* study consisted of all patients having the diagnosis of neurosis or personality disorders who were attending an outpatient clinic in England over a six-month period. Ratings of social inadequacy were made by two psychologists and two psychiatrists. One of the psychiatrists made his ratings on the basis of a clinical interview and from psychometric tests and other questionnaires. The other psychiatrist made his ratings on the basis of case notes. The two psychologists made their ratings on the basis of observations of the patient during an eight-minute social-structured situation. For the purposes of this study, all four raters had to agree that the patient was socially inadequate in order to be included in that category. Interrater reliability between the four raters was .76. The percentage of those nonpsychotic outpatients classified as being socially inadequate was 16.3%.

The Curran et al. survey was conducted on an American inpatient population. The source of data surveyed consisted of the patients' assessment and treatment plan formulated by the patients' attending physician and other members of the patients' treatment team. This treatment plan was formulated five days after the patient had been hospitalized. The subjects were the first 779 consecutive admissions to the inpatient unit during the course of the study. Coders trained by another investigatory team systematically went through each patient's chart and coded all of them for 240 distinct problem behaviors. The coding system was organized into ten major problem areas: physical, sensory, thought and cognitive functioning, affect, overt behavior, sexual behavior, social behavior, social-role relationships, life-task roles, and environmental problems. Within each major problem area, the code is hierarchically organized to account for varying degrees of specificity within the assessment and treatment plan (e.g., physical problems → excessive mobility → pacing). One of the problem codes listed under the major heading of social-role relationships was social-skills deficits. In order for the coders to code a patient as having a social-skills deficit, it had to be recorded in the patient's chart that the patient appeared to have long-standing generalized difficulties interacting with people. Neither the attending physician nor coders were aware of the survey exploring the incidence and nature of the problems associated with socially deficit psychiatric patients. In the Curran et al. survey, approximately 7% of the inpatients were characterized by the coders as having social-skills deficits. The incidence of socially deficit individuals in the Curran survey was less than that found in the Bryant survey. Numerous factors could account for this discrepancy, including the following: the subject samples were from two different countries and patient populations (inpatient vs. outpatient), there were different definitions of the term social inadequacy, different data sources, and so forth, but perhaps most importantly, the Bryant *et al.* survey involved a specific attempt to make the diagnosis of social inadequacy.

In neither survey was any systematic relationship found between the problem of social inadequacy and any of the traditional psychiatric diagnostic categories. In the Bryant *et al.* study, no relationship was found between social inadequacy and any clinical measure used, such as diagnosis, symptoms, and length of illness. Symptoms of depression and anxiety were as common in inadequate patients as in adequate patients. There was no association between the diagnosis of inadequate personality and the label of social inadequacy. In the Curran *et al.* survey, of the 58 patients who were judged as socially deficit, approximately 22% had a diagnosis of schizophrenic, 22% had diagnoses of major affect disorders, 21% were labeled as neurotic depressives, 10% were labeled as adjustment reactions of adolescence, 7% were labeled as alcoholics, and 3% were diagnosed as personality disorders. In the Curran survey, not one of the individuals labeled as having a social-skills deficit was diagnosed as an inadequate personality. As in the Bryant survey, Curran found little relationship between the label of social-skills deficits and any of the traditional psychiatric diagnoses; that is, there were no differences in percentages of socially deficit patients and those patients not so labeled in any of the traditional diagnostic categories. In the Curran survey, the label of social-skills deficits appeared to be related to length of stay in the hospital. For those patients who were labeled as socially inadequate, the average length of stay was 29 days, while the average length of stay for those patients not labeled as socially inadequate was 21 days.

In both the Bryant and Curran surveys, an attempt was made to differentiate socially inadequate and socially adequate patients along a variety of dimensions. In the Bryant survey, raters observing the patients during the social interaction test rated the socially inadequate patients as more cold, unassertive, socially anxious, sad, and unrewarding than the socially adequate patients. On specific behaviors, the socially inadequate patients were rated as having less expression in their face, voice, and posture, less frequent eye contact, producing a less spontaneous and interesting flow of speech, and were less able to manage a conversation than a socially adequate patient. Socially inadequate patients, in contrast with socially adequate patients, tended to talk too much and allow their personal problems and moods to intrude inappropriately in the conversation. With respect to psychometric testing, inadequate patients were significantly higher than other patients on measures of introversion, but not on neuroticism. Inadequate patients tested out as less dominant, sociable, and self-adapting than the other patients. With respect to reports of social difficulties, inadequate patients were described as more likely to have had a history of poor mixing with others and a failure in dating, and reported considerable difficulty in a wide range of social situations, particularly those involving contact with strangers, especially those of the opposite sex. They were judged by the clinic psychiatrist to have had social difficulties long before their current illness. Almost all of the inadequate males were single, whereas approximately 60% of the males in this survey were married. There was no association between marital status and social inadequacy for the females. In the Bryant survey, social class did not appear to be related to social inadequacy; however, there was some suggestion that individuals without siblings or from small families may have been more likely to be labeled as socially inadequate.

In the Curran et al. survey, the frequency of socially inadequate individuals falling within the other 239 problem codes was calculated. Those problem categories which exceeded 20% for patients labeled as deficient in social skills were: hypermotility (27.6%), thought problems (20.7%), nondelusional, negative ideas about self (56.9%), other-directed sadness (70.7%), other-directed anger (31%), other-directed anxieties (27.6%), alcohol abuse (20.7%), suicidal ideation (34.5%), insufficient social contact (25.9%), overly assertive (20.7%), excessive dependency (22.4%), lonely (24.1%), family problems (39.7%), and strained relationship with parents (22.4%). Interestingly, only 6.9% of the socially deficient patients were also coded for insufficient assertiveness. In fact, more of the socially deficient individuals were labeled as being overly assertive (20.7%). Clearly, in this particular population, those individuals who were labeled as being socially unskilled were not synonymous with the definition of low assertiveness. Consistent with previous theorizing, social-skills deficits were associated with anxiety, depression, low self-esteem, insufficient social contact, and social difficulties, especially with family members.

A stepwise multiple discriminant analysis was conducted in order to determine whether the problem codes could significantly differentiate the unskilled from the skilled subjects in this sample. Problem behavior frequencies which differed in the skilled and unskilled samples by more than 5% were used as predictors, with the two groups of patients, skilled versus unskilled, as the criterion groups. A significant discriminative function was established. Those problem codes contributing significantly to the discriminant analysis were: emotionally distant, anxiety associated with thought disorders, insufficient social contact, excessive social behavior, negative ideas about self, mutism, excessive assertion, socially inappropriate behavior, problem with spouse, inadequate work performance, and other anger. Although the discriminant analysis significantly differentiated the two groups, the derived function was less than satisfactory in correctly classifying patients into the two groups. While 95% of the socially skilled individuals were correctly classified as belonging to the socially skilled group, only 36% of the socially unskilled patients were classified as belonging in the unskilled group.

Another analysis was conducted to determine whether the total number of problem behaviors coded within each of the ten major problem areas employed in the coding system differentiated the socially deficient patients and those patients not so labeled. Socially deficient patients were found to have significantly greater frequency of problem behaviors coded than the other patients for the three primary social codes (social-behavior problems, social-relationship problems [excluding social-skills deficits], and life-task role problems) and the mood problem area. No other significant differences were found.

One conclusion is evident from this survey, and that is, patients perceived by their therapists as having social-skills deficits are a heterogeneous group of patients, both with respect to their social-behavior problems and other problematic behavior. While some proportions of the socially deficient individuals in this survey conform to the stereotypical patient thought of as inadequate—that is, as having insufficient social contact, being emotionally distant, excessively dependent, and insufficiently assertive—other patients clearly did not fit this stereotype. Other patients labeled as socially unskilled were described as overly assertive, engaging in verbal abuse, rebellious or resistant, engaging in socially inappropriate behaviors, and being a social-behavioral problem. Parenthetically, in the Bryant et al. survey, there was a group of patients about whom the judges disagreed as to whether they should be labeled socially inadequate or adequate. These patients were described as speaking too much about themselves and too loudly for too much of the time, and as too controlling and treating the other person as an audience rather than as an individual. These patients were rated as being more aggressive and assertive than inadequate patients, but almost as cold and unrewarding as the inadequate patients. Results of the Curran *et al.* and the Bryant *et al.* surveys would seem to indicate that at least some clinicians feel that overly aggressive, overly domineering individuals should also be regarded as socially unskilled. With respect to the other problem behaviors coded in the Curran survey, some of the unskilled patients were described as being hyperactive while others were described as being hypoactive. Some of the unskilled patients were described as having a flat affect while others were characterized as having large mood swings. Some socially deficient individuals were described as being depressed, others angry, others anxious, and still others fearful.

It appears from these two surveys that an individual may be labeled as socially inadequate for a number of diversified reasons. A socially inadequate individual may or may not be socially anxious, may or may not be self-deprecatory, may be unassertive or conversely, overly assertive or aggressive. No one socially inadequate individual would be likely to manifest all of the behavioral, clinical, and social attributes which fit the stereotype of socially inadequate individuals. Furthermore, it is also possible that some of these factors may be present in adequate individuals. To regard individuals who have been labeled socially inadequate as a homogeneous group would be an example of what Kiesler (1971) has labeled as the "uniformity myth" and could have serious detrimental effects on social-skills research. We wish to caution researchers that unless they become more specific regarding the particular behavioral deficits of socially inadequate individuals, they are in danger of replacing traditional diagnostic labeling for a new label which will have many of the associated problems of the old labeling system.

It is our hope that in discussing the various theoretical–definitional issues, etiologic factors, and the nature and complexity of social-skills deficits, we have sensitized readers to the enormous difficulties involved in the assessment of social-skills deficits. It is our opinion that no one assessment strategy is capable of yielding all the pertinent information needed to determine the myriad reasons underlying skillful or unskillful social performance. In the next section of this chapter, we will propose a classificatory model of assessment and attempt to indicate the relative merits and liabilities behind each assessment strategy with respect to providing data relevant to the different factors involved in social-skills performance.

Assessment Issues and Models

As has been evident in recent years (Curran, 1977; Hersen & Bellack, 1977), assessment in the social-skills area has received an increasing amount of attention. For a substantial period of time, treatment methods seemed to outstrip the actual measurement and delineation of the constructs of social skill, social inadequacy, social anxiety, and so forth. This has been a troublesome period for researchers and clinicians because we have been struggling to deal with issues that, as yet, have not been defined or clarified. It has become apparent that the definitions and means of assessment in this area must receive much more attention if any meaningful, accurate predictions relevant to social skills are to be made. We would like to point out here that our immediate concern in assessment is toward predictive issues (assessment *for*), rather than complete understanding (assessment *of*) (Prelinger & Zimet, 1964). Naturally, we hope to be able eventually to understand the myriad factors affecting any given individual's problems. Realizing our limitations, though, our more modest goals relate to identifying specific behaviors or patterns of behaviors that will enable us to accurately classify patients for proper treatment.

In many ways this is similar to the traditional decision-making issues that involve selection, classification, incremental validity, and discriminative efficiency (Cronbach & Gleser, 1965). That is, we are trying to classify patients in the most effective, accurate manner we can, to provide the best, most compatible treatment. To use decision-making terminology, we must focus on correctly identifying the "valid positives" and minimizing the "false negatives" to ensure that all those socially inadequate patients we assess are assigned to receive treatment geared to their types of problems. Incremental validity refers to the degree of improvement our newly developed assessment program has over already existing programs. This will be addressed later in this section. Discriminative efficiency indicates how precise any method is for enabling us to make correct decisions. Obviously, without a formal all-encompassing definition of social inadequacy it is difficult to know in every case whether correct decisions are made or not. This creates a bind in which we must continually develop our definition, assessment, and treatment in a somewhat circular manner, relying on new evidence in each realm to build onto the other realms. This is called "bootstrapping" and is similar to the process of building a "nomological network" (Cronbach & Meehl, 1955), wherein we use the findings from more concrete levels of a constructual system (indicants) to refine our understanding at more abstract levels (constructs). Our focus in this section is on some of the various strategies used to assess socially inadequate performance, including a proposed multidimensional classification plan. We would like to discuss these strategies in general, first, and then to deal with some of the specific methods now used.

Many of the various factors affecting social performance were discussed previously in this chapter. These included skills deficits due to failure to learn or lack of opportunity to learn, poor performance due to interference by anxiety, faulty cognitive appraisal, and the like. Given the level of understanding we have about social inadequacy and our concern that its definition may become so broad so as to be unmanageable, we choose to limit our current discussion to overt, publicly observable (at least in principle) behavioral performance. Obviously, emotional and motivational factors play a central role in social behaviors, but they are not the focus of this chapter.

Much of assessment to date in the field of social inadequacy can be characterized as lacking clear guidelines for adequate conceptualization. This is due partially to the less than adequate definitions employed and partially to the failure of investigators to follow basic psychometric principles such as developing and using reliable and valid instruments (Paul, 1969). Many research and treatment studies have relied heavily on self-report measures without proven criterion relevance. Findings from such work only lead to contradictions and confusion with regard to a better understanding of the phenomena under study. Hersen and Bellack (1977) summarized things nicely when they stated that most of the easy (treatment-outcome) studies have been done and that it is now time to do the hard (assessment) ones.

This is not to impugn all investigators in the field. On the contrary, several noteworthy attempts have been made to take into account both the multidimensional nature of social inadequacy and the numerous considerations of measurement techniques. Trower, Bryant, and Argyle (1978) and Freedman, Rosenthal, Donahue, Schlundt, and McFall (1978) are among recent investigators to address these matters. The Trower *et al.* survey was discussed earlier in this chapter.

The Freedman *et al.* study comprised two phases. Phase 1 involved empirically developing a measure to assess various problem behaviors with delinquent boys. Phase 2 focused on validation of the measure with different samples and different formats. Each of these groups of investigators attempted to empirically specify a wide range of behaviors related to ratings of adequacy (although each used different populations), and to identify specific subgroups with the use of those measures. What may have been lacking in these and other previous studies is a clear, practical conceptual system to enhance measurement and identification of the multiple and often extremely complex variables underlying social inadequacies. Indeed, Freedman *et al.* stressed the need for basic taxonomic research to better classify individuals with respect to specific behaviors or combinations of behaviors. This, of course, reflects our general concern with arriving at clear definitions of what we are assessing and treating.

Classificatory Models for Assessment

Multidimensional schema are not uncommon in any field of investigation, and such is true in the area of social competence or inadequacy. For example, one 2 × 2 table has already been presented in this chapter to point out an individual's possible combination of skill repertoire and interference characteristics. Cone (1978) has offered a rather complete Behavioral Assessment Grid (BAG) that purportedly covers, in general, the organizational and theoretical needs of behavioral assessment. This grid consists of three dimensions: (1) methods (e.g., interview, self-report, observation), (2) behavioral content (cognitive, physiologic, motor), and (3) universes of generalization (e.g., score, item, setting). While such an attempt at classificatory organization is commendable, we suspect that it may not be practical for use with typical behavioral problems needing to be routinely assessed. We choose to view it as a potentially useful device for classifying a given assessment procedure or instrument, and not primarily suitable for identification or classification of specific client problems. That is, it would not be very helpful for delineating problems in a way that could be readily usable by clinicians to plan an appropriate program of treatment. Cone's assumption that measures can be reliably assigned to the grid categories must be supported for the system to have any practical value. Only empirical results will provide a test of the grid's characteristics. Despite its possible inappropriateness for the types of issues we are addressing, it is nonetheless a step in the right direction for providing a necessary organizational framework for assessment.

With a lack of clear conceptual guidelines as a major shortcoming in the assessment and understanding of social inadequacy, we would now like to offer one possible framework as a potential guide for future work in the area. Though perhaps more modest than Cone's (1978), it is nevertheless, we hope, a more practical proposal for a conceptual framework. It is based on the dimensions that we think are most relevant in dealing with social inadequacy. Although its development has been independent of Cone's model, it does nearly fit into a subsection of the grid development he discussed. Specifically, the present proposal may be seen in some ways as a behavioral grid broken down for the use with the specific response class characteristics of social inadequacy. Keeping in mind the issues previously discussed about the focal point of observation (self vs. other), and the unit of observation (molar vs. molecular), and adding the facet of setting (naturalistic-immediate, naturalistic-retrospective, controlled, and contrived [Wiggins, 1973]), the reader can perhaps anticipate the model we would like to use as a guide. With two levels of each of the first two facets, and four levels of the third, a $2 \times 2 \times 4$ framework is developed (see Figure 2). Before proceeding with a discussion of how we think this model will be useful for purposes of assessing social inadequacies, it is important to clarify each of the levels of the facets.

Earlier, we briefly discussed which behavioral units were more appropriate for measuring social inadequacies. Our feeling on this issue is that the level of analysis (molar vs. molecular) depends primarily on the questions we are asking and the predictions we want to make. Numerous molar measures have been used; usually an overall rating on skill, anxiety, assertiveness, and the like; is made by observers with varying degrees of experience and training. These types of measures are often employed because they are easier to obtain than more discrete, specific ratings or frequency counts. Though there are problems related to their use (e.g., raters having different training or implicit criteria of what constitutes social adequacy, raters "drifting" over time so that the relative level of their ratings changes among subjects, and selection of raters who lack an understanding of the value system of the ratees), molar recordings are useful for a number of

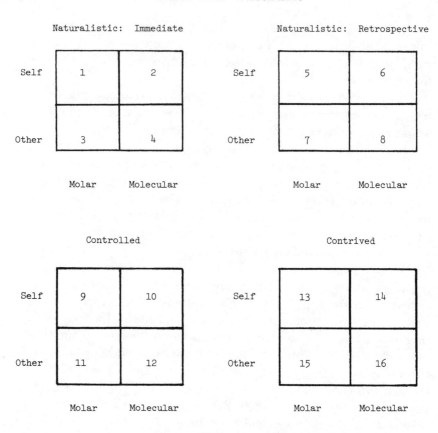

Figure 2
A classificatory guide for assessing social inadequacy.

reasons (Curran, 1979). First, molar ratings are more likely to be obtainable in actual criterion situations than are molecular recordings. Second, the global rating may be more appropriate for an accurate index of a person's general social functioning because of the ease of sampling many situations with global scores as opposed to discrete frequency measures. And third, global evaluations are more like the actual judgments made by those in the ratee's environment than are molecular-level recordings. All three of these advantages of molar ratings must necessarily be empirically investigated.

Molecular-unit measurement involves more precise, well-defined assessments of specific target behaviors. For example, many investigators use response latency, eye contact, smiles, and so forth, as separate indicators of adequate performance. Their primary advantage is a higher degree of precise and reliable observations. However, the criterion relevancy of such distinct behavior has not been consistently demonstrated. In fact, important parameters of the timing and sequencing of behaviors are often ignored in molecular-level recording (Fischetti, Curran, & Wessberg, 1977). Thus, their utility must be empirically examined. If substantial correlations between ratings of these micro-behaviors and outcomes in criterion situations can be shown, then they are potentially an excellent means of assessing for prediction—our primary emphasis. Thus, either the molecular or molar level can be appropriate for assessment of social inadequacy only to the extent that it is shown to relate to relevant criteria.

We realize that the unit of observation usually comprises a continuum with molar and molecular levels as endpoints. For the sake of clarity and to stay within the scope of the chapter, however, we will not discuss some of the intermediate levels of analysis. The model being discussed is thought of as a guideline and an aid, and thus we choose not to try to introduce into it all of the complex determinants involved with social inadequacy assessment. This is in line with suggestions by other investigators to avoid making distinctions so fine that meaningful categorizations are precluded (Weick, 1968). Actual use of the model in any given situation will dictate which factors must be added.

On the dimension of observational source (self vs. other), the levels appear quite clear-cut. Self-observations, reports, and recordings have often been the source of information commonly gathered from interviews, diaries, and behavioral monitoring. Though we would ideally expect a high degree of agreement within the self-report mode, different methods of self-report do not consistently yield convergent results. Evidence from Farrell, Mariotto, Conger, Curran, and Wallander (1979) and Curran, Monti, Corriveau, Hay, Hagerman, Zwick, and Farrell (in press) suggests only a moderate level of dependability from one type of self-rating (prediction of behavior in a specific situation) to other types (self-rating immediately following participation in the situation and self-rating of a videotape of the behavior therein). "Other" sources include information collected by clinicians in traditional interviews, family or peer ratings, confederate ratings, and ratings by observers in the natural environment. These sources also produce varying degrees of agreement on a particular patient's behaviors. This is to be expected because of the different context in which the behaviors are seen, along with the assumption that behav-

ior is situationally specific (Mischel, 1968). The various types of information obtained from the patient or from others are taken into account in the proposed model by means of its multidimensionality.

The last facet of the model, settings, is broken into four levels
based on the immediacy of the behavioral rating and the constraints
under which it occurs. Other investigators have noted the continuum
of situational settings that exists in any measurement attempt. For instance, McReynolds and DeVoge (1978) have discussed different
levels of behavior which might dictate the types of assessment methods employed. These include real-life behavior, pretending behavior,
vicarious behavior, and dreaming. Assessment of each of these would
be accomplished by means of naturalistic observation, improvised
role playing, paper-and-pencil measures, and fantasy material, respectively. As McReynolds and DeVoge (1978) point out, the primary
concern of psychologists is usually with the prediction and understanding of real-life behavior. We agree with that appraisal and again
emphasize that our current focus is on prediction. Thus, the four settings we choose to use are at the real-life end of the continuum, relying on observation and self-reported behavioral assessments in favor
of more traditional "personality trait" measures, or analyses of unconscious factors that could be seen as falling on the fantasy end of the
spectrum. We will now describe the types of settings used in the proposed model.

The naturalistic-immediate level encompasses behavior assessed
in the absence of artificial constraint (*in situ*). Examples of this level
include field studies using naturalistic observation of subjects in their
natural setting, with or without their awareness of an observer's presence. This type of assessment is characterized by preprogrammed
plans for specific observations and by little or no control by the observer over the behavior observed. When behavior has occurred in the
past and is being recalled or summarized, we speak of the second level
of setting, naturalistic-retrospective. This type of observation imposes
no preconceived structure on the original behavioral observation. Behavior is simply recalled or reconstructed as it naturally occurred. A
clinical interview yields observations from the patient in a naturalistic-retrospective manner. Peer ratings, peer nominations, and family
interviews are other examples of this setting level. A controlled setting
is one in which the observer assesses behavior under special conditions
over which he or she has control. By manipulating the stimuli in the
subject's environment, the investigator is able to increase the prob-

ability that a certain response class of behavior will be emitted, and to decrease the range of behaviors possible, thereby allowing for easier categorization of responses into a preplanned coding system. Also, controlled settings can reduce extraneous influences which reduce the dependability of measurement across times and situations. One commonly used method is the role-playing technique, in which subjects are asked to behave "as if" they are in particular situations. Though some of these role-play assessments may be charged with being artificial, there is an increasing body of literature to support their value for controlled observations of behavior which are not easily measured in the natural environment (Greenwald, 1977; McReynolds & DeVoge, 1978; Wessberg, Mariotto, Conger, Farrell, & Conger, 1979). The last level of settings, contrived, includes attempts to retain the laboratory control without including its artificial nature. Contrived situations are those that the subject believes to be natural when really they are under the investigators' control. The television show "Candid Camera" is an excellent example of a contrived situation with naive subjects and hidden observers. In general, methods that rely on observing subjects without their knowledge or consent are not favorably accepted by the general public or investigators in the field. Use of such measures is not a settled issue, with the advantages of observing more criterion-relevant behavior consistently being weighed against the risk of unfavorable public and professional reaction.

Now that the levels of the facets making up the proposed model have been defined, we will briefly outline each of its categories and then focus on several categories that seem most relevant to us for the assessment of social inadequacy. The listing of cells includes: Cells 1 and 2: self-monitoring of social functioning; Cells 3 and 4: naturalistic observation in the social environment; Cells 5 and 6: the patient's self-appraisal of past behavior; Cells 7 and 8: family or peer interviews; Cells 9 and 10: role-play self-ratings; Cells 11 and 12: role-play ratings by a confederate; Cells 13 and 14: rating by patient after being in a contrived situation; and Cells 15 and 16: ratings by a hidden observer. Odd-numbered cells correspond to assessment at the molar level, that is overall ratings of the patients' adequacy. Even-numbered cells comprise categories which would include molecular-level recordings, that is, ratings of specific, discrete behaviors.

Not all of these 16 cells lend themselves equally well to use with existing measurement instruments. For example, no measurements are currently available to enable frequency counts of specific, discrete behaviors that have occurred in the past (Cell 6). Of course, whether or not such measure would even provide information that related to any external criterion of social inadequacy is not clear. However, given the present state of the art of assessment within this area, no cell should be ruled out without evidence that it is not useful.

There are some cells in our model which seem especially relevant for our purposes. These include Cells 1, 3, 5, 7, 9, 10, 11, 12, 13, and 15. Again, we must stress that the actual level of measurement used will ultimately depend on the question being asked. If a particular patient complains of having problems in only one small area of functioning (e.g., being assertive around his or her spouse), a selected few of the measurement devices might be adequate to assess the specific nature of those problems: perhaps self-monitoring of the patient's behavior in assertive situations with his or her spouse (Cell 1), interview information from patient and spouse (Cells 5 and 7), and ratings by a confederate in a role play dealing with assertiveness situations (Cells 11 and 12). Our contention here is that currently no single method is as good as a combination of them. While an extensive clinical interview should ideally pick up the specific nature of a patient's inadequacy (Peterson, 1968), time limits imposed upon professionals working with psychiatric inpatients prevent them from conducting as thorough an assessment as might be desired, and the self-report data must be validated by some other method. In those instances, some of the various alternative methods listed above would be useful. In addition to the time bind on clinicians, a patient's interview data are not always accurate (e.g., poor memory, covering up, failure to understand important components of the problem situation). Hence, other methods of assessment are indicated to give a broader picture of the patient's inadequacies. More than one method is also urged because if there are discrepancies among them, they can help indicate what further investigation is needed. For example, if the patient reports poor performance but a family interview and confederate rating indicate adequate performance, then we might see the patient's problem as more of a cognitive misevaluation than a performance deficit. This would be an appropriate point for a therapist to examine cognitive, emotional, and motivational aspects of the patient's problem. As we mentioned earlier, these covert determinants are not as directly related to the assessment of inadequate performance as are specific skills; nevertheless, a thorough assessment should tap all areas that might be potentially relevant.

Up to this point, we have been primarily discussing the cells of the scheme as they might generally apply to a wide range of client populations. Our work with psychiatric inpatients has revealed advantages and disadvantages with the use of various methods, and we think there are notable advantages in each of the ten cells previously listed. In each of the four settings, molar-level ratings are generally attainable without special training of raters. In all four situational settings, patients usually divulge evaluative information with a fair amount of ease, as do the patients' relatives and friends (Monti, Curran, & Corriveau, in progress). Molecular-level observations are difficult to obtain in naturalistic settings, but relatively easy to obtain in controlled or contrived ones. Our own preference, within the limits of our research resources, is to use short interviews and role plays representatives of situations faced by patients when interacting socially. We rely heavily on global ratings made by trained raters who watch videotapes of patients' responses. The major advantage of this approach is that it allows overall evaluations of overt interactional behaviors in the context of common, everyday situations. The major disadvantage is that it is still unclear how well a patient's role-play behavior matches his or her behavior in real-life settings. Such verification is an ongoing process. Recently, much attention has been directed at the correspondence between behavior in both controlled and contrived situations with behavior in more naturalistic situations (Bellack, Hersen, & Turner, 1978; Bellack, Hersen, & Lamparski, 1979; Greenwald, 1977; Wessberg et al., 1979). Numerous problems have marred these studies (Curran, 1978), but the overall pattern of results has suggested only a fair amount of behavioral similarity between settings. Future use of role plays should move in the direction of specification and development of meaningful (to the patient) role plays and increased interaction potential (longer time, more latitude of confederate behavior). A combination of methods should enable investigators to delineate the different etiologic factors pertinent to any given patient's problems. For example, combining judges' ratings of the patient's behavior in role plays with self-report interview information might provide a means of discriminating poor learning from anxiety-induced inhibition. Neither method alone would provide this important information. Similarly, demand manipulations in the role plays (e.g., "Give the best response" vs. "Give your normal response") (Nietzel & Bernstein, 1976) might make the distinction between skills deficits and inhibited performance, but a single role-play format would not allow the distinction to be made. Other differentiating questions can be answered with further combinations of the appropriate cells.

We now return to the issue of incremental validity mentioned earlier in this section. The question is: To what extent does any method improve upon existing ones? In the area of social inadequacy, many methods of assessment are sorely lacking in reliability and validity. Therefore, almost any psychometrically sound instrument would provide some degree of improvement. Freedman *et al.*'s (1978) use of a discriminant analysis to classify adolescents on the basis of their responses on an empirically developed role-playing measure is exemplary. Given the multiple determining and maintaining factors of social inadequacy, we urge a careful analysis of specific assessment questions which may be relevant to individual investigators. We work primarily with inadequate psychiatric inpatients, whose problems generally stem from gross instances of inappropriate social behavior. Hence, our focus is on overall ratings of patients in the context of common social interactions. Naturally, the accuracy of these ratings must be independently verified for confidence to be placed in them. In practice, the independent validation may actually be some convergent means of confirming various sources of information, necessitated by the absence of firm criteria for what constitutes social inadequacy. The following case history illustrates some of the issues we have been discussing.

Case History

Mr. C. was a 26-year-old single male who sought treatment for what he described as his inability to meet and date females. In the initial interview he reported a history of minimal social contact with females and feelings of anxiety when interacting one-to-one with them, although he claimed to be comfortable in social situations in general (i.e., at parties and bars). His last date had been at the age 23, with a girl introduced to him by his mother. He was unable to recall specific details of the date, but remembered feeling awkward and uptight. Mr. C. was unable to clearly state what he thought treatment should include. He simply stated his desire to be more relaxed around females and to start dating instead of "sitting at home most of the time." Apparently the precipitant for his coming for treatment was the firm insistence of his mother, with whom he lived.

Because of the role of Mr. C.'s mother in urging him to seek treatment, she was briefly consulted about his problem. She confirmed the information he had given, and suggested that her son just didn't seem to know what to say or do after the introductory stage with females. She said he always seemed to stare at the ground when he talked to females, but not when he talked to his male friends. We had seen Mr. C. when he was greeted by our clinic secretary, and also had the impression that his eye contact was poor. Thus, his mother's general assessment corresponded with our clinical impression.

On Mr. C.'s next visit, he was asked to engage in two role plays to allow examination of his behavior in simulated social interactions. First he was seated in a room with a male confederate and instructed to start a conversation with him, and to keep it going for four minutes. In the second role play, he was seated next to a female and told to imagine that they were together in a restaurant waiting for their meal to be served. The second role play also lasted four minutes. The confederates were trained to be pleasant, but to be uninitiating and only moderately responsive. In each situation, Mr. C. rated himself on overall skillfulness and anxiety. The confederates and two raters viewing the interactions through a one-way mirror also rated him on the global scales, in addition to making judgments about discrete behaviors such as smiles, eye contact, and response latency.

Mr. C. rated himself as highly anxious only with the female, and low on skill in both situations. The confederates and observers rated him as highly anxious and low on skill with the female, but gave him average ratings on his skill and anxiety with the male. Hence, some skill misappraisal by Mr. C. was inferred. The pattern of discrete behavioral cues also differed in the two role plays. He smiled more, had better eye contact, and maintained a more continuous conversation with the male.

It was unclear whether the high anxiety was a result of being in social situations or of being viewed through a one-way mirror in a role play. Therefore, two contrived situations were developed in which Mr. C. participated; one was with a male and one with a female. Both involved accompanying a member of the staff on an errand during which time the staff member persuaded Mr. C. to stop in the cafeteria for coffee. During each "coffee break," a third staff member sitting nearby observed the interaction. At the time, Mr. C. was unaware that the stops had been preplanned and that he was being observed.

Ratings by staff members immediately following the interactions suggested high anxiety and low skill during the coffee break with the female, and low anxiety and average skill with the male. After being informed of the "setup," Mr. C. rated himself in the two interactions similarly to his self-ratings in the role plays. The results in the contrived situations supported those from the interviews and the role plays, suggesting that Mr. C. lacked skills to get beyond the initial stages of a conversation with females. His conversational skills with males seemed adequate.

When presented with this information, Mr. C. was pleasantly surprised that he was evaluated as adequate in his interactions with males. Until then, he had suspected he was probably inadequate in that domain also. Fortunately, we were able to assure him that many of the same skills were useful for interactions with both males and females, with only some moderate variations on topics discussed in each. The treatment in Mr. C.'s case consisted of a skills-training group format in which he refined the skills he needed with both sexes and was taught new skills appropriate more for male–female situations. Throughout the skills training he was given feedback by group members to aid him in more accurately appraising his performance. His anxiety in the role plays slowly diminished, until he eventually reported feeling comfortable enough to talk to a female he had seen several times on the bus. Several of the discrete behaviors such as eye contact with females improved as his anxiety decreased.

Mr. C. discontinued treatment at the completion of the skills training group. Subsequent incidental contact and second-hand reports revealed satisfactory progress, with an average of about two dates per month and a generally more active social life.

Treatment of Social Inadequacy

Although the major focus of this chapter has been on the assessment of social inadequacy, we would be remiss if we did not say a few words about treatment. The most obvious statement we can make regarding the treatment of social inadequacy is that it should be tied as closely as possible to the nature of the factors responsible for the inadequate social performance. If the faulty social performance appears primarily due to an emotional state such as anxiety and not to a deficit of social skills, then the method of treatment should comprise anxiety-reduction procedures. If the inadequate social performance appears to be due to cognitive factors such as illogical assumptions and negative self-statements, then the method of treatment should be some type of cognitive restructuring technique. If the deficit appears to be due to poor ability to perceive social cues or lack of ability to generate alternative responses, then the treatment should focus on the appropriate reading of social cues and response generation. If there appears to be an actual response deficit, then the focus of treatment should be on response acquisition. A thorough criterion analysis would need to be undertaken in order to specify, both at the molar and molecular levels, the behaviors required in the criterion situation. We should keep in mind that correcting an individual's obvious social-skills deficits may not be enough to provide the patient with the minimal skills needed in a given situation. That is, getting a patient who fails to make eye contact to make eye contact in a criterion situation may not be sufficient enough to have his or her performance judged as adequate. In some cases, because the particular social unit with which the person is interacting is also dysfunctional, it may be necessary to treat the entire social unit.

Summary

In this chapter we addressed the adult disorder generally termed social inadequacy. We pointed out its central importance in a wide variety of behavioral problems, and mentioned some previous treatment approaches over the last decade. We discussed the major theoretical and definitional issues associated with social inadequacy, stressing its complexity. Next, we focused on predominant etiologic and maintaining factors, and then moved on to present evidence of the widespread incidence and multifaceted nature of social-skills deficits in clinical populations. Some of the fundamental issues in assessing social inadequacy were described, along with a proposed classificatory model to be used as a practical guide for conceptualizing, assessing, and treating this disorder. Finally, we mentioned the preferred methods of treatment for various forms of social inadequacy.

Social inadequacy is a contributing factor in major forms of psychopathology, in addition to being associated with dysfunctional behaviors such as sexual problems, alcohol abuse, drug addiction, heterosexual social anxiety, and marital dysfunction. To help alleviate these difficulties, a social-skills training approach has been adopted by many therapists. Though differing theoretical assumptions and treatment strategies are involved, there is a fundamental need to develop reliable and valid assessment methods to measure social inadequacy.

Social inadequacy, social competence, social skills, and the like are mega-constructs. This affords organizational simplicity in one sense, but poses problems in another sense. We can see a variety of different behaviors as falling into general response classes subsumed under the social inadequacy mega-construct. Nevertheless, these must not be mistakenly seen as representative of invariant dispositional units. Personal, situational, cultural, and interactional variables influence the likelihood of responses as well as the evaluation of behaviors or patterns of behaviors as adequate or inadequate. Thus, the manner in which social inadequacy is assessed depends heavily on the types of questions a therapist or researcher wants to answer. Inadequate social performance, adequate minimal social performance, and adequate optimal social performance may differ; this mandates adaptability in the type and level of behaviors examined.

Social skills are response capabilities inferred from performance. They can be lacking in the socially inadequate patient for numerous reasons, including poor learning, deterioration, and anxiety-induced inhibition. In general, assessment is focused on delineating which factors or combinations of factors are involved with a given patient. Primary social failure is the result of faulty socialization or lack of social experience (poor learning, deterioration). Secondary social failure stems from biological, cognitive, or dynamic disturbances (inhibition). Adverse cognitive and emotional states can be the cause of, or the result of, a lack of social skills; the distinction is difficult to make without a thorough functional analysis.

The evidence to date provides a picture of social inadequacy as characterized by a diverse array of problem behaviors in heterogeneous patient groups. Socially inadequate patients seem to fall into numerous traditional diagnostic categories, but not in any apparent systematic fashion. Also, socially inadequate and socially adequate patients are equally represented in those categories. Patients who are described as inadequate display a wide variety of behaviors, ranging from cold, unassertive, and socially anxious to angry and overly assertive. To some extent, the clinician making an assessment decides which behaviors are appropriately classified as socially adequate or inadequate.

In light of the numerous etiologic and maintaining factors underlying it, and because of the myriad questions clinicians and researchers want to answer, assessment of social inadequacy is exceeding complex. Assessment methods must not only attempt to clearly define the specific nature of patient problems for understanding and treatment, but must also be cost-effective in terms of discriminative efficiency and incremental validity. Again, the issues of reliability and validity become important when determining the usefulness of assessment methods. To help organize the variables involved with assessing social inadequacy, a classificatory scheme is presented as a practical guideline. The major facets in the scheme comprise focus of observation (molecular and molar), source of observation (self and other), and setting (naturalistic-immediate, naturalistic-retrospective, controlled, and contrived). Specific assessment methods within the framework depend on the cells of interest and the nature of a given patient's problems. A case history is presented to illustrate the advantages and disadvantages of the various cells. Overall ratings of adequacy are generally the easiest to obtain, in addition to being ostensibly the most criterion-relevant measure of social inadequacy. Though interviews and role-play measures provide some information about patients' inadequacies, development of more naturalistic-immediate means of assessment is urged. This approach would, it is hoped, result in firmer, independently verified criteria of social inadequacy.

Treatment of social inadequacy must obviously be closely tied to specific etiologic and maintaining factors. In this regard, identification of those patient behaviors lacking in a given situation is essential. With the potential complexity of personal, situational, cultural, and interactional variables involved, the classificatory scheme discussed in this chapter may serve as a useful guide for performing the necessary assessment of social inadequacy needed to offer adequate treatment.

References

Argyle, M., & Kendon, A. The experimental analysis of social performance. In L. Berkowitz (Ed.), *Advances in experimental social psychology* (Vol. 3). New York: Academic Press, 1967.

Barlow, D. H. Increasing heterosexual responsiveness in the treatment of sexual deviation: A review of the clinical and experimental evidence. *Behavior Therapy*, 1973, *4*, 655-671.

Bellack, A. S., Hersen, M., & Lamparski, D. Role-play tests for assessing social skills: Are they valid? Are they useful? *Journal of Consulting and Clinical Psychology*, 1979, *47*, 355-342.

Bellack, A. S., Hersen, M., & Turner, S. M. Role-play tests for assessing social skills:
    Are they valid? *Behavior Therapy*, 1978, *9*, 448-461.
Bryant, B., Trower, P., Yardley, K., Urbieta, K., & Letemendia, F. J. A survey of
    social inadequacy among psychiatric outpatients. *Psychological Medicine*, 1976,
    6, 101-112.
Callner, D. A., & Ross, S. M. The reliability and validity of three measures of as-
    sertion in a drug addict population. *Behavior Therapy*, 1976, *7*, 659-667.
Cone, J. D. The Behavioral Assessment Grid (BAG): A conceptual framework and a
    taxonomy. *Behavior Therapy*, 1978, *5*, 882-888.
Cronbach, L. J., & Gleser, G. C. *Psychological tests and personnel decisions.*
    Urbana, IL: University of Illinois Press, 1965.
Cronbach, L. J., & Meehl, P. E. Construct validity in psychological tests. *Psycho-
    logical Bulletin*, 1955, *52*, 281-302.
Curran, J. P. Skills training as an approach to the treatment of heterosexual social
    anxiety: A review. *Psychological Bulletin*, 1977, *84*, 140-157.
Curran, J. P. Comment on Bellack, Hersen, and Turner's paper on the validity of
    role-play tests. *Behavior Therapy*, 1978, *9*, 462-468.
Curran, J. P. Social skills: Methodological issues and future directions. In A. S. Bel-
    lack & M. Hersen (Eds.), *Research and practice in social skills training.* New
    York: Plenum Publishing Corp., 1979.
Curran, J. P., & Mariotto, M. J. A conceptual structure for the assessment of social
    skills. In M. Hersen, R. Eisler, & P. Miller (Eds.), *Progress in behavior modifi-
    cation.* New York: Academic Press, in press.
Curran, J. P., Miller, I., Zwick, W., Monti, P. M., & Stout, R. L. The socially in-
    adequate patient: Incidence rate, demographic and clinical features, hospital
    and post-hospital functioning. *Journal of Consulting and Clinical Psychology*,
    1980, *48*, 375-382.
Curran, J. P., Monti, P. M., Corriveau, D. P., Hay, L. R., Hagerman, S., Zwick, W.
    R., & Farrell, A. D. The generalizability of procedures for assessing social skills
    and social anxiety in a psychiatric population. *Behavioral Assessment*, in press.
Eisler, R. M., Miller, P. M., Hersen, M., & Alford, H. Effects of assertive training
    on marital interaction. *Archives of General Psychiatry*, 1974, *30*, 643-649.
Farrell, A. D., Mariotto, M. J., Conger, A. J., Curran, J. P., & Wallander, J. L.
    Self- and judges' ratings of heterosexual-social anxiety and skill: A generalizabil-
    ity study. *Journal of Consulting and Clinical Psychology*, 1979, *47*, 164-175.
Fischetti, M., Curran, J. P., & Wessberg, H. W. Sense of timing: A skill deficit in
    heterosexual-socially anxious males. *Behavior Modification*, 1977, *1*, 179-194.
Freedman, B. J., Rosenthal, L., Donahue, C. P., Schlundt, D. G., & McFall, R. M.
    A social-behavioral analysis of skill deficits in delinquent and nondelinquent
    adolescent boys. *Journal of Consulting and Clinical Psychology*, 1978, *46*, 1148-
    1163.
Gladwin, T. Social competence and clinical practice. *Psychiatry*, 1967, *30*, 30-44.
Goldsmith, J. B., & McFall, R. M. Development and evaluation of an interpersonal
    skill-training program for psychiatric patients. *Journal of Abnormal Psychology*,
    1975, *84*, 51-58.
Gottman, J. M. Toward a definition of social isolation in children. *Child Develop-
    ment*, 1977, *48*, 513-517.
Gottman, J., Gonso, J., & Rasmussen, B. Social interaction, social competence,
    and friendship in children. *Child Development*, 1975, *46*, 709-718.
Greenwald, D. P. The behavioral assessment of differences in social skill and social
    anxiety in female college students. *Behavior Therapy*, 1977, *8*, 925-937.
Hersen, M., & Bellack, A. S. Social skills training for chronic psychiatric patients:

Rationale, research findings, and future directions. *Comprehensive Psychiatry*, 1976, *17*, 559-580.

Hersen, M., & Bellack, A. S. Assessment of social skills. In A. R. Ciminero, K. S. Calhoun, & H. E. Adams (Eds.), *Handbook of behavioral assessment*. New York: John Wiley & Sons, 1977.

Homans, G. C. *Social behavior: Its elementary forms*. New York: Harcourt, Brace, & World, 1961.

Kiesler, D. J. Experimental design in psychotherapy research. In A. E. Bergin & S. L. Garfield (Eds.), *Handbook of psychotherapy and behavior change*. New York: John Wiley & Sons, 1971.

Kraft, T. Social anxiety model of alcoholism. *Perceptual and Motor Skills*, 1971, *33*, 797-798.

Lentz, R. J., Paul, G. L., & Calhoun, J. F. Reliability and validity of three measures of functioning with "hard-core" chronic mental patients. *Journal of Abnormal Psychology*, 1971, *77*, 313-323.

Liberman, R. P., Vaughn, C., Aitchison, R. A., & Fallon, I. *Social skills training for relapsing schizophrenics*. Funded grant from the National Institute of Mental Health, 1977.

Libet, J. M., & Lewinsohn, P. M. Concept of social skills with specific reference to the behavior of depressed persons. *Journal of Consulting and Clinical Psychology*, 1973, *40*, 304-312.

McReynolds, P., & DeVoge, S. Use of improvisational techniques in assessment. In P. McReynolds (Ed.), *Advances in psychological assessment* (Vol. 4). San Francisco: Jossey-Bass, 1978.

Miller, P. M., Hersen, M., Eisler, P. M., & Hilsman, G. Effects of social stress on operant drinking of alcoholics and social drinkers. *Behaviour Research and Therapy*, 1974, *12*, 67-72.

Mischel, W. *Personality and assessment*. New York: John Wiley & Sons, 1968.

Monti, P. M., Curran, J. P., & Corriveau, D. P. Comparability of procedures used to assess social anxiety and social skill with psychiatric outpatients. Study in progress, Providence Veterans Administration Medical Center.

Nietzel, M. T., & Bernstein, D. A. Effects of instructionally mediated demand on the behavioral assessment of assertiveness. *Journal of Consulting and Clinical Psychology*, 1976, *44*, 500.

Paul, G. L. Behavior modification research: Design and tactics. In C. M. Franks (Ed.), *Behavior therapy: Appraisal and status*. New York: McGraw-Hill, 1969.

Paul, G. L., & Bernstein, D. A. *Anxiety and clinical problems: Systematic desensitization and related techniques*. Morristown, NJ: General Learning Co., 1973.

Peterson, D. R. *The clinical study of social behavior*. New York: Appleton-Century-Crofts, 1968.

Phillips, E. L. *The social skills basis of psychopathology: Alternatives to abnormal psychology and psychiatry*. New York: Grune & Stratton, 1978.

Prelinger, E., & Zimet, C. N. *An ego-psychological approach to character assessment*. New York: The Free Press, 1964.

Rose, Y. J., & Tryon, W. W. Judgments of assertive behavior as a function of speech loudness, latency, content, gestures, inflection, and sex. *Behavior Modification*, 1979, *3*, 112-123.

Sullivan, H. S. *The psychiatric interview*. New York: W. W. Norton, 1954.

Sylph, J. A., Ross, H. E., & Kedward, H. B. Social diability in chronic psychiatric patients. *American Journal of Psychiatry*, 1978, *134*, 1391-1394.

Trower, P., Bryant, B., & Argyle, M. *Social skills and mental health*. Pittsburgh: University of Pittsburgh Press, 1978.

Trower, P., Yardley, K., Bryant, B. M., & Shaw, P. The treatment of social failure: A comparison of anxiety-reduction and skills-acquisition procedures on two social problems. *Behavior Modification,* 1978, *2,* 41–60.

Weick, K. E. Systematic observational methods. In G. Lindzey & E. Aronson (Eds.), *The handbook of social psychology* (Vol. 2). Reading, MA: Addison-Wesley, 1968.

Wessberg, H. W., Mariotto, M. J., Conger, A. J., Farrell, A. D., & Conger, J. C. The ecological validity of role plays for assessing heterosocial anxiety and skill of male college students. *Journal of Consulting and Clinical Psychology,* 1979, *47,* 525–535.

Wiggins, J. S. *Personality and prediction: Principles of personality assessment.* Reading, MA: Addison-Wesley, 1973.

Zigler, E., & Phillips, L. Social competence and the process reactive distinction in psychopathology. *Journal of Abnormal and Social Psychology,* 1961, *65,* 215–222.

13

Assessment of
Marital Dysfunction

NEIL S. JACOBSON
RICHARD W. ELWOOD
MERCEDES DALLAS

The behavioral assessment of marital dysfunction exemplifies many of the dilemmas of current-day behavior assessment. For example, investigators have had to grapple with the question of what behaviors should be measured. "Marital distress" does not immediately translate into a set of behaviors, and the fundamental assessment question has become: "What are the behavioral determinants of marital distress?" But in order to answer this question, a theoretical model of marital distress is required. Thus, the behavioral assessment of marital distress has become inextricably linked to a behavioral model of marital distress (Jacobson, 1979a). It has also become necessary to create laboratory analogues, quasi-observational checklists, and self-report questionnaires, rather than relying exclusively on the direct observation of behavior in the natural environment. These analogue measures have required a number of assumptions and semiarbitrary decisions regarding construction. The state of the art is such that efforts to evaluate these assumptions are just beginning.

In this chapter, our goal is to examine the critical issues in the

Neil S. Jacobson. Department of Psychology, University of Washington, Seattle, Washington.
Richard W. Elwood and Mercedes Dallas. Department of Psychology, The University of Iowa, Iowa City, Iowa.

behavioral assessment of marital problems. Assessment techniques have been developed for a number of different purposes: to test hypotheses derived from behavioral models of marital distress, to assess the efficacy of behavioral marital therapy, and to aid the clinician in conducting a behavioral analysis of the distressed relationship in order to formulate an intervention strategy. We attempt to address issues which are relevant to all three of these assessment tasks. In the first section, the relationship between behavior-exchange theory and behavioral assessment is elucidated. The purpose of this section is to outline the types of information that a clinician needs in order to complete a behavioral analysis of a distressed marriage, and to illustrate how the goals and tactics of such an analysis follow from a behavioristic conception of marital distress. The next three sections each examine one source of assessment information: behavioral observations collected by trained raters; spouse observations; and spouses' subjective reports. In each instance we begin by describing a widely adopted assessment instrument representing the modality under discussion. The instrument is discussed within the context of more general considerations in the evaluation of any instrument within that modality. Thus there is an attempt to evolve from the specific to the general. Since many of the important contributions to the behavioral assessment of marital dysfunction come from the collaboration between the Oregon Research Institute and what is now called the Oregon Marital Studies Program (Patterson, 1976; Weiss, Hops, & Patterson, 1973; Weiss & Margolin, 1977), much of the discussion is focused on their instruments. A fifth and final section concerns itself with a conceptualization of marital satisfaction–distress which takes into account all of the various sources of assessment information.

Behavioral-Exchange Theory and Behavioral Assessment

The earliest articulation of a behavioral framework for understanding marital distress was in a paper by Richard Stuart published in 1969. According to Stuart, marital distress results from a low rate of positive reinforcement mutually exchanged between partners. This functional definition of marital conflict placed the analysis of marital distress securely within an operant framework, although it said nothing about the development of marital distress over time, nor did it speculate about the content or topography of marital reinforcers and punishers. From this conception it followed that the task of a behavioral assessment was essentially an idiographic one, that is, to identify the rewarding and punishing behaviors in a particular relationship. More specifically, assessment seemed to necessitate (1) pinpointing these potentially reinforcing behaviors that are occurring (if at all) with insufficient frequency, (2) pinpointing those punishing behaviors that are detracting from each partner's overall satisfaction, and (3) determining the factors which seem to be responsible for both the deficits in rewarding behavior and the excess in punishing behavior.

A number of instruments have been developed to facilitate the task of pinpointing rewarding and punishing behaviors. Some of these are self-report questionnaires. Spouses have also been asked to collect pretreatment data in the home in order to provide information regarding the day-to-day exchanges of rewarding and punishing behaviors. The most useful available checklist for this purpose is the *Spouse Observation Checklist* (cf. Weiss & Margolin, 1977). Since this checklist instructs couples to record a global daily satisfaction rating (on a 1-7 scale) in addition to daily frequencies of "pleasing" and "displeasing" behaviors, it is possible to derive from this checklist an empirically based list of rewarding and punishing relationship behaviors. This is accomplished by correlating the frequency of various response classes with daily satisfaction ratings over a period of days, and discovering which behaviors are directly and inversely related to overall satisfaction.

Patterson and Hops (1972) hypothesized that marital conflict was the result of dysfunctional behavior-change skills on the part of spouses. In particular, it was alleged that distressed spouses relied on aversive control strategies in their efforts to induce desirable behavior in one another. Over time, spouses shaped one another into a gradually increasing tendency to rely on punishment and negative reinforcement in their behavior-change efforts.

This addition to Stuart's formulation lead to a focus on the direct interaction of the couple, especially when engaged in attempts to resolve conflict in their relationship. Attempts to quantify and measure couples' problem-solving interactions lead to the development of a behavioral coding system called the *Marital Interaction Coding System* (MICS) (Hops, Wills, Patterson, & Weiss, 1971), which has been the most influential attempt thus far to measure marital behavior within a social-learning framework.

Attention has been devoted elsewhere to a critical analysis of these theoretical principles (Jacobson, 1979a). The relevance of these assessment devices is dependent upon the validity of the theoretical model. Any examination of the assessment strategies that occurs outside this theoretical context begs the question. At present these behavioral hypotheses have not been adequately tested. For example, although considerable research supports the existence of a relationship between marital satisfaction and various indices of rewards and punishments (Birchler, Weiss, & Vincent, 1975; Gottman, Markman, & Notarius, 1977; Gottman, Notarius, Markman, Bank, Yoppi, & Rubin, 1976; Vincent, Weiss, & Birchler, 1975; Wills, Weiss, & Patterson, 1974), the direction of the relationship remains unclear. Only one study has followed couples longitudinally to demonstrate that rates of reported rewards and punishments were predictive of subsequent satisfaction (Markman, 1979). Similarly, there is no direct evidence that behavior-change skill deficits place couples at risk of developing marital distress.

Finally, although a number of studies have shown that a portion of the variability in day-to-day satisfaction within a relationship can be accounted for by the frequency of rewarding, and especially punishing, behavior that was reported on that day, these studies are open to a number of interpretations, not all of which support the behavioral hypotheses (Jacobson, Waldron, & Moore, in press; Wills *et al.*, 1974).

In recent years, the behavioral model of relationship distress has expanded (Jacobson, 1979a; Jacobson & Margolin, 1979; Weiss, 1978). This expansion has highlighted new areas to focus on during assessment. In some cases, currently available assessment instruments can be applied to these new domains of inquiry. In other cases, assessment has to be conducted less formally. In many instances, the relevant instruments simply do not exist, and the clinical interview has remained the primary source of assessment information.

RELATIONSHIP SKILLS

The behavioral model views maintaining a marital relationship over a long period of time as requiring a series of skills (Jacobson & Margolin, 1979; Weiss, 1978). A skill deficiency in one or more critical areas can be sufficient to produce significant conflict. A thorough behavioral assessment will survey these various areas to determine which, if any, constitute a deficiency for the couple. The most pertinent areas include problem solving, supportive communication skills, sexual capabilities, parenting skills, financial-management skills, domestic and related maintenance skills, and interpersonal skills as directed toward areas outside of the relationship. In those instances where the skill area involves direct social interaction, the assessor can rely on observational procedures to acquire the information. In most other instances, the interview will be the primary source of information.

SOCIAL ENVIRONMENT EXTERNAL TO THE MARRIAGE

Recent revisions of the behavioral model have considered the role of each spouse's alternatives to the present relationship in determining whether or not he or she remains in it (Jacobson & Margolin, 1979; cf. Thibaut & Kelley, 1959). A very attractive alternative to the present relationship may produce or exacerbate marital conflict. Therefore, it is important that the assessment produce information regarding the attractiveness of each partner's nonrelationship environment.

RELATIONSHIP RULES

Recent behavioral formulations have emphasized the importance of a consensually agreed-upon structure of rules for the smooth functioning of a relationship (Jacobson & Margolin, 1979; Weiss, 1978). Rules refer to lines of decision-making authority, agreements regarding appropriate and inappropriate behavior, and the like. During the pretreatment assessment phase, there is an attempt to elicit an explicit, comprehensive set of rules. At present, the interview is the primary tool for uncovering this information, although a section of the *Marital Precounseling Inventory* (Stuart & Stuart, 1972) asks couples to survey the various areas in which decisions need to be made in their relationship, and note who makes the decisions, and whether the current situation is desirable or undesirable.

RELATIONSHIP STRENGTHS

Many of the self-report instruments developed by behavioral marital researchers are aimed at ascertaining the reinforcement potential currently available in a relationship. This reflects a basic tenet of behavioral marital therapy, namely, that the emphasis in therapy should be on enhancing couples' already existent strengths. Couples are asked to identify those desirable behaviors that are already occurring as well as common interests and recreational activities that they both enjoy.

Thus, a comprehensive behavioral assessment attempts to cover a wide range of potentially relevant areas, both within and outside the context of the couples' direct exchanges. Theoretical predilections lead to an attempt to thoroughly define the environmental domain in which the couples' exchanges occur. The focus on environmental determinants of each spouse's satisfaction with the relationship leads to hypotheses regarding where the controlling influences are located. The events which serve to maintain undesirable relationship behavior could include reinforcers and punishers provided by the spouses themselves, the environmental context outside of the relationship, or cognitions each spouse holds regarding the relationship.

The still uncertain status of behavioral-exchange theory makes the task of evaluating assessment techniques derived from that theory more difficult. In the critical review of behavioral-assessment techniques which follows, we will try to consider a number of different angles. Both the psychometric properties of various instruments and their clinical utility will be considered. While the latter is more difficult to determine objectively than the more concrete psychometric questions involving reliability and validity, the extent to which these techniques can be used by practicing clinicians are an important justification for their existence. In the next section which examines observational coding systems, the MICS will be discussed in detail, since it represents the most widely used system for coding marital interaction.

Behavioral Observations of Marital Interaction: Marital Interaction Coding System (MICS)

The MICS was originally adapted from the coding system used by Patterson and his associates to code family interaction in the natural environment (Jones, Reid, & Patterson, 1975). The original MICS consisted of 29 categories of verbal and nonverbal behavior (see Table 1). The 29 codes were combined a priori into six summary categories:

Table 1
Marital Interaction Coding System (MICS)[a]

Verbal code name	Nonverbal code name
AG Agree	AS Assent
AP Approval	AT Attention
AR Accept responsibility	CO Compliance
CM Command	LA Laugh
CP Complaint	NC Noncompliance
CR Criticize	NO Normative
CS Compromise	NR No response
DG Disagree	NT Not tracking
DR Deny responsibility	PP Positive physical contact
EX Excuse	SM Smile
HM Humor	TO Turn off
IN Interrupt	
NS Negative solution	
PD Problem description	
PS Problem solving	
PU Put down	
QU Question	
SP Solution (past)	
TA Talk	

Combined codes for levels

Verbal codes	Nonverbal codes
I. Problem solving (AR, CS, PS)	V. Positive (AS, LA, PP, SM)
II. Problem description (NS, PD, SP)	VI. Negative (NR, NT, TO)
III. Negative (CP, CR, DR, EX, PU)	
IV. Positive (AG, AP, HM)	

[a]Reprinted by permission from Weiss *et al.* (1973).

problem-solving behaviors, problem description behaviors, negative verbal behaviors, positive verbal behaviors, negative nonverbal behaviors, and positive nonverbal behaviors. The MICS has been used both as a pre–post outcome measure (Patterson, Weiss, & Hops, 1976; Jacobson, 1977a, 1978a; Harrell & Guerney, 1976; Margolin & Weiss, 1978) to assess change that occurs in marital therapy and as a clinical tool for developing a profile of couples' problem-solving strengths and weaknesses.

The MICS can be applied to a wide variety of interactional situations, but most often it has been used to code the behavior emitted by couples in a standardized, laboratory problem-solving situation. For example, one couple identified "initiation of sex" as a problem in their relationship. The therapist presented them with the following instructions: "I would like you to take 5 to 10 minutes and try to reach agreement on what you can do to solve this problem." The therapist then left the room, and the spouses' discussion was taped. The MICS was applied to the 10-minute interaction. As an example to how the MICS is used, let us examine a brief segment of interaction by the couple discussing "initiation of sex." The appropriate abbreviated code is designated at the end of each behavioral unit.

> WIFE: I brought up this problem because I feel like I don't have the right to initiate sex. (PD)
> HUSBAND: That's not true. (DG) You're always worried that I'm not going to be attracted to you and so you don't initiate. (CR) But don't put it on me. If you. . . . (NS) (Wife: AT)
> WIFE: (*Interrupting*) I admit that I don't take risks in our sexual relationship. (IN/AR) But how do I know whether or not you are going to be receptive? (QU/PD)

Each segment of verbal and nonverbal behavior is coded; certain behavioral units are given two codes (QU/PD; IN/AR). In evaluating the MICS, we will consider three issues: reliability, validity, and clinical utility. The considerations discussed below apply not only to the MICS but also to any multicategory observational coding system attempting to code sequences of dyadic interaction. Thus the MICS is being used to exemplify the critical concerns in evaluating the utility of any attempt to assess the interactional behavior of couples.

RELIABILITY

Although few would argue with the need to determine whether or not the data that emerge from observational coding systems are reliable, there is a startling lack of consensus regarding both the definition of reliability and the statistical techniques used to measure it. The questions relating to the determination of an instrument's "accuracy" and "stability," commonly accepted as the referents of reliability, become exceedingly complex when the instrument is a multidimensional coding system such as the MICS. First, the MICS consists of 30 categories. Second, these categories are not mutually exclusive. Third, and most problematic, the categories do not all share the same class-defining characteristics. (1) Some categories are defined by content (PD), some by grammatical properties irrespective of content (QU), some by an emotional state (CP), some by an emotional state which the speaker *intends* to induce in the partner (PU), and some are defined by the exclusion of other categories (NO). (2) Definitions also vary on a nomothetic–polythetic continuum. (3) Certain class-defining characteristics are directly observable, while others are highly inferential (CP, PU). (4) Some codes refer to verbal behaviors, while others refer to nonverbal behaviors.

These complexities complicate the task of determining the reliability of the MICS. For one thing, MICS categories vary greatly in the extent to which they can be coded accurately. An overall agreement index of .80, taken across all 30 categories, might obscure the fact that some categories can be coded to unanimity whereas others may be coded with virtually no agreement. Thus, a minimum criterion for assessing MICS reliability is the calculation of an agreement index for each category, a practice which has not been adopted in behavioral research on marital interaction.

Another unfortunate consequence of the complexity of the MICS is the impossibility of computing the likelihood of two coders agreeing by chance. In any observational coding system, an acceptable agreement index must substantially exceed that which would be expected by chance alone (Hartmann, 1977; Hollenbeck, 1978). Normally, the probability of chance agreement (p_c) is a relatively straightforward computation. If each behavior unit of couple interaction was given a single code, and all code protocols were mutually exclusive, chance agreement base rates would be a joint function of the frequencies of the various codes, and total number of codes available.

But because the MICS is comprised of a number of taxonomies, p_c becomes impossible to compute. Behavior units can be given more than a single code and many codes are not mutually exclusive of other codes. Moreover, once the reader selects a first code, the domain of logically possible conjoint codes is not only restricted, but restricted differentially across codes. That is to say, codes differ in the extent to which they are exclusive of or contrary to other codes. Thus the term "number of available codes" in the earlier equation is constantly changing. Also, given that a first coder applies a conjoint coding and the second coder elects to do likewise, a disagreement by the coder on the first code results in a different domain of possible second codes.

Thus in determining the reliability of the MICS, agreement indices which depend on a calculation of p_c such as kappa (Hartmann, 1977), cannot be used.

To summarize, once it is recognized that the MICS is a system of behavior taxonomies, several problems emerge which bear directly on its reliability: (1) the wide variations in the nature of these taxonomies preclude the derivation of meaningful chance agreement base rates, (2) the same variations almost assuredly produce rates of agreement which differ across categories and (3) these variations in categories, and their effect on both chance and achieved rates of agreement, confound the establishment of an adequate criterion for reliability. Indeed, adequate levels quite likely vary by codes. Thus a MICS reliability based on overall agreement is clearly inadequate. A minimum requirement for assessing MICS reliability between calibrations is agreement for each category.

An additional barrier to assessing the reliability of the MICS is the insufficient specification of procedural details in published studies using the MICS. For example, strategies for preventing and controlling observer drift (Johnson & Bolstad, 1973) are seldom specified. Distinctions are seldom made between initial training of coders and calibration once data collection has begun; it is often unclear when reliability data were gathered. Finally, we are seldom told how or whether raters are kept blind as to when reliability is being assessed. We know that reliability figures can be spuriously inflated by observer drift as well as by knowledge on the part of the coders of when accuracy is being assessed (Johnson & Bolstad, 1973; Reid, 1970; Romanczyk, Kent, Diament, & O'Leary, 1973). Unless proper safeguards are implemented, the reliability assessments cannot be considered valid.

In order to evaluate the adequacy of the procedures by which coders are trained and reliability is assessed, procedural details must be reported. In regard to the procedures themselves, we recommend some explicit safeguards against the problem of observer drift. We know from previous research on consensual coder drift (cf. Johnson &

Bolstad, 1973) that high accuracy during training does not insure high accuracy during data collection. We also know that high inter-rater agreement may be disguising two inaccurate coders who have simply "drifted" into committing similar errors. The common solution to this problem is to have a calibrator randomly code a portion of the data. But the calibrator is also susceptible to drift; in fact, this approach may similarly disguise observer drift amidst high interrater agreement percentages since observers are able to match calibrator idiosyncracies (Romanczyk et al., 1973). To minimize the problem of observer drift, we recommend that accuracy be assessed by agreement across multiple pairs of observers, and by discrepancies between within-pair and across-pair agreement indices. By utilizing multiple-coder pairs, accuracy can be assumed to be representative of a larger population of observers employed under similar training and data-collection conditions. Furthermore, by alternating members of observer pairs and monitoring agreement scores for each observer as she or he alternates with other observers, deviant coders would be identified. A further advantage of this procedure is that it tends to control observer drift, since alternating observer pairs are afforded less opportunity to either learn the idiosyncratic protocols of their partners or jointly devise new ones of their own. For a smaller number of observers, a single calibrator could be floated among observer pairs, and the resultant pattern of agreement scores could be used to disclose deviant coders. Superior accuracy would not be attributed a priori to the calibrator; indeed, she or he may well be judged deviant.

Finally, it is difficult to ascertain the reliability of the MICS from previous research because the common choice for an agreement index, percentage of interrater agreement, is insufficient for a number of reasons (Hartmann, 1977; Hollenbeck, 1978). In addition to its inability to correct for the rate of agreement expected by chance, percentage-agreement statistics possess no metric properties amenable to further mathematical analysis (Hartmann, 1977; Hollenbeck, 1978). Such properties would allow for a formal analysis of error variance both between and within coders (Costello, 1973).

Ideally, a reliability index will partial out the probability of chance agreement. However, we have argued that p_c cannot be computed from data coded by the MICS. Our choice of a reliability statistic for MICS-coded data follows from our earlier discussion of accuracy. In a matrix of agreements formed by alternating coder pairs, we recommend that either the product–moment correlation coefficient or one of its several linear transformations be used. The criticism that the correlation may be inflated by one coder's overestimates of behavior rates (Johnson & Bolstad, 1973) applies primarily to binary coding schemes (i.e., occurrence or nonoccurrence of a single class of behaviors). The correlations would permit further analysis, given that the investigator published, or otherwise made available, the statistical data used to derive the correlations.

SUMMARY AND CONCLUSIONS

The point of this discussion is that, on the basis of the information published in studies which have used the MICS, and to the extent that the conventions for determining reliability proposed in the MICS manual are adopted, the reliability of the system cannot be determined. We have recommended three changes which would improve existing practices: (1) using at least two alternating pairs of raters, and preferably more, (2) calculating separate agreement indices for each category, and (3) using a variant of the product-moment correlation as a reliability statistic.

VALIDITY

The MICS in its original form, and for that matter any observational coding system constructed a priori, is not a *measure* at all but rather an attempt to *describe* behavior. Its creators claimed only that its categories provide "an adequate accounting of the behavior which takes place in a problem-solving session" (Hops *et al.*, 1971, p. 1). In this statement there is no presumption that MICS-coded performance relates to constructs such as "problem-solving ability." However, subsequent investigations by the Oregon Marital Studies Program (Billings, 1979; Birchler *et al.*, 1975; Vincent *et al.*, 1975; Royce & Weiss, 1975; Vincent, Friedman, Nugent, & Messerly, 1979) and others (Gottman, Notarius, & Markman, 1976; Gottman *et al.*, 1977; Haynes, Follingstad, & Sullivan, 1978; Resick, Sweet, Kieffer, Barr, & Ruby, 1977; Robinson & Price, 1976; Resick, Welsh, Zitomer, Spiegel, Meidlinger, & Long, 1978; Margolin, 1978a, 1978b) suggest that the intent of the observational coding systems is more ambitious than mere description. At least two distinct intentions can be detected. The MICS, or alternative coding systems have been used to measure conflict-resolution or problem-solving skills in couples. Alternatively, it has been used more generally to assess the rate of reinforcement and punishment exchanged between spouses.

Since the MICS has been used to measure constructs such as "problem-solving skill" and "rewardingness," construct validity becomes a critical concern. In addition, criterion-related validity must be evaluated, since in the case of both constructs, the behaviors of interest are typically measured in the laboratory rather than the natural environment. Moreover, the methods used to combine the frequencies of various codes to yield an overall score become critical. Since the MICS does not provide an overall score, each investigator has developed his or her own a priori strategy for summarizing the specific codes. Before discussing the construct validity or representativeness of laboratory-coded couple interaction, we will review the predominant research strategies. These are aimed at establishing *discriminant validity*, by looking for differences between distressed and nondistressed couples in the frequencies of "positive" and "negative" behavior, and *concurrent validity*, by correlating MICS-derived measures with criterion measures of marital distress.

CONTRASTING GROUPS

Vincent *et al.* (1975) compared the communication of distressed and nondistressed couples while problem-solving in the laboratory. Couples were instructed to resolve hypothetical conflicts of fictional couples, using standardized vignettes from the *Inventory of Marital Conflicts* (Olson & Ryder, 1970). Combining specific MICS codes a priori into summary categories of positive and negative behaviors, Vincent *et al.* found that distressed couples, compared to nondistressed couples, employed a greater frequency of negative behaviors and a reduced frequency of positive behaviors. Birchler *et al.* (1975), using the same sample of couples, replicated the differences for negative behavior in a "casual conversation" task, although the two groups could not be differentiated on the basis of positive behavior. Klier and Rothberg (1977) utilized some of the MICS codes, combining them into their own a priori version of the summary categories of positive and negative behavior. These authors found that distressed and nondistressed couples could be differentiated on the basis of negative behavior, but that the two groups did not differ in their frequency of positive behavior. Regardless of the degree of distress, couples emitted an increased frequency of positive behaviors when discussing "issue-oriented" as opposed to "relationship-oriented" problems. Finally, Billings (1979) was able to discriminate between distressed and nondistressed couples on the basis of both "positive" and "negative" behavior.

Vincent *et al.* (1979) replicated the findings of the earlier Vincent *et al.* (1975) study. More importantly, their findings pointed to the importance of task and instructional variables in mediating the discriminability of MICS summary codes. When couples were instructed to "fake distress" or "fake happiness," verbal summary categories no longer discriminated between distressed and nondistressed couples, whereas nonverbal negative and positive behaviors retained their discriminatory power. That is, couples' verbal behavior was sensitive to instructional cues, whereas nonverbal behavior was relatively invariant across different instructional conditions. It appears that nonverbal categories (turn off, not tracking, laugh/ smile, and so on) are less sensitive to demand characteristics, and therefore may be more useful than verbal cues in discriminating between distressed and nondistressed couples.

Gottman *et al.* (1977) have reported findings which shed further light on the importance of nonverbal behavior in discriminating between distressed and nondistressed couples, although they used a different coding system. Spouse behavior was coded both for speech content and for affect (positive, negative, or neutral); affect was coded on the basis of voice tone, facial expression, and posture. With the exception of the ratio of agreements to agreements plus disagreements, which was higher for distressed than for nondistressed couples, verbal behavior categories did not significantly discriminate between the two groups of couples. Only when verbal codes were accompanied by nonverbal affect codes were successful discriminations made. Compared to their nondistressed counterparts, distressed couples were less likely to express agreement with neutral affect, and more likely to agree, mind read, and express feelings—all with negative affect. In addition, the nonverbal behavior of couples was generally predictive of satisfaction: the nonverbal behavior of dissatisfied couples was generally less *positive* and more negative than that of satisfied couples. Since many of the MICS categories, particularly those which are thought to reflect negative verbal behavior (such as criticism, complaint, put down), include both verbal and nonverbal cues in their definitions, it is impossible to differentiate between the two sets of cues in MICS research. On the other hand, Gottman's findings, although seemingly consistent with the Vincent *et al.* (1979) study using the MICS, may not be generalizable to the MICS, since the two systems employ different content codes. It should also be pointed out that there is no guarantee that Gottman's observers were relying exclusively on nonverbal cues in their assignments of affect codes.

Collectively, these studies provide some support for the discriminant validity of couple interaction coded by the MICS, and, more generally, suggest that distressed and nondistressed couples can be distinguished using behavioral observations. However, none of these studies suggest that the MICS, or any other behavioral-observation index, is sensitive to or reflective of either *problem-solving skill* or a general dimension of *interactional quality*, if quality is defined as the rewarding or punishing impact of the interaction on the partners themselves. Several issues need to be kept in mind when evaluating the implications of this research. First, each study arrived at its summary codes through a different linear combination of specific behavioral codes. Therefore, although the findings collectively suggest promise for the discriminatory power of behavioral observations, no specific observational index has been consistently validated. Second, the studies offer considerable testimony to the influence of task and instructional cues on the behavior of couples. Since the discriminations are task-dependent even across various laboratory analogues, it is extremely hazardous to assume that behaviors which discriminate in the laboratory also do so in the natural environment. Third, none of these studies has attempted to relate observed behaviors to a criterion representing "successful problem-solving outcome," or looked at the relationship between various behaviors in the problem-solving setting and successful conflict resolution in the natural environment. Fourth, the research cited thus far does not address the extent to which these behavioral codes accurately measure the valence or impact of the behaviors in question on the spouses themselves. If the MICS, or any other observational coding system, is really a reflection of the rewarding-punishing value of interaction sequences, then categories labeled as "rewarding" or "punishing" by observers should correspond to the ratings given to the same behaviors by the spouses themselves. None of these issues has been adequately dealt with in research conducted thus far.

CONCURRENT VALIDITY

The distinctions between concurrent and discriminant validity are not clear cut. Studies comparing distressed and nondistressed couples must employ some selection criterion when assigning couples to groups. When the selection criterion involves an established psychometric instrument, any subsequent demonstration of discriminant validity also shows that the two measures—the selection measure and the measure serving as the independent variable—are correlated, thus establishing concurrent validity. The studies reviewed in the previous section all used multiple criteria for designating couples as distressed or nondistressed, including the *Locke–Wallace Marital Adjustment Test* (Locke & Wallace, 1959), a self-report questionnaire which yields a global measure of relationship adjustment. Thus the primary distinction between research which correlates behavioral observations with standard measurement criteria and research attempting to discriminate between groups of couples is the criterion for the establishment of validity: correlational research places all couples on a continuum of distress in the terms of the criterion measure, whereas the "contrasting group" approach classifies couples into dichotomous categories. Unless one assumes that satisfaction and dissatisfaction are qualitatively distinct states, correlational research of the kind to be described should be more sensitive to the correspondence between the two measures in question.

Margolin (1978a, 1978b) looked at the relationship between self-reports of marital satisfaction (Locke–Wallace, Areas-of-Change) and "positive" and "negative" behaviors, based on summary codes from the MICS, in a sample of distressed couples. There was no correlation between observed positive or negative behavior and either of the self-report satisfaction indices. These data should be interpreted with caution since the client sample was comprised of a restricted range of couples on the criterion of interest. However, the findings suggest that although the MICS can identify distressed and nondistressed couples with reasonable accuracy, within the population of distressed couples degree of subjective distress is unrelated to MICS summary categories of positive and negative behavior.

CONSTRUCT VALIDITY

What is reflected in the summary codes derived from observing couple interaction? What do they measure? Let us consider three possibilities which have been suggested in the literature, and evaluate the evidence supporting each of the three.

First, the summary codes, or more specific codes therein, may measure problem-solving skill. Certainly the tasks in which couples have been evaluated consist primarily of problem solving or conflict resolution. The MICS has also been used to assess the amount of change occurring as a function of treatment programs placing a heavy emphasis on problem-solving training (Jacobson, 1977a, 1978a, 1979a). Using the MICS in such a way implies that the MICS is sensitive to changes in problem-solving effectiveness. However, there is no evidence that the frequency of any MICS code is associated with effective problem solving. One deterrent to the conducting of such research is the dearth of available criteria for determining effective problem solving. According to definitions of problem solving that have been used by behavioral marital therapists (Jacobson, 1977b; Jacobson & Margolin, 1979), effective problem solving means overcoming a conflict and agreeing on a change in the relationship. Although one of us has speculated that such changes are more likely to occur following desirable problem-solving interaction (Jacobson, 1978b), supporting data do not as yet exist. In order to determine whether an association exists between MICS-coded behavior and problem-solving competencies, it would be necessary to observe and objectify the outcome of problem-solving sessions, and investigate the relationship between observed problem-solving behavior and the desirability of the outcomes.

One could argue that if behavior in a problem-solving situation improves from pretest to posttest with a treatment program based on problem-solving training, the observational coding system must measure the construct "problem-solving" ability. Unfortunately, there is circularity involved in this kind of argument. How do we know that couples were successfully treated? Because they evidenced change on an observational coding system. But how do we know that the observational coding system is a valid measure of change? Because couples manifested change on it after the completion of therapy. It should be clear that independent evidence for the construct validity of the MICS as a measure or problem-solving skill must be provided before changes in therapy can be said to provide such support. Moreover, the observational coding system may reflect some other construct which changes as the result of successful therapy. Overall increased satisfaction may be associated with positive changes in MICS categories, without necessarily proving that these changes reflect improved problem-solving ability.

Another possible construct which might be reflected in MICS summary codes is "effective or desirable communication." There seems to be an underlying assumption in much of the research using the MICS that its categories are sensitive to the quality of communication (Birchler *et al.*, 1975; Vincent *et al.*, 1975, 1979). The quality of communication can be defined in numerous ways, but certainly it refers to the impact of the communication on the partners themselves. The empirical question can be phrased as follows: do couples who receive a relatively high frequency of "positive" codes on the MICS, and/or a low frequency of "negative" codes, also rate the impact of the communication as positive? The answer to this question involves an examination of the association between observer-coded behavior and the impact of the communication, based on ratings by the spouses themselves. Again, Margolin (1978a, 1978b) has reported the only data directly relevant to this question, and these data were collected on a sample of distressed couples. She found little agreement between observers and the spouses themselves regarding the quality of communication. With the exception of wives' communication skillfulness, as measured by observers and husbands, no significant interobserver correlations on measures of communication were found. Thus, behaviors coded as "positive" or "negative" on the basis of MICS summary codes bore little relationship to the behaviors that distressed spouses rated as positive or negative. Once again, because these investigations were limited to a sample of distressed couples, the results may not be generalizable to a more representative sample of couples. But neither can they been seen as supportive of the hypothesis that MICS-coded behavior measures the effectiveness or quality of communication, as experienced by the spouses themselves.

Finally, data coded by the MICS might be regarded as a reflection of the overall exchange of reinforcement and punishment be-

tween spouses. However, it is by no means self-evident that problem-solving exchanges in the lab elicit frequencies of rewarding and
punishing behaviors which are representative of the rewarding and
punishing exchanges that occur in other areas of the relationship.
Couples exchange rewards and punishments in a variety of ways
other than by direct communication (cf. Jacobson, 1979a): they ini-
tate and withhold sex, they share pleasant and unpleasant activities,
they do favors for one another, and much more. It is an unjustified
leap of faith to assume that the exchange of reinforcement in a relationship can be understood simply by counting the frequency of
positive and negative exchanges that occur in a brief laboratory interaction. The empirical question again requires a substantial correlation between such laboratory exchanges and the gamut of exchanged rewards and punishments in the natural environment. Such
correlations have not been forthcoming. In Margolin's studies,
couples tracked the frequency of "pleasing" and "displeasing"
events on a daily basis (using the Spouse Observation Checklist),
and these frequencies were correlated with MICS-derived measures
of positive and negative communication. Frequency of "pleases"
and "displeases," as measured by the spouses in the natural environment, were unrelated to frequency of observer-coded positive
and negative communication.

OBSERVATION IN THE NATURAL ENVIRONMENT

Since the behavior of interest in the assessment of marital interaction is ultimately behavior that occurs in the natural environment,
all laboratory-based assessment procedures are analogues, and their
relevance to real-world marital interaction must be demonstrated
rather than assumed. Vincent et al. (1979) have shown that instructional cues can have powerful effects on the frequency of many of
the behavioral categories coded by the MICS. Other research has
shown that the nature of the task or the type of problem being discussed can also exert a powerful influence on couples' performance
(Birchler et al., 1975; Klier & Rothberg, 1977; Gottman, Notarius,
Markman, Bank, Yoppi, & Rubin, 1976; Resick et al., 1978). Given
the abundance of research demonstrating the variability in couples'
performance across different task, instructional, and topic variables, it would be premature and extremely hazardous to assume
cross-situational generality between any or all of the laboratory

analogue situations and communication in the natural environment.

There have been no investigations which demonstrate the criterion-related validity of laboratory-based assessments of marital interaction. However, there have been attempts to systematically code marital communication in the home and relate these codes to other measures of marital distress. Robinson and Price (1980) had observers code marital interaction in the homes of four distressed and four nondistressed couples. Nine behavioral categories were used, all of them very similar to the categories embodied in the MICS summary codes of "positive behavior." The frequency of these behaviors was uncorrelated with global measures of marital satisfaction (e.g., Locke–Wallace), although two of the codes were highly correlated with daily measures of relationship satisfaction. Haynes *et al.* (1978) reported a similar study comparing the interaction of seven distressed and six nondistressed couples, as recorded by observers in the home. Haynes *et al.* borrowed twelve categories form the MICS, sampling from both "positive" and "negative" summary codes. Their results were puzzling, to say the least! Although distressed couples engaged in some negative behaviors (criticism, interrupt, disagree) to a significantly greater degree than did nondistressed couples, distressed couples also exceeded nondistressed couples in their emission of categories normally comprising the category "positive" behavior (eye contact, agreement).

Thus, the only two studies which have systematically observed behavior in the homes of married couples found results which are inconsistent with the laboratory-derived data. Although it is impossible to determine the sources of these inconsistencies, it is highly probable that the discrepancies have multiple determinants. A few hours of observed marital interaction are unlikely to provide a representative sample of what transpires between them. The constraints imposed by the presence of the observers and the task instructions might also lead to a restricted range of behavior, limiting opportunities for the discovery of reliable differences between couples. These problems are common to naturalistic observation, and have been articulated in other contexts (Johnson & Bolstad, 1973). In order to collect meaningful data in couples' homes, the minimum requirements are the collection of numerous samples at different times, on different days, and in different parts of the home. In addition, steps must be taken to minimize the reactive effects of observers. For now there does not seem to be a cost-effective way to collect valid, nonreactive data on marital interaction in the home. Laboratory-based tasks are the preferred modus operandi at the present time, although one can never be sure that tasks produce behavior that is representative of and generalizable to the natural environment.

CONCLUSION

By most standards, the validity of observational data coded by the MICS or by other similar coding systems remains undetermined. It is not clear what aspects of marital interaction are measured by the MICS, nor what the relationship is between observer-coded data and the constructs which are central to behavior-exchange theory. However, distressed couples can be differentiated from nondistressed couples using criteria from either the MICS, coding systems derived from the MICS, or an observational coding system developed by Gottman et al. (1977). Discriminant validity offers some cause for optimism, but it is not enough to justify the expensive, cumbersome process of coding observational behavior. The gross discriminations of which the MICS is capable can be equaled or even exceeded by a number of simple paper-and-pencil questionnaires (cf. Jacobson & Margolin, 1979).

Problem solving plays a central and pivotal role in behavioral marital therapy, both in theory and as an intervention procedure (Jacobson, 1979a). The MICS, or some similar coding system, provides a way to address the specific mechanisms of marital problem solving. Since current research has not exhausted the potentialities of observational coding, its original and still unfulfilled promise may prove to be its vindication.

CLINICAL UTILITY

Most practicing clinicians do not have research assistants, videotape equipment, or other resources necessary to make use of observational coding systems. Except for the rare clinical research setting which may include research as part of its *raison d'être*, the utility of observational coding for clinical practice is minimal. However, the assessment of communication and problem-solving effectiveness can and should be an important part of the clinician's assessment repertoire. Clinical strategies for evaluating marital communication have been described elsewhere (Jacobson, 1979a; Jacobson & Margolin,

1979; Weiss & Margolin, 1977). Certainly couples can be given problem-solving tasks; direct observation, as a strategy for evaluating their
capabilities, is far superior to simply asking them to describe their
communication. Although the methods used by the clinician to assess
the communication may be less systematic and less formal than the
coding procedures which we have been discussing, clinicians can approximate the rigor of a research setting by rating couples on a variety
of dimensions relevant to communication effectiveness.

An example of a behavioral checklist which has potential for the
practicing clinician is the Verbal Problem Checklist (VPC) developed
by Thomas and and his associates (Thomas, 1977; Thomas, Walter,
& O'Flaherty, 1974). The checklist includes 49 categories of verbal

Table 2
Response Categories for Verbal Problem Checklist[a]

1. Overtalk	26. Topic content avoidance
2. Undertalk	27. Other content avoidance
3. Fast talk	28. Topic content shifting
4. Slow talk	29. Other content shifting
5. Loud talk	30. Topic content persistence
6. Quiet talk	31. Other content persistence
7. Sing-song speech	32. Poor referent specification
8. Monotone speech	33. Temporal remoteness
9. Rapid latency	34. Detached utterance
10. Slow latency	35. Positive talk deficit
11. Affective talk	36. Positive talk surfeit
12. Unaffective talk	37. Acknowledgment deficit
13. Obtrusions	38. Acknowledgment surfeit
14. Quibbling	39. Opinion deficit
15. Overresponsiveness	40. Opinion surfeit
16. Underresponsiveness	41. Excessive agreement
17. Excessive question asking	42. Excessive disagreement
18. Pedantry	43. Dysfluent talk
19. Dogmatic statement	44. Too little information given
20. Overgeneralization	45. Redundant information given
21. Undergeneralization	46. Too much information given
22. Excessive cueing	47. Negative talk surfeit
23. Incorrect autalitic	48. Negative talk deficit
24. Presumptive attribution	49. Illogical talk
25. Misrepresentation of fact or evaluation	

[a]Reprinted by permission from Thomas (1977).

behavior (see Table 2). Each category is carefully defined. On the basis of direct observation of couple interaction, each category is rated from 1 to 4, with a rating of 1 equivalent to "not at all," and a rating of 4 equivalent to "a large amount." In addition, the categories are given problem ratings on a 1–3 scale, corresponding to the extent to which each category comprises a problem area for the couple. The VPC provides one example of guidelines that a clinician can use in surveying the important components of effective couple communication. Thus, while the direct observation of marital interaction will remain an important area for future research investigations, for the present it is unlikely to be particularly useful to practicing clinicians. The legacy for clinicians is that communication and problem solving should be evaluated as carefully as possible, despite the implausibility of producing the kind of data depicted in research investigations.

Spouse Observation

Spouses in a distressed relationship are at once the most qualified and least qualified sources of assessment information. They are eminently qualified since they observe each and every exchange that occurs, and are therefore the only possible source of comprehensive information regarding the relationship. In addition, they are uniquely qualified to report on the *impact* of particular behaviors that occur. For these reasons, as well as for the practical advantages of using spouses as observers, spouse observation is and will continue to be a popular tactic in the assessment of marital dysfunction. The other side of the coin is their inherent biases, their dual roles as participants and observers, and the possible reactivity of the observation process (cf. Weiss & Margolin, 1977). In this section, we will review the strategies for spouse observation that have been developed for use in both the clinical-laboratory setting and in the natural environment.

SPOUSE OBSERVATIONS IN THE LABORATORY

Gottman, Notarius, Markman, Bank, Yoppi, and Rubin (1976) describe the use of a "talk table" which allowed couples to code ongoing communication along a five-point Likert Scale (1, super negative, to 5, super positive). As each spouse finished speaking, the listener immediately rated the *impact* of the speech, while the speaker rated his or her *intent*. The *impact* ratings, which occurred concurrently with ongoing conversations, were effective at discriminating between distressed and nondistressed couples. That is, distressed spouses reported a greater number of statements having a "negative" impact, and a fewer number of statements having a "neutral" impact, than nondistressed couples. In one of two studies, these differences were confined to high-conflict tasks.

Markman (1979) used the Gottman, Notarius, Markman, Bank, Yoppi, and Rubin (1976) procedure to study the predictive power of "impact" ratings from a sample of couples planning to marry. Partners also rated the "intent" of each speech. Although neither impact nor intent ratings were correlated with global relationship satisfaction at the time in which the ratings were taken, both were highly predictive of marital satisfaction two-and-a-half years later. The correlations were $+.61$ and $+.60$, for males and females, respectively. Male intent ratings were also highly correlated with relationship satisfaction at the two-and-a-half-year follow-up ($r = +.55$). A cross-lagged panel correlational analysis suggested that impact ratings were causally related to subsequent satisfaction ratings.

These two studies demonstrate the potential utility of having spouses rate the quality of communication as it occurs, both with respect to identifying marital conflict and predicting subsequent distress. Clearly, spouse ratings have a number of advantages. If they are interpreted literally as ratings of the "impact" of the partner's communication, their face validity is appealing and seems to obviate the need for a demonstration of construct validity. An additional advantage of spouse ratings is the ease with which they could be employed by practitioners.

Unfortunately, the utility of spouse ratings is limited by the inevitable investment which each spouse has as a participant in the interaction. With spouses as raters, one can never rule out the confounding influences of observer bias. This limitation is significant even when spouses are carefully trained as observers to count the frequency of specific behaviors enacted by the partner; here, for example, Robinson and Price (1980) reported marginally significant or nonsignificant correlations between spouse frequency estimates and observer-coded behavioral frequencies. When the task is more subjective, such as the impact ratings used by Gottman and his associates, the interpretative difficulties are even more severe. A "positive impact" rating may be a function of many factors, including the intrinsic properties of the rated behavior, the rater's interpretation of the behavior (which may be highly unstable), the rater's overall cognitive set regarding the relationship at that point in time, or demand characteristics (Jacobson, 1979a).

SPOUSE OBSERVATIONS IN THE NATURAL ENVIRONMENT

In the clinical-laboratory setting, criterion-related validity must be demonstrated for any behavioral observations, whether the sources are observers or the spouses themselves (Jacobson, 1979a). Communicative exchanges are only a small portion of the universe of pleasing and displeasing exchanges that occur in a relationship (Weiss & Margolin, 1977). In an attempt to develop a comprehensive checklist which would assess these exchanges, the Oregon group developed the *Spouse Observation Checklist* (SOC) (Patterson, 1976; Weiss & Margolin, 1977). The SOC consists of approximately 400 behaviors divided into 12 categories: companionship, affection, consideration, sex, communication, coupling activities, child care and parenting, household responsibilities, financial decision making, employment-education, personal habits and appearance, self- and spouse independence. Each spouse is instructed to peruse the checklist each night and denote all behaviors emitted by the spouse during the previous 24 hours. The task can be assigned in a number of ways, depending on the type of information which the assessor desires. For example, one revised form of the SOC further divides the behaviors in each of the 12 categories into 2 subgroups: pleases and displeases. This division was done a priori, and it was an attempt to categorize the events according to their typical *impact*. Spouses were instructed to record only those events which were experienced as either pleasing or displeasing. This assignment calls not only for the tracking of spouse behaviors, but also for an experiential report on the valence of the behavior. An alternative set of instructions asks couples simply to record all behaviors that occur, without regard to valence.

The SOC has a number of potential uses. First, it produces a profile of the day-to-day exchanges in relationship. If couples are simultaneously recording daily satisfaction ratings, it is possible to pinpoint those behaviors that are most useful in predicting each partner's degree of overall satisfaction with the relationship. Second, the SOC provides a baseline for the occurrence of a wide variety of relevant relationship behaviors. This baseline can be used to evaluate the effects of therapy if part of the therapeutic strategy involves increasing or decreasing behaviors that are included on the checklist (cf. Jacobson, 1979b; Weiss & Birchler, 1978). Third, SOC data can form the basis for a number of behavioral interventions; a variety of clinical strategies revolve around the task of prompting couples to increase positive behavior (Jacobson & Margolin, 1979; Weiss & Birchler, 1978). Couples can use the SOC to become more adept at pinpointing desirable and undesirable behaviors, and to monitor the effectiveness of attempts to modify these behaviors. Finally, the SOC can be used by practicing clinicians, although clients often report that it is an onerous task. If it is presented effectively and strategically, and the assignments regarding its use enforced, compliance tends to be very high (Jacobson & Margolin, 1979).

Birchler *et al.* (1975), using the original form of the SOC, found that distressed couples reported significantly fewer pleases and a significantly greater frequency of displeases than did nondistressed couples. The ratio of daily pleases to displeases was 4:1 for distressed couples, and 30:1 for nondistressed couples. These findings were partially replicated by Robinson and Price (1980), who used a modified form of the SOC which listed only pleasing events.

A preliminary form of construct validity has also been demonstrated for the SOC. These studies have examined the relationship between reported daily frequencies of pleases and displeases on the one hand, and overall daily satisfaction on the other hand. Wills, Weiss, and Patterson (1974) examined this association across twelve consecutive days of spouse observation for each of seven nondistressed couples. From the spouse-recorded data, five predictor variables were derived: affectional pleasing and displeasing events, instrumental pleasing and displeasing events, and quality of outside interaction. The criterion variable was a global daily satisfaction rating (DSR). Each time an affectional or instrumental event occurred, it was given a pleasantness or unpleasantness rating. These weighted frequency counts collectively accounted for 25% of the variance in DSR across the entire sample of couples. Displeases were better predictors than pleases. Among the categories of pleasing behavior, a sex difference emerged: affectional pleases were significantly related to DSR for wives only, whereas instrumental pleases were predictive of DSR only for husbands. Quality of outside experiences were not associated with DSR.

In our laboratories at The University of Iowa (Jacobson *et al.*, in press), we have replicated and extended the findings of Wills *et al.* (1974). Our predictor variables included shared activities, positive interaction, negative interaction, positive physical contact, negative physical contact, instrumental acts, and instrumental failings. Items from the SOC were classified a priori into one of these seven categories. A sample of distressed spouses was instructed simply to note whether each item occurred or failed to occur during the past 24 hours. The best single predictor of both husbands' and wives' DSR was the partner's frequency of negative verbal interaction ($r = -.40$). Of the total variance attributable to spouse behavior, 57% of the husbands' and 79% of the wives' was attributable to negative response classes (response classes which were inversely related to DSR). In other words, distressed spouses were happiest on days when there were the fewest aversive events, and the absence of such events was more important to a satisfying day than the presence of positives. We have found in subsequent research that happy couples exhibit quite the opposite pattern. For them, DSR is primarily a function of the frequency of positive events, with negative events playing a small role. Thus distressed and nondistressed couples can be distinguished not only with respect to frequencies of spouse-recorded behavior, but also on the basis of those events which are most predictive of daily satisfaction.

Despite the obvious benefits of spouse observation, instruments such as the SOC are also plagued by a variety of interpretative problems. Let us first address the issue of reactivity. Just as the self-monitoring literature suggests (Ciminero, Nelson, & Lipinski, 1977), therapeutic goals may be in conflict with the goals of precise and accurate measurement. Since the SOC provides information to a couple, it constitutes an intervention procedure which may, in and of itself, produce changes in the relationship (Jacobson & Margolin, 1979). Although it is impossible to assess the reactivity of the first few days of data collection, since there is no suitable baseline with which to compare these data, the temporal stability of daily tracking can be examined to provide an index of any gradual change brought about by the process of data collection itself. Wills *et al.* (1974) and Robinson and Price failed to find trends toward change in the frequencies of pleases and displeases over a two-week period. Thus, the extent to which the process of spouse observation affects the frequency of spouse behavior is not clear. Moreover, to the extent that frequencies of reported behaviors change over time, there are at least two major ways to interpret these effects. First, the behavioral frequencies might actually be changing. Second, the spouse-observer's criteria for recording either the occurrence or the valence of a behavior may change over time. This potential for an alteration in observer recording biases can also affect the interpretation of SOC data when used as a pre–post outcome measure. Since behavioral marital therapy involves teaching couples to become more accurate at pinpointing behavior, and since cognitive restructuring is often included to alter spouses' maladaptive labeling practices, any changes that occur in the frequency of pleases and displeases, as measured by the SOC, may simply reflect cognitive changes on the part of observers rather than actual behavior changes on the part of those observed.

This leads to the central interpretive dilemma imposed by data derived from spouse observation: should these data be regarded as behavioral observations or should they be regarded as simply another type of self-report information? When the SOC is used to record behavioral frequencies, this dilemma reduces itself to a question of accuracy. Although there is very little evidence regarding the accuracy of spouses as behavioral observers, Robinson and Price (1980) reported very low correlations between observer ratings and spouse ratings of the same behaviors. Moreover, distressed spouses were significantly less "accurate"; that is, they agreed with observers less often than did nondistressed couples. Specifically, distressed couples underestimated the frequencies of positive behavior. The lack of correspondence between spouses and observers casts doubt on the accuracy of spouse observations based on the SOC. Moreover, the tendency on the part of distressed spouses to underestimate the frequency of positive behavior suggests that increases over time in reported frequency may reflect, at least in part, modifications in recording biases. It should be pointed out that Robinson and Price had couples estimate behavioral frequencies retrospectively, whereas observers were engaged in ongoing behavioral tracking. Thus the tasks were not comparable, and the low correlations may be attributable to these task differences. Clearly, definitive data on the accuracy of spouses as observers remains to be collected.

The question of reliability must be phrased somewhat differently when spouses are recording the pleasing or displeasing impact of spouse behaviors in addition to their occurrence. Are spouses (1) simply reporting their momentary evaluations of behaviors whose valence varies depending upon the observer's cognitive state, or are they (2) actually reporting behaviors that usually carry the same impact, when they occur—and to what extent? To put it another way, are spouses reporting the frequency of rewarding and punishing behaviors or simply spreading their global-satisfaction ratings over all behaviors that occur? The only way to answer this question is to examine spouses' consistency over time in the valence which they report upon the occurrence of particular spouse behaviors. To the extent that behaviors are valued consistently from day-to-day, regardless of overall mood, the ratings are likely to reflect relatively stable reinforcing and punishing properties of the behaviors. But to the extent that valences of particular behaviors seem to covary with overall mood on a particular day, less significance should be attached to the intrinsic properties of the behavior, and more to the mediating effects of cognitions.

CONCLUSION AND CLINICAL UTILITY

Spouse observation plays an extremely important part in the behavioral assessment of marital dysfunction. The use of spouses to define their own reinforcement preference is consistent with the idiographic emphasis in behavioral assessment. Spouses provide access to these idiosyncratic behavioral preferences to a degree that standardized coding systems cannot match. Spouses also offer the potential for continuous observation. Finally, one does not need a research grant to utilize spouse observers in one's clinical practice. Given these advantages, plus their utility as stimuli from which to launch intervention strategies, it is easy to overlook the significant interpretive problems posed by data collected from spouses. At present, it is probably most prudent to regard spouse-collected data as a subjective report of what happened that day. To the extent that clinicians and researchers recognize that these data are reflective of each spouse's view of the world rather than reality in an objective sense, data derived from spouse observation will be extremely informative, useful, and often therapeutic.

Thus in our clinical work with couples, we have found the SOC to be extremely useful for both assessment and treatment. First, the SOC provides each partner's appraisal of the positive and negative behaviors she or he is receiving from the partner on a daily basis. The fact that the recordings are conducted daily, and the degree of speci-

ficity entailed by the task, combine to yield assessment information
which cannot be duplicated by general self-report questionnaires. For
example, although it is important to know that, in a general sense,
both spouses are unhappy with the frequency and quality of their sex
life, such information is uninformative in regard to the specific behaviors that do or do not occur during sexual encounters, the impact
of those behaviors, and so on.

Second, since the SOC asks couples to record global daily satisfaction ratings along with the frequency of pleasing and displeasing
behaviors, it is possible to assess the degree to which various classes of
behavior predict daily satisfaction ratings. Through such correlational analyses, conducted either formally or informally, one can develop
an empirically derived measure of the reinforcing or punishing value
of particular response classes. It is reasonable to assume, at least as a
working hypothesis, that events which are positively correlated with
daily satisfaction serve reinforcing functions in the marriage, whereas
those which are negatively correlated with daily satisfaction function
as punishers.

Third, with minor modifications, the SOC can provide vital information regarding interspouse consensus. To what degree do
spouses share the same perceptions regarding what behaviors are occurring? If one spouse uses the SOC to track his or her own behavior,
and the other uses the checklist in the usual manner, than both
spouses are recording the behavior of the same partner. It then becomes possible to assess their tendency to agree on what has happened
that day. Along the same lines, if the self-monitoring spouse is recording the "intent" of each spouse-directed behavior (positive, negative,
neutral) while the other is recording the "impact" of those same behaviors, it becomes possible to assess discrepancies of the type reported by Gottman, Notarius, Markman, Bank, Yoppi, and Rubin
(1976) between the intent of particular behaviors and their impact.

Finally, the SOC provides a mechanism for monitoring the state
of the relationship and the ongoing effectiveness of therapy. After a
therapist has grown accustomed to using the SOC, she or he can tell
at a glance how satisfying the relationship was for both spouses during
the previous week. A more formal functional analysis can be added
simply by graphing target behaviors on a cumulative basis from one
week to another.

As we have already mentioned, the SOC is a lengthy checklist,
and for any given couple, a vast majority of the 400 items will be irrel-

evant. Although we have developed procedures for assuring compliance from the vast majority of couples (cf. Jacobson & Margolin, 1979), a viable alternative would be to reduce the length of the checklist by eliminating items that are irrelevant for a particular couple. The primary caution here is that such a reduction not be undertaken prematurely. Events that never occur during a two-week pretreatment baseline may nonetheless be salient behaviors, that is, desirable behaviors which may become targets for behavior change. A final caution in using the SOC concerns the way SOC data are to be interpreted. Some recent data from our laboratories (Jacobson & Moore, submitted for publication) suggest that spouses are not particularly accurate as data collectors; indeed, one of the concomitants of marital distress may be the tendency to selectively track negative behaviors. Thus the SOC may provide little more than each spouse's phenomenological account of what is happening in the relationship. This account, we would assert, is highly significant despite its lack of correspondence with "objective reality," since, for the distressed spouse, the reality of his or her perception may have more to do with the overall level of satisfaction than the actual state of affairs (Jacobson, 1978b).

The Use of Self-Report Questionnaires in Behavioral Marital Assessment

Self-report instruments are again on the ascendance within behavioral-assessment circles (Bellack & Hersen, 1977). Opposition to self-reports in the early years of behavior therapy stemmed from a number of factors: inventories and questionnaires tended to be constructed for the purposes of psychodynamic and trait theorists; they did not seem pertinent to a behavioral analysis; they seemed vulnerable to various biases and distortions. Recently, prejudice against self-report instruments has eased. As any recent textbook on behavioral assessment will document (cf. Ciminero, Calhoun, & Adams, 1977; Cone & Hawkins, 1977; Bellack & Hersen, 1977), self-report questionnaires which address assessment questions more relevant to a behavioral analysis have proliferated.

A number of self-report questionnaires have been constructed in recent years by behavioral researchers. All of them address questions of primary interest to a behavioral analysis. One of the most useful is the *Areas-of-Change Questionnaire* (A-C), developed by Weiss and his associates (Patterson, 1976; Weiss *et al.*, 1973). The questionnaire is described in detail elsewhere (Jacob, 1976; Jacobson & Margolin, 1979; Weiss *et al.*, 1973), and we will confine ourselves to a few comments here. Essentially, the questionnaire elicits from each spouse a list of spouse behaviors where change would be desirable, along with a specification of how much change, and whether each spouse views each particular area as "major." In addition, each spouse is asked to predict how the partner will respond — that is, what change the partner will desire — thus the assessor can see at a glance whether or not communication regarding these problem areas is clear. Couples' scores on the A-C effectively discriminate between distressed and nondistressed couples, and are highly correlated with scores on the Locke–Wallace Marital Adjustment Test (Birchler & Webb, 1977; Weiss & Margolin, 1977). Although the A-C is sensitive to marital distress in much the same way as other self-report questionnaires are, its use transcends the global score because it provides a behavior therapist with specific information regarding the target areas.

Another example of a self-report inventory which has been designed to aid in the task of a behavioral assessment is the *Marital Precounseling Inventory* (MPCI) (Stuart & Stuart 1972). This inventory comprises an assessment package in and of itself. It is divided into nine separate questionnaires which elicit information from spouses regarding such diverse areas as the identification of target problems, common interests, satisfaction with communication, rules for decision making, reinforcement power, general satisfaction, and optimism regarding the future. The inventory is oriented toward the specification of desires for change in concrete behavioral terms. It is also designed to elicit the strengths and resources of the relationship as well as its problem areas. Although the psychometric properties of these questionnaires have not been documented, the MPCI is the most comprehensive and thorough self-report package yet to be assembled for behavioral marital therapy.

A number of additional self-report questionnaires offer great promise in aiding the behavior therapist. The *Marital Activities Inventory* (Weiss *et al.*, 1973) elicits information regarding how spouses distribute their time (alone, together, with others outside the relationship, and the like), and how they would like to see these time distributions change. The *Marital Status Inventory* (Weiss & Cerreto,

1980) was designed to measure each spouse's behavioral proximity to legal termination of the marriage. The 14 items consist of a series of steps which vary in terms of their proximity to divorce. The more items that are answered in the "divorced" direction, the closer the spouse is to ending the relationship. LoPiccolo and LoPiccolo (1978) have developed an inventory for assessing spouses' dissatisfactions and preferences regarding sexual behavior.

Despite the emphasis on direct observation in behavioral assessment, self-report questionnaires will continue to play an important part in the assessment of marital dysfunction. Considerable work still remains to be done in establishing the psychometric properties of particular instruments. Although most of the questionnaires can effectively differentiate between couples who are generally satisfied and dissatisfied, whether or not the measures can be considered to be valid indices of the specific information which they seek remains an open question. For example, do couples respond to the A-C simply on the basis of their overall level of distress, or do they actually endorse the items representing their true complaints? Can distressed couples be classified according to their presenting complaints on the basis of A-C responses? Or similarly, are couples scoring high on the Marital Status Inventory more likely to divorce than distressed couples who score low, or is the MSI simply another questionnaire measuring general distress? To what extent do social desirability factors play a role in these various instruments? Pending the answers to these and other empirical questions, self-report questionnaires will continue to be popular because they are inexpensive, quick and easy to administer, and they address questions which are critical to the formulation of a treatment program.

In our standardized pretreatment assessment at the University of Washington Psychology Clinic, we rely heavily on self-report questionnaires, in addition to the interview, the SOC, and behavioral observations of marital communication. Below is a list of the instruments we use, and the particular information acquired from each questionnaire:

1. *Areas-of-Change Questionnaire.* As we stated above, the A-C provides a statement by each spouse regarding the particular behaviors emitted by the spouse which are occurring at either an insufficient or an excessive frequency. It also results in each spouse pinpointing the "major" behavioral problems in the relationship.

2. *Marital Precounseling Inventory.* We use portions of this comprehensive inventory. First, we have couples enumerate ten behaviors emitted by the partner which are "pleasing" when they occur. Second, we have each spouse enumerate the common interests, and new interests which they would like to acquire in the future, either alone or together with the partner. These items appear near the beginning of the assessment battery so that spouses are immediately introduced to a basic premise of one treatment program, namely, that our focus is on increasing positive behavior and building on relationship strengths. These items also provide important information regarding the current status of each spouse's reinforcing power vis-à-vis the partner. Third, couples complete the subscale which asks for an enumeration of decision-making authority in each of the important domains of married life. This subscale aids in the delineation of relationship rules, and sheds light on whether each spouse is satisfied with the status quo distribution of power and decision-making authority.

3. *Marital Status Inventory.* This inventory is given specificially to assess each partner's proximity to divorce, operationalized by the number of concrete behaviors undertaken in the path to separation and divorce.

4. *Marital Activities Inventory.* We use this questionnaire in order to assess each spouse's reinforcement preferences, and, in particular, the extent to which spouses prefer relationship activities (as opposed to either independent activities or social activities with people other than the spouse) as a primary means of attaining benefits from life. We are particularly interested in any discrepancies between the spouses, that is, a tendency for a spouse who depends on the relationship for reinforcement to be paired with a partner who derives most reinforcement from independent activities.

5. *Dyadic Adjustment Scale (Spanier, 1976).* We use this scale simply for a global index of marital distress. It does not provide much discriminating information for a behavioral analysis, but it does yield a score which reliably places couples in a standardized continuum of marital distress.

6. *Sexual Interaction Inventory (LoPiccolo & Steger, 1974).* This inventory provides valuable and specific information regarding the quality of various aspects of a couple's sex life, as well as preferences for various sexual activities. We have found that many spouses find it much easier to respond to a sexual questionnaire than to discuss their sex life during an interview.

Marital Satisfaction–Distress as a Multidimensional Construct

We have discussed the behavioral assessment of marital dysfunction, and in the process have identified three distinct measurement strategies: self-report, spouse observation, and observation by trained, uninvolved coders. The fact that all three types of measures possess discriminant validity suggests that each measurement mode has a contribution to make in the assessment process. However, correlations between the three modes are often quite low, and at times nonsignificant (Margolin, 1978a, 1978b; Robinson & Price, 1980). For example, Robinson and Price (1980) reported that a global self-report measure of distress was uncorrelated with observed frequencies of positive behavior in the home. Although spouse observations were correlated with observer observations of the same behaviors, the correlations were quite low.

In an area where no response mode has achieved preeminence, no class of measures are sufficiently well established to serve as criteria for the validation of other classes of measures. Thus the low and at times nonexistent relationships between various measures cast aspersions on all three types. However, these low correlations are not particularly surprising, and are not necessarily cause for pessimism. There is a well-established precedent in behavioral assessment for low correlations between different measures of the same construct. For example, it is now uncontroversial to regard "fear" as a construct consisting of three distinct response dimensions—physiologic, motoric, and cognitive—with little expectation that the intercorrelations among these dimensions will be particularly high (Lang, 1968). In the same way, there are a number of different vantage points from which to assess marital distress. Rather than regarding one response channel as preeminent or as a criterion by which to judge the adequacy of other measures, we suggest that all three be viewed as components of the construct *marital distress*.

How do we know that a couple is distressed? Clinicians infer a dysfunctional relationship on the basis of the spouses' subjective reports of distress, spouses' reports (which are actually biased perceptions) of and judgments regarding the partner's behavior, and the clinician's observations of the couples' interaction. At times, as any marital therapist knows, these data sources provide inconsistent information. For example, it is not uncommon for a couple to enter into inadvertent contact with a mental-health professional (e.g., because of a behavior-disordered child) and to appear, on the basis of external observation, to be distressed. Yet the couple may report that they are perfectly satisfied. Another common example involves the spouse who reports that she or he is unhappy with the present relationship, yet she or he reports a high frequency of positive behaviors, and few negative behaviors, from the partner on a day-to-day basis.

The goal of behavioral assessment is to evaluate all three response channels as components of the same construct, and to determine the variables which are functionally related to each channel. To some extent, these channels may be synchronized, but in most cases, stimuli outside the satisfaction–distress constellation will account for a substantial proportion of the variance. Wills *et al.* (1974) found that 25% of the variance in couple's daily subjective satisfaction was accounted for by their reports of frequency of pleasing and displeasing spouse behaviors. However, this leaves 75% of the variance still to be accounted for. A behavioral analysis forms hypotheses regarding how to apportion the variance accounting for all three components of distress. The treatment plan is ultimately based on these hypotheses.

The outcome of a particular assessment may be the hypothesis that increasing one component of satisfaction will lead to a corresponding increase in other components. For example, a therapist may instruct a particular couple in the enactment of certain behaviors, based on the assumption that the enactment of these behaviors will produce changes in both their respective reports of pleasing and displeasing exchanges, and in their overall satisfaction with the relationship. However, it might also be that factors outside the relationship—such as the opportunity for involvement with an attractive new partner—may limit the possibile impact of these behavior changes on one or both spouses' perceptions of the relationship. Ultimately, consumer satisfaction requires that global satisfaction be increased before therapy can be considered successful. But a broader view of the construct of satisfaction–distress better accounts for the data presented in this chapter, and, we would argue, helps to structure the assessment process in a meaningful way.

As we have already stated, although the practicing clinician has insufficient resources for approaching the rigor of the research setting, it is still possible to assess the progress of therapy using many of the assessment procedures outlined in this chapter. A behavioral assessment of marital dysfunction aims to conduct a functional analysis of the distressed relationship by pinpointing those behaviors which correlate with distress, and then identifying the controlling variables for the identified target behaviors. By manipulating those variables and observing the impact on the identified target behaviors, one can ascertain the validity of the behavioral analysis. Moreover, by observing the impact of these behavior changes on each couple's global satisfaction, it is possible to assess generalization across dimensions of the marital satisfaction construct.

There are many ways that a behavioral clinician can approximate functional and analytic procedures in his or her work with couples (cf. Jacobson & Margolin, 1979). For example, in past studies (Jacobson, 1977a, 1979b) we have used multiple-baseline designs based on data collected by couples in the home. If the therapist can identify response classes that are independent of one another, it is possible to demonstrate a causal connection between specific treatment interventions and positive relationship changes. If spouses are also recording daily satisfaction ratings, the therapist has a way of monitoring the importance of specific behavioral changes in improving the overall quality of the marriage.

Future research in marital behavioral assessment will shed further light on the reliability, validity, and clinical utility of all three sets of assessment instruments. Additionally, we hope to see the development of new assessment instruments which take into account the broadening of behavioral theoretical formulations (Jacobson, 1979a; Jacobson & Margolin, 1979; Weiss, 1978). For example, a number of factors have been pinpointed as possible antecedents of marital distress. None of these factors are easily measured by currently available assessment techniques (Jacobson & Margolin, 1979). The "rules" of the relationship, the reinforcement power that each spouse has vis-à-vis the other, and the reinforcing value of the social environment of each spouse outside the context of the relationship are all areas which can only be informally assessed at present. Moreover, we would hope to see greater attention paid to the ability of various assessment instruments to predict the likelihood of a positive response to marital therapy. Although we have tried to be objective and critical of the current state of the art, our overall view is that a considerable amount of creative work has been initiated involving the construction and initial validation of behavioral assessment instruments to assess marital dysfunction. With the growing appreciation for the importance of adhering to psychometric standards, and a continuing dedication to empirical research, one can be sanguine about the future of the enterprise.

References

Bellack, A. S., & Hersen, M. *Behavior modification: An introductory textbook.* Baltimore: Williams & Wilkins, 1977.

Billings, A. Conflict resolution in distressed and nondistressed married couples. *Journal of Consulting and Clinical Psychology,* 1979, *47,* 368–376.

Birchler, G. R., & Webb, L. J. Discriminating interaction in behaviors in happy and unhappy marriages. *Journal of Consulting and Clinical Psychology,* 1977, *45,* 494–495.

Birchler, G. R., Weiss, R. L., & Vincent, J. P. A multimethod analysis of social reinforcement exchange between maritally distressed and nondistressed spouse and stranger dyads. *Journal of Personality and Social Psychology,* 1975, *31,* 349–360.

Ciminero, A. R., Calhoun, K. S., & Adams, H. E. (Eds.). *Handbook of behavioral assessment.* New York: John Wiley & Sons, 1977.

Ciminero, A. R., Nelson, R. O., & Lipinski, D. P. Self-monitoring procedures in behavioral assessment. In A. R. Ciminero, K. S. Calhoun, & H. E. Adams (Eds.), *Handbook of behavioral assessment.* New York: John Wiley & Sons, 1977.

Cone, J. D., & Hawkins, R. P. (Eds.). *Behavioral assessment: New directions in clinical psychology.* New York: Brunner/Mazel, 1977.

Costello, A. J. The reliability of direct observation. *Bulletin of the British Psychological Society,* 1973, *26,* 105–108.

Gottman, J., Markman, H., & Notarius, C. The topography of marital conflict: A sequential analysis of verbal and nonverbal behavior. *Journal of Marriage and the Family,* 1977, *39,* 461–477.

Gottman, J., Notarius, C., & Markman, H. *Couples Interaction Scoring System (CISS).* Unpublished manuscript, University of Illinois, 1976.

Gottman, J., Notarius, C., Markman, H., Bank, S., Yoppi, B., & Rubin, M. E. Behavior exchange theory and marital decision making. *Journal of Personality and Social Psychology,* 1976, *34,* 14–23.

Harrell, J., & Guerney, B. Training married couples in conflict negotiation skills. In D. H. L. Olson (Ed.), *Treating relationships.* Lake Mills, IA: Graphic Press, 1976.

Hartmann, D. P. Considerations in the choice of interobserver reliability estimates. *Journal of Applied Behavior Analysis,* 1977, *10,* 103–116.

Haynes, S. W., Follingstad, D. R., & Sullivan, J. L. *Assessment of marital satisfaction and interaction.* Unpublished manuscript, Southern Illinois University, 1978.

Hollenbeck, A. R. Problems of reliability in observational research. In B. P. Sackett (Ed.), *Observing behavior* (Vol. 2). Baltimore: University Park Press, 1978.

Hops, H., Wills, T. A., Patterson, G. R., & Weiss, R. L. *Marital Interaction Coding System.* Eugene, OR: University of Oregon and Oregon Research Institute, 1971. (Order from ASIS/NAPS, c/o Microfiche Publications, 305 East 46th Street, New York, NY, 10017.)

Jacob, T. Assessment of marital dysfunction. In M. Hersen & A. Bellack (Eds.), *Behavioral assessment: A practical handbook.* New York: Pergamon Press, 1976.

Jacobson, N. S. Problem solving and contingency contracting in the treatment of marital discord. *Journal of Consulting and Clinical Psychology*, 1977, *45*, 92–100. (a)

Jacobson, N. S. Training couples to solve their marital problems: A behavioral approach to relationship discord. Part I: Problem-solving skills. *International Journal of Family Counseling*, 1977, *5*(1), 22–31. (b)

Jacobson, N. S. Specific and nonspecific factors in the effectiveness of a behavioral approach to the treatment of marital discord. *Journal of Consulting and Clinical Psychology*, 1978, *46*, 422–452. (a)

Jacobson, N. S. A stimulus control model of change in behavioral marital therapy: Implications for contingency contracting. *Journal of Marriage and Family Counseling*, 1978, *4*, 29–35. (b)

Jacobson, N. S. Behavioral treatments for marital discord: A critical appraisal. In M. Hersen, R. M. Eisler, & P. M. Miller (Eds.), *Progress in behavior modification*. New York: Academic Press, 1979. (a)

Jacobson, N. S. Increasing positive behavior in severely distressed adult relationships. *Behavior Therapy*, 1979, *10*, 311–326. (b)

Jacobson, N. S., & Margolin, G. *Marital therapy: Strategies based on social learning and behavior exchange principles*. New York: Brunner/Mazel, 1979.

Jacobson, N. S., & Moore, D. Spouses as observers of the events in their relationship. Submitted for publication, 1980.

Jacobson, N. S., Waldron, H., & Moore, D. Toward a behavioral profile of marital distress. *Journal of Consulting and Clinical Psychology*, in press.

Johnson, S. M., & Bolstad, O. D. Methodological issues in naturalistic observation: Some problems and solutions for field research. In L. A. Hamerlynck, L. C. Handy, E. J. Mash (Eds.), *Behavior change: Methodology, concepts, and practice*. Champaign, IL: Research Press, 1973.

Jones, R. R., Reid, J. B., & Patterson, G. R. Naturalistic observations in clinical assessment. In P. McReynolds (Ed.), *Advances in psychological assessment* (Vol. 3). San Francisco: Jossey-Bass, 1975.

Klier, J. L., & Rothberg, M. *Characteristics of conflict resolution in couples*. Paper presented at the Annual Meeting of the Association for the Advancement of Behavior Therapy, Atlanta, December 1977.

Lang, P. J. Fear reduction and fear behavior: Problems in treating a construct. In J. M. Shlien (Ed.), *Research in psychotherapy*. Washington, D.C.: American Psychological Association, 1968.

Locke, H. J., & Wallace, K. M. Short-term marital adjustment and prediction tests: Their reliability and validity. *Journal of Marriage and Family Living*, 1959, *21*, 251–255.

LoPiccolo, J., & LoPiccolo, L. (Eds.). *Handbook of sex therapy*. New York: Plenum Publishing Corp., 1978.

LoPiccolo, J., & Steger, J. C. The sexual interaction inventory: A new instrument of assessment of sexual dysfunction. *Archives of Sexual Behavior*, 1974, *3*, 585–595.

Margolin, G. A. multilevel approach to the assessment of communication positiveness in distressed marital couples. *International Journal of Family Counseling*, 1978, *6*, 81–89. (a)

Margolin, G. The relationships among marital assessment procedures: A correlational study. *Journal of Consulting and Clinical Psychology*, 1978, *46*, 1556–1558. (b)

Margolin, G., & Weiss, R. L. A comparative evaluation of therapeutic components associated with behavioral marital treatment. *Journal of Consulting and Clinical Psychology*, 1978, *46*, 1476–1486.

Markman, H. A longitudinal investigation of couples planning to marry. *Journal of Consulting and Clinical Psychology*, 1979, *47*, 743-749.

Olson, D. H. L., & Ryder, R. G. Inventory of marital conflicts. *Journal of Marriage and the Family*, 1970, *3*, 443-448.

Patterson, G. R. Some procedures for assessing changes in marital interaction patterns. *Oregon Research Institute Bulletin*, 1976, *16*(7).

Patterson, G. R., & Hops, H. Coercion, a game for two: Intervention techniques for marital conflict. In R. E. Ulrich & P. Mountjoy (Eds.), *The experimental analysis of social behavior*. New York: Appleton-Century-Crofts, 1972.

Patterson, G. R., Weiss, R. L., & Hops, H. Training of marital skills: Some problems and concepts. In H. Leitenberg (Ed.), *Handbook of behavior modification*. New York: Prentice-Hall, 1976.

Reid, J. B. Reliability assessment of observation data. *Child Development*, 1970, *41*, 1143-1150.

Resick, P. A., Sweet, J. J., Kieffer, D. M., Barr, P. K., & Ruby, N. L. *Perceived and actual discriminations of conflict and accord in marital communication*. Paper presented at the Eleventh Annual Convention of the Association for the Advancement of Behavior Therapy, Atlanta, December 1977.

Resick, P. A., Welsh, B. K., Zitomer, E. A., Spiegel, D. K., Meidlinger, J. C., & Long, B. R. *Predictors of marital satisfaction, conflict and accord: A preliminary revision of the Marital Interaction Coding System*. Paper presented at the Annual Meeting of the Association for the Advancement of Behavior Therapy, Chicago, November 1978.

Robinson, E. A., & Price, M. G. Pleasurable behavior in marital interaction: An observational study. *Journal of Consulting and Clinical Psychology*, 1980, *48*, 117-118.

Romanczyk, R. G., Kent, R. N., Diament, C., & O'Leary, K. D. Measuring the reliability of observational data: A reactive process. *Journal of Applied Behavior Analysis*, 1973, *6*, 175-184.

Royce W. S., & Weiss, R. L. Behavioral cues in the judgment of the marital satisfaction: A linear regression analysis. *Journal of Consulting and Clinical Psychology*, 1975, *43*, 816-824.

Spanier, G. B. Measuring dyadic adjustment: New scales for assessing the quality of marriage and similar dyads. *Journal of Marriage and the Family*, 1976, *38*, 15-28.

Stuart, R. B. Operant-interpersonal treatment of marital discord. *Journal of Consulting and Clinical Psychology*, 1969, *33*, 675-682.

Stuart, R. B., & Stuart, F. *Marital Precounseling Inventory*. Champaign, IL: Research Press, 1972.

Thibaut, J. W., & Kelley, H. H. *The social psychology of groups*. New York: John Wiley & Sons, 1959.

Thomas, E. J. *Marital communication and decision-making*. New York: The Free Press, 1977.

Thomas, E. J., Walter, C. L., & O'Flaherty, K. A verbal problem checklist for use in assessing family verbal behavior. *Behavior Therapy*, 1974, *5*, 235-246.

Vincent, J. P., Friedman, L. C., Nugent, J., & Messerly, L. Demand characteristics in observations of marital interaction. *Journal of Consulting and Clinical Psychology*, 1979, *47*, 557-567.

Vincent, J. P., Weiss, R. L., & Birchler, G. R. A behavioral analysis of problem solving in distressed and nondistressed married and stranger dyads. *Behavior Therapy*, 1975, *6*, 475-487.

Weiss, R. L. The conceptualization of marriage and marriage disorders from a behavioral perspective. In T. J. Paolino & B. S. McCrady (Eds.), *Marriage and marital therapy: Psychoanalytic, behavioral, and systems theory perspective.* New York: Brunner/Mazel, 1978.

Weiss, R. L., & Birchler, G. R. Adults with marital dysfunction. In M. Hersen & A. S. Bellack (Eds.), *Behavior therapy in the psychiatric setting.* Baltimore: Williams & Wilkins, 1978.

Weiss, R. L., & Cerreto, M. C. The Marital Status Inventory: Development of a measure of dissolution potential. *American Journal of Family Therapy,* 1980, *8*(2), 80–85.

Weiss, R. L., Hops, H., & Patterson, G. R. A framework for conceptualizing marital conflict, technology for altering it, some data for evaluating it. In L. A. Hamerlynck, L. C. Handy, & E. J. Mash (Eds.), *Behavior change: Methodology, concepts, and practice.* Champaign, IL: Research Press, 1973.

Weiss, R. L., & Margolin, G. Assessment of marital conflict and accord. In A. R. Ciminero, K. D. Calhoun, & H. E. Adams (Eds.), *Handbook of behavior assessment.* New York: John Wiley & Sons, 1977.

Wills, T. A., Weiss, R. L., & Patterson, G. R. A behavioral analysis of the determinants of marital satisfaction. *Journal of Consulting and Clinical Psychology,* 1974, *42,* 802–811.

AUTHOR INDEX

Abel, G. G., 32, 39n., 254, 259, 261, 262, 301, 326, 368n., 389, 393, 394n.
Abrams, D., 275, 299n.
Abrams, R., 112, 113, 125, 125n., 128n.
Abramson, L. Y., 154, 164, 170n.
Achterberg, J., 265, 266, 267n.
Adams, H. E., 28, 39n., 469, 476n.
Adkins, D., 287, 299n.
Adler, C. S., 262, 268n.
Adolph, E. F., 338, 394n.
Agras, W. S., 150, 174n., 179n., 183, 185, 194, 195, 197-199, 201, 203, 204, 205n., 207n., 231-233, 235n., 237n., 309, 314, 326n., 378, 389, 392, 394n.
Ahles, T. A., 248, 266, 268n.
Aitchison, R. A., 413, 437n.
Aitken, R. C. B., 148, 150, 170n., 179n.
Ajuriaguerra, J., 50, 84n.
Akhtar, S., 213, 216, 217, 235n.
Albaum, J. M., 335, 361, 396n.
Albee, G. W., 51, 83n.
Alexander, F., 242, 267n.
Alford, G., 150, 174n.
Alford, H., 286, 297n., 406, 436n.
Allen, J. J., 229, 235n.
Allen, R., 185, 203, 204, 207n.
Allman, L. R., 275, 297n.
Alpert, R., 190, 205n.
Alpev, T., 155, 156, 160, 175n.
Amenson, C., 155, 165, 175n.
Ananth, J., 212, 238n.
Anderson, C., 306, 326n.
Andrasik, F., 255, 269n.
Angle, H. V., 16, 30, 35, 39n.
Anton, J. L., 166, 170n.
Arconad, M., 169, 175n.
Arkowitz, H., 157, 160, 171n.

Askenasy, A. R., 168, 172n.
Armstrong, W. H., 335, 397n.
Argyle, M., 405, 421, 435n.
Arthur, R. J., 243, 269n.
Ashwell, M., 339, 394n.
Astrand, P. O., 358, 394n.
Atwater, W. P., 358, 394n.
Ault, M. H., 30, 39n.
Ax, A. F., 198, 205n.
Azrin, N. H., 283, 284, 297n., 314, 326n.

Babigian, H. M., 385, 400n.
Bailey, G. M., 337, 379, 398n.
Bailey, P., 49, 83n.
Baker, B. L., 190, 205n.
Baker, L., 392, 400n.
Barker, W. J., 308, 326n.
Bandura, A., 3, 5, 11n., 161, 171n., 184, 191, 193, 194n., 197, 204, 205n.
Bank, S., 442, 457, 461, 462, 468, 476n.
Barber, T. X., 195, 205n.
Barlow, D. H., 26, 32, 34, 35, 35n., 36, 37, 41n., 150, 179n., 185, 195, 204, 205n., 231, 233, 237n., 301, 303, 305, 307-309, 311, 314, 326n., 330, 389, 394n., 405, 435n.
Barr, P. K., 450, 478n.
Barth, J., 82, 83n.
Bartko, J. J., 118, 125n.
Barton, R., 156, 175n.
Bassiakos, L., 223, 233, 235n.
Bastien, S., 34, 40n., 158, 173n.
Beck, A. T., 102, 103, 125n., 128n., 132, 136, 145, 147, 154, 161-163, 166, 170, 171n., 176n.-179n., 319, 326n., 379, 394n.
Beck, R. W., 147, 171n.
Becker, J., 136, 171n.

480

SUBJECT INDEX